SECOND EDITION

the journal of
David Q. Little

R. Daniel McMichael

A publication of

National Institute Press®

2012

Published in 2012 by National Institute Press®
9302 Lee Highway, Suite 750
Fairfax, Virginia 22031

Library of Congress Cataloging-in-Publication Data

McMichael, R. Daniel, 1925-
  The journal of David Q. Little : / R. Daniel McMichael. -- 2nd
ed.
     p. cm.
  I. Title.
  PS3563.A318945J68 2012
  813'.54--dc23
                                        2012032967

For my father, the late Ross D. McMichael,
who taught me the existence of honor and truth, intelligence and
diligence, and the perpetual challenges of youth and achievement;
my mother, Katherine McMichael Carpenter, who lived these virtues
throughout her entire ninety-two years

and dedicated to all those who still care, wherever they may be.

Contents

Foreword
William J. Bennett

The first time I picked up *The Journal of David Q. Little* I thought about what it was my old boss President Ronald Reagan saw in it. Why did he send a copy to Margaret Thatcher on the eve of her election as Prime Minister, before he himself would be elected president, and over a decade after it had been published? What did he see in this little known novel that it would be one of only a couple of books, we now know, that he ever recommended to prominent people?

Ronald Reagan was a man deeply shaped by his experience with communists in the 1950s. He had seen firsthand their tactics and their methods of intimidation, including threats against himself. He had given speeches about the Soviet Union as he witnessed its domination of Eastern Europe, its expansion in the Third World, and its penetration of Hollywood and other American institutions.

Ronald Reagan also knew the power of nuclear weapons. He had been intimate with the intellectual debates surrounding the use of nuclear weapons in the 1960s and 1970s and the warnings of many on the right, including the Committee on the Present Danger. Indeed, go back to his impromptu speech at the 1976 Republican Convention and you will see how such issues were always on his mind. And, Ronald Reagan especially understood the vulnerabilities of the United States, since we did not possess a national missile defense. These concerns formed the basis of his Strategic Defense

Initiative as president, and, to this day, the push for a national missile defense lives on as a result—with the need for it as urgent as ever.

I had always thought that Ronald Reagan's push for missile defense was born, in part, from *The Journal of David Q. Little* and the ease with which, in the book, the United States was made to surrender its sovereignty. Reagan understood the power of ideology and how a free people could be corrupted. *The Journal of David Q. Little* presents such an ideology and the consequences of a free people succumbing to a centrally planned state in return for physical and economic security, however specious such "security" truly was.

This wonderful book by R. Daniel McMichael presents an America that no one would ever want to see or experience. Dan knows, and has spent his adult life explaining to leading policymakers, that absent the ability to provide for the common defense—the most basic of constitutional duties—there will be a terrible loss of faith in a free society. And, with that faith so lost, even the greatest of nations will descend into corruption, totalitarianism, and ultimately barbarism.

I did not first read *The Journal of David Q. Little*, a novel after all, to take my mind off things. It was, and is, serious work. Although the writing is excellent and the reading pleasurable, it hits you between the eyes, it gets your attention, and it does not let you go. Ronald Reagan believed that freedom was never more than one generation away from extinction. *The Journal of David Q. Little* will show you what that looks like.

> Dr. Bennett is the former secretary of education under President Ronald Reagan; the Washington Fellow of the Claremont Institute; and the host of the nationally syndicated radio show *Bill Bennett's Morning in America.*

Foreword
Brian T. Kennedy

I grew up during the Cold War.

My father told me stories of those fateful days in October of 1962 when, during the Cuban missile crisis, Americans went to bed at night not knowing if there would be a tomorrow. I was just a child when the U.S. naval blockade turned back the Soviet ships and nuclear war was averted.

As a young man the thought of losing a war was unbearable, indeed unthinkable. My father and his friends had fought in World War II like many men of his generation. I heard few stories of what had transpired there in the South Pacific. It had no doubt been bloody. The men who came back were heroes to me even if they did not think that of themselves.

After dinner talk centered on the Vietnam War and what the Soviet Union was doing around the world. The prospect of nuclear war seemed real, as did the animosity between the United States and the Soviet Union.

When the United States withdrew from Vietnam there was an amazing sorrow that enveloped me. Anti-war protestors seemed cowardly and even as a young man there seemed something unreasonable about the United States "losing" a war to the Vietnamese. We had nuclear weapons. They did not. But what they had, I realized many years later, was an ally in the Soviet Union and Communist China that possessed nuclear weapons and we had neither an air or missile defense that was adequate to defend the United States. We accepted a political defeat because American policymakers did not think it worth prosecuting the war in such a way that American interests would be served or, more precisely, that would escalate tensions between the United States and the totalitarian powers. For the communist world it was a great victory and it demonstrated the power of nuclear weapons to fundamentally alter the strategic balance between nations.

It was with this mindset I first read *The Journal of David Q. Little*. It is a book both beautiful and disturbing. To read it is to enter a world devoid of that spirit of American exceptionalism that won WWII and has animated our nation since our first days. Instead it is a nightmare: a world where American freedom has been lost and is no more.

R. Daniel McMichael is, for those who know him, a philosopher and strategist of the first order. This will seem like an odd combination. But he has written with this book a philosophical treatise of how to dismantle a free people: how to dispirit them; how to break them down; how to take them apart. For it is not enough to destroy the United States militarily, it must be done spiritually and morally.

The Journal of David Q. Little is, in its most lucid prose, an explanation of how the international radical left could destroy the United States. McMichael presents a world where men who had the constitutional duty to defend the United States chose instead surrender in the face of thermonuclear war. How that surrender caused the demoralization of the United States and therefore its destruction. How effortlessly political organization emerged to administer a new regime, with new principles to replace the old ones that had, by necessity, to be destroyed, and perhaps most importantly, how so many could go along with it.

McMichael had studied how the communists had operated in the Soviet Union and in the communist satellites, most notably Czechoslovakia and in the writings of Jan Kozak. It was here he saw that the radical left has to win at the level of philosophy as well as force. For it is not enough to conquer a people and intimidate them militarily, as the Soviets did in Eastern Europe, but the people must be made to comply—to be complicit—in their subjugation. For this to be achieved one must first demoralize a people, undermine their constitution, and finally manipulate their leaders and their lawmakers to limit their freedom in the name of some higher justice. This recreation of a public philosophy where people willingly give up their freedom is no easy task and one that McMichael spent years studying.

But McMichael knows America even better. He knows the American spirit and why Americans had achieved their freedom and why they were not willing, are not willing, to let it go lightly. McMichael understands as well as any writer in the twentieth century that America is a country built on the self-evident truths of the Declaration of Independence: that all men are created equal and endowed by their creator with the inalienable right to life, liberty and the pursuit of happiness. Theoretical to some, these ideas take on a powerful spirit, one that has moved Americans to create the greatest nation in the history of the world and to defend their freedom anywhere and anytime their liberty is threatened. So the task for McMichael was to construct a world where that spirit of freedom had to come into conflict with a radical leftist ideology that would put security over liberty. This is the tension of the book and one reason it is such a compelling and thought-provoking story.

Many thoughtful young people read Ayn Rand and *Atlas Shrugged* to see the dangers of big government and modern bureaucracy. It is my sincere hope that they will read McMichael and *The Journal of David Q. Little* the same way and see a more accurate portrayal of what their world could look like, and how nuclear weapons and nuclear blackmail, not to mention radical leftist ideology, could be our undoing.

Despite its dark themes, *The Journal of David Q. Little* is the story also of hope and it is here we find McMichael the patriot for he presents to an American reader both the dangers and the way out.

For many it has served as a cautionary tale. It is a story that so horrifies you that you are forever changed by it.

In this masterwork of philosophy and politics, *The Journal of David Q. Little* shows why America is worth defending, now and forever.

Mr. Kennedy is president of the Claremont Institute for the Study of Statesmanship and Political Philosophy and the publisher of the *Claremont Review of Books*.

Foreword
Keith B. Payne

As Benjamin Franklin emerged from the Constitutional Convention in 1787 an onlooker asked him what type of government America would have. "A republic, if you can keep it," he responded. History following that convention has revealed the stark reality behind the implicit warning in Franklin's challenge, "if you can keep it."

For example, Western democracy was in a precarious state in 1939 when two equally-brutal totalitarian systems, one communist and the other national socialist, separately claimed the future and based their identities in large measure on hostility to democratic institutions and traditions. The "greatest generation" of Americans successfully met Benjamin Franklin's challenge at that time and America emerged from World War II as the global center of economic, technological, industrial, cultural and military power.

The Soviet communist threat to Western democratic civilization following World War II became blatantly obvious as the Soviet Union and local communists installed new regimes in Central Europe via a combination of subversion, coercion, and military force, and Soviet Premier Khrushchev declared to Western ambassadors in 1956, "Whether you like it or not, history is on our side. We will bury you." The greatest generation again rallied, and met Franklin's challenge by orchestrating the peaceful collapse of the Soviet Union and its empire.

Nearly every generation of Americans now seems compelled to confront a claimant to the future who demands power and authority at the expense of individual freedoms and democratic institutions, and again confirms the stark reality behind Franklin's 1778 warning. These aspiring tyrants typically hope to beguile, distract, confuse, deceive and otherwise shape the thinking of those who might otherwise oppose them, and deal ruthlessly with those who cannot be so controlled. They seek to mold thinking so that peoples will give up control of their lives willingly, even with relief that they no longer have the burden of responsibility for their lives. This idea, said Joseph Stalin, is more powerful than guns. Adolf Hitler essentially said the same, "How fortunate for governments that the people they administer don't think."

With the benign conclusion of the Cold War in 1991, many sanguine American academics and policy makers claimed that given the global appeal of democratic governance, individual liberty and opportunity, history in the Hegelian sense had come to an idyllic conclusion and that a new more benign "world order" had arrived. Had systemic threats to the Republic come to an end with the fall of communism?

Unfortunately, within the decade, Harvard professor Samuel Huntington's dark prediction of a coming "clash of civilizations" appeared to be the new reality: brutal, authoritarian spoilers again emerged to claim the future and pose a new challenge to the existence of democratic civilization. Militant Islamic terrorist organizations now wage war against Western liberal democratic institutions, rule and populations. They too place supreme importance on the war of ideas and allegiances. The future of state-based threats from China and Russia is unclear, but current trends are not encouraging as communist China in particular appears to be vying for its "place in the sun" at the expense of the United States and its allies.

In this emerging environment, the re-release of Daniel McMichael's compelling book, *The Journal of David Q. Little*, offers timely and important insight for a new generation of Americans who generally lack the schooling in adversity and harsh reality that so benefited the "greatest generation." Although originally published in 1967 as a gripping tale qua tutorial about the lethal reality of communist ideas and subversive tactics, the author also focuses on broader questions that remain as current as today's headlines. Indeed, these questions appear to be timeless: Are peoples to be free citizens or subjects of those who seek centralized authority and power via attractive but ultimately vapid promises? That was the Cold War's defining question; indeed, it always is and will be the defining question when authoritarian aspirants to power confront democratic traditions and institutions, as Benjamin Franklin well anticipated.

When one recognizes the ongoing reality and significance of this war of ideas, the full meaning and value of *The Journal of David Q. Little* becomes clear. Its re-release is a boon for contemporary students who generally are unfamiliar with the history of past systemic threats to the Republic, or even the possibility of such threats, and will benefit from a greater understanding of how tyrants seek to win wars of ideas via subversion, guile, distraction and deceit.

The Journal of David Q. Little is an exceptional work of fiction that is informed by author Dan McMichael's deep knowledge of the actual strategies and tactics employed by communist organizers such as Vladimir Lenin, the leader of the communist revolution in Russia, and Jan Kozak, who brought communist rule to Czechoslovakia. They exploited the moral sentiments of "fellow travelers" and the naiveté of "useful idiots" (Lenin's term) to appropriate power and authority and thereby suborn governments. *The Journal of David Q. Little* is a fictional account built on stark realities. In one particularly pertinent passage, the author explains via dialogue the tyrant's preferred strategy for gaining and retaining power: "The trick... the real adventure in life... is to acquire the skills of motivating someone without his being aware that he is being... controlled." Dan McMichael leads the reader through a riveting story of the slow decay of liberty to remind us that apparently "good intentions" can lead to catastrophic consequences.

As such, *The Journal of David Q. Little* offers fair warning to those who are attracted by utopian visions and promises that ultimately will cost them dearly, or simply are too apathetic or indolent to resist such promises. It chronicles the deadly actions or passive inaction of those who fall prey to the aspiring tyrant's promises, those who think that political freedom is a birthright that needs no protection, who are easily distracted, or who simply prefer the ease of watching someone else pay the costs for their own liberties.

Dan McMichael captures the aspiring tyrant's inevitable claims and corresponding empty promises that if individuals relinquish their liberty and freedom for the tyrant's centralized power and authority, the tyrant will "protect you, [and] keep you safe, productive, happy and secure." As the author's protagonist, David Q. Little discovers, the truth is that these promises are not kept and watchful citizens who courageously demand truth from power are indispensable to preserving a free society in the face of aspiring tyrants and those sympathetic to or duped by them. Unfortunately, however, as Father Herbert, the book's model passive onlooker laments, it often is the case that "people hate truth more than they hate tyranny."

The Journal of David Q. Little spoke to readers of its time and promises to do so again today. Its lesson is critical for contemporary students because they will not have the luxury of avoiding Franklin's challenge, "A republic, if you can keep it".

Dr. Payne is the department head of the Graduate Department of Defense and Strategic Studies, Missouri State University (Washington, D.C., campus) and co-founder and president, National Institute for Public Policy.

Foreword

Robert L. Pfaltzgraff, Jr.

In *The Journal of David Q. Little* R. Daniel McMichael describes how a country lost its freedom and spiraled downward into chaos, tyranny, poverty, and barbarism. That country was the United States of America. Fortunately the characters are allegorical, although the author utilizes history as well as his profound understanding of strategy and tactics, in this case Vladimir Lenin and Jan Kozak, to frame his narrative. As a result, the reader gains a haunting depiction of how a country – like the lobster in a pot in which the heat is gradually increased until the lobster is boiled – finds itself transformed beyond recognition as its freedom, together with the Constitutional traditions and values that sustain limited government, are eventually eroded and destroyed. The result is a grotesque entity called the United Socialist States of America (USSA), based on a new tyranny in which the individual is submerged in a faceless Orwellian collectivist society.

Although the scenario set forth here has the Cold War as its context, the themes that surround the descent of a once great nation are timeless. They transcend the Cold War era. As described in *The Journal of David Q. Little*, they include the loss of sovereignty and liberty as a result of gradualist efforts that circumvent Constitutional principles; the increasing centralization of power that restricts liberty and makes larger numbers of people dependent on the state; the pursuit of redistributionist policies that sap individual initiative; impoverishment through the imposition of crushing taxes and regulations that diminish productivity, while lowering wages and increasing permanent unemployment or underemployment; the loss of national freedom and independence to an international order that is overtly hostile to American values; and the surrender of sovereignty to an international body that is controlled by an outside power – in the Cold War the Soviet Union.

In addition, the journey down this darkening path is spearheaded by homegrown, domestic supporters seeking fundamentally to transform society, together with the emergence of an ethos that prefers short-term gratification while postponing the longer-term grief and tragedy that are the consequence of their actions to be addressed by a future generation. It is left to the reader of this foreword to determine the extent to which these themes strike a resonant chord in the twenty-first century.

Despite the unfolding tragedy, the story set forth in *The Journal of David Q. Little* ends on a note of renewal. Forces such as those that helped to destroy the Soviet Union contribute to the demise of the USSA. The forces that dismantle the USSA bear an uncanny resemblance to those that helped to bring down the Soviet Union and the Soviet empire, namely the fact that "geography and distance made centralized control extremely difficult, since there was no longer an economic base capable of supporting a highly automated technological society that might have been able to enforce the discipline of the state. Most important of all was the growing resistance that swept over the land in thunderous waves." (Think, for example, of the surging throngs of East Germans who literally tore down the Berlin Wall in 1989.) In the final analysis what doomed the Soviet Union also itself spelled the end of the USSA. Both shared a fatal set of structural contradictions.

The triumph of the human spirit over seemingly insurmountable obstacles and odds is the ultimate theme of *The Journal of David Q. Little* – a message that adds to its timeless quality about the quest for liberty that is central to American exceptionalism. However, the price of liberty is a willingness to expend blood and treasure in support of the values that sustain freedom. As one of its heroes who commands the guerrilla forces who help to administer the *coup de grace* to the USSA puts it:

> There will always be those who care; those few who carry it on, this thing we call civilization; those few who have always been with us, whom adversity and failure only strengthen... They are the tiny bands of resolve who, as did their forbears, struggle to rise up again; who have dotted the landscape since the days of the mastodon...

Such is the spirit that both informs the life work of the author of *The Journal of David Q. Little* and leads to the triumph of good over evil but does so, as the pages that follow reveal, at a vast human and material cost that could have been avoided by timely action in defense of the values that once sustained the United States. Salvation comes, thanks to those "tiny bands of resolve," who fight back against the forces of tyranny and barbarism to begin the long journey to restore the United States of America.

Dr. Pfaltzgraff is president of the Institute for Foreign Policy Analysis, Inc. and Shelby Cullom Davis Professor of International Security Studies at the Fletcher School, Tufts University.

Author's Introduction

Over the years I've been asked how I came to write *David Q. Little* and most particularly where I got the idea.

It came from two interrelated sources that surfaced in the aftermath of World War II, which, some of us would argue, was the last major conflict of a hot war – at least in the twentieth century and so far in the twenty-first. It was to be replaced by a new form of conflict – except that it wasn't really new but upside down, which made it new largely because it didn't make any sense to most people.

It was George Orwell who apparently first used the name for it as a general term – *Cold War*. This appeared in a 1945 article that looked at the prospect of nations being coerced under nuclear blackmail into the "reimposition of slavery" brought about by an "unconquerable" power that was in "a permanent state of 'cold war' with its neighbors."[1]

Within a year the Orwellian concept became more and more real as a handful of policymakers and opinion leaders began to see the edges of a new form of growing conflict but in an almost surreal setting – conflict based on contradictions and non sequiturs steeped in ideology about who owns what and who does what and for whom. In 1946, as the USSR was hammering its political and military domination into the Eastern Bloc, Kennan did his Long Telegram from

---

1   George Orwell, "You and the Atomic Bomb," *Tribune* October 19, 1945, http://tmh.floonet.net/articles/abombs.html.

Moscow and his celebrated X article, while musing (along with Orwell and others) whether or not the dark forebodings of James Burnham were being taken seriously enough.

And then Churchill immortalized the emerging scope of the Cold War in his March 5, 1946, Fulton Missouri speech by declaring: "From Stettin in the Baltic to Trieste in the Adriatic an *iron curtain* has descended across the Continent . . . Behind that line lie all the capitals of the ancient states of Central and Eastern Europe . . . and the populations around them lie in what I must call the Soviet sphere . . ."[2]

Events were tumbling like an avalanche upon American and western populations, alike, even as people were struggling to restart their lives again. In 1947 Truman – already socked with an unexpected presidency and the burdens of the a-bomb – dove into the deep end of the pool to create the Truman Doctrine of containment against further Soviet expansion; this as the Soviets created the Cominform to tighten their political and ideological control of the Eastern Bloc and also of the international communist movement, and then to unleash the Berlin Blockade in 1948, which subsequently boomeranged when the West in turn countered with the airlift followed by the North Atlantic Treaty in April 1949.

The game was on, a giant three-dimensional chess game, and suddenly Americans were thrust into a new world of conflict, about which they knew virtually nothing as to how or why it was conceived or organized or prosecuted or for how long it would last.

Also in 1948 came the brutal fall of Czechoslovakia as the last remaining western-style democracy to be coopted behind the Iron Curtain. Some would count it as the first conquest of the newly minted Cold War, in that all previous members of the Eastern Bloc were essentially the territorial spoils of the hot war of WWII ceded to the Soviets by the U.S. and the other allies. The Soviets wasted no time into forging them into Soviet-style regimes.

All except for Czechoslovakia, where at this point in time any visible means of military coercion (tanks and troops) would have

---

2   *The Collected Works of Sir Winston Churchill, A Centenary Limited Edition*, Post-War Speeches, Volume I (The Library of Imperial History: 1975) p. 80.

severely compromised the new Soviet image that went with its emerging "peace offensive" now bursting upon the world in a bold bid to persuade Americans to give up their atomic weapons to point the way to a world peace without fear of a "nuclear holocaust."

A way was found quite in keeping with the enigmas of the Marxist-Leninist world of dialectics. For the Czech problem: just turn everything upside down. Keep the military on the sidelines, stationed in other Bloc satellites but close enough to pose a frightening threat. Then, activate a concerted effort to break the will of the non-communist Czechs against a peaceful solution, this through the arts of propaganda, subversion and intimidation – components of which included: use of popular fronts, protest committees, disinformation, discrediting and decapitating non-communist leadership – all designed to generate loss of national confidence to resist the "inevitability of history and the will of the people."

The means employed was the continuing use of the strategy of "pressure from above, pressure from below" projects and the application of the "salami" technique to isolate leadership and institutions (such as bankers and banks) from lay public support. Targets involved leadership penetration of parliament, civil service, police, judiciary, as well as the electorate. The instigators were the Communist Party of Czechoslovakia (KSC) and the largely covert Soviet cadres brought in by their Ambassador Valerian Zorin.

A concerted blitz involving all of these ploys began in deadly earnest following the Czech election of 1946 and ended with the May 9, 1948 elections that approved a new constitution for the Czechoslovak Socialist Republic, this without any military shots being fired or any boots on the ground.

In 1957, after participating in a major conference in Chicago that was devoted to Cold War issues, an ad hoc group of us began to look at some of the key issues and how to deal with them. Things were not going all that well for the guardian of freedom – helped along by the constant drumbeat of the Soviet peace offensive. One of the nagging problems was that very few Americans understood the dynamics in play, except that Soviet-led actions were not a good thing, which all kinds of horror stories from fleeing defectors confirmed again and again. But trying to explain the upside down nature of this kind of conflict was extremely difficult. Impossible, for the most part.

Then, also in 1957, a member of the Czechoslovak communist party, Jan Kozak, presented a strategy paper at a closed meeting of the Inter-Parliamentary Union (IPU) in London that explained in detail – like a field manual – all of the ploys taken to achieve the Czech revolution. Although it was not intended for non-Marxist eyes, I managed to secure a copy early on and studied it carefully. And with the help and encouragement of my ad hoc colleagues, I proceeded to adopt Kozak's treatise as the matrix from which I constructed this story – a blend of historical precedent unfolding in a fictional setting that few really wished to know about.

It took me seven years to write *David Q. Little* – over a year just to construct historically verifiable plot lines, as well to create a credible venue. For this I developed biographies on each of my principal characters, going back at least two generations for each, so that I could write about them as people I actually knew. Then, I turned them loose in the story lines to do their own thing.

R. Daniel McMichael
Pittsburgh, Pennsylvania
August, 2012

Note to reader: All characters in this story are allegorical and thus entirely fictitious; any similarity between persons living or dead is purely coincidental. The use of Pittsburgh for the story location was merely a matter of convenience in selecting a setting familiar to the author, since he resides in Pittsburgh, and has no specific bearing on the story which could have been set just as easily in any other major industrial center in the United States.

the journal of
DAVID Q. LITTLE

Edited by Jason A. Doyle

Published by

A·A·GRACE, LTD
PUBLISHERS
SYDNEY, AUSTRALIA

A.D. 2223

There webs were spread of more than common size
And half-starved spiders prey'd on half-starved flies.
Churchill—Prophecy of Famine

The Publisher's Preface

There perhaps is no more popular and intriguing study of history than that of Americana. The strange, oftentimes unpredictable behavior of Americans has fascinated much of the world for centuries. Ever since they pitched their tea over the sides of sailing vessels in the old Boston harbour some four-hundred-odd years ago to set off their first revolt, they have been a rich source of conjecture for a watchful, sometimes hopeful, sometimes sorrowful world. The most consistent thing about them has been their very inconsistency. Their history is both strewn with the wreckage of supreme folly and illuminated forever with magnificent monuments of unparalleled heroism. Whether one despises them or merely wonders at them, the people of the North American continent catch at the heart as much today as at any time in the past.

Twice now during the past fifteen hundred years or so the Western Civilization has allowed itself to be overrun by the barbarians. The first time its most advanced civilization, Rome, was destroyed, and it took nearly a thousand years for the West to recover. The second time was the Great Crisis of America, so named by modern historians and not yet 250 years past. That Australia escaped most of the crushing waves of terror that swept throughout the world cannot be particularly credited to our forebears, for the web of tyranny had not yet encompassed our land when it crumbled under its own weight. But then every school child knows what has been the outcome, the incredible triumphs and tragedies of these last two centuries.

As has been well publicized, a task force of human-behaviour scientists recently returned from the North American continent. The study group spent nearly a year there observing the peculiarities of this culture. This is the sixth such group to have visited there during the past forty years.

One of the tasks of this most recent exercise was to examine certain elements of Christianity and other religions as currently practiced. It was in respect to this effort that Dr. Jason A. Doyle and Dr. Edison Tyler, the two noted scholars from our distinguished Churchill University who headed Study Group VI, came to find the *Journal of David Q. Little*. This occurred during a visit to an obscure Christian mission secluded on the western slopes of the Rocky Mountains. Known as St. Luke's Mission of Hope, it is located not far from the summit of Mt. Victor, part of the Wind River Range of the Wyoming Federation. The Head Disciple, apparently convinced of the goodwill and sincerity of the study group, revealed the presence of the Journal, which had been in the possession of the Mission for a very long time. No one knows exactly how it came to be there, since the narration is set nearly two thousand miles to the east.

Edited by Dr. Doyle, the Journal is published here in light of resurging public interest in Americana. The footnotes are the work of Dr. Doyle and are a tribute to his scholarly labours. The publishers hope the reader will find the narration as colourful and interesting as did they and that it will help shed additional light on conditions of life during the Great Crisis that engulfed the nation once known as the United States of America, which twice during the twentieth century saved the world from tyranny only to succumb to its own mystique.

—A. A. Grace, Ltd.

Sidney, Australia. July 4, 2223

1

The First Month

"Thank God it's over and we can begin to live again!"

"That's what you think, lady. It's only the beginning, and you've been offered up on a platter."

Both voices were soft, but the crispness of the air gave them a peculiar clarity that cut through the loudspeaker. And the speaker was louder than usual, which is saying a lot for the mayor of Pittsburgh, because he always speaks in a booming, sincere voice. But today he was twice as booming and three times as sincere and four times longer than usual, and everyone's feet kept getting colder and colder.

You could tell by the way people kept shifting around that they were wiggling their toes. A two-and-a-half-hour ceremony is exactly two hours too long unless you want trouble. That they should have known. When you make a sales pitch keep it short and sharp.

The two were standing in front of me. I had not really noticed the woman until she spoke her prayer of thanks. But I became sharply aware of the kid in the jacket shortly after the limousines arrived at the reviewing platform. The jacket, of course, was leather—genuine leather—a rarity these days, which means he must have stolen it. He had the mark of the streets on him. It was the general set of him that gave him away—arrogant nonchalance with an underlying wariness. Slender and tall, like so many I have seen huddled under street lights. But his hands and eyes made him different from others. It was not so much the cold blue but rather the way his eyes took in things in irregular flicks that made you feel almost naked. He had the habit of looking straight at things. He looked at me only once and then away as if I were of little consequence. His hands were larger than they should have been and looked as if they would be comfortable wrapped around an iron bar. He kept flexing them slowly, absently into fists as he listened and looked and looked and listened. He wore no gloves and did not seem to mind. He was not wiggling his toes.

And then the pale woman in black spoke out loud to herself in answer to the mayor's promise of a "better tomorrow that will erase away the fears and bitterness of the dark days now past…"

The boy's retort—he could not have been over twenty-one—snapped like a pistol shot that stirred the crowd to an uneasy, silent tenseness, as if all were watching a high wire act, wishing it were over, yet morbidly curious as to what the next move would bring.

"On a platter, lady. You've been surrendered. We've all been surrendered."

His voice rose, not shrilly, as would be expected with youth, but firmly, with a resonant openness that commanded unwillingly a growing segment of the crowd.

"Hush!"

I sought his arm for fatherly restraint but he shook my hand away.

"You've surrendered us! Do you hear? You've surrendered us, and we'll all pay. You'll see."

He was in full cry now, and the crowd drew away as three patrolmen slipped swiftly and silently about him. And with a movement so quick and skilled that the few who might have seen it would doubt their eyes, a powerful blue arm jammed the end of a night stick deep into the boy's flesh well below the jacket, while other blue arms pinioned him and then supported him with tender care as they half dragged, half walked the sagging body out of the crowd, its tight-lipped face lolled in agony.

Still the woman had not spoken but only stared hypnotically at the wake in the crowd. The mayor droned on, too far from the scene and too caught up in his prepared script to notice. And the crowd went back to wiggling its toes, while the woman slowly moved away bewildered and weeping.

The whole scene could not have taken more than three minutes. Yet, strangely, it seemed to alter the emotional flow of the crowd, which had assembled slowly beginning about nine-thirty, with calm and purposeful expectation. The ceremonies were scheduled for ten a.m., and there had been the usual confusion around the speakers' platform—a tangle of high school band uniforms and instruments, newsmen, dignitaries, mobile T.V. units, all directed into final positions by a corps of harried men and one tall, bony woman who seemed to be running everything at once.

The crowd was not as large as I had thought it surely would be. But then what could you expect for a New Year's Day? Judging from the morning newscast, the city had been on a New Year's Eve binge even worse than the time when the Pirates won the pennant years ago. Twenty-eight traffic accidents, eleven of them involving fatalities, and nearly three hundred arrests, the radio said, for drunkenness and disorderly conduct. I am glad we stayed in the neighborhood, which was noisy but safe.

Still, Point Park was nearly filled. Most people, like myself, had come alone. I had not wanted to waste gas by taking the car, and Nancy had not felt like coming. So she and the children stayed home to watch the TV coverage, which I would have liked to have done. But just before I left the office Friday the boss had told me that he hoped I would make a point to attend the ceremonies in person. "We've got to show them that we in business are behind them one hundred percent," he told me. So what could I do?

Of course, the caravan from the airport was late, but no one seemed particularly irritated, which was unusual as crowds go. Everyone seemed pleasant, almost too pleasant. It was as if all of us had gone to a stranger's wedding reception and covered our sense of guilty boredom with elaborate displays of formal, noncommittal politeness that gave us the look of pristine robots.

There was little conversation, as if by mutual consent or perhaps for mutual protection. A common, instinctive understanding warned

3

us that if we visited too much we might either reveal more of ourselves than we should feel safe in doing or, even worse, accidentally think about things we did not want to think about. Silence was the safe way, the easy way to greet the new year, and everyone observed it with masks of confident serenity.

Instead, most of us studied the speakers' stand with unflinching pleasantness… though inside it seemed my blood pounded more than it should have. But then who would not be keyed up? The nightmare of these past six months, climaxed with the news that we would not be destroyed, had left most everyone with an explosive kind of giddiness that fluctuated without reason between tears and laughter, anger and goodwill, guilt and pride, fear and confidence. It was everywhere: the stenographer who giggled and then sobbed in the middle of a letter ordering baseball tickets for the coming season; the store clerk who flung an arm load of neckties into the face of a customer; the woman driver who held up traffic through five light changes, until the patrolman convinced her that she would not hurt the feelings of oncoming motorists by making them wait on her left turn; the drunk who emptied his pockets into the Salvation Army kettle begging forgiveness; the steadfast parishioner who stalked from a bowed congregation, muttering that he no longer needed God.

The times have been hard on us, and perhaps we do not know any longer how we should act. We are told that we should be calm, proud and happy; that our dangers are gone and that we are still among the free and the living. We see this. We know this is true. Why is it, then, something inside makes us unsure of everything—ourselves, our work, each other?

The sight of the speakers' stand seemed to heighten this feeling of being mixed without knowing why. The stand was made of gleaming new marble balustrades featuring sculptured doves set upon a pedestal of steps serving all sides. A tall, stainless steel shaft rose gracefully from the rear side, atop of which sat the American eagle, cast from a gold-colored alloy—its head turned toward peace—and framed within a flaming red metal outline of the Star of Russia, fully six feet in diameter. A staff rose above this from which flew the flag of the World Order of Nations.[1] A cross spar set below the eagle carried flags of our country and the Soviet Union in equal positions fluttering from snapping halyards.

Set against a deep blue sky and served by brilliant sunshine, the Peace Monument, as it was christened two days earlier, gave the park an imposing point of reference visible from every direction— from the ice-clogged rivers, from the row houses on Mount Washington, from the offices of Gateway Center and the tangle of streets that serve it.

It had been built hurriedly but with great care. The day after the Treaty of Friendship was signed a civic commission was appointed by the mayor to design and build the monument as a "fitting center where we can meet from time to time in the cause of peace and brotherhood." Its progress had been thoroughly reported, from the glowing details of its design by Vasili Petrovitch, one of the exchange art professors at William Penn University, to the final feverish hours of setting the shaft plumb and securely into the frozen earth. It was a feat accomplished in a little over seven days, each man donating his labor, skill and equipment, "overwhelming proof of what men can do when they pool their skills and work unselfishly in the common cause," as the *Pittsburgh News-Journal* pointed out editorially. It is rumored that three lives were lost— one at a railroad siding, another in

---

1   Three times during the twentieth century conscientious men had sought to banish war as a means to settle disputes and to create in its stead an international body that could both arbitrate and articulate the wishes of men living under the rule of law. The League of Nations was the first of these attempts, created in 1921. But American isolationism and the apathy of Western Europe toward fascism made the organisation ineffective to prevent World War II. In 1945, a second attempt was made with the creation of the United Nations. Although more strongly structured than its predecessor, the provisions of its charter, nonetheless, were sabotaged by the growing Sino-Soviet sphere of influence in the latter half of the twentieth century. In the chaos that followed, the statesmen of the West made yet another valiant effort to establish a parliamentary body known as the World Order of Nations (W.O.N.). This time, the founders representing 126 nations vowed to eliminate mistakes of the past by creating an organisation with broad, supranational powers to settle disputes "by rule of law" through a system of world courts and, where necessary, "to raise, maintain and place military forces in the field to keep the peace."

a fabricating plant and one at the construction site under the flood-lights late one night. But the rumor was never confirmed, and one hears so many rumors that it is better not to believe them.

It was the sight of the eagle within the star that was most difficult to get used to, though it was by now a familiar sight. For the Peace Seal had been reproduced in all the newspapers and magazines over and over since the treaty ratification. Even so, seeing the symbol now in its bold and coldly real dimensions against the sky left all of us, I think, feeling that we had passed by some point in our lives where there could be no turning back or away from the future; that the past was no longer ours to cling to; that what happened yesterday and last night would never happen again; that change was upon us and the future was to be forever our mortal enemy.

Yet, the words from the loudspeaker, the spirited music, the creaseless W.O.N. color guard and the cheering student section mocked these feelings and made one acutely and silently ashamed for thinking them. For it was all quite logical. A war had been prevented, and two nations, once sworn to outwit and outdo the other, had been brought together into a foolproof agreement that guaranteed peace beyond any doubt. The price, of course, was a high one. Each nation was required to give up equal amounts of its sovereignty but—unlike past treaties and agreements—not to each other. This is what made it all different. The Russians were surrendering just as much to the World Order of Nations as we were. We each were disarming. We each were turning our entire productive efforts to strict peacetime use. And our human rights were now fully protected by strongly armed W.O.N. troops made up of people from all nations to insure justice for all. Nowhere in all history has there been anything quite like this!

Our alternative to this—as everyone knows—was death, the special searing kind that comes with the nuclear bomb. We had only two choices. There was the emotional, irresponsible and ungodly way that meant fighting a war to try to preserve outworn traditions of unworkable nationalism; a war in which there could be no winner; a war that could have reduced millions of innocent people to atomic ashes...

6

Or there was the wholly logical, mature, peaceful way, in which each side in the true godly tradition could give of themselves each unto the other; could abolish petty nationalism in return for life and freedom in the service of mankind everywhere. ...And thank God our choice had been the right one or else this very ground might now be a smoldering, water-filled crater marked with ragged bits of stone and steel ...

These were the words coming from the loudspeakers as the crowd wiggled its toes in the clear cold and responded with polite enthusiasm when, one by one, the members of the Joint Committee for Local Action were introduced—one representative for each township, municipality and county in the newly established Southwest District of the state. Each wore a neat dark suit and topcoat and a distinguished hat. Each smiled and waved. Each sat down promptly except the District Chairman, a former New Yorker and social science teacher named Smith Armstrong, who gave the keynote address.

A sense of relief, a sudden relaxation of tension, swept through the crowd when it soon became apparent that only one Russian was among the JCFLA group, the rest being mild, banker-type Americans. And he looked more like a jovial St. Nicholas, square shaped and grinning under a heavy fur cap, than the enemy we had been first taught to dread and more recently to love. In fact, Chairman Armstrong even joked about it, a bit brazenly, I thought, considering the peril of these past months.

"Well, ladies and gentlemen, here's that terrible Russian that the Belltollers[2] have been screaming about. I could only bring one with me, since there are so few here in this country. In fact, we had trouble getting Nick away from his wife, three married daughters and five grandchildren so he could come over here and live up to that treaty.

---

2   According to historical records the term "Belltoll" was a popular expression to identify supporters of Jason B. Bell, senator from the state of Virginia, who bitterly opposed the "co-existors" in a 37-hour filibuster which he conducted entirely alone. A stroke took his life a week later. Wags of the day referred to his supporters as "the Belltollers of our doom."

"His only regret is that we don't have some flowers for him. That's a custom in warlike Russia.... Well, what do you know! Nick, they've fooled us. Look what they've got for you."

The crowd had tittered shyly and then chuckled more comfortably when they saw Nicholas Syerov, now revealed as the Vice- Chairman of the W.O.N.'s sponsored committee, beam at the Chairman. Then he winked at the youngsters in the band up front, smiling and nodding while a purposeful, pigtailed tot of six flounced up the marble steps clinging to a huge bundle of mums which she promptly gave him, along with a peck on the cheek, and then bounced back down to the arms of the tall, bony woman. This brought unrestrained laughter and applause—the only time during the wearisome ceremonies. But it was too hearty, too prolonged, too much like the response to comedy lines in a stage tragedy when the audience gratefully accepts the excuse to escape the harshness of the play.

It was at this point that the mayor rose to read his prepared response pledging the wholehearted cooperation of the city of Pittsburgh and the "fine, wonderful, dedicated people, who, as do I, devote their every effort to the continued well-being of people everywhere..."

It was here that the shouts of "surrender" had echoed above the loudspeakers, and by the time most people could look, all they saw was an obviously drunken youth being gently led to a discreetly parked paddy wagon.

But the interruption had broken the spell of impassive pleasantness. Here and there whisperings inquired of each other when the show would be over and they could go home; home to safety, warmth and comfort in the tangible things; to see the old homestead still there, still unaltered, still just as it was yesterday and would be tomorrow... and would be tomorrow...

It seemed to me the county commissioners were introduced and then a choir sang the "Star Spangled Banner" and some Russian song, probably their anthem, and then everyone started moving slowly, vacantly away.

8

The boy in the leather jacket blocked out all the rest of what was said, done and sung, and I found myself alone with myself when I did not want to be alone with myself—there in a crowd at Point Park.

And it was that way shuffling away and then waiting my turn for the bus. Even standing on the bus with chatter in my ears, the boy was still there—flexing his hands and screaming at me—and I hated him, as I hate him now, because he makes me think, and I do not want to think. It was that way when I got off the bus along Washington Road and half ran up the road leading away from the highway.

He only left me momentarily when I reached the top of the hill and looked down to see that the house was still there, exactly as I had left it, safe and secure and real and all mine.

All mine.

2

My name is David Q. Little. The "Q" stands for Quincy, after my Grandfather Little, a carpenter who came to Baltimore from England in 1884. I can think of no particular reason why I started this, shall I call it, Journal? I know of no secret passions or hidden ambitions or shining motives that would cause me to do this. I can think of nothing splendid or noble about it, except that for reasons not known to me, sitting here in my basement fall-out-shelter-now-turned-den with a ledger book in front of me and a ballpoint pen gives me an ease of self I have never known.

The idea struck me some months ago right after the ultimatum.

We had tried to have a normal weekend, but between the headlines and all the special statements and bulletins that kept blaring at us, we all were pretty upset, especially Nancy. But that is not unusual for women. They cry when the washer is broken or when we are on the verge of war with about the same degree of hysteria. Playing golf as usual that Saturday had not helped matters. And Sunday I scorched Nancy's best pan when I left the barbecue sauce on too long. Then I tried to settle the children—they were cutting up around the grill—and I had to face more tears for "denying them their few remaining months of happiness." All in all it was a bad weekend, and after everyone had gone to bed with their headaches and upset stomachs I sat out back alone in the cool June-night air.

I do not believe I ever really listened to the quiet before. Most of the lights on the block were out, except one or two dimmed kitchen lamps where people, like me, were still in their yards. Occasionally with the breeze came soft but earnest murmurs from the hedges down the line—once, I thought, a sobbing sigh. People scrambling with their emotions to meet the no longer certain future; people talking themselves in circles, as if back yard discussions offered up in a churchlike atmosphere would somehow banish the crisis; people afraid.

But I was listening to the quiet, intrigued with the thought that even in times of crises a person can make a discovery, can learn something new. Or was it that crises generate discoveries? For it was I alone in the night and there might just as well not have been a single person within a million miles. Somehow, in my muddled fatigue, I had, after many, many years, once again come face to face with myself. And I found it pleasant to drift with the tides of my thoughts, to move with them, rather than to make them move with me.

Instead of the prospects of a nuclear war, I was thinking of what a change it was to be alone with no other purpose in mind except to be alone; to trace patterns in the stars, patterns of my own invention and not another's; to count lightning bugs; to contemplate the neighbors' cat; to ponder the materials flow intricacies in the growth of a new leaf.

For a moment I felt guilty that I should know such ease of mind. Instinctively I looked around unobtrusively to be certain that I was not being monitored by some unseen social force that might frown upon me. For a person, I learned long ago, never actually admits right out loud that sometimes he likes to be alone. A working buddy of mine dropped this thought casually at lunch one day—the kick he got out of occasionally being alone. I was about to agree when a flicker of puzzlement crossed our boss's eyes, and I remained discreetly neutral. It was a good decision, for afterward the boss mused half to me and half to himself that he hoped "Hank wasn't doin' a lot of drinking and running around, too ..."

I tried this being-alone stuff a few times in the early years of our marriage. But Nancy had been hurt because I was obviously escaping from her, and I felt badly that I had let self-centeredness get the best of me. The psychology and the sociology professors at school used to warn us about the dangers of wanting to be alone, a grave symptom of chronic escapism and an unwillingness to participate in society. But with our doom supposedly only a matter of months away, it did not seem to matter now whether I was antisocial or not.

The tide eddied on. Often I have thoughts that do not seem to fit anywhere. Either these thoughts are too self-centered, too opinionated, too biased, too presumptuous, too self-effacing, too revealing, too immoral, or too controversial. You do not discuss them at the office or at home or at parties or in letters or, above all, with customers or other influential people. And this certainly is as it should be. But still, a person gets these thoughts from time to time.

This is why people keep diaries, I suppose, and the thought on that June night amused me. A rather zany idea but why not? Here I could express fear, joy, doubt, confidence. I could boast or complain—tell lies if I like—do whatever comes to mind mentally with no one the wiser. The idea gave me a sense of daring, of adventure, of creating something selfishly mine for no other reason than that it would be all mine and no one else's. A rakish, immoral act to lift me out of a rut, like playing the horses or keeping an exotic, all-knowing woman on the side.

I went to bed relaxed and slept soundly all night.

By noon the following Monday the whole idea seemed a madman's dream. Too much new and completely unreal was happening each day. The atrocities in Mexico, the military call-up, rationing, allocations, labor drafts, that mess with the fallout shelters— and trying to keep the family, company brass and customers calm —kept me numb at first and, later, when it really looked as if we would try to fight, scared like I have never been scared before.

The straw broke when they began evacuating the children in August. Poor Nancy was nearly out of it by then. But my job kept me from being called up, and they put Nancy to work in the BWP,[3] which they expanded to keep profiteering down as much as possible. That helped keep her mind off of things. She even joined a citizens' group[4] late in September, an outlet that, I am convinced, enabled her to keep going.

October was real bad. By this time all of us had learned that the children were having a pretty tough time—heavy rains; food shortages; illnesses, flu mostly; living in tents. Letters back and forth were almost impossible. And it was apparent that Russia was serious about us recognizing Del Mingo,[5] yet Washington continued to refuse. Neither Nancy nor I slept much.

---

3   Bureau of Wages and Prices, Department of Commerce. Created a few years earlier under the Federal Fair Wages and Prices Act in the United States to approve wage and price increases and/or decreases in the basic industries of the times—drug, motor vehicles, steel, etc., "consistent with productivity norms of such industry weighed against standards based on gross income, gross national product and dollar valuations…"

4   Probably Mr. Little was referring to one of the popular groups that sprang up in the United States during this period to press for a peaceful settlement of issues in order to avoid the consequences of nuclear war.

5   Francisco Del Mingo was leader of the Mexican Reform Revolution and provisional head of the People's Democracy of Mexico. The Soviet Union had demanded in a six-month ultimatum that the United States officially recognize the new government or the USSR would consider this an act of aggression and would act to defend itself and "other peace-loving peoples democracies around the world through the use of every kind of weapon necessary to assure victory in the shortest possible time." It was a creditable ultimatum. Ample scientific evidence exists to indicate that at this particular point in the 20th Century the USSR had gained a clear superiority over the United States and the West in the development and deployment of highly sophisticated strategic nuclear weapons. This was done secretly under the very noses of the West in clear violation of a number of treaty agreements between the USSR, USA and other nations, i.e. treaties prohibiting: (1) the testing of nuclear devices; (2) the deployment of nuclear space weapons, including a ban on orbital nuclear bombs, and (3) the proliferation of nuclear weapons. Specifically the USSR had secretly developed: (1) a comprehensive civilian nuclear bomb shelter program; (2) anti-ballistic missiles which had been deployed widely to protect her military and industrial centers from virtually any type of nuclear ballistic mis-

Thanksgiving was "Pray for Peace Day." I don't recall that we prayed, but we certainly got drunk. DD-Day[6] was less than a month off, and there were no turkeys to be had anywhere, even if we would have wanted them. We ate baked beans. It was a neighborhood get-together, just the adults, of course. The party got a little out of hand.

We also celebrated on December 13, barely three weeks ago, but it was for a different reason. The Russian Premier was the first to crack under the strain and offered real concessions to the World Order of Nations. Then you should have seen Nancy tie into things. We all did. Washington never got so many telegrams. We worked around the clock for two days doing nothing but phoning people to wire the White House and the Congress. On December 15, the summit conference was held, and the Treaty of Friendship was signed just two days before Christmas.

How they ever got the children back between the thirteenth and Christmas—in fact, how they ever resolved the whole terrible event before Christmas—we will never know. But they did, bless them. And what a Christmas it was.

They did not have time to get the lights up downtown, except for makeshift decorations in Hoffman's, Barnes', Gay's and some of the smaller stores. And there was not much to choose from. Merchandise was in short supply, but thanks to the BWP prices were kept under control. Crowds were enormous and never let up. Stores stayed open around the clock, and most people were reasonably good-natured,

---

sile; (3) 100- megaton nuclear warheads capable of inconceivable destruction; (4) a vast array of fully deployed earth-to-earth nuclear missiles that were either mobile, underseas or fixed types; (5) orbital space vehicles which on signal from earth were capable of firing clusters of nuclear bombs at different targets. At the time of the Mexican Ultimatum the USSR announced that twelve such orbital vehicles already were in orbit.

6   Newspapers used this expression in referring to the December 20 "destruction deadline" set by the USSR; the day on which she, presumably, would have exploded nuclear devices over 24 United States cities. Fairly reliable records indicate that during the period she had a nuclear superiority of about 20,000 megatons capable of rapid delivery, compared with the U.S.A.'s rapid delivery nuclear capability then of only 2000 megatons—down from a previous high some years earlier of about 53,000 megatons.

all things considered. Our whole family fanned out, each assigned to find two gifts for the others. With five of us on the loose we made out very well. The Christmas morning we had lost hope of ever seeing turned out to be, as the papers put it, "the greatest Christmas of all time….Peace comes to the world at a time when we celebrate the birth of the Prince of Peace!" I do not expect we will ever see the likes of it again.

I was able to get Nancy a white blouse in her size, soiled from the counter beating it took but with washing as good as new.

Found some blankets, too, to replace the ones the children had to take away with them. I located some ice skates for David, used but in excellent condition. Two pounds of assorted chocolates was the best find of all.

Nancy came home with a jewel box for Peggy—wood, oriental design—a watercolor kit for Ann and flannel nightgowns for both, along with socks for David and me.

The children found a light-green shirt in my size, except the sleeves were a little long, which Nancy fixed, and three new golf balls and six used ones and a pretty head scarf for Mom.

Nancy fixed a huge meatloaf and baked some bread and a small cake. We had unlimited powdered milk rations, too. It was our first real feast since June.

Most impressive of all were the churches, jammed and overflowing, so much so that the regulars were almost pushed out. We had six services, as did many others. It was inspiring. A lot of us cried without shame as we offered up our thanks for knowing the joy and security of a permanent peace and for being united with our children once again.

With all of this happening it is no wonder that the idea of jotting down some of my thoughts from time to time was completely lost, until this New Year's Day at Point Park. Since then the idea has grown stronger. I am bothered about something, and I do not know what it is. There is really no one I can talk to about this uneasiness. Someone might misunderstand, and I could end up being tagged an extremist, and I cannot risk that. I should be on top of the world.

14

Everyone else seems so sure and confident of the future. Why am I the only one? Or *am* I the only one? They say "writing things out" sometimes helps a person see where he is going, like taking inventory. So I bought a big, thick ledger, and I am going to try it.

My key problem, of course, is to be sure no one reads this. Even thinking of such a possibility would ruin the whole purpose, for I would immediately be on guard and would write only those things which I think other people would understand and approve of. We have already been told at the office that while no major changes are expected it would, nonetheless, be wise to keep to our own affairs and not get involved in any questionable activities.

I have fixed up the shelter so that it is quite comfortable. The folding picnic table makes a nice desk, and I can keep my things in the old footlocker. I have kept one of the cots up, covered with an old duster that is still plenty good. A couple of knickknacks also add a lot. I feel like a twelve-year-old working on his first tree house.

Nancy did not react quite the way I expected. She did not seem really to care when I told her I wanted to convert our four-thousand-dollar white elephant into a little den—when I think of that second mortgage I could slug that crooked contractor. Do what you want, she said, and do it I did.

The only time Nancy is ever suspicious of anything is when she thinks someone is hiding something from her, and then her imagination runs wild. I learned that the hard way and this time went the opposite direction. I told her I was going to write about my observations on life and that I hoped she would read my creations.

She merely shrugged.

So now I need not worry about Nancy. And the children are too busy at play and catching up in school to be curious. The footlocker, inside under my old yearbooks, is a good storage place for the ledger.

There has been a change in Nancy that is difficult to trace. She wants to keep on at the BWP, even though she now is eligible for release. The work pays very little, "an emergency patriotic service" job classification.

"I want to feel useful," is her reason. When I mention we all need her here at home, she points out that, after all, the children and I are away during the day and she does not, apparently, want to be left alone.

She has lost weight, which has not hurt her. In fact, she looks prettier than I have seen her in some time but in a melancholy way, unlike her. She has always been somewhat strong-willed and likes to be fussed over. She has always been a good mixer, who likes to be well-dressed, a source of more than one argument between us. You cannot have a new home, a new car and a new wardrobe all at once—not on my salary and with the inflation, taxes, shortages and high prices. Probably it is wise that she keep working.

3

I think I am a reasonably nice guy who likes nice people. I like simple things. I like to mind my own business, and I like people who like to mind their own business. This sounds smug cut out like this in words.

It is strange seeing yourself on paper. In front of the pen there is nothing but blank space with no guideposts to tell you where to go, what to do, what to say. An eerie feeling because of the uncertainty of the nothingness ahead. Yet, the pen moves with a will of its own to leave footprints of thought which begin to uncover an image that is barely recognizable. It is not because this self-image conflicts with anything I know of myself, but because I have never paused long enough to draw out of myself that which I really am.

What makes a man what he is? Why am I what I am? Indeed, what am I? A steel salesman, thirty-nine years old. I am as successful as I want to be. My salary, all things considered, is adequate for our needs, though we could always use more. I have a good wife and three fine children—two daughters, sixteen and six, and a son, fourteen. We live in a three-bedroom split-level in a fairly new subdivision, Southern Estates, twenty-one miles south of Pittsburgh. The house could be larger, but it is comfortable enough, although Peggy complains about having Annie in the same room. Her emerging vanity no longer tolerates the bunk beds, even though she sleeps on the bottom one now that Ann is old enough.

My territory is the tri-state area, upper West Virginia, eastern Ohio and western Pennsylvania. I am luckier than most salesmen in that I am home most evenings. I am active in scouting and teach a Sunday-school class. I can break a hundred in golf and enjoy fishing. We have a little twelve-foot fiberglass outboard, fine for Youghiogheny or Deep Creek. We stay off the rivers. I am not good at hunting and so do not do much. I like baseball but dislike pro-football. Nancy and I bowl on a neighborhood team. My average used to be 168 but it is down to 127 now. We socialize mostly in the neighborhood—bridge parties, cook-outs and the like.

Occasionally we entertain customers, which gives Nancy a chance to get out to the boss's country club or to the Royal Room downtown, something she fusses about days beforehand. Nancy belongs to an afternoon bridge club and is active in the PTA and Women of the Church. We are both moderate drinkers, although we perhaps do more than we used to.

That covers what I am. It can be simply listed in a few lines. But to explain, even to myself, why I am what I am is a different matter.

How do I explain that Nancy is the pusher, or would be the pusher if I would let her? Probably I could be a district manager by now had I dug in a little more, accepted a transfer or two, and got to know more of the right people. In this I suppose I have been a disappointment. I sense this, rather than know it, for Nancy says very little, to me at least.

Occasionally over a hand of bridge she will make a casual reference, such as "at the club the other night" or "chateaubriand for two at the Royal Room," and then sigh, "I'm so glad David's boss takes pity on us and gives us a night on the town every now and then. ... Maybe someday David's ship will come in. One heart..."

Always there is the little this-is-among-friends laugh, but always it carries a telltale high pitch that betrays a wistful longing for a prestige and natural elegance we do not have.

It is the same when she says "David." Until I started dating her in college I was always "Dave." I wanted to call her "Nan." She would not hear of it, and before very long it was "David" and "Nancy." It has been that way ever since. Even Mother calls me "David" now. My brother, Harry, does not. It is still "Dave." His brashness and candor irritate Nancy and sometimes even me. But they have served him well. He flies his own plane and does not need to rely on a boss for country club outings. He is four years younger than I and already is vice president of a small electronics firm he helped start from nothing. I think he spends all of his life at the place. Yet for all her snorting about Harry, Nancy still speaks well of him in front of others.

He reminds me of Dad and will probably end up as he did—dead of a heart attack at forty-two. Usually the elder son follows in the footsteps. But I was too close to the struggle to become a "chip off the old block."

My father was a grocer. We lived in Cleveland out off West 117th Street. Our first store was a remodeled yellow house. We lived upstairs, and about all I remember were early breakfasts, disorganized lunches and late suppers around an oilcloth kitchen table. Someone always came into the store during mealtime, and Dad would slip from his chair, clump down the stairs and slice off a few pieces of lunchmeat or grind some roundsteak and then climb back to a cold plate. We always waited dessert for him, usually an orange or apple, or, if business was good, ice cream, nuts and syrup. We were open Sundays between one and four—except when people banged on the door either before we were open or after we were closed, and then Dad would clump down the stairs, still struggling into his "store" jacket. Saturdays we were open from nine to nine. After that there were the receipts, books and bank deposits to make out. The house always seemed too warm, too close, too cluttered with bits of paper, handbills, posters and coupons. I was always glad to get outdoors and play in the park.

By the time I was seven I was helping Mother and Dad with chores—sweeping, stocking shelves and making deliveries at twenty-five cents an hour, fifteen cents of which went into the bank. A

18

year later I began taking turns with Dad, leaving my supper to "see who is there."

"Call if you need help, son." For a while I did, until I learned how to run the slicer and grinder. My pay was boosted to thirty-five cents.

I was nearly ten when Dad moved farther south to open a fine new brick store. He had saved his "two-thirds," as he always called it, and the bank cheerfully supplied the rest along with a sound, manageable mortgage. Save your money, he would say. Build solid, work hard and make sound investments and "don't go against the banks and try to live beyond your means."

That was a favorite sermon of his. Don't go against the banks. Dad had a reverence for money. Not in the sense of the ill-getting and ill-use of it but in the sense of making every penny count to the maximum for himself—his "legacy of the future." He talked of it often. How Grandfather Quincy came as an infant to Cleveland, brought from England by his father who became a Great Lakes seaman. How Grandfather Quincy became a carpenter, "a very good carpenter." How the whole family saved and Grandfather Quincy built a house, "all by himself, on our property. In England we did not have property." How Grandfather Quincy went on to become manager of "the lumber yard" (I never knew which one).

How Grandfather Quincy saved for his wedding, saved for his own house, saved for his family, saved for his future and owed "not a man anywhere." How my grandfather, Quincy, died under an ill-stacked pile of lumber, toppled by the thundering vibrations of a nearby speeding freight train. How Grandfather Quincy's legacy had provided the means for a family of six to live—with all hands working—and with enough left over to launch Dad into the grocery business at the age of nineteen.

"Your grandfather, Quincy, always said, 'Oak is hard to work but it stands solid against nature, while easy pine is soft and splinters with every blow. A thrifty man chooses the oak.'"

This, along with fried chicken, was a steady Sunday diet, and Grandfather Quincy, in his grave long before I was born, became my patron saint of virtue. He went proudly with me to the savings bank each week. He cheered me on while I sorted rotting potatoes on stifling August Saturdays. He scowled whenever I splurged on a date and fidgeted every time I passed Morrison's Men's Store, Inc. And in college he nearly had me expelled from Economics 201. Puzzled by a comprehensive explanation of booms and busts and the value of expanded credit, I brought up the question of oak. Against the background of snickers and outright laughter, I learned quickly:

1. That the United States has changed since the nineteenth century from a backward agrarian nation at the mercy of the elements and unenlightened people to a major world power with grave and far-reaching obligations—in case I didn't know it.

2. That probably Grandfather Quincy could have lived much more easily had we had economic enlightenment in his time—in case I didn't know it.

3. That probably Grandfather Quincy did more harm than good by not circulating his earnings more freely to provide a broader base for jobs to increase national wealth, and so contributed, as did all of his contemporaries, to the boom-bust cycles that have plagued us since the beginning of the Industrial Revolution—in case I didn't know it.

4. That all of us were living in a new era, and we cannot afford the luxury of thinking as our grandfathers did—in case I didn't know it.

Even though I buried Grandfather immediately after class, it was too late to avoid the repercussions. A girl in class broke a date. I was dubbed the "Economic Wizard of Alpha Beta Alpha" by song at dinner that night and later received a casual visit from the chairman of the ABA Scholarship Committee, and then was given a few extra pledge duties by our trainer the next day. Six weeks later I redeemed myself nicely by preparing a theme paper on "The Myth of Thrift," which on request I read aloud in class. I pulled a "B" in the course.

During my senior year, Dad collapsed while shifting empties in the storeroom and was dead when the firemen got there. It hit Mother hardest, although Harry was very close to Dad, closer than I was, which I do not like to admit to anyone, not even myself. I have

20

often felt that if Dad had been a little less narrow in his thinking, a little more available to his family and a little less hard on all of us, things might have gone better.

Our differences came to a head when I was fifteen. Supermarkets were springing up everywhere and the independents found it increasingly more difficult to stay in business. Dad recognized that self-service markets based on huge volume were the answer to higher costs. He decided to remodel and expand the store, but he insisted on saving his "two-thirds" so as not to "overextend." Mother argued with him. My uncles argued. His friends argued. But it was a matter of principle, I suppose. He did it his way, although it took three years longer of extra effort, three years longer of "making do." They were my last three years of high school. I missed the Washington, D. C., tour—busy in the summer. I missed the football squad—busy Friday nights in the fall. I missed a senior play part—busy nights with construction details.

Not that I ever begrudged working for Dad or did not feel genuine affection for him. But if there is an easier way, why deliberately take the hard way? At least, Dad was able to pay most of my way through school, and there was enough left for Mother to live on comfortably. For this I am grateful, of course. But I cannot shake the feeling that had Dad not pushed quite so hard and so unnecessarily we could have had more leisure with him, more time for self-development, and he probably would be alive today—this in spite of the doctor's feeling that work in itself did not greatly affect the final events.

I resolved long ago that the welfare of the family must come first and that I owe it to my wife and children not to push them out of my life; that I should hold a good, solid job; do my work well and yet keep my perspective. Nancy does not fully understand this, but she did not spend twelve years of her youth behind a counter, either.

4

Other things likewise shaped my outlook. Don't meddle where you don't need to. Good intentions and noble causes are idealistically fine.

But as a practical matter, beware of controversy and beware of the friends you try to "help." I learned that one at the age of eight in the dim halls of Bluff School.

The rain had stopped by the time school had let out, and I was halfway home and partially through a standing mud puddle when I remembered my rubbers, still in the school locker. Of course, I returned to get them with a sense of reprieve, a move which properly done could chew up better than a full half-hour—that much less store duty at home.

It was fine adventure. I had just escaped on foot from the Indian camp. I could not risk stealing back my horse. My books, of course, were important Army dispatches that had to get through to the yellow brick fort in the distance. Problems were many, but I had come through before. I was forced to move back up the path along the ravine so that I would leave no footprints. Neither could I risk any movement that might alert the dozen or so war parties riding hardby. It was slow going. Leaping, crouching, creeping from one pebbled surface to another, checking with considerable suspense to see if my last step had left a print. Once disaster nearly took me when I dropped one of the dispatches, but fortunately it landed in the soggy weeds and after a bit I found it still mostly readable. I reached the edge of the clearing, which earlier in the day might have been confused with a school play-yard. I had been discovered, and a blizzard of arrows was unleashed. No choice but to keep my body low and run for it. I made it through the great double doors in the nick of time and was on my way to the general's quarters when I heard the voices around the corner.

They came from in front of Miss Lee's room midway down the junior high corridor, which intersected the elementary section. Except for that room, the lights were out, and I paused in the shadows to worship Miss Lee from afar as she stood talking with three boys. For Miss Lee was my absolute favorite. She was the most beautiful lady that ever was. She came to our room every Thursday for a whole period to show us how to draw pictures. She always smiled at me, and once she even squeezed my hand, because I did such neat work.

Her hand was cool and clean and soft, and I thought about it before I went to sleep that night. Miss Lee always smiled and laughed and said nice things. Everybody liked her, but I liked her best. She was special. Ideal for an Indian fighter.

"I really must get on with my work." Her voice seemed especially cheerful. "Perhaps tomorrow…"

"Come on, teach, we wanna learn art." The boy's voice was deep, smooth and chillily confident. One hand rested lightly on the knob of the open door, while he pleaded with the other. Two other boys flanked their taller spokesman. The young woman, small and lithe, stood against the doorjamb clutching a black grade book— hugging it.

I knew them by reputation only. The bigger one was Red Alberts, known behind his back as Flunky. He had failed sixth grade but somehow had managed to make the ninth grade without further setbacks. The other two, likewise ninth, were his devoted companions. Most everyone feared them, especially those of us in elementary. I knew little about them except that you stayed away from them. Once I dreamed Red chased me behind the school, and I woke the entire household.

"Yeh. An' I'll bet you're a good teacher," a more adolescent voice added bravely.

"At least let us look at some of your pictures," Flunky smirked. He planted his palm on the doorjamb near her shoulder and leaned into her face.

"Yeh. You got a book in there I hear has n…"

"Tomorrow, boys. I really must…"

"Why not now?" Flunky shifted his body slightly. All wore bright sweaters and T-shirts. "Ain't many teachers we'd stay after school for."

His hand grabbed her shoulder and lie pulled her to him, grinning at his companions. She twisted away clutching harder at her book.

"Come on… baby . .

"Stop! Please! I'll call Mr. Thomas. I'll . .

"That old wart. My old man'd fix him real good. Besides, he's gone."

"Yeh. We watched."

The boys giggled softly.

"I'll scream. So help me I'll scream, and the coach and janitor will…"

"You bitch." Flunky suddenly straightened and stared hard at the grade book. "I've seen better 'an you down on Poplar Street."

And then he struck her, sharply, viciously, his fist against her upper arm.

"You no good whore. Come on, guys, let's go over to Gert's."

And before Miss Lee could cry out or move, the trio swaggered into the dimness, hard heels ringing in unison, while brash voices echoed and echoed again in the empty school until the clanging of metal doors brought complete stillness.

I had not moved. Afraid and completely bewildered, I had held my breath. With a low sob Miss Lee lurched back into the room and I ran after her, tears beginning to blind me.

She was at her desk staring silently out the window, hands still clutching the book, knuckles white. She seemed glad, relieved, angry and disturbed, all at once, seeing me at her side—a smeared, wet trembling face gaping into her own. For a second I think we both cried, then smiled and finally laughed. Yes, she was all right and those boys hadn't hurt her and no it wasn't nice at all and she knew I'd never be that rude and surely Mother must be terribly worried and hadn't I better scoot on home.

A monumental hug and a cool, soft hand flicking the hair out of my eyes finally sent me back down the path, both elated at my good fortune and deeply troubled at what caused it. I was an hour late getting home, and my rubbers were still at school.

The full meaning of what had been said and done, of course, was beyond my scope. Even so, I must have felt the full naked obscenity. For a nameless guilt of seeing and sensing more than I should have—not unlike peeking in someone's medicine chest and then wishing you had not—had left me feeling unwashed, even though I scrubbed my face and hands twice before dinner. Instinctively, without knowing why, I related only the bare essentials of the incident at home, and this only after the most insistent prodding. Three big ninth-graders had been mean to Miss Lee and even hit her right on the arm, and they ran away, and Miss Lee cried, and I helped her, and she thanked me and sent me home.

Mother was upset, and Dad was proud. "Doubtless, Mr. Thomas will take care of things and, of course, Davey, you must be very careful to tell the absolute truth, just the way you saw it, understand? Now don't invent things, but stick to the truth. Be fair and honest. ..." Dad was pacing the kitchen like a coach in a locker room at half-time... "Just remember that, when Mr. Thomas sends for you. Mother, be sure Davey wears a white shirt and his good, blue coat-sweater tomorrow. He'll probably send for you first thing. Better get to bed in good time, son. Now don't worry a bit. Mr. Thomas knows how to handle these things. It's a mighty good thing for Miss Lee you were there to see it."

Twice during the night I awoke with a cry. Flunky was after me, and Miss Lee was standing on top of her desk screaming. Mother put a cold washcloth on my forehead, and I finally slept.

Mr. Thomas did not come to the classroom door. No one came to interrupt Miss Kynal to tell her Davey Little was wanted immediately in the office on important business. The lessons droned on uninterrupted—dull, unimportant lessons. Maybe Mr. Thomas couldn't find me. Maybe Miss Lee forgot which was my room. Or—maybe they were waiting for me? Recess. I would go and see at recess.

The few times I had been sent to the Great Office to pick up or deliver various class messages always had been very important events for me. But this time I could hardly breathe as I pushed cautiously through the glass door and asked if Mr. Thomas wanted to see me. The square and greying lady steeped in filing looked up, nodded and waddled to the corner office.

"That boy you wanted is here."

"What boy?" a muffled voice asked.

"What's your name, boy?" the woman called.

"David Little."

"David Little."

"Oh, am I supposed to see him?"

"Is Mr. Thomas supposed to see you, boy?"

Whatever it was I stammered in reply apparently was good enough, for in another minute Mr. Thomas was saying, "Oh never mind, Miss Beale, just have him come in..."

I had never been in the principal's office, and it was even more grand than I thought anything could be. Seeing Mr. Thomas up close—his creamy white cuffs and collar, his rimless glasses and thick gold fountain pen—momentarily blanked out the purpose of my mission. We must have sparred verbally for several minutes, each under the impression that the other one had called the meeting. Somewhere in the confused exchange of words came, "Miss Lee... hard with the fist on the arm... Flunky, I mean Red Alters, I mean Alberts... and Dad said...." Mr. Thomas lowered his voice and then listened, finally removing his glasses to polish them slowly as he summoned Miss Lee.

She did not smile when she saw me. Neither did she say hello. She only frowned and half opened her lips as though she would say something if only she knew what to say.

"Could you tell me please what went on here yesterday afternoon?" Mr. Thomas did not get up but nodded her into a wooden armchair. "David said some boys ... hit you with fists?" His voice rose in an incredulous question.

"I..." Miss Lee looked searchingly at me for what seemed a long time. "More or less. It was just a minor incident. Nothing... nothing. Not really."

Mr. Thomas sighed, a long and tired one. He removed his glasses, inspecting them for dust.

"Who were they?"

"Helmet Alberts, Malcomb Winter and Russell Jones," she said softly.

"I might have known."

The summons went out, and I wanted to run.

They were neat in their bright sweaters... and polite little boys. The inquisition was on, Judge Thomas presiding with fatherly concern, while Miss Lee, looking first at the trio and then at the Judge, fumbled for the right words which added together said, "It was nothing, nothing at all." The trio nodded in unison, explaining—as little boys explain soaping windows on Halloween—that they were merely "horsing around in the halls," and Miss Lee had come out to quiet them, and someone had pushed Red, I mean Helmet, and Helmet, well, he did bump Miss Lee, but he didn't know he'd hurt her. Did you, Red?

"Naw. No. No, I'm awfully sorry, Miss Lee." But Flunky was looking at me.

Tell them. Tell them. Tell them now. Now is the time to tell them. Tell them.

"Is that about right, Miss Lee?" the Judge said, about to close the case.

"That's… about… right, Mr. Thomas." It was the only time she bit her lip. But she looked him straight in the eye.

The trio was found innocent of wrongdoing, save for loitering in the halls after school—you know the rules, boys—and released.

Then Mr. Thomas turned to me, and Miss Lee closed her eyes. He was polishing his glasses again.

"Now, David, we know you meant well, and sometimes little boys imagine more than they see, eh, lad? Now, I think you'd better get back to your room. And—ah—we know you were only trying to be helpful and—ah—that's fine but—ah—may I suggest that—ah—in the future you—shall we say—do a little less helping, eh, lad?"

The laugh and the pat on the head were of an understanding, patient father.

I had long since lost my power of speech.

She looked at me then and spoke her only words to me; low, sad, reproachful words, that left me staring back at her, simply because I could think of nothing else to do.

"Oh, David… how could you…"

"Now then, Miss Lee, before you leave, perhaps we had better discuss this unhappy situation. Now, Miss Lee, you know my policy about teachers who are unable to handle their own problems. And while I sympathize with your personal situation with your mother's illness and all, still I must ask myself the question that if you can't

27

handle discipline problems how on earth can you continue to teach here... ?

"David. You...may...go...now." Mr. Thomas had lost his fatherly decorum.

I was kept 25 minutes after classes to make up time lost, so the path behind the school was deserted, the others having long since gone home. Except three boys, sauntering casually toward me across the weeds.

Three boys—fifteen, fifteen and sixteen. Three boys who put their arms around me and squeezed my shoulders until the tears came. Three boys who patted me on the back, on the chest, on the arms with brotherly fists. Three polite boys who taught me a new game, "out of the circle," who joined hands and danced around me, bouncing me back and forth like a volleyball. Three comrades who picked me up by the heels and swung me wide. Three human beings who had me walk the edge of the mud-caked bluff along the ravine; who watched gleefully as the turf gave way, and I tumbled end-over-end, sliding, rolling, scraping down the steep side, over rocks and brush to the creek below.

One eight-year-old who limped home to a warm bath and bed and who was chided gently for playing too near the cliff. "It was bound to happen to him sometime, Mother."

One eight-year-old who never again enjoyed art on Thursdays and one art teacher who never again enjoyed teaching it.

One eight-year-old who learned not to meddle where you do not need to.

5

It has been a very long time since I have thought of these incidents—the store, Dad, Grandfather Quincy, Miss Lee. That I recall them so clearly now without effort is a surprise, though not a very agreeable one. That I should recall them at all, much less put them down, is even more surprising. And it has the effect of pulling a loose thread. The more you pull, the more there is.

Geometry class, for instance. There is very little I remember except a vague picture of cluttered blackboards, a room always stuffy, and that I usually was asked to clean the erasers. I would take them out one of the back doors and pound them against the brick. The dry chalk dust always choked me, and my hands were gritty and dry the rest of the day. Mr. Hall was younger than other teachers, with dark wavy hair, and both boys and girls thought him the answer to perfect manhood—a perfect balance between physical attractiveness and all-knowing wisdom. The boys tried to emulate him, and the girls plotted to lure him with their studied sophisticated ways. Even the other teachers seemed to like and respect Mr. Hall, particularly Miss Berg in speech and Miss Lamb in home economics.

Mr. Hall could do no wrong.

Geometry was a problem for me right from the start. I was confused with the infinite maze of it and yet awed that men somewhere out of the past had discovered it. I was particularly struck with Pi. The thought that a man had actually concocted it—that he did not get it out of a book like I did but took it out of nothing and actually created it—made a deep impression on me. Lying in bed nights I used to try to imagine who he was and why he did what he did. Why 3.1416? Why not 3.6114 or 6.1413? Why that particular number? Who had told him? Or if no one told him, where did he get it? Was a teacher like Mr. Hall writing some numbers on a blackboard one day and in a brilliant flash did he suddenly calculate the area of a circle while the class looked on in disbelief at this great genius? Or maybe he was a grocer's son and noted math student. Maybe one day he went casually to the blackboard while the teacher stood humbly aside as the handsome young man quickly demonstrated a new theory that had come to him in the night, while the class looked on in disbelief at this great genius.

Dad always said never to be afraid to ask. Remember, teachers know the answers. That's why they teach. And nothing pleases them so much as the student who wants to learn, Dad had said.

I resolved to ask Mr. Hall about the origin of Pi. I mapped out the whole scene before I fell asleep. Mr. Hall pleased, his head nodding with increased pleasure and understanding as I unfold my searching question. Mr. Hall wise and handsome, as he commends me for my scholarly interest and then begins to unfold the Historic Discovery. Mr. Hall clasping my shoulder after class to ask if I had considered studying advanced mathematics under his personal supervision— while boys and girls alike hover in admiration as the great master and his budding young student hold their First Great Meeting. Goose bumps, as I thought of Gwendolyn Price asking if she might walk back to my locker with me. I should be the talk of the school!

Mr. Hall, it turned out, indeed did smile and nod when I started to ask the question. But the smile faded before I was finished, a frown replacing it. It was terribly still, and I wanted to sit down. He kept tossing the chalk in his hand and then to my relief smiled again.

"Davey, do you know what makes electricity flow through a wire?"

"No, sir."

The smile broadened, and the girl next to me sighed. "Have you ever seen electricity flow between a switch and a lamp?"

"No, sir."

"Yet, you turn on the lamp when you need it."

"Yes, sir."

"Why?" The smile pivoted slowly around the room.

"Why?"

"Why."

I had not expected this approach and no longer felt like the bright young student. I felt awkward, aware of the leather elbow patches on my sweater. "Because a lamp gives light."

"Excellent deduction, Davey. A lamp gives light because of the flow of electrons, which no one can see. Yet, we know electricity is there because it works. Science never has learned precisely why electricity works but it does work even though we're not exactly sure why. Now doesn't this tell you something?"

"No, sir. I mean, yes, sir. That is, I don't know, sir. I mean, does Pi... Wh ..." I stopped in utter confusion.

"The important thing for you to know, young man, is how Pi works. The why is unimportant. It is a number. It is to be memorized and used in formulas, likewise to be memorized. And your work performance tells me you need to do more memorizing and less speculating. Math is a precise subject, and it demands precise thinking."

"I know, sir. I was just wondering why it is 3.1416 and not something else?" I wiped my hands on my trousers.

"Davey." The smile was gone, replaced by scholarly sincerity. "We'd all like to know more about the why of things... why a bird flies and we don't, why a flower grows or why our football team loses when it should be winning."

A ripple of amusement, a respectful ripple, swept the room.

"Now, I could take the rest of the period to try to explain why Pi is what it is. But it is very, very complicated, and I doubt very much that you could even begin to understand it." He paused to take in the rapt expression of the class and toss the chalk a few times.

"Davey, if we had to stop to explain all the whys of this world, we'd never get our class work done. 'Theirs not to reason why, theirs but to do and die.' Remember that great quotation? Well, Davey, sometimes we are not privileged to know all the whys. We must fall back on faith in superior minds and take from these great minds the knowledge they give us and use it properly. Pi works, and that's all we need to know. Now, young ladies and gentlemen, let us return to our assignments..."

I made one last try after class. Could I stay after school and that way learn about Pi? Again, the voice of reason patiently explained heavy commitments and obligations—advising the school paper, pep rally plans, the Junior Prom Committee, papers to grade...

I am not sure what made me do it. Perhaps it was because Mr. Hall was shuffling through his papers over and over and over without ever looking up. A feeling of confidence came over me, revealing that somehow I had the upper hand, that I had detected a flaw in Mr. Hall and that he knew that I knew that at least one of his feet might be of clay.

"Mr. Hall." My voice was calm, steady and sure. "You don't know why Pi is 3.1416, do you?"

He rose slowly from his chair, no longer looking handsome, no longer looking wise. His eyes bore into mine with an intensity I can still feel. His voice was quiet and cold with a quality of ruthlessness I have not heard since. I never knew before that words could bite, could cut, could shatter, could bring chilling fear.

"Get this," his voice hissed, "you mention Pi to me, or anyone, ever again and I shall take you by the scruff of your dirty neck right down to the principal's office, and once there I shall proceed to have you expelled from this class as an unruly, undisciplined time-waster, who spends his time disturbing and disrupting my entire teaching schedule ... a boy so insolent, so ill-mannered, so low in his thinking as to be a disgrace to this school."

The words, "principal's office," had done it. The confidence left. They were the magic words, and Mr. Hall recognized them in my face the moment he spoke them. His face hardened even more.

"Pi is 3.1416. Say it."

"Pi is 3.1416."

"I do not need to know why Pi is 3.1416. Say it."

"I do not need to know why Pi is 3.1416."

"Say it again."

"I do not need to know why Pi is 3.1416."

"Again."

All told I repeated it a dozen times, each time with increasing humility, until I was the one who could no longer look at Mr. Hall.

"Now get out of here, you filth."

Never again was I ever so bold. For a long time it affected me, I suppose. Once I overheard Dad talking to Mother about the way I "seemed to resent being asked to help out at the store."

"Surely, he must know why you need him," she had said.

"I don't know. I don't know what's got into that boy. So different from Harry..." He had sounded very tired.

Later, in college, I came to understand Mr. Hall better. I found it easy to memorize and let it go at that. I became quite good at it. I found that professors were flattered when you recited—out loud or on paper—their key phrases. It did not matter what the subject was or who the man was. The reaction was always the same, a shucks-you-shouldn't-have-done-it modesty. It was the same when you called them "Doctor," when, of course, they were not. "Not *quite*." Heh, heh, heh. "But soon now." Heh. Heh. Heh. Except for the horror of Grandfather Quincy, college was much easier than high school, which in turn was a little less difficult than junior high and grade school.

It is easy to tell what I am. It is difficult to describe why. I have learned to get along in this world. I know how to keep my nose clean and stay out of the way, without sacrificing the well-being either of myself or my family. While it is perhaps interesting to speculate as to why I am what I am, it really matters not at all.

So long as it does not conflict with my morals I do my job as I am told to do it and I live my life as I think I should live it, without complications and with faith enough in myself to adjust to any situation. I feel I am skilled at this—better than most.

While there are uncertainties about the future, there is less to feel uncertain about today than there was two months ago. And while we may not get along with the Russians quite as easily as we would like, as some people have been saying, still, it is much better than seeing your family, your home, your whole way of life vanish in a flash.

My family lives, and I live. What can be more precious than this? Certainly there are details to be cleared up and resolved. But they are insignificant when compared to the stark realities of either you live or you die. I have learned to take one thing at a time and not build straw men by thinking too far ahead. Tend to the present and the future will take care of itself. The world has existed for a long, long time, and so long as there are reasonable men, practical men, logical men, we need not be concerned with things.

We are the wealthiest nation on earth. We have a tremendous future, and I plan to do just as I have done in the past. Do my job well, mind my own business and do my best to "cooperate in achieving the adjustments still facing us," to quote the President's State of the Union Address, one of the most stirring speeches I have ever heard. Certainly it will rank with the Gettysburg Address.

Some people—the ill-tempered and dissatisfied, those who want it all their way—some of these doubtless will get hurt.

But I will not, because I understand what needs to be done so that things will stay about the same for me. In fact, with new world markets opening up and full employment almost realized even now—how can I lose?

II

The Second Month

The thing I admire most about Larry Best is his deep sense of understanding. If ever a man has learned to turn the other cheek it is he. Certainly he is among the most brilliant in the city. That he puts up with such shoddy stunts without anger or bitterness makes me all the more conscious of how inadequate I am. I could not do it. I would create such a stir that the authorities would have to track those hoods down and put them behind bars for a hundred years. Yet, Larry remains calm, in spite of what happened to his house. But then, that is Larry, always giving the other fellow the benefit of a doubt.

We have been pals ever since college. He is the only one I have ever bothered to stay in touch with. Of course, he is the only one out of our class here in the area, except Lard Williams, down at Wheeling, who is as much of a loudmouth as he ever was. Larry had called me early the other afternoon for dinner, a long shot that I would be in. And I was, pulled in off the road yet again for yet another meeting on the new operations schedules, regulations and regulations on top of the regulations. He caught me in the middle of a ten-minute break. I had a choice of taking his call or returning any one of six other calls, all from unhappy customers. Talking with Larry is like a breath of fresh air—even-paced, always the same, a solid man, usually with something both practical and sensible to say. This time he made lots of sense.

"Look, old boy, we've both been at it pretty heavily what with those damn seminars and all. Mary's off to Philadelphia to try to retrieve her book. Can you get out for dinner?"

"The one about *Nellie, the Talking Horse*? I though it was already out." I was glad to shake the heavy atmosphere of heavy business. Mary, his wife, writes children's books and had finished that one months before.

"Yes. The publisher somehow lost interest during the latter part of the year. I don't think they were too confident that they would have a market." His humor was so dry that unless you listened carefully it would escape you. I think that is why people always are so attentive when Larry speaks. They do not want to miss anything.

"And when we regained our senses, Babcock lost his and wanted to cancel the agreement. Mary's gone to try to talk them out of it," he added between puffs that revealed difficulty in firing his pipe.

"Won't take no, old boy. Haven't seen you since the holidays. Give Nancy a break. With Mary gone she'd be bored if she came along and probably would like a nice quiet evening after facing all those people at the BWP day in and day out."

As it turned out, Nancy had planned to be home on time and seemed quite pleased. She admires Larry almost as much as I do. Once or twice recently she had commented that, now that Larry was really on his way up, she hoped he would not forget us. She was referring to his appointment as Regional Coordinator for the month-long JCFLA Activation Seminars,[7] begun in mid-January and held at Dome Center. All adults in the area were required to attend two night sessions, seven to eleven, or one day session, eight to

---

7   While data is sketchy, apparently mass meetings were held throughout the United States to explain purposes and functions of the Treaty of Friendship, including its national, state and district committee structures used to carry out its measures. It is not known whether similar meetings were also held in the USSR. See Appendix for excerpts of the Treaty and committee diagrams. While too lengthy for reproduction here, a full copy of the Treaty can be found in Edison Tyler's *Treaties of the Past and Their Roles in Shaping World Events*, Musk and Musk, 2181.

four-thirty. The purpose was to learn details of how the JCFLA will operate here.

We had been among the first to go, the invitation coming from our civil-defense block coordinator who had been asked to remain at his post full time by the JCFLA. Of course, the papers had carried a story about Larry so it was no surprise seeing him on the platform with the others. All the same it was a thrill to watch the elegant way he introduced the meeting. Dome Center was jammed, a breath-taking sight. A giant bowl of faces mixed with flecks of red seat-backs, all hushed as Larry, looking rumpled as he always does, explained the purpose of the seminar with a simplicity and ease that made me truly proud of my old friend. He introduced Smith Armstrong and Nicholas Syerov as if he had known them all of his life. Nancy's eyes were shining. She could not resist the impulse to whisper, "He's our very close friend," to the woman on the other side of her, who either did not hear or understand, because she kept on staring straight ahead without even so much as a nod.

It was a long two nights. One ten-minute intermission was all they allowed, hardly enough time to fight to the refreshment stand and hardly worth the trip either. All you could get was a warm, watery "Fruit Delight," certainly not worth sixty cents each, but at least they were beginning to serve refreshments again.

Both Nancy and I were surprised to learn of the number of bureaus that had been established to help the JCFLA supervise portions of the Treaty. If I recall correctly there are eight. A Bureau of Employment. A Bureau of Education. One for protection. I don't yet understand why they need one for culture, but the man giving that lecture in the seminar referred to Article Five and Article Ten of the Treaty and said something about culture being vital to freedom, especially if we are to keep on boosting the standard of living to meet national and world goals. It was difficult to understand everything he said, he was too close to the mike, and whenever he raised his voice everything got jumbled. Then there is a Bureau of Justice, Health and Welfare, Finance and the Bureau of Property. Why they think they need all of them I do not know. A number of them duplicate the federal functions we already have.[8] Larry explained it nicely saying that, after all, these bureaus are here only as concerns the Treaty—and nothing else. The bureaus therefore cannot conflict with our regular domestic government. In fact, he did an effective job squelching a lot of loose talk about the Treaty.

"There have been some extremists," Larry had said in introducing the seminar, "who are doing a great disservice to the cause of lasting peace by darkly implying that somehow the Treaty of Friendship is going to change the Constitution." He took a slow sip of water and looked calmly about the bowl of people. It was terribly still, and Larry was at his classroom best. "Larry Best is best" had been the campus election slogan years ago, and it was just as true here.

"My fellow citizens, I have been nearly twenty years studying and teaching the role of government. One of the first things we discuss in the classroom out at William Penn is the fact that the Constitution cannot be changed unless either it is amended or a Constitutional convention is held." He paused to rumple his hair, thinning brown.

"Now, have you people heard even a suggestion that someone—some mysterious, unnamed person or persons probably wearing black cloaks—is out to tamper with that beloved instrument of

---

8   In addition to Bureau of Wages and Prices, Department of Commerce: Department of Urban Development—Bureau of Construction (to supervise maintenance of federal standards for all urban monumental, multi-dwelling, highway and street construction); Bureau of Property (to approve all types of home loans, mortgages, building permits, and to acquire and lease "reclaimed" land for private use, in accordance with standards of the Private Property Act); Department of Health, Education and Welfare—Bureau of Health (various medical programs); Bureau of Public Welfare (community funds, various unemployment and assistance programs); Bureau of Studies (supervision of curricula to meet federal standards of all schools, colleges, universities receiving federal grants); Bureau of Educational Facility Plans (construction and/or modernization of schools); Bureau of Culture (federal support of literature, art, music, in keeping with "national goals"); Department of Agriculture—various bureaus to control production of food, fibre and livestock, as well as land use, purchases and leases: Department of Justice; Department of Defense. Foregoing only a partial listing. For complete and detailed data on the full aspects of United States federal government during the period immediately preceding the Treaty of Friendship refer also to Edison Tyler, *An Historical Look at Central Planning*, Musk and Musk, 2197.

freedom? Maybe I missed something in the newspapers, or maybe I didn't hear the President's State of the Union Message correctly, but he didn't say anything about changing the Constitution, did he?" It was a reasonable question, reasonably put.

A few scattered no's echoed from the audience.

"Could it be that about the only people who might have an interest in such sly tricks would be those dedicated patriots themselves? Those giants of selflessness who profess such superior devotion to their country that they would be glad to sell you either into oblivion or poverty, whichever suits their egotistical minds and greedy fingers? Just who do you suppose would like to change our government? Now, think hard." Larry's voice was soft so that you had to work to hear him. He was half-smiling and shaking his head, feigning a puzzled dolt, and the crowd loved it.

"David, he is simply wonderful." Nancy had said over the laughter and applause.

"My fellow citizens . . The quiet fell again almost as if someone had pulled a lever.

"If you remember nothing else, please remember this. The Treaty of Friendship was created to assure peace and freedom. Please read the summaries of the Treaty so you will understand that the purpose of this splendid document is to protect you, to keep you safe, productive, happy and secure. Nowhere in the Treaty is our Constitution even referred to. And nowhere has there ever been the slightest suggestion that we alter our own Constitution, not even at the summit conference last December. Even Mr. Syerov, who was at Geneva, will tell you that. The joint Committee For Local Action is merely an instrument of the Treaty, and its duties and functions are confined strictly to the Twelve Articles of the Treaty—and nothing else."

The meeting had been closed with "God Bless America,"[9] and I think all of us went home feeling reassured and pleased. At least there were no demonstrations.

One improvement was the traffic situation. A great many people were on foot, bundled tightly against the cold, moving downhill to

---

9   A patriotic-religious popular song of the day composed by Irving Berlin.

busses, I suppose. Nancy had commented on how few women wore heels these days. Flat shoes, instead. A coming and sensible trend, more and more noticeable almost everywhere. I never could figure why women wanted to ruin their feet. Probably the results of rationing. We all walk more. A good thing, really. As Regus Peoples[10] points out, "Even in adversity there is good; for what better way to keep physically fit than to return to the time-honored discipline of walking." However, I am lucky enough to have a leased company car with a brand new "U" card, so we are now unrestricted in gasoline. Since the emergency ban was lifted, we can drive most anywhere we please. The company lets me use it for personal needs, for which I reimburse them. So we had driven to Dome Center, pleased at finding plenty of room to park so close and quite impressed with the smooth way traffic was handled. The new police chief seems to be doing an effective job in streamlining the force and strengthening it to cope with mounting crime problems, in spite of what the critics say.

The night we had completed our seminar, we decided to take a long way home by stopping on top of Mount Washington. It was a cold, clear night, and the moon was bright on the Monongahela. We took the Liberty Bridge and McArdle Roadway to the top.

When we first came to Pittsburgh, the view from Mount Washington had captured and held us. During the first year or so we always managed to stop every now and then at the rustic observation pavilion and lean on the rough railing to look out over the city, to talk and to look some more, oblivious of the others, some native, some tourist, who likewise came to see, to sense the dynamic magnetism of a city mighty in its rugged beauty.

Pittsburgh at night. To savor unashamedly the grandeur of its winking mountains and glowing mills, the jeweled serenity of its rivers, the confidence of its lean, clean buildings, the patterns of its bridges—all etched in hues of starlight, moonlight, electric light and flickering fire. A colossus of energy; a citadel of will; distant and untainted like a toy town in a store window with the purity of a child's

---

10 Regus E. A. Peoples, United States Secretary of Health, Education and Welfare at the time of the Treaty.

dream. But only a half-dream because you wanted to reach out and touch it but could not reach it. Pittsburgh sanctified in the velvet vestments of night.

Here with Nancy I had celebrated my first raise; I learned of my first child; planned for our future. Here, too, we had come at first to nurse our anxieties and confusions; the doubts and indecisions, where the daylight mind conditioned by practical realism clashes at nighttime with another kind of mind, unsupervised, untutored and unwanted; where inner gnawings and unexplained feelings crowd against and then finally overcome the pat, comfortable feelings that black is black, white is white and everything fits a pattern, a norm, a trend, a group, with no loose ends to be concerned with because they—and there are many "theys"—already have the answers for you.

In the span of years since then, the times changed. For, while the Golden Triangle still looks new and prosperous, the empty faces of vacant buildings—a fabricating plant and trucking terminal here, a hat shop and dime store there—tell a different story. Somehow we have grown weary. Somewhere in the shadows of everyday life, the energy and the will of the city, once so clearly evident to Nancy and me, began, at first, to falter and then, later, to fade almost completely. A dying city, some have said.

So it had been a very long time since we had wanted to pause at the mountain top. Perhaps the mountain had demanded more of our inner thoughts than we were willing to give up. Perhaps it demanded answers to questions which we had asked of ourselves without, wanting to ask. Perhaps we were simply too busy meeting the glittering demands of the complex daylight world to take time out to try to discover whether this world was right or wrong. Or maybe we had grown too far apart—Nancy, dissatisfied with her role in life, and I, resolved to stick to mine. Anyway, we stopped going there.

But now the secure reality of Dome Center with its promise of the future and the close, hard, physical downtown with its stream of people fanning out into its narrow, harshly lit streets had given us the assurance we needed. The world was righting itself again. Pittsburgh would grow again. Mount Washington no longer was a symbol of personal doubt but looked as secure and inviting as Dome Center. Nancy sat close in the chilled car, not seeking warmth so much as seeking to renew an intimate companionship, long since eroded away. We were sure enough of ourselves and of our future to be confident that the mountains-eye-view would prompt the same hopeful thoughts as those generated in the heart of the city.

Except for a muffled figure walking a dog, the street was deserted. There were fewer cars parked along the curb than I had remembered. Occasionally, draped lights still shone from frosty windows. Our footsteps crackled like miniature firecrackers. The low roof of the pavilion made it seem warmer than it was. The city stretched before us mile on mile, hill on hill. Up river, a pulsating glow that danced on the black water and tinted the sky—the cast of a blast furnace. Down river, lonely headlights speeding over a lonely arch bridge—someone in too much of a hurry. And across from us the building blocks of a city nearly ready for bed.

"It's still here. We're still here." The moon played tricks on Nancy's face. She looked like a coed about to accept a fraternity pin. But she only half looked at me.

"David, it was right, wasn't it? Is it so terribly wrong to want to live, to want your children to live, to want to hang on to what you've got?"

"Of course it's right."

"Then what's the matter with everyone?" Her gloved hand played along the railing until it found an icicle. She broke it off and examined its luminous facets. "Why doesn't everyone feel the same?"

"Most people do."

"Not all of them. You can see it every now and then in their eyes. The way they look at you—or don't look at you. I don't think I'll ever forget Mr. Grant." She snapped the icicle in two and let the pieces slip from her hand. In the silence you could hear them tick the brush far below.

"So that's it. Nancy, that was months ago. I'm sure Mr. Grant didn't mean what he said."

White-haired, stem, unyielding Mr. Grant had stopped Nancy and me in the church corridor after service one Sunday just before the

Treaty was signed. He had addressed us with cold, blue eyes and thin, quivering lips. "Communists! May God have mercy on you." Then he stalked away, while onlookers pretended they had not heard. A senior member of church council, Mr. Grant was also chairman of the Allegheny Committee for American Action,[11] part of a national group that had called for the impeachment of the President and six or so members of the Congress as being "Communists or instruments of Communism." Mr. Grant owned his own metal fabricating plant. I know little about him, except what I have seen of him in church. He was against redecorating the parsonage. He was against buying a new typewriter for the church office. He was against putting in a parking lot. He objected to the Couples Club hayride, a year or so ago. I do not recall hearing that he has ever been for anything. I had shrugged off his comment, but apparently Nancy had not.

"It was so unfair, David. Neither one of us likes Communism and we don't want it here. No one in their right mind does. And we won't have it here, either. But how can we ignore them? We can't pretend they don't exist. What other, sensible choice except the peaceful way? And, David, Larry is right. It is a good treaty and it will keep us safe and secure, won't it?"

She was like a little child seeking comfort in a thunderstorm. She drew close to me, trembling slightly in the cold. A warmth filled me, alien at first, then recognizable as the same warmth I had felt toward her on our first date more than twenty years ago. The feeling of elation mounted with the warmth. We were regaining a plateau of understanding and mutual need that had slipped from us sometime in the past. A great crisis had forced us to sift our values and look again at each other, this time more closely.

"Darling, how many times have I told you not to take these Belltollers too seriously. People like Mr. Grant are against everything. So why shouldn't he be against this, too?"

---

11 Again factual data is sketchy, but newspapers and some newsfilms of the day referred to various local committees for "American Action" as "archconservative... fascistic, actively seeking war against the Soviet Union and drastic changes in our form of government."

"I know, I know," her voice was low, pensive now. "It's just that sometimes they—not Mr. Grant, particularly, but some of the others—seem right, almost logical."

Then she grinned like a coquette. "Why, David, you said darling. What's come over you?" For some reason, her perkiness at my unconscious use of the dusty term embarrassed me. I could think of no answer and so went on as if I had not heard.

"I think you mean mushy idealism. Sure we can all look back to the nineteenth century and try to wish things as they were then. But that's not being practical."

"Yes," she sighed. "Off with the old and on with the new, or as they say, 'We are living in a new world, where man's selfishness must be controlled with new ideas if we are to bring freedom to all peoples.' We hear it often enough, don't we? Oh, here I go getting confused again."

"What are you trying to do, incite riot?"

We looked at each other soberly for a minute and then laughed. It was easygoing, soft, honest laughter. It was beckoning laughter, that broke the tension and called a recess. I pulled her close and we kissed, gently, exploratory at first, then deep and savage as we rediscovered each other. My hand sought her coat button, skillfully and smoothly—a long forgotten reflex come to life. The warmth of her body through her sweater was electrifying.

"Your hand is cold," she nuzzled.

"Can you think of a better way to warm it?"

She pulled back and searched my face intently. Remarkable how young and worry-free she looked then. A sensitive, heart- shaped face, porcelain in the pale light. Easily broken, I thought, which shall not happen.

"Perhaps I can." Little Miss Coquette, again. "Why don't you take me home and see."

The rumble of a freight train on the tracks along the river below ended, for the moment, the recess.

"Oh David, it just has to be right. There's so much ahead for us, if only we play our cards right."

"And keep our noses clean, as they say at the office."

"Yes, that too, I suppose." She found another icicle along the railing and broke it off.

"But there's nothing wrong in that. Tom says there are plenty of opportunities ahead for all of us. Employment already is rising and under the new treaty we'll all be so busy producing things to go to other countries that we're really going to have our hands full."

"By Tom, you mean Tom Shade at the BWP?" There was incredulous doubt in my question. "Do you know *him* that well?" "Uh huh." She let the second icicle go.

"David? Have you thought any more of changing jobs ... to get a higher classification."

Somehow I did not resent the question. Perhaps it was the mood of the mountain and promise of the warm sweater. She had not raised the issue for more than a year, and issue it had been. Under law, all jobs, including management positions, are classified with both minimum and maximum pay scales. I had reached the top of my class more than two years before and, except for occasional "job ceiling adjustments" to allow for inflation, was ineligible for raises. There were no immediate promotional prospects, and Nancy had wanted me to look elsewhere for a job with a higher classification. It had been a stormy session, but I had won out when I reminded her of the loss of seniority and resulting benefits.8 The subject was dropped until that night after the seminar.

"Tom said he might be able to turn up something, say a number eleven or even a number twelve." She was pleased with her news, like a child bringing home a gold star for the first time. Mine was a number nine, "Salesman, steel—general."

The details tumbled out. The Mastersmeld Steel Company had two sales openings coming up,[12] retirement vacancies. Furthermore, the Mastersmeld Company, as everyone knew, presently was being examined for possible price violations. While no grave wrongdoings

---

12 The BWP by law reviewed all management vacancies and candidates for salary and job classifications based on "Federal Management Responsibility Standards."

were expected to turn up, the company had been most cooperative with Tom Shade and his staff at the BWP. Tom was sure that a friendly tip from him might help give "David a fair hearing, if he wants it."

It was hard even to think about saying no. While smaller than ours, the company was an old one with prestige. The thought of being an assistant sales manager or director of marketing services was pleasing, and I must admit that never before had an opportunity like this been presented. As a rule, it is rare that a person in my level of management would ever come to the notice of the BWP, unless it was in a negative sense, such as being caught padding expense accounts. This, I was reluctant to admit, I owed to Nancy and her job. I could think of dozens of company officials who would give much for this opportunity. In fact, I had heard talk a day or two before about a "move to get closer to Shade before he eats us up." Everyone, of course, knows of Tom Shade, probably the single most important person in Pittsburgh. I had seen him only once at a Chamber of Commerce Industry Day dinner. He spoke on the "Dollar Versus the Public."[13] I recall him as a short, neat man who did not smile much. I was proud that Nancy knew him as well as she apparently did, since the BWP offices occupy several floors of the Federal Building and employ several hundred here.

"Oh, I've been doing some special work for him, pulling all the price records of Whiteside Electric Corporation. Something big up, I think. But he likes my work and sometimes we talk." Her reply was bright.

"About," I searched for casual words, "what do you talk?"

"Oh, just things. You know. People, places, things. He's a brilliant man, David, with so much on his shoulders. I don't see how he stands the constant pressures. He thinks I have, well," she fumbled self-consciously, "abilities and the, well… talent to understand the demands of our age."

I had never heard Nancy use such scholastic terms. Their coming from her seemed out of keeping with her love for lace, appliances and polite, therefore meaningless, conversation.

---

13 At the time of the Treaty, the United States dollar equalled sixteen cents of the 1939 dollar, and the gold-backed Russian ruble was preferred as world currency.

"David, you do see what this could mean, don't you? Before you say no, hear me out." She paused to gather her forces of persuasion. She did not look down at the city, but away from it, toward the close-up of realism of the street along the pavilion.

"First, Tom tells me that if you're successful, which is virtually certain, he'll approve payment of the benefits you would lose. And," she was moving in for the kill, "*both* positions call for company-sponsored country club memberships, *and* their benefits are almost as good as what you have now, but the salary increase will more than make up the difference. You won't have to travel much either."

This time I peeled off an icicle. Surprising how much beauty there can be in frozen water. I looked down at the city and wondered who, how and why it had been built, what had given it its soul.

"What about the others?"

"What others?" Her voice held a tense puzzlement.

"Somewhere in this city there are others who hope for a crack at those two job openings. Somewhere there are men, maybe a dozen for all I know, who have been working twice as hard as I, hoping twice as hard as I and praying twice as hard as I for a promotion. They're all probably there right in the company, at least counting on one of *them* getting the good word. And they may be twice as good as I am. Besides I'm not a marketing specialist."

"What on earth has that got to do with your taking a job?" There was budding frustration in her tone.

"I mean, have I earned the right to apply... and get ... a job one of *them* should have?"

"You don't know that's the case. You're a good salesman, aren't you? And this marketing business. You could learn that."

"Yes. I do my work and . ."

"Mind your own business. Yes, I know David, I know. But you don't know for *sure* that any of them are as good as you."

"No. Of course not. But, on the other hand, I don't know whether I'm as good as any one of them, either."

"That's right, David. Be sure to take the negative side." Her voice was low, icy fury. "Never mind that for fourteen years you've been a good salesman, not a blemish on your record and never once cited by the BWP. Never mind your wife or your family. Never mind how we've had to scrape through the years. No. Never mind! Just stand aside and let someone else take it away from us. You've earned the right, David. A practical man exercises his rights when they are given to him.

"Who is it that is always talking family obligations? The family comes before everything. You've said it again and again. All through the war scare you said it, and now that we have peace and a future," she paused to gather air, "now of all times, you start becoming noble about people you don't even know exist, at the expense of your own flesh and blood who do exist. David, how can you!"

She was all fury, and I couldn't dispute her logic.

"You're right. I don't know what's come over me. It's this silly place, I guess."

She pressed in close, happiness breaking on her moonlit features.

"Oh, David, I know." She was a mother, tending the young now. "But don't you see these are the ways things are done. And it isn't as if Mastersmeld would be getting someone *bad* for them. Remember how your boss was picked."

"I had forgotten that."

He had come from the outside, and I suppose with some sort of BWP recommendations. Some of the men had been unhappy, but, of course, I had not cared, since I did not want that damned headache.

"And has Frank been mean to you?" Her smile was a mother gently chiding a small child.

"You know better."

"But do *you*, David? How do you know someone else could have been a better boss than Frank?"

"We'll never know."

"No, we'll never know. But we do know that he is a kind, considerate man, interested in our welfare. This is fact. This is real. So let's go on facts, not some silly myths. The BWP perhaps isn't the greatest, but it tries to be fair and helpful to deserving people. No planning system is ever perfect, but we know it's best for us."

48

I looked back at the city.

"Is it?"

"Please, David. Let's not get into *that*. What's here is here."

She nuzzled close and fed my hand against her warmth.

"Please say yes."

Her logic was cold and real. The doubts vanished, replaced by a kind of harsh satisfaction that by taking the job I would somehow get even with someone, although I knew not who. I had only felt that way once before. During military service, years ago, someone had stolen my mess kit just before chow time. It had hung on a crude rack with a dozen others to dry between meals. I was incensed at the injustice and lack of fair play. A buddy soothingly urged me to steal another and go on to chow. "Don't worry," he had laughed, "the guy who's missing one now will swipe another, and it'll keep going until somebody has to get one from the supply tent, but the Army has plenty of mess kits." So, for the first time in my life I stole something not mine, secure in the knowledge that no one would be hurt and pleased that I had so easily revenged the thief who had preceded me.

"Yes, indeed." I said to Nancy through clenched teeth.

She was truly happy. Her kiss was hot with a ceremonial fire celebrating her victory. We abandoned ourselves for a furious minute and then she broke with a laugh.

"I can hardly wait to tell Tom." She giggled.

Tom Shade, the jarring note. It was still difficult to realize that Nancy actually knew him.

"Just what is Tom Shade to you, anyhow?"

She searched my face for a clue to my thoughts.

"Tom Shade is a brilliant man of great poise and sureness, a dedicated man. He is ambitious and devoted to his career. He has an answer for everything. He can pinpoint our ills and name our cures. I admire him greatly, David. I feel both flattered and honored even to be in the same room with him." She spoke quietly, reverently.

Perhaps I should have been angered or felt twinges of jealousy. Instead, I felt a curious kind of respect for this person—any person for that matter—who could draw this out of Nancy.

"Tom Shade is not a person you would want to love. He is a person you want to serve in every way you can." Her tone was hypnotic, more disquieting than a passionate declaration of eternal love.

She clutched my coat. "Please hold me very, very tight."

After a moment the spell broke, and we both were in high spirits. Moments of doubt had been conquered and great decisions made. We had reached a turning point in our own lives that paced itself to the new order of things in the world. I do not recall that we had ever been closer in mind, spirit and body, heavy clothing notwithstanding. And suddenly we were cold, eager to be home, each acutely aware of the other physically and of the exotic promises this held. We were high-pitched and heady with the nonsensical and mildly lewd as we turned off the pavilion.

Nancy saw him first and dug her fingers deeply into my arm, the lilt of her laugh dying in the echoes.

"David!" Her whisper was a scream. "That person coming toward us..."

"Keep walking. Stay calm, but be ready to run."

He had come out of the shadows and was crossing toward us, the street lamp playing tricks on his slim features. He moved soundlessly, with an underlying wariness, his face fixed toward us.

My ears pounded. I steadied Nancy, tense and wooden as she walked, ready to push her aside and swing my body into him. That way she might make it to the car. I was no match, as my rubbery knees told me. What could he want? Money or Nancy? A sadist bent on a little light-hearted fun?

But he passed by, and sagging relief swept us. He was not looking at us but at the sleeping city below. He moved into the shadows again toward the pavilion to stand as a lone silhouette against a railing and the clear night.

Nancy still trembled as we drove away, our headlights bright on ancient trolley tracks and frost-slick bricks. We were silent quite awhile, alone with our separate thoughts.

"A boy in a leather jacket at midnight on a deserted street. It's a wonder he didn't slit our throats ... or worse." She slipped her feet from her snow boots and rested them against the heater. She smiled sleepily and closed her eyes.

I did not tell her I had seen the boy before on New Year's Day. Neither did I tell her that my hands trembled on the steering wheel. I could find no reason for it, except that I did not like him and hoped I would never see him again.

2

All of this had occurred two weeks before Larry Best called me at the office for dinner. I was relieved and flattered that my old friend had not forgotten me. I was amused, too, at Frank's face when the secretary had interrupted us to say, "Mr. Best is on the phone for you, Mr. Little." That, plus the knowledge that Tom Shade was looking into Mastersmeld, gave me a considerable sense of well-being.

"That's right, David, I'd forgotten you and Best are buddies. He's certainly doing well, I would say. We ought to get together— the three of us—for lunch one of these days. Or perhaps grab up the gals—he's married, isn't he—and head for the club."

He said this as we walked back down mirror-waxed, clinical- looking corridors to the meeting, which had to do with new production schedules. Federal funds, formerly allocated for defense, now are being channeled into new forms of foreign aid for underdeveloped countries. Increasing quantities of steel plates, strips, sheets and bars are being purchased by the government for shipment overseas to feed new industries that supposedly are being developed.

Already we can see the effects. We have been in a state of recession for nearly four years, our mills operating anywhere between forty and sixty percent of their capacity to produce. This is largely due to the loss of world markets, the fact that much of our equipment is old, and a general national slowdown.[14] In the last five weeks

---

14 A number of historically accurate sources substantiate Mr. Little. Situation just prior to the Treat)': European steel capacity was high, relatively cheap and more than enough for its own "domestic" demands. To take up its excess production of steel and other items, the European community created numerous trade agreements with the USSR and China, as did Japan, Canada and most

alone, mill production is up to an eighty percent average. We have hired back hundreds and expect full employment soon. Our "problem" now is we may not have enough of some steel products to meet our regular customer needs—most notable at the moment being Whiteside Electric, since over half of our February sheet production is to be shipped to Poland and will cut into the usual order requirements for domestic appliance production. So even in the midst of a business upturn there are problems. Now it looks as if we will need to start allocating certain steel items. So, meetings—more and more it seems—are being held with new sets of instructions, new forms, new policies to learn each time.

I was glad when five o'clock came. The cool, solid, confident decor of the conference room had failed to keep the meeting from becoming particularly confusing and contradictory. How were we to keep our customers happy by cutting back on some of their orders? The new priority forms—A,B,C,D—were even more confusing. How do you split carload orders, or do we ship partly empty? Mr. Lemon—the veep who called the session and then gratefully adjourned it—looked especially cool, solid, and confident as he tidied his papers into a rich, brown briefcase, straightened his flawless blue suit and left on the high note that he would explore all details and aspects of the situation with respect to all parties concerned and advise us with suggested approaches to the problem which we might wish to use, and that we should hold steady, use good judgment, keep calm and keep our perspective. Smile boys.

It had warmed some, the air wet with mist, putting halos around street lights and signs. I even rolled the window partially down as I drove out to Le Gourmet, a restaurant near the University, Larry's favorite place and the scene of many gay evenings when Nancy and I had been invited to small get-togethers. The damp air felt good. Real good.

South American countries—thus essentially creating a new balance of trade that worked against the USA. Along with a weakening dollar, twice rescued from oblivion by the International Monetary Fund, the USA was faced with a sharp reduction in capital investment, a 50 percent reduction based on the 1950-60 average. This plus high production costs and a weakening credit system appears to have helped perpetuate a recessed economic condition.

Traffic was slow, as it always is with even a speck of moisture, in spite of the few cars. Busses were jammed with weary-looking people, bunched solid, while others waited patiently and silently for busses they knew would be long in coming. Bigelow Boulevard was a hopeless tangle. A bus had broken down in the center lane, a common sight which most people accept philosophically. So it was nearly an hour before I made it to the serene interior of Le Gourmet.

Larry was there in the plush, red corner booth at the back of the lounge. There were a scattering of couples and a few strays at the bar, not at all crowded as it used to be.

"Come on in, the drinks are fine, old boy." Tall and lanky, Larry looked quite English, complete with pipe, mild tweeds and rumpled hair. He had studied in London for two years and was an open admirer of English intellectuals. He extended large, bony fingers in a firm handclasp and ordered drinks from a pert waitress, provocatively dressed. We sipped in silence, both of us, I think, letting the atmosphere wash away the world outside. "Pretty beat, I suppose?" I asked finally.

"A bit, but no more than the others."

"Others?"

"Smith, Nick and all the others at JCFLA. They have cut themselves a large piece of pudding. I hope they can manage without spilling any." He fired his pipe placidly, deliberately holding the match until the flame reached his thumb. He waved it out slowly and puffed.

"We're going half crazy with new directives," I replied, lighting my own cigarette. I put the match out right away and, strangely, regretted it.

"I don't wonder. The world runs on directives, but at least the world runs, eh?"

"Nancy and I were mighty proud of the way you handled those seminars. Congratulations."

"Ah, Nancy. How is the dear? Understand she's working directly for Tom. Saw them at the Royal Room the other noon. Didn't have a chance to say hello." I must have looked at him sharply, for he added dryly, "They were with four other people." We both laughed and fell into small talk, laced with rounds of scotch and bourbon. The waitress: "If she keeps on she'll have two more cheeks to powder." A nearby couple: "She's ready if I've ever seen one." The President's economic message: "Personally, old boy, his new two-hundred-billion-dollar budget is too low considering the job ahead of us." Nick: "Don't ever try to outdrink him." Smith Armstrong: "Quiet, like a fish, like he's listening to sounds from outer space." The weather: "Would you believe it, they want eight bucks for Brazilian rubbers!" Drink: "Let's have another from old four-cheeks." Economics: "On me, old fellow. Very well, dutch if you insist."

The sense of time was gone, and the mellow mood was full upon us. Larry was easy to listen to. He could talk about anything and make it sound significant. His voice was firm, sure, clear, without exaggeration or affectation. Whenever Larry enters a room heads turn, as if on a master string, to appraise this man who is rumpled in well-cut clothes, without being sloppy; casual, without being rude; at ease, without being flippant. He is the man of letters come unspoiled to those of lesser letters with devastating humanism. As someone once remarked, he is like an old shoe, but an elegant one of unexcelled quality. And when Larry speaks, everyone listens. Not because he demands it or forces his way, but because people want him to speak, want him to settle an issue or round out this tidbit or embellish a point or two. Larry is the final word.

Ultimately the talk, with its flecks of wit, whimsy and ribaldry came to rest on "the situation." People do not refer to current happenings by specifics; this by common, unspoken agreement. No thinking person openly asks another's opinion on anything, since it might betray some sort of flaw in the questioner's make-up and so harm his personality image. Similarly, no one probes directly for your views on business, the crime rate, inflation, taxes, the Treaty or whatever is the top news of the day. Yet people are expected to converse. To say nothing is as bad as saying too much. The happy compromise then is to inquire about "the situation." You remain uncommitted and the burden of sociability falls on the other fellow. Occasionally there is an effort to dodge, and the question is bounced right back. "I don't know. What do you think of the situation?" Or worse still, "Which situation do you mean?" Then the burden once more is on you, and you must contrive to give it away again. It takes real skill to be sociable. And while such thought-bargaining is unnecessary with Larry, the habit was too ingrained to shelve in honor of the evening.

"Tell me, Larry, what do you think of the situation?"

Larry did not dodge. He chased a dying ice cube with a swizzle stick from the empty glass to his mouth.

"The situation couldn't be better," he crunched. "Consider this. No war. The Reds—I mean Russians—damn, I've got to kill that habit. The Russians are being remarkably good sports. Employment, up. Gross National Product, up. Personal income, up. Personal spending, up. Gross corporate earnings, up. Federal revenues, up. Social reforms, continuing uninterrupted. And," he paused for emphasis, "our prestige throughout the world, at an all-time high." He had ticked them off with the swizzle stick one at a time and the come-hither waitress had edged in at the signal. We ordered another round.

"Don't you think we'd better eat?"

"Soon. Soon, old boy. But back to the situation."

"What situation?" The drinks had warmed me to a rich comfort and unaccustomed boldness. My attention had wandered to two women now perched at the bar obviously out hunting.

"*The* situation. Not *that* situation." There was a trace of sharpness in his tone. Larry did not like interruptions, and I flicked back.

"You asked *me*, remember?"

The frivolous mood vanished, replaced by an increasingly bold desire to expose nebulous back-mind wanderings to the floodlight of Larry's tailored perception. With Larry I should be safe and not at all sorry. Maybe he would know the answer.

"Larry, you know how I hate details."

"Sure, old boy." His smile was understanding, big-brotherish. It warmed me almost as much as the alcohol.

"Yet, I seem to want details." I paused to marshal words. "All I have ever wanted out of life is to stay out of trouble and get along with people. I don't want the world on a string. I just want to live and let live. Right?"

"Right." He was puzzled, but so was I. My voice sounded far off, as if taken out of my control and made to do the bidding of an unknown power.

"What's so wrong with that?"

"Nothing. In fact, it's Utopia, the ultimate of man's goals. Plato, don't you know." He rapped out his pipe, eyes narrowed and heavily underscored by the wavering candle lamp.

"Look here, David, are you in trouble? Has someone been talking to you?"

"No. No more than people talk to people, or you hear things and read things and... think things." It was a lame answer but the best I could provide. I rushed on.

"Somehow I feel I've missed something along the way, that somewhere something is wrong. Cold, hard logic says that we are right in doing what we did. The proof is everywhere I look. In all the things you mention. In the integrity of our leaders. In the findings of the experts. Yet in spite of all this ..." I took a deep breath to cut out the splinter of thought that had festered within me for months.

"Larry, I cannot fully convince myself that we *did* do the right thing. I have doubts... pin pricks that jab more and more each

day. And that's what bothers me. I can understand having doubts a few months back, or at Christmas or even a month ago. But now... with the Treaty in effect for nearly two months and with much less strain and sacrifice than any of us ever expected... you'd think the doubts would go away.

"But they don't go away, Larry. They... don't... go... away. They grow instead." I was not looking at him. Instead, I was watching an elderly man move through the entrance and the calm, sure way he closed his umbrella, removed his dark, moisture-speckled hat and coat and gave them over to the hatcheck. It was a gentle ceremony, not unpleasant to watch. The hostess smiled warmly and led him to a small table against a wall bearing a nineteenth-century Parisian scene, while the bartender with a solemn nod delivered up a snifter

56

to a waitress who set it before him as soon as he was seated. It was a smooth and orderly operation. They obviously knew him well and held him in a kind of reverence, as one might a priest. But he was not, for he wore a plain, somewhat dated suit which looked durable and well cared for, giving him the homeyness of someone's granduncle. A hidden ceiling light pinpointed his pure white hair, a well-brushed mane. His face, while deeply creased about the eyes and mouth, was ageless, as if he had already lived a long time but would live even longer. He savored the golden liquid as if he, himself, had created it and knew each element and each moment that had gone into the brandy. There was quiet simplicity about him that said he believed implicitly in each move he made. He had at once suffering and triumph stamped upon him.

"Ah, yes, of course. The work of the minorities. They've gotten to you, haven't they?" Larry had turned to follow my gaze, and having broken it, took a quick draught from his glass. His face was impassive.

"For a moment, I thought something serious was wrong." He chuckled and shook his head. "But I see you are suffering from a feeling of guilt... which you can't pinpoint, can you?"

"No," I answered, feeling a gradually growing sense of comfort.

"Has it ever occurred to you why you can't?"

"No."

"Because you have nothing to feel guilty about..."

"But why?"

"Because you are *made* to feel that way," he went on smoothly.

He had settled back, as one who had seen the light and knew what to do next.

"You are simply a victim of the minorities, that's all. If somebody tells you something long enough, no matter how illogical, sooner or later you'll begin to believe it. That's why we've got to do something about these damn crackpots who still insist on stirring things up. They're beginning to have a bad effect on you and a lot of other sensible people. I've even got a couple of bad cases in my classes. Their work has slipped. They've become surly, restless, and I don't know what I'm going to do with them. Probably I shall have to report them to the Dean's office, and it could go badly for them." He seemed genuinely concerned.

"Expulsion?"

"At least. The Dean is required to report such situations to the JCFLA. The new Bureau of Education."

"Come on, now. For something as simple as that?" Sometimes Larry's humor is so dry that it's obscure. But he was not joking.

"Not quite so simple, old boy."

"But for a purely domestic..."

"Not domestic at all," he replied. "What happens here at home affects our abilities to live up to the Treaty. Disorder in our educational process can impede our abilities to meet national and world goals. But, back to the point. ...Consider this. And maybe this will clear up a thing or two for you.

"The world was in turmoil. War was certain. Now, who was at fault?" He was bent earnestly over the table, eyes bright and searching. He was on his favorite topic.

"The Communists?" I felt somehow I was giving a wrong answer.

"Well, yes. They've never been easy to get along with. But we have to accept part of the blame, too, you know. After all, when they were getting started we had everything—productive knowhow, wealth and a completely favorable balance of trade. Right from the start we made things pretty miserable for them. We wouldn't recognize them for years, and when we did we treated them with suspicion. We've always criticized what they've been trying to do. Then after they had been torn to pieces by the Nazis in World War II, what did we do?"

He gulped the rest of his drink and waved me silent when I started to respond.

"Boxed them in. We boxed them in with air and missile bases, built NATO[15] and refused to trade with them. And all of this after hundreds of years of oppression under the czars, when they knew nothing but brutality, starvation and slavery.

---

15 North Atlantic Treaty Organization. A military alliance of Western European countries and the United States.

"Now," he edged in still closer and smiled, his voice low but unerringly firm. "What would you do if you were hungry and boxed in from every side?"

"Well, I don't.. ."

"You'd fight, that's what. You'd fight with any means available. I tell you, old boy, if we had slowed down in going our own pet, selfish ways and taken a *little* time to *understand* them... well, we'd all be a lot better off today. It's no wonder we couldn't get along. Could you feel nicely relaxed and comfortable with me... could you trust me, if I held a gun to your head?"

Larry leveled his pipe and jabbed it in my arm. Out of the corner of my eye I saw the ageless man still coveting his snifter.

"No. Of course not."

"Then how in the name of all that's logical could we expect the Reds... Russians ... to sit down and jolly it up with us over a conference table? So, who was the one who created much of the world tension?"

"We?"

"Right." He leaned back and signaled for another round, brushing aside my comment about dinner.

"In a minute. Let me finish. Now." He pondered, one eye sighting down his pipe stem. "Here we have two nations in conflict, but is this just a simple matter of differences between two countries? No. A couple of hundred years ago, perhaps. But today... when they've got military space stations and orbiting missiles, and we have one station; when they have ICBM missiles, and we have them, too; when we both have all sorts of nuclear equipment; *and* when they've perfected an anti-missile missile[16]... it's no longer two countries involved in petty dispute. No. It's just the whole world that's involved, that's all."

There was a trace of bitterness in his voice, which he quenched from a fresh glass.

---

16 The U.S.A. interestingly had developed an effective anti-missile missile some years earlier but never incorporated the device on a mass scale into its North American defense system.

"So," he continued, "the whole world is involved in *our* quarrel. Millions upon millions of helpless, underprivileged people are at our mercy."

I nodded, anxious that he continue.

"Now, I'm all for nationalism in its proper place. But too much of this kind of patriotism can blind a people, can make them forget their higher obligations... obligations above self, even above family and the country. Our obligations to mankind involve not just one part of the world, but all parts of the world."

His eyes stayed bright, an eloquent smile playing on his face. There was something almost holy about it.

"So, David, old-fashioned patriotism was fine for the horse and buggy but much too narrow for today's world. Some people just haven't seen that yet and, unless they're watched, they'll sure as hell kick the whole thing off again. Yes, we could have gone to war. There would have been no winners. But we could have gone through with it, and you and I would be ashes tonight. Millions of other innocent people would be ashes, too. And still more millions would be waiting for the fall-out to get them. Now, does *that* sound logical? Can you find anything moral in *that* kind of social crime?" He leaned back and expelled a long sigh.

The thought chilled me. I looked up to be certain where I was. The man with the brandy was looking—even in the dim light I could tell— at Larry. His face was placidly expressionless and motionless. Larry sensed it, turned slowly and started ever so slightly. Both looked at each other without a sign of anything—the tall, urbane man of letters at the erect, older man of quiet stature. They were locked in a duel— of what kind I knew not. I know only that Larry lost. For he finally broke first and turned away. In that fleeting second his composure left his face, and he was a small boy caught stealing apples. He looked at me sharply, but I am skilled at hiding thoughts, and he relaxed again.

"Let's go eat," he growled.

Ordinarily I would have considered it impolite, but the liquor had made me bold.

"Know him?" I asked, as we moved into the dining room. It was nine, and the tables were nearly all deserted. I felt somehow I had caught Larry in a vulnerable spot in which I was the dominant force, a new role for me. But by the time the head waiter had greeted him as a much coveted patron and we were seated, Larry had reassumed the role—a burden I was glad to give up, even after so brief a possession. Still, he did not answer until he had thoroughly cleaned and filled his pipe. He hugged its bowl and smiled.

"Yes. I thought from the way you stared at him earlier that you knew him, too."

"Never saw him before."

"Well," he laughed easily now. Back in command of the ship. He had passed by the iceberg, and the seas lay before him calm and unobstructed. "He's the thorn in your side. He's what ails you."

He grinned at my puzzlement. "We were talking about social crimes. Let me go on, and you'll see what I mean. How about beef. A filet, maybe?"

The thought of a nice thick cut of beef blotted out all else. Meat is still rationed and probably will be for some time. Between that and the high cost we have had nothing that elegant at home since June. Neither have we dined out since this past spring, before the emergency. Restaurant prices have been almost prohibitive. For a while the BWP had tried to enforce price controls, but quite a number went out of business. "If they can't have their way, they just quit, pick up their marbles and go home," Nancy had said. Anyway, Le Gourmet had survived, as had a few of the better places, under a special BWP directive. The dinner was $21.75, and I wasn't sure I wanted to spend it. But the drinks were cheap, and besides, I reminded myself, there is Tom Shade and the new job. I ordered grandly. We talked as we ate.

"Now, tell me just how that oldster ails me when I've never seen him before," I said, after biting into the shrimp cocktail. I was so hungry I could scarcely sit still.

"Oh, I don't mean him, as such, but what he is... what he represents. Old Stone Age is typical of the reactionary element that keeps trying to sow seeds of suspicion. You know, an S-S Man... sowers of suspicion."

"Stone Age?"

Larry laughed and gestured lightly with a fork. "Stone Age Rodgers, as the kids—and a few of the rest of us, I'm afraid—call him. Doctor Hamilton M. Rodgers, professor of philosophy on campus and self-proclaimed scholar in economics, political science and English literature," he said between hefty bites.

"He's an agin'er. Against everything. A harmless old coot, if it weren't for the delicate situation we're in today. But we can no longer afford the luxury of quaint old characters."

The name, of course, was familiar. I had heard it from time to time over the years, as one does with community leaders, mostly through scattered newspaper accounts—never front page though. A speech here, a committee appointment there, usually concerning economics in some way, but I cannot recall anything specific about him, except this past fall when he did stir up some attention for a day or two during the Jason Bell Senate filibuster by circulating some sort of an open letter. It was a hazy impression that took me exactly nowhere, except that he was not quite the same attention-getter as was Mr. Grant and his Allegheny Committee.

"He makes a mighty good first impression," I replied. Larry dismissed my comment with a negating shrug.

"Well, old boy, most of us do for a first look, but.. . ah ... that second look. Why, old Rodgers is so conservative that, if they ever put up a statue of him, they'll have to set him on the damn horse facing backwards. Had he lived in the Stone Age, I'll bet he would have been against the wheel." He used low, machine-gun tones.

I laughed in spite of my effort not to.

"So, how has he harmed me or anyone else?"

"How does a cloudburst wash out a bridge? First the raindrops form into rivulets, which turn into streams, which cascade into the river to build a wall of water and…swoosh…no bridge." A fork went over the side with the sweep of his hand. He retrieved it with an ease that somehow made dropping a fork seem quite the thing to do. He continued smoothly.

"Rodgers is a raindrop. Taken by himself he's harmless. Put him with a lot of others, and he could become part of an instrument to erode the foundations of our society."

"But why should that give me—I think you said—a guilt complex? I've never had any contacts with him. Is he dangerous?"

"No. No. Oh, he's a nuisance, right enough, but they keep him pretty confined. Has a permanently endowed chair, you know, so getting rid of him would be a bit sticky. Has one seminar, I think, maybe two. Only a few ever take him. Of course, those he does influence can make things awkward. Well, like the problem students I mentioned."

"Students of his?"

"Indeed, yes. He's like a two-year-old. In the jam all the time. Gums things up, but I'd scarcely call him dangerous."

"Then if he does mind his business—fairly well—what does it matter what he does?" There was a trace of edginess in my voice, one I wanted to control but could not. I felt a fundamental kin- Dred ship to the man minding his own business. The pins were beginning to prick again.

"Oh, come now, David. You've missed my point entirely." His voice gave hint of a disdainful rebuke.

"All I meant," he said with elaborate clarity, "was that old man Rodgers is a *symbolic* cause of the guilt feelings you expressed a while ago. What he thinks, what he does has no direct bearing on you. But he does think, feel and act the way other reactionaries do, and when you put them all together they constitute an unwholesome force that could do us harm. Look at yourself, for instance, getting jittery when you should be calm, happy and secure. I merely singled out Rodgers because he was here, and you seemed to take such an interest in him."

Larry's long-suffering expression—almost like a boy about to cry—made me feel stupid and sorry I had attempted to pull things apart. Yet the unknown power was still tugging at my voice.

"Well," I paused lamely under Larry's careful eye, "there's no question that we did the right thing. To have condemned millions to death is unthinkable. But if it is that logical, why can't these extremists see it, too? Take this Doctor Rodgers. He wanted to stick it out. Now, either he's stupid, or he knows something you, I and a whole lot of other people don't know. That, Larry, I think is what has been disturbing me all along. Do these people have some knowledge we don't have?"

I was relieved that, finally, the festered splinter was located. This was my fear—hounded down and cornered, at last. Larry saw the change as quickly as I felt it. His eyes closed to slits and he chewed his beef slowly, as if he expected to find ground glass in it. Carefully, he cut himself several pieces and devoured them one by one. A smile grew slowly across his features. He drank deeply from his coffee cup, wiped his lips thoughtfully and folded the napkin away like it was his last act on earth.

"David, old boy, you have found the key." The captain was back in command of the ship yet again. "I don't mind confiding in you that I've been a little concerned myself about underlying attitudes and feelings of far too many people.

"In fact," he looked carefully around and leaned forward, "I wouldn't ever mention this but Nick, Smith and I were discussing this very point today. People aren't responding quite as they should. We know they're bothered. But we don't know why ... or we didn't, until you supplied the key."

I was touched with this expression of confidence and pleased to be allowed to share some of the problems of the inner circle. Already the burden was lifting.

"Now, hear me out. I want to be sure I've thought it through exactly right. Let's see, I'll lecture on it tomorrow and by the next day I'll have it pat enough to lay the whole thing out to Smith and Nick. This is just what I need to get me in with them permanently. Of course, I'll let them take the credit with national..." I might as well have not been there, for Larry was speaking only to himself, his eyes centered on some faraway vision I could not see.

3

As faithfully as I know how, I shall try to set down here highlights of Larry's thoughts. That the President delivered an address on all networks four days later containing these thoughts is a source of overwhelming pride to me.[17] For the President's message has pointed the way forward for all of us. And while it is Larry's thinking, I was the one who triggered it. How magnificent it is to feel useful.

Peace once more has settled upon this great land. With it has come some discomforts, many adjustments and a few doubts. The discomforts and adjustments in time will be met and made in the true American traditions of courage and sacrifice. But what of the doubts? Suppose they are not met and conquered? Then what? For is it not true that a man can only work well when he is free of worry?

So let's look at your doubts. Oh, we know you've got them. We can even tell you what sort they are. First, let me say, there is absolutely no need to feel badly at having them. So be at ease. Know that your leadership understands—so deeply so, in fact, that we want to help you overcome them.

Now, let's look at the kind of doubts you have. Can you pinpoint them? We suspect that you cannot, save only that you feel some shapeless, nameless guilt that defies your own logic, your own common sense. Now, usually, doubts stem from outside forces. In recent months we have had two principal forces play upon all of us. One is the voice of the majority—the voice of democracy at work in the most lofty traditions of government. That voice has said it is sinful to kill. The other is a minority voice—the voice of reaction at work undermining progress which we have so painfully built, stone on stone over the years, the foundation walls of security and happiness. That voice has said we must ignore broad human wants for the sake of a select few.

All of us know, at least, someone who voices reaction, who wishes to conserve all that he can for himself without regard to the other fellow. Now, I know that most of us—most thinking people—promptly discard such self-centered thinking in favor of the logic of the majority. We do this consciously, forgetting that we have subconscious minds, too, which can be influenced without our even realizing it.

---

17 Mr. Little is correct. See *An Historical Look at Central Planning*, pp. 874-882, for full presidential text.

How is this possible, you ask? Through conditioned responses. For one, we traditionally respect whatever appears to be the voice of reason, and some of the reactionaries sound reasonable—if you do not examine carefully what they say. For another, the world moves so fast these days that it often takes us years to adjust old habits and old thinking to new happenings. There's a mental-image lag that sometimes confuses us when we are confronted with new situations. We like to think of the good old days, simply because we know what they were like, and we never know for sure what the future holds. So there is a natural tendency to look backwards, because it is easier and more comfortable. Some even delude themselves by thinking history is a minor, a blueprint to the future. But how could something past materially affect something that has not happened yet, especially when change is ever with us?

So, the reactionary can subvert our subconscious, can question our logic, by simply referring over and over again to the past. He uses words like freedom, honor, truth as if they belonged to him alone and the rest of us were interlopers. It is not surprising then that certain extremists arouse our conditioned responses, particularly if they are persons you have known as reasonably good citizens.

Let us give you an example of one such person. We do this because we suspect that you know of someone very much like him—who, whether you realize it fully or not, may be partially responsible for creating a feeling of guilt in you. We will call him, Mister X.

Mister X is a respected, influential citizen in the educational-social-business complex of his community. He opposed the Treaty of Friendship on the grounds that the Soviet Union is not trustworthy. He cites examples which seemingly give evidence of such distrust. But he conveniently ignores that we ourselves may have generated much of that distrust. For you cannot ring a nation with hostile arms as we have done and expect them to love you for it. Mister X also cites examples of violence and upheaval in other countries which have adopted the Communist form of government; nations which, admittedly, did have severe internal adjustments. Again, he uses half-truths. For one thing, he conveniently ignores the fact of cultural differences between our nation and, let us say, Czechoslovakia or Hungary, where the make-up of their people differs entirely from our own. To compare what happened there to what *might* happen here is like comparing apples and oranges.

And finally, Mister X refuses to acknowledge that if a nuclear war had developed between ourselves and the Soviets, millions upon millions of totally innocent men, women and children would have been destroyed, perhaps even the human race itself. In his frantic reach for the past, Mister X has forgotten that "private" wars solely between two or three nations are a thing of the past. Advanced weapons make this kind of conflict impossible. For, like it or not, the whole world becomes involved in the destruction. While a nation does, we suppose, have the self-determining right to commit its own people to destruction, it does not have that right with innocent parties. Hence, partisan nationalism must give way to a much higher moral responsibility to all peoples of the world, in that total war must be permanently eliminated at all costs, even including the sacrifice of some nationalistic traditions to the greater good for the greater number. This is the highest calling of democracy—to let the majority rule for the common good.

Even so, Mister X protests over and over again. While logic tells us he is wrong, still, Mister X stands firm, and Americans traditionally respect the man with the courage of his convictions, be he right or wrong. So, while you and the rest of us cannot accept his beliefs consciously, our subconscious minds are less sure and doubt begins to eat at us, affecting our happiness, tampering with our peace of mind and causing us to take our minds from our work. And constructive work is desperately needed from all of us to set the world right.

But subconsciously we ask ourselves, does Mister X have some special kind of knowledge none of the rest of us have, which somehow makes him *right* and the rest of us wrong? This is the core of our selfdoubts. We have been led to believe that we do not have the full facts. We have been led to believe that only the reactionaries have the skill to lead us from the jaws of death. And, mind you, the reactionaries have proposed to save us by carrying us to the brink of war, not away from it. Does this sound logical? But some of these are respected people; so how can we be *sure* that they should—*indeed, must*—be discounted?

Well, first it is necessary for you to know in your *own* minds that these self-styled "experts" *do not* have special knowledge of our world affairs. Indeed, they are among the most poorly enlightened when it comes to government and the world about us, as the record so clearly shows.

Then, it is also necessary for you to know, beyond all doubts, that these extremists are not creditable people. They are misguided—as respectable as some might be. They have spent their lives focused upon themselves. They forget that if there is no world, there is no nation, and that if there is no nation, there can be no society—and if there is no society, there can be no individual. The individual must place his welfare last, with the common good first.

Returning to our example of Mister X, who is a real person, let us examine his character.

Is Mister X merely against a peaceful solution to world problems? Oh, no! For Mister X has spent a lifetime being against everything. For instance, Mister X was against the BWP, predicting all sorts of dire things. Yet, we are closer to wage and price stability than we have been in a generation, and there has not been a single major strike since the BWP was formed. Mister X was against the Private Property Act. Yet, new federal property standards are curbing abuses of the landowners and industrialists. He was against boosting our teaching standards; against the right of men to have employment and security; against abolishing the House Committee on Un-American Activities.[18] He was against profit controls, agricultural standards, construction standards, welfare standards, and federal standards of all kinds, including even medical standards. He was against tax concessions to the underprivileged; against loans to failing businesses; against cultural subsidies; against the patent-restriction laws;[19] against federal stocks and bonds subsidies.

18 A Congressional Committee established in the 1940's to examine "un-American" activities which was abolished three years prior to the Treaty.
19 Patents under a revised law expired after five years and became "public proper-

Mister X has never been "for" anything—except to return to outmoded and ineffectual traditions of the past. Thus, by his own acts, Mister X reveals himself as one who has spent a lifetime keeping opportunity away from others, people like you. This is why we call him, and others like him, "reactionaries." And have you ever known of a *poor* reactionary? We doubt that you ever have. Reactionaries are against social change because it cuts into their wealth. They are "conservatives," because they want to keep things for themselves. Their creed of greed would take us back to the oxcart days where private property was completely without controls, where businesses made any profit and charged any price they chose. *They* are the ones who would change our way of life, our improved form of government, in order to bring the power back to the profiteers. This could only lead to fascism, and dare this nation allow itself to forget the terror of fascism that once shook the world under the murderous Hitler? Do you wonder why the Treaty of Friendship outlaws this evil as treason? Do you wonder why unemployment—until the Treaty—kept rising year after year? Do you wonder why private business year after year fell behind in the competitive race, leaving the federal government faced with the necessity of saving business? The answers lie in the Mister X's of our nation. The reactionaries who live for their own profit and thus dry up our economy.

And what do they propose? They would add more burdens to you. They would have you worry about not only your jobs and your families, but they would weight you down with the complicated and intricate tasks of handling educational problems, economic problems; labor, business and medical problems; cultural and national-goal problems. Most of us work to eliminate our problems. For is it not true that a man burdened with complex cares is not happy and cannot do his best work? And what other way is there for us to achieve our Golden Age? But, the reactionaries would increase our burdens and, given the chance, probably would create a 48-hour-long day so we all could work and worry longer!

ty, available for the welfare of all the people..." See, *An Historical Look at Central Planning*, p. 648.

Are these the safe, sane, wise, logical people with whom you would entrust your futures, your very lives? Do you think it healthy for the nation to condone their petty protests; to let them keep on resorting to all forms of irresponsible emotionalism, in order to make decent people like you feel guilty and in some way responsible for our plight in world affairs? Is it in the best interests of this country— indeed, in the best interests of true democracy the world over—to continue to allow these undemocratic forces to inflict themselves upon us, to ignore the will of the majority, to poison us with distrust, to abolish love and understanding, to set brother against brother?

We say no. We say "Down With Mister X." We say this because he threatens our domestic tranquility and the peace of the world. We say this because this is what you want us to say. For we are your servants and you are our masters; because you are the majority, in which all men are of equal voice in exercising the final will of our society. Will you let yourselves be destroyed by a minority? How you respond to the challenges ahead will give us our answer. Freedom in a new world, or slavery in the backwashes of the past? Which will it be?

4

We were in the highest spirits when we left Le Gourmet. After Larry completed the dry-run of his dissertation, during which time I sat as still as stone, we had several more drinks to celebrate. For the first time since the emergency began, I felt confident, secure and bubbling with good cheer. We had peeked into the lounge. I had convinced Larry we should buy a cup of hemlock and have it

served on the rocks to old Stone Age, but he was gone. So were the two women, a source of grief to us both. For the call of adventure was racing through us, and this was the night of all nights when fears were buried and a man could walk fully upright again. And what is more manly than the conquest of a beautiful woman? The two at the bar were not as appealing as we would have liked, but, under the circumstances, they would have served the purpose of rounding out our egos.

"Have to be good, my dear, splendid, brilliant old fellow. Have n' other choice." Larry's diction had slipped some. Mine was no better. "Know some coeds, but that's big trouble."

"Big, big trouble," I echoed, pontifically.

We decided to walk the two blocks to Larry's home, a fairly new red brick colonial in the heart of the once grandiose East End of Pittsburgh. I would return for my car later, hopefully better able to drive. It was past midnight, and the streets were empty, washed clean by the rain. Along the way we spotted some garbage cans awaiting an early morning collection.

"Remember when we were in New York that one weekend," I mused.

"Huh. Never forgot. Senior year."

"Naw. Junior year."

"Senior year. We went to celebrate my class presidency."

"Oh. Well, remember the garbage cans on... 69th street?" I asked, steering Larry around a puddle.

"Thank you. Saved my life. No, Donna lived on 78th street. That's where the party was."

"Some party."

"Wonder what happened to Donna?"

"I can guess."

"We kicked garbage cans all the way down 78th."

"When it's three o'clock in the morning..."

"A garbage-canning we'll be a-going ..."

"Not so loud!"

"Hap-py New Year."

"Shall we?"

"Anyone around?"

"Nope."

"Can't be messy. Here. Empty this one into this one here. Now we got a nice loud empty." "After you."

"No, old boy, I insist. After you."

"To the Queen."

"To the King."

"Long live the Republic."

"Amen."

In a toast to the dear, dead days of the past, a tired, galvanized steel can went rolling, tumbling, scraping, screeching, spinning across the sidewalk and into the street. The operation was repeated a second time. The uninhibited noise; the grating, nonconforming racket; the very uncouthness of kicking garbage cans provided our highest sense of achievement for the evening.

We were still chortling when we rounded the corner into Larry's street. We were still discussing Donna and cans generally when we turned into the front walk and looked up at the house front bathed in the quiet light of the street lamp.

Right then the small talk stopped. Right then the happiness- binge ended in sharp intakes of breath and a choking protest against an unseen force.

On the walk at our feet; on the red brick front, neatly placed high under the upper windows. Big, black letters stained forever in the pores of the brick. Big, black letters over and over again. Big, black letters put there sometime recently by unknown hands of unknown enemies. Big, black letters that made you rage at the injustice.

Yet, Larry remained calm. Larry showed a power of love and understanding I cannot show. Larry would forgive.

"Easy, old man. We must have patience. This sort of thing will end soon, I promise you." He even smiled.

For someone had painted the word "TRAITOR" over and over again. In the brick, leaping at us.

TRAITOR! TRAITOR! TRAITOR!

III

The Third Month

Never have I seen such activity as in these past few weeks. Everywhere people are on the move. Bus and air terminals are jammed. Even the railroad stations are packed, for during the emergency they brought back all the passenger equipment still remaining to handle evacuations, and they have been kept busy ever since. Every kind of person imaginable seems in a hurry either to leave or arrive. Whole families clutching parcels and juggling suitcases; brisk, older men, with trim attaché cases and struggling porters; alert, younger men, mostly in jackets and with little luggage, hovering in tight groups, eating hot dogs or doughnuts, waiting for a flight, a train or a bus to be called; sleek professional women of all ages moving with queenly assurance to and from government limousines; uniformed police and W.O.N. militia, the latter hastily organized from remnants of rapidly disbanding armed forces, either keeping order or swinging purposefully toward unnamed objectives; tired old ladies with swollen ankles and worn shopping bags; unshaven derelicts of undetermined age moving listlessly with the human tide. The old and new. Some doubtless fleeing imaginary foes. Others rushing eagerly to new adventure and the release from boredom.

The streets, too, are jammed. There are long lines snaking into the government buildings, as people rush to beat the deadline to register for the new cards we must have. Elsewhere, throngs of people wait their turn in bright new offices for their permits. And in still other offices neat, confident-looking businessmen wait in hallways and on hard benches to receive their federal authorizations.[20] Stores turn away coveys of women, square-shaped, pear-shaped and lusty-shaped, who come too late to buy non-rationed stockings, slips, bras, toiletries and other items still in short supply. Teams of youths swirl in and out of Dome Center to patriotic rallies, cultural programs and physical fitness competitions. Battered taxis, official-looking cars, transcontinental trucks and clanking buses choke the streets during noontime. Strings of barges—many rusted from retirement and long neglect—now begin a new life, sliding downriver with cargoes of steel, appliances, raw plastics, machine tools, mill equipment and coal for various parts of the underdeveloped world. Plant gates at shift-time disgorge rivers of men and lunch buckets, as employment booms under the impact of new trade and aid agreements signed under the Treaty.

It is as if we have awakened from a long sleep of apathy and indecision and been transformed into people with purpose and action. Our leadership has begun to assert itself. Where no clear goals had existed and direction had been unreliable, we now have been given both goals and direction. The voice of government— no longer as encumbered with the squeaks of the die-hards—has become firm and resolute, speaking with unity and confidence. Although I do recall something very much like this after Pearl Harbor, I was then too young to appreciate fully the excitement and clarity of purpose that comes to a nation aroused. One would think we are entering upon a great war, and in a sense we are—a "war against war," as the President put it the other week. His speech was just what the nation needed, beautifully timed to cope with the doubt and confusion. Not only did

---

20 Judging from various records of this period, Mr. Little is referring to identity cards, ration cards, work classification cards, social service cards and voting cards; meeting permits, mortgage and credit permits, real estate permits and travel permits; federal authorizations for businesses to change location; requirements to buy or sell products or property, to boost prices, to secure credit expansion and tax concessions, to relocate plant equipment, change power and freight rates, rearrange work shifts, adjust production norms and apply for profit subsidies.

he draw fully upon Larry's lecture, but he laid out his "Plan for Total Peace," with such sureness and fire that almost overnight things began to happen so rapidly that it has been difficult to keep pace.

In his hour-long, all-networks address he gave us back our lost perspective. Drawing first on Larry's thoughts, he called on the nation to reject the "seeds of fear and suspicion sowed by the Mister X's of our land." It is they who "seek scapegoats rather than solutions to our problems. This has been their historic lot: never to trust the will of the people." Is it any wonder that "the private sector of the economy has failed more and more each year, as the extremists become more and more preoccupied in seeking greater profits—the evil fruits of greed and gorging—at the expense of wages and the public interest.

"And what have been the results of this outrageous social injustice?" the President had asked. "Powerful corporations still try to dictate prices, without considering the public interest, simply to increase profits. They and other reactionaries have consistently fought every program this and other administrations have developed to help them and you; refusing to accept the cold facts that the more complex and productive we become the more we must plan production and prices together. Such foot-dragging has caused us recession after recession, each one more and more prolonged and idling more and more of our capacity to produce. This blindness to our national purpose and welfare has cost us hundreds of billions of dollars in national production and millions upon millions of man-years of employment opportunity—despite efforts of your government to speed up national growth.[21] The extremists would have us cut spending as the means to stimulate growth, completely bypassing the fact that demand can only be created by spreading purchasing power, not only here at home but over the world. We no longer can afford the luxury

---

21 Some vital statistics uncovered concerning the United States during the fiscal year of the Treaty, all figures approximate: Population, 300 million; Gross National Product (a term used by their government for measuring annual productive wealth) 890 billion dollars; "employable work force," 124 million; "unemployed but eligible for employment," 26.8 million; National Debt, 498.9 billion dollars.

of such narrow-minded views. For we must once and for all succeed in bringing production and consumption into proper balance by improving still more the relationships among profits, prices, wages and investments both private and government-sponsored. This final effort must have the absolute consent of all people, not only as to economic principle but also to practical economics applied in all industries.

"Through our Treaty of Friendship we now have the means to develop fully our human capital. Our efforts must center on opening up markets in the underdeveloped nations and boosting our trade with our new friends.[22] Our first move must be to re-define again the cooperative efforts of business, labor and your government to strengthen our American Economic Performance Budget for World Peace. Out of this must come a great new national economic purpose which will permit us to use our resources to vindicate America's promise to the world.

"And we have the means. Our ninety-billion-dollar defense budget is being rapidly cut back to give us a whole new source of funds, which already are being channeled into foreign aid through government purchases of domestic goods for shipment overseas and to South America. We expect an ultimate freeing of thirty billion, the remaining sixty billion to be paid each year to the World Order of Nations for our share of maintaining the Peace Army. Beyond this, our Russian allies in peace and progress have advanced us gold payments to cover future purchases of capital equipment and grain we have agreed to sell them, the result of the trade agreement signed two days ago.[23] We

---

22 In the period immediately preceding the Treaty, the United States government had pushed for the increase of trade with Communist countries including: France, Belgium, Finland, Denmark, Sweden, Germany, Japan and the Philippines (Communist-Socialist coalition governments at that time) and the total Communist countries of Cuba, Brazil, Peru, Venezuela, Ecuador, Dominican Republic, Haiti, Panama, Costa Rica, Guatemala, Colombia, Puerto Rico, Korea, Laos, Vietnam, Thailand, Cambodia, Pakistan, China, Indonesia, Burma, Greece, Poland. Czechoslovakia, Hungary, Yugoslavia, Romania, Italy, Bulgaria, Albania, Turkey, Austria, Algeria, Congo, South Africa, Tanzania and, of course, the USSR and Mexico.

23 Surprisingly enough this is the only reference Mr. Little makes to any of the three "Peace Loans" granted by the USSR to the United States in an eighteen-

therefore look forward to a stabilized dollar able to regain its place in the world. With these new resources, of course, there will be temptations for us to create a budget surplus, which we cannot let happen lest our economy once again fail in its purpose."

In rapid succession the President then called for an expanded federal budget, a revising of the national debt limit to 510 billion and strengthening of the Bureaus of Agriculture and Wages and Prices with broader powers to bring us into "full productive balance." Farm land previously retired from production is to be plowed up again for crops, and institutional advertising by business or rightist groups is now prohibited as subverting our national interests.[24]

"Within the year we shall have full employment. Within the year we shall know the full rewards of a lasting peace. But even so there doubtlessly will be cries of protest from the Mister X's still in our midst. Cries to divide us. Cries that breed disharmony and loss of purpose. Cries that terrify and set brother upon brother. But let us not heed these counsels of doom. Let us, instead, heed the call to action to bind up the economic wounds of our nation. Let us create confidence, not suspicion."

Within hours after the President spoke, the mood of the city began its change from quiet ploddings to vigorous action. For later that evening people, seemingly out of nowhere, began to gather at Point Park around the Peace Monument. They carried flickering torches, placards and banners. "Down with Mister X!" they cried, while the

month period following the Treaty. Mr. Tyler reports the first one was made to help the United States meet foreign claims against its dwindling gold reserves pressed by England and Switzerland. The other two were to help protect against the "disintegration of the dollar." Loans were to be paid off through agricultural products, basic and consumer goods, capital equipment and skilled labour.

24 Historian Edison Tyler spent weeks researching this line and concludes Mr. Little was referring to one of the agricultural plans that took land out of production and turned it into recreational areas, this to offset earlier food surplus problems. Apparently the plan was eliminated and the land brought back into production. Regarding advertising, Mr. Tyler believes this decision stems from earlier tax legislation which made "institutional" advertising a non-deductible business-expense item, which curtailed most of this kind of advertising even before it was outlawed as "contrary to the intent and purpose" of the Treaty.

cards and banners screamed: Don't let Mister X X you! Let's X Mister X! Down with Mister X!

The impact of the mass gathering was instantaneous. Both TV stations switched to live coverage of the scene as soon as its full import became apparent. For it was not a matter of a few irresponsible people out for a wild night. Rather, as the commentators described it, there was "a drama building here bigger than perhaps any of us realize; not men and women gathered to work hooliganism, but citizens both concerned and moved to express themselves in the only effective way open to them, collective action …"

Word of the event had cut through to us in the midst of "Tomorrow's World: Hungary, Part II," a documentary on improved living conditions in Budapest. We had tuned it in at the suggestion of Larry, who, along with Mary, had come to dinner so that together we could see the President speak. It was our first dinner with them in over six months. Nancy had done well, using the extra coupons she picked up through Tom Shade; an elegant prime rib-roast, real butter, crabmeat and frozen strawberries, which along with vegetables—still in good supply—made quite a meal. Other than casual contact with neighbors, we had had no other dinner guests.

So Nancy went to considerable effort. The sterling was unwrapped and polished. We had buried it in the yard near the evergreen clump, and, though it had been dug up, it had not yet been used. The good tablecloth was brought up from the basement, washed and ironed at one a.m. ("Nancy, why *don't* you come to bed." "David, please quit bickering… oh, damn! You made me scorch it! Pul-ease, go to bed…") She even fixed a centerpiece of artificial flowers, resurrected from some mysterious source within the house. ("Just stay away from the table. Just *stay away*, David.") It was good to sit at the head of a formal dinner table again. Softly groomed Nancy, serving with deft grace; perky Mary, bright with chatter and dancing eyes almost too large; the rumpled Larry, lounging benevolently in the creaky straight-backed chair; the ebb and flow of gentle conversation between leisurely bites—all framed in candlelight. Straight out of a "gracious living" ad in a slick magazine, I suppose, but enjoyable all the same. For it conveyed the image of the life we all seek, one of kindly affluence, justly won and reverently preserved through the Grace of God and our own intellect; an image not easy to create and, thus, most difficult to let go of.

Talk had centered mostly on Whiteside Electric Corporation, which—even in the face of the BWP, the President, Congressional Committees and the JCFLA—still continues to press for a price increase.

"And they even had a 1.6 percent return on their sales last year and—" Nancy paused significantly to butter a piece of roll, "out of it paid a handsome dividend of seventeen cents on the common." She spoke crisply with elaborate casualness, a hint of pride filtering through her half-smiling, thoughtful face. For Nancy to have expressed such a thought a year ago would have been unthinkable. In her short time with the BWP she has come a long way. Even Larry was impressed, for he looked at her hard for several seconds with bright, unblinking eyes and then responded with a one-expert-to-another air that brought a warm glow of triumph to Nancy's cheeks.

"Exactly what I was saying to Smith Armstrong this morning." He nibbled as he spoke. "Some companies haven't paid a dividend in two, three years, but they manage to keep going. They manage to do their part, and more power to 'me. But these sticky-fingered pirates!"

"I know," Nancy cut smoothly but eagerly into Larry's sure, swift, and silken tones, "more profits they say to... uh," she floundered, her new-found knowledge temporarily fogged by a faulty memory. Larry beamed:

"To invest in new plant equipment. Their stuff is wearing out, and I suppose they're right about that but..."

Her fog cleared, and Nancy picked up the thread with determined vigor. "But if they need new equipment why do they want to take it out on the poor consumer by raising prices against the public interest in time of emergency when they can apply for a capital improvement loan, which Tom says he'd give them in a minute on the One-Hundred-Year Mortgage Plan." She finished in a rush, as if she had been called upon to recite a poem she had not yet had time to rehearse.

"And, old girl, don't forget special tax considerations, which, I've no doubt. Shade could arrange, if they were really serious about the public interest. ...I say, these strawberries are elegant, simply elegant."

Mary had watched with pixie silence, a touch of secretive amusement dancing in her eyes as she studied us one by one.

"I doubt Whiteside will be a nuisance much longer ... do you really think... my dears? Certainly someone somewhere has readied a plan to help them out of their miseries." Her voice, soft and light, had a pleasant tingling as always. But with Mary there usually is a two-edginess in her words that hints at—but never confirms—an untraceable cynicism, never actually exposed but covered with infectious gaiety. For Mary is never sad, which makes her well-liked. She seldom monopolizes conversation, nor does she ever try to change its flow. Rather, she always seems to have something appropriate to say at just the right moment, even though one is not always sure of the full meaning. This ability to mystify seems to delight her. As someone once remarked, "Mary has a secret—a joke on all of us— that she keeps to herself." And once at a cocktail party years ago she told me in a moment of semigravity, "The spring-fed stream always is clearest nearest its source; while far away the rivers and oceans, which it feeds, become muck-laden, cruel and salty, enslaved by tides and currents.

That, dear David, is why the spring is best for me and why I write for children." She had spoken it as a ballad, her eyes crinkled in humor over the rim of a martini glass, which she quickly drained and then moved away abruptly to get another. I have often wanted her to elaborate on her riddle but she always changes the subject. And now her soft voice had floated between the spirited exchange between Larry and Nancy, both of whom looked thoughtfully at her.

"Mary, my love and light of my heart, plans there certainly are, as our little beady-eyed friends at Whiteside shall soon discover." There was banter in Larry's response—the kind that comes of the unrestricted, dependent love the man has for his wife. And if he caught the double-edge of Mary's words, he was content to let it pass, as he always does.

80

"Sort of like the horse that learned it was stronger than the fence, and so it would smash right through, barbed wire and all." She popped a spoonful of strawberries between her pert lips and closed her eyes in an elaborate show of ecstasy. "Hm-m-m! Nancy, where did you find them?"

"There's a small grocer out near the government apartments who's able to get them from some place. Tom put me onto it. Lot of the government people buy there," said Nancy, still glowing at the obvious success of her carefully planned dinner. We ate in silence, until dessert was finished.

"And the horse?" Larry had pushed back and was lighting his pipe. He had waited longer than usual for Mary's punch-line.

"Here, let me help you, dear," Mary rose as Nancy got up to clear away the plates. Then she turned full on Larry, an impish smile on her face.

"We simply shot him and sold him for fertilizer." Her tone was flip. She looked at us one by one, face still smiling but searching each of ours. Nancy dropped a cup. Larry burnt his fingers on a match. I snickered.

"Really, darling," said Larry, striking another match, "sometimes I think you lived too long on the farm. You can be positively brutal at times." His tapered hand reached out to encircle her wrist, and he tugged her closer.

"Daddy still wants us back, and you'd look awfully cute driving a tractor. And I wasn't being brutal, just realistic. King was a lousy horse." She flounced into the kitchen, chattering after Nancy.

"Speaking of horses, how about *Nellie, The Talking Horse*"? I called, remembering suddenly that we had heard nothing about Mary's trip to Philadelphia.

"It was shot, too," she sparked. Liqueur glasses had been set, richly filled with Drambuie, and she settled back in her chair with a bounce. "Didn't have enough of a message to it, they said." There was no reproach, no disappointment in her voice.

"Remarkably fine old girl here," Larry said. "Took it right on the chin. Remarkably decent of her. Publisher must be out of his mind. But you'll get him next time, eh, dear."

"Perhaps, old thing-thing. Perhaps." She had lost her perkiness, but only for an instant. She will never write again, I thought. I do not know why, but she never will. The "Talking Animal Series" that has delighted children for over twelve years, too, has been left behind. I closed my eyes for a moment in silent toast.

The children had been farmed out to neighbors who had been anxious to help once they knew who our guests were. The three returned at seven-thirty, as they had been instructed, to "see the Bests, and please behave, and then upstairs to your rooms." They filed in gravely—tall, slender Peggy, wearing the new "Friendship Hair-do," two honey-colored braids criss-crossed up over her head to give her a much too worldly look to suit a father; David, more thickly set, but nearly as tall, trousers too short and shirt too small, a crooked grin on his face; and wee Annie, picture-pretty in a crisp yellow dress, a remarkable six-year-old, with grace and radiance well beyond her years. I love them all, and they made me proud as they greeted "Uncle Larry" and "Aunt Mary" with exacting measures of properness. Nancy has done well with them. Then they were gone, pushed on their way by the President's approaching telecast. We wanted not even the slightest distraction to mar Larry's greatest moment, when the highest office in the land would reflect—in part at least—the genius of the man now seated so much at ease in my favorite armchair.

We watched in complete silence, carefully absorbing each word the President said. Mary had seated herself on the floor, cheek resting on arms folded over Larry's knees. Once, near the end, she looked up at Larry, somber and searching—and if I didn't know better, with a touch of pity. When she saw I was looking at her, she flicked quickly to her impish grin.

Of course, we discussed the message afterwards. Certainly this would affect things with Whiteside, Larry reported, and quite a number of other people, too.

"No one believes more in freedom of action than I do," he stated stoutly, "but when one person's freedom of action infringes upon the public welfare... well, no choice but to blow the whistle."

Then it was time for "Tomorrow's World," one of several new television shows that have replaced the old-fashioned adventure- fiction kind. I must say this is an improvement. Photography and the commentary are nearly always flawless, crisp and to the point, with no foggy statements or pictures. Everything is neatly capsuled and summarized. I never thought the process of learning could be made so easy and enjoyable—although, I must admit, I miss the old nonsense kind where you do not really learn anything. But that, too, is part of the past. Larry had just been saying that, given a chance, intelligent planning can work wonders ("Just look at how those new apartments have brought both life and fine line appeal to Budapest.") when the grave voice of the announcer broke in:

"Ladies and gentlemen, we interrupt this program for a special bulletin ..."

From the scholarly setting of the station's news center we learned of the rapidly growing gathering at Point Park, "what appears to be a spontaneous response to the President's special message earlier this evening." Then came the "remote switch direct to the scene," and for the next two hours we watched, hypnotized by the spectacle. At first there was nothing but chanting, singing and yelling—a bubbling sea of sounds, signs and people, all screeching for the hide of Mister X. It was both chilling and exhilarating to watch.

"To think that one man's words could have such an effect..." Nancy had said, awed by the seething majesty of the crowd.

The roar of the crowd and the stentorian tones of the breathless commentator, as he gulped out a rapid-fire description, had a dulling effect upon my senses. My eyes grew dry from staring, and my ears ached with the screech and rumbles. But Larry was transfixed. His eyes, small and glittering, never left the screen. There was a peculiar tightness about his jaws and nostrils. His breathing was measured and heavy.

"There is no greater sight, no greater moment in life than this... to see... to feel ... to taste of the power and the glory of the people aroused... and to know you helped them achieve their will." Larry said it only half-aloud, to no one but himself; yet all of us heard. It was a mystical, unreal sound, so soft as to be a whisper, and yet it drowned out all else.

"Larry, dear..." Mary's hand shook his arm with tender concern. Only then did he arouse himself to sink back to his casual manner.

By this time some of the leaders had gained the speakers' platform at the Peace Monument. They wore jackets and short coats against the raw March night, men and women alike, eight all told. Leaders representing workers of Homestead, Millvale, Carnegie, McKeesport, McKees Rocks and Pittsburgh; leaders speaking out on behalf of the "employed and unemployed alike... patriotic men and women who ask for nothing more than to work in the cause of peace and prosperity." Leaders demanding the end to the "social injustice of never-ending poverty and degradation, calling on the irresponsible barons of reaction and tyranny to vacate their seats of power this very night and return the conduct of business, education and government to the hands of responsible people." Leaders exhorting the "peoples of the world to hear our plea for brotherhood and work with us through the World Order of Nations to banish once and for all the Mister X's who tarnish the escutcheon of the free world, those fascists who bring dishonor upon our lives, our fortunes, our sacred honor..."

"People, this is getting just a little rough, isn't it?" Nancy asked. She had broken the hypnotic spell and was looking around nervously.

"Come, come old girl," Larry was grinning with unconcealed pleasure, "It's about time the almighty Got Rocks got theirs and that goes for the sanctimonious Uriah Heeps that serve them. The Privileged are having the privilege of seeing themselves as they really are... courtesy of the underprivileged. You can't blame them, Nancy. For years they have suffered one recession after another, with wages not even able to keep pace with inflation, and loss of jobs everywhere you turn ... all because small-minded people still clutch their stock certificates and hang on to the past.

"Besides, see? The police are on the scene. They'll keep order,"

Larry added, still flushed with the excitement of history in the making.

"Enter the police, summoned from their happy hearths, doubtless, to protect one and all alike, even Mister X. How lucky we all are." Mary said, though neither Larry nor Nancy heard her. "David, I'll have something to drink. Gin with anything."

By the time I returned with drinks for everyone, the new Chief of Police had moved to the Peace Monument and had the P.A.- system microphone in hand, attached earlier to a sound truck that had been parked adjacent to the Monument for use by the group leaders. Gradually the crowd quieted, as platoons of uniforms— some police and some World Order of Nations security police— took positions in and around the assembly. In tones of full authority, the chief warned against violence and pleaded with the workers to return home "and let the process of democratic justice act" for them. But all he drew were jeers, and the chanting began again, this time calling for the mayor. It started as a low, rhythmic moan, growing louder until the roar echoed and re-echoed against the hills. "We want the mayor. Give us the mayor. We want the mayor. GIVE US THE MAYOR. WE WANT THE MAYOR."

The din lasted twenty minutes while the police chief tried to restore silence. Yet, no violence broke out. There was no motion, save only the swaying of three thousand bodies to the rhythm of the chant, the scattering of torches held high in the night. Then the chant ended in a mighty roar of approval, as the squat figure of the mayor, surrounded by even more police, broke through the throng and puffed up onto the speakers' stand to greet the leaders.

Silence fell on the group—silence punctuated only by cheers of approval. Leaders of the "Patriotic Workers of Allegheny County," as they called themselves, made known their "demands in the true spirit of rational men seeking rational and lasting solutions to the problems of the county, the nation, indeed, the world," as the television commentator movingly pronounced. The workers, the mayor was told, could no longer sit idly by while a selfish few continued to threaten the peace and security of good people everywhere. The Mister X's must be removed, by force if necessary. And to dramatize this need, they, the workers, would strike for freedom if necessary. Hapless, harried and visibly ill-at-ease, the mayor countered feebly with the thought that, to his knowledge, the extremists—while morally wrong, understand—had broken no laws that he could think of, and, while he sympathized deeply with the workers' patriotic concern ("and I, too, was as deeply moved by the President tonight as you") still he was powerless to act.

This brought angry protest, and the crowd surged closer, precariously close to becoming a mob. The mayor was grateful as one of the leaders restored order, and then suggested that a commission be appointed to study the Peace Treaty to determine whether any local citizens stood in violation. Amid cheers, the much- relieved official promised to discuss the matter with the JCFLA.

Then as suddenly as it had begun, the demonstration melted away, and the cameras returned to the studio for a round-up summary of earth-shaking events here in Pittsburgh, and elsewhere around the country. Only then did we learn that similar demonstrations had occurred in Cleveland, Albany, Chicago, Los Angeles, in fact, 34 cities in all. To cap off the evening, Smith Armstrong appeared in the news center long enough to state that he and Nicholas Syerov would consider an appeal by the city and county governments to conduct World Order of Nations hearings to see if there had been violations of the Treaty—although he, himself, personally doubted that any serious wrong-doing had occurred.

"Let me stress," he concluded soothingly, "that the JCFLA does not wish to interfere in your local affairs. We prefer that local issues be resolved where they properly should be, at the local level. However, we are mindful of the fact that certain local citizens still take exception to the decision of the United States government to conduct peaceful relationships with the Soviet Union, the People's Democracy of China and other nations through the instrument of the World Order of Nations. Even so, we should prefer to remain out of local entanglements. But if we are called upon to assist in your local affairs, be sure that we shall engage in no witch-hunts nor foster vindictiveness…"

Larry was buoyant. Mary was gay. Nancy was pensive, and I was weary. The day had been long with many twists and turns. I was still deeply affected by all that had been blared into our home, even after the Bests drove off into the night, their thanks-for-a- perfect-evening ringing in our ears. That men could be so stirred by words; that men could act in such potent unison; that a quiet, apathetic city could be transformed into seething action in a few short hours, action that has continued at a terrifying pace; that the JCFLA and local authorities were moving—not to encourage— but to restrain the workers from violent action ("What did I tell you, old boy. What did I tell you," Larry had cried, lost in some unnamed victory); that these things could happen here!

I did not rest well during the night. I kept seeing myself in some sort of a mob—the noise crushing my eardrums—wondering how I got there. A silly thought, I said to myself, for I am not a joiner and certainly not one to rah-rah around Point Park.

2

To stand alone with Truth; to know at last the evil of deception and to see yourself as part of that evil; to plunge headlong into the trap you, yourself, helped to build; to know there is nothing now you can do or say or cry out to, save only yourself.

This is Hell, and I have entered it.

The forces that sprang the trap began their subtle play a few nights after the workers' demonstration. Dinner—cabbage and boiled beef—was over and Nancy was tending to some PTA program chores, while I was on the phone lining up some help for an April Scout outing—David's troop, of which I am Assistant Scout Master. Annie was asleep, exhausted from a tumbling afternoon of play, brought on by an unusually balmy day. Peggy was grumbling over a history theme, due on the next day, on "The Negative Effects of Nationalism in a

Free World," and David was struggling with mathematics, a subject for which he has no gift. It was the end of a day in which all of us were struggling hard for normalcy to keep things as they used to be, as if in clinging to past habits the present and future would go away. The doorbell rang three times before anyone answered, this done by loud voice votes echoing irritably throughout the house. David, resplendent in a loosely flopping T-shirt and grotesquely shaped corduroy trousers, was elected.

It was Mr. Jamison, our former Civil Defense block warden, now assigned to the JCFLA. Not yet sixty, he volunteered for the chore two years ago when he was prematurely retired as an accountant for the old Sanders Window Company, now out of business. A dour man, he is almost completely bald, which, with his reedy frame, makes him look like a tired skeleton much of the time. He lives eight houses away with his wife, Maude, who is unbelievably fat. He takes his job seriously, a fact we came to appreciate only last fall. Since then, though, Mr. Jamison's role as keeper of the block has become the source of much neighborhood jesting. For he still continues to make his rounds, checking attendance and reactions to the Treaty seminars and delivering endless streams of flyers, newsletters, brochures and pamphlets furnished by the JCFLA, which no one reads. For the latter he has taken to using a battered red coaster wagon with a handle much too short. Small children seem attracted to his plodding mannerisms, and he seems not to mind pulling them about on his semi-weekly tour of duty. But he was off schedule this particular evening and graver than usual.

"Mr. Little."

I never could get him to call me by my first name. He waited patiently in silence until I concluded my phone conversation, not even wishing to comment on so much as the weather to Nancy, who had joined him in the living room. I answered an appropriate, you-got-the-right-man, "Yes."

"Need your signature," he replied, flourishing a packet of white papers. "And your wife's too."

"Whatever for?" Nancy smiled at me, shaking her head ever so slightly.

"Requesting hearings," he said, smoothing the papers out on the coffee table. As an added touch, he produced a pen with solemn politeness.

In dry, clipped tones he explained that a South Hills Citizens' Committee was circulating petitions requesting that hearings be held immediately by the JCFLA and that the JCFLA had offered the help of its block wardens in circulating them to local residents "for their interest." Mr. Jamison added hastily that the JCFLA was only trying to help "a local group exercise its democratic prerogatives without attempting to influence either side of the issue."

And issue it had become. The papers were full of stories and photos reporting the demonstration and subsequent local moves to form other protest groups representing merchants, students, housewives and management. Feelings were running high, and there had been talk of imposing a ten p.m. curfew to keep budding mob demonstrations from getting out of control. Neither Nancy nor I sympathized much with the demonstrators. "After all, David, these Mister X's, as they keep calling them, aren't criminals. You'd think this was the French Revolution or something," Nancy had said earlier over dinner. "But then, as the paper said tonight, we can be thankful that the JCFLA is helping us keep our heads."

Mr. Jamison crackled on. He placed one of the petitions in my hands and pointed with a knobby finger at the key phrase. "We request that the below-mentioned persons be examined at public hearings to determine whether or not any have committed criminal acts as defined under the articles of the Treaty of Friendship..."

Then I read the names listed. With each, as my eye moved down the long list, the lump grew in my chest. With each—the name of a minister here, a physician and banker there—came an ever- increasing urge to shake my head violently, as if by so doing Mr. Jamison, his papers and the undefined terror surrounding them would vanish. With the name of each industrialist, labor leader and educator that blurred before me, the roaring in my ears increased, and I thought I heard my father calling for me to come help him in the store.

Nancy took the paper from me and scanned it anxiously, lips tightening and eyes widening, as mine must have done. Discreetly, Mr. Jamison was looking the other way, admiring a corner of the room.

"Why, David, this can't…"

"Yes, 'tis, M's Little," Mr. Jamison whistled softly through his teeth. "They picked 44 of them. Big wigs, mostly. Pen's right there…"

"But, see here, my own big boss is on that list and he's no more a criminal than …" I could not find the words that in any way could do justice to my indignation and the almost hysterical desire to convince Mr. Jamison how wrong this was.

"Surely you can't mean this; I mean Avery A. Brown is chairman of David's own company!"

"You can sign right there. Right underneath the Williams's," Mr. Jamison prodded. "Most everyone's signed. Just you and the Clarks and…"

"And old Mr. Grant. I know he's outspoken and downright mean, but he's never broken the law. I mean . . Now Nancy searched for words.

"Kruger, Nancy." I think I began to giggle, if a grown man can giggle. "Did you see Kruger?" She stared hard at me, wondering, I think, if I was going to cry. "Kruger. President of Mastersmeld. My new job, Nancy. That lovely, shiny, rich new job." I laughed at the joke. I laughed hard and loud, and then the children were there, pinched and curious. We sent them back upstairs. "Nothing my dears, Mr. Jamison just told Daddy an extremely funny joke …"

Then my mind righted itself. A spark of righteousness shone brightly as I handed back the paper.

"No."

"Sure you mean it?" Mr. Jamison's lower lip quivered slightly. An old patsy of an excuse for a man, I thought, and a heady feeling of pleasure came over me, as I realized that I was standing against the tide of the majority. It had been long in coming, for my wants and, I suppose, my principles have been simple and uncomplicated. But

there it was. I had gone along with—indeed, had vigorously supported—all of the moves that had brought World Peace to us. But now
someone had overstepped the boundaries of logic and human welfare.

"I see nine… maybe ten … on that list who might be considered
extreme in their opposition to social progress. Control them, yes.
Call them criminals, no. And the rest… true, they opposed our peace
moves, and they still criticize to some extent the way things are being handled. But they have done so without violence and within the
bounds of democracy. They merely have exercised their right to disagree. And while, personally, I don't think they always have acted
wisely, still these men are builders and leaders, whether you agree
with them or not. They helped—along with all the others—to keep
Pittsburgh alive. Misguided in some ways, perhaps. But to persecute them, No!"

It was a good speech. It felt solid and good to say it, rather than
think it. And Nancy saw it and felt it, too, for she nodded firmly. But
the words fell short of their mark. Mr. Jamison was unimpressed.

"Good-night," he rasped, and plodded out the door, a skeleton
clutching a sheaf of papers that shone white in the still balmy night.
There was one name on the list I had not mentioned—Dr. Hamilton
M. Rodgers.

The rest of the week passed without any repercussions. Nancy and
I both, I think, expected some sort of a reaction from some quarter,
but we never spoke of it. Instead, we were super-gay and super-con-
siderate of each other. (Here, let me get it. No, I'll get it. No, no, I'll
get it…) Two people frightened and inhibited by a nameless guilt but
quite unable to admit it, even to themselves. Public pressures continued to mount. Mr. Grant's house was stoned one night, and Avery
Brown very nearly did not make it to his limousine parked in front
of our office building one evening. A group of "Youths for Freedom,"
students from William Penn, they say, surrounded him, and it took
both our building guards and the police to get him into the car. Then
the mob screamed all the louder and began rocking the car, kicking
huge dents in the sides and fenders. I shall never forget the stony,
impassive Mr. Brown, completely unruffled in his Homburg, staring

straight ahead as the car finally pulled away down the street. The issue was not discussed at work, either with company people or with customers. There seemed to be a determined effort to pretend that things were the same as always, and so, within the confines of increasingly complex allocations, forms, directives, complaints and countercomplaints, it was business as usual. Neither did Nancy report any particular change in the BWP save only that she was taken off the Whiteside Electric case and put back in central filing. Nothing, we decided, to get alarmed about.

The weekend, too, passed uneventfully. Some of the men in the neighborhood and I spent most of Saturday looking for fertilizer for our yards. The chemical kind in handy bags no longer is available, except to farmers on limited rations, the rest going overseas someplace. We used my car, since I still have unlimited gasoline. We only found one farmer willing to sell us some manure, but counting the cost for delivery, he wanted too much money, and renting a truck now is hopeless. The yard will have to go without.

Mr. Grant was at church Sunday, the same as always, and Reverend Sandmire went out of his way, I think, to preach on compassion, love of mankind, evils of materialism and turning the other cheek. After church I learned Mr. Grant had been requested to resign from the Council. Nancy made some nice soup from a real meaty bit of ham bone she had found on sale and navy beans, which are plentiful.

On Monday everything fell apart.

I had gone to work as usual, checking in at the office for our weekly staff meeting. It was easy to sense from the all-too-hearty greetings of the office that the morning was not to go well for me. Experience has taught me that when daily intercourse is brisk and impersonal all is well. You are accepted as a matter of course, one of the inner family. But when conversation becomes too planned, too casual and too considerate it is time to beware. For you become the stranger, the man relegated to amenities accorded to outsiders. This usually means someone knows something you do not and is waiting for the humane moment to let you have it. There has been a death in the family since breakfast or a salary cut or a monumental management blunder. But always it is something, and Frank does not usually come calling at my desk at 8:15 a.m. on Mondays.

"Ah, there, David, my boy. See you're bright-eyed and ready to move the tonnage!"

"Yes, sir."

"Heh, heh, heh. Yes, sir. ... Nice weekend?"

"Yes, sir."

"Kids holdin' up and growing like weeds, I'll bet. And I'll bet that pretty Nancy is really bloomin' in the old spring air. Fine family, David."

"Yes, sir."

"David, wonder if you'd help me out of a bit of a jam? ..."

"Yes, sir?"

"What with staff this morning and all, thought maybe you wouldn't mind bein' first down at the JCFLA."

"Yes, sir?"

"That World Order of Nations Bureau of Employment wants to chat with all of us... nothing formal... just wants to get better acquainted, and... well ... a nuisance, but we all have to cooperate with the W. O. N. and all that, and I thought you might just as well go first and get the thing out of the way so's you can really get out and move that old tonnage and rack up those orders! O.K.?"

"Yes, sir."

"Nothing to be concerned with. Just a little visit. Just keep it low-key. You know."

"Yes, sir."

"Fine, boy! Got to put our best foot forward, and you're our man, O.K.?"

"Yes, sir."

"Lemme know how you make out."

"Yes, sir."

There was no point in mentioning that my job since January was not to sell tonnage but to allocate less and less of it to our regular customers. There was no point in inquiring why Frank was perspiring, it being only 67 degrees in the office because of faulty equipment.

There was no point in asking why the assistant manager—clearly designated as the favorite son—did not represent us for the maiden voyage before JCFLA. It would only have embarrassed us both, an unforgivable breach of etiquette. My fortunes had been pre-selected, and that was that.

I looked at the slip of paper that Frank had given me, still damply crumpled from his sweaty palm. Leon S. Tidings, room 407, the Skyway Building. I looked at my co-workers, stenographers and salesmen, silently hustling into a busy week. No one looked at me—not even to say good-bye.

Mr. Tidings had a small office, with a small desk and two small chairs and one small bookstand. He wore tinted, rimless glasses, topped with heavy, black eyebrows. His hair was not combed. His heavy facial features were marked with signs of stomach distress. He was shorter than I. He did not like me from the moment he saw me, and I did not like him. The way he puffed out my name—like a judge—told me he very much wanted to be a big man. The sureness with which he marked his papers and settled himself for the interview told me one day he would be.

"The 'Q' stands for?"

"Quincy."

"Ah, yes. We didn't have that." He made a brisk note. "You know why we are here?"

"To carry out the Treaty," I said, not sure just what "we" meant.

"To *enforce* the Treaty, Mr. Little. To enforce it at all costs. That is our job." His tone was measured and coldly casual.

"The JCFLA Bureau of Employment has been given the all-important task of helping you live up to your obligations under the Treaty." He fitted a cigarette into an ornate silver holder, a jarring contrast to a plain man in a plain room. He did not offer me one.

"Me?"

"Your country, I mean. This country." His voice showed disdainful impatience, and it stirred a deep hostility within me that had not yet been tempered by fear of the man. He still remained an unknown quantity.

"I had thought you, too, were a citizen of this country... my country," I said as calmly as I knew how. Perhaps I gave as good as he had given me, for his heavy brows rose, and his tinted eyes looked into mine. But they were cool, unruffled, as if to say, "Well put, but you will not win."

"Mister," he glanced deliberately at the papers on his desk, "ah, Little ... a most appropriate name, by the way," he smiled, sleepily as if he held in his head a whole field of knowledge completely foreign to me. "I am an American by the fortunes of birth. To love this country either for its traditions or for its present degenerate state does not mark a citizen as a true patriot. If America ever is to fulfill its dream for the millions upon millions of people who have been exploited by the capitalists, it must first learn that it cannot put itself above the higher demands of the worldly purpose. Perhaps some of us have learned this sooner than others. You, and I—all of us—are intricate and important parts of the whole of mankind. How well we perform our respective duties determines the extent to which we can have an orderly and fully productive society. Would you disagree to that?" The question was kindly put, as if Mr. Tidings already knew my answer.

"I..." but nothing more came. My mind drew a blank picture.

"You don't know how to answer, because you don't quite know what I mean, do you, Mr. Little." There was not even a hint of a question in his tone.

"I'm not sure." The small office had been close and too warm when I first arrived, but now the temperature seemed suddenly to shoot yet further upward. "I suppose you mean we must all work together and all of that sort of thing." I was beginning to despise myself, first, because he was right, and, second, because instinctively I wanted to save my face, which I was rapidly losing, and so was beginning to answer with any platitude that came into my head. A frantic gesture, like filling in the mystery-laden blanks in a college exam.

His smile grew frosty, like a banker about to refuse someone a loan.

"You don't play chess or study much, do you?" The voice was silken, and all signs of stomach distress had vanished from his face.

He settled back, as if he had consumed a thoroughly enjoyable meal.

"No."

"Ah," he sighed, "the American people. You make it so easy that it almost spoils the challenge." He righted himself again and swung briskly back to his papers. "But, on to the matter at hand. You sell steel for Mr. Avery A. Brown, and you must like him."

"Well, I don't know him."

"Don't know him? Don't know his habits? Don't know his beliefs? Don't know his activities?" His voice dripped incredulity.

"Well, that is I don't know him personally…"

"But you do know his habits, beliefs, and activities."

"Not exactly. Yes and no. I mean his statements and the newspapers … I suppose I know a little about him." My forehead felt damp, and I wanted to wipe it dry.

"Like him?" Mr. Tidings snapped harshly.

"Well. …" I was not used to direct questions which required direct answers. It seemed as if my mind would cease entirely to function at any second. "In a way. That is, I can't really say I dislike him." I finished in a burst of new confidence. I had found a way out.

"You don't dislike Mr. Brown. Thus, you don't dislike his stand on the… Treaty of Friendship," he rolled the words out slowly, almost to himself, "or his rather interesting views on profits, or his unwillingness to cooperate…"

"But that's not true." Now I knew I had the way out. "We've all been directed by him to cooperate to the fullest. The directives… and there have been dozens … are all signed by him. Why, he calls regularly on all the government bureaus and JCFLA just to keep things …" I paused, not knowing for sure where the road of words would lead me.

"Smooth," he finished. "To keep the business seas calm. To arbitrate. To conciliate. So that your business can continue to operate as it has in the past, which has not been too good," he added in helpful tones.

"No. Not exactly that."

"Oh?" It was a politely asked question, as if he were guilty of some terrible misunderstanding. "Then, perhaps we've all misunderstood Mr. Brown's statements and basic attitudes toward us. I thought he was… shall we say… not entirely favorable toward the Treaty." There was a long pause while I tried to think of something appropriate to say.

"I take it then that Mr. Brown is in favor of the Treaty?" he prodded once more.

"Not exactly."

"Then he's against the Treaty."

"In a manner of speaking, but he's never been… violent… like a lot of others. It's just his personal opinion. It's . .."

"Are you against the Treaty?"

"Good heavens, no!" I cried, tired of the twisting and turning of his words. "Everyone knows Nancy and I pushed and worked hard …" Now my suit coat was beginning to stick to my back.

"I know, Mr. Little. On this you have a splendid record." His tone was now gentle, brotherish. "Cigarette?" I took one, relieved that perhaps the interview would settle into a more normal pattern.

"You will agree that Mr. Brown is against the Treaty?"

"He's not against—just like that—I mean he probably doesn't like it and therefore…"

"He's against it. Yes or no, Mr. Little? Now surely you can answer at least one simple question?"

"But you don't understand. He's not like all the others. He's simply expressing an opinion. Good Lord! Look how hard he's trying…"

"I am fast losing my patience. Yes or no?"

"Yes."

"Yes, what?"

"Yes, he's opposed to the Treaty." I was beginning to feel unclean.

"Mr. Brown calls on all of us in order to feather his own nest, isn't that also true?" The voice was almost a whisper.

"Absolutely not. He goes to the government and he meets with the JCFLA people to cooperate. He wants to get along with you. He wants peace." My voice had risen to a shrill plea. Somehow I would convince this man that all we want is to work together and get along. Yet, regardless of what I said or how convincing it sounded, I was failing to get through to Mr. Tidings. An unseen barrier was between us, and it was as if he never even heard me. It was like trying to dent a pillow that kept returning slowly to its original shape after you hit it.

"What is it Mr. Brown seeks?" "Well…" My mind was whirling, trying to grasp onto something concrete. "He wants to keep things going. He needs more loans for new plant equipment…"

"He wants to keep things going so he can keep the old system, doesn't he? He wants to keep the stockholders and Wall Street happy, doesn't he?"

"Yes. I suppose…"

"Which all is based on private profit, isn't it?"

"Well, yes. But you see he's not the really greedy kind like…" "But he does favor profits?"

"Yes."

"Do you?"

"In a way. But only …" I was stuck. My mind seemed about to explode. Think. Think. Think of something. Don't sit here like this.

"Has the profit system worked?"

"Well, if we only… "

"If we only had the chance, I know. But you and I know that it hasn't worked in a hundred years, has it? Look at your bankruptcies, unemployment, depression, inflation. Yet you say another chance?"

"But…"

"Mr. Little…"

"I don't know. Maybe it hasn't worked. I don't know anything about these things." My throat was dry, and my head began to ache. I was no match. And he knew that I knew.

"Yet, you favor this antiquated system of exploiting workers… and even people like yourself. At a time when America needs fresh leadership and a new way of doing things… when our full productive abilities are needed as never before … do I understand that you intend to obstruct our progress under the Treaty by adhering to an

98

economic system that can't possibly work?" His voice now had risen, and his teeth were clenched in fury.

"I ... no ... of course, I won't obstruct the Treaty..."

"Has the profit system worked?" Again Mr. Tidings drove forward.

"Maybe ... I don't know... maybe it hasn't done what it should have. I just don't..." Oh, God! Oh, God! How can I defend something that I do not know how to defend!

"Now, Mr. Little," his voice had softened, and the brotherish tone was back. This pleased me. It was a relief. "Think carefully for a moment. Let's be logical. Avery Brown is against the Treaty. Now, can a person really work in favor of something he doesn't believe in? Can you? Could I?"

"I guess not."

"So if Mr. Brown is not in favor of the Treaty how can he work effectively for it?... and don't forget he's head of one of the most important steel companies in the world."

"Maybe he can't but..."

"Now if he can't work effectively, is it in the best interest of the Treaty—and all that it stands for—to allow someone as strategic as Mr. Brown to stay where he is? Now, the fact that we've already suggested this to him, and the fact that he has refused to vacate his post voluntarily... wouldn't you say that's being uncooperative?" "I ..." I must have blinked my eyes, for the room suddenly became blindingly bright. The small man was small no more. He moved so fast with words and thoughts that I could not keep up.

"Let me try again, Mr. Little. I'll make it easier this time. Would you dare deny that Mr. Brown is uncooperative?"

"I suppose not." My voice sounded far off, as if from another person.

Mr. Tidings made a few more brisk notes in silence. He hummed some tuneless tune to himself as he refilled his cigarette holder. He smiled and breathed a long sigh.

"Mr. Little, this job is not easy. The Bureau of Employment perhaps has the most critical task under the Treaty. For the root of all production lies in the hands of those who do the producing— the people. The workers and the managers. An ineffective person —be he a mill hand or a man like you or Mr. Brown—can only impede the progress we are making toward world-wide peace and prosperity. Production is the key. Without adequate production the Treaty will fail in its purpose. Is that what you want? Do you want more war, starvation, illness?"

"No."

"Neither do we. And my job—as it is with others in the bureau — is to see that it doesn't happen. The only way we can do that is to weed out all of the obstructionists we can find. To do this we conduct hundreds of interviews a week to search out those who will hinder the Treaty and have them removed from their jobs and put either where they will perform better or where they cannot harm the great work going on."

"But how can you do this? The Treaty is not supposed to interfere with local affairs..." Slowly, a new awareness was spreading over me.

"It doesn't, except where local affairs affect the Treaty. And if a man is not working up to his job, this then affects the nation's performance under the Treaty..."

"But how can you remove...?"

"Your Federal Bureau of Wages and Prices has no other alternative but to help us remove the incompetent and the obstructionists. And neither does a company or union, unless they wish to be prosecuted for open violation of the law."

"But our laws allow us the right..."

"Your Constitution requires you to honor all treaties signed by you—*regardless* of their content." He spoke with sureness and with unconcealed triumph.

I do not know how long the silence lasted ... a second or an eon ... it makes no difference. The awareness had burst full upon me.

"Except where local affairs affect the Treaty," I repeated numbly half aloud. Somehow we ... all of us ... had fallen into a pit with no possible chance of escape. Somewhere, something had gone all wrong.

"Precisely that," was the crisp answer. "You've tumbled to a rather intriguing thought, haven't you, because nearly everything that

100

happens in Pittsburgh affects the Treaty in one way or another." His voice was silken again, and his tinted eyes grew heavy-lidded.

I could only nod.

"Has the full impact reached you, yet? Have I made myself clear? For all practical purposes—and I suggest you get used to this—you no longer are a citizen of the United States in the same way you once were. You are a subject of the World Order of Nations." He spoke in open triumph, as if he could no longer contain within him the *good news*. But that was not what brought the chills and a whole new set of fears. We had long anticipated the day of world government. Rather, what left me frozen in my chair was the dawning realization of the kind of world government this was.

"And the Soviet Union? They are also subjects of the World Order of Nations?" He read it in my eyes. He saw what I feared to say. I wanted to scream and throw myself at him. I wanted out. I wanted to go home and be a little boy again. I wanted to hide my head in my mother's lap and have it all go away—like after a bad dream. Only Mr. Tidings would not go away. The small desk and the small chairs and the small room—they did not go away either. The voice cut through, cold, sharp and vicious. It sang of power supreme and vengeance completed.

"Not quite," the unmasked face pronounced. "You see, the Soviet Empire is the World Order of Nations, and the whole world is the Soviet Empire."

3

How does it feel, David Q. Little, to betray yourself deliberately, knowingly for the very first time? How does it feel to shave in the morning when you must look squarely into your own face to see what others cannot see? How does it feel to drive alone, even when you keep the car radio tuned loud? How does it feel to eat lunch, the sandwich suddenly dry and wooden? How *now* does it make you feel to be alone with yourself—in the long hours of the night or in the brightly lit conference room rigged for Teamwork?

It makes me feel sick.

It is a basic illness. The senses no longer are as they were. The March rain does not wash as clean. The children's kisses at bedtime are not as intimate. The water-cooler jokes are not as funny. Crisp white shirts do not feel as good. People do not look at me in the same way—or is it that I no longer look at people as I used to?

It is not so much the idea of betrayal, as such, for we all engage in betrayal. Rather, it is the thought of *conscious* betrayal of *self* that drugs the spirit. To betray another person; to fool the other fellow; to con the victim—one can bargain with himself in these. For we can always find a palatable motive if we search long enough. I betrayed my first blind date when I promised to call her soon. Kindness was my motive. I betrayed brother Harry when I promised to fix him up with my fraternity his first year in college.

Forgetfulness was my excuse. I betrayed my customer when I promised an order delivery date that no one could meet. Expediency was the rule. I betrayed my family when I got slovenly drunk with a harsh, crude, tramp of a woman in the dimly lit booth of a wretched bar in Johnstown. The weakness of mankind was my shield. These and many other betrayals I have learned to live with.

For, regardless of whom I might have betrayed, I kept always a little patch of honor for myself; a small place swept clean of deliberate fraud, where at least I could say, "Fool others if you must, but never yourself. When it comes to basic things, never sell yourself to any man."

The petty thief who steals but a little; the upstanding citizen who betrays but a little; in the end they become the same—robbers and killers, both.

I am one, because I marched the other day. I am one, because I carried a sign, held high in the noon sun. I am one, because I cheered loudly and jeered viciously when they told me to. I am one, because I damned Mister X when I did not want to. The little patch of honor is gone.

It began to fade when Mr. Tidings sketched the alternatives facing me under the new order of things. I had not seen fit to join with my friends and neighbors to protest the fascist activities of Avery Brown, Mr. Grant, Mr. Kruger, Dr. Rodgers, and the others; rather, I had turned reactionary, turned traitor against world peace, turned my back on humanity—and the welfare of my family. "Or have you forgotten why you fought so vigorously for peace only a few months ago ... ?"

He wore smoothly on, noting only with a flicker of his tinted eves my growing fear—and fear is all I can call it.

"One thing you should know, Mr. Little, with respect to my... ah... observations about the role of the Soviet Empire in the World Order of Nations. No one will believe you, largely because they will not want to believe you. On paper, at least, there is absolute equality between this country and the Soviets, and they shall prefer to keep to this illusion, which we have so painstakingly created for them. You can speak out, but I assure you, it will do no good. You'll succeed only in having yourself branded as an extremist. I scarcely need tell you that others have tried... and failed.

"On the other hand, if you cooperate to help make this new world of ours *really* work, then... perhaps... there is a place for you.

"You are free to act as you wish. The choice is yours, and free choice does have a place in society—so long as it does not interfere with the public interest. Only then must the forces of free men act collectively to prevent aggression and preserve an orderly society. We had hopes for you, but it is plain that you have revealed yourself as an unreconstructed capitalist, a willing tool of the exploiters. This makes them no worse than you. So, you stand equally guilty as a fascist and a traitor to liberty. You, of course, must be added to the list, to the detriment of your wife... ah... Nancy and... ah... three youngsters. I don't say this, for it will be up to the people to decide. But I know how they will decide. They will see you as an obstructionist to peace and all worthwhile effort. They will demand your removal from the important job you hold, and we will have no choice but..."

The toothy smile held mock sympathy. The shrugging shoulders conveyed helplessness against impossible odds. The Will of the People was at work.

Yet all hope was not to be abandoned, the heavy black eyebrows wiggled upward to say.

"You can re-establish your integrity with the people. You can re-establish the bonds of brotherhood with those who so earnestly seek peace and prosperity. You can rebuild the trust we once had in you. You can assure a place in the new scheme for yourself, your wife… ah… Nancy and those… ah… three fine youngsters… ah… Peggy, David and Annie, who I see is only six. Or is it perhaps that you have independent sources of wealth? But then your bank records don't reveal it, and I see your credit rating is not too good. And you're not a union man, and goodness me, a rather tidy home mortgage, too! Seventeen thousand, four- hundred-and-eleven dollars and sixteen cents. But then you have twenty-four more years to pay it. Nice. Nice. Hm-m-m-m. Tax assessment is particularly low. Could it be you're doing a little exploiting on the side? I note, too, several most interesting income tax returns. Well, well! Mr. Little, this is a most interesting file for one who guides Boy Scouts and teaches Sunday school…"

His head bobbed in wonderment. I had the distinct feeling that Mr. Tidings would enjoy his coming lunch hugely. More by instinct than by any wisdom, I now knew it would be useless to explain anything about anything. The tide would take me where it wished.

"Now, Mr. Little, we suggest you think things through carefully. I shouldn't be surprised if Mr.…." he paused to run his thick finger down a long list of names neatly typed on pink paper, "… Jamison, a fine man by the way, may call on you again, doubtlessly expressing the hope you'll sign that petition."

I started to speak, remnants of protest still on my face—the little patch of honor still struggling for its life.

"Be kind to yourself, Mr. Little," Mr. Tidings interrupted. "Think first. Speak later, and you'll be a much happier person."

I rose to leave, my trousers and coat damp and sticking to the small wooden chair. My aching legs were weak with strain, as if they had been encased in lead. It was difficult to stand erect and make my feet move with a confidence I no longer had. And still he was not finished.

104

"By the way, Mr. Little. A considerable number of management people—responsible citizens like you—have really become quite concerned with all of these Mister X's in Pittsburgh. They've been begging to organize into some sort of a protest group... not that we want anything of the sort, understand... but there it is. What can we do when people everywhere want action. Anyhow, they need a chairman, and it occurs to me that a man with your natural reluctance to become involved in civic affairs ... if you were suddenly to become involved... might give such a group the, shall we say, stamp of sincerity that it needs to be wholly effective in the cause of peace. Why don't you think it over..."

I closed the door and moved unseeingly to the elevators.

How do you express fear, panic, terror? How do you convey on paper the grief at knowing not what to do, not how to act, not how to think. For I have not been taught how to think. You clutch, instead. You clutch to instinct, and instinct says "walk." And you walk fast, blindly, through crowded streets and drab dime stores. You pass flower ladies and peanut vendors without smelling. You are deaf to the cries of the city—the giggles of shoppers, or the commands of traffic cops, or the frantic horns as you cross against an unseen light. You clutch to the small patch of honor, still flickering inside your sick breast.

Then you go have a drink.

The dim, quiet mood comforts you. The ghostly figures—and there are many for 10:10 a.m.—are friends requiring neither introductions nor conversation, not foes to abhor. The bartender is the Mother Ship in a white apron that turns light blue, then green, then red as it moves under the soft, neon gaiety rimming the bar— on errands of mercy to bind up the walking wounded. Somebody's Lounge at 10:10 a.m.—all that is left for a cradle or a womb to crawl back into. Warm, dark and far away, where a man might rest for just a bit. Rest past lunch. Rest into the early afternoon. Rest past the boundaries of time and on out into the black space of quiet emptiness to drift. To float on in suspension, where mind and matter become fluffy fog banks. The juke box is the Heavenly Host to strum you along, and the cool glass is the Magic Flask of what might have been. The world is left behind, rocking in the wake of forgetfulness.

Until something—ah, yes, it is the Mother Ship standing by in heavy seas—nudges you gently into another kind of darkness; less pretty, with cars, buses, bright lights and late evening strollers whose faces you can distinguish, more or less. And the siren song fades, as you seek manfully to moor yourself to this strange new place. A lamp-post does fine as the stanchion, while you check the landscape for clues. Somebody's car keys in your pocket. Shucks, they're yours! And the ominous shadow towering across the way? The Skyway Building. The iron door of reality clangs shut behind. David Little is back.

The dime does not fit so well in the phone coin-slot, and the dial holes are a little too small, and you are forced to try three or four times. When she finally answers even Nancy is impossible. So a fellow wants to stop for a drink or two, so what's all the tears and that crap...can't a guy have a little old snort without havin' to post it on the billboards? You hang up and sway indignantly from the booth. Dumb women. Vanish for a couple of hours, and they want to start draggin' the river. And the drive home is no better. Crazy drivers! And the stupes who invented stop lights. People. How I hate 'em! I'll show the dirty...

Then comes the nausea, followed by the tears—for the first time. Finally comes the most universal and ancient ritual of absolute despair. It is the Prayer of the Hopeless: Oh, God! Why me?

Then you are standing in the driveway, steadier, but weak and wondering how you ever made it. In the front doorway, framed in the lights of home, is a drawn Nancy and the concerned face of

Larry—summoned to soothe the fears of a bewildered family. Hot coffee and tell-me-about-it-old-boy serve to unleash a torrent of words that reveal the villainy of Leon S. Tidings. It is Larry who applies the magic balm of practicality.

"Look at it this way, old boy. For years we've talked cooperation and mutual trust with the Soviet Union as the only way to achieve lasting peace. Now, we've always known that sooner or later we and the Soviets would have to join forces against Red China... the really big threat to peace[25]... now, just a minute, David ... I know the Soviets have been a little loose with promises in the past...let me finish... But remember, the climate hasn't been conducive to stimulating their better instincts....Wait, damn it....But now, how the climate is all changed! They no longer have any cause to mistrust us. We can get along with them so long as we show our good faith by cooperating and working together. It'll work, you'll see. Besides, that creep, Tidings, is overstating his case. Sure, the Reds...Russians...have power in the W.O.N. But so do we, and I'll never believe that the neutral nations would deliberately turn their backs on us... not after all we have done for them.

"Now, about that petition. Has Avery Brown really done all he can for peace? Has he now really ... I know, David, now just a minute... No! No, of course I don't like power tactics, and maybe that Treaty was a bit one-sided. But did we have any choice... you see!

"Always, wherever there is social change there must be some dislocation, some hardship. Why, that's true throughout history. And in these past two-hundred years it has been the capitalists who have caused the most hardships. Look what automation has done to millions of families, and did these creatures give a hoot. Why, old boy, they practically rolled with glee in the aisles of their plush clubs. And now it's their turn. So what has Brown or Grant... and you don't even like him... ever done for you? So maybe they lose their rich jobs. So what about the steelworker who lost his?

"What do you mean, not fair? What's fair? Give me an example. See? Do you think it's fair what you'll be doing to Nancy and the kids? What do you mean... never be able to look at yourself in the mirror again. My God, you must still be drunk as a billy goat. Do you think you're pretty or something? That's better.... See, Nancy, we got the old boy laughing again.

---

25 The Asian Communist Bloc during this period, in addition to China as the leading nation, included Korea, Laos, Vietnam, Burma, Indonesia, Thailand, Cambodia, Pakistan.

"Fair, old boy? Oh, feathers! Let's put it another way. Do you have any other choice? There, now do you see what I mean? The choice has been made for you. So why worry ..."

Hot pancakes and plenty of oleo and sugar water—the heck with the food stamps. Forgiveness to a naughty boy. A hug from Nancy and a pat on the back from faithful Larry, buoyant to the last. The hot shower, and then the soft, cool folds of bed. Merciful oblivion, hiding the small patch of honor, now doomed.

That is how it was. You clutch for awhile at familiar things and then let go when weariness wrings from you what little it was that made you eligible to walk upright as a man.

For I signed the petition the next night, Mr. Jamison having waited discreetly until then. And I accepted, with proper humility, the "call to action against those who would destroy our efforts to lasting peace" by volunteering to "accept the will of your fellow citizens and colleagues in industrial management ... to serve as Chairman of the Greater Pittsburgh Industrial Association For Peace. .. ." This came to me in a letter from a man I never heard of, who lives in the North Hills and works for an ornamental iron works.

4

But the actual divestiture of honor did not begin to take place until eleven days later, at noon on a side street behind the county building. By forces unseen and unknown, all of the signs were there—stored in a battered green truck parked in a no-parking zone. A sign bearing Avery Brown's name with a big X through it, and one for each of the other 43. Other signs, banners, flags bearing a host of slogans calling for JCFLA hearings; for peace; for punishment of traitors and fascists; for prosperity and for working together—all neatly at the ready. And upwards of a thousand bright young men and distinguished older men, some fat, some lean, in their business suits awaited me—along with Leon S. Tidings. Topcoats were forbidden for image purposes. The suits had to show. A demonstration, a march through the city, was about to take place with myself at the head of the column. The preparation and assembly had been made easy for their honorable chairman. I had done nothing except sign two letters—reproduced in quantity—detailing the "protest demonstration" and sent to "my fellow citizens who must share with me my grave concern...." That and be there on time.

By now I had been reinstated in the office as one-of-us. People were looking at me and even smiling. Frank had become a real pal. No one seemed particularly upset that I was—on the surface at least—a ringleader conspiring to blast our own very dear chairman and 43 others clean out of the sky. To the contrary. I was something to be held in awe for I had made it with them. Apparently, neither the men nor the women ever look at themselves closely in the mirror of a morning. For them, life goes on seemingly without a flicker of— anything. In their cool, detached and flawlessly fixed faces I see not the serenity they want me to see, but rather the complacency of oxen, and in place of their bright and brittle chatter of small things, I hear only the Voice of Immortality come thundering from the Chambers of the Ancients—still unheeded now as then:

As in the days before the flood
They were eating and drinking
And knew not until the flood came
And took them all away...

So I had been given time off for the spontaneous, noontime demonstration. "Take your time, my boy. Got to cooperate in these things. You certainly must have gone over big with that fellow Tidings. Sure had some nice things to say about you ... a natural leader when really aroused by something you believe in. That's what he said...."

It is strange, numbing—tramping in the streets; not on familiar sidewalks and across friendly intersections, but stumbling and slipping along unfamiliar car tracks, ankles wobbling as slick shoe-soles fight to grab rough and worn bricks. Strange to see the city from here. Strange to sec the mixture of faces. The little Negro boy in a faded, ragged sweater, tugging gleefully at his mammy's red coat of many years. The old man with no teeth, smiling. The traffic cop, respectfully aside. The fat and sloppy. The lean and worried. The trim and triumphant. The neat and nervous. The happy. The anguished. A swirl of faces, all—to a man, to a woman—focused on you, because you are first.

Initially, the words simply do not come. You try, but nothing happens. So at first there is silence, underscored by the shuffling quiet of two thousand reluctant shoes, steered only by blank minds obediently following the leader—doing no more or less than he. If there was to be spirited protest, let it flow from him, the Great Leader now at the head of his Legions of the Oppressed! Let my indignation spark their mood; this was the signal flashed to me from the tinted eyes of Leon Tidings, who moved inconspicuously down the sidewalk abreast of me. I wanted to bolt, to run into another dimension where I would vanish into safe nothingness. It was like that time in army basic when I was ordered to crawl on my stomach under a screen of live machine-gun fire. Would that I could have done that again, instead of this.

Let me see. How did it go? You cannot kill, until you hate your enemy. So, you cannot yell, until you make yourself hate those who—I was getting it now—those who *caused* you to be here. Hate Avery Brown! Hate Mr. Grant! Hate the sinful ministers and greedy doctors! Hate them all! Hate them for selfish reason and blind stubbornness! Hate them for poverty, fear and all like ills! Hate them for bringing *this* upon your innocent head! Clench your fists; grind your teeth; roll your eyes and hate!

"Down with Mister X." My voice sounded too high-pitched and watery. My embarrassment now was my outward image. I must please Mr. Tidings, and I must preserve the illusion of crusading manhood—the clear-eyed, fearless Angry Young Man of Pittsburgh.

"Down with Mister X." There was a ring this time that brought a flick of approval to Mr. Tidings' half-hidden face.

"Down with Mister X." Better yet, and now I was no longer alone. The choir lurching along behind me had also found its voice. The Leader had spoken and made his wishes known.

The chorus wavered, slid off cadence a few times as it sought confidence. By the time we had reached Grant and Fifth, we were in tune and in step. Power surged through us, vicious and exhilarating. For we were venting ourselves of an animal kind of meanness, the kind that hits you on a sizzling-hot day during a traffic jam. We were, for a moment, the big kids on the block. We could swagger and shout, and all of Pittsburgh could do nothing about it, except watch in fearful silence. That was the magic potion. Fear. We had transferred it to those huddled on the sidewalks. An old lady, particularly frail, complete with traditional black shawl, apparently misjudging our gait, darted across the street in front of me. Halfway across, fear spread over her face—fear that I would trample her. I must have grinned horribly at her, as she minced grotesquely out of my way. I found, too, that whenever I looked directly at someone, their eyes returned fear and a plea—please, not me. By the time we had gained Liberty Avenue I was a pro. All was now delight. I will crush you, people. Out of my way. Hate! Ah, there, you bitch. Stand aside, you miserable old man. And you, smart kid, you'll get yours if you don't wipe that smirk off your face.

The mood carried me into Point Park and up the steps of the Peace Monument and the waiting television camera crew. Ah! The magnificence of it. Acres of heads and more heads—eager now. For their Leader had risen and would speak.

I had read the speech they gave me aloud in the men's room earlier, before the demonstration, so I was only a little nervous, the flush of the march still on me. It was mercifully short. I read it well into the P. A. system—not at all displeased at the tenor of my voice echoing back. My Message by now was quite familiar, and it had its usual effect. "It was a simple, eloquent plea," the paper recorded later, "of a modest, unassuming man in a white collar, who desires neither power nor riches but only peace for himself, his family and the peoples of the world.... Surely, the JCFLA can no longer ignore the wishes of the people.... The hearings must be held without further delay ..."

The entire operation took less than an hour. Less than an hour to change from one kind of a man to another. Less than an hour to sever forever my ties with the past. A relatively long time by the standards of the universe; for it takes but a moment in which to be born and another in which to die.

Then I was alone, all having departed in an unseeming silence, even Leon Tidings. The deed was done.

The pain and sickness crept over me slowly, as the evil drug of animal aggrandizement wore away. I turned my back on the city—even as I turned my back on myself—and walked mechanically under the overpasses toward the point where two rivers die and a third is born every second upon the second. The quiet was awful, the emptiness of the park worse. The day had turned gunmetal grey, and there were no shadows, so I should have seen them sooner than I did.

Young men—four of them under the bridge in the posture of measured waiting. One wore the leather jacket and stood easy, his big, knotted fists resting on slim hips. The other three were also young, but less cleanly tapered and more tousled and anxious. They were not twenty feet away, and I could see hate in their eyes—a kind different from that which I most recently had conjured up; the deep long-lasting kind that generates relentless purpose and furious strength.

He was the one who had known on New Year's Day when he cried "surrender," and they dragged him away. He was the one who had moved silently past me in the night to brood upon Mount Washington. Now, he was the one who read me for what I had become. This youth—hardened to perfection, a mercenary of the streets—dared to stand as a judge might stand, as if it were his natural right to do so. He did this without elaborate show, as if he were the rightful heir to all mankind and was simply claiming an inheritance justly due him. The cold fury of his face revealed that he had seen not only the demonstration, but my own betrayal and my flash of savage pleasure in it.

From the depths of his fists came the gleaming knife, which flicked open with a low click. Three other clicks followed, and the quartet moved in silent unison. It was the schoolyard all over again, and Miss Lee had just kissed me and sent me home.

I ran.

A slightly balding, slightly overweight man in a neat blue suit—the Great Leader and Angry Young Man of Pittsburgh now dispossessed from his throne—running awkwardly, pantingly back to the city.

A grown man blubbering and sweating.

That is what I see in the mirror these days.

And the voice I hear is not my own or the chatter around me. It is the voice that reached out after me as I fled Point Park—soft, clear, deliberate.

"Someday I will kill you."

IV

The Fourth Month

While I still do not know what moves me to keep this journal, I do appreciate what it has come to mean to me. It is the sounding board for my reason, whether or not I reason correctly. It helps me retain my sanity, so that I can get on with things, as forbidding as they are. Out of this there begins to emerge an image of me as I must really be, though it is yet too blurred to know what it is. It is difficult to record my thoughts honestly. For there is the constant mental habit of many years to recast the thoughts of others as my own. This would be less tiring; easy, like going to sleep when you are so weary and want so badly to sleep. Except, often I cannot sleep. Rest, even the pitiful bit I do sometimes get, is slow to come. My insides fight to come apart, and I want to smash at the placid, expressionless crowds who seem to flow so effortlessly. I am haunted by some unnamed will that drives me on an equally nameless search.

I face two distinct worlds, each in growing, more violent conflict with the other. The one outside these basement walls demands that I give myself up to its will, while the other—this inner world—lures me by its comforting solitude to seek Truth, surely the least rewarding of all quests. The one says I am of no consequence. The other says I am and that I must search out why. So, here in this small room the fight rages.

To set down what I feel, I find, has forced new habits upon me. I have become more observing and more cunning in hiding what it is

I begin to see in myself and others. I have been forced to think. As to what it is I observe, I still do not know which portion of it is Truth and which is illogical rationalization.

I write only as I am moved. Sometimes it will be two or three weeks between jottings. Other times it may be a steady string of nights, when I become so immersed that only the rising sun and a stirring household above stop me. The value is in writing impressions of the moment. Having done so, my mind then is cleared, shored up to face that other world once again. It is a means to take my measurements as of a given moment, like a meteorologist reading his instruments six times daily.

Mr. Tidings was right. They do not want to believe it, not completely, anyhow. They prefer to cling to what they want to believe.

Several times during these past couple of weeks I have tried to convey the sickness within myself and to sound a warning. But it is like fighting your own shadow.

Nancy: "You don't fight when you can't win…"

Larry: "Surrender! Bosh! Let the Tidings and the other pipsqueaks have their little illusions of grandeur. Let them think they have the upper hand. That, m'boy, is politics. How have we handled labor power over the years? Scramble the tax structure a bit and inflate the dollar and their egos! Let them think they've got what isn't there and make them love you for it. Don't sell us short, David, we're not dumb to political strategy…"

Mary Best: "The quick brown fox jumped over the lazy dog. Problem: Which one is the dog? Larry, won't you please see to more drinks?…"

We were at Larry's place the Sunday after my "remarkable display of leadership of the spontaneous demonstration." Nancy and I already had been over the ground a couple of times—once at supper and once staring into the blackness of a bedroom ceiling as we talked into the night—without successful conclusion. While I had no intention of trying to escape the course set for me, still I had wanted the people closest to me to know exactly how things were. And now we were in Larry's small study upstairs, a room of old leather and scarred furnishings, looking as rumpled as its keeper. Mary was sitting on a tired, lopsided hassock in a floppy blue sweater and skirt, looking like someone's teenager. Larry was knotted into an equally weary smoking coat and was fussing with drinks, coasters and napkins, like someone's maiden aunt. Nancy and I were neat in dress and suit, like students visiting a college dean the Sunday before registration, trying to hold ourselves erect on a sagging sofa. Nancy was at once sympathetic and exasperated.

"People, I can't get him to stop worrying. You'd think the situation was all his doing. I don't think he's slept soundly since that night I had to call you, Larry. And by the way, I don't think I ever did thank you properly."

"Quite all right, m'dear." Larry had found room on the floor by a stack of battered books long overdue for some storage closet. His bony frame was jackknifed into a distorted kind of comfort that only Larry could enjoy. He gestured with exaggerated hopelessness, nearly spilling his drink, and looked at me intently.

"David always has been something of a sober-sides. I don't think he's ever trusted the intellect of the human race very much, and without that..."

"Oh, hell!" I growled. "Look, doesn't it mean anything to you that my job... my whole future... was threatened, that I was made to do something I did not want to do? Doesn't this tell you something? What if the next time..."

"Who's to say there'll be a next time?" Nancy asked, plainly convinced that there would be no next time; that I had "done my part," as she had kept saying.

"Yes. Who is there to say it ... or hear it?" Mary echoed, so softly and so much to herself that she was unnoticed by the others. I must have looked at her sharply, for she caught it and our eyes locked, but she was without a sign of anything, save only a studied passiveness with an overriding film of wry humor. Even so, for once at least, I caught the full meaning of her words. She knows, I thought. She knows and she understands! Elation began to work through me but was checked with the thought, does she care?

116

"Sure, some heat was put on you, and sure you did something you didn't want to do. I suppose this has never happened to you before. Never had to carry out the garbage! Lucky fellow!"

Nancy's laugh skirted the edge of Larry's mild ridicule and then slid upwards in an uneven treble. "Didn't you know, David never does anything that disagrees with him." When she saw me flush she added hastily, "Oh, I know, I didn't like what you had to do any better than you."

Her hand sought mine. "Who encouraged you to stand up for your beliefs? Who stood by your side all the while that awful Mr. Jamison kept coming around?"

"And we all admire you... both of you," Larry added, like a judge giving out a second prize to somebody who also ran.

"You tried your very best, but the odds were simply too much, and a person can just go so far," Nancy soothed. "This is what I've accepted, and you must too. In the long run it could be the best thing that ever happened to you. Larry's right. Things have to change, and you've got to have more faith in our leaders. After all, who is this Tidings? I've seen better than he working as a file clerk at BWP..."

"That's what I mean! You didn't see him, neither of you! But I did! Can't...

"Oh!" Nancy bounced forward, frustration contorting her face. "Must I become a lawyer to talk with you any more? Of course I didn't actually see him, but you know what I mean."

"David." Larry's tone was grave and deep, and the whole room stopped, save only the ignorant antique clock, which ticked on much too loudly. The voice and manner told all of us that the time had come to put an end to this nonsense, once and for all.

"We can win."

His voice was soft and sure, like an "Amen" breathed in hushed confidence. The clock beat notes of punctuation into the silent room.

"You can win ... I can win... All of us can win ... if we use our wits." He spoke in unison with the clock.

"You've let Tidings get under your skin, and in the game of life you don't do that."

117

"I suppose you ignore him." I consciously put acid in my voice, a warning that my own wits were being crowded to their limit.

"No-o-o." Larry shifted and extended a long leg into the middle of the room with thoughtful care, as if sudden motion might crumble it. He studied the toe of his still faintly elegant loafer and then cocked his head in a bird-like gesture. His pale blue eyes were bright pinpricks of hard thought, oblivious to anything in the room —a particular trait that always gives Larry the seat of command in any gathering whenever he has something really significant to say. One always has the feeling that he is painfully collecting the sum total of his intellect to unleash a mighty bolt of wisdom to burn away the fog of doubt. This is the cornerstone of his appeal. Instinctively you feel Larry is giving everything he's got, his mental shirt right off his back, all for you. So overwhelmed are you with this supreme effort that you want desperately for him to succeed— if for no other reason than that your own sense of fair play would have you do or say nothing that might cause him to fail.

"You don't ignore children. You mold them, badger them, flatter them, scold them, cajole them… and when it suits your purpose, occasionally you give in to them. But never do you lose control. A good parent doesn't ignore his brood."

"And of course, Larry, Tidings is part of the ever-growing brood. Is he the raucous teenager or the baby in burlap?" It was Mary who asked the question.

Larry's eyes lost their vacant glint and crinkled into his face. "Eighth grade. Old enough to lord it over the younger pups but out-classed by the boys—and menfolk—up the line," he said with good humor.

"But he still could be marble champ, better even than his parents."

"Marbles are harmless."

"Unless unleashed from a sling shot. And boys can use sling shots rather well. Take David and Goliath. David, who was but a boy, felling a full-grown man three or four times his size. Larry, you're slipping," she teased.

"Ah! But you forget that David and Goliath were but legends, and most legends of the past are now forgotten." Larry spoke in a surgical way that put a chill on the repartee that was supposed to be effort-less and gay. It revealed his often expressed skepticism of religion as "a crutch for the weak" and his general coolness to anything historic as being "of little importance in the grand scheme of things."

"True. Great legends of the past are dead, and we have shiny new legends of the present… like the fifteen-year-old lad who raped that woman in the parking lot in broad daylight last week. Now, that takes a bit of fortitude, wouldn't you say?"

"Proving?"

"That not all parents keep control."

"Not all parents are good parents."

"And which are you?"

What had started out as an attempt to lighten the somber mood, like a fledgling in flight, faltered and tumbled to the ground. The game of chase, as Larry and Mary call it, had ended before it started. The two are likely to lapse into their game at any moment, regard-less of who is around. The object simply is to out-wit each other with quick thoughts and clever phrases. It is an instinct with them and usually ends in some sort of draw in which each wins some form of satisfying recognition from the other. It is a form of chemistry that has existed between them since they first met; a means, I have al-ways supposed, for each to test the worth of the other to themselves. Usually this fast-paced exchange of tumbling, often unrelated words is stimulating to witness, and it leaves them flushed and happy, like children finished with a romp in the yard. It is part of what makes the tall, sure husband and his small, tom-boyish wife exceedingly popular at every kind of social gathering and why hosts never seat them too far apart, lest the game be spoiled and the spectators cheat-ed. But not so this time, for Mary's question had the sharpness of a plea, as if she had become lost in the twists of rhetoric, and wanted to call the game off.

"Which am I?" Larry shifted lazily to look more fully upon her. "I am the good parent, and I know how to handle the brood. You know that, don't you?" His voice was that of an understanding father.

"Dear, dear Larry. You never fail me, but then that's why I married you." She smoothed her skirt over thoughtfully, while Larry beamed pleasantly at us momentarily, and then set his face in concentration.

"You know, David, there are a lot of people who never grow up, or never succeed in adjusting to life." He reached up backwards to a sagging book shelf, long arms, searching like giant feelers for an ash tray, tapped out his pipe. "Either they can't—due to lack of knowledge or intelligence—or they won't—due to their environment. It makes no difference in either case."

"Some people are dumb, is that what you mean?"

"Bluntly put, but generally correct, I'm afraid." He stuffed his pipe and lit it, squinting at me through the smoke. "Only, I choose to think that all of us are dumb. It's just that some of us are more dumb and possibly more mentally warped than others, as well as less fortunate and perhaps less gifted than others. It's up to those with the greater advantages to help those whose lot is more difficult, an oftentimes unrewarding experience."

"Like the Sarah Long case."

"Precisely," Larry chipped. He smiled ruefully. "I had forgotten that one, but that's exactly what I mean."

I was thinking of Larry's first professional experience some years before with the PAP tests.[26] He had been appointed test counselor by the Federal Bureau of Studies and assigned to work off the William Penn campus with South Hills Public High School. He had uncovered some rather bizarre findings about a seventeen- year-old girl—plain-looking, in fact fat as I recall—who, even though scholastically superior, apparently had formed rather strong attachments to her father that "quite possibly bordered on incestuous tendencies," as Larry had judged it, plus a host of other clues to emotional disturbances that made her a poor risk for college. He had summoned the mother, Sarah Long, in an effort to help untangle the girl, and the woman, distraught by the news, had tried that night to burn the school. The public hearing that followed was a real ordeal for Larry,

---

26 Personality and Adjustment Profile, a series of standardized nonacademic psychological tests given under law in both public and private schools at all levels under jurisdiction of the Federal Bureau of Studies.

who asked that the mother not be prosecuted. The girl, if I recall the right one, never was able to readjust to finish out the year and was confined to a mental institution. The father tried to bring suit against Larry, but it was thrown out of court.

Larry rolled on, the case of Sarah Long resolved and forgotten many years before. "M'lad, m'whole life has been centered on trying to find the key to liberating the energies of human beings. Few people have either the capacity or will to make the most of themselves. They're forever getting tangled in a maze of contradictions and all sorts of unpredictables that just simply run contrary to what ought to be. A regular chamber of horrors!"

"They don't know any better, do they, Larry?" Mary had risen as if she had heard this many times before and had suddenly become too weary to hear it again. She began collecting glasses for refills from the kitchen store of liquor. "Here, David, Nancy, time to tap the keg. Bourbon and .. ."

"Beer, this time, if it's cold," Nancy said, flexing her shoulders, her back, I suppose, aching as badly as mine. The edge of a sick sofa is no place to sit rigidly for very long.

"Well..." Larry appeared rueful; as if apologizing for the whole human race; as if he personally must assume all the blame. "No, they really don't know any better." He spoke with a long sigh.

"You try and you try. You try to show them the way, but somehow they just never seem to get it." His eyes lost their momentary despair and hardened to blue flints. "That's what has always angered me. To see them helpless and..." his voice rose in hopeless fury as he sought the right words, "degraded and exploited by the shrewd and selfish who, somehow, are forever in the way.

"I have wanted nothing more in life than to help people save themselves from themselves, by curing social injustice and by helping them to understand the role that is theirs to play... if-they-would-but-play-it! And I think I have learned a great deal."

His voice was somber now, as if he had made an irrevocable decision to reveal the sum total of himself by straining every mental muscle of his being. This is too holy a thing to watch; to see another of your species divest himself of the earthly habit of doubt and self-effacement to acquire the robes of divine, unwavering purpose engrained by some monumental force in the very center of his soul.

I wanted to turn away, but the force of Larry's trance held me still.

"People can become beautiful beings if they are helped... guided... and kept from their awful weaknesses. They are as children, right enough, and must not be allowed to stray... lest they hurt themselves.

"They need only an understanding climate to lift them to a... a glorious nobility. This is society's destiny, and I must help mankind to meet it...

The mystical thread was broken by the muffled footsteps of Mary on the carpeted stairs and glasses clinking on a metal tray, leaving Larry still unto himself, for he had left us, the room, everything tangible.

"How, Larry?" I sought to restore him as I have always known him, slightly flip and brightly confident.

He came back, from whatever his vision, and grinned. He took Mary's offering and drank deeply, as one who has labored long and hard in the hot fields of thought. He rose and stretched, windmill arms flexing.

"People must be motivated in the right direction." "Controlled. Tom Shade comes right out and says it, Larry," Nancy uttered with a trace of daring.

"Exactly. Nancy, you're becoming a first-rate strategist. I think you'll see what I mean." He spoke directly to her, as a teacher who suddenly touches a responsive chord in a questionable student.

"The trick... the real adventure in life ... is to acquire the skills of motivating someone without his being aware that he is being..."

"Controlled."

"Exactly. This is not easy but it is necessary, because the human tendency is to resist any kind of..."

"Control."

"Exactly. So he must be motivated ... no, let me finish... must be channeled in the right direction, and the trick is to let him think he thought of it himself."

Nancy's eyes were bright.

"Now, the more childish the person, the more you must resort to the stratagems of good parenthood." He turned quickly to Mary, who watched in thoughtful silence. "You see, Mary, that's what I meant."

Mary nodded, started to speak, but smoothed her skirt some more instead.

"Now," Larry was pounding into the home stretch, "The Communists, both Russian and Chinese,[27] are especially childish. They are immature, petulant, and at times downright foolish, though cunning, in spite of it all. If we are to cope with this sort of thing we must be coldly realistic.

"First, consider that the very fact they are impatient and peevish is, in itself, the key reason why we simply cannot antagonize them, lest in a moment of blind rage they trigger a war."

The cool, urbane manner of the lecture hall—earthly reality—once again was in full possession.

"If little Johnny deliberately locks himself in the bathroom in order to dump the contents of the medicine chest down the toilet, I doubt very much that you'd panic the little brat by taking an ax to the door!"

"Anyone knows better than that." Nancy spoke with a growing sense of participation. "You coax him. Remember, David, when Annie did just that?"

There seemed little point in reminding Nancy that Annie had been thirty months old and had been concerned only with a dirty, stuffed bunny, not a medicine cabinet. Nor did she deliberately lock herself away. It was an accident, due to the innocent lure of a shiny doorknob.

"Precisely. Little Johnny must be humored, must be diverted from his mischievous intentions, must be given other things to think about..."

"Ice cream awaiting in the hall, or perhaps papa's big gold watch to play with," Mary added.

"Something like that," Larry breathed into his glass as he took a quick gulp. "So it is with our Russian friends, and especially the

27 During this period, the Russians and Chinese had patched up their on-again-off-again interparty feud. In the middle and latter parts of the twentieth century the Chinese generally favored violence as the means to achieve "revolution," while the USSR, largely through strategic necessity, favored "revolution" through a softer parliamentarian approach.

Chinese. We buy time by humoring them with little face-saving devices of no consequence, to keep them from dumping the world down the toilet. We let them win a round or two where it doesn't count, but we stay firm where it does count.

"And… then…" He rolled the words out slowly to gain emphasis. "Gradually … a little here, a little there … we begin to reconstruct them, which, once they understand that we mean them no violence, should not be too difficult, for in the end they want the same as we."

"Let them think they've mastered you, but you master them through your wits," Mary spoke the words almost sorrowfully, and for an instance our eyes locked again. No hint of encouraging understanding in them this time; instead, a look of passiveness.

"Yes, m'love. But the job is not to destroy them and the rest of the world, as some would have us do. The job is to save them and ourselves. To put them back on the track. Motivate them without their realizing it. To do that we must win their trust, and to do that we must put our own house in order, too, y'know."

"Be more clever than they, is that not so?" Nancy asked, the triumph of understanding on her face.

"You've summed it up beautifully," Larry chortled.

And he turned full upon me, beaming as one very dear old friend to another.

"Be more clever, David. This is your worry, if you feel you must. Don't waste your energy on things you cannot control. Instead, focus on things you can control. Get along with them, David. This is the one great ability you do have. Use your wits and you can win."

2

From there we moved to small talk, little of which I recall, for my eyes were increasingly on Mary. There was something different about her now. I had a new awareness. She, better than anyone, had understood my fumbling efforts to reveal a growing conviction that we somehow are doomed to an unnamed fate more terrible, more degrading than death itself. She seemed to know of that awful sickness that comes with a feeling that, unknowingly, we have infringed in some sort of way upon God Almighty, Himself—the same kind of sinking sickness that must have seeped through the Romans when the heavens turned black and the earth shook and the rains came to wash away Blood from a Cross. What puzzled me, though, was that she seemed to have known all along that which I have only lately come to. And the more chilling puzzle was that she seemed to know, too, that I would fail to convince anyone; that, indeed, it would be I who would be convinced instead. Her look had been one of "welcome to the club" and "forget it." Then she seemed to do a mental double-take, as if reconsidering something. For her look had brightened with thoughtful alertness, with a mixture of curiosity and, I thought, hope.

She had lifted a corner of a veil to reveal a new dimension to herself—as deliberately as a harlot might raise her skirt and caress her spread thighs, in order to lure a hot-blooded youth to new heights of understanding. And, like the youth, I could not let the veil close again. So it was that I looked at Mary not as Larry's girl-later-wife; not as a kid-sister-pal to be platonically smooched, patted and half-heeded; but as a whole person, complete with a wisdom, a spirit, a body all unto herself. She saw this and did not mind, while Larry and Nancy talked little things quite without us.

She saw that I looked at her honey-colored hair, tousled by a flip disregard of what others might think of her nonconformity to style. She saw that I looked without apology into her large green-grey eyes that were clear, steady and warm with some kind of inner peace made long ago. She saw me examine her oval face and button nose and full lips, perked most of the time in open inquisitiveness but now set in a relaxed softness. She saw me move down her body and then quickly back to look again at the tips of her breasts poking out in matter-of-fact clarity from beneath the floppy blue sweater—small breasts, easily discounted as too boyish to hold much promise of anything, until one looks again closely and sees, instead, exquisite, sensuous works of sculpture. She saw me examine with thoughtful care the rest of her, eyes coming to rest on the fullness of her legs—also easily discounted as being slightly over-proportioned for any real appeal, until one sees for the first time that really smooth skin covers really well-molded muscles that are firm, healthy and unafraid. She saw this mixture of new awareness of both her mind and her body. She saw it, because she straightened herself on the lopsided hassock, smoothed her skirt carefully, folded her tapered fingers in the hollow of her lap and waited until I was done.

And when I was done she looked at me no more, but to the outside, where the late March wind blew hard against the study window, cracked open to ease away the closeness. It was a warm, moist wind that churned fleets of great sunlit clouds across an ocean of blue. Still naked trees and shrubs danced to the wind song, against a backdrop of moving shadows that played upon once grand houses and impressive apartments, now peeling and drab; upon streets once smooth, now pocked with neglect. Somewhere, children laughed and footsteps slapped hard against soggy brown ground. A nervous squirrel darted in and out of view— gone in a flash—busy with "very important things." A kite fluttered bravely; its ragged tail too short; its string lost in the jumbled horizon. Who held it, man or child? And what dreams went with it? The promise of spring. Everything expectant, restless for the new chance. The kind of a day that begs for understanding.

She got up abruptly, as if suddenly infected with this restlessness of nature.

"I need a walk. Who's coming?"

"Out of your mind, m'dear. Wind gives me the jitters. Ought to close the bloomin' window." Larry and Nancy were looking through frayed photo albums of his graduate days at Oxford. Nancy, engrossed with the trappings of scholarly grandeur, could only shake her head. I could read her dreamlike concentration. I had seen it before in country club lobbies, given over to the likes of us once a year; in orchestra seats freeloaded from a benevolent employer; and in the back seats of occasional company limousines. It said: "If only it had been David…" She had not succumbed to it in months, and now she was becoming more her former self, a sign that she was convinced that all of us would soon return to past ways. It contradicted me and made light of my struggle with reason. It rubbed me wrong.

"David?" Mary's voice was soft with expectancy, and I warmed to an increasing awareness that she actually wanted me with her.

I protested sincerely enough, I think, and of course was urged to go by both Larry and Nancy. An act of cleverness on my part, that had so lately been commanded of me.

So, we walked, and the conversation ambled pointlessly, as did we. This was due to an inherent bashfulness on my part, a product —and here I must stop to think.

Do I mean shy? No. Afraid? No. Unworthy? Yes. But unworthy about what? My work? No. My dress or habits? No. My knowledge? Maybe. Try intelligence. Not quite. Myself! I somehow feel unworthy as a person! But why? I do not know, but I feel it, all the same, and as I look back I now begin to see why Mary has stirred me so deeply, for she has ignited within me a spark that gives me a new will. She makes me feel worthy.

It came about as we neared the underside of the great stadium that hugs the hill above the University, made all the more vast because it was empty. Neither was there anyone about it. We had been gone nearly an hour—precious time, I now realize, miserably wasted! We were standing in the growing shadows beneath the Romanesque columns that towered upward in the deserted stillness like patriarchs of an ancient world, long forgotten but still there for anyone who cared enough to pause, look and feel. We were very much alone, as if we had stepped across a threshold into timelessness.

She had her face to me. The pink aureole of setting sun smothered in tumbling clouds bathed her in gentle light; while eddies of damp, scented wind rinsed her uplifted head and laid her loosened coat away so that her body, too, might be anointed in pink and revealed in clean, fresh lines—to offer, no longer the mate of another, a half-equation, but a woman-child, the sum total of nature and innocence and youth, set free under the giant columns. A transfiguration that had mercifully included me, though by what new standard she measured me, I could not then know—save only that she must have seen what it was that I now saw.

To touch her with brotherly care—as had been so often my unconscious habit—could not be ever again. I must now dare to touch her, lightly on the arm, a timid feeler to speak half hope, half despair. So did I seek her, and she moved ever so slightly, so that our hands could meet by chance that was planned by two minds, two wills; not one.

Warm hands, each growing stronger in the keeping of the other; eyes that searched, then closed in deep, agonizing effort to bring forth yearnings long ago laid to rest; lips that parted in silent cry of the liberation of self; arms that encircled to weld tightly the warm flesh of two wholly living beings. Only then did our lips meet, and neither poetry nor song nor cheap novels nor lofty prose could have captured the might of it. Every man has his secret kiss. Every woman has hers. We had ours, and only the great stone patriarchs knew.

Her body—warm, soft, violent—became partner to my hands, as mine to hers. It was a ritual of motion, whose rhythm was broken only once when I paused to arrest my hand in trembling uncertainty on the taught curve of her stomach. Then, finally, did she speak, a whisper-cry.

"No, don't take your hand away! Please. Be strong! Be firm! Be sure! Oh, Davey... may I call you Davey... you are my hope!"

And she fed it downward, nails dug deep in my wrist, while her legs shifted apart, and we both swayed against the stoic solidity of a massive column which both held and hid us.

The ritual of motion continued, until there was very little more of us to be discovered.

The street lights winking on in the chilling dusk and the dying of the wind roused us to start back. Only then did we talk—the kind of babble that comes as the aftermath of an intimacy that knows neither shame nor regret. A verbal dam had burst, but I was still too much within the transfiguration to fit what we said into any sort of a meaningful pattern then.

Our return was uneventful. Larry and Nancy were still at it, talking about trust, Oxford and the wisdom of using the JCFLA to perpetuate social justice.

128

"Don't forget for a minute, the Russians need us, and they would never be so foolish as to bite the hand that keeps them," Larry was saying.

Both scarcely noticed us; nor did they see the soft, casual brush Mary gave my hand as she pressed by me to resume her place on the lopsided hassock, looking once again like someone's teenager; nor did they see that I no longer cared. The world and everyone in it, save one, could go hang. What counted was now concealed beneath a floppy blue sweater and skirt that folded innocently between legs slightly parted.

Of course, we met the very next morning while Larry was in class and I was supposed to be selling steel that no longer needs to be sold. We used her guest room.

"I want you here, in this room, in this bed that will become ours, completely uninhibited by anything." She did not let me undress her. Instead, she slipped unclothed from a soft housecoat, her body still faintly damp and sweet-smelling from a morning bath. She helped me with my clothes in gradual stages and in teasing interludes—"I want to feel the roughness of you against me first." Warm discoveries grew warmer and more rewarding. Violence begot greater violence. Peace came again and again to give greater peace. And freedom of self grew, nurtured by the sureness of the other. It was a form of birth in which mind, body and spirit burst forth to give unrealized power its glory. Indeed, the intensity of our freedom was such that we wanted to conceive; to make a special child that would grow bigger and stronger and more beautiful than anything that is now; a special child that would grow into a giant to sweep away the chains that hold ordinary men. How we have tried! The next day and the one after that and the one after that—these past couple of weeks.

3

From where does it spring, this new awareness? Is it the delayed reaction to forces long dormant; a time-capsuled chemistry only now released by an unfathomed mechanism? Or are we only now sufficiently grown to be fitted to one another?

The first time I saw Mary O'Neil Best was on the train platform at Carthage Center, Ohio. It was a hot September Thursday. She stood in a whirlpool of baggage carts, trunks, suitcases, parcels and endless varieties of students. She was one of the new ones. You could tell by the way she stood bravely still against the human tide that swept toward the half-dozen taxis assembled by a distraught dispatcher to execute the nightmare shuttle service from train to campus. She seemed terribly small. To a sophisticated senior it was obvious that she was ill-equipped to cope with such worldly confusion. For she bore the marks of a country girl, a fresh, unpainted sweetness that glowed. Only her eyes moved, dancing grey-green hues caught in a spectrum of moods by the late sun. She watched with forthright honesty and waited with a ladylike poise that did not quite cover the tomboy curiosity. She was measuring the new environment against the old. Look before you leap.

Even then she looked as if she belonged exclusively to someone —to a big, burly brother, perhaps, who would poke your eye out for tampering or, maybe, to bent, aging parents who had staked their meager fortunes, dug from stony soil, upon this little girl in a cotton print dress. Whatever it was, some force outside of my reach had already claimed her. This was how I imagined her to be—never an entity unto herself, free to accept any outsider's bid; rather, the closely guarded secret of another. She had impressed herself deeply upon me, and the image stuck from then on. I wanted to be her friend and nothing else, but then I wanted nothing else, for Nancy and I already had reached an understanding.

I had moved up the platform toward her, somewhat disdainful of the feverish competition for taxi seats. For I was being met by no less than the president-elect of the Senior Class, the president of the Student Assembly and immediate past president of the Debating Society, of the Student League for World Peace and of Alpha Beta Alpha. Only he was not there. Lawrence A. Best was late.

Her look was frank and puzzled as I neared her. Was I, perhaps, some forgotten acquaintance? My amusement must have shown, and I spoke to her.

"No. We haven't met," I said.

"Do you always run counter to the pack?" Her eyes spoke a warm welcome, as she nodded her head toward the bedlam through which I had just emerged.

"Only when it benefits me, and a friend is picking me up," I replied.

We introduced ourselves and became friends at once. She had come from a farm, northeast of Lima, and wanted to learn to write. I was unfolding some valuable information on living habits at Western College when he arrived.

He swung a trim black convertible expertly around the comer, cut a path smoothly to the far side of the station, and dipped to a noiseless stop. His pipe flopped carelessly from clenched teeth, bared in a painful grimace from the heat and sun. He stretched around to look, his features taut with mild discomfort. He seemed unaware of the faces that one by one had turned to follow him in. There were scattered greetings of "Hi, Larry," which he acknowledged with casual waves of a bronze arm. But his eyes were intent on the search—a trim young man erect, sure and decisive. In a moment he saw us and broke into a grin.

"Come with us." I steered Mary and our assortment of luggage to the car.

As always it was a warm greeting, and as always it was good to see him. It was particularly so this time. The summer had been drably spent at the store, and Dad and I had quarreled repeatedly —a fact that lately has begun to bother me again, for I never saw him alive after that. But Larry was quick to make me forget my concerns.

"Dave. You look pale and in need of beer." He had not yet been taught by Nancy to say "David" nor had he yet been to Oxford.

I do not believe she took her eyes off him from the moment he came into view. Her gaze was neither moonstruck nor aloof. It was thoughtful concentration. He did not pay her any particular attention, until we were close enough for introductions. Then he must have caught the full sparkle of her, for he sobered momentarily and then brightened to booming good humor, as we packed into the car and drove off.

"Another jewel added to the crown of Western College," he said.

"I'm a mess, and you know it." Her face was flushed and damp from the still heat of the dying afternoon, and her cheek was smudged.

"Mary O'Neil. O-o—T'is a foine naime!"

"Ah, thankee, sor-r-r."

And we were at the freshman dorm too soon. I doubt any first year student had such knightly porters. A growing pall of homesickness had begun to spread over the walks and courtyard, which were strewn with first-time-away-from-home girls and their puffing parents, younger brothers and grandmothers, each toting something. But Mary—flanked by two Very Important Seniors, each bearing a portion of her mismatched effects—moved as one whose transition from one environment to another had been smooth, indeed.

A week passed before I saw her again. This time it was in the littered quarters of The Arc, the weekly school paper, the motto of which was "Let the Arc Lamp of Truth Light the Way." I was the assistant advertising manager, and the student management had gathered to select their respective staffs for the coming year from the assembled group of freshmen and some upperclassmen. After a normal amount of confusion Mary was duly assigned special events reporter and a spot on the copy desk every other Thursday. She had remained as unaffected as when I first saw her, still appraising everything in sight with an openness that already had begun to charm a growing number of the more dashing boys, who became even more dashing whenever they thought she might be watching. Even the newly appointed city editor, a mighty junior who barked out the pep talk, perked up under her eager eyes— slouching in an ancient swivel chair so that he could prop his feet on a beat desk with just the right amount of disdain for conventional behavior, a must for anyone seeking to become a Lion of Journalism. And she loved it. She had the rare trait of being able to look at anyone or anything as if he, she or it were the most important thing in the world to her. She did not

132

do this consciously, a fact readily apparent to anyone exposed to her, which made her appeal all the stronger.

Even the girls liked her. Nancy, perhaps, put it as well as anyone could. She had stopped by after the meeting, and the three of us had gone to the Raven Haven for snacks. Ordinarily a bit standoffish—in fact a bit snobbish, as I look back—Nancy seemed to take to Mary almost immediately. She had said later, "Mary doesn't make you feel as if she is competing with you. She makes you feel, somehow, important to her...."

I do not know that Mary saw Larry again until the night of the Debating Society's first meeting. It was her initial reporting assignment, and she took notes feverishly. She sat in the front row of the physics classroom, the battleground for a debate entitled, "Resolved: That Compulsory National Health Insurance Is Vital to a Growing Democracy." Larry took the affirmative. I do not even recall the name of the student who took the negative, only that Larry cut him to pieces.

I can still see him pacing back and forth across the creaking platform, hands thrust deeply into his trousers' pockets, head bent in a kind of controlled anger and his voice held so low that the small audience had to strain to hear him.

"Freedom, I believe that's the word my most... worthy... opponent said... over... and... over... and over," Larry had said. "Freedom to what?"

"Why," he mocked, "to pay bills! What else! Name me one family that has not had at least one major illness to cause the most terrible kind of economic hardship. If this is all this country is good for in terms of freedom, then we had better throw in the sponge. What worries the responsible citizen more than the health of his loved ones. What greater gift of freedom than to lift the burden of crippling medical payments from the people. This is freedom with meaning...."

Ordinarily, I would not have gone. Controversial gatherings of that sort sometimes used to give me headaches. But this time Nancy was busy with sorority, and I went with Larry to kill time. Mary, late in arriving, had slipped silently into the nearest seat. While neither she nor Larry gave open signs of recognition, each was acutely aware of the other. It was sensed, rather than seen. It was in the way Larry became twice his usual self. Everything clicked. A flawless performance of a super-sharpened mind keyed to quick body reflexes which charged the room with moods of his choosing. It was in the way Mary responded with a singleness of purpose to record and report as if a great human monument were in the making. Each worked at total capacity—not, I am sure, as a means to show off but as a kind of silent salute to the other. It was the first firm sign of mutual admiration.

The second sign came later at the Raven Haven. We sat over coffee in the rear booth. It was a good scene, full of the warmth and cheer one always ties to college days: the long, low building crowded with chatter and laughs, the smell of sizzling hamburgers, the clink of spoons and china, short-order commands, smoke and the juke box ever booming away. It was a room vibrating with the busy process of youth.

Against this background, Larry talked of many things with boldness and sureness. He did this without bragging, as one who believes deeply in things and so dedicates himself. His bearing was that of a perpetual winner. Mary listened, her eyes fixed unwaveringly on his face. Her response was not giddy. Not coated with superficial words. Not angled to win praise or thanks. Not calculated to win anything. It was silent, simple appraisal that ran deep within her and did not miss a single word spoken or gesture made or line of his face. He had captured her. For the moment, at least, she belonged to him, because she believed in him, as one might believe in himself or a god. Larry must have known this, and she must have known that he knew.

I remember this so well, because—my God!—how I envied him. Not because it was Mary, but because few women could ever have the capacity to look at a man as she did. You grow up to accept this, ruling out any other thoughts as romantic fantasy. But here fantasy became real.

He turned suddenly silent, and his finely featured face softened.

"I will take you home now." Not a command. Not a question. It was merely a spoken confirmation of mutual thought.

134

"Yes." She moved with smooth, unhurried certainty as if she had been walking home with Larry all of her life.

"See you back at the house, Dave."

"Good night, Dave… and thanks . .

And I sat alone in the booth long enough to finish a cold cup of coffee.

Thereafter, the two were seen together with increasing frequency; not without paying a price initially, though. For a time Larry's popularity with upper-class women suffered somewhat. He had skillfully avoided serious attachments and so had enjoyed a rather remarkable dating career. He was a symbol, I suppose, to the beautiful and elite corps of campus queens who apparently regarded him as quarry entirely worthy of them. Were one of their own to nail him—fine, indeed, and may the best gal win. But for a freshman baby absolutely from nowhere to get away with it—well! Such poor taste for him! Mary got some lumps, too. Her fellow freshmen proclaimed that she had gone uppity and deserted for ill-gotten social position. Sly digs from some of the boys suggested that she must have p-l-e-n-t-y on the ball to stop a smooth mover like him.

But they kept their good humor, and gradually people got used to the idea. If anything, this encounter with public opinion drew them closer together than might have occurred otherwise. Yet, they did not compromise their respective activities. Larry continued in his normal ways, while Mary plunged into her studies and her assignments on The Arc with impressive energy. Her reporting was thorough and remarkably objective, even to the point of offending Larry a couple of times.

"Look, you didn't have to give him equal attention," he said once after he had beaten another debate opponent. "You didn't even weight the story to disclaim his logic or support mine, almost as if my beliefs had no special significance. You'd think I won only because I was smoother."

"You were smoother, and you did win—because you know how to win. What does anything else really matter? Besides, one can't have everything…"

Mary even turned down the fall sorority-rush, not to prove something, but simply because she could see no point in "hasty decisions." She stuck to her own affairs with zestful contentment. By the end of the semester she had begun writing for The Forum, the college magazine. Her first effort was a poem about "The Brave Little Field Mouse" that outdid "Elmer, the Cunning Barn Tomcat." Done with a light, warm touch, it was the first of a long list of writings that gradually won for her an affectionate place in campus life. Her subjects were animals and nature—like, "The Tall Grass," "The Green Leaf on the Spring House Wall" and "Mr. Kramer's Mule." From poems she moved to essays and then to short stories from which came the raw beginnings of a most entertaining horse, named Nellie. She used simple words in simple phrases. Underlying them was a sensitivity that revealed her keen awareness of things close to the soil.

During the spring of her first year, Mary was persuaded by Nancy to pledge the same sorority to which she belonged.

Larry's star began to rise again, too. Early in the second semester he received the fellowship that would take him to Oxford for graduate studies. Phi Beta Kappa came next, and before the school year was out, Western College applauded with genuine delight when "Larry pinned Mary." The Senior Prom was the scene of romantic triumph for them. Warmly greeted and admired by all, they moved together, danced together, laughed together, as if their every wish had been answered.

Graduation came for Larry, Nancy and me, and we went our separate ways for a time—Nancy and I to be married and to start life in Pittsburgh, Larry to rattle the world of letters with distinguished work at Oxford, and Mary to remain behind until the end of her junior year. She and Larry were married after his return. William Penn University took him as an instructor, and Mary finished her schooling here with him.

Now, time has altered the course of events, and the old images are gone. They are gone largely because they never were valid. I began to know this when Mary and I stood in the shadows of the great stone columns. Since then, I have come to know it more and more.

"How carefully we have been taught to hide ourselves," she had said to me on our first morning together.

"Taught?"

"Can you think of a time when you haven't been weighed against a norm, a standard... some kind of yardstick where your deeds, your thoughts—if you are unwise enough to let your face show them—your every move come under some kind of scrutiny? How many times, Davey, have you wanted to feel or say or do something, only to pull back, to stop short of being yourself? How many times have you grown listless at the world because it seems to offer so little to you personally? How long has it been since you laughed deep down and meant it? How long, Davey, has it been since you've fallen into bed at night exhausted, but feeling warmly rich and at peace with yourself because you had given your very best to some difficult task?"

My mind groped at fragments of the past, sorting through this and that, looking for something to hold up to Mary in answer to the flood of questions. But nothing came except faded images of small boyhood. Happy weariness the night I mastered the meat slicer. Mom, Harry and I playing dominos around the kitchen table. Dad hunched over his cash register in the little store, logging receipts and humming softly and with terrible flatness to himself. We none of us had fitted any particular norm or standard then; or if we did we had not yet been told.

"Maybe things were different when I was a kid. I don't really know," I replied. "But I don't recall ever being taught."

"Not like geography or math." She smiled. "We are not born with fear. The world instills it in us. Was it your father?"

"I don't ever recall that my father was afraid of anything." I spoke before I thought, as a reflex. Never had I thought of him in a light quite like that.

"How lucky you are."

"Lucky?"

"To have had a father to be proud of."

As close as we had become, I could not tell her of my disappointment in him. I doubt she could have understood. For it turned out

137

that her father was a product of fear, and this is the key to Mary and the fallacy of my images of her.

For the pattern of Mary becomes clearer with each new moment with her. Ours is a setting in which the world outside stands still. And in our quiet times we talk.

Thus, the first image to be shattered was that of her parents. Hardly to be considered self-sacrificing, they did not even want her to go to college. "It was my grandfather, who left me a legacy, and they even wanted me to give them that…"

The vision of Grandfather Quincy rose before me. I must have shuddered, for she looked at me questioningly.

And her brother was not big at all. He had left the family farm at age twenty-one to enlist in the army after he wooed a local barmaid into trouble. Moreover, he left with the blessing of his father. He was caught in one of the police actions but managed to keep from going overseas. Afterward he went to Washington to take a job in the Department of Agriculture. He is still there, "arrogant and sneaky… caught at least a dozen times in scandals but always wiggles out with a better job…"[28]

It was Mrs. O'Neil who ruled both the farm and home. "She was older than Daddy and taught school before they were married. She never let him forget she had the education. Daddy never got past high school."

But Mary did belong to someone, or rather something, as I have always suspected. She belonged to the soil and still does. "From as early as I can remember, I spent every available minute away from the house, even on the most foul days, poking around the yard or the orchard or in the barn. My earliest memories were of the trees. How tall they were, swaying up and up. And, oh, Davey… the animals! I swear I loved anything that moved—homely caterpillars, dogs, horses and . . her voice dipped, its brightness gone, "… even pigs."

---

28 With increased centralized government and a corresponding rise in welfare spending, scandals involving fraud became common. Public officials at all levels arranged illegal payoffs to private citizens "applying" for various forms of aid, particularly in agriculture, industry and labor. Edison Tyler refers to this period as producing "a new class of elite, the politically powerful bureaucrat and his all-willing subject who fed themselves at public expense."

I should not have laughed. Her rebuke was painful, because it was so gentle.

"To love a pig does sound silly, doesn't it? Yet, have you ever held one, a tiny baby pig, that is? No, I didn't think so. So you can't know. I was awfully small. I had climbed into the stable where they were ... a new litter, eight or so, probably. At first the mother wouldn't let me near, and I started to cry. Then one scrambled over to me—like a drunken toy—so confused and wanting to be friends, and he worked so hard to get to me. I sat right down in the straw and held it. Soon all of them were crawling all over me, bristly and wiggly with sad little squeals and eyes squinty and bright with trust. Once, the mother rose up, and I was scared. But she lay down again. We had such a wonderful time! Then Daddy was there. Mother, too. And they dragged me away. I must have been a sight. Can you imagine a little me in coveralls, smeared with tear stains, dirt and straw, and the confused hurt that must have been on my face. They shook me and spanked me. Rather, Mother did. Daddy just stood there. I think they must have argued that night. I know I cried. The next morning Mother told me I could help Daddy raise the pigs. How unbelievably happy I was. Soon they became 'Mary's pigs.' I must have spent hours with them. Daddy fixed us a place in the manger, and he'd set us all in for a time, safely away from their mother. Have you forgotten a child's world, where even the most common objects are bright, new frontiers to explore? The wonders of a leaf, a bent twig, a flower and an old wooden potato masher dressed in rags for a doll. How then must a child have delighted over the discovery of life! Life that tumbles through pudgy hands and snuggles warmly against chubby legs. Does it sound silly for a little girl to love pigs? To discover the miracle of nature, its beauty, its balance, its struggle and magnificence, courage and bravery? Oh, Davey, why do we rule against it so!

"An eternity passed. Time set adrift in a manger full of dreams. Then one day a man came. He said Daddy would have to kill my pigs to help the country. Daddy said no. Mother said yes if we were to get the money.[29] The man went away angry, and I hugged my daddy.

---

29 Probably public funds for an agricultural subsidy of some sort.

But the next morning my pigs were gone. And, Davey! Daddy promised! He promised!

"He did it because of fear of *her*. He sold out a child's world for a miserable few pieces of silver!" Her voice was agony. "He knew it. He was never the same again.

"See how lucky you are."

The incident apparently affected her development from then on. "Bit by bit I saw my father lose—lose his self-respect, lose his dignity, lose everything worth having. I saw him beaten into a whining old man long before his time, dependent on everyone, me, my mother and the government—for some kind of a favor. Always he was going to see someone for a favor. He was so miserably weak that I had not the heart to rebel against him. So I just bit my tongue and learned the art of pleasant silence. After all, I couldn't very well run away from them or the world."

So, she turned even more to the land and its creatures, building close friendships wherever she wandered. "Once I even made friends with a deer…" Gradually her private world came into conflict with the more powerful world at school and elsewhere. "They said I was uncooperative and all sorts of things." The memory of Pi reappeared, sharp in its detail.

Slowly she began to believe that nature was being defied and even defeated. It was as if men—she could only suppose they were heady with their victories in material science—had risen up to mock nature, as ungrateful children will spurn their parents. She had an overpowering sense that nature's ways would be lost for a time—and she with it, weakened into a faceless person, as her father.

"How was I to survive as a whole being and yet live in a hostile world?" It was a plea she spoke, not to me but to herself, as she must have done a thousand times.

"Weakness became my greatest fear, strength my greatest hope."

She devised her own weapons for survival, drawing upon nature, herself, for guidance. She adopted protective coloration. In her communication with others she learned to camouflage her truths and make them socially acceptable—available to those who wished to hear them and comfortably hidden from those who did not.

"I wanted to be true to myself without hurting anyone or fighting losing battles. I wanted to win and, so, live."

"Your double meanings. I never knew why," I said.

"A game of hide-and-seek, I suppose. Even before college I was quite skilled at it. It became a reflex with me. I had to live in this world on its terms, and I had to live inside me, too, on my terms. At any rate, a strange peace came over me. I found I could enjoy life. I could look at people openly and not be afraid."

And so she searched out the strong.

It was Larry who provided the final answer to her war against Man's world.

"I knew from the first that he would never be dependent on anyone—that people would be dependent on him. I knew he was strong, stronger than you or me or my father or anyone. And while he was of the material world, still he was the best that it offered. If anyone could survive, he could. I saw in him a winner. Even nature loves a winner.

"Yet," she smiled sadly, "he was a paradox. He preached against survival of the fittest, but he was the most fit for our time. He was all-important to me. Without him as my shelter I would die inside. So I truly loved him."

"You say 'was' ... as if he were ..." I simply could not form the word.

"Dead."

The word was spoken in cold hopelessness, and I could not comprehend it. Not Larry. Anyone but him.

She saw my protest.

"Because he has not survived after all. He does not see that they have won and that they will kill him. He believes too much in himself to see. Even if, by some miracle, he were to see, he would no longer be able to believe in himself, and this would kill him.

"Either way he is dead." She spoke in flat, matter-of-fact tones, as if the shock of it still had hold of her.

"I don't see how I can accept that."

"Davey," her voice was a quiet plea, "you must."

"Even if I could, it still doesn't explain ..." I gestured wordlessly, trying to find a kind phrase.

"Us?" Her grey-green eyes were unwavering in their openness. "I'm not sure," she added. "I have never thought that I could love you, yet sometimes... now ... I think I do or that I could. I don't really know. On the other hand, I'm not a harlot, or am I? Have I deserted Larry, or has he deserted me?" A wry smile swept her earnest face.

"Perhaps it is simply that you bring hope back into my being. The sweet, trouble-free, nice David I have always known has shed his cocoon to emerge another being ever so much more glorious." She spoke in a soft murmur, a whisper, as pines sighing in the spring balm.

That I breathe heavily at the memory of her words—someone please forgive me. For who is the man who has not dreamed the heady dream of dreams—the vision of a woman's adoration? To be adored, and so to be swept along in a violent updraft to the noblest of heights. It is the force that moves men to create and build or to plunder and destroy—Man at his best or worst, never in between but an absolute. Artists call it inspiration. Psychiatrists call it ego. The rest of us—plumbers, bankers, salesmen—call it by no particular name. But all men search for it. Some find it early in high-school marriages or in Parisian mistresses. Others still seek it —the quiet loners, wandering and lost, eyes never still, probing street corners, office lobbies, theaters and cocktail lounges; the good-time-Charlies traveling in packs, sweeping noisily into night spots with fat rolls of bills and bold, bragging, puffing conversation to wow stag spinsters and automated B-girls and strippers; and finally those who simply give up the search for adoration and forget the dream altogether—fellows like me. Then—there it is. The face looking into yours, a carbon copy of your particular dream. And the impossible becomes in this instance possible. For some a war is won, an invention is achieved, a book is written—to leave an indelible mark upon the world. For David Quincy Little to be adored by Mary O'Neil Best, it meant the birth of raw courage mixed with leaden lumps of panic.

"After all this time... me?" I spoke an inane response, like a line from a cheap movie.

"Yes, dear, you." There was pride in her voice, as one who has witnessed a personal fulfillment.

"You've changed, Davey. You see our danger, now, and you want to resist..."

"I want to fight it... them... whatever it is... this web that I'm stuck in." I spat the words out, angry at everyone, everything, save only Mary. "Only I don't know how ... or even why."

"Let me help. Oh please! Let me!" She hitched herself up, her face alive and expectant. "We can do it... together! Don't you see!"

"No, I don't see."

"We'll go away."

I had not considered such a thought, simply because it had never occurred to me to leave behind the familiar for something unfamiliar.

"How? Where?" The specter of Nancy and the children— home, car, office—shattered the sanctity of the special world Mary and I had created.

"The hills. We could go there."[30]

"And starve."

The expectancy in her waned momentarily, and then she brightened.

"Canada! I heard you still can get in!"[31]

"You know how the roads are watched." I replied.

"I know, silly," she teased, as a child might cajole a tired and unwilling parent, "but there are boats..."

"Sure, if you happen to know someone."

"And airplanes!" she exclaimed, the meaning dawning on her. "Your brother, Harry. He still has his, doesn't he?"

---

30 Later records indicate many citizens fled to remote areas to begin armed resistance. Apparently some already had begun to flee at the time of this journal.

31 Canada had grown increasingly hostile toward the United States. For instance, it had signed trade agreements with Communist countries prior to those with the United States, closed out U.S. capital inflow and Canadian outflow through heavy taxes. Passports and armed border guards did not come until some months later.

143

"I don't hear from him much. I don't really know ..."

"Davey, find out. Think! Canada!" And she was off in a word world of her own filled with clear streams, tall grasses, brilliant trees and a wood-smoked cabin. But I only half-followed her joy.

"And what of Nancy ... and Larry?" I asked.

Her word song stopped, and the dullness returned. "I tried. I begged. I even cried… and I never cry… and he only laughed and patted me, and then lectured me… and I just sat there like I always do…." Her voice trailed to nothing. She had been sitting cross-legged on the bed, perked like Peter Pan, and now she slumped, her hair hiding her face, lonely in her despair.

The quiet of the guest room—our room—was as intense as her thoughts, a woman struggling for her dignity and her honor—even as I groped through a crazy quilt of elation, fear, guilt and elation all over again, a mad cycle that took me nowhere.

"Let Nancy come with us." She spoke at last, voice and face still muted by tousled hair. "I will give up any thoughts of you. Only just let me come with you."

"She would never do it. You know that."

"Yes."

The silence returned for a time.

"We must take your children."

"She wouldn't allow it."

"Damn her!" She jerked her body rigid, moist eyes flashing. "Steal them! Don't let them stay! Don't murder them! Not children! Not the wee ones I worked so hard to comfort with my little stories. Don't trample their souls, Davey! You brought them into this world, and you can't abandon them… not when you're so close to the answer… our answer! Until now, I could never bear the thought of having my own children, because I was afraid for them. But now all that is changed. I want babies, but away from here… but not if yours aren't with us. I wouldn't want you then, and I can't lose you now, not when you are beginning to grow strong and alive. Davey, you still have time. Let Nancy and Larry stay. This is what they want. This is their dream! Let them live it… together! They haven't gotten to you all the way yet. You can make it."

She flung herself at me. "Oh, God, you have to!"

The heady dream of dreams rolled over me.

"I will try," I said.

And so I will. I will not let them get me.

God keep me strong.

4

It came in the mail two days ago—the summons. I am legally bound to testify at the JCFLA hearings "to determine whether or not there has been any wrongdoing on the part of certain local citizens with respect to the Treaty of Friendship in sufficient degree to bring misconduct citations before the World Order of Nations…"

The hearings open on April 27. Nancy naturally expects me to cooperate. (What do you mean it's starting all over again? So they want you to complete something you're already involved with…) Mary counts on something different. (Fight them! Testify… but your way. Tell the truth, and before they can do anything about it we'll be out of the country…,)

I could not think what to do, so I went to see the Reverend Arthur Sandmire.

The Reverend Mr. Sandmire wears round—perfectly round—horn rimmed glasses. He looks like an owl, and I have never particularly cared for him. But I go to his church simply because one always goes to the church one is born to. This is doubly true, since it is Nancy's denomination, too, and it has never occurred to either of us to desert. Besides, the Reverend Mr. Sandmire came after we did, and we worked hard to get established there. (David, I've talked with the new minister to arrange for you to teach Sunday school. Be sure to have the BWP put that on your activity card.[32] It will help…) I am

---

32 The Bureau of Wages and Prices kept accurate records on all wage earners as to "civic, social and cultural activities" and had devised a system of credits or "merit points" for those who participated in "approved welfare betterment activities."

not sure quite how my religion helps me. It always has been simply something that one does, like eating or brushing teeth. I have never been able to fit it to me so that it makes too much sense, and the BWP certainly was not impressed. Not only did they refuse to put anything on my card but they accused me of mixing church and state affairs for personal gain. I have always believed in God. My difficulty is in trying to understand how He is supposed to help me as He apparently helps others. No one I have ever tried to talk with seems to know either.

I know it is more blessed to give than to receive and that violence is wrong. I know I must serve mankind—to help others—and that I should turn the other cheek. I know that nothing I have is mine and that it is evil to keep more than I need. I know I am a sinner but that when I die my soul can be saved if only I Believe.

But what do I do in the meantime?

That is what I asked the Reverend Mr. Sandmire, and he went "ahem," like he always does whenever he starts to say something, or moves to another subject or merely whenever he pauses in his speech. He does not do it loudly. Rather, it sneaks in, barely audible and not too distracting, unless the sermon is long.

"You endure, ahem, even as our Savior endured." His smile was peaceful. His hands were peaceful, fingernails flawlessly clean and well shaped with big half-moons. The church study, desk, papers, and books—peaceful. Even the blue paint on the concrete block wall behind him had peeled in long, lazy strips that in themselves suggested overwhelming peace. I might well have been struck by heavenly lightning at that moment, for I felt anything but peaceful. I had told him only of my dilemma about Mr. Tidings, the demonstration and the hearings to come. This was enough, I decided. Mary could keep until he proved himself as understanding as he was peaceful.

"How?"

"Ahem. Of course. You are wary of the future, and so we all are. You fear it because you can't see it. This is the great strength of the Christian religion ... to buttress us ... to light the way: *The Lord is my light and my salvation; whom shall I fear?*"

146

"Right now I fear Mr. Tidings, because he can pull the rug out from under me."

"Ahem. Yes. Now just how has this man harmed you ... or blasphemed God?"

I tried to explain that no one had harmed me yet and that God was not even mentioned. But I had the sense of floundering in a vast sea of muck. I am not accustomed to summing up newly found feelings, themselves alien to all previous patterns. My mind gives me no cleanly cut path to follow. What began as a hesitant trickle grew into a tumbling torrent of words as I fought to bring clarity to my thoughts. At first he tried to follow them, his round glasses intent on me, but it was too much, too fast and likewise too alien. He waved me down.

"Ah..." His eyes blinked, and he cleared his throat again. "You have feelings of guilt now, because of the demonstration you organized. Well... ahem... natural enough, I suppose. Only, I shouldn't feel too badly. I thought you handled yourself rather well leading all those businessmen, and, ahem, certainly your speech was not intemperate. Saw the whole thing on TV."

I curbed the impulse to heap another jumble of words upon him. Instead, I enunciated slowly and with vicious care. I did not organize the demonstration. Mr. Tidings did. Mr. Tidings threatened to have me removed from my job unless I betrayed the 44 citizens by making it appear that they had done something terribly wrong. But the Reverend Mr. Sandmire waved me silent again with a gesture not unlike a papal blessing.

"Doubtless this Mr.... ahem..."

"Tidings."

"Tidings was a considerable help... indeed, as you keep stressing, doubtless he had to do a little persuading, but... ahem... mustn't let your own modesty overcome you, David. You deserve some of the credit..."

"Credit. These men are being framed."

The peaceful composure of the Reverend Mr. Sandmire began to slip. He hitched himself up, fingers now restless. "By whom?" "That W.O.N. group—the Joint Committee."

He began to chuckle softly to himself. It was a kind chuckle, void of any criticism. "David, where have you been. They didn't even want the hearings. It was people like you who…"

"That's just it!" I was getting someplace now. "They really want the hearings. They used me to make it seem that way."

"But I've heard nothing of this." The Reverend Mr. Sandmire was beginning to show slight traces of excitement.

"Of course not." I spoke wearily but with understanding. How could he know. "They don't tell people."

"Then how do you know?"

"I told you… through Tidings."

"Well, why wouldn't they put it on the news? After all, if the W.O.N…. ahem… did want to hold some hearings, why wouldn't they just say so? Quite understandable and fair."

"They want to keep *that* a secret."

The Reverend Mr. Sandmire's whole being abandoned peace entirely and took the form of a huge question mark, eyebrows even rising above glasses. "If it's a secret, then why are they making the hearings public?"

I rested for a moment to clear my mind and then tried another tack.

"Does the idea of holding hearings bother you?"

"Of course not." A slight tinge of color touched his softly rounded cheeks, as if I had accused him of sleeping with the devil. "Public discussion—best tonic in the world. Men of good will gathered…"

"Is Communism bad?"

"It is one of our prime evils, and we must all of us work, ahem, together to erase it from the face of the earth."

"How?"

"Through understanding and the regenerative powers of our Savior. *We who… ahem… are strong ought to bear with the failings of the weak, and not to pleasure ourselves.*"

"Give in to them."

"Certainly not." Several "ahems" followed. "We can never stand for Godless, militant Communism here or anywhere else. But things

148

are changing, David. Things are changing." His voice began to hum, peace settling back upon him once more.

"They are not as godless as they once were," he continued. "Why... He swung his modem, chrome swivel chair around and poked among shining volumes in the cantilevered book shelves behind him. He pulled a slim book to him and, with a quick nod of the head, flashed the title: *How the Peace Was Won.* He thumbed to a heavily marked section.

"Just listen to this—none other than the Soviet Premier on the day he sued for peace at the World Order of Nations: 'I am no theologian, but as far as I remember, according to the Gospels, Jesus Christ preached peace not war. Christians surely will want to work with us for peace and the security of peoples.' Now, how about that for progress!"

"How can we trust them?" I asked.

"How can you trust anyone except through faith? All of us are untruthful at times, yet the Savior forgives. Can we do any less?" He slapped the book shut and returned it to the shelf with studied care.

"Communism is not the only evil, David. We forget the evils of capitalism. And as far as goals are concerned, Communism is much more humane. No. What is wrong is the godless, ruthless means of militant Communism and unfettered capitalism. Our task is to temper both of these evils with the third force of God, and then we shall have everlasting peace on earth. Who can say? We know that mankind can set up an international world authority to preserve peace only after human beings have first been regenerated, and maybe this is God's way." The speech was liberally sprinkled with "ahems."

"Supposing," I said, "the hearings are not God's way. Suppose ... just suppose .. . that the godless Communism is in control..." I held up my arm as he began to protest.

"All right." I sighed. "Let's suppose—I'm just pretending now — some Communists are still godless, militant and in power someplace. Would it be right for anyone... you ... me ... to help them?"

"Absolutely not!"

Relief flooded over me. At long last, a straight answer. Uncompromising. Real. Solid.

"Then it would be right to fight them." I said it mostly to myself.

"No-o-o-o," the peaceful voice drawled. "*He that leadeth into captivity shall go into captivity; he that killeth with the sword must be killed with the sword.* Here is the patience and the faith of the saints.

"This means Christians who ... as you choose to suppose... happen to be under the yoke of godless Communism are forbidden to act with animosity. Instead they would be required to prove themselves by suffering what God has ordained."

"Then a person would flee... perhaps to another country?" It was a timid question, upon which much depended.

"Oh, no-o-o." He meditated for a moment. "No. One doesn't run. It could only mean that a person, out of purely human considerations, would be escaping a test of his faith instead of accepting such a test at the hands of God."

"Let me see." My head was beginning to ache terribly. "You don't help them. You don't fight them. You don't try to escape. What do you do?"

"Endure."

"Try to get along, is that it?"

The Reverend Mr. Sandmire moved uneasily. "Well... ahem ... the Church cannot engage in political judgments. We can only offer guidelines. One would have to make his own decisions," he smiled in a peaceful way, "secure in the knowledge that his sins are forgiven if he is bound to God's will and knows of his responsibility to the Savior."

"Supposing they try to force you to do something for them?" "Godless?"

"Yes, of course. Godless."

"You must say no!"

"But..." My voice stuck.

"Say no!" He wagged a neat finger at me. "And be prepared to suffer the consequences. A Christian... ahem... should never condone the godless ways of militant Communism. But this does not mean that political resistance or flight would be the answer. It is, rather...

ahem… perseverance in Christian faith and Christian patience in a condition which has been ordained by God. In this faith the Christian, were he caught in the web of such godlessness, would live and suffer and even die."

"But you might be condemning… perhaps millions of people to slow death."

"The will of God."

I rose to leave. He rose quickly with me and edged gravely around the desk, which wobbled slightly on frail, chrome legs. A brotherly hand reached out to my shoulder. "Ahem. Mustn't fret, David. We all exaggerate our problems. Come and see me again whenever you think I can be helpful."

I thanked him and left.

Out in the churchyard I stopped again before the Message of the Week handsomely posted on the church board. I studied each word carefully to be sure I had read it right. It said:

"I love my country too much to be a nationalist."

5

I braved the Den of the Devil this morning. The office was every bit as small as I remembered it, and the man there still seemed to suffer from stomach distress.

"Come in, Mr.… ah… Little, I believe." Leon S. Tidings did not get up, did not look up, did not offer me a chair. I took one anyhow, which cost me a scowl that fleeted across his face, as if a gnat were buzzing in his ear. He was busy making notes, the aftermath, probably, of the weary, desperate looking man in blue coveralls who was leaving as I arrived. There was only one small change in the room. A newly framed object hung impressively behind him. It was a richly lettered Citation of Merit complete with the Treaty of Friendship Seal and signed by Lester A. Foil, chairman of the Pennsylvania JCFLA. At length, Mr. Tidings straightened his notes into a bulky file, laid it carefully aside, selected another folder and began leafing through it.

"Hm-m-m. Brown. Brown. Let's see. Ought really to have them alphabetized," he murmured, looking up at me, his pink glasses almost friendly. "They're arranged by priority, and Brown's along toward the bottom. Most all the corporate executives, at least, are already pretty much discredited, so we don't worry too much about them," he explained absently, as if I were some new and dedicated initiate.

"Ah! Here we are. Avery A. Brown, chairman of that splendid, aggressive company of yours, Mr.... ah... Little." He paused to study a sheaf of notes written on yellow legal paper. He hissed a senseless but cheerful melody through his teeth while I waited. Up until a half-hour previous I had been with Mary, and I could now look at him without fear. "How well did you say you know Mr. Brown?"

"Not very well."

"Any personal dealings?"

"No."

"None at all?"

I made an honest effort to recall. "Once, three or four years ago I met him at a dinner. It was a sales meeting, and I got to say hello."

"What did he say to you?" Mr. Tidings asked. He pulled a yellow pad to him and held his pen expectantly.

"Keep up the good work."

"He would have made a dinner speech, of course. What did he say?"

"Keep up the good work."

Mr. Tidings shook his head and sighed. "Nothing much here. Certainly can't use you on the personal stuff. Well," he brightened, "we've got Saunders and Grimm, at least... though I kind of hoped for someone else down the line."

Saunders and Grimm are two of our vice presidents. So they got them, I smiled inwardly to myself.

"Very well, Mr.... ah... Little, we'll just have to work you in elsewhere."

"Work me in?"

"Naturally. At the hearings. Wouldn't be right for you not to show. Let's see." The small, dark man pondered and then leaned back and smiled. "Of course. We'll use these." He flashed a number of small booklets, laying them out on the desk one at a time like a blackjack dealer. "You're the ideal person. Recognize them?"

I had seen them before. They came in my home mail every three or four months, at least they used to. Distinctive type, dignified border and always with the corporate insignia. They were speech reprints. "Yes," I replied, "Mr. Brown's speeches." Only the highest officials are allowed to make speeches.

"Correct, Mr. Little. You'll do nicely, I think. Been a bit of a problem. You see, we only had half the equation. We've traced the men who wrote these speeches, and they are quite anxious to be at the hearings to explain how Mr. Brown inflicted his will by threatening to fire them if they didn't write his vindictive half-truths.

"Our real need, however, is to dramatize how this... poison," he jabbed a thick finger viciously at the distinguished looking booklets, "has eaten away at the minds of unsuspecting people."

He turned slowly in his chair to gaze fixedly at the Citation of Merit and then rocked slowly back. "Beautiful," he said softly to himself. "A quiet, struggling employee ... a good employee... anxious to cling to his job so that he can feed and clothe his lovely wife and children... influenced by company propaganda during the day... only to come home, weary and frightened, to be confronted by these half-truths. The sanctity of the home invaded. A Bob Cratchit pitted against a Scrooge with power over money, mind and body. And so," he leaned forward to level his pen at me, "David Q. Little, you read avidly each of these, forcing yourself to memorize key words and making yourself believe every thought written so you could please the bosses."

He paused, with heavy-lidded eyes half closed in an effort to complete the scene. I returned his gaze unblinking.

"So, you and thousands of others become the unwitting tool of unbridled capitalism, of ambitious bosses and exploiters. And were the issues not so critical, perhaps, we could excuse this. But!" Mr. Tidings rose from his chair and strode three steps to his window, hands clasped behind him, like a skipper pacing the bridge in the heat of battle—one which he was winning. "Look at what this man, Avery A. Brown, has had the audacity to cast into print."

One by one he picked up the booklets and slapped them in my hands. "Profits can be as important as public spending. Money can be a worthwhile incentive. Private investment can create jobs. Government need not be in all areas of business. Military force can be useful. We should trade with Communists but go no further . .. that one is a real dandy!

"Can you imagine, Mr. Little, that we ever could have had a friendship treaty with Avery A. Brown running this country? Can you imagine his obstructionist tactics very nearly wrecked the peace?"

"Yes. I can imagine it... imagine as much as you want," I replied, thinking of Mary.

Mr. Tidings returned to his seat. Two dozen booklets were jumbled in my lap.

"Of course we only went back the last ten years, but there's enough here, I think, for you to do a good job."

"Which is?"

"Study them carefully... particularly the marked passages and you'd better memorize those. Then simply respond to the prosecutor's ... I mean the hearing chairman's questions. We'll see that you have an opportunity to meet him. That, along with your statements made last month—which we of course will ask you to repeat—should be sufficient. I shouldn't think you should be on the witness stand more than five, six minutes, certainly no more than ten. Mustn't make it appear phoney. And we'll put you on toward the end, I think." He paused again to make brisk notes, and hissed a silent tune. "Won't get to you for, maybe, four or five days. Better plan to attend each session, all the same, at least until after we've heard from you. I'll arrange a pass."

He finished writing and looked at me thoughtfully, as if somehow, I was the last piece to the puzzle. "Any questions?"

"Yes. One." I replied.

"Go on."

"Do you believe in God?"

"What!" He tilted forward, a stunned disbelief covering his dark face. He was not angry. He was simply thrown off balance, as if no

154

one had ever asked such a question before, as if I had asked him if he believed in J. P. Morgan. "What the hell are you talking about! Of course not!"

"Do you believe in violence?"

The question apparently touched a more familiar chord, for he smiled sleepily.

"I love violence, Mr. Little," he said softly. "The art of violence is the most exhilarating of all human acts. Were I not fettered by... ah... considerations of strategy I should love nothing more than to unleash violence upon this place." He sighed and began straightening his papers. "Maybe someday... when this part is over..."

V

The Fifth Month

I tried. I honestly tried. Whatever my feelings for Mary; whatever my resentments toward Nancy; whatever my shaking bewilderment toward Larry; I let love of my children rule.

"They love their mother. She must go with us, too," I had said to Mary the morning after Leon Tidings.

She gave me no argument, but then I expected none. She showed neither sorrow about what our future would have to be nor regret for these past weeks. Instead, she was perky and alert to the prospects of a new life. She was—on this morning—more a child than a woman. I was her knight and miraculous deliverer, more godlike than human. I was pleased with my decision. I reached it the minute I left Tidings' office, and I swear I will not weaken.

"Canada." Mary had spoken it as a small child might proclaim Santa Claus. Her pride in me was unmistakable. It was in the way she pulled her boyish figure erect as she sat cross-legged, with slender arms and tapered fingers extended outward to my hands. It was in the tilt of her head and in the scrubbed freshness of her face. But mostly it was in her eyes. Wide and more green than grey, they spoke of things that only the young and unspoiled dare feel. It was my moment of triumph; my moment of supreme bigness. For once I would act, rather than be acted upon. For once I would redress the balance, rather than slip deeper into the pit I had helped to dig.

The plan was simple enough. Harry would fly us over in his plane. I still had one more legitimate trip to Cleveland—a customer complaint on strip quality that had been routed to me, one I had been reluctant to follow up, because nothing can be done for him. I have recently been given the added responsibility of coordinating complaints on coiled strip-steel products for the northeast area. The gossip is that I am best qualified because of my "in" with Tidings (How can they object to you, David, old pal). I would simply take Mary, the children and Nancy with me. The passes are general enough.[33] I would leave the company car in Cleveland. Leave behind everything and we would go…

Here the reasoning ran afoul of practical considerations. Money. All told I have a little over eleven thousand dollars to my name. Better than eight in my home, another twelve hundred in a savings account and the remaining fifteen hundred is the present market value of my company stock, now worth less than half of what I paid for it over the years.[34] I cannot sell the house. The minute I tried they would know.[35] The stock is out, too. They will not let me have it until I retire, unless I can show "dire and immediate need" as certified by the BWP, and that usually takes months.[36] But I have a realistic chance with the savings account. While there is talk of freezing all such accounts, no official action has been taken that I know of. I have heard that all withdrawals are reported to the JCFLA, but I think that is rumor.

---

33 A tight system of travel passes existed during this period. A rigid checkpoint system had been created governing passage from one region to another.

34 Employee "stock savings" plans were common during Mr. Little's time. Usually employing companies withheld a modest percentage of the employee's wages and also matched this sum with company funds to purchase shares of its stock. Most plans were oriented to employee retirement and prohibited premature withdrawal of the stock, which was held in trust.

35 All home sales were conducted through a Property Bureau under the Private Property Act.

36 Apparently the powers of the Bureau of Wages and Prices were quite broad, even into employee affairs where wages already had been approved and paid, a fact which is contrary to the belief of some authorities on Americana who believe the BWP was largely "political window dressing and not particularly effective."

"What would we live on?" I had asked, a knot beginning to grow in my stomach.

"The land. What else," Mary had replied. I do not know if it was irritation or growing panic, but whatever, in that instant Mary had become a threat quite as terrible as the one I sought to escape. Then the feeling was gone, and I wondered if I had nearly betrayed her, too.

"Davey, have you forgotten? Our ancestors came to this country with very little, and the land was good to them. It will be good to us, too, if we just give it a chance to help us." The hope in her eyes was too much.

"We'll have only twelve hundred."

"That's all we need to get us there. Here, let me show you." She was gone as she spoke, a flurry of energy and purpose. She returned a second later, bearing a battered atlas stolen from Larry's study, and turned quickly to a map of Canada.

"There." She indicated a point northwest of Calgary, Alberta. "I've been reading about it…"

How realistic her book of dreams I do not know, but in listening to her the logic of escape once more became firm.

There was no real physical contact between us on that day. We spoke not at all of it. Neither of us apparently expected anything differently. It was as if a major turning point had been reached; that the new life lay directly ahead if we could hold firm to the resolve not simply to run away but to take with us the hearthstones of society. It was the yearning to do right by the world and in so doing make the world right again. We had tasted of the nobility of lasting purpose and found it satisfying enough to deprive ourselves of that which in good conscience we could no longer have.

We would, of course, leave before the hearings—just two weeks away. Only two things remained; tell Nancy and Harry. Neither was insurmountable; not after Mary on the day after Leon Tidings.

But things did not work out that way.

I decided first to set the stage for my departure by discussing the unhappy Cleveland customer with Frank. It was he who pointed to the fine print of the W.O.N. summons which prohibits my leaving the state until I have made my appearance, and "how can we issue you a travel permit with that!" the boss had boomed in rare good humor. Tidings must have advised him of this provision. After the hearings? "Fine, old pal. I'll handle the paperwork personally. Glad to have you get over there, too. Drivin' me nuts, he is." I put aside for the moment precisely how I would deal with the hearings and moved on to the next objective—Nancy.

She would not hear of it.

At first she thought it all a joke. Initially, I decided not to mention Mary or Larry but refer only to us and the children. I even found Calgary in our own atlas and—I think with some degree of warmth and expectation—tried to unfold the vision of near wilderness, untainted skies and streams, bountiful land. This was an error, because I was out of context to Nancy. For the David she knows never emotes. He never bubbles. He never dreams aloud. He never makes little plans. He never pitches out the known for the unknown. Risk and adventure are not household words; not because Nancy has decreed Thou Shalt Not, but because David, himself, knew not.

And she could not possibly know that her David stood now on the threshold of deliberate, joyful self-destruction to make way for the new; a man to be known henceforth as Davey, who first had found inspiration and from this the will to dare, to think, to be and finally, in a blinding flash of courage, had achieved the pinnacle of human meaning—the unyielding urge to act. She could not know that the words I spoke were ones I now felt and in which I now believed. That I spoke them awkwardly was not because of doubt —and I must believe this—but because this was my solo flight. I was invading the familiar, old domestic world with something new, something untried. I was injecting nobility of lasting purpose into her stark world of washing and ironing, monthly bills, peeling paint and a job at the BWP. Davey Little was unveiling himself before his most potent critic—an emerging artist, who has dared to create an unorthodox, socially unacceptable piece of sculpture, now running back the curtain, anxiously reading the first flickers of reaction from his carefully selected audience that will make him or crush him.

159

I spoke alien words. I talked forcefully of children and the responsibilities of parenthood. I referred reverently to the inner spirit, to reason, to logic. I spelled out the fearful consequences of slavery, elaborating at length my recent meeting with Tidings. I pictured a new start in a land still remote to the nightmare about us; outlining the virtues of a simple, uncomplicated life where one learns to work with his hands and one's mate cheerfully takes her place at the rustic hearth. I shrugged off the value of money and worldly possessions—even going so far as to reach back deep into my head for one or two Biblical quotes left over from boyhood Sunday-school days. Somewhere I even used the word individualism. With Mary and the memory of her so nobly pushed aside, I pumped my heart out.

Nancy snickered. I would have preferred that she had laughed or grinned. Anything but a snicker. It died when she understood I was not joking, and for a moment her face was a blank. Then disbelief swept her posture, peaking in the depths of her widened eyes. The audience had reacted.

"You…" she fought furiously for words, "are… insane!" It was no flip comment. She meant it, because she truly believed it. "Leave this," her arm swept downward, "for that!" She pushed at the atlas, and it tumbled to the floor. We were in the kitchen, and the hour was late. From dinner time on I had stalked her, waiting for the right moment, which came only after the dishes were done, the children sent to bed and two television seminars on unemployment and cultural exchanges carefully monitored. I had suggested some hot powdered milk, tea and coffee now being too precious to waste on non-social events. I did my unveiling at the kitchen table.

"You call parental responsibility dragging me and the children off to… god only knows where! Chopping wood! Pine trees! Have you ever heard of snow? Would you feed us logs for lunch or perhaps trap a rabbit?" She spit the words out. It was hate that had hold of her now, a deeply entrenched hostility that exploded out of context with anything known of Nancy.

"Listen… you…" she was groping for the term, a name, a phrase to do justice to my lowly state. "For years I stood it while you spent

160

your time going exactly nowhere… letting other men your age get ahead of you so far that sometimes I could cry for the shame of it! Our only friends either are younger than we… people on the way up who haven't passed us yet … or older people who never did amount to much." She paused in her gale of anger to add thoughtfully, "Except Larry, bless him, and why he's put up with us…" Words left her entirely. She moved her head slowly from side to side, blinding tears rolling grotesquely down her face.

There was a hollow sickness inside of me now, eating away as she unburdened herself.

"David! Why now? Why… when for the first time in our lives things are beginning to go our way? No! Let me finish," she said, cutting off my interruption.

"For weeks now you've talked some kind of mysterious threat to all of us when the facts just simply don't match. And don't give me that Tidings stuff again. Both Larry and I have told you he's nothing more than an insignificant nut. Besides, the disarmament is almost done,[37] so what possible danger could there be? There is nothing logical to support what you say. I don't like the hearings, but they're not that dangerous. After all, they're only to see if any laws and things have been broken, and it'll all blow over. Even Larry says that, and he ought to know. He's with Armstrong and Syerov nearly every day, and they deplore the whole thing. You've got it all wrong. David, think! You are actually being asked to testify against someone else… not yourself! Why, you're becoming an important man! People are beginning to look up to you. Even Tom Shade has mentioned you. On his own, too, without so much as a single hint from me. Larry is right. We can win, David. Think of it! You cooperate at the hearings,

37 Very few of the United States military were actually disarmed and mustered out of service. Rather, existing Army, Navy and Marine units were in effect transferred over to the World Order of Nations "to help enforce the peace." This was accomplished by, first, deactivating a particular unit, then granting honorable discharges from the United States services and, finally, giving each man the "opportunity" to enlist in the World Order of Nations Peace Forces. Military equipment and facilities were transferred over by written agreement.

and I just know there's a new job in it for you. Tom as much as said ... in fact, he even suggested I tell you."

The shock and hysteria had gone. She was caught up in her own vision now, and the words she spoke were the ones she believed in. And they tore at me, because they were familiar words. They spoke of warm, comfortable security in a world shorn of its capacity for violence. They spoke of the possibility of a new, larger home bought with a better job. They spoke of a new kind of recognition among friends, neighbors and the community at large. They sketched David Q. Little—leader; David Q. Little—the man with the ability to temporize conflicting views and so help to reestablish order and purpose in a sorry world; David Q. Little— beloved family man through whom his children would wax useful citizens.

"Or are you so obsessed with this thing that you have become an..."

"Extremist?" I finished, somehow expecting to hear it.

"Yes." She was quite grave now. "Up to a point I could go along with you, David, but don't you see, you've become an extremist. You've let *them* get to you! You frighten me, David. Even Larry is worried, because it could go badly with you... badly with us."

So the tag had been pinned on me, too. I was not angry and did not even try to protest. Had someone so labeled me six months earlier I would have shrieked bitterly and been hurt and stunned. But now I was more awed than injured; more clinically impressed than indignant. Society for years had warned—with the consent of the majority—of certain dangers. Had I given voice to these concerns, say ten years ago, instead of today, my beliefs might have been tolerated, possibly even heeded. Only now, society has decreed that the dangers are passed, this too, with the consent of the majority. So the matter is closed and is not to be reopened, unless the majority so orders. Thus, once accepted views now are extreme; off limits; without credence; the mutterings of a twisted mind. It is an interesting cycle, and I think there is something important in whatever it is that I have observed here.

I did not reply to Nancy, not for very noble reasons. I simply could think of nothing appropriate to say. In terms of our world, the only

162

one I have ever known, she made sense. She had pitted the known against the unknown, and I might have gone along with it had it not been for an incident the next evening.

We went to a party at the Leroy Silkmores'. Leroy and his wife, Beth, are part of the *desirable* group. Both of them are our age, only Leroy is well out in front of me. He is an assistant vice president of ACD Oil Company, belongs to three clubs and has a ten-room house further south of us on a full acre of ground. We know them casually through church, and shortly after my forced march through the Golden Triangle, Beth had invited Nancy to fill in at bridge. And now, this was to be our maiden voyage to the Silkmores' for cocktails and a buffet supper. I was not looking forward to it. For one thing, Nancy had used the invitation as Exhibit A in the People's Case against my irresponsible frame of mind. Also, I did not particularly care for them. This is based on my association with Leroy through the church building-fund committee a few years ago. He was chairman and I was vice chairman. He made a big speech before the congregation one Sunday, calling on everyone to do their part. It was a beautiful job. He has that boyish, all-American, dedicated manner that one envies. Unfortunately, he was too busy to do much on the fund drive, which had a goal of two hundred thousand dollars with three years to pay. So he left the details to good-old-David, which consisted of organizing eighty men into teams and following up on all of the strays—something like one hundred families that I called on myself, my teammates likewise being too busy. It took me better than four months. The drive was a ninety percent success, and Leroy received a handsome certificate lauding him for his Christian stewardship which he accepted with boyish humility and a deft touch of grandeur in a little speech that outdid his pep talk. I was not mentioned in either one. Leroy was able to pledge only fifty dollars, payable over three years.

The party, nonetheless, was impressive. Plenty to drink, which is not unusual. But the food was outstanding. Shrimp, enough so that I had four of them without appearing impolite. There were two different kinds of cheeses. Someplace they had found soda crackers and some rye bread cut thin which was delightfully fresh. Also, peanuts, lots of peanuts, and a whole baked ham that was so good that I would have given anything for a second slice. Potato salad loaded with eggs, celery and onion. And real coffee with fresh cream. How they came by this, I can guess.[38]

It was an intimate party. Counting the hosts and ourselves, only nine couples were present. I knew only one, the Peters, and then by name only. He is with a small electronics company. I had heard of none of the rest, but they were either department heads, assistant vice presidents or vice presidents outright, each from a different company. They appeared to know each other well. They golfed together, played bridge together and even went on vacation together. The men played poker, and the women went—or used to go—on chummy shopping tours. Their children grew up together, played together and went steady with each other, depending on ages. They were fresh-looking and confident couples, lively with good cheer. They welcomed us into the group with ease and warmth. It was as if we were the missing link, as if only now could their group really be called complete. Nancy liked this. Within minutes after our timid arrival—we were last—she was glowing with rich, deep pleasure, as a woman does when she has achieved a measure of fulfillment. Within an hour she was one of the girls. She was smooched by the men and patted coyly by the women. I was consulted repeatedly about the steel business, the stock market[39] and "the situation." We were VIP all the way.

It was also a party that flopped.

Most of the action took place in the huge game-room wing that jutted out from the back of the house onto a large yard with an impressive swimming pool, now empty. The room was at ground level

38 "Luxury foods came from two sources. Special "AA" food ration coupons, made available to selected government authorities, entitled holders access to "premium" stores operated by the World Order of Nations, which offered an unlimited variety of fresh foods at low prices. The other source was the black market, which flourished to serve the up-and-coming, reasonably well-paid individual.

39 On the New York Stock Exchange, the industrial averages stood at about 1900 during this period, highest in the nation's history, and carried to that level primarily by electronics and communications industries, which offset the depressed state of some basic industries, such as steel.

with walls of floor-ceiling glass and an elegant view of meandering estates belonging to still other bright young men. The room was casual in an expensive sort of way, with rich mahogany paneling and rugged-looking furniture, all polished.

Nancy got drunk. Not badly. Not so that she differed particularly from the rest of us. People do it all the time without meaning to. It usually happens when we become over-confident, over-eager, over-buoyant. The sailor on shore leave; the proud new father; the man who has just been promoted; the housewife turned office worker who senses that she and her mate have arrived. We all do it. But Nancy let the barriers slip out of place, and she blew the whole evening. It happened after dinner, and we had settled down on concentrated sociability. I was being consulted once more on "the situation" by about half of the group—a bright array of male and female faces that were beginning to resemble a roomful of manikins, all fashioned with the same carefully groomed expression of pleasant, sometimes eager, interest. Nancy was similarly surrounded.

"Tell us, David, old boy, just what is the real score?"

"The score?"

"About the hearings..."

"Yes. Tell us, old man. I hear there's going to be hell to pay..."

"I hear that Hank Barnes and Jeff Lang are really going to get it..."

"Huh! That's nothing. Look at old man Wright!"

"Yeah. And there's a lot of talk about Zanhorst, who apparently wasn't really behind the Treaty at all, even though his editorial support..."

"Why don't we let Mr. Little talk?"

"David, Martha. He likes to be called David, don't you, David?"

"Sure. Call me David."

"O.K."

"You know, fellas, there are going to be some big changes, I do believe..."

"That's right! I understand ... and this is pretty straight stuff... that there's a lot of pressure being put on some of 'em to get out. You know. Resign!"

"Yeah. A lot of the old bloods are on their way out..."

"We-l-l-l. That's not so bad. Not really. There's plenty of talent around, and I always say that all of us, sooner or later, outgrow our usefulness and have to make room..."

"What do you think, David?"

"Well, I..."

"Yes. Especially about... well... you know. Ave Brown over at your place?"

"Well, I..."

"I'll bet there's some *real* scrambling goin' on over there. Who's got the inside track?"

"Say. I understand you're going to be part of the hearings. How'd you manage that? You must have a real in. Why don't we have lunch..."

"Why don't we let Mr. Little..."

"David, Martha."

"David, that is, talk?"

"What do you think, old man?"

The discordant symphony of voices stopped as if a conductor had suddenly cut them off. Eight pairs of eyes searched me, expectantly, hopefully.

"I think the hearings will prove," I paused to gather courage, "nothing, except that a lot of people got all worked up over a few little things. I think it will all blow over," I mumbled, the blood pounding in my ears. The image was wrong. I should have spoken out clearly, with calm authority and firm conviction. I should have been unruffled, a man of granite. It did not come out that way, but at least I said—partially—what I really felt. My intention was to proceed, to tell all, to warn and to ask support.

But the silence was overwhelming. The eight pairs of eyes registered instant disappointment, as if eight shutters had been tripped simultaneously. Then it dawned on me. All of them wanted these 44 hearings victims comfortably removed. Each had a target in the form of a newly created job vacancy. Each was riding on the expectations of better days to come with the old-timers out of the way. Heirs sitting around in the family library waiting for someone to die. Vultures perched on a dead tree limb.

And in the stillness we were irrevocably tuned to the group around Nancy. The spirited exchange there compelled us to listen.

"You must be very proud of your husband," a female voice was saying fervently to Nancy.

"Yes, my dear," another voice rushed in, "and such a modest, nice man, too."

"He must be in all sorts of meetings and things..."

"How on earth did he get so lucky," a male voice cut in.

"He probably works a lot harder than you, Sam," a shrill voice bit back.

"I told my husband weeks ago to get down to JCFLA and offer his services, but would he? Oh, no…"

"The way he handled that demonstration, Nancy . ."

"Handled. What do you mean. It was a masterpiece of administration and programming. Took real skill to organize that bunch!" Another male voice interrupted.

"A very smart man."

"He's a fool!" It was Nancy who spoke in trembling rage. Not by design but by reflex. An unfortunate blunder wherein a person's inner spoken thoughts are mistakenly switched to the wrong channel, like a mike left open by mistake in a radio studio.

The silence was complete. Even the waiter passing drinks stopped dead in his tracks. I do not believe that even then Nancy knew that she had spoken aloud, or if she did then she had lost all sense of anyone being present. And she was too deeply immersed within herself to care anyway. She looked not at me or anyone. Her eyes were fixed at some distant point and revealed a blend of stupor and defiance—the result of mixing drinks and gnawing despair together to create a new kind of cocktail. I should have been alert to it, whenever Nancy overdrinks it most always is because she is ill-at-ease with people and, thus, usually falls shyly silent, which is hardly a social storm signal. But the pattern was different this time. She had grown progressively more bright and talkative in what was for us an alien setting. She was chipper, self- assured and bountifully outgoing—until the conversation turned pointedly to me, and the pressure became too much. She had to set the record right. She could not bear to see the world hoodwinked. This is the thought that must have driven her words outward.

"He's scared to death." Her voice sped on flatly and with quiet sureness like a beam of light that can never be recaptured. "He wants to run away. They frighten him, just as everything frightens him. He's a nothing, and he wants to stay that way."

Tears came in an absent sort of way.

"Proud of him, you say? I..."

Then she became aware. It was wretched to watch. The dawning look on her face, suddenly pale with panic and fragile looking, as if it would shatter if anyone so much as breathed. And no one did for a long moment.

Leroy Silkmore rescued her. He could hardly have done otherwise. For, after all, he had picked us for this group. So he was, in a sense, on trial before his peers, and one dare not be guilty of poor social— or business—judgment. One never admits to picking an unreliable employee or married couple. One never makes mistakes, or if one does he never admits it. This is the iron law of our day.

"You have a rare little bird here, David," he chuckled admiringly. "A wry sense of humor . .

"Just to keep you awful men from having things go to your head," Beth Silkmore added bravely. "Every time Roy even looks like he needs a larger hat... it's pow! Remember that time, Eileen, he was boasting about his golf score, and I let him have it right in the middle of cocktails..."

"Do I ever!" Eileen replied. She was a plump woman, well equipped to be jovial when events required it. "Oh, that was funny." And she spun into a hearty gale. Soon the whole group was laughing.

The team was pulling together.

Nancy, flushed now, was able to stammer appropriately, "Sometimes I do overdo it, but David gets so much attention these days, and I just simply can't have him spoiled." Her laugh was high-pitched but passable. She moved with openly displayed tenderness to my side and plucked at my sleeve. "Poor humor. Forgive me, all. I am very proud of him," and she managed a smile that conveyed adoration to the untutored.

"Charming," someone said.

It was a superficial rescue, but it served all of us well. It enabled conversation to be resumed on light topics for an acceptable period of time, which in turn allowed people to become suddenly tired or worried about the dog or the baby-sitter; so that good-byes could be said without embarrassment to the hosts. It got us all out the door in one piece. We will, of course, never be asked back.

But that is not the real tragedy.

The tragedy is the cold fury I feel. It is bitterness, hurt and dismay all balled up inside of me. So that is what she really thinks of me. A nobody, she says. We shall see about that! This is what I said over and over to myself on the way home. Two grim and shaking people staring straight ahead into the oncoming lights of other, perhaps happier, automobiles. It was that way all the rest of that night, as I lay sleepless in bed, rigid with rage.

By morning I had reached my decision, and by that evening I had formulated my plans. I will take the children and Mary to Canada. That Nancy and Larry will be left behind leaves me unmoved.

2

During these past few days I have been alive with details. Perhaps I should be grim and filled with misgivings. But I am, curiously, happy and, so far, unafraid. They say an infantryman knows the fear of battle most when he is away from it, but in the heat of conflict he is too busy to worry. I have been too busy to worry.

First, I contacted Harry by phone. It was neatly done, if I do say so. I was able to by-pass the monitors with surprising ease. It was accomplished simply by dropping Harry a chatty letter which told him absolutely nothing, except one thing—a specific request to telephone me at a particular number at noon on a certain date (last Tuesday). It was a pay phone in the arcade near the office. I warned him to place the call from another pay phone in Cleveland and that when I answered to go along with anything I might say. By writing only that much, and there was no way around this, the censors could only get part of it. My assumption, of course, was that the censors would alert the FCC, who in turn would have ample time to do a special tap into the number I gave Harry and monitor the call that way. Naturally, when Harry called (I got there fifteen minutes early to be sure the phone would be free) I merely asked him for the number he was calling from and told him to hang up and wait. I walked quickly through the arcade to another pay booth and called him back. The FCC could never have moved quickly enough to set up another tap, so I would be able to speak quite freely.[40]

"What are you up to now, big brother?" Harry asked. His voice manifested the same unperturbed cheerfulness that I have always associated with him, a certain brashness and never-ending optimism in it that spills over into a lean, hard jaw and brings into play a pair of icy blue eyes. Though I could not see him, I knew he would have a pork-pie hat jammed on the back of his head and that he would be leaning, half-standing, half-sitting, against the phone booth taking in everything about him in roving, searchlight glances. For Harry never quits at anything. Even in his sleep his mind must continue to grind away on some thought, whether it be the shape of someone's head

---

40 In the year prior to the Treaty, legislation was enacted authorizing the Federal Communications Commission to monitor all telephone calls emanating from any commercial enterprise, and, if deemed necessary, private residences of commercial employees, in order "to safeguard the public interest from possible monopolistic practices, customer discrimination and discriminatory purchasing practices which might tend to stifle competition, as well as from unlawful lobbying and/or the use of public communication facilities to seek special favors from persons not legally connected with the allowable commercial transactions of a particular enterprise as specified by the Bureau of Wages and Prices." The law also authorized the FCC to relay any evidence of wrongdoing to the Justice Department and Internal Revenue Service for appropriate action.

Regarding censorship of mail, evidence of when and how this began is sketchy. No records have yet come to light to give clues to the specific legislation. It can be reasonably assumed that legislation empowering the Post Office Department was probably similar to the FCC authorization.

or some kind of production problem. An idea a minute. That is what they used to say about Harry. I have never cared particularly for his cocksureness. Indeed, I used to criticize him for it. But on this day I was truly glad to know that, apparently, he was much the same as always—alert, tough and quick.

"We can talk freely now," I replied.

"Yeah," he mused, "a pretty smooth operation!" There was honest admiration in his words. "But you'd better check the booths beside you...

"This is the only booth. Made sure of that," I said.

"Then be on the lookout for any strangers leaning against your booth. The walls have ears."

"Not a soul."

"Yet, they may have a tail on you. They do me," he said. "Look for a man with big ears!" He laughed with light-hearted contempt.

"You're being followed?" I cried.

"Sure. They're holding some kind of hearings here in a couple of weeks, and some burly baboon gave me a summons. .. ,"[41]

"You're going to testify against someone. That's exactly..."

"Hell, no!" he snapped. "I'm one of the ones. People are going to testify against me, or so they tell me!" He might have been talking about gossip at a tea party for all of the concern he showed. "I told 'em to go shove it down someone else's throat and to quit bothering me. That made them sort of mad, and now they've got a couple of grey-looking characters following me around. They take turns."

There was a pause.

"What's on your mind?" He read my silence and added, "Don't worry, my friend can't hear us. He's across the way. He can't use his electric snooper in public. Attracts too much attention, and every time he tries to sneak up I just stare at the bastard. It's remarkable. All you have to do is to face up to these piddling little rats, and they don't know what to do."

---

41 Neither David Little nor his brother apparently realized that such JCFLA hearings were organised and held in over a hundred cities at about the same time, including New York, Boston, Miami, Chicago, St. Louis, Denver, San Francisco and Los Angeles.

"Don't they make you nervous?"

"No-o-o, big brother. They're really not very bright. I can lose them any time I want. Fact is, yesterday I lost one just for the hell of it and then followed him around while he looked for me. You should have seen his face when I tapped him on the shoulder. Even invited one to join us for dinner last week, but he turned me down. I think he was afraid." Once more Harry's laugh showed more glee than gravity.

Quickly I outlined the whole situation. I left out Mary and my differences with Nancy. That could be explained later. All Harry needed to know was the basic plan to escape into Canada and the number involved—a man, woman and three children, referred to simply as the family.

"Well, I don't know what's happened to you. Not like you to uncork a scheme like this. It's intriguing, and frankly I've been kicking the idea around myself..."

There was a faint click on the line, but Harry gave no sign that he had heard it.

"...of taking a bit of a vacation, too," he continued smoothly. "Now, of course, there are some likely spots in upper New York State, but I'm ripe for something a little more south. For example, the Carolinas are nice in June. I assume that's where we'd all like to go—after school is out. Of course, there's the problem of gas rationing, and we'll have to think of something sneaky... and it was sure smart of you to call this way..."

Again, a faint click, and Harry's tone instantly became sharp and his words quick.

"They've traced us. That was the operator on to be sure. Next they'll cut us in on someone's extension. Now listen! I'll phone your office later... regular way... give you phone number, but I'll give it to you backwards. Call me tomorrow noon. Got it?" "Yes. I'll do just as you say," I replied. There was a click once more and this time my voice had a strange echo. We were being piped into some kind of listening device. "I'll see if I can get some booklets on places where we could go. I'll try to figure an angle on how we can get extra gas rations, too," I added thoughtfully.

"Fine!" Harry boomed. Then he paused and added softly, "very fine, indeed... Dave."

We hung up. I swung briskly from the phone booth and quickly lost myself in the noontime crowd. The arcade floor, with its rows of shops brightly lit in brave efforts to lure buyers, was packed with competing forces of people all hurrying in different directions. Few people were in any of the shops, there being little merchandise of sufficient quality and reasonable prices to attract much of anyone. I found an apathetic but stationary group of onlookers clustered about a tired, threadbare pitchman who was trying to sell a new can opener. The world may change, but there will always be pitchmen selling new can openers. I worked my way to the front of the group just in time to see a nondescript man working his way hurriedly through the arcade entrance past me to the phone booth. I let myself sneak a look as he stood staring at its emptiness, while he fished savagely for a cigarette. My heart pounded loudly in my ear as I turned into the street. It pounded not because of the disappointed man behind me but because Harry had called me Dave, instead of the biting, mocking phrase of "big brother" he sometimes used. For years there had been little between us that could pass for respect and admiration, but in these past few minutes a bond had been re-established. A void inside of me was being filled. I had a comrade! No fancy words of explanation. No excuses or qualifiers to seek understanding. Just action between two men who once again could begin to call themselves brothers.

This triggered another thought. My mother. From college days on, the warm relationship between us had withered away. This was not entirely my doing. For, from then on, she, Dad and Harry were more closely drawn together than any of them with me. When Dad died, the bond between her and Harry, who was still at home, grew even stronger. He seemed to take charge of things almost instinctively. He sold the store at a handsome profit, even though he was not yet eighteen and Mother and I had to sign all the papers. He made it his business to find out all about trusts and had one set up for her. When his turn in college came, he went home every weekend. Of course,

I was relieved, because Nancy and I were building our life together, and it was most unhandy to be obligated to go home all the time. After college Harry returned to Cleveland to be near her, which is the way it has been ever since. He did not even marry until he was 29, but I think that was because he was helping to build an electronics company, more than anything else. Two years ago Harry built a house large enough for Mother to live in, too. Of course, there is only Harry, Margaret and their little boy, Charles. So it was not too much of a burden to take her.

But now I wondered about her. What would we do with her? It had been months since we had written, not, in fact, since the Treaty was signed, and Nancy had sent a long letter, happily reporting on the well-being of the family. Somehow, we would take her with us.

I spent the balance of the day between phone calls and filling in allocation forms. I worked mechanically, my mind focused instead on perfecting the plans to escape. The children, for instance, how to get them away without revealing the plan either to them or to Nancy. The fact that Nancy works from nine until five at the BWP, I decided, would make the operation fairly simple, although it would mean running in daylight. Actually, this will be better. People appear less suspicious than at night. When the time comes I can drive home during the day and lift the children right out of the school with an excuse that they are needed to participate in a student demonstration at the hearings. No one would have the courage to question it, for fear of becoming involved. Once I had them in the car, I would tell them that we were going to Cleveland on a little holiday. I could explain Mary's presence by saying that she was coming along to look after Annie. This would please the two older children. We would be in Cleveland long before we were missed, provided I could start early enough.

I also reasoned that the travel permit will be easy. Frank likes things done for him, and as soon as the exact time I testify at the hearings is known, I can have the permit pre-dated and signed, so that I can leave immediately. He will want me to hit the road as soon as possible anyway, and he likes advance planning.

Having sorted through these details, I came reluctantly at last to grips with the biggest question of all—my conduct at the hearings. To cooperate with Tidings, and so do an injustice, or to shoot holes in a carefully staged play? Which? I doubt that they would arrest me or otherwise put me out of commission, at least not for a few days, because it would ruin their impartial image. Still, the safest way would be to cooperate. Except...

And my mind began boiling up fragments of the past. In one respect, I argued, Nancy is right. I have been a nothing. Nowhere have I distinguished myself. My pattern is one of compromise based, I am beginning to see, on fear rather than reason. Not fear for my life or of physical harm or other forms of retaliation, but a worse fear. The one born to him who is convinced he does not possess the ability to live on his own and so places his lot in the hands of others willingly, gratefully. It is the fear of being wrong and so being isolated from the world. It is the desire to please others, lest they become angry and desert you. One cannot alienate. In school, to alienate means failure in the classroom or in the fraternity house. Neither can the adult alienate, unless he is prepared to lose a wife or suffer neighborhood ridicule or be cut from a promotion or incur a penalty fixed by some kind of law—and there are many laws. Behave. Cooperate. And life will be good to you. Never mind your instincts, and forget your questions. This has been my creed. And in return for the faithful practice of it, there is nothing really concrete. No deep-down satisfaction about anything. So now, I allow myself one tiny thought. If I have been nothing, will more of the same make it any different? Once I was called upon to memorize the formula Pi, an insignificant act. Today, I am called upon to conspire against other men, significant to say the least. This is the measure of the distance I have traveled. And what of tomorrow? What then is the price for the good life? To take a man's life? To rob or steal openly? Where does compromise end?

Now! It ends now, I thought. I looked about my office, an eight-foot-by-eight-foot cubicle formed by head-high steel and frosted glass partitions. I have one small steel desk, a plastic covered swivel chair, a filing cabinet and a guest chair, also plastic covered. The plastic is light green and the metal is chrome. The desk is grey. My walls are cream colored, but the whole building interior is cream colored. The floor is a beige tile throughout. There are nine other cubicles where I work exactly like mine. All feed neatly into three big offices which have floor-to-ceiling partitions, doors, carpeting, at least one window, and which house Frank, the boss and district manager, and his two assistants. The fluorescent lights give everything a surgical cleanness, and because the executive offices block most window light, one cannot judge time without looking at the clock. The big, round one on the far wall, peeking above the cubicles like a full moon, told me that better than four hours had passed since I had talked with Harry. I listened to the muffled clatter of typewriters, rolling file drawers, high heels clicking and the pitches on the telephone by salesmen like myself telling some tired voice on the other end of the line why he could not have steel.[42] Absently, I reached across to my calendar and wrote in bold pencil: "It ends now… 4:44 p.m."

A wheel within a wheel within a wheel within a wheel. A flawlessly machined resource to be used as others see fit. That is me, I told myself angrily. I drew big, black circles around the message I had just written. My mind was clear. I would begin now to square myself. And I thought of how the hearings would be when I tell them, quietly and plainly, precisely what Mr. Tidings does not expect to hear. Push a man just so far, and watch out! My invective included Nancy, as well.

The phone rang. It was Harry.

"Hi! 5932365. Got it?" the cheery voice asked.

"Got it." I repeated the number.

"Bye."

---

42 Under Treaty of Friendship agreements, the United States was obligated to contribute as a form of foreign aid approximately thirty percent of its semifinished and finished steel production to the World Order of Nations for allocation to "underdeveloped countries, such as the Ukraine, Poland and China…." The U.S. government would purchase the steel from the producers, as in earlier wartime actions which, of course, created a severe shortage of the metal for use by "nonessential" domestic fabricators. The quota was later upped to forty, then fifty percent.

Noon is a good time to make phone calls. No one misses you, and the crowds are wonderfully thick. I will talk to Harry tomorrow, and we will see how foolish I am. I mused this over as I drove home. For once, I was not bothered by the stalled busses that in ever-increasing numbers make the rush hour nearly impossible. It was raining as it had been for several days, and green was beginning to carpet the earth. The air was exotic with the smell of rain mingling with the dust and cinders of leftover winter. I felt heroically alive. The lightness of spirit lasted until I was home and even carried through the dinner hour. We had boiled potatoes and carrots cooked with fragments of stew meat. Nancy was red-eyed when I arrived, and I knew she had spent the afternoon thinking, too. She brightened when she saw that I was in truly good cheer.

"David, you've come to your senses. I knew you would."

"Yes. I've come to my senses."

"Thank God!" Relief swept her.

"Yes. Thank God," I said, wondering whether we, perhaps, had two different Gods.

The next morning I spent in the East End calling on small metal- fabricators. I had good news for one. We could provide him with enough steel to see him through another six weeks. He makes industrial siding. For another it was bad news. The allocation had not been approved. This one made stampings for car radios and small accessories now considered non-essential. He ordered his payroll closed out. I had not been near Mary for several days. Larry was home with a cold. Besides I thought it would do no harm to stick close to the job and give as active an appearance as possible. I could not be absolutely sure that I was not being followed. I found a phone booth in the rear of an old drug store, with shelves and bins half empty, sprinkled with dusty hardware items and cheap soaps, cosmetics, a few medicines and used magazines.[43] A weary, dusty man in a smudged white coat

43 Under the Treaty there was a considerable push to "upgrade" all publications to include more "balanced educational material and less reactionary propaganda and decadent fiction stories...." The reading public therefore began to reread older magazines not printed under the new edict, and there was apparently a considerable market for used books and magazines.

pointed the way back behind a faded display of electric light bulbs. I called Cleveland exactly at noon. Harry answered immediately.

"I shook the tail!" he greeted me. "Now, suppose you explain yourself."

I did a recap, including my decision to play things straight at the hearings. There were no clicks or hollow sounds on the line. Our plan had worked. Harry was impressed, for his voice lost its customary brashness. There were, instead, the soft sounds of respect.

"I never knew you had it in you, Dave. Nancy... how does she feel about this?"

"I haven't told her."

"Good God, man! How do you expect..."

"You let me worry about that," I replied. In the snug safety of the phone booth I was finding new measures of confidence.

"But if you bring her..."

"There'll be five of us. One man. One woman. Three children," I parried.

"Good," the voice came back. "Now, you'll have to get out immediately after your hearings, or they'll nail you for sure. Look, Dave, why not just cooperate with them? Say what they want you to say."

"No!" I barked, the words biting sharply in my own ear. The specter of Nancy in her drunken trance seemed to crowd into the booth with me. "Harry, I've got to. I've got to show them that they can't push me around any further. None of them!" I breathed. "Besides, I've a debt to pay to you, to Mom... and to Dad ... as well as myself. Don't ask me to explain, because I can't. But I will not leave this country by paying yet another price of betrayal."

There was a long pause, and then the voice became softer.

"I think I understand." Then it hardened into crisp efficiency. "O.K. Now. I'll fly us out, but we'll have to get out right after you testify. Obviously, I won't be able to come back. So I'm taking Margaret and Charlie with us."

Charles is five, and I have only seen him twice. "Mom, what about her?" I asked.

"We'll take her, of course, along with Sam Burns our flight engineer and Tony Long, you know, the president of our outfit. He's a widower and Sam's a no-good bachelor so there's no problem in their skipping out."

"But your plane only seats four."

"Ah-ha! We're going to heist the company jet and leave mine here, along with the company pilot, who's a no-good bastard. It seats nine, counting the jump seat. Someone will have to hold Charlie and Annie, and we'll have to take it easy on luggage. I figure about ten pounds per person. That aircraft can zip us across Lake Erie in about twelve minutes... low, under radar. Now, I'll need one day's notice. Think you can do it?

Harry then gave me the rest of his plan, a masterpiece of timing. If I testify before noon, I am to leave immediately afterward and be at the company hangar on the far side of the Cleveland air terminal at exactly four-thirty p.m. Harry in the meantime will visit one of his plants, lose his tail and come directly to the hangar. Margaret, Charlie, my mother and the others are to rendezvous at the hangar. Sam Burns is the key. Since he's on duty at the hangar, the flight preparations will arouse no suspicion. He will notify the tower of a routine flight pattern instrument check with the take off scheduled for four forty-five p.m.

"That way," Harry added, "we get off the ground without questions... and away we go before they know what happened. Now, there's one other thing. I know I can lose my tail. I do it regularly to keep in practice. But I'm good for no more than about forty-five minutes. Whenever they lose me they always check my office first and then they check the hangar next. Last time I vanished they were at the hangar in forty-one minutes. I'm sixteen minutes from plant to hangar. Allow another four for traffic problems. So if I duck them at four twenty-five, we can be in the air at four forty- five and in Canada by five... providing everyone is on time. Dave, you must promise, once you've given me the day, that you'll be on time. If for any reason you can't, call Sam. I can only do this once, and to wait past take off time almost surely will mean that they'd trace us. Even if we got off the ground, they'd shoot us out of the air for sure."

Of course I promised, grimly aware of the risk.

"What if I testify in the afternoon?" I dropped my voice to a whisper. The dusty druggist had moved close to the phone booth to rearrange a display of used hair pins. The bird-like tilt of his head told me he was trying to listen.

"Same plan," Harry answered, "only you should leave first thing the next morning, and we'll take off at twelve-fifteen. But remember I must have twenty-four hours' notice. When you know the date write it out numerical style and add your arrival time on the end. Then call me and give it to me backwards."

"Will do. And ..." A lump formed in my throat. I wanted to say something profound, but all that would come was a pitifully inadequate "Thanks."

"Maybe we should thank you, Dave. You see, I used to think ... that is... never mind," he faltered. "Let's just say that when a guy like you can find the guts to come through, well, maybe we'll all of us make it all right... the country, I mean. Maybe one day we can come home again."

We hung up then, the bonds of understanding firmly in place.

3

I saw Mary today but only long enough to explain the plan in detail. We have agreed to keep our personal feelings under strict control so as not to risk detection. We will see each other when necessary to finalize details of our departure. I do not believe I am being followed.

Mary is the happiest person I have ever seen. How wonderful she makes Canada sound. How she aches to be free. She is like a small, furry wild creature who is about to be released from captivity by some noble passerby. The gratitude, hope and pride that come with victory all are in her large grey-green eyes. When she looks wholly at me to unleash the full measure of her feelings, it is almost more than I can bear. She trusts me so completely now. It is a burden, not unpleasant, mind, but still an added load. She has cast her lot with me, and I cannot escape the thought that one mistake in judgment on my part could destroy her. I hold her life in my hands. Sometimes I think I have been handed too much, too fast; that I am too unsure afoot and could easily stumble and crush her in the fall. I do not know enough. I am untaught to deal with the unknown. I wonder at the future. But we must escape. Escape from power. To be free of being constantly watched and measured against a standard, and to be able to match our inner thoughts with outer actions. Power! Everywhere, power! Except in the remoteness of Canada. Surely they could never reach out to us there? Surely it must be so.

4

Only a week left, and my throat grows dry thinking what it is I still must face. Leon Tidings sent for me today. He took me personally to see Smith Armstrong, who will conduct the hearings. The top floor of the Skyway Building. That is where he lives. I hear he never leaves. He has an apartment, they say, more lavish than such as I could imagine. I believe it. For what I saw of his office on the floor below confirms even the wildest rumors. Carpeting, beginning at the elevator, so thick and unmarked that I hated to walk on it. Walls of rich woods and subtle fabrics. Huge potted plants arranged in striking groupings. Low armchairs luxuriously covered. Art objects— sculptures, paintings, ancient teak cabinets and tables bearing relics of silver, pewter, copper and bronze. Occasionally a huge desk swept clean and polished to mellow hues, behind which sat magnificently groomed young women looking unhurried, yet busy with paper and telephones. All of this in the reception area I was led through. All of this bathed in the softness of indirect lights and, occasionally, hidden spots. All of this unfolding before me without sound. For our footsteps were no more than rustles, and even the typewriters— the few I noticed— were muffled. The quiet was enormous, as if the process of breathing, itself, was banned. To speak, to cough, to let change jingle in one's pocket was unthinkable.

It spoke of pure power, a low purring giant. I walked on my toes.

We entered Smith Armstrong's office through massive double doors that were opened noiselessly by another flawlessly groomed woman, possibly 30, who wore a black, silk suit that swished suggestively with each move of her trim body. She seemed to know who we were without asking, yet I had heard no one announcing us. His office bit out a huge corner of the building. Three independent sofa-and-chair groupings were set around three of the walls which appeared to be covered with a light-green silk fabric. Original paintings—Picassos, Renoirs, and Goyas—were tastefully hung about the huge room. The papers a month or so before had announced that the Art Museum had presented them to Smith Armstrong "as a token of welcome to the city." In the center of the floor stood a massive conference table ringed with great high-backed chairs of wood—oak, I think—and brown leather. And in a window-end of the room stood the biggest desk I have ever seen, oak also, with upholstered occasional chairs formed in a perfect crescent around it. And behind sat the man, not yet fifty years old. He had coal black hair which was thinned out at the top of his head. His sunken cheeks accented his black eyebrows and lashes. Even the pupils of his eyes were so black that they reflected pinpoints of light. He rose noiselessly from a smoothly gliding swivel chair, higher in the back than any other in the room. He was of medium height and build, slightly rounded at the shoulders. I had only seen him three times before; once bundled up in a heavy coat standing beside Nicholas Syerov at the Peace Monument last New Year's Day; a second time at Dome Center when the Treaty was explained, and once on television. At no time did he look particularly imposing, but rather, quite average. Of course, I had not seen him up close. He looked then nothing like he did now, neat in a quiet, dark suit with pencil fine stripes. His every movement was quiet and unruffled with not a wasted motion. He did not tap a finger or adjust an arm or shift his stance. He simply stood quietly still, his head inclined toward two chairs immediately across the desk from him. After Tidings and I seated ourselves, he continued to stand for a long moment, silently contemplating us both with equal attention. I was compelled to look him in the face, to watch for an expression, a sign that would betray whatever it was he was thinking. I dared not turn away for fear of missing something which might give me a clue. But there was no expression to monitor. There was neither pleasure nor displeasure, humor nor ill-humor, like nor dislike. His face revealed only how absolutely calm he was, void of any anxiety or doubt, and that he knew secrets, many secrets. It was a terrible ordeal—to sit there in complete silence and watch at once nothing and everything. A phrase kept up a steady sing-song through my head: The seat of power.

This was power unassailable and enduring. I was sitting in the vortex, in the very center of the web, not as a participant but as a victim.

Tidings must have experienced this sense of power, too, but in a different way. He must have felt privileged, awed to be summoned yet again—I think he comes often—to the wellspring that sustains him. For he looked refreshed, almost inspired with a hint of breathlessness.

Smith Armstrong sat down noiselessly. Only one item was on his desk, a slim file folder. He opened it noiselessly. His hands moved with perfect smoothness. Finally he spoke. His voice was neither loud nor soft nor accented nor hurried nor slow.

"You are nice to come, Mr. Tidings."

"Thank you, sir," was the soft reply.

"And you are nice to come, Mr. Little."

How I despise myself that I did not answer him! I could only nod. My breath began to stick in my chest, and I licked my lips.

"Mr. Tidings has briefed you on the hearings." He did not even allow himself sufficient emotion to phrase it as a question.

"Yes." My reply sounded too high-pitched and loud.

"You are clear on your role."

"Yes."

"I shall ask my questions rapidly and in a particular order." His words were cut by the soft buzz of his phone. Only then did emotion overcome him. A slight scowl creased his face. He lifted the receiver soundlessly and listened for a moment, and then in tones powerfully low and icy he answered what was doubtlessly a query put by the trim woman outside.

"You may tell the President not to call me again under any circumstances. I will telephone him in due course... and don't you ever disturb me like this again."

He replaced the receiver without so much as a bump.

"I do this out of consideration for you, Mr. Little," he continued as if the phone had never rung. "I trust you will give me the same consideration in return. I do not take unnecessary risks or make the same mistake more than once."

Not here, I thought, I cannot be brave here. I will be different at the hearings, but not in this place.

"Yes." How weak a reply, but how safe.

Then there was silence. He looked at me. Not once did he blink. I began to stir restlessly, feeling someone had to say something.

"Yes. Yes, Mr. Armstrong. I see what you mean. I see . . I was beginning to babble, seeking safe words to say, anything to combat the awful silence.

"Good day, gentlemen." He cut me off softly, as if he had learned all that he needed to know.

Again he rose silently, as we stumbled up and out of our chairs. For Tidings, too, by this time appeared to be slightly unnerved and relieved to leave.

"Good-bye, sir," he said, too lightly, too fervently.

But there was no answer. All that spoke were two cold black eyes that followed us through the door.

I could feel them in my back.

I still feel them in my back.

He haunts me.

My god, how can anyone oppose him! I had no idea what he would be like!

5

I have struggled with myself tonight. Only three more days until the hearings begin, and I have not really settled down to planning specifically how I shall carry it off. Should I make a speech, and will they let me finish? Or shall I let them question me and use my answers to reveal how this all really came about. I keep trying to imagine how it will be. I see Smith Armstrong all right, and I know just how he will phrase his questions. The vision is terrible enough, but even worse, I draw a blank when I try to imagine myself answering. Have I the wit and wisdom to do a good job? Perhaps Harry is right. Maybe I should play it safe. But something else will not let me. I keep seeing Nancy again and again at that miserable party. "He's a fool! He's scared to death. He's a nothing, and he wants to stay that way." Why did she have to say that?

Because she is right, but not in the way she thinks. I am weak, and this awareness bears hard upon me. I must fight them. The almighty THEMS and the THEYS who have stalked me all of my life. How I hate them—the THEMS and THEYS! Except I have not known who they were. No one ever says, "Pete Jones says" or "Tom, Dick and Harry say..." It is always THEY say. But now I know who some of the THEYS are, and before I leave I must have my day, my hour to get even.

But what shall I do?

I will play it by ear. I have always been good at that. I will adapt to the situation as it unfolds. I will keep my head and not overdo. Keep it low key. No, I will say. No, I enjoyed reading those speeches of Mr. Brown's. No, Mr. Armstrong, Mr. Brown has been as cooperative as any American citizen. In fact, Mr. Armstrong, he should be commended for the great efforts he has gone to. No, Mr. Armstrong, I'm sorry, sir (I will say sir every so often, but not overdo it), Mr. Brown is dedicated to the welfare of all. No, Mr. Armstrong, I had nothing really to do with the demonstration. No, Mr. Armstrong. No.

6

Tomorrow is the day. Eight a.m. Hotel Royal. Grand Ballroom. Why there? I might as well face it. I am scared. I went to the bank today to withdraw the money. I went three times. Once the line was too long. Then I could not decide how much to take away, since I must leave

Nancy something. The third time back I realized it would be far wiser to withdraw the money on the day I leave. Less suspicious. Of course, I have no intention of backing out. I stopped to see Mary for a minute. Larry is over his cold. There was not too much to say. She is so happy and does not seem in the least anxious. You would think she would be more on edge. But then, she does not have to face what I must. She plans to attend on the day I testify. I objected to this, but she already has the pass. She says she cannot bear to miss me. She says it will be the proudest moment of her life.

And now Nancy is nice to me. Fortunately her work will keep her away. She sees I am upset. She baked a lemon pie today. Went to four stores in order to find the lemons. Curse her hide! Why does she have to complicate things this way? If I am so damn worthless, why does she bake lemon pies?

7

Two hours per person. That is all they get. Some of them do not even take the full time. Others plead for more, only to be gaveled and shouted down into their chairs where they sit numbed, unseeing and not listening any more. With each "presentation," as they call them, a little bit more of Pittsburgh dies. One hallowed name after another is sent crashing to disgrace and oblivion. Sinners all— brought to light by the swift and sure machinery of "social and international justice" which, as Smith Armstrong stated quietly in his opening remarks, "must be served if world peace is to be preserved."

It has been awful to watch. The flawless perfection of it makes it so. The aura of certainty and power supreme is present everywhere. The Grand Ballroom of the Hotel Royal is a ballroom no more. It is a mammoth courtroom, half-a-block square, jammed with better than two thousand people who sit at hushed attention and gaze steadily at a huge tier of platforms draped in blue velvet. On the first tier sit the 44 "subjects" in armless, straight-backed chairs, eleven to a row. And the four rows are arranged to feed symmetrically into the second tier, upon which sit six "examiners," members of the Southwestern

186

Pennsylvania Joint Committee For Local Action in what appear to be white leather swivel chairs. Three each share a common bench of polished wood. And both benches flank the third tier, upon which sits one man at a particularly imposing bench, also of gleaming wood, which bears the bronze emblem of the World Order of Nations. His chair is white, too, but bigger. He is the chairman, Smith Armstrong. Behind him is a huge backdrop of gold cloth bearing a cutout of the Treaty of Friendship Seal. The red star and eagle within it must be fully ten feet in diameter. The witness box is located to the left on the first tier. Witnesses must stand facing the opposite side of the platform so they are clearly seen by spectators, as well as those conducting the hearings. Television cameras and the press table are discreetly set opposite the witness box in a wing off-stage which is almost completely shielded by a masking curtain, also of blue. Platform lights are arranged so that each figure is sharply illuminated. The spectators are bathed under softer house lights bright enough to read a program, take notes and move around by, although guards stationed at the exits are quick to accost persons who move around too much. For the most part the spectators wear wooden expressions, except whenever demonstrations break out. With each "subject" examined, as Smith Armstrong keeps referring to the 44 men and women, one section or another of the acre of faces erupts into angry invectives directed to the person then being examined, and guards move hastily to the trouble spot to restore order, while Smith Armstrong bangs for order, "or I must clear the hall." And usually within ten minutes quiet is restored. The people in our area had been advised by word of mouth to demonstrate against Joseph Vendurella when his turn came to be examined.

The hearings begin at eight and adjourn at noon. They resume at one and adjourn again at five. I have been there seven straight days now. After a time one becomes numb and in a half-conscious daze from staring at one place for so long. There are no windows. We are tightly packed. The man sitting next to me actually believes this whole thing to be purely spontaneous in every respect. He has even discounted our word of mouth orders to demonstrate as merely a sign of healthy interest. He watches, listens and comments from the edge of his chair like it was the seventh game of the World Series. He is fat and takes up too much space. No smoking is permitted, which bothers him considerably. I am glad, because I do not smoke much.

We have programs. The official name is "agenda," but it looks like a program and that is what we all call it. It lists all of the subjects and examiners. It also points out in italics that "This session has no right to prosecute but is empowered only to recommend prosecution by the World Order of Nations through the due process of the World Court."

The spectators are about three-quarters men. All kinds are here. Suits, work clothes, shirts and ties, sport shirts and jackets. The women wear everything from tight skirts, sweaters and loafers to heels and elegant suits and dresses—even a stole or two. Both sexes range from super-neat to unbelievably sloppy. It is a cross-section of humanity that leaves very little unrepresented. Everyone has a pass, which is a badge of one color or another bearing his photograph, name and seat number.

Spectator moods vary. Most of the time the mood is passive and noncommittal. Occasionally hostility breaks out, as I mentioned. Sometimes there is laughter but only when Smith Armstrong or one of the examiners makes a reference that is obviously intended to ridicule the person being examined. Actual jeering occurs rarely, usually only when the demonstrations take place. I live in constant fear that I might be asked to lead a demonstration and so try to stay in the background, far away from Leon Tidings. Since everyone checks in and out, he knows I am here but has made no contact, yet.

I shall carry with me always the memory of that first Alice-In-Wonderland morning. I arrived a half-hour early, only to find most of the spectators already milling around in the lobby, coffee shops and plaza. It was a bright-blue May day, the kind that should make people feel good. And most did. The atmosphere was festive. Nearly everyone there was absent from work with pay. And after all, it was someone else—not the happy spectator—who was getting the axe. It was a combination of relief, the sense of playing hooky and the feeling of being in on something big. I did not sense the presence of fear.

I felt terribly alone.

Larry, of course, was on hand but was working behind the great curtains with members of the JCFLA staff. I have seen him only once, from a distance. We waved. He looks as buoyant and confident as ever. Oddly, it was good to see him. For through all of this he still remains the most familiar object in my life. One cannot very well crush 21 years of close association just like that, even though very soon this friendship must be irrevocably destroyed.

There was some confusion in checking in and finding assigned seats, so that the proceedings did not begin until nearly nine. A person I never heard of called the hearings to order. All rise! Including the subjects now prominently displayed on the first tier. They had filed onto the platform shortly before. It took them several minutes to find their seats. What made it terrible to watch was the sheer number of them. Forty-four men and women, each one commanding varying degrees of eminence; each one a figure who had known elements of respect, envy, stature and admiration in other days; each one now of subdued bearing—shamefaced, like drunks being herded into night court, squinting with uncertainty under lights that glared from every direction so that no shadows were upon their chalk-white faces. Their obvious embarrassment was shared by the spectators who became hushed. They moved to their places with awkward obedience—all except two persons: a lean, bony man of 60 who had stem, set features and whom I knew to be Mr. Grant of our church, and Dr. Hamilton Rodgers. Mr. Grant was flanked by two police officers who ushered him in firmly by his arms. He moved rigidly, looking straight ahead. White-headed, ageless Dr. Hamilton Rodgers, unlike Mr. Grant, moved passively but with quiet dignity, as if he were seeking a place at a college commencement. Of the group, he was the only one who sparked within me an unwanted feeling of sorrow. As for the others, including Avery Brown, I could feel only impersonal pity, as one does when meeting a crippled stranger on the street.

189

And so we stood as the six examiners filed soberly to their benches, followed after a long pause by the highest judge of all— Smith Armstrong. All wore black robes, by what right I do not know. After this a minister led us in a prayer beseeching "Almighty God to guide our steps this day, as we continue our quest for the fulfillment of mankind's oldest aspiration—peace." The prayer is a daily occurrence, as is the Pledge of Allegiance. The Pledge is a new one and so most of us had to read it from printed slips of paper. I had it memorized by the third day.[44]

Then, finally, came the first call.

"By the Grace of God we are met here today to honor the petitions of thousands of citizens of the several counties comprising southwestern Pennsylvania who desire that this body conduct an examination into the affairs of...." So spoke Smith Armstrong, and he read gravely and with flawless pronunciation the names of the 44. "It is our solemn task to determine if there is just cause to remand any one or all of these citizens to the World Order of Nations Department of Social Justice for consideration as to whether anyone or all shall be brought to trial under the jurisdiction of the World Court on charges of violating articles of a Treaty of Friendship lately signed by the United States of America, the Union of Soviet Socialist Republics and members of the World Order of Nations."

A wave of expectancy swept across the two thousand spectators, as Chairman Armstrong paused to adjust the papers on his bench. The six examiners did likewise and also fingered their table microphones. Slowly the rustle grew into murmurs which flowed from a group seated near the front. "Down with Mister X!" The murmurs grew into a soft chant. Then came a few whistles and catcalls, and the chant grew louder. Smith Armstrong scowled down at the noise and rapped vigorously with his gavel.

"There will be order here!" he cried over the din. "Guards. Kindly restore order." When quiet did come he added with chilling firmness, "Let us understand that we are not here to persecute or prosecute.

---

44 "I pledge allegiance to the World Order of Nations and to my country as a co-operating member; I pledge my loyalty to peace and my contributions to the progress of all the peoples of the world."

This body recognizes and… indeed sympathizes… with the wishes of conscientious citizens to have done with these weeks of charges and counter-charges and seek out the truth. But we can tolerate no disorder. We have an obligation to those summoned here to insure fairness and impartiality. We, therefore, will brook no further outbreaks." And he paused yet again to examine his papers. The stillness was total, save only the crackling of the papers, which was repeated harshly through his microphone. Finally, we were on our way.

"We will examine first the conduct of… Richard . .. Malcolm ... Grant. Mr. Grant, will you please assume the witness box?"

Mr. Grant did not move or speak. A few boos and hisses rose from yet another group of spectators, only to be quelled by the gavel.

"Will the Sergeant-at-Arms kindly escort Mr. Grant to the witness box?"

Two blue uniforms, W.O.N. police this time, flashed smoothly across the platform, and Mr. Grant again was escorted. There was a cold, bitter smile on his face. He stood straight and stiff in the box, looking at no one.

"For the record, kindly state your name and occupation," the chairman instructed.

No answer. A low rumble began to sweep the spectators, and again the gavel was sounded.

"Very well," Smith Armstrong said evenly. "Will the Sergeant-at-arms please verify the identity of this man?"

One of the blue uniforms pulled the floor microphone in the witness box toward him. "Mister Chairman. I verify to this assembly that the person on my left is Richard Malcolm Grant, founder and chairman of the board of R. M. Grant and Sons, metal fabricators. He resides at 11706 Ross Lane, Fox Chapel."

"Let the secretary of these hearings so note. And now, Mr. Grant, your peers have charged you with violations of Articles

One, Four, Five, Six, Eleven and Twelve under the Treaty of Friendship. Are these charges true or untrue?"

The silence was deep, and the waiting was the highest suspense. One of the most outspoken opponents of the Treaty stood before us. He was the acknowledged leader of the highly vocal Allegheny Committee for American Action which for years had bitterly assailed the World Order of Nations, our government, labor power and organized crime.

Mr. Grant spoke at last in a thin but unwavering voice that revealed not fear but overwhelming contempt.

"Anything I say to you…" he paused to pick just the right words, "ungrateful, treasonous snakes will be perverted to your own dirty purposes!" And he waved his stick-like arm to include the entire assembled room. "It is you who have violated our Constitution. It is you who sold out your country to become Communists who would…"

He got no further. Spectators erupted all over the room, roaring protest. From one near me came, "Kill him!" His teeth were clenched in awful hate. Even I felt resentment. It was the way Mr. Grant had spoken, rather than so much what he said that rubbed very much against me. For I wanted Mr. Grant to succeed. But he ought to know, I thought bitterly, that some of us here are not Communists or snakes. Some of us care, too.

"Silence!" the chairman roared. "Let him speak."

And Mr. Grant spoke. I got sweaty as I listened, wishing he would be still. His fellow subjects progressively dropped their heads lower and lower as if hoping the floor would open up and swallow either him or them. Only Dr. Rodgers continued to watch with polite interest.

"Well! This is a switch!" he cried. "Speak I will, as I have again and again. You are traitors. You deserve to rot in hell. You are parasites who suck the blood of honest, decent people. You have been bewitched by shysters of sin and corruption." With regular sweeps of his arms, eyes and body, he continued to take us all in as equally guilty. "You elect corrupt, power-seeking politicians who are really Communists at heart. You … all of you… are every bit as bad as he is!" And he shook his fist at Nicholas Syerov.

There was no holding back the spectators now. Chairs were overturned. Men and women leaped to their feet in violent protest. The gavel did no good this time, and a cordon of W.O.N. guards moved quickly into the fray. Even Mr. Grant lost his composure. He swayed

192

slightly in the witness box and gripped the handrail. His stern face took on growing proportions of disbelief. It was nearly ten minutes before order was restored.

This time Smith Armstrong's quiet voice was even more chilling due to its contrast with the bedlam. "Mr. Syerov. This hearing begs your understanding and patience." The applause was instant and deafening, as the Soviet representative nodded with the benevolence of Father Christmas.

"How say you, Mr. Grant? Confine your remarks to the charges."

The old man still faced the spectators. His voice was lower now and carried traces of disbelief. "So. It is too late. You are beasts already." Then he turned stiffly to face the examiners. "I oppose the Treaty. I do not recognize its existence. I do not recognize this mockery. I can only thank God that I am not as you." Once again the sweep of his arm included us all. The chairman turned to his papers and dismissed Mr. Grant with a matter-of-factness that was sterile of any emotion. Clearly, the seat of power could not care less about what Mr. Grant thought.

While the guards escorted the brittle figure back to his seat, Smith Armstrong continued in a flat voice. "While Mr. Grant has left little doubt as to the validity of the charges brought to bear by his fellow citizens," here there were more boos and catcalls, "still, I do not believe we can in good conscience conclude this examination. I hope my associates agree that more facts are needed before we can render an honest judgment."

And the six robed forms nodded gravely.

I struggled to kill the growing feeling of gratitude toward the chairman. Gratitude! It was like my first encounter with Leon Tidings when he became suddenly almost friendly. I had felt gratitude then, too. My god! If they can make me feel this way, then what of the others who know less about this than I? These are devils at work.

The first witness summoned to "tell us something of your relationship with Mr. Grant" was president of a union local. Under quick, surgical questioning by the chairman and others, he revealed that Mr. Grant had threatened to close the plant unless workers wrote to their senators demanding that they vote against the Treaty ratification; that following this—indeed up until the past week—he had continued to bombard employees with "bitter letters designed to turn honest, hard-working men and women against the Treaty in an effort to kill their sense of responsibility as free citizens working in a free society to build a peaceful world;" that he ordered the W.O.N. flag hauled down from the plant flagpole; that he promised huge bonuses to any employee who would resist the "tyranny" of the Treaty, "this at the expense of American taxpayers and the needy people of the world who the people of the United States now are committed to help."

Following this came Mrs. Clinton Lowell Snyder, vice-chairman of the Allegheny Committee for American Action. A plump, widowed housewife of some substantial means—she has three fulltime maids, one butler, a chauffeur and gardener, which was brought out skillfully by Smith Armstrong—she was called as "possibly one, at least, who could speak on behalf of the distinguished gentleman." For an instant I was certain that Chairman Armstrong had assumed more than he should have. For Mrs. Snyder's devotion to Mr. Grant was well known, along with her ability to speak bluntly. But on this day she was docile, polite and anxious to please. She minced into the witness box and proceeded to slice Mr. Grant into thin slivers. She revealed that Mr. Grant had conceived of the Allegheny Committee as a "militant, fascist group seeking to destroy" the World Order of Nations, as well as our own national government; that Mr. Grant misled her and "a lot of other well-meaning, patriotic citizens;" that he has been purchasing fire-arms;[45] that he has been meeting secretly with people to organize a resistance; that she—Mrs. Snyder—was grateful "for the opportunity to speak openly and freely."

She received a standing ovation. Not once did she look at Mr. Grant. Not once did she pause or become confused or show anything resembling sympathy for him. In a voice that permitted some small show of emotion, Smith Armstrong commended her as a "woman of remarkable courage to whom the world owes a deep debt of gratitude."

---

45 Some years prior to the Treaty of Friendship, the United States enacted legislation prohibiting the possession of firearms by its citizens "in order to assure greater public safety." A few citizens were permitted to use—but not own—government arms under highly specialised circumstances. The JCFLA under the Treaty sought to re-enforce this law.

194

And Mr. Grant? It caved him in. Three times he leaped to his feet in wild fury to deny her words. Three times he was firmly replaced in his chair by the two blue uniforms that flanked him. Finally, he slumped.

Still it did not end.

Smoothly, impassively, the well-oiled machine continued its flawless performance. For next came Mr. Grant's two sons, Richard, Junior, and Sanford J. Grant. Both worked in the family business as president and vice president-sales, respectively. They tied the knot tighter. Richard, Junior, went first. He revealed that his father had ordered him to pad production cost data-sheets in order to realize a profit for the first quarter of this year; that he ordered the falsification of raw materials inventory records, even to the transfer of inventory (strip and sheet steel) to a secret warehouse to escape his assigned quota restrictions; that he, Richard, Junior, was heartsick at what he had to do to the father he loved but that he had a higher duty to perform.

He then burst into tears and fled from the witness box with the visibly sympathetic understanding of Smith Armstrong. There was more applause.

Finally came the younger brother, Sanford. Boyish and unsure, he stammered through gently put questions that revealed that his father had forced him to make illegal deals with longstanding customers to supply them with black market products.

"Do I understand that your father deliberately falsified his reports so that these customers could continue to line their pockets with fat profits on a business-as-usual basis while the rest of the world was deprived its rightful share of steel?"

"Do you really mean to suggest a black market here?" one of the examiners asked harshly.

The young man licked his lips and looked for a second at the hunched figure of his father. "Yes, sir. I... tried... that is..." he shrugged unhappily, misery oozing from every pore.

He was gently released and allowed to slip quickly behind the curtains.

Then came the twist. Nicholas Syerov had remained silent throughout. Now he called for the floor and in faltering, broken

English proceeded to praise these "two wanderfuls boys... 'n I haf son... who haf did mos difficult of tings ... we bless tham." And he blew his nose vigorously.

The spectators were deeply moved. The big man beside me began to eat his lip and sniff. Nearby, a woman began to weep. No catcalls now. Mr. Grant had been snapped in two like a toothpick. He was bent over in his chair, too dazed and uncaring to move. He made no sounds. He was all anguish. The two uniforms lifted him from his seat and supported him off the platform.

Total elapsed time for Mr. Grant: sixty-three minutes, well under the allotted two hours, but then they were running late. Now they were right on schedule.

At precisely 10:05 they called out the second name—Benjamin Zanhorst, the much respected and, until now, unassailable publisher of the *Pittsburgh News-Journal*. He required no escorts. A heavy-set man of square build, he was the perfect image of solidarity and impartial integrity that one associates with the reporting of news, even down to the heavy shell-rim glasses. He stood in the witness box with quiet dignity that spoke confidence that all would be well. For he had an enviable record. No scandal had ever been connected with him. He had supported almost all worthy causes and served on more civic committees than most. He supported the summit meeting preceding the Treaty, as well as its ratification. From time to time his editorials, however, had questioned certain measures being taken under the Treaty, but always done in moderation and in a way that demonstrated willingness to cooperate "to make the thing work," as he had said on countless occasions. His posture in the witness box plainly said, "I am not a Mr. Grant type, as you can see." His fellow citizens deemed otherwise. For he was charged with violating Articles One, Two, Six, Seven and Ten. And the moment Smith Armstrong made this known, yet another demonstration broke out among spectators in yet another quarter of the great ballroom.

"Down with Mister X!" they screamed, and they were pounded into silence by the gavel.

To say Mr. Zanhorst was taken aback is an understatement. His bulldog face with its firm lines of relentless courage became in an instant nothing more than a flabby, fat face with jaws sagging open, as with Mr. Grant, in utter disbelief. Aside from this he reacted differently. With considerable effort he struggled hard to exercise "reason and calm in an atmosphere charged with the understandable emotions of serious-minded citizens concerned about Pittsburgh's role in the future," as he said. Taking but a moment to re-establish his lost image and to reset the glasses that had slipped down his nose, Mr. Zanhorst proceeded to give a speech. It was relatively short and polished. He pointed out in a well-modulated but powerful voice that his entire life had been dedicated to the preservation of a free society "not on paper in the form of empty lip service but a truly free society with equality' and prosperity for all… and I am proud of my liberal record." Then he cited the "precious heritage of a free press" so that "issues of the day might be honestly weighed in the cause of social justice.… Surely these acts of mine of raising honest questions about relatively minor things… surely this meets both the spirit and intent of that magnificent instrument so lovingly created by men of good will and deep purpose—the Treaty of Friendship."

He got no further. Someone yelled, "Liar!" Another, "Traitor!" Then in unison, "Down with Mister X!" He tried to say something more, but a curt nod from the highest bench of all dismissed him. He had no choice but to resume his seat.

Phase two involved six witnesses: the chief editorial writer of the paper, the managing editor, a reporter, a copywriter, a pressman and an advertiser. In orderly fashion they recounted how Mr. Zanhorst issued various instructions that resulted in the newspaper misleading the public by saying that (and several items were quoted) the Soviet Union might prove not fully trustworthy unless carefully watched; that under certain circumstances a nation might need limited arms to defend itself; that comments of certain reactionaries should be reported even when they were trying to foment fascism; that domestic allocations should be redrawn, a move that could only further fatten the profits of American capitalists at the expense of all mankind;

that business firms which advertised in the paper would enjoy personal gain from slanted stories contrary to the public interest; that the World Order of Nations might not be the final answer to world government; that people should have more of their earnings; that international gift quotas should be cut, and that wages should not be reduced.

The six examiners, especially Nicholas Syerov, and the chairman, at various points during the lengthy questioning, conveyed a growing sense of indignation at "what appear to be the wanton and irresponsible acts of a man who holds a key position of trust within this community."

"I find it difficult to believe that we—all of us—could have been so cunningly misled," Smith Armstrong commented wearily. "I simply cannot allow myself to think that this man, of all men, could actually be… dare I even say this … a fascist subtly at work to destroy what we are trying to do."

Again and again came the demonstrations, followed by the banging of the gavel.

Mr. Zanhorst sat very still throughout. He sat very still the rest of the day and the one after that, too.

So far, now, there have been 26 others. People like Justin Wright, president of the Bar Association; Dr. S. Lawson Murry, president of the Medical Association; Dr. David O. Harmes, superintendent of schools; Bishop James D. O'Brien of the Catholic Diocese; Elizabeth Robbins St. John, president of the Federation of Women's Clubs; Ernest B. Good, president of an accounting firm and chairman of the Community Fund; Henry G. Gates, Boy Scouts of America; H. H. Barnes III, the merchant and president of the Chamber of Commerce; Lester E. Simpson, Republican county chairman, and Adolph H. Kruger, president of Mastersmeld. The balance also were prominent in business, industry, labor, banking, women's organizations, government, law, and medicine.

Through all of this the pattern seldom varies—the subject proclaims his innocence and anywhere from six to nine witnesses show him guilty as charged and then some. Occasionally a prostitute, gambler, or bartender will appear to give evidence of lurid love or reckless betting, or acute alcoholism. It was this tack that caused Henry Gates to collapse, shrieking denials, as a fellow scoutmaster implied that Mr. Gates might prefer boys to girls. Smith Armstrong did not need to show any indignation, because the spectators went wild screaming for Mr. Gates' blood.

The conclusion of each subject's examination seldom varies either.

"Are there any more witnesses?"

There is silence.

"Very well. Any more questions, gentlemen?"

Pause.

"Let me remind you that we are obligated to give the subjects of these hearings every advantage we can in keeping with our responsibilities. If you can think of any question that will shed further light upon these shocking revelations, then I urge you to ask them. Spectators, have you any?"

Pause.

"Very well. This concludes the examination of [fill in the name, any name]. We will advise you of our decision."

And the subjects follow a pattern too. They slump in their chairs, unless they are led away as were Messrs. Grant and Gates. As was Elizabeth Robbins St. John (alleged use of male prostitutes).

This is the awfulness of it. To see them crumble. To see a whole human being who, two hours later give or take a moment or two, is no longer whole. To see them all stripped and picked clean without a stitch of clothing being removed or a finger laid upon them, unless someone needs help.

I cannot strike the image from my mind and, worse, I am haunted by something else.

How much more terrible to be the betrayers.

8

Harry has been notified that the day will be Thursday, day after tomorrow. I testify between eight and ten, which means that we must be at the plane in Cleveland at four-thirty. We should be across the border by five o'clock. Not one witness has yet testified in favor of a subject.

9

This has been my last full day in the United States. All is ready. Tomorrow I will go to the bank immediately upon my release from the hearings and meet Mary in the parking lot at noon. We will pick up the children after that.

Nancy suspects nothing. I fight to restrain myself. My disgust with her grows each day. She has been watching the hearings on television at the BWP, and tonight at dinner, for instance, she remarked again about her shock at what has "been turned up... blue-nosed citizens always pretending to be so proper and upstanding..."

The hearings today were particularly bad. They finally got to Jeffrey Wilmington Lang, one of the most honored and respected men in the nation. He is quite wealthy and is a director of at least a half-dozen large corporations. He also is a philanthropist and a symbol of Pittsburgh. There is not a university or trade school or medical center or park or library that has not been touched by him and so helped. There is not a man more modest than he. While people have always joked about the Langs—sometimes with cruelty and envy—still they hold an uncompromising reverence for the man and his family. It is as if the city has always sought to return its thanks by putting up a protective screen about him. Newspapers never press him too hard. Civic groups never inflict upon him the usual trappings of plaques, long luncheon meetings or very long speakers' tables. Salesmen never bother him, unless he calls them, and then it is a privilege to sell to him. Businessmen never slap him on the back or tell dirty jokes in his presence. He is that kind of a man. He is *the* symbol of both benevolence and power wisely used. He is every mother's dream for her son and every son's dream for himself. There have always been Langs in Pittsburgh, just as there have always been three rivers and Mount Washington.

Smith Armstrong called him to the witness box without a trace of any emotion. And Jeffrey Wilmington Lang came, a gentleman of 71 years who walked without assistance, though he moved slowly. But a spectator could not match the emotionless chairman. Someone started to yell, "Down with Mister X!" Only no one picked it up. The great room stayed silent. Awe was in the air.

And I thought to myself, dear God! Now! He can hold them! They will not get away with this with him. He will speak out and take it all away from Smith Armstrong. Strength, hope, and embarrassment at his being there all began to flood into me. I sensed this same response in others around me. A small, nervous woman in front of me stretched forward in her seat and gnawed her fingers. A college student behind me cracked the knuckles of his hands and chewed gum loudly. Even the fat man next to me bit his lips and closed his eyes momentarily, while Mr. Lang completed his long, slow walk to the witness box. All was silent, like watching television with the volume turned down. Everything seemed to hang in some sort of balance, as if Time itself were waiting to see the outcome of an old giant pitted against a new and completely different giant. One generation ranged against another.

Chairman Armstrong's voice was like the crack of thunder, even though he spoke softly, when he asked Jeffrey Lang how he pleaded to charges of violating Articles Two, Three, Nine, and Ten.

Mr. Lang considered for a long time, and the silence hung on. Then he spoke in a voice dry with age but strong still.

"Mister Chairman. Gentlemen. I have never engaged in public discussions that are partisan in nature. This is borne out by my constant impartiality towards both political parties and in my longstanding belief that I should never take sides in partisan issues. I leave such things to others. So there is nothing on record to indicate that I either favor or disfavor the Treaty of Friendship. However, for your records let me state that this Treaty... while it perhaps causes some dislocations and readjustments... will in the long run, very likely, prove a better alternative to nuclear war. I shall continue to do my best to cooperate." The unconcerned manner in which he spoke left

201

no doubt that he expected his position to be thoroughly understood and that he would be gracefully returned to life within the tightly drawn circle of selected friends and the gentle surroundings of his estate, his office, and his club.

And he did it with such grace, as if his bearing and his manners were more important than the words he spoke. He stood as a great benevolent monarch who, having been threatened with the loss of his throne, reacts in a dream-like way, detecting neither the danger nor the solution and still assuming that his subjects love him—just as before; that the guillotine might be for others but not for him, because after all he was the monarch, was he not? That was how he stepped down from the witness box, and while he did not say it aloud his manner screamed to the spectators: "I am still Jeffrey Wilmington Lang, Protector of Pittsburgh. I have been a gentleman all of my life, and I will be one now. The people will continue as before, for they see that I am good, just and wise."

Only the people did not see it that way. There was a rustle among the spectators, due more to growing anger than to tired muscles. The rustle turned into murmurs. The aura of respect that had silenced them now was being courageously overcome. Brashness returned. The King is dead, long live the King! Someone again yelled, "Down with Mister X!" This time others responded, and soon the acre of faces was screaming back at him, loud and vicious. A barrier had been reached and overcome. A hope had been rekindled, allowed to bum for a moment and then snuffed out. The progenitor of the old life had betrayed us all by refusing to speak out for himself, for us, and for our ways; so the new life was on, after all, for sure. So live with it! Cooperate and maybe we will be spared. That is what we were really screaming—for I was yelling as loudly as the fat man next to me. And the monarch stared hard at us, complete incredulity on his regal face. He seemed not to comprehend. Because of this he was pitiful in his lingering grace and simple dignity. He continued to wear them as was his long habit, as was his breeding; a man from the courtly world of the past thrown into the violence and hate of the present. And he knew not why.

So followed the witnesses—a son, a congressman, three clients, one customer and an Internal Revenue agent. In less than an hour they left no doubt that Jeffrey Wilmington Lang profits wrongly; that he would willingly engage in world warfare to protect his vicious financial empire; that he still holds a priority feeling for the United States, and that he refuses to help merge the productive resources under his control with the Soviet Union—aircraft, trucking, fabrication, chemicals, and agriculture.

The crowd roared and booed and hissed, and Jeffrey Wilmington Lang grew feeble.

The Sergeant-at-Arms helped him away.

But he retained his stately presence, like a dispossessed monarch who numbly accepts his fate and goes to the guillotine with all the dignity of attending his coronation.

Then it was Joseph Vendurella's turn. He is a youthful 40 and has slender, handsome features with thick black hair and flashing dark eyes that stood out even from where I sat. He is a ward chairman from the southside near the river and is candidate for the State Senate. Rumor is that he was asked to withdraw from the primary election but that he refused.[46] Some say he is part of the rackets, but it has never been proved. He is a lawyer—the laborers' lawyer, as he is called. Most of his practice involves lawsuits against corporations, utilities and, every so often, the government. He was one of the leading proponents of the Treaty of Friendship. He also is prominent in the ADR and Council on Citizens Rights.[47] He did not walk to the

---

46 While legislation and the courts permitted the Communist Party of America and its members to operate openly in the United States, the party still was very much in the minority. It had not yet attracted sufficient support to become a major party. Therefore, pressure techniques were applied through the JCF-LA to discourage "undesirable" candidates from the two existing major parties (Democrat and Republican) from participating in the primary elections. Only "desirable" candidates were expected to remain, i.e. communists or sympathisers, who through pre-planned action had filed candidate petitions earlier in the year to have themselves included on the primary ballots. (See Appendix, excerpts from *Achieving the Revolution in America*.)

47 Both the Americans for Democratic Reform and the Council on Citizens Rights, according to their own statements, regarded themselves as "militant leftist or-

witness box. He stalked darkly with tough, resolute anger—the kind you would never want to meet up with in a deserted alley. There was silence among the spectators when Smith Armstrong summoned him. It was a different kind of silence from that initially given Jeffrey Lang. It was a salute to two-fisted power. For slender though he is, Joe Vendurella is a fighter, equally good with fists or words, and he usually wins over his opponents whether in a courtroom or elsewhere. None of the spectators wanted to start anything just yet; not until the witnesses would at least give them a pretext. The mood was different, too. It was not one of budding hope. It was one of smirking expectation—like the half-grins that spread over the faces of a street gang when two leaders are about to slug it out. How would he make out in this fight?

Smith Armstrong read the charges of Treaty violations under Articles One, Three, Four, Five, Six, Eight and Ten. And Joe Vendurella unleashed stilettos of wrath.

"Mister Chairman and gentlemen." His voice was as soft as Armstrong's but more swift and with a razor edge. "I don't know who these citizens are who have made these so-called charges, and I want to see them… here in front of me. Unless, of course, it is you, Mister Chairman, who makes these accusations?" There was no trace either of fear or hysteria in his voice.

"You should know better than that. We accuse no one of anything," the chairman shot back. "And as far as seeing your accusers, there are too many of them to crowd into this area. Further, this is not a court of law where formal charges have been made or, further, where the accusers are required to be present. However, it may be that certain witnesses might be able to accommodate your wishes," he finished with silken smoothness.

"Very well. Be sure I'll find my accusers anyway."

"How say you to these charges, Mr. Vendurella?" the chairman asked flatly.

"A bunch of bull!"

---

ganisations" each calling for nationalisation of all industry, banking and utilities, unilateral disarmament and the abolition of the United States Senate.

The spectators stirred excitedly. "Continue," Armstrong said. "Let's cut out this crap. Everyone knows I supported the Treaty right down the line. 'Deliver the support,' they said, and deliver I did. Eighty-seven percent of the families in my ward signed petitions, because I told them to. Twelve percent sent at least one person to Washington for the Peace Marches, because I told them to. I helped to get you that fancy job, Mister Chairman..."

"Out of order!" the chairman rasped. "Leaving aside your last remark, we'll agree that your work has not gone unnoticed, and this is all the more reason why we are sorry that your peers have found other causes to have you brought here."

"Not gone unnoticed!" the steel voice replied. "Hell, you're trying to frame me with a lot of doubletalk. And don't try to tell me differently. I know what a frame is. I've done it often enough."

In spite of themselves, the spectators tittered, which brought a deep flush to Armstrong's face, and he banged furiously for more order.

"Mr. Vendurella, I can cite you for contempt, which carries a prison sentence. But I am inclined to be lenient if you will answer the question. How say you?"

"How say I? I say you're not going to prove a damn thing. I say you're not going to scare me like you have the rest of these cottonheaded suckers. I know why I'm here!" and he turned full upon the spectators, dark eyes flashing under the white lights. "Because I went ahead and ran in the primaries, and I won, that's why..." Smith Armstrong rapped for silence. "I think we've had enough. Your own county chairman and your county commissioners and your governor asked you to withdraw from the election because you are unsuited as an honest candidate. And nothing else."

"Nuts! Maybe you think you're smart. But out there," he made a short, quick jab toward us all, "things will be different. My people aren't going to buy this stuff, and then you're going to be real sorry." And Joe Vendurella stalked back to his chair.

There were more witnesses than usual—thirteen. The first was a square-shaped woman who wore a print dress bearing a bold floral design. She had a babushka over her head and looked to be in her early sixties. She was Joe Vendurella's neighbor. She was a widow. Her four sons worked in the mills, one a department superintendent. She disclosed meetings in the Vendurella house after the curfew.[48] She mentioned the existence of firearms, a shotgun, a rifle and a pistol.

"Did your neighborhood not receive full instructions as to the disposition of privately owned weapons?" one of the examiners asked.

"No understand. No sure what..."

"All people must turn in... give up firearms... guns. You, your friends and neighbors did this?"

"Ah! Yes! My sons turn guns into authorities during winter," the woman croaked nervously.

"Then Mr. Vendurella should have done the same?"

"Yes, sirs." She looked at Joe and was on the verge of panic.

"He knew of the ruling, and he deliberately broke the law?"

"Yes, sirs. He break law."[49]

The woman—with gentle prodding from the examiners—then exposed Vendurella's opposition to the Wage Adjustment Program[50] and the fact that he spoke openly to workers in the area about it. This brought the subject to his feet, declaring that this was not under the province of the World Order of Nations' Treaty. He was restrained by the Sergeant-at-Arms while Smith Armstrong cited Article Five, saying that both the Soviet Union and the United States had pledged more products to the rest of the world and that costs had to be brought into line so that "these goods will be more readily available to the underprivileged of the world."

"But you can't deliberately cut a man's wages ..."

---

48 The JCFLA enforced a "civilian curfew" requiring all citizens, except authorised personnel, to be off the streets between 10 p.m. and 5 a.m. daily as a "means to safeguard the public safety."

49 See Appendix, excerpts from the Treaty of Friendship.

50 The Wage Adjustment Program was sponsored by the JCFLA with the cooperation of the Bureau of Wages and Prices in which "all wages, salaries and commissions would be reduced by twenty percent of the gross amount paid in order to promote more efficient production."

"Silence!" the chairman shouted, and the whole room jumped. "A fair adjustment has been made, leaving the American working man still with the highest wages on earth."

"But the cut was too much!" Vendurella bellowed. Three blue uniforms once again restrained him.

"You say it was too much. Others say it wasn't enough. I suggest it was a fair decision ... or are you one who chooses to line his pockets with wealth that should be shared with others... like a fascist or a capitalist?"

"Don't call me a capitalist. I never..." but the blue uniforms cut him off.

"You act like one," Smith Armstrong replied with super softness.

That did it. Groups within the sea of spectators at last found their opening and their courage. "Down with Mister X!" they screamed over and over. Several demonstrations took place over the great room, and they ran for nearly fifteen minutes, the chairman being slow to respond with the wooden hammer.

The other twelve witnesses—workmen, lawyers, a plant foreman and another housewife—not only substantiated the testimony of the elderly woman but described how Joe Vendurella's "tactics of harassment" had sown seeds of discontent so that production in area plants had dropped off, which in turn was seriously affecting Pittsburgh's participation in the Materials Allocation Program,[51] "clearly obstructionist tactics against the Treaty."

We heard no more from Joe Vendurella.

The next subject was the man who, three months earlier, had done nothing more than stop by Le Gourmet restaurant for a sip of brandy, while Larry Best and I pondered our respective concerns—mine about the rightness of the Treaty and Larry's about how to win support for it; the man whose very presence that night had triggered a whole chain of rationalizations that was now being climaxed with these hearings; the original Mister X—though he could not know

---

51 The Materials Allocation Program, organized by the JCFLA and administered by the BWP, classified by priority needs the use and disposition of all ferrous and non-ferrous materials including petroleum and chemicals.

this—Dr. Hamilton Rodgers, professor of philosophy at William Penn University.

He was booed instantly the moment his name was called. He is a fairly big, lumbering man, more so than I remembered, but not particularly overweight and standing about six feet tall. He is slightly stooped, and the most striking thing about him still is his well-brushed mane of pure white hair. He had not lost the quiet simplicity that had so impressed me. His face, even under the bright lights, still held the quality of agelessness, in spite of the deep creases about his mouth and eyes. The clamor of the spectators did not appear to affect his serenity. His movements as he approached the witness box were slightly stiff, probably due to arthritis. The fat man beside me cursed obscenely and mumbled, "Hurry up, you old..."

I performed my first bit of bravery. I told the fat man to shut up. He did, and I felt a sense of victory and kinship to Dr. Rodgers. I prayed—honestly I did—that he would be spared the humiliation and defeat that had marked all of the others, 36 of them now. In spite of his cumbersome size, he stood small against the vastness of the setting with its angry sea of faces and tiers of black robes jutting up like jagged rocks of granite, but not as small as the others had appeared.

Smith Armstrong read the charges: violation of Articles One, Two, Three, Five, Eight, Eleven and Twelve. He had quieted the spectators with little effort. After all, Dr. Rodgers was an anticlimax.

"How say you, Dr. Rodgers?"

He spoke in a voice deep and strong. He articulated his words with simple, unaffected clarity. He spoke with conviction that was neither forced nor modest. It was simply there. And the people listened, not because they wanted to but because they were compelled by his presence to remain still.

"Am I permitted to make a statement, Mister Chairman?"

"Of course," was the curious reply. "Only please be brief. We have witnesses to hear yet."

"I quite understand your problem, sir," came the equally polite response. "You have a time problem, and I shall be content to keep my statement brief. Further, Mister Chairman, it may well be that the witnesses you have appointed to analyze my behavior may be unnecessary." The great room became absolutely hushed, and I felt that we were on the threshold of even more disillusionment. Doubtlessly, he was going to give up.

"Under the Treaty of Friendship as ratified, I am, of course, guilty of violating the Articles just now cited." The spectators stirred, plainly mystified and disappointed. The examiners, too, seemed puzzled, and Smith Armstrong became wary as he pulled himself forward.

"And if I may," Dr. Rodgers continued, "I should like your records to be more complete. For I stand in violation of all of the Articles. For example, I still possess firearms. One is a Colt .45 manufactured in 1872, but it is in perfect working order. Also, I have a twelve-gauge shotgun which I use to hunt ducks. Further, in my lectures on Constitutional Government, I refer repeatedly to such points as the advantages of using both popular and corporate bodies in the legislature and the meaning of consent of the governed. Also, as late as last week, I have lectured ... to a private group ... on the strategy of militant socialism. I have opposed having my stipend reduced and recently approached members of the government and the World Order of Nations to ask them to oppose the Materials Allocation Program, which was so pointedly referred to a moment ago. I think these will suffice to broaden the scope of the original set of charges." And Dr. Rodgers paused, obviously waiting for the chairman to speak.

Wariness spread still deeper across Smith Armstrong's face. He pondered a moment and finally nodded. "Will the secretary so record. Does that conclude your statement?" There was a faint trace of expectancy in his voice, shaded with apprehension. He wanted Dr. Rodgers to sit down.

"In part, Mister Chairman, but I wonder if I might have the privilege of asking a question of you?"

Smith Armstrong obviously wanted very much to deny the request but even with a stacked audience, to say nothing of stacked witnesses, he would not have dared to refuse such a simple request from one who had so willingly confessed his guilt.

"By all means," came the soft reply. The spectators rustled with un-abashed interest. Something was different. The pattern had changed. The familiar landmarks of fear, defensiveness and well- programmed spontaneity were gone.

Dr. Rodgers paused a moment and with simple dignity removed a rather large white handkerchief from his pocket and blew his nose gently. Then he turned so that he faced both the spectators and the television cameras.

"As some of you know, I am something of a student of the applica-tion of pressure techniques designed, first, to isolate an individual and then to alter the credibility of that person, thus lessening the impact of that person upon society. While this stratagem is quite old… probably as old as Man himself … it has only been during the present century that this technique has been so skillfully and effec-tively applied. I am, therefore, moved to compliment you, Mister Chairman," and he turned his great, white head momentarily to-ward the benches, "your examiners and members of your staff for this most successful operation."

Chairman Armstrong's face was beginning to darken. Few, if any, of the spectators caught the full significance of Dr. Rodgers' academ-ic references. But the chairman knew, as did the examiners, a couple of whom began to fidget.

"This brings me to my question. If the purpose of this hearing is to isolate and, thus, destroy the credibility of my fellow… subjects… and let me say that you have done this most uncommonly well… and if the reason behind this purpose is to lessen our impact upon society … by that I mean remove us from positions of leadership in Pittsburgh, which is a must if your plans are to succeed, then, Mister Chairman, why me?"

And before the startled Smith Armstrong could answer, Dr. Rodgers continued.

"For consider this. The efforts to apply pressure to me began years ago. My credibility as a teacher and scholar has been questioned for nearly twenty years. Indeed, within the academic community,

my credibility over the past four years has been almost completely destroyed."

The words of Larry once again flashed through my mind about
Stone Age Rodgers. A harmless old coot.

"Further . ... with respect to my position of leadership within the
community, that, too, has been completely neutralized. The process
began six years ago when the University switched me to teaching
night school courses in current events. I was allowed to continue
to teach but one course involving my specialties of philosophy, economics and political science, this under the requirements of my chair.
Student enrollment in this one course has dropped from forty-four,
three years ago, to nine last year, and none had the courage to enroll
in my course for this current term beginning just a few weeks ago.

"Therefore, unlike the other subjects summoned here, I hold no
further positions of leadership that must be wrested from me. It is,
therefore, unlikely that I can serve any useful purpose to you, since
there is no more that can be taken away from me. Were you to hold
me for trial before the World Court I am afraid that it would only
serve to water down the effectiveness of the very thing you are seeking to accomplish. World opinion would only laugh at you for making
a pretentious show at beating down an old dog like me.

"So ... I simply ask... why would you weaken this masterful presentation by summoning me here?"

In the instant of silence that followed, it was plain that Smith
Armstrong was at a complete loss for words. Much of what Dr.
Rodgers had said had gone over the heads of the spectators. But
the gist of his thoughts had stuck. I could sense it all about me. The
chairman was at a verbal crossroads. To ignore the question with
its rambling preamble would in effect give credence to the Doctor's
words, since they would go unchallenged. But to engage in rebuttal
would only focus more attention upon them and in the process even
clarify some of the academic obscurities which certainly the Doctor
had deliberately left hanging.

Someone had fumbled. I hoped it was Leon Tidings.

But Smith Armstrong recovered to make the best of a bad play.

"I am not academically equipped to discuss your several personal and arbitrary observations, Doctor, but I can say that you are here at the will of the people who petitioned that you be summoned." The chairman spoke firmly. "Now kindly resume your seat."

"Of course. I am finished now," Dr. Rodgers replied. Then he turned his creased face to search the great room, and his voice rang clear. "The will of the people. You are the people. Aren't you pleased and proud, too, that these hearings are in your hands and not in the hands of unscrupulous men of power!"

He turned to gaze steadily at the tiers of benches and the robed figures sitting frozen behind them, and all eyes followed his. Then he moved slowly, stiffly back to his seat, while Smith Armstrong offered his summary for the day in a voice much too brisk and uncaring to suit the mood. The examiners had become quite busy shuffling papers, making notes vigorously and calling pages to dispatch these schoolboys on important but unannounced errands. Even the spectators now were terribly busy stretching in their seats, blowing noses, tying shoelaces and looking anxiously in the direction of the restrooms. All were too busy to look any longer upon Dr. Hamilton Rodgers.

They were even too busy to shout, "Down with Mister X!"

So it is that Dr. Rodgers has been the only one to win anything that might be considered some sort of a victory. But in winning it, he has already lost everything.

This then is the terror.

Must I give up everything in order to win?

And what is it I will have won?

Tomorrow.

Where will I be at this hour?

VI

The Sixth Month

It still burns in my head, in my eyes, in my stomach—the memory of my last day at the hearings. The day had come brightly without a cloud anywhere, with the sun rising in huge gold. I had slept not really at all, this journal keeping me up until the faint light of dawn. Then I packed a suitcase with the barest of essentials for the children and me and locked it in the trunk of the car, careful to press the lid down so as not to make any noise. Then I did manage to stretch out in bed to become aware of little things.

Nancy lying beside me in heavy sleep, her body warming me, for I had grown cold and cramped in my basement room. A taken-for-granted thing, warmth from another person. Regardless of the daylight conflicts between us, we still did warm each other in the night bed—not as lovers any more, perhaps, but as two living creatures giving off heat to the other for material comfort. Selfish, satisfying comfort, but comfort that was there night after night, year after year, to be grown accustomed to. Comfort that would cease to exist after this night was finished. Comfort that would not come my way again. Comfort that would be discarded in favor of another comfort that would give both warmth and love. But what happens to the old comfort that had been mine for nearly nineteen years? Where goes Nancy who, in spite of everything, always has meant well enough and who has never intentionally harmed anyone? One does not discard so easily those things that have served reasonably well.

But when that which has served, however well, no longer serves—indeed begins to destroy—then it must be discarded. The plan had to be carried out, but the pang and the sadness were both there in those still hours. Then something creaked, a door or a floor board, and I thought of the house. The storm windows still unpurchased. The split gutter-spout out in front. The crooked wallpaper in the front hall. I had put it up none too well some years ago when the days were good days; when the bomb had been banned, and we thought we had all the answers.[52] The day we bought the house in an area with others fresh from the carpenters and bricklayers—a Sunday special with a procession of cars loaded with families straining out the windows to look at the "latest thing in estate planning." The signs had said: "Your one home in a lifetime. The Baxter Life of Dreams." And now my dreams had outgrown this. Or was it that I had only now begun to dream; to dig down deep within myself and come up with golden nuggets of promise? And the children were sleeping now. Annie, who would be a tight little lump burrowed deep in her covers. David, my image as I was a generation ago, sprawled doubtlessly spread-eagle in his bed. Peggy, with the trace of a pout on her round, pretty face and neatly covered like a Hollywood queen with a satin quilt that hints of her maturing body resting beneath. Children at peace in the only place they have ever known, a city called Pittsburgh. Children to be uprooted and planted again. Once I moved a shrub so that it would grow better. The dog, Peppy, a sort of beagle, would be chasing in his sleep at Annie's feet. He would stay behind and be bewildered. Mary O'Neil Best. Would she be sleeping? Is her spirit of rebirth with her now? Does she smile in new-found peace? Or is this dimmed by creaking floors and a man who sleeps heavily in her

---

52 For a number of years Americans were subjected to an intensive education campaign assuring them that there was absolutely no danger of a Communist takeover, since the Communists "had fully realized both the strengths and intentions of the United States to protect its national interests and the interests of free nations everywhere and had no wish to test our superior strength"; thus the only real danger was the possibility of nuclear war. As one editorial stated, "Eliminate this danger and Americans at long last will realize man's oldest dreams of both peace and prosperity."

room? Does she stare at the dawn, too? And what of the office; what will be their reaction at my empty desk? Forget that! How will the spectators be today? Will they scream at me? Will they recall the dignity and message of Dr. Rodgers? Surely they will. Surely they will have thought through that which he has said. Surely things will be a little easier today.

The new David Little. In a few hours it will be over. I will have redressed the balance. And all of this will pass away.

The alarm went off at six, early enough to get me into town for a breakfast meeting with Mary. She was to be at the hearings, despite my pleas to the contrary. We were to reconfirm everything. I showered, shaved and dressed for what was to be the last time—without emotion. The years of habit. Then I woke Nancy. We had arranged school rides for the children so I could leave early. We discussed some laundry problems, and she asked me to locate some chocolate candy. Then I left, closing the door into the garage for the last time. My feet moved as if they were set in concrete. I did not dare to look back.

The sun was burning away the dew, and the gasoline station attendant looked especially good to me. He was alive with energy, his breath visible on the cool air as he spoke cheerily. One man fully alive and busy in a world still half-asleep. One man who would own the universe for another half-hour, until the rest caught up with him. One man who was an island of reality in the misty stirrings of early morning. We chatted about nothing much, and I drove off forever.

Mary had a booth in a small restaurant near the Royal. She looked up brightly, her grey-green eyes sparkling. She was dressed in a durable looking dark green suit, ideal for a long journey. I seated myself next to her, feeling self-conscious, like a high school boy during the first five minutes of a blind date. I wanted to say something dramatic that would become a historic marker upon which both of us could look back in later years. Instead, all I could manage was a hello and a brief description of where I had parked the car. We would meet there at noon and then go after the children who would be in the school cafeteria. We ordered hot powdered milk and two not-so-sweet rolls.

215

The restaurant was beginning to fill rapidly with a cross-section of business suits, dressy dresses, work clothes and tight sweaters. They were the spectators, and today I would not be among them. Instead, I would report to the witness section to await my turn to testify. The place was noisy, and everything was too bright. The walls were white. Chairs, tables, booths—white and chrome. The help was all dressed in white. Coffee cups and voices clattered. It made a good screen. No one could hear us, and so I related Dr. Rodgers' brave and wise stand of the day before.

"Speak of the old angel, there he is!" Mary cried.

He was moving through currents of people haltingly to dodge an elbow here and a shoulder there as he searched the faces about him, like an ancient philosopher on an urgent mission. His neat but dated dark topcoat and suit made him stand out in the relatively unkempt human sea. His white head was bare, and he held his hat protectively at his side. As he passed, people looked at him and then grinned and made sly quips to one another.

"Oh, Davey, the poor dear has no place to sit. Let's ask him." Before I could answer my pleasure at this, she waved. He did not see her at first, but when he did the heavy lines of concentration brightened. He nodded and, all of a sudden, there he was—the original Mister X, the man I had helped to condemn on that rainy night in February, the subject of Larry's lecture.

He reached across me to clasp Mary's hand into both of his, which were large and worn with work that must have included everything from picks and shovels to books and pens. But they were kind and competent. Honest hands. She held them a long moment and tiny tears grew from her upturned eyes. Quickly she pressed her cheek against them in a silent tribute. I had not realized that she knew him so well, but I should have known. For they were two of a kind, a father of nature with his daughter. She released him and smiled at me, while he pulled from his coat.

"You didn't know, Davey, that we are long and dear friends." Once again she looked at the old gentleman. "The hours we have spent…"

"Walking, talking… exploring all of this." Dr. Rodgers gestured significantly to the crowded restaurant. His voice was low and un-hurried, but alive with meaning and resonance.

"I used to go to his rooms, usually in the late afternoon, and we'd read sometimes or just talk about… oh," she paused, excited to be showing him off to me, "all sorts of things. He would help me some-times, or we'd take long walks, or… back before all this… I would sit in his classroom and just listen."

He chuckled pleasantly and once again took her hand in his. "Is he the one?" he wagged his head at me.

"Yes," she replied with simple, unashamed pride. I could not have been more moved had she spoken a paragraph of eloquence.

"Then, he knows?" I asked.

"Yes, Mr. Little, I know."

He extended his hand, and I rose to greet him. It was a warm handclasp. It spoke at once of sureness and understanding.

"And you approve?" I asked, as he seated himself opposite us,

"How can I approve or disapprove? For some it would be wrong. For others it could be right. How does one man judge another? I only know that this is God's creature," he looked at her, "and she yearns to be free. Indeed, she will die without it, I think. A man … or a wom-an… can only do what he believes to be right. She sees in you the same yearning and the potential to grow. Man is on earth to grow. It is his nature to want to grow … to want to stand tall and firm."

"But how do we know we are right in what we do?"

"No one can tell you, Mr. Little, though many try, doubtlessly, to tell you." He shifted thoughtfully in his seat, trying to fit his large frame more comfortably to the box-like booth. "Right is whatever is within us that sets well. To be right, oftentimes, is to suffer pain. It is the absence of shame in spite of the pain. Right is harsh more of-ten than kind. Right, sometimes, is even unjust, but less unjust than wrong. Right takes strength … great strength. That's why it is diffi-cult to be right, for we are often asked to pay too great a price."

"And how you have paid." Mary spoke not with pity but with the compassion of low anger.

"No-o," he mused. "I have not had the flesh torn from me or been fed poison to burn my insides away. And my students... the one or two ... I have them, and they are all that matters. I am a rich man so long as I have one young mind to teach, and there will always be at least *that*." He looked at us both for a long moment, as if he would try to say something else. His big, creased face was not unkind in looking at you or unkind to look into. His eyes were clear and alert and seemed to be soaking up every bit of detail of us. I did not feel uneasy. I could look him in the face without fear of betraying myself or fear that he would betray me. I was comfortable with him but not complacent. With him I felt that I counted for something. Whatever it was, he decided not to say it but reached for a worn menu. He squinted in the harsh light and poked into his breast pocket for heavy-rimmed glasses which needed a good cleaning. He flipped them onto his nose and began to read. "I suppose I'll never see kippered herring with scrambled eggs and muffins again, but I keep looking," he sighed. The waitress happened by, and he motioned to her. "Very well. Some hot tea..."

"No tea, sir."

"And, of course, no coffee at a dollar-ten a cup ... so, hot powdered milk and... English muffins?"

"Oh, no, sir. Not since last summer."

"One of *those*, then," he replied, pointing to Mary's half consumed roll. "Ugh!" He sighed again and once more looked about him. "I'm to meet someone. A young student. But, of course, he's late. If you should spot a reasonably presentable young chap who looks as if he's looking for someone, tell me." And he settled back to look again at us. "The boy is concerned for me. Can you imagine this? When, at least, I have a decent roof over my head . ."

"But they are going to retire you, and what will you do?" Mary interrupted. "Is it to be soon?"

"It has been done."

"On what grounds?" I snapped.

"Age, Mr. Little."

"You can call him Davey," Mary said.

"Of course. Davey, they have a rule. Any time past 65, they can lift the contract or not… depending… and I am over 65 now. I depart the end of this month." And catching the pained look that flashed across her face, he added, "But don't worry. I have my pension and some savings that will keep me well enough."

I saw him first. He moved smoothly through the crowd with an arrogant nonchalance that caused people to step aside to accommodate his search. For he was looking hard at everyone and everything with quick, irregular flicks of cold blue eyes. His movements revealed underlying wariness, as if he could spin around and strike instantly at anything that would threaten him. His hands were extra large, and he had them balled into fists. He was in hostile territory, his body seemed to say, and woe to anyone who got in his way. Yet, he did not look the bully. His triangular-shaped face was smooth and sharp with youthful purpose that combined deadly realism with rigid discipline. He would give no quarter, nor would he ask for it. I had almost forgotten him in the rush of these past weeks. The memory of his screaming "Surrender!" at the throng gathered around the Peace Monument in Point Park; the start he had given Nancy and me at the observation pavilion on Mount Washington the night we thought we had squared ourselves with a new world bright in its promises; the terror of meeting him, knife in hand, the day I led the demonstration down Liberty Avenue and betrayed myself—all flooded back to me. Both Mary and Dr. Rodgers left their talk in mid-air to follow my look, which must have been frightening, for the doctor scowled as he turned, expecting, doubtlessly, to see armed guards or something equally sinister making for us. Then he saw the tall, slender youth—still in a leather jacket—and his big face flashed an instant smile that spelled both relief and pride.

"Ah!" he cried. "There you are, Chip. I had given you up."

The young man had spotted me as quickly as I had seen him. He had tensed and slowed, puzzled to see the doctor's beaming face in my company. He approached with narrow eyes which flicked back and forth from me to Mary to the doctor.

"Come. Sit. I want you to meet these people," the doctor added, half rising so that his big and slightly stooped frame was awkward and rather precariously poised above the table.

The youth hesitated uncertainly. In this instant the anxiety in me melted. He was only a young man—but surely a man—looking for a friend, a very dear friend. A young man, hardened perhaps beyond his years, thrown by something unexpected. Just a young man lost for a moment.

"Sorry, sir. I had some problems."

"Tommy?"

"Yes. He got worse. I was up most of the night getting a doctor. The one on duty at the clinic was busy. But I found one."

"Who? Come. Sit." Dr. Rodgers motioned beside him. Only then did the young man seat himself, but he was still wary.

"Dr. Miller. The old man who's retired."

Dr. Rodgers nodded his approval. "Used to know Lester. He's a good man. What's the verdict?"

"Pneumonia."

"Bad?"

"Yes, sir. Got to try to hurry up the medicine. Things open up at nine o'clock and maybe I'll get lucky."[53]

"Chip, why don't you and your boys come to my place?"

"You know we can't do that, Dr. Rodgers," the youth replied. His face was too serious for his age.

The doctor looked at Mary and me. Hopelessness was stamped on his face. "You see? Chip, I guess I should introduce you. This is Charles Comer Baker, better known as Chip." He spoke our names, and Chip nodded. "He's a student of mine," the doctor continued, "not in the school officially now but, all the same, my most promising

---

53 The Bureau of Health handled all applications for medical care. Because of a shortage of drugs, among other reasons, a priority system was adopted in prescribing and dispensing drugs. Chip apparently had no such drug permit and had to rely on the slim supply of drugs still available at the few privately owned drug stores that still operated. Also most of the sick were required to use government clinics which were usually overcrowded and understaffed because of a severe shortage of doctors.

student. He lives with four other young men in a most wretched place. Actually, he looks after them. They can't get jobs ..."

"The BWP!" the young man said between clenched teeth.[54] "We're too risky!" He broke into an odd smile.

"But I want you to come with me." the doctor said.

"There isn't enough room. Besides, you couldn't afford to keep us...even if we would let you. And we get work enough." "Trashmen and muck shovelers!" Dr. Rodgers retorted. "With your minds and talents..."

"Let's skip it, Doctor," Chip cut in sharply. He refused the offer of a roll and powdered milk, saying he already had eaten, obviously not so. All through the conversation his cold blue eyes had returned again and again to my face to look boldly without apology. "Why are you with him?" he said to the doctor.

"He's a friend," was the soft reply.

The young man shrugged and shook his head. "Some friend. I've seen him before. He's some friend, all right."

"He's not like the others." Mary spoke for the first time. "Why, just you wait. In another hour or so you'll see."

"Yes, Chip. Mr. Little has decided to do a very fine thing. You see, he's a witness supposedly against Avery Brown... only he's going to speak the truth," the doctor added. There was sprightliness in his voice with an underlying tremor of gratitude.

"He really wants to do it, Chip. May I call you Chip?" Mary asked. Her face was soft with a maternal warmth, as if she wanted desperately to reach out and touch his cheek. The young man nodded and looked at her with somber eyes. Slowly his lean body was drained of its tenseness, and his chiseled face began to relax into a half-smile. "No one is making him, but he wants to..." She paused to gather the right words.

"To square things." I spoke for the first time. "I really want to do this one small thing."

Chip Baker surveyed all three of us with a face that froze out all emotion. Where has he been and what has happened that could cause

---

54 Apparently Chip Baker had a bad record with BWP and, therefore, was ineligible for anything but common labour work.

such unbending hardness, I thought. The image of my own son came before me. What would he be at 21?

Chip rose from his seat. "Got to leave." He paused warily, as if he were reluctant to give away any more of his personal secrets. "Uh ... Doctor ... I'm having a tough time with the Stoics. I can't get that paper done by tonight."

The doctor scowled. "This is the third time that we have postponed this assignment. Now are you interested in learning or not?" His voice had taken on a gravel quality of disgust.

"Of course, sir. Only with the illness and .. ."

"The great men of the world have had their crosses to bear, too, but that has not kept them from their work. Weak men can always find excuses, Chip. I expect better things than excuses from you." Dr. Rodgers' tone had dropped to soft reproach.

And Chip stood ramrod straight, struggling to control the flush of anger that was trying to take over the lines of his face. "Very well!" He bit his lip. "I haven't got my work done, and I don't have any excuses!"

"Be at my rooms at eight tonight. Bring your work with you. Also, be sure to return the *Madison Papers* which I loaned you. If you lose that book, I'll upend you for sure!" the old man growled.

A trace of a smile stole across Chip's face. "Don't worry, sir." Then he took us all in once more with a flickering glance. His body tensed again, and he stared at me. "I hope you're right about *him*."

He turned to go, hesitated and then spun back to Mary. "I think you're nice, ma'am." He shot the words out harshly, I think to cover the embarrassment at having revealed yet another deeper personal feeling. But he looked Mary straight into her eyes and, turning abruptly again, left as he had come, fists balled at his sides as he shouldered his way to the door.

Dr. Rodgers gave a long sigh. "You must forgive him. He has little cause to trust any of us. He has a raw mind yet, but his potential is most amazing ... if I can just get the bitterness out of him."

"Aren't you a little rough on him?" Mary asked. "After all, if he works and if he looks after the four other boys, how can he find time to study?"

222

"I'm rough on him deliberately. It keeps him alive. Don't you think I know what he is faced with? If he ever gets to feeling sorry for himself, he's finished. Besides," the doctor mused, "I have picked him to cram as much knowledge into as I possibly can. He is my last remaining hope, and there is so little time left."

So little time left. I looked at my watch. Ten minutes to eight. Time to leave. Time to cast off into a strange, bold, new world. I bit my lip hard. An old man and a still young woman had said I was doing a very big thing. Ordinarily, I would suppose these to be words to uplift a person. But they were lead lumps in my stomach. I had committed myself not through wisdom and knowledge but through an unlooked for, unreasonable, unwanted instinct. A vague yearning to be free pitted against the cruel realities of achieving such freedom which, even in Canada, may not exist. A life of relative ease and safety to be swapped for a life of unknown consequences. Why cannot a person be content with his lot? No harm has yet come to me. I only think it might. I am in this only because the principle of fair play is being violated, and something inside of me resists. I rebel without fully knowing why, and there is no time to find out. Surely, everyone will think me mad, so I must be mad. Am I right or wrong? Everyone would say I am wrong. Even Dr. Rodgers will not say. Nothing sets well within me. Always there have been guidelines to tell me when I am right or wrong. Now they are no longer there, so how can I know? Yet, I have committed myself. I cannot back out.

These were the thoughts that pounded inside of me, as I searched the dial of my watch for some answer.

"Davey? Are you all right?" Mary's cool, soft fingers closed firmly upon my hand.

"Yes. Of course. It's just that I'm ..." I fought to find the courage to say the word.

"Scared." Dr. Rodgers spoke without condemnation.

"Yes," I replied.

"You should be," the doctor said.

"Are you ever scared?" I asked.

"Frequently," he replied. He spoke simply, without apology. "But people aren't supposed to be scared."

"Where did you learn that?" he asked gently.

"Well… everywhere, I guess. In school or church," I groped for words, while trying to run my whole life in front of my eyes. It was like jamming a two-hour motion picture into a split second. "Everybody says…"

"Yes. They do."

"It's just that I don't know how I will do. Yesterday… listening to you … it was … I wanted to rise up and shout then and there. Today, I don't know how good I'll be standing there alone. You see, I've never done this before."

"This is the great tragedy of our age," Doctor Rodgers said. There was a faraway look in his eyes. "Davey, you'll end up doing what you are capable of doing. It can be no other way. You can't be more than you are, but," he smiled, "don't you see, with your determination you won't do less than you are able to do. Maybe this is the test that will help you know yourself."

The words were soothing but brutal in the challenge. I rose and looked down at Mary. "Bear with me, please. I will do my best."

I see her smile yet, and the youth in her eyes. "I know you will. You'll make it, Davey. You'll make it because you've got to."

2

The witness area was partitioned off from the rest of the great ballroom by heavy blue curtains. It was like an opulent tent, with heavy armchairs set so they faced a TV monitor tuned to the hearings out in front. There were two sections, each curtained off from the other. Section A housed the witnesses on behalf of Henry C. Biggerman, who was to be first on the morning schedule. I was ushered into Section B, reserved for witnesses summoned to testify on behalf of Avery A. Brown, the chairman of the board of my company. There were seven of us. I had nodding acquaintance with three—Alvin Sanders, our vice president of production; Sam Grimm, vice president of sales, and

Mrs. Tuttle, secretary to Avery Brown. I recognized the others and closed my eyes in near panic. One was the Governor of Pennsylvania. Another was the United States Secretary of Commerce. My god! Them! The other man was a Mr. Croate, a company customer. Two women, dressed to show off especially beautiful shapes, served as hostesses. They bid us to be comfortable and offered hot coffee, the real stuff, and rich-looking sweet rolls. Also, brandy, bourbon and scotch were available. I took brandy mixed with coffee to steady me. Everyone else had a shot of something, too. The area was dimly lit, except for the single eye of the TV screen which glared at us. No one spoke, save the hostesses who kept moving among us.

At precisely eight o'clock the call to order came, and Smith Armstrong moved briskly into the first subject for the day, Henry C. Biggerman, president of the Amalgamated Workers of America. He was probably more powerful and important than any of the other men and women in the hearings lineup.[55] This, in itself, was terribly unnerving, because it dramatized the enormous power wielded by Smith Armstrong. Still, hope began to well up inside me. Perhaps after yesterday with Dr. Rodgers, things would be different. Maybe this time Chairman Armstrong would go down in defeat. For Biggerman was no man to trifle with. He is a tough but well-schooled labor leader. He has led strike after strike and has won victory after victory, except recently. He is one, at least, who always has taken vocal positions on major issues. He was, for instance, a vigorous supporter of the Treaty and fought long and loud for its ratification. He was just as vigorous an opponent of the Wage Adjustment Program and did not hide it. His bitter attacks were reported in great detail during the three months preceding the hearings. Better than three hundred wildcat strikes across the country had been credited to his opposition to reducing wage scales. He is a large man with powerful shoulders, a

---

55 Correct. There is considerable information on Henry C. Biggerman, at one time one of the most powerful labour leaders in the world. For nearly three weeks, during this period, members of his union struck hundreds of basic metals, fabrication and manufacturing plants, which threatened to paralyse the nation. World Order of Nations peace troops intervened, and the strikes ultimately were broken but not without considerable violence.

thick chest and hefty hips. He is in his late fifties. He had more sheer guts than any person I have ever seen, and for a moment I thought he had them on the run. But the pattern turned out to be the same as the others—except that at least he fought hard.

"You think you can do anything to get me to back down." he belted at the chairman. "You think I'm gonna throw away better than a hundred years of blood. Look, I know the score. You guys, the government, the W.O.N.—all of you built yourselves up on the backs of labor, and we're not going to give in."

One is conditioned to expect cheers and whistles and stomping of feet to accompany fighting words such as Biggerman slugged into the big room. But nothing came, and the stillness stood as a terrifying rebuke, which had its effect. For the fighting words stopped, and the battered face looked less and less fierce. He stood there dumbfounded that his oratory which had stirred thousands of men to action now fell upon wooden ears. Finally, he went voluntarily to his seat.

Then came the witnesses. Seven were officers and staff members of the union. Three were businessmen flown in from New York, Chicago and Los Angeles. One was the Secretary of Labor. One by one, this distinguished array of "dedicated patriots" took the edges off "President Hank," as Biggerman was known across the world. Gradually, demonstrations began to break out here and there until— by the time the last witness had testified about his morals, treason, graft and violation of nearly every provision under the Treaty—the huge hall was seething with angry faces and harsh voices. But he did not keep his silence. Rather Henry Biggerman rose in mighty wrath to fight some more. Chairs and bodies flew from his path as he made, not for the door, but for the milling crowd in front of him, arms swinging like crane booms. It took a dozen blue uniforms, but they got him and dragged him away to jail, where he sits now under charges of contempt.

It was an awful thing to watch. What helped to make it so was the apparent unconcern with which my fellow witnesses watched the action over the TV monitor. Once, during the height of the debate between Chairman Armstrong and Biggerman—when the latter

226

had jumped from his chair to protest—one of the hostesses slid onto the arm of my chair and, leaning very close, asked if I had any questions about my role as a witness and then in a low, breathless tone, asked if there was anything she could do for me. I said no as coldly as I could, and she moved on to Grimm who was sitting close by. Out of the corner of my eye, I saw him grin as he reached for her hand and placed it on his thigh. I turned away in sick disgust. On the other side of me the other hostess sat very close to the Secretary of Commerce, and I thought for a moment that I would become violently ill. The scene still is too unreal to make any kind of sense. The image of a fighting-mad Biggerman flickering in front of me in garish blue light, and the figures around me shrouded in the gloom of a nightmare setting. The human race, busy in the art of consuming one another.

Order was restored all around the minute Biggerman was hauled away. The subjects and their chairs were set right again. The guards had ordered milling spectators to their seats, and the hostesses had gone back to serving coffee.

Then Avery A. Brown was called. He moved as if he still had his Homburg hat on. He is a mild-looking man. He is not meek. He is not pushy. He is not loud. He is not milquetoast. He is a grey sort of a man. He does not command any particular sense of presence that can be identified. One cannot say he is weak appearing either. About all I can say is that he has always struck me as being a nice guy, and one who gives the appearance of being intelligent. He is not quite 60 and is of average height. He is mostly bald and his face is more or less round. He wears heavy glasses which make him look dignified, studious and a bit unassuming, all in one. He was calm and respectful as he approached the witness box.

"How say you?" Smith Armstrong asked after reading a long list of charges.

"I should like to have my specialists in corporate affairs present," was Mr. Brown's reply. There was something in his manner that made him ridiculously naive. He actually believed that he would be granted the privilege.

"The request is denied," the chairman snapped. "Now, Mr. Brown, this is not a United States court of law or a congressional hearing. This is merely a World Order of Nations hearing, and such representation is neither provided for nor desired... else we would be here until doomsday as the victims of wasteful, verbal gymnastics designed to confuse not clarify issues and subject us to obstructionist's tactics. I do not want to cite you for contempt. Please answer the question."

If Mr. Brown felt any emotion he did not show it. He did not show disappointment. He did not show fighting anger. He did not show defeat. He displayed "even temperament." It is the key to corporate success. I suppose that no less than two dozen times during my career with the company I have heard my superiors expound on the quality of "even temperament." The successful manager, a training director told a group of us many years ago, must see all sides to any given question and be broad-gauge and mature enough to display "even temperament" at all times. On another occasion my present boss told me that one must lead without appearing to lead; that a true manager never solidifies his position in anything, because all things are relative to the moment, and, of course, no one moment is like any other moment; that a log-roller keeps his balance by constantly shifting his position; that in the complexities of our life we achieve the same through "even temperament." When Avery Brown was appointed chairman seven years ago, much was made of the "rare ability to display even temperament even under the most trying circumstances... the mark of a true leader."

So Mr. Brown replied mildly, "Please understand that I willingly accept the conditions set forth by the distinguished members of the panel. I am sure you gentlemen are cognizant of my deep and earnest desire to cooperate in every way possible in the common effort to win for men everywhere peace and freedom and the prosperity to which so many of us strive daily to . .."

"Will the subject please answer to the charges!" Chairman Armstrong interrupted icily. A low rumble of impatience spread through the spectators.

228

"Mister Chairman, the complexities of this situation," Mr. Brown wore on smoothly, "are such that any answer I might give would... indeed must... reflect a host of considerations that are properly centered about my responsibilities and loyalty to the general public welfare of this great, dynamic nation of ours, as well as to our employees, our stockholders and our customers. In the discharge of these grave duties, I cannot see that I have violated any Treaty provisions that could be termed significant..."

A mighty roar let loose from the spectators, and Chairman Armstrong banged for order.

"On the other hand," Avery Brown continued without visible sign of discomfort, "I recognize that there are some few persons who, because of their admirable zeal and humanitarian dedication, might be inclined to feel that certain Treaty provisions have been violated. Let me assure you that I quite understand—indeed fully sympathize—with these sincere people but hasten to point out that the true facts, if we can arrive at them here sensibly and logically, will reveal that these fears are nothing more than misunderstandings. I have long championed the important role of teamwork, of getting along together, of..."

A wave of titters began to roll over the spectators, and the hall noises began to grow as people blew their noses, coughed and carried on extraneous visits with their seat mates. The chairman rapped them to silence, and wearily he turned to Mr. Brown. "I quite understand your concern. Now, sir, will you please answer the question."

"Of course, Mister Chairman, and that is precisely what I was leading up to. I simply want all of us to have a clear idea of the issues..."

"You have made yourself clear..."

"...involved and that is why I should like to take the liberty of reading a prepared statement which I am sure will clarify the atmosphere... and I quote," Mr. Brown produced a sheaf of papers with a flick of his hand and at once began reading in a low, flat, evenly paced voice: "America is great because free men working shoulder-to-shoulder in the free market place and in cooperation with the federal government have wrought great miracles of productive might that have given us the highest standard of living on the face of the earth. The result has been true people-to-people wealth that has benefited us all and now we are embarked upon a great crusade to carry' our skills and know-how to the far-flung places of the earth. The task is a mighty one. It involves the total cooperation of millions upon…"

"Mr. Brown!" the chairman snapped like a bull-whip, which brought, at last, instant attention from Avery Brown and the waning spectators who had begun to visit and move about with bold disdain. "Never have I heard so many words that say absolutely nothing."

And then they laughed. Two thousand variations of laughter. Not rigged but genuine. The first real laughter since the hearings had begun. Deep laughter. Gasping laughter. Tear-releasing laughter. Howls. Back slaps. Knee slaps. Quaking.

Through it all, Mr. Brown kept his even temperament, as a banquet speaker might await the subsidence of an audience that has been charmed by his extremely funny story.

When silence was restored, Chairman Armstrong said, "This . .. ah . .. statement is the same one that was distributed this morning to the press, is it not?"

"Why, as a matter of fact, yes." Mr. Brown replied.

"I have already read it. It does not answer the question. Please say yes or no to the charges, and step down. Will the Sergeant-at-Arms please assist Mr. Brown."

"See here!" Mr. Brown lost his evenness in favor of righteous indignation and hurting disbelief that no one wished to listen to him with breathless attention. "I demand that my remarks go into the records of these proceedings. I demand that I be placed clearly on record so that all might know…"

"Yes, yes, Mr. Brown," Chairman Armstrong replied with true weariness spreading over his features. "We will insert your remarks in the record, and let the record show that Mr. Brown has failed to answer the question."

There was laughter again, as Avery Brown moved evenly to his seat. Not once during his testimony had anyone bothered to shout "Down with Mister X!"

Avery A. Brown, apparently, was not worth the effort.

And all the while I raged inwardly.

I am going to stick my neck out for *him*? For a bumbling dreamer? For a man so taken up with his own importance that he ceases to see that which is real? For a hunk of jelly that draws a salary of four hundred thousand dollars a year, because he is supposed to have talents and skills that the likes of me lack? I am going to risk my future for *him*? Let him go to hell. I hope they give it to him good.

These thoughts pummeled me as the first witness "on behalf" of Mr. Brown was ushered out of our waiting area to the witness box. He was Alvin Sanders, our vice president of production. He is the only one of our high-ranking executives for whom I have had any particular respect. Once he told a group of us salesmen that "contrary to what many people say, a machine or a system still is only as good as the men operating it." I always liked him after that. For he had spoken at a meeting at which much had been made of an expertly conceived quality control system that, one gathered, was a cut or two above the ability of any of us assembled. The covey of experts who sat in godlike poses at the head of the conference room had not liked what he had said. And now he stood in the witness box waiting. He is a tall man. He appeared to be without fear. His rugged features also revealed that he had resolved exactly what he would do and say. It was soon apparent that he would neither defend nor warp his testimony to condemn Mr. Brown. He had determined to play things absolutely straight and go no further than the circumstances required. He did not offer gushy remarks about the peace treaty, nor did he say anything detrimental. He merely said that he was a production man and had no interest in politics. He had no intention of revealing what sort of pressures must have been applied to make him serve as a witness. "Business and politics do not mix. There are unpleasant things in politics that are better forgotten," he said.

The examiners tried to pin him down on Mr. Brown's efforts to bribe BWP officials for higher price schedules. "Did Mr. Brown engage in price bribes?" they asked.

"I never knew of it."

"Could Mr. Brown have engaged in trying to bribe BWP officials?"

"I couldn't say."

"You didn't hear the question. I said could Mr. Brown have done such a thing?"

"Well, I suppose he could, but I have no proof ..."

"That will do. Thank you. The record should show that Mr. Sanders agrees that a bribe attempt could have occurred."

Then they came again to a familiar stretch of questioning. It concerned whether or not Avery Brown favored the Treaty.

"He did nothing actively to oppose the Treaty," Mr. Sanders said in answer to *the* question.

"He did nothing to help the Treaty, did he?"

"No."

"He is on record as not in favor of the Treaty, isn't he?"

"A very cautiously worded statement... just one statement in answer to a press query made before it was even signed... and even then he indicated his willingness to cooperate if the majority so ruled."

"That statement clearly stated... quote ... I do not favor the Treaty... quote."

"But the complete sentence said: While I do not favor the Treaty I will cooperate if..."

"That will do, Mr. Sanders. We cannot dilute the quality of our search for fact by dragging a lot of extraneous detail into the record. The fact remains that he did not favor the Treaty."

"That is correct."

"You are one of the largest steel producers in the world. Does it seem logical that your board chairman, who is against the Treaty but upon whom so much responsibility rests for the common public good, should continue in his present post where he can obstruct the will of the people at every turn, where he can deliberately slow production, where he can continue to line his own pockets with the wealth of others... does this seem logical?"

"But no one has proved this."

"As chairman he has the power to do these things, does he not?"

"Yes, of course."

232

"And if he's against the Treaty, isn't it only logical to assume he would obstruct wherever he could, as other witnesses will show he has done? Is this not logical?"

I could not see Avery Brown's face, for the TV screen showed only Sanders, who had remained cool throughout his interrogation. I could imagine, though, that the symptoms of shock would by now have consumed Brown's features; that the studious look would by now be replaced by a stupefied expression.

"I am not qualified to answer."

"You mean that a man in your position who must govern the production of millions of tons of steel, who must handle a work force of thousands, who must deal with hundreds of complicated mechanical and engineering problems ... do you mean that you can't tell us whether or not Mr. Brown very logically could, in his present position of unbridled power, sabotage the Treaty and the efforts of millions of people? It is a most alarming situation if a man of your responsibility feels unqualified." Smith Armstrong had posed this question. He asked it quietly and with the underlying implication that perhaps Mr. Sanders might need some investigating, too.

The spectators responded with precision, uttering a forest of boos and catcalls.

And Mr. Sanders got the message. I could see it on his face—the flicker of final decision. The flicker of the eyes and of the facial muscles that said he was thinking. About momma and the kids. About a country club membership. About a very large office, very nicely furnished. About a lifetime of getting there. "If you can't lick 'em, join 'em." He had said that, too, once at another sales meeting, and his face said it now.

"Yes," he said over the noise. The chairman banged for order.

"Yes—what, Mr. Sanders?"

"Yes, it's logical."

"Thank you. Let the record show that Mr. Sanders believes that it would be illogical for Mr. Brown to continue as board chairman in light of his unbridled power to destroy the effectiveness of the Treaty of Friendship. Is that correct, Mr. Sanders?"

"Yes."

"You may be excused."

Mr. Sanders departed by another exit, and we did not see him again.

There was a hurried change in the pattern. Mr. Sanders had been cooperative, but still it was apparent that the examiners had been put on edge. They had had to work too hard on this one. A brief recess was called, and the examiners moved off the platform obviously for a hasty conference.

Had it not been for this interruption things might have been different. Had there not been an unplanned ten minutes of nothingness, perhaps I would have acted differently. Who is there not to say? Certainly not me. But there it was. Time to think. Time to wonder anew. First came the thought—what are they up to? Secondly came again the growing awareness of power. Off and on, as I have already written, a sense of the power they possess had been inflicted upon me each time with more and more intensity. And here in the witness waiting room the sense of it was stronger than ever. It was in the affluence of the room itself and in the trim, flint-eyed women who guarded it with absolute disregard for the human play on stage. It was in the stifling closeness of the atmosphere, in the folds of the thick curtains. And it was what was behind those curtains—the sea of faces out in front, the tiers of platforms, the vacant expression of the 44 once respected men and women, the bright lights, the aides, helpers, assistants and technicians moving about with a crisp efficiency that was without trace of fear and which seemed to say, "The world will run without you; we have everything well in hand; go with us and you win—go against us and you perish." Efficiency. That was it. Power to make or break with no escape. By now, counting both subjects and witnesses, hundreds of persons had been caught up in its soft, invisible net and swept into the fiery furnace of betrayal which feeds upon the fuel of expediency and the drive to survive at any cost. The last to go was Sanders, and he was no different from the first. Power was the great leveler, and soon my turn would come.

In this ten-minute pause the seeds of panic were sown.

Then the examiners came back, and the seeds began to take root.

Chairman Armstrong—with just the right touch of grave importance and thanksgiving carefully mixed into the tone in his voice— felt "moved to make known to all of you certain matters which have only now come to our attention." He flashed before the assembly several pieces of paper. They were letters, he explained, from seven of the forty-four subjects. In each case, the chairman went on to say to a now still audience, the writers had confessed to "poor judgment" and had conceded that they had been "unwittingly guilty" of obstructing progress under the Treaty and wished to thank "their fellow citizens" for this "regenerative experience" and—finally—to pledge their "full cooperation."

He quoted liberally from the letter which Mr. Grant had written from his hospital bed. "It has been difficult for me to face the truth," the letter said, "and that is that the witnesses who spoke in my behalf were essentially correct. I regret that I have erred and wish all to know that, henceforth, I shall work diligently to foster true peace throughout the world. Toward this end I feel the most constructive step I can take at the outset is to retire as chairman of the board of R. M. Grant and Sons and turn my responsibilities over to younger leadership whom I feel to be better equipped to steer the company to a more effective role in the affairs of peace. Also, I feel that the Allegheny Committee for American Action has outlived its usefulness, and so I resign all connections with this organization and urge my associates therein to do likewise . .." Benjamin Zanhorst, distinguished publisher, also advised in similar language that he had seen the light. His initial contribution to world peace was to resign from the *Pittsburgh News-Journal* as "unworthy to carry on the work that must go on at all costs."

Then there was David O. Harmes, superintendent of schools—resigned; H. H. Barnes III, president of the Chamber of Commerce—resigned; Adolph Kruger, president of Mastersmeld—resigned; Elizabeth Robbins St. John, president of the Federation of Women's Clubs—resigned, and Justin Wright, president of the Bar Association—resigned.

It was all so kindly done that the terror of it still stalks me.

For they gave the seven repenters a standing ovation.

First came Smith Armstrong's eloquent statement after the letters had been read. "These are no ordinary men and women... but courageous... highest patriotism... unselfish ... to whom we owe an enormous debt of gratitude ... for they have given hope that peace can and will be attained in our time ..."

Then came Nicholas Syerov, which drew deathly still attention, for he seldom participated in the questioning and so each word he did utter was considered a rare collector's item. "Mister Chairman, I am mos touched by such wondersfuls peepul. I beg my associates that ve mus... dismiss all charges agains thees peepuls . ."

One of the examiners seconded the motion and, by unanimous vote, then and there, all charges against the six lucky people—plus the bedridden Mr. Grant—were summarily dropped, and in place a Resolution of Commendation was read into the record so that officials of the World Order of Nations and "indeed the people of the world might know of the unselfish spirit of Pittsburgh leadership in achieving peace and prosperity for all."

After this, the ovation. Cheers, clapping hands and stomping feet shook the room as one by one the Enlightened Six were ushered from their seats and out into the bright new world.

Six Pittsburgh leaders cited for leadership.

Six Pittsburgh leaders without jobs to go to, castrated of their virility and turned out to pasture.

And the cheers rang louder and louder.

The seeds of panic had grown into tough, thorned vines and had broken through the soil of my resolves and had begun to strangle me. They have given up. They have seen the light. They are smart.

The next witnesses against Avery Brown went quickly. Smith Armstrong had restored order with mechanical precision and swung smoothly into the pattern again. Sam Grimm was next and before he had spoken a full minute the excitement had died out, and all was as before. Grimm is the big boss of sales at the company. He is a hearty kind of a man of medium height but overweight. He established

236

that illicit relationships existed between Avery Brown and certain "pet" customers—one of whom was Mr. Grant. Mrs. Tuttle, Brown's secretary, was next and smoothly revealed illicit support of both political parties; pressure phone calls to the White House; attempts to bribe BWP officials—who, of course, had refused; more customer hanky-panky; and the fact that he tried, on numerous occasions, to seduce her. Mr. Croate, a customer, then entered the witness box to reveal black market attempts to sell steel to him for unpatriotic uses. The Governor of Pennsylvania—under most respectful questioning—revealed a long list of pressure tactics applied to him by Avery Brown. The Governor concluded by expressing his appreciation at being "invited here today to set the record straight." He was cheered. Finally came the United States Secretary of Commerce. Out of respect no questions were asked but, as Smith Armstrong said, "You were invited to come only if your busy schedule permitted and only if you would wish to speak out in this matter. Would there be anything you wish to say to us, sir?" And indeed there was. The secretary pulled from his pocket a short, damning statement which he read in most willing tones. He revealed more of Mr. Brown's transgressions in seeking "privilege to escape his clear-cut responsibilities under the Treaty..."

Then it was my turn.

3

This is the moment I have dreaded over these past several days; to put down forthrightly on paper an appraisal of my last hour at the hearings; to face the facts by looking at myself as I would another person. When a man falls from his horse he knows that he must get up and ride again quickly before fear overtakes him. So it is that I must here force myself to relive the events so that my mind will accept—make peace with—myself as I am and will continue to be. To write as it was, not as it might have been.

As it was I approached the witness box in a frozen state of panic. From the platform it looked as if the entire human race had been assembled just to watch and judge me. And the benches, particularly Smith Armstrong's, towered at such awesome heights that I had difficulty remembering that I was a full-sized human being. The lights were everywhere, painfully blinding and hot. I could see nothing clearly—only vague forms moving, shifting, whispering, coughing or issuing muffled instructions. The eyes of the TV cameras stared unblinkingly at me, metal monsters with x- ray vision that had been ordered by a great super-power to tear me open to reveal every fibre of me—body, mind, spirit. *I can't fool them. They will know.*

"Will you please state your name and occupation for the record."

Name. Yes. Is it David or Davey Little? There's a difference, you know. One is the old me. The other is the new me. Also, do I mention Q? That's for Quincy. He was grandfather. You see, he worked very hard and saved money back before there was any peace. Strange, since the peace I have found no peace. How interesting!

"Your name, please."

"David Quincy Little." *Ha! Fooled them! One up on the monsters. I gave my full name as it is on all my records. Cant be blamed for that! Perfectly natural. That way they can't tell whether I'm really David or Davey. A wise move. Keep them off balance until the very last moment. That way...*

"Occupation, please."

"Salesman. I sell steel." *And I'm planning to steal away. Ha! Ha! Bet you didn't get that, metal monsters!*

"You are employed in the same company with Avery Brown?"

"Yes." *Do they have steel jobs in Canada? Or are all of them there, too. But who cares. You'll do something. But I don't know how to cut wood. Learn! Then what? It's been a pretty good job ... this one. So I'll make out. Sure you will! No, you won't.*

"Do you know Mr. Brown personally?"

"Only slightly." *If I had a gun I'd shoot him! Know him? Hell, he doesn't know me from a drinking fountain. And I'm up here to sweat for him. All the Big Boys are smart. They know how to stay on top. I'm the dumb one here! It figures. I've never done anything right. How do I know this is right?*

"But you are familiar with his professional position on various matters?"

Oh, God, here it comes!

"What is your opinion of Mr. Brown's general reaction to the Treaty of Friendship?"

They call it The Moment of Truth. It *can* be a phrase easy to say. For it rolls grandly off the tongue, and properly applied to conversation in a world that judges words for the sake of words alone, it can be used to beef up shallow thoughts and lackluster deeds. But to *face* the Moment and *live* with it in the dark hallways of the mind, where the doors and windows to life are locked against all outside things, and you tremble alone in this darkness; where small voices echo like the scamperings of unseen creatures at prey; where you pound on the walls of sanity to be let out and no friendly footsteps come to undo the door; and the unseen creatures dart in to nibble in squeaking triumph and then away before you can crush them; thoughts like bats swooping and calling in your face; noble vows and shining resolves once made now turned to sharp-toothed rodents that attack again and again; and though you writhe and plead, they do not go away. To live through the d.t.'s of conscience or lack of conscience; of will or lack of will; of courage or no courage at all. This is the terror of the Moment of Truth faced. A man, therefore, does not face truth often. And when he does, it is because he is forced to, if only to keep from being eaten alive by the creatures of reality.

I could not go through with... any of it.

I fought. I must give myself that. In that long moment I knew I could not defend Avery Brown. For a second it seemed that I might compromise; say what they wanted and then flee. Mary, the children and I could escape just as we had planned. Mary would understand. Dr. Rodgers would, too. After all, I owed Brown absolutely nothing. But a rodent of truth bit me just then. My noble plan had not been some altruistic move to defend the likes of Avery Brown at some great personal sacrifice. That others might conceivably have benefited from my resolves to speak out fearlessly was beside the point. My soul-lifting urge had been to stand before this slum of reason as a

239

whole man. All of this I was doing for myself, to test the degree of my own inner strength against the pull of the tides about me; to discover how deep I dare wade in the surf before my strength would fail and so be swept to my doom. Brown and Canada were one. The terror was that I could not flee, because I did not *want* to flee. The procession of d.t.'s that brought me to this truth carried me, first, through the burning desert of hate—and as one delirious from thirst who flails out desperately. Had it not been for *Them* I would have been spared all of this; the *Them* being everyone from my parents and teachers to Larry, Nancy, and—horribly—Mary. In one sweeping mental invective I included the bulk of the human race. Were it not for *Them!* Oh, god, how I hate *Them!* Then the delirium scene changed to utter darkness and complete stillness where I saw, heard and felt nothing. And a voice from somewhere deep inside me thundered in the darkness. *You cheat! You do not want to flee because you do not have the courage to flee!* "Yes!" I screamed back to myself. "It is true! God help me, but it is true!" Only I did not scream these words to myself. I screamed them aloud over the P.A. system, and the shock of my own voice, bursting like a shell over the great room with its regal trappings, shook me free from the dark hallways of my mind. I had endured the terror of Truth and stood now dimly conscious of my surroundings and numb with the realization that I would do—after all of this—exactly what they who towered above me wished me to do.

The room was alive with noise and there was the banging of a gavel.

"Mr. Little! Kindly control yourself! I merely asked what your opinion was concerning Mr. Brown's reaction to the Treaty. You shout that it is true." The voice paused from somewhere out beyond the unbearably bright lights and then went on soothingly. "Now, would you please clarify what you mean…"

I draw a blank every time I try to remember precisely what I said or what was said to me or how I acted or how I looked or how I felt. I sense, rather than recall clearly, that I was among the most cooperative of any of the witnesses who appeared at the hearings. It seems I was quite positive that Mr. Brown firmly opposed the Treaty and that a great injustice could occur if Mr. Brown were allowed to continue his position of leadership. It seems that I recited correctly the concerns for my family and my professional well-being, due to Mr. Brown's outrageous demands that I read his speeches and follow his beliefs without reason or compromise, that is if I wanted a monthly pay check. It seems that somewhere in the midst of my performance voices out behind the bright lights screamed "Down with Mister X!" I cannot be sure that Smith Armstrong complimented me on my courage for "speaking the truth so boldly at the risk of incurring the wrath of your employer." Yet, I recall I was pleased about this—somehow. I do not know how I came to leave the hotel or how I came to the parking lot—at noon exactly.

But I do know she was there. This is certain. For I still see her face. Eyes large and dry and looking far away. She stood in a sea of automobiles at honking high noon, her trembling gloved hand playing absently along the sleek lines of the chrome hood ornament of our get-away car. She was all slender and twisted with silent sorrow. She was a waif without a home. Without hope. Wilted. A thing of beauty no more. She knew my mind.

"You're not going." She managed a crooked, slim little smile and lowered her eyes.

"No."

And so it ended.

She fled into the noontime scramble, her hurried steps fading…

From somewhere near came the blare of a car radio.

It was a commercial.

It was an invitation to enlist today in the Peace Enforcement Corps.

4

Thank goodness, we still have a family doctor. Most people use the clinics for everything, but we have not gone that far yet. He has diagnosed me as having a virus flu in his reports to the BWP. Otherwise, it would have been difficult to explain my prolonged absence from work—more than two weeks now. As it is, I can probably take another week without arousing suspicion. Of course, I did not tell him very much; only that the hearings had exhausted me and that I simply could not go back to work. Not just yet. But, we both agreed, it would be unwise to report this fatigue. Reports of this nature often are interpreted as a sign of a person's inability to adjust properly to his environment and thus he becomes a poor employment risk, something I can ill afford now. I had a friend once who gave out in the corporate struggle to have a directive of some sort approved. He had tried for seven months and one day quietly fell apart, too tired to care. A week of rest had him back in shape, but they still transferred him to a lesser job. Our doctor understands these things. When Nancy summoned him after I was released by the police, he shut her gently out of the bedroom, sized up the situation and then gravely pronounced to her that I had a severe virus infection. His prescription was sedation and rest. A personal doctor is well worth hanging onto if one can possibly afford it.[56]

So it is in this sixth month of June that I have the days to myself to rest, to write and to rest some more. In the evenings I watch TV or just sleep. I am still not able to join in with the normal pattern of family living, but everyone—even little Annie—seems satisfied that I have been too ill to spend much time with them. I have still much yet to clear away in my mind before I can rejoin the outside world. The impulse is to push all thoughts out of mind of these terrible months and sleep. But the instinct to survive tells me that I must grapple with them one by one. So each day a little bit of them goes on paper. Each day the weight lifts as I become accustomed to that which now is passed and done with forever. Each day I gain strength but only after suffering the ups and downs of memory.

Thus, I remember Harry; not because I want to but because only by forcing myself to remember him can I ever hope to forget him and so gain peace of mind.

I see him best as a kid, from around the time he was eleven or so, until I left for college. He is most clear to me as he was then. He was

---

56 Nearly all medicine had been nationalised, but physicians were allowed to keep private patients on the side.

such a nuisance that I simply took more notice of him then than at any other time. Although he was four years younger than I, he possessed twice the energy and ability to get into trouble—this in the midst of Dad's three-year struggle to make our store into a supermarket, a bad enough burden to bear in my closing years of high school without putting up with a brother who was the talk of the school, the neighborhood and on occasion the entire city. I do not recall that he was clumsy as most boys usually are at that age. He was perpetually agile, never still. But his movements were not the aimless putterings of awkward youth. Quick, sure, determined but, oddly, never pushy, he circulated through his world of tree- houses, baseball, junk parts, home chemistry sets and electronic devices with a rhythmic sense of purpose. He was always lean about the face and of moderate stature. His limbs were tough, and his cool blue eyes already had begun to develop humor lines. For his manner was easy, though he was never easygoing, and his delight in the things about him never ceased. He would devour the contents of *Popular Mechanics* with the same eagerness as he would spring home for his ball and glove after school or pick a marooned cat out of a tree, such as happened one Sunday morning at the cost of a new suit only minutes before Sunday school.

He was a pest: collapsing a giant pyramid of jelly in glass containers at the store on a crowded Saturday; wondering aloud in the dead of night, "Hey, Dave, where does the wind come from?"; dismantling my bicycle to use it to drive a homemade generator; using my toothbrush to clean his fishbowl.

He was embarrassing: riding the neighborhood with the junkman in search of treasure; attempting to scale the outside wall of the school, using nothing but fingers and tennis shoes dug into rough brick (he made it almost to the second story before he fell into some expensive shrubbery below); trying to make a synthetic diamond out of coal dust, which nearly cost the sanity of school officials, and any number of corporate officials to whom he wrote repeatedly, as the newspapers reported in a gay Sunday feature.

He blew our house fuses regularly, two or three times a week, due to one experiment or another that constantly cluttered up the house. He must have blown a hundred trying to transform the coal dust in a homemade electric arc kiln. His first electric circuit maze nearly burned us out. He used a penny in the fuse box. He tried to electrify the driveway so the heat would melt the snow. But both his electric eye and motorized birdbath, however, caused relatively little difficulty, and his various homemade radios were all successful.

He was always in business. Dad would not let him work in the store. We were, by this time, large enough to have outside help, and while I was still a year under age, the clerks were agreeable to my working, since I was there before they were hired. An eleven-year-old would have been too much. But Harry did not mind. He simply went into business for himself. First, it was a wake-up service, beginning at five-thirty every morning. Then came handy work. He purchased a power mower and hired himself out to take care of lawns, wash windows, cultivate gardens and wash walls. Later, he added a delivery service using a bicycle, later a motor scooter. Then he began selling ads for the local weekly newspaper. He made his first purchase of stock at age fourteen and took a beating, losing eighty-six dollars. By the time he was fifteen he had made it back with a little to spare. He was taking flying lessons when he was sixteen.

In between, he went to school and, surprisingly, stayed mostly in the upper ten percent of his class. He had the gift of intense concentration, which is what probably saved him from expulsion. For he was forever in trouble with his teachers. "Failure to adjust" and "obstructing class procedures" were the charges consistently lodged against him. He had to ask the question—the one that brought the well-ordered teaching machinery to a dead halt, the one that reversed the trend of thought, the one for which the teacher seldom had an answer: "How can you be so sure Jefferson would have changed his views if he were alive today?" "Solutions can too be simple, else how do you explain Einstein's formula $E = MC^2$?" "How do you spend something that isn't?" Still, he did well in his exams. "The questions are easy," he used to say, "and if that's all I have to do to make them happy..."

He was in trouble elsewhere, too. Most particularly it was with professional gardeners. They did not like the way he offered himself at something less than the prevailing adult wage for lawn work. He had sixteen customers at the peak of his operations, which represented a sizable hunk of business for a fourteen-year-old. While nothing was ever said to his face, he did lose two mowers. One, which Harry had left in a customer's yard while he went to lunch, somehow had rolled up a small rise into the street. At least that is where he found it hopelessly smashed, apparently the victim of a truck. The other suffered a dose of sugar in the small gas tank, done while we were all away at a movie.

He was in dutch with the baseball coach for being late to practice or missing it entirely. Yet he played especially well as an infielder and seemed to revel in the keen competition of a tight game. He teased girls, which gave him no end of trouble. He bothered librarians with odd requests for information and bugged brokers for stock tips. He was in trouble with me constantly for borrowing my pens and paper, sweaters and socks, half-read magazines, flashlights and penknives, belts, slippers and even my textbooks. To make matters worse, we shared the same room, ninety percent of which was occupied by Harry with his electronic devices, business invoices and roughly a ton of sketches, blueprints, wire, tools, books and assorted parts, including gears, switches, wheels and plugs.

At least, as I see now, his troubles were honest troubles. I do not believe he ever cheated, although he was stubborn in his determination to see a thing through. He never complained, either, even after the lawn mower incidents. Always he had a backlog of humor. He could laugh at himself—and his failures, which were many—as well as at the rest of us. He had a disarming kind of charm, a certain brashness born of his curiosity for things, which, coupled with his easy humor, made him difficult to dislike for very long. He neither asked nor gave quarter. At times he could be amazingly polite, especially with his elders. But that did not keep him from asking his endless stream of questions. What made it difficult was that he put them in such nice, respectful ways that would leave you defenseless.

Thus did Harry grow to become a master inventor, salesman and business executive for whom all life was one grand adventure.

I do not see him so clearly in adult life. We saw little of each other after Dad died, both of us busy going our separate ways. But I am kidding myself. We lost contact largely because I wanted it that way, for during those early years he irritated me with his constant prying into things. He made me uneasy with his endless energy. His ease of self—an infernal, perpetual confidence expressed without any visible effort—left me darkly hollow. Whenever he succeeded at something—a project that worked, a fruitful day's work, scoring the winning run (he could hit as well as he could field and peg a ball)—I was secretly sorry. And whenever he failed—whenever the lights went out or the neighbors would take after him with their cracks ("Made any diamonds lately?"), or he missed a catch—I was gloatingly glad to myself. But the glee would be watered down with my disappointment that Harry never seemed to mind defeat. He never seemed to learn his lesson. He never seemed sorry. He did things his way, oblivious to criticism and yet bearing no grudges. Still, he was liked and respected. Perhaps, he may even have been feared, because he could be different and not care, because he could be different and get away with it. He did not seem to need people or their approval in order to exist. This rubbed me raw inside.

For a while during those young years he followed me around, to wait patiently for me to notice him. He seemed anxious to share some new-found bit of knowledge or an observation fresh and new to his ever-widening world. To tap me on the shoulder, with a crude, newly made gadget in his grimy hands; to wait for me after school with some useless bit of news; to offer me part of a crumbling, gooey peanut butter sandwich. Scram, I'm busy.... Oh, for Christ sake, what do you want now.... Ugh! You expect me to eat that! The words of brotherly love, spoken in anger, boredom and revulsion, because I was so overwhelmingly busy shaping myself to get along in a world based on brotherly love. Gradually, Harry began to go his own way. At fifteen he began calling me big brother with a metallic, biting twist.

To leave home, store, Dad and Harry for the good, really worthwhile and important things of college—what relief! I wrote only when I had to and kept home visits at the absolute minimum. And so it had been ever since. Harry and home synonymous with too much drudgery, too much effort and too much of swimming against the tide. Harry's wedding, an occasional holiday, once in a while a letter or post card or a casual reference by a mutual acquaintance passing through—that is all there was of Harry in his adult years to be remembered.

Then there is my mother. The images are less sharp. I cannot summon up any great plateaus of likes or dislikes about her. She was always quiet; simply there. If I was sick, she was there. If Dad was shorthanded, she was there. If Harry needed someone to help him wind an armature, she was there. She was medium in everything. She was of medium height and build. Her voice was medium, not loud or soft. Her interest was medium, neither weak nor strong. I am sure that I loved her, but I cannot seem to grasp onto any concrete emotion. I know I used to enjoy her reading me stories just before bed. I believe she used to sing to me or at least sing around the house. But I begin drawing emotional blanks when I try to think further. I recall quite clearly after the three boys had pushed me over the cliff behind the school that my mother had tried to comfort me and that she had chided me gently for playing too near to it. I am certain that I had tried very hard to explain the awfulness of what had happened; first in the principal's office with Miss Lee angry at me and then later when the boys in bright sweaters knocked me about. But I never got through to her, or to Dad for that matter. From then on I seemed to be more conscious of the outside world and whether or not I could deal with it. Whatever magic there usually is between a boy and his parents was gone before I was nine. Later, when Dad died, Harry took over with an unconscious ease, as if it were the most natural thing to do. I was never asked to help, but then I was seldom around. Military service accounted partly for this, and getting married and starting a career in Pittsburgh was part of it, too.

The rest of Harold Little is even more vague. I knew hardly at all his wife, Margaret, except that she was suited to him. She was a tall, lively redhead with as much energy as Harry. And their son, Charles, was a daring four-year-old the last time we saw him. That was a year ago Christmas. We had wanted, this time, to make the trip—mostly, I must confess, to see Harry's new home, a rather large one. They were truly glad to see us, and I was particularly struck with how pleased and happy my mother appeared with her "tight little family" as she would call them. She had her own apartment, complete with separate entrance in one wing of the house. We had a pleasant enough time seeing part of Harry's world, including a trip to the airport to see his plane. But I was glad to leave and even gladder to get home, out of the car and into bed. For Nancy and I had a discussion most of the way home, while our children squirmed uneasily in the back seat. "David, why can't you get on with things the way Harry has? Not that I like Harry, but…"

This is about all I can recall of the Harold Little family. In these recent weeks, as I have noted, I had begun to look again upon them. In the whirlpool of events that tore at my mind, I had begun to reappraise my brother and to think again and wonder about my mother. I had been, I think, on the brink of discovering something: a new sense of strength and being that comes with the reunion of kin; an urge to pick up again the mislaid threads of mutual understanding; the desire to return home for a second chance. To start fresh together in Canada; to bind together, Harry and me, our respective loved ones and move forward in a new world of freedom and purpose; to see our mother at peace in her twilight years; to love our mates and shape our children to be lean and strong. What a glorious dream! But it was not strong enough to sustain me through my Moment of Truth.

So, I return—here on paper—to that last day at the hearings, to put it behind me so that I need never think of it again.

After my encounter with Mary in the parking lot I became violently sick, retching horribly, grasping with slimy hands the car door to keep upright. I was dimly conscious of people gathering to look. When I raised my head, one little girl who hovered with her parents looked at my sick face and buried herself in the folds of her mother's skirt. I shall never forget the revulsion on her sweet face or the grim disgust of her parents. It was as if I were looking upon all of the tomorrows which, in turn, were looking back at me in somber, silent rebuke; for I had bargained them away. Coming as this did, on top of everything else, purged my mind of the last vestige of normal and reasonable behavior. All of what happened, what I thought, felt and did over the next few hours still remains a blur.

Surely, I must have been half mad. For I spun out of the parking lot—God knows how I got out without tearing the place to pieces—as if all the creatures of heaven and hell combined were after me; a crazed man in an automobile charging into the blaring jungle of metal and people at high noon. I do not recall exactly where they picked me up—somewhere on the eastern outskirts of downtown. I had driven blindly and without purpose through a circus maze of honks, screeches, screams, oaths and, finally, through the arm flailings of a policeman who leaped in panic from his post in the center of an intersection. Then there was the ominous moan of a siren and the heart-stopping wink of a red dome-light as a police cruiser closed in. For a long moment we were fender to fender and florid face to sick face. Finally, with the street shrunken to nothing, I stopped. The cop approached slowly with an I-got'cha-now-Buster walk.

Things might have worked out differently, a whole lot differently, if he had not made me step out of the car. He cannot be blamed, of course. I must have looked pretty desperate and, as was coldly pointed out, I had crashed six or so stop lights, along with a broken trail of other violations beginning back at the parking lot. So, "Outside, Buster." Even that would have been all right, except that he put his hand on my shoulder. Maybe he was going to search me. Maybe he was only trying to steady me.

It was a heavy hand. It had the weight and sureness of unquestioned authority. It had the power to stop; the power to end flight; the power to stifle will; the power to crush hope; the power to force absolute surrender. A heavy hand to tell me the end had come; the end of months of searching, planning and dreaming. It held me as a net holds a butterfly, as a trap holds a bear. A heavy hand to tell me that there was no compromise, no way to deal, no way to rationalize or plead. It said: "The world wants you back now." It was the end of the line.

And I struck out at the beefy, florid face. I kicked and pitched. I punched and pummeled. But the Law stood firm. We rocked in the street, three of us now, with the brother officer hurrying into the fray to restore order; quickly and neatly done with a night-stick jammed into the lower belly. What magnificent pain! It stops everything.

Somehow they got me back downtown to the gleaming new Justice Building. The corridors were terribly long, dazzling bright and slick with wax. Echoes from shoes, shrill voices and typewriters reverberated again and again inside my head. I wanted to close my eyes and sleep but they would not let me. Arms, hands and faces came and went out of nowhere in a spinning blur. At length came quiet. The light was dim, and I could sleep. I dreamed I was in a box. At first I thought it was a snug hole in the ground, and I was a rabbit. Then I knew it was a coffin and I could not get out. I fought to get the lid up, but it was closed tight. I was running out of air. From beyond someone was singing, "Jesus Wants Me for a Sunbeam." From somewhere near a voice said, "Take it easy."

I was on a canvas bunk, barren of blankets. Above me another bunk. Across from me still more. There were men in them. The floors and walls were icy white. I was in a large cell.

David Little had made jail.

I took inventory. My limbs moved. The throbbing in my head had slowed. Some semblance of reason had again taken possession.

"Thas more like it," a voice breathed. It belonged to a battered, dirty, whiskered face and reeked of stale whisky. "The animals got you?"

"The what?"

"Animals. The slippery critters. It's hell, ain't it?" The voice soothed. "D.T.'s kin kill you. Mine's always bats. Come at you from everywhere."

"I'm not drunk, if that's what you're talking about," I pulled myself up. "How long have I been here?"

"Just a couple of hours."

I sighed my thanks, relieved that I had not been there a day or a month or a year. The dirty face slipped away to another bunk. From a point above him another form broke again into a drowsy verse of

"Jesus Wants Me for a Sunbeam" while from above me came broken sobs and the blubbering vow, "never do it again if I can come home…"

For another long moment I rested, trying to piece together all that had happened, beginning with my breakfast meeting with Mary, Dr. Rodgers and Chip Baker, struggling through the eerie half-dream of the hearings and my flight from the parking lot. I was too spent to feel much of anything except weariness and an underlying something. I should be doing something, I thought, but what? Nancy will kill me when she finds out where I am. I mused on this point for a time before I realized that I had not planned to see Nancy again.

Harry!

He was expecting me at the airport in Cleveland at four-thirty, and it was three-forty now!

His words, given sternly over the phone weeks ago, rang loud and clear in my head: "Be sure to call if you can't make it, and don't be late! If we're late getting off the ground… missiles…

The next hour was the climax to all of my nightmares. The horror was my helplessness. At first I yelled to be let out, and in time—precious time—someone came, a surly guard. He only laughed and went away. So I yelled again, more frantically because it was nearly four. The guard came again in a very black mood. I begged him to let me use the phone. I had the wild idea of calling Mary and telling her what to do. He would do it—and my spirits rose in praise and thanksgiving—for a hundred dollars, he finished. Hope gave way to rage. Even if I had had such a sum, they had taken my wallet. The guard thought it great sport and called another guard into the steel corridor to watch the monkey perform in the zoo. Then other monkeys in the cage began to protest. So there was a fight, me and a bunch of drunks. Soon came the man in the white coat and black bag. Then came the force of arms with the bunk under me once again. Finally, the needle. "There, that'll quiet him." Drowsiness and space creeping up fast. One last effort to look at my watch. The time: five-o-five. Too late now.

Sometime later came a crescendo of footsteps, clanking of iron and the calling of my name. Hands fumbled for me, and I was lifted up gently and set on my feet. Soothing tones and a cool wash cloth wiped away the traces of imprisonment. Cheerful voices and helpful hands sped me out of the building, down long steps to a waiting automobile.

And then I was home in bed with the doctor there to order me to take this long rest.

I had been sprung from jail. Someone had fixed it up with the Law. I was square again. I was an overworked hero, too ill to carry on. "Surely you fellows understand his great responsibilities as a leader in the hearings that have been going on for weeks..." It was easy to recognize the confident and buoyant voice of my deliverer, who once again had tracked me down.

Larry Best brought me home. In this irony of ironies, who else?

And brother Harry and wife Margaret and son Charles and Mother Little... what of them?

They are dead. They died in flames over Lake Erie.

The newscasts the next day merely referred to an "unidentified passenger aircraft exploded in mid-air over..."

I was not officially notified—I am next of kin, you see—until the day after that.

No explanations were given. No inquiries were held.

But then, none were needed.

Harry had waited for me once too often.

5

The iron collar of betrayal begins to fit more comfortably now. I am like the newly trained dog; the innocent pup that has a choker chain forced over its head for the first time. For a while it struggles to remove the collar, rolling in the dirt and digging with its paws until, finally, it accepts what is inevitable. So I, too, accept the inevitable.

Larry, of course, is right. *Be more clever. Don't waste your energy on things you cannot control. Get along with them. Use your wits and you can win!*

VII

The Seventh Month

I returned to the office this week and was delighted with my reception. Thanks to Larry, my difficulties with the police were resolved without any record being made. The cost was light, only three hundred and fifty dollars sprinkled around a bit. Until now I have never fully appreciated the value of knowing the right people. Fortunately, Larry always has. Fully half of his energies have been devoted to this pursuit over the years. He drags himself to the most boring affairs and spends hours over drinks or lunch with persons in whom he has absolutely no interest. (Whooee, old boy, what a horrible lunch! But that mushhead works at the Internal Revenue Service, and I'm weak on contacts there.... Always arrange to have as many persons obligated to you as possible. That's Double-I, m'boy, Ironclad-Insurance!)

Now I'm schooling myself in the art. The first thing I did back at the office was to dictate a note to Leon Tidings expressing my willingness to cooperate further should he think of any way in which I could be of additional help. It was a smooth letter. Not too long, with just a touch of familiarity. His reply, while short, was prompt and courteous enough. Of course, word got around. I find my popularity with the other fellows, including our boss, Frank, has not suffered in the least. I have not had to buy lunch all week.

The company is reorganizing all over. Avery Brown resigned, as did the president. The new chairman is a man named Dobbs who was the company economist, and the president is someone new from the outside, a banker from New York. Nancy said her boss, Tom Shade, at the Bureau of Wages and Prices had a hand in the selection. W.O.N. brass even came to see him, and he went over to Washington several times. But, then, we are a mighty big company and, I think, will have an important role to play in the whole scheme. The mills continue to operate at full capacity, with better than forty percent of our products being shipped overseas. There is plenty to do. Very little in actual sales solicitation—in fact, none. It is all allocation, now, which has become quite complicated. The processing of orders takes considerable research. Each customer has a different priority classification and a sub-priority rating within that. For instance, a manufacturer of surgical instruments falls under Priority Classification F-Medical; Sub-Priority 6-Equipment; unit point two-Surgical Instruments; so that F- 6.2 is the complete designation. F-6.1 (Surgical Appliances) is higher in priority and therefore takes precedence. The A Classification, which is agriculture, is the most important priority of all. There is more to it than that. In determining who shall receive an order for steel, we must also determine the risk. If the customer is attempting to produce a new product of some sort, one of our tasks is to determine whether the product will be successful. If there is a possibility that it will fail, that people or governments will not want to buy it, then we do not allocate the steel, regardless of the priority. Waste of resources will not be tolerated anywhere. This gets to be a bit sticky.[57]

For instance, I spent most of yesterday on a small customer who certainly was not worth the effort. But it was a particularly fine day—in fact, the Fourth of July. I suppose I wanted to escape the boredom of the office as much as anything. Besides, the Fourth always had been a holiday, and so it is still something of a reflex not to

---

57 Presumably Mr. Little means that the problem of determining what is or is not a risk was not as easily solved as the written directives might have suggested. Unless one could have perfect foresight in predicting the whims and behaviour of both customers and various bureau planners the situation could, indeed, become sticky for anyone charged with the responsibility of making such decisions; hence probably a great deal of "buck passing." In addition, research and development work must have suffered considerably.

want to work.[58] Also, there is the matter of hanging on to the company car. They are beginning to recall them. No need to be on the road. Besides, gasoline is increasingly short, and rationing is stricter than ever. So I must justify keeping mine by looking for every opportunity to make a call.

It was good to be behind the wheel again. The heat was intense and the air sluggish with July closeness, but I could not complain even if I did not rate air conditioning. I was alive and sure. To perspire because of heat and not because of fear or indecision— what a feeling! Traffic was light, as it is now during most of the business day. People must walk or ride bicycles (if you can get them) or use buses. The city stretched all about in receding waves of valleys and hills dotted with traces of green, solid and neat. Even those unkempt buildings and homes that blurred by me looked trim in the dazzling light. To see the world again! To feel relief and thanks all in one deep breath; relief that you still have a job, a car, a home; relief that you have been able to preserve all that you have spent years achieving and holding; relief that the darkest hours have ended and that you can still pick up the pieces and go on. Like the man who has had a serious illness and has recovered to look again on life's offerings with new perspective. Out the expressways, past the mills, some of them our mills, strong and mighty against the white-blue sky. Out a quiet residential street past parading young mothers dressed in summertime briefs, square- shaped grey women, tottering old men and brawling children; the smells, sights and sounds of life that somehow go on, whatever. Out past bumpy railroad tracks to a plot of modest buildings covering the area of a football field—the Rug-Bilt Company,

---

58 Independence Day. On July 4, 1776, the American colonies declared themselves free and independent of Great Britain. Following ratification of the Treaty of Friendship, the national holiday was abolished on the grounds that "the Founding Fathers had only begun the process of true independence, which is the liberation of all people from the chains of the past, and it becomes our calling to complete the task. What better way to honor the Founders than to make the Fourth of July a day of work and dedication in the cause of peace and justice!" Quote from an editorial in the *New York Call*, an internationally read and respected daily newspaper.

manufacturers of truck bodies (priority H-6) and custom-built ambulances, hearses (priority U-5).

I parked in a cinder lot and entered a dingy but busy looking little building labeled "Office" in peeling gold letters. The reception area was covered with worn and splintered floor tile and over-furnished with three battered metal chairs and a bent desk, grandly designated: "Information." But no one was there. A window air conditioner of ancient vintage wheezed a stream of tepid air. From behind a half-open door came the sounds of bedlam.

"Easy. Here now, once again. Ah, Jennie, move that stuff. O.K., fellas, gently! Ow!"

The floor, none too substantial, shook to mysterious thumpings and scrapings.

"My foot!" the voice gasped.

"Sorry, boss."

I pushed my way in. The room was crammed with shelves of blueprints and scale models of trucks and cars, and several drafting boards were set haphazardly about. In the center stood five men, four in wilted white shirts and one in tired overalls. A trim young lady in a crisp print dress hovered nearby, holding a drafting stool as if she were not quite sure where to put it. In their midst stood a huge metal box, freshly painted white. All looked at me with mild surprise.

"Hello," the girl said. She set the stool down and moved with stately care to the door and ducked primly by me to assume her post at the information desk. "May I help you?" she inquired, as if she were a YWCA housemother.

"Mr. Krenski, please."

"Who shall I say is calling?" Her voice and manner were all pluck, a serious but not unfriendly little lady trying hard to hide her youth under the mantle of girl-Friday professionalism.

I gave her my card. She drew her breath in ever so slightly and smiled with unconcealed warmth.

"Oh, Mr. Little! We hadn't expected you quite so soon. Won't you be seated, and I am sure Mr. Krenski will be with you in just a moment!"

She popped back through the half-open door, only to emerge seconds later from yet another door that had been tightly closed. "This way."

Then I was in Mr. Krenski's office, marked in more faded gold: "President." It was small, stuffy, but had the lived-in look of a busy, somewhat harried man—one of those in the white shirts. He was of medium height but quite thin and not yet 40. His face was tired, and his mussed brown hair gave him the look of one who moved from one battlefield to another. But both his voice and dark eyes snapped with energy and optimism. He shook a chair loose from another pile of drawings and offered it to me with simple hospitality. Then he spun himself into a creaking seat behind his desk and sat for a moment to collect both his wind and his thoughts. He poked at his shoe.

"Thought for a moment my toe was busted, but it's all right, I guess." He settled himself with a bone-weary gesture. "Mr. Little, I'm in a jam. I hope you can help me."

I knew the problem. Mr. Krenski was broke. Being a small manufacturer his overhead was high in terms of the wage scale set by the BWP. Also, steel used to make truck bodies—particularly for light-duty commercial trucks—was difficult to get. In light of more urgent needs, steel for this purpose had been assigned a low priority, since there was an "adequate supply of light trucks to meet domestic demands for at least two years," as the directive stated. Further, his custom-built ambulances, hearses and special buses were out of the picture entirely "unless for highly specialized purposes authorized by government." Also, recent price reductions enforced by the BWP had thrown him permanently into red ink. Finally, larger companies were able to compete more effectively for what little business there might be for non-essential equipment such as this.

He went over the ground again, as he had done earlier in the week on the phone. He had even tried for a government loan but new rulings made him ineligible (non-essential). Commercial banks were out of the question and had been for some time.

"But I've found a way to keep going!" he announced, in a tone that spelled victory won after many sleepless nights of some kind of monumental effort.

I knew the answer to that one, too. He wanted to break into the container market, manufacturing big steel boxes to be used to ship all kinds of products—plastic materials, textiles, machine tools, parts, paper—almost anything. But there were already too many manufacturers of containers, and the BWP, even before the Treaty, had ruled that authorization of additional manufacturing facilities would "work a hardship upon existing concerns and so threaten free competition." And since the Treaty, more foreign manufacturers, particularly Russian and Czechoslovakian, had become involved in container production, using steel allocated from the United States as part of the program to help developing nations and boost the world economy. Also, containers are made to standard specifications, internationally authorized now, and Mr. Krenski was not planning to follow these specifications. I am up on this because I spent most of the day before researching all of the data, which is why each order or potential order for steel takes so long to process. He had created something new, and he had begged me to come to see him.

"I don't have to tell you, Mr. Little, that one of the big problems with containers is the deadhead problem. A fella in St. Louis makes a widget of some sort and ships it to a customer in Berlin or Omaha. That's fine, but what happens to the container afterwards? Well, sir, most probably it'll be shipped empty to some other place in the world to be reused. Right?"

"Right."

"Why, that's just like moving freight car empties. Containers consume a lot of shipping space on a flat car or truck bed. That's O.K. when they're full of something, but when they're empty," Mr. Krenski said in growing indignation, "why that's wasted space, and wasted space is expensive and that means wasted money. Right?"

"That's right."

Mr. Krenski brightened considerably. His frame shed its tired lines and took on a new posture of energy and hope. I heard a slight rustle along with a soft whisper from beyond the half-opened office door and caught a glimpse of a print dress hovering expectantly. The staff was waiting in the wings, hoping, too.

"Well, Mr. Little, that's why we're so excited! We've developed a fully collapsible container! Our design is so efficient that four— mind you, four—empty containers can be deadheaded in the same shipping space occupied by one standard empty. Why, imagine what this can mean to the whole materials-handling industry. Imagine!"

"Well…"

"Here. Let me show you." The lean man moved briskly out of his chair and urged me toward the door, while the staff outside scurried discreetly away, so that when we went again into the drafting room the three white shirts were serenely busy at their posts, and the young girl, Jennie, was helping the man in coveralls, whom I found to be the master mechanic, busy checking the white metal box.

"One man. Just one man is all it takes." Mr. Krenski explained. "Here, let Pete show you." And like a magician working a huge, magic box, the man in soiled blue deftly undid a series of locks, bolts and catches. The container was folded silently into a neat, square shape on the floor, occupying about one-fourth its former height.

"You can stack three more collapsed ones right on top of this one— notice the ribbing—and they can all be strapped together, and you have a package the size of the original container," the president of Rug-Bilt finished proudly. He and everyone else in the room faced me and waited. It was like a motion picture being stopped on the screen. The faces were fixed with half-smiles mixed with half-frowns; the looks of desperate hope—our-last-chance-we-gotta-make-him-see looks.

They made me see. For a moment I fought the reflex to grin in open admiration. They had worked hard and lovingly to create something new. But I knew the rules, regulations and directives. The chances of approval would be slim.

"How do you know it will work?" I asked, anticipating in my own mind the barrage of questions that would be fired at me, should I decide to carry this to the BWP, Commerce Department and the JCFLA.

"But... didn't you just see?" Mr. Krenski cried.

"Of course. What I mean is, have you market-tested the container?" I asked.

"No. Don't you see we can't, until we get enough steel to make... say a hundred prototypes. I'm sure we can test them. I know several companies that would be willing to use them. This is the only one we've got... and we had to filch enough material just to make this one."

"But if your container isn't proved in shipping tests, how can anyone be sure this product will make the grade? You must know the regulations. Steel allocations simply are not permitted when this kind of risk is involved. The rule is quite specific: Products must be thoroughly tested and proven for purposes intended before priorities can be assigned and materials can be allocated for sale."

Gloom settled on the room.

"Yeah, I know, I know," Mr. Krenski sighed, mostly to himself. "They also say that companies wishing to alter their product mix or enter into the manufacturing of a new product line must first submit their proposals in writing to the Bureau of Wages and Prices for evaluation and approval."

Now everyone looked tired, weariness born of losing a battle. I mentally sorted through my contacts at the BWP and decided there was one man, a little more friendly to me than the rest, who might at least give me a hearing.

"Let me try," I said, and the room burst into cheers. They crowded around like children seeking candy. Informality broke through the aura of renewed hope. I was introduced to young Jennie (Thank you! Thank you, Mr. Little. Golly, we sure had our fingers crossed!) and the other men, each of whom in his own way fumbled words of more thanks.

As I was leaving, Mr. Krenski called me aside. He made no pretense of hiding his fatigue now, as he spoke in soft, earnest tones. "Anything you can do... today, still. It's almost a matter of hours before I'll have to close down. Mr. Little, you're our last hope. I have 106 employees out there," he waved solemnly, "who simply won't have

260

jobs if I can't get steel sheets for my containers. I'm licked on trucks and the special autos. Unless I can switch to another product that shows some promise of success, I'm through. And so are they. One hundred and six people with families to keep. We've worked on this project for nearly two years… nights, weekends, every spare minute… me and my boys, here. Please, sir. Give us a chance."

The drive back downtown was not quite so enjoyable. I picked a neat little restaurant and stopped for some lunch. It was crowded with people, most of whom were government employees of one sort or another. I phoned the BWP and was lucky to catch Jim Thomas in time to make an early afternoon appointment. Then I found a small table for a single and ordered a hamburger, liberally laced with bread crumbs, but tasty. I had cold powdered milk and some sort of gelatin dessert.

At one-thirty I arrived at the BWP and found Jim at his desk deep in the middle of a huge open room jammed with other desks just like it. The place was crisscrossed with bustling women and men clerks on various errands of mercy while unhappy looking clients waited patiently in straight-backed chairs adjacent to each desk. Nancy works several floors above, but there is no legitimate reason to visit her, which is probably just as well, and I would not dare to risk pulling any strings through her.

Jim Thomas is a nice enough fellow. He is about 30 and athletically handsome, with even white teeth and a perpetual sun tan. Judging from the female climate around his desk, or wherever he happens to be, he must fare well with the ladies. He does as well on the golf course, from what he says. He is somewhat easier to deal with than most of the others. He tries harder to be genuinely helpful, even though he may not always have firsthand knowledge of some of the problems that face us in steel. He cannot be blamed for that. He was trained as a hospital administrator under the Government Career Scholarship Program, and actually spent most of his professional life with the hospitals. But last year he was transferred to BWP as a steel specialist. From time to time I have tried to help him become familiar with our business and he seems to appreciate this.

261

I outlined the Rug-Bilt problem as Jim sorted through the thick file he already had on his desk. His reaction was about what I expected. "This bird Krenski already has hounded us half to death. He's had one ... no, two conferences here and ... let me see... three more phone interviews and," he searched some more, "three letters of application."

"I know, Jim, but he really has an interesting idea."

"Oh, god!" he sighed. "Don't they all. We get some real strange ones in here. Not that some of them don't have some pretty good ideas, but they usually involve so damn much! I mean the paper work and revamping that would have to take place right across the board to accommodate them. Why, it would take an army of specialists and a ton of paper to get things going. Then, of course, there's no real way to know if they're going to succeed and right now ... with all the changes, really important stuff .. . readjusting the whole foreign trade stuff and all that... we've got more than we can do. You know I had to work past five twice this week?" "Yeah, I know," I sympathized. "Same with me."

"People just don't understand how complicated things are. They seem to think... you know... that allocations can be whipped up just like that. They have no idea of the work and decision making that must occur on every change." I nodded as he talked. "Just reprinting the directives, not counting putting out an availability tracer that goes back to the steel mills and cross-checking standing orders and... ah... what's that word?"

"Which one?" I asked.

"You know. The one that means how soon you deliver ..."

"You mean lead time?"

"Yeah. Lead time. Cross-checking lead time of everyone who needs steel sheets, too, you know. All that forecasting to see if we can fit it in." He shook his head as a doctor does when he gives up the patient.

"Well, look, could he get a temporary allocation... just for prototype work, I mean," I asked, trying to get back to the problem.

"Gosh. I don't know. That's decided at another level, in fact, even over my boss, and that's usually government stuff. Very little of the private sector, if you really want to know. Unless," he perked, "Krenski knows somebody in Washington or the W.O.N. If he could get someone like that.. ."

"I don't think so."

"Well, David, I don't know what to say. You're always pretty helpful with me. But, hope you don't mind my saying this, you've got a tiger by the tail. I don't know much about this container stuff, but you did say he wasn't planning to follow the international specs. You said he was going to make these things different?"

"So they collapse."

"Well, whatever. The thing is, it could screw up the whole… ah…"

"System."

"Yeah, right. The system. And I don't think our people would go for that. Not *now* with all this other work. And let's face it. That container thing hasn't been market-tested. Supposing no one liked it. Who do you think would hold the bag on that?" Jim asked. "Besides there are the regulations, not too clear always, but we gotta live with them."

There was a long pause. I glanced across the big room. Nearly every desk was like a small stage featuring two performers, acting out their own private play. A middle-aged woman in tears. A beetfaced man pounding a desk top. Occasionally there was a happy grin and a vigorous handshake. But mostly it was people versus the people, the government careerists who sat unruffled in their chairs with polite, sympathetic expressions on their otherwise immovable faces.

"Can't we at least try? The guy has 106 employees. He's dead broke."

"O.K. Let's give it a whirl. A temporary allocation. Good thing I know Mr. Fox's secretary," he grinned.

Jim flipped the phone receiver to his ear and dialed briskly.

"Hi, Emma?" His voice was soft with a touch of restrained eagerness to it. "Yeah, me…sure…busy…oh, lordy yes, I know. I've been meaning to…no, I haven't forgotten…of course, honey." Jim grinned even more broadly and winked at me. "Sure I meant it.. . next Saturday? Why… ah" his face clouded and he shook his head at me. "Why, I'd love to! Sure I mean it… eight o'clock… right… right…

listen, honey, I've got somebody here. Can you help me on a temporary allocation... sheets... wait a minute."

He cupped his hand over the receiver. "David. What kind? Carbon or what?"

"A-440, I think."

"A-440, hon ... yeah ... private sector... minute."

He turned to me. "How about just plain old carbon."

"Won't work."

"Nope ... he doesn't have any friends in Washington. Strictly private... minute."

He cupped his hand again. "Helluva pile up. Fox is in Europe for two more weeks. He's got better than a hundred high-strength steel applications to review, nearly all government, which takes precedence. Doesn't look so good."

"Try, will you?"

"Hello, Emma ... look, lover, for me. Just slip it in the stack ... well at least the second stack... yeah, baby," he purred. "So turn the date stamp back! Sure. Do it all the time. You will! Love you. Minute."

He laid the phone aside and smiled, enormously pleased. "She'll fix it so Fox gets the application, and he'll probably approve it. He never looks at them too closely. They're screened ahead of time by the likes of me."

Contacts are beginning to pay off, I thought, delighted that I would have good news for energetic Mr. Krenski.

"I'll give you the forms... he'll need new ones... and you have him fill them in. And get them right back."

"How soon can he get the approval? I'll start things rolling at the mill."

"Can't be sure, of course," Jim said, "but probably eight weeks or so."

"Eight weeks!" I cried.

"Well, sure. Not soon enough?"

I explained once again, and Jim scooped up the phone.

"Emma, doll. How about maybe the first stack ... I know, baby, but this is real important to me," his voice dipped in a soft coo. "For me,

264

honey. Ah! That's my little girl… sure, honey, eight o'clock… this Saturday. Right. Bye-bye."

Jim sat back and shook his head again. "Boy, the price you have to pay." He grinned wryly. "Cost me a date … to go to her girl friend's party. Wouldn't be so bad, except she's a real witch. She has a face not even her mother could love. But it's done. Four weeks. How do you like that! Don't ever say that old Jimmy Thomas doesn't deliver for his friends."

There was no point in telling him that this would be too late, for he had honestly tried. It was a grim reminder that I would have to upgrade my contacts to include Fox, for example. With appropriate thanks, I returned to the office and phoned Mr. Krenski.

"Four weeks!" he cried. "I'll be out of business in a week!"

"I know but, believe me, I did everything I could. The BWP man is in Europe and there's no way around him."

The pause on the other end of the line was long and eloquent in its plea.

"Mr. Krenski," I said finally and firmly. "There is no other way. Four weeks."

"I know … I know you did you best, Mr. Little."

For a moment the past came at me again.

"Yes, I did my… my best."

"Forget it. Good-bye, Mr. Little. Forget the whole thing."

There was a soft click before I could say any more.

So that was my Fourth of July. One cannot be bothered by these things. Some of us, perhaps, are more fortunate. I have much to be grateful for, more than I have realized. I have a job, still, and a nice home.

I am thankful I am not in Mr. Krenski's shoes.

2

Saturday Nancy and I went to a cocktail party. It was a very important party for me, because it put me permanently back among the living. For the party was hosted by Larry and Mary Best. It was the first time we had seen them, socially speaking, since that March Sunday now so long ago when Mary and I first became fully aware of each other. Mary had telephoned Nancy to invite us. I had answered the phone. It was a shock to hear her voice again, and for a moment I was not sure how it would go. But she was just like the old Mary, brightly asking to speak with Nancy. I paced anxiously as they talked. Nancy was plainly delighted and chattered with obvious good humor. I could sit down with relative ease, once I found that only a party invitation was involved. It could have been other things. It was to be a garden party. The Best's yard is small but neatly screened in back by tall shrubs and a weathered fence to make it into a courtyard of sorts which, in times past, has been kept colorful by a forest of bright flowers, a sparkling bird bath fountain and uneven patio stones. They were having a few friends in which, as Nancy happily explained, meant the works. "You can bet half of Pittsburgh's finest will be there. Oh dear! What shall I wear?"

I was nervous about the whole idea. How would she be? Soulful or perhaps cold and embittered? And Larry. What did he know? Damn, I thought, all I need now is a screw-up! Just when things were beginning to go my way.

As it turned out, there was nothing to worry about. Mary greeted us at the door, looking cool and pert in a gay print dress. Her grey-green eyes were bright with pixie cheer. She looked at me only fleetingly without a flicker of anything and devoted her attention to Nancy whom she greeted warmly. She led us through the house to the garden with an impersonal kind of gaiety and sought Larry, who detached himself from a mixed group that reeked of affluence and intellect to greet us.

"Ah! You are late, m'dears." Larry was all smiles and neat in an open-collared, bright white shirt, sharply creased blue walking shorts and matching knee socks. His pipe was carelessly clenched in his teeth, and he held a frosty glass of gin and tonic cocked with equal carelessness—the image of coolness in sharp contrast to a hot, sticky day. The eternal Larry, master even of the weather. "Say now, David, you do look splendid! Don't you think, m'dear?" he chirped, turning

266

to Mary. "Must have had the same bug you got. Knocked her out for a week almost."

"But my bug wasn't as bad as what must have hit poor David," Mary replied. She looked at me with a half-smile hovering around her eyes which, finally, met mine. They said nothing, but I looked away anyhow. "You do look well, David. It is good you could be here. You deserve it. For these are Pittsburgh's finest," she gestured to the filled garden. And then she excused herself and moved quickly into the casual ebbing and swaying group of perhaps 40 men and women; a busy hostess seeing after her guests with youthful energy. She had made it easy for me, and for a moment I felt pangs of regret. Then it occurred to me that perhaps she, too, had managed to forget.

The waiter arrived with cold, soothing drinks. After two quick ones I felt at ease. It had been just a year ago that nuclear war had been threatened, and all of us had begun the six-month vigil to await our doom. Only doom had not come, after all. Here I was today, alive and well. Larry was introducing us about, and Nancy and I were moving with calculated care from one knot of persons to another, learning names, memorizing faces and listening to the latest commentaries on "the situation."

Perhaps it was just as well Mary had forgotten.

It was a group well worth remembering. For these were the survivors of the new order of things. None had been touched by the hearings, save a few who, like myself, had testified against some poor soul. All, like me, were intact. All, like me, were still gainfully employed and secure in the midst of a changing world. We, all of us, had something very much in common then. Contacts! Most were from the University. Two deans, four assistant deans and three professors, all with wives. There were five refreshingly smooth and witty lawyers, three of them right out of the Blue Book, and two distinguished medical doctors, also listed in the ranks of Pittsburgh society. One congressman and two wealthy heirs. All were young, by my standards these days, between 30 and 50. All had sparkling wives dressed in cool and, occasionally, quite revealing dresses. Nowhere was there gloom or despair—only gaiety laced with traces of intellect as some

267

one or another of them made an observation or revealed a bit of inside information about any number of situations.

There was plenty to talk about.

The two main streams of interest centered on the World Court and the growing influence of the Communist Party here. Because of the Biggerman Case and some forty-odd others, it has become necessary to establish World Court districts across the country to handle an increasing number of cases. This has caused some considerable excitement. The addition of a whole new legal system has created a furor of activity here in the city, since a new World Court building is being constructed near Dome Center. There will be four judges to start, appointed, I think, by the World Order of Nations. One fellow is from India. Another, I think, from England. One is from Poland and one from either Cuba or Venezuela. They arrive in August. They will use the Hotel Royal ballroom for temporary court rooms.

But by far the most interesting is that the Communist Party is fast becoming a major force, having won universal acceptance of its right to function. It had to happen, of course. As the papers have been pointing out, how can world peace be pursued if Americans continue to be hostile toward a philosophy of government practiced by the very nation we signed a peace treaty with? We are supposed to be "world leaders in tolerance." How then can "we, the pace-setters for democracy, set an inspiring example before the peoples of the world if we continue to discriminate against those who practice democracy in a different way?" an editorial had asked. "Let us remember that there are many similarities between the ideals of Communism and our traditions of liberty," a TV commentator had intoned the other night. "The United States cannot allow the bigotry of hostility to continue any longer. We must prove our faith in the Treaty of Friendship by allowing the free and open exchange of ideas right here at home before we can expect to be heard anywhere else. Narrow-minded extremists who rigidly tout but one way of life—their way—can no longer be tolerated. An unfettered Communist Party will no longer feel the need ever to advocate distasteful violence. Indeed, it has said violence is a thing of the past. Let us have open competition between

268

these two ideas of government!" Maybe things have changed for the better all the way round.[59]

A third but much less exciting topic was the growing effort to nationalize the steel, aluminum, transportation, oil and power industries. There has been some talk of this for years. Now, however, a bill is in the works and some expect passage before next fall.

I should mention the elections, too. The parties are going through the motions of holding conventions in a few weeks to pick presidential candidates. But that fellow in the White House has it for certain.

"He can't miss," a distinguished looking man in a sharp crewcut was saying to a couple of well-groomed women, as Larry ushered Nancy and me into the group. He was none other than Dean Butterfield, Larry's immediate superior. The two women belonged to Dr. Crossingham and James Larson Howe, III. "With Congress finally on the ball with the Reorganization Act, we'll be able to retain the leadership we must, I say, simply must have!"

"You don't think they'll be able to put anyone decent up against him?" Mrs. Howe III asked. There was just a trace of concern. Actually, it was more curiosity than concern.

"Dear lady," the Dean swooshed, "I am charmed by your party loyalty in searching for a worthy candidate to run against the President, and I admire you for it… even though I don't always share your views. But surely, who would there be who would have the experience in world affairs, especially treaty affairs? After all, the President negotiated the Treaty. We need him now more than ever to carry out the Treaty. Wouldn't you say so, Mr…. Biddle?"

"That's Little. David Little."

"Of course, Mr. *Little!*" the Dean cooed. "You were rather prominent at the hearings… wasn't it on Avery Brown?"

"That's right. I had a little to do with his … retirement."

---

59 By this time the Communists the world over had mounted a massive propaganda campaign once again aimed at reassuring the world of their "peaceful intentions." Only now, because of the political and nuclear military power international Communism then exerted in world affairs, even the most creditable thought leaders in the United States and elsewhere became vocal adherents to these proclamations of "peaceful change."

The Dean responded beautifully, slightly embarrassed. "Little. Ah, yes. Forgive me for mispronouncing your name. Heh, heh."

"It's all right. But you are quite right, Dean Butterfield." I emphasized his name with extra clarity. "The President should run again. He's the only man who can handle the rather sizable period of adjustment ahead."

The good Dean beamed. "Yes. Just as I was telling the ladies. Yes." He paused to pick some drinks from a floating tray which he passed all around. "I suppose you're still working closely with the JCFLA. Any more hearings lined up?" There was a trace of anxiousness in his voice.

"Oh," I lied with studied calm. "We're in a bit of a lull. Been days since I heard from Leon... Leon Tidings. I work through him. But we'll be getting the call one of these days. Can't let down, you know. We're all needed."

"Yes, of course. Well. Well."

It was a pleasure to visit, to talk, to listen. A little half-truth here and just a bit of a fib there. That is all it takes. People build their own image of the people they meet. The Dean, and through him the ladies, had created an image of me as an unknown quantity of some kind of power and influence. I imagine they saw me as being in close contact with the officialdom of world affairs. It was easy to go along, in fact, to help them along.

"Didn't you feel rather sorry for Mr. Brown?" the wife of Dr. Crossingham asked. She was a small thing, and for a second she reminded me of Mary.

"Duty can never know sorrow, ma'am. The burden of making command decisions can be a heavy one. True, I had great personal friendship for Avery. (I did stretch that a little.) Still the truth had to be told." How easy it is to speak when one puts his mind to it. One can say anything and, if one is careful, be believed.

And so we chatted.

"You must come see me," the Dean said.

I said I would be delighted, and the good Dean beamed full upon me, a happy and satisfied man.

270

Contacts. Must have contacts. Add Dean Butterfield.

A slight lift of the body, involving a deft half-turn, accompanied by a broad, warm smile brimming with understanding and good will. Follow this with a feigned expression of surprise at seeing an old friend that one simply must say hello to. This is how to extract yourself from one group and inject yourself into another. But first you scout the scene out of the corner of your eye. Pick the most promising new group closest at hand. Then make your move. Nancy and I did, not too awkwardly, bidding farewell to the Dean and ladies at his side.

Under the cool shade of a locust tree stood an immaculate gentleman, not yet 40, with the stamp of Harvard unmistakably on him, even down to the perfectly round shell-frame glasses he wore. His straw-colored hair was combed flat and uninterestingly and his summer coat was flawlessly cut of a cool-looking fabric. He could be nothing but a lawyer. He was talking with quiet sincerity to a more rumpled-looking person wearing a heavier-than-air coat, obviously selected for year-round sportswear. The latter was a bit older and looked to be the scholar. Two passing-fair women stood with them but not listening too intently. Their wives, of course. We joined them in the midst of some grave talk about Joseph Vendurella.

I should note that Joe Vendurella—who put up such a whirlwind fight of it at the hearings—was shot dead a week later by the W.O.N. Peace Force. Official published reports gave no details other than that he was shot while resisting arrest. But the rumor pretty generally circulated was that, following the hearings, where he had been pronounced guilty of wrongdoing, he was served with a summons to face formal charges before the World Court for Treaty violations. The same was true for Henry C. Biggerman, the labor leader. These, it turned out, were the only two out of the original forty-four citizens tried, who were found guilty and assigned to the World Court. With the exception of Dr. Rodgers, the remaining forty-one ultimately submitted letters confessing their guilt to charges lodged against them. Each of these offered to resign from his professional and community responsibilities in return for clemency, which was granted. Virtually every major area of city life was affected by these en-masse resignations, ranging from businessmen like Avery Brown, who left the company, and assorted bankers, to Scout leaders, ministers, teachers and women in civic life. Wholesale promotions and appointments resulted, with people most of us never heard of assuming broad new positions of leadership in finance, steel, aluminum, oil, youth, civic and church groups. Only Joe Vendurella and Henry Biggerman held out, and when Joe saw them coming with a summons, apparently he swung hard and often at the blue uniforms. When he saw he could not lick them he ran but was gunned down before he could reach the sidewalk. Even when hit again and again he would not quit. It took four slugs in the back to bring him down. His wife and five children saw him die, as did most of the neighborhood.

With Biggerman it was different. He accepted the summons, vowing to fight, "to carry the torch of free labor to the doorstep of the world." His trial at Geneva, Switzerland, attracted a great amount of attention. I did not follow the news accounts particularly, so I have no details, other than that he was found guilty as charged and was sentenced to life imprisonment, somewhere in Poland.[60]

"Vendurella deserved it," Round Glasses was saying. "To flout the law when he had been given every chance..."

"But violence, Lester, is not our creed," the other man replied. The two wives were making a valiant attempt to appear interested. None of the four had as yet acknowledged us, and we had no desire to stop the flow. So we listened.

"What choice had they? The man obviously was fleeing to the hills. I don't like violence either. World order through law. My creed for years..."

"True. True. But to shoot a man in front of his family .. ."

"Or let him escape to god knows what kind of activity that goes on up there. Andy, you couldn't want that, now! How could you? More murder and plunder. We must take every precaution. Look at

---

60 Most World Order of Nations prison camps were in eastern European countries, the Soviet Union, China and Africa. Prisoners were sentenced usually to hard labour and were used in various kinds of mines and massive construction work, such as roads and dams.

Biggerman. Of course, he's not one of those crazy ethnics who's half-cracked to begin with. I knew Henry, you know. Tough fella, but at least he didn't want to run to the hills."

"Only because he thought he could win," the rumpled man said. "God, I hated his guts. I handled an arbitration matter for him. I was the referee and really threw him a bone. So what does he do? Gets on television and kicks the hell out of me!"

The man in round glasses laughed pleasantly enough. "Andrew, you just don't understand the beauty of power politics."

They chose to notice us then, for we smiled, too—an unavoidable proclamation that we were already party to the conversation. Introductions could not longer be postponed.

"I'm Lester Miller." The man in round glasses offered a brisk, British handshake and proceeded to present Andy Murphy and their respective wives. In due course, we learned that Miller was a lawyer and Murphy taught economics at William Penn University.

"Little. Of course! Did a fine job at the hearings. Really had Brown's number." Lester said.

"Indeed, he did! A very smooth and I must say forceful presentation," Andy added. The two women murmured soft, halfhearted approval, but it was enough to relax Nancy, who had begun to fidget, into the spirit of togetherness.

For a while we followed the same conversation route we had taken before. My good friend Leon…getting his wind…doubtless back in harness soon….Heh heh. Yes. Of course. Then a pause to lift glasses from another floating tray. Snacks came by, too. Wedges of cheese and succulent little sausages. I wanted to take a dozen of each and would have, except for Nancy's nudge. Refreshed, we plunged on to more word games.

"How will the World Court affect your operations, David?" Lester was referring to his image of me, that of an official, functioning under the wing of the JCFLA. Selling steel was of little concern, since I had succeeded in conveying the impression that my steel job was a cover for my real operations.

I took a moment to answer, deliberately pausing to sip my drink. I have seen Larry do this many times with excellent effect. They all waited. So I took another sip.

"Well, you're a lawyer, Lester, and I'm sure you're better qualified to answer that... but from where we sit, it's certainly going to help having a district here. Geneva is simply too impractical..."

"Oh? Were you perhaps to Geneva on the Biggerman case?"

"No-o-o. Brown was my man. Besides, I couldn't contribute very much..."

"Sure you couldn't!" Lester grinned. "You're downtown, aren't you?"

"My offices... office, that is ... is there."

"Why don't we have lunch sometime..."

"I would be delighted."

Contacts! Must have contacts. Add Lester Miller. Forget Andy Murphy. Just a professor.

Time to move, like over there.

It was a large group, eight or so, gathered around a weathered redwood patio table which was home base for some cheese dip and crackers. The center of attention was none other than Congressman Johns, now completing his second term in the House. Lean, dark, young, sincere and hungry-looking, he was widely known as the "Poor Man's Representative." During his campaigns much was made of the fact that he rose from the slums to overcome his poverty—by what means has never been fully recorded. Two other men were engaged with him in rather far-ranging animated conversation. We soon found they were Thomas Lambeck, the dashing and energetic heir to the Lambeck fortune (early steel) and a Doctor Post, a physician of some sort of social standing. The balance of the group, which included three smartly dressed women, stood as rapt spectators. I did not get their names. But everyone got mine and that was fine.

"At the hearings, did I hear you say?" the Congressman inquired with more than casual interest. His triangular face narrowed still more in concentration. "Sorry I missed that. I understand from the

274

Secretary of Commerce that it was well handled. And wasn't the Governor there?"

"Yes, and as a matter of fact, I worked with both the secretary and the Governor... the Brown case," I replied, feeling a tingle.

"Ah, yes. Now I place you." Lambeck said. "I knew Brown socially... not now, of course... and I always felt that he could have done a great deal more for humanity, instead of scheming all the time how to make more money. I don't think he had a bit of social conscience. It wasn't very often that I ever heard him apologize... well, for anything..."

"Arrogant type," the doctor said. He was nearing 50 and well-fed, but he had a thoroughly professional look.

"No real humility. No real feel for his obligations toward the less fortunate. We're well rid of him," the young heir said.

"The rich bastards are all alike," the Congressman growled, and then grinned quickly. "Except you, Tom." And he gestured magnanimously to Lambeck. "Not this fella. He's supported every welfare measure I've ever put up... even when he knew it would cost him. Yes sir. Here's a real humble, dedicated man."

Lambeck smiled apologetically. His face began to flush, as if he had been caught peeking down a woman's dress front, which would have been easy to do. "Least a guy can do to help compensate for... well... the unfairness of it all," he finished indignantly. "You can always count on me, Congressman."

"And don't think I won't... election coming up, you know!" he roared. And the group roared back, delighted with this good-natured exhibition of sportsmanship and mutual accord between classes.

The conversations took many twists, focusing finally on the "most dramatic development in our generation," as the papers had said, "the emerging role of the Communist Party."

"America has had her great moments in the pursuit of true freedom and justice. And the House of Representatives can take great pride in helping in these things. But, truly, our finest hour came when we unshackled the last vestige of discrimination against the beliefs of men." The Congressman had embarked upon a speech, a natural thing for

275

one used to making speeches. "I wasn't there. ... I hadn't been discovered by my constituents yet ... but the moment was magnificent when the law was changed to bring full political emancipation to our nation by freeing Communism to compete openly with our traditions. And the debate! An ugly handful of self-seeking opportunists would have killed the whole thing... would have killed... mind you... the only sensible step that the Congress could have taken and still preserve true freedom. But we beat them! You may have read all of the accounts when it happened..."

"Indeed."

"Excellent, too."

"Harmony," the Congressman wound on, "the beauty of harmony. Think. The two greatest powers on earth... now united in a spirit of mutual trust ... a mutual respect for the other fellow's point of view. This...*this* is the true meaning of tolerance. The whole world has learned the United States *means* what it says."

Drinks floated by. I had to go to the bathroom but did not dare leave. To eavesdrop on the fringes of *this* conversation was worth minor discomfort.

"A magnificent record. Congress has a right to be proud," the doctor said.

"Oh, we've had good sessions in other areas, too, particularly this one I'm in."

"And how." Lambeck stated. "Most effective Congress we've ever had."

"I think so," the Congressman replied judiciously. "Yes... yes. When you think that in this session alone we've moved the Reorganization Bill, which of course will finally curtail some of the ineptness of the Senate and strengthen the Executive... and this is a must if we are to get this country moving on reforms."

"That tax bill was a little rough, though," the doctor mused.

"Come now, Doctor! So your taxes will go up a little. So right now in committee is a bill to nationalize, finally, *everything* in medicine... and the fee breaks we're giving doctors..."

276

"Think it will pass? I heard they might knock the fees down and put a restriction on the number of patients we can have."

"That's only some of the wilder liberals squawking," the Congressman soothed. "We'll keep 'em in line. May have to do a little sham compromising...but you'll have it pretty good."

"Nationalization doesn't disturb you, then?" I asked, curious to know how Dr. Post would respond.

"Socialization... nationalization... whatever you want to call it... bound to come," the doctor shrugged. "Why not face it. Besides," he added with a glint of frank satisfaction, "I've always had it pretty good, and I'm making more money now than I've ever made in my life. Most of that green stuff already comes from government programs. Why not all of it?"

Maybe, Doctor. Just maybe. The good doctor, I decided, was too narrow in his scope of influence to be much of a contact. But the Congressman and boyish, trusting Mr. Lambeck, an entirely different matter. I pressed into the conversation.

"How does it look with steel?"

"Pretty good," the Congressman replied. "You're steel, didn't you say? Well, the bill is being drawn right now. Be several months before it's out of committee. But most people are reconciled that nationalization is the only way to get a very sick steel industry back on its feet. Doing well now with the aid programs, but the equipment is shot, and the owners just don't have enough to buy what's needed."

"Space," someone said. "Is that new station ever going to get off the ground?"

The Congressman narrowed his face and gulped his drink thirstily. The sun had slipped well below the trees, but it was still hot. "Well, that last failure . . ,"[61]

---

61 Even during this period of unrest, the space exploration program continued. The accent was on space posts "to keep the peace." But the Soviet Union had developed more know-how on space weapons than the United States because of a continuing crash research program which for many years had been kept secret. At this time elements of United States technology had begun to stagnate. There is ample documentation that either carelessness or sabotage was responsible for more than a dozen major failures, including one massive explosion that

277

"The fourth in a row..."

"Well, yes. Only the second one wasn't really a failure. The station just didn't go into proper orbit. We learned a lot, you see..."

"But will the Soviets pay their share, and can they really get a big thing like that off the ground?"

"Sure. Next February at the latest."

The bathroom was not going to wait much longer. I had not yet scored any points. So I hauled out the JCFLA again and was successful in conveying the impression that the Secretary of Commerce, the Governor and I would doubtless be collaborating on yet another assignment.

Both the Congressman and Dr. Post invited me to play golf. Post is not worth it.

And young Mr. Lambeck invited me to call him for lunch some time.

Then—mercifully—the bathroom.

We met unexpectedly in the lower hall by the stairs. As sometimes happens in crowded places, there was a momentary lull with complete silence, insulated by the distant babble that came from the garden. She was hurrying toward me, head bent in solemn concentration, bearing several crisp-looking guest towels obviously meant for the powder room. In this unguarded moment Mary Best had lost her youthful, tomboyish energy. She looked frail, as if a sharp blow might shatter her into a thousand pieces, and her face was drawn with weariness. Her spirit that had turned so many admiring heads in the garden that afternoon had abandoned her, leaving a vacuum— absolutely nothing to convey her inner thoughts. She moved as an overtired automaton might. Though I must have surprised her, she gave no sign of being startled. We both stopped within a foot of each other, and wherever her thoughts had taken her, it took several seconds before she gave me any sign that they had brought her back. It was the halfhearted beginning of a smile. The words of Dr. Rodgers roared in my ears, "She will die unless she is free!"

"Are you ... all right?" I asked.

---

took over a hundred lives, around the time Mr. Little writes.

"Of course." She continued to look at me. Her smile hung on as if she had summoned every last bit of will to keep it there.

"Mary... I..."

"Tried."

"Yes. Oh, yes!"

"I know," she replied gently. She placed her hand lightly on my arm. And for a moment I knew again her warmth. It reminded me of the life in her and that life particularly suited her and that some day her life would end and there would be no more warmth in her. I thought of how it would be if she were dead. No more dreams. No more talking horses. A world lost forever. A world bound up in her tiny body. Mary's world born again in the warmth of her finger tips. Let nothing happen to her. Larry and I will see that nothing does. She does not understand that our way is the only way. We can win over them if we're smart, and Mary will be safe. She can write again— have her world back, if she just trusts our way. Those were the words I wanted to speak but, of course, did not.

"Some day, you will understand," I said.

"You think you can lick them this way, don't you? You really believe it!" She spoke with soft emphasis, without bitterness or ridicule.

"Yes."

"Have you ever seen cattle slaughtered?" she asked, as if evading my answer.

"No. Why?"

"It is of no importance."

"Can you forgive me?" I asked. The recently healed wounds were beginning to crack a little.

"It was I who led you on. Can you forgive me?" It was a completely honest question.

"No. No. It was I..."

"Hush, David!" And she placed her forefinger at my lips as a mother soothes her young.

"But I'm worried about you!"

"Sh-h-h. People will hear. Don't worry about me." She managed a bright smile. "You must forget all about me, now. You must promise. Don't you see I am truly all right. The trees have said so."

"The... trees?" I asked.

"Yes. At night when it's quiet and there is a breeze, the trees talk to me." The tired lines of her face softened and her grey-green eyes became far away again. "They have promised to care for me. They have promised me... all sorts of wonderful things. But I must be patient. They have said that, too. I must wait until they are ready. I should have known all along that it would be the trees... and nothing else. So, please, you would only sadden me by worrying ... or remembering." And then she was gone, up the stairs and out of sight.

In that instant I thought perhaps Mary's mind had begun to slip. But when Nancy and I saw her again ten minutes later to say goodbye, she was her sparkling self. I will never fully understand Mary —her closeness—her never-ending closeness to nature. As it was when I first saw her so many years ago, I had the feeling that she belonged again to someone—or something—else; that she was already taken by another who was neither Larry nor me.

"Good-bye, good people. Come again... and soon!" she cried.

"Keep up with the good work, m'boy," Larry echoed.

Both stood framed in the white doorway. The tall, lanky man with arm draped carelessly over the boyish shoulders of a trim little girl who looked like someone's teenage sister.

On the way home the sun cast long wonderland shadows from the edge of the horizon. I drove absently, my mind contemplating a host of random thoughts. The sweat-smudged, sunburned faces of a bobbing file of Boy Scouts trudging doggedly along the roadway, homeward bound. Here and there bright dots of people moving about on a hillside backyard. Bicycles and motor scooters wheezing slowly upgrade only to catch up with us on the downgrade. A fine Saturday afternoon—all things considered.

I turned to look at Nancy. She was pretty in the late glow. The sun on her face gave it a golden brightness. She had been looking at me, I think, for some time. It was a kind look.

"You know, David. The way you handled yourself... I'm proud of you." There was a slight catch in her voice, as if some great victory had been won.

And then she settled back in the seat—a woman content with things as they are—to let the cooling wind blow full upon her.

3

Another good week with remarkably few annoyances. Under more normal circumstances I would have begun my vacation, but I canceled it voluntarily. With so much to do these days, nearly everyone followed the suggestion of the President of the United States that we all continue at our jobs to get everything moving again. Even the brass at the top of the heap are doing their "fair share to make all of our resources count for the fullest," as the TV commentator said the other evening. Any number of business meetings are being held with all kinds of government and W.O.N. officials to iron out new programs for production and employment. I am amused because most briefing conferences are held at the big resorts in Wisconsin, Michigan and, well, all the big places. Still, as an editorial said, they have to meet someplace, and "the use of resorts is a splendid example of conducting business while at the same time keeping the resort industry economically sound."

They say rank has its privileges. Some day I am going to have rank. But in the meantime, I am broke, and I will have to tap my savings to get caught up a little. World Relief nicked me the other day for a pledge of ten dollars per week for the next year. Tax increases have not helped either, and of course food and other necessities become more expensive every time we go to the store. I am also being pressured to sign up for more Peace Bonds (Do Your Share By Sharing).[62] So, we could not have gone any place anyway. When the President

---

62 In addition to punitive taxation, one other highly successful method of confiscating private wealth was to force employees to buy World Order of Nations Peace Bonds. At this point employees were expected to apply fifteen percent of their income to the purchase of bonds which could not be redeemed for cash until maturity in fifteen, thirty and fifty years, depending on the type.

issued this Vacation Gift Plan, I was the first one in the office to renounce time off as a "perfectly good waste of my talents."

The boss was impressed, because he had anticipated some resistance to the idea, but after me everyone came around. It earned me a personal note of praise from the Personnel Department, copy to the BWP. Not too bad, considering. By scheduling my customer adjustment calls in the afternoon I am able to get home earlier than otherwise. Ideal for hot days. And ideal, too, for another reason. I am coming to know my family again. I look at my children as they busy themselves with a whole new summer program and give thanks for their happiness.

Monday, for example, was Annie's birthday. Seven years old! She is my favorite. David and Peggy seem remote and at times ill-tempered with me. But one must expect this of teenagers. Annie is different. She is always happy to see me, and while I was sick she was ever so careful about playing too loudly. Her hair is still long, and it is golden in the summer sun. Her eyes are very blue and innocent. She is a generous little bit, so much so that sometimes other children take advantage of her. She takes everything seriously and tries hard to please. Yet, she is far from somber. She has perpetual good nature and almost always is in high spirits. She has a way of looking at you as if you are the most important person in the world, and maybe that is why she is special to me. Or maybe it is because her home is still number one with her. No slumber parties or movies or other outings to take her away, yet.

So her birthday was a big event for me. I knew she dreamed of owning her own roller skates, the real ones with ball bearing wheels, not the plastic kind that simply do not work well. And I found them.

Shopping for quality toys can be more tiring than trying to find foodstuffs or clothing. The toy departments in the big stores, of course, did not have them, or the hardware stores. It was a pawn shop in McKeesport! I was on a customer call (another closing out) and I walked right by the place before I realized they were right there in the window. The ankle straps were rotted, but the rest of the skates were in perfect working order, the wheels showing remarkably little

282

wear. All that was needed were new straps and a little rust remov-
er, some of which I still had at home. I bought the skates on the spot
for only twelve dollars.

Getting the straps proved a little more difficult. I wanted real
leather and went to two shoe repair shops before I got wise. No one
would chop up good leather for a pair of lousy straps. So I went to a
men's store and bought a belt, boy's size. That was another fifteen dollars, but it was worth it. I talked the shoe shop into cutting the belt
into straps. I gave them the rest of the belt in exchange for the labor
and two dollars. It was a nice feeling—to be doing something special for a little girl who had no notion of the surprise in store for her.

I was not disappointed. How she loved them! She hugged them
as a mother does her newborn. She has taken them to bed with her
every night since.

Nancy found extra sugar—how, I do not even want to know—and
she baked a magnificent chocolate cake. I do not want to know where
she found the chocolate either. No stinting on the ingredients. We ate
the whole thing in one sitting. To watch Annie blow the candles out;
to see her clutch the skates; to see her eyes alive with overwhelming
delight; to hear her say, "Daddy, I love you so!" To have her sticky kiss,
while her frosting-covered fingers trace abstract patterns across my
shirt front; to hear her coo softly from her bed, "God bless you, and
sweet dreams!" and then ask for another drink of water. These are
the rich moments that a man can reflect upon over and over again.

But I imply unfairness to the other two. This is not so. On Tuesday
I made it my special business to help David review and memorize his
new Boy Scout Manual. As with fourteen-year-olds, he had put it off
again and again, until he brought home a written notice from his new
scoutmaster, a Mr. Simmons, or someone, who has replaced old man
Thomas as an aftermath of the hearings. I arrived home early. David
was not back from Scouts yet. They meet three afternoons a week. It
is part of a crash program to update the whole Scout movement to be
more consistent with current happenings. I have been an assistant
scoutmaster, but because of the hearings and so on, I have not been
asked to any meetings. I am sure this is just out of consideration for

me and nothing else. There are some changes being made that I am not entirely happy with. The merit badge system has been greatly revised, with the ruling that each Scout must be reexamined on his last Scout rank. David, for example, is a Star. In order to requalify he must re-do certain of the revised merit badges. World Citizenship is completely new. Another one is Brotherhood, plus one in Economics. In all, David has seven exams to take before Labor Day. It is a tough schedule, but they are insistent that all boys join the Scouts and that the boys do as their elders—sacrifice part of their vacation time to improve themselves. But I know better than to complain.

So I was home in time enough to relax with a shower. I let the water run, ice cold, just for the hell of it, until Nancy banged on the door for me to stop. We have a three-minute honor system, clocked by an old egg timer, that helps keep water waste down. Nancy complained that I went better than six minutes, which I doubt. It put us in a bit of a bad mood, Nancy saying, well, *she* would skip her shower, and me saying expense and shortage be damned. We settled over some gin on ice, and I said I ought to take a shower in that, it's cheaper. She surprised me by laughing. Then David came in the drive on his bicycle, too fast of course, and he banged into the rear of the car. His brakes are none too good. He hurt his wrist, which took more cold water. The bicycle tire, naturally, went flat, and I got dirty all over again fixing *that*. Then Peggy and Annie bounced in from separate directions— Peggy mad at a new boy friend and Annie in tears because someone had stepped on her new plastic ball, another birthday gift. She was not skating just then because of ankle blisters from the straps. Dinner was late but good. There are plenty of fresh vegetables if you know where to look, and Nancy had found some new sweet com, an ear apiece, and some tomatoes. She also had ground beef patties and cold potato salad.

After dinner there was more play until darkness, except for David. We went to work on Scouting. It's nice to be with your son, the perpetuator of your name and perhaps your image. We sat on the back patio in the shade of early evening and studied the new manual; reading a little, discussing a point, practicing a sign; two menfolk, each momentarily respecting the presence of the other, seated on an island of calm in the center of a sea of sounds created by children and adults at play and in leisure work up and down the neighborhood. The whirr of a lawn mower. The crack of a bat. Alle alle in come free! The ideal environment for a man to contemplate his son. A full face, more oval than mine, set in heavy concentration. Brown eyes betraying restless energy, zeroed in on a printed page. Full lips the girls, if not now, one day would think sensual, shaping words with halting care. Restless hands that would rather be wrapped around bicycle handlebars. Feet. My lord, his feet! If they get any bigger, no amount of money will keep them shod. He must be ten pounds overweight and not at all neat. Yet here he is, a person complete in every detail. He thinks, or tries to. He feels things, like the rest of us. He must have problems that I do not even suspect. I wonder how he is away from home. Sweet or brash? Does he show off in front of girls and tell dirty jokes? How does he really do in school? Is there a Miss Lee, and bullies in bright yellow sweaters? Does he lie awake at night and wonder? Is he a Harry type, like the Harry Little who is dead? Or is he my type? Beneath that soiled shirt beats a heart that pumps blood, my blood, all the way through him. Under that mass of messy brown hair—I ought to clip it tonight, too—there is a brain of some sort that records his world, probably at the expense of my world. All of this is wired together with a soul which, if we are to believe, makes him a special creation of God. He is a mystery and so the object of criticism and uncertainty. He is a clumsy oaf who never seems to do anything right. This fourteen-year-old, bigger-than-britches boy is my son. He is the next in line to take up the reins. What in heaven's name will he be good for?

No matter. He is all mine, and I love him. I wish I could tell him so in a way he could really understand. But the gulf is too wide. His energy and his headlong dash to manhood are directed away from me. He moves with the speed of light, and I can never quite catch up to him. There is the urge to reach out and touch him and even be so bold as to draw him close, so that he might be sheltered and kept in check long enough to instill in him some of my world. But somehow the time never is just right. So you do the next best thing. You help him learn his new Scout Manual. You stop him on his way out the door to Charlie's house, and you lead him firmly back to the patio and hand him his book. He does not fight or complain much, but you know what he thinks about it all, be it Scouting, geography, math or washing the car. You feel for him, but you know what happens to him if he does not learn to make his way in this new world. Your son must live and succeed, perhaps where you have failed. So we begin on page three with the revised Scout Oath.

" 'On my honor I will do my best to do my duty to God...'" "No, son. Here, look again. See, '... Do my best to do my duty to the world and to my country.' "

"'To do my duty to... the world and to my country and to obey the Scout Laws....' "

"Good!"

"Can I go now, huh, Dad? Charlie's waiting."

"Let's have the laws."

"Aw, gee..."

"Now."

"O.K."

"Pages six and seven... no... six. Did you write them out like I said to do?"

"Write them out?"

"This morning at breakfast. Don't you know I said . .."

"Oh, gee! I guess that's right... I... what did you say, Dad?"

"Nothing. Just read them aloud to me."

"A Scout is... uh... obedient to his leaders ... an' loyal to his government ... an' ... "

"Leave out the ands. Now, you don't see them there, do you?" "Uh... dedicated to peace, cheerful in his giving... uh... kind to world friends, disciplined in his habits and... that belongs there, see ... denying of himself in all things that are selfish."

"All right. Let's start at the top. A Scout is.. .."

"Trustworthy ... I mean loyal... no... obedient to his leaders, loyal to his government..."

286

Dusk with my son on a Tuesday in July.

On Wednesday there was a night baseball game. We lost, as usual.

Thursday I started out to work with my eldest, Madame Queen Peggy, who teeters on the verge of being seventeen. David is an open book compared with her. She will not cooperate with her mother. She is nasty to Annie, and she ignores David. She thinks I am a tyrant, largely because I do not approve of the way she chases boys or the late hours. Nancy thinks I am too harsh about this. "She's not a child any more, and besides she's dating some rather eligible boys." True. Three or four, at last count, and every one the son of somebody important—a BWP official, a newly appointed veep from Whiteside and one with the JCFLA. So I cannot make too much of a fuss. Somewhere along the route we lost her, I think with the evacuation last year. She left home still a little girl, even though she had filled out rather noticeably. But she returned home with the air of a woman. It was in her eyes, in her walk, in her mannerisms, in her voice; a kind of flip sureness; a maidenless insolence which betrayed to me, at least, that she knew all there was to know and, perhaps, then some. Evacuation Camp must have been for her a variety of experiences which she found not at all unpleasant. I never learned for sure, but I sense it strongly. I sense it the way she slips too quietly into her room after a much-too-late date. I sense it in the boys who come to call. Their eyes betray them, and the way she holds herself upward and outward reveals more to me than simply her near-perfect anatomy. For she is a well-shaped woman. Her face is strikingly beautiful, like that of a kitten. She spends hours on herself, so that her dark hair shines in an endless number of styles, from girl-next-door 'dos to a vamp straight out of New Orleans. But she does not overdo. She exaggerates nothing, be it makeup or posture or clothing. She has the knack of displaying herself so that she is aesthetically pleasing, yet potentially possessable. While I am openly curious about how David behaves away from home, I have no such desire to know about Peggy. The less I think of it the better.

But she is bright and quick. She speaks with some slight affectations, but generally her tone and inflections are truly hers. She is persuasive, a mixture of the skilled debater and the helpless kitten. She can be cross when it suits her and quickly put adversaries on the defensive. She has little original humor but listens and responds well to the humor of others. She knows how to organize things. She has goals in everything she does, which one is not fully aware of until she has achieved whatever it is she wants. Thus, she is a natural leader. When she changes her hair, the dozen or so girl pals do likewise. When she tackles a job, she does do it well and with remarkable ease. She is always president or secretary or something significant with a seemingly endless parade of organizations—the church Youth League; the choir for awhile; the debating society, four ribbons; "sorority," I forget what it's called; various class offices; swimming team; class plays, usually lead parts; the school paper. She draws a B-plus average, too. She has spirit, purpose and know-how, and except for the sexual side and her prima-donna behavior at home, there is a lot to her that a father can be proud of. But they say one must accept sex away from home and ill-behavior at home as part of growing up. And I must admit that Peggy's reputation and record are good ones. So maybe these are unimportant concerns. Sex is here, and every parent accepts it. So who is there to complain or gossip?

I have never been concerned about whether Peggy will succeed in the world. She can scarcely miss. Still, I worry about her. Women are at the mercy of men, and men are at the mercy of systems. Left to herself, Peggy can adjust to the world ahead, which after all is for her generation, not mine. Yet, what would happen if she were somehow trapped? She has dignity now. What might she become if she were ever bent beyond her will? She is a woman newly come alive. She must never become degraded to something much less than she is now. For I love her, too. She is my muscle, bone and blood. She is my elder daughter in whom I take great pride.

Occasionally we look over her shoulder when she lets us, to help if we are capable of helping, and on Thursday night I was able to help. One of her current activities involves serving as Secretary General of World Order of Nations Student Assembly, District Four, which is headquartered at her school. Actually she assumes the post next fall when she is a senior. It is considered a singular honor to be so chosen (a faculty committee appointment with student approval) and it usually means a four-year W.O.N. scholarship to any one of several dozen universities here and abroad, including the University of Moscow. One of Peggy's goals is to win a scholarship. Part of her plan is to call the mock W.O.N. Assembly into session a full month before the school year begins. She is doing this as "evidence of our deep desire to cooperate with the President of the United States in his Vacation Gift Program." The school authorities themselves had not thought of this as a useful summer activity and are delighted. Peggy even received a letter of commendation from the JCFLA with a carbon copy to the school and the W.O.N. Secretariat. Her new principal, Aram Kosokowski, has stopped by our house three times in the past week or so to confer about the program. He has been most solicitous of us all, even to the point of inquiring whether I had ever considered running for the school board.

So, there she was on the patio after dinner. The same setting as it had been before with David. A clear, hot evening, punctuated with the busy sounds of neighborhood relaxation. Nancy was in the family room off the patio watching television. It was the only comfortable place in the house, which is not air conditioned, a real blunder on my part. I could have had it easily enough, but I wanted to keep the mortgage down. Peggy of course was not alone. She was seated at the redwood table littered with newspaper clippings, books, magazines and paper. Nearby, a long, good-looking young man was stretched the full length of a chaise longue watching her through half-closed eyes. Whether he was observing her paperwork or just her was difficult to determine. Peggy was wearing spotless white brief shorts and a pale green blouse, low and loose cut, with the top buttons somewhat casually unfastened. She was tanned, even to her plunging neck line, and trim with the suppleness of youth. I swallowed the urge to kick the young man off his perch and send her end-over-end to her room. But parents are warned against showing anger toward their children. Better to win their confidence through friendship.

"Hi, Pop! You remember Buck. Buckley Valentine. He's helping me."

" 'Lo, Mr. Little." The long form stirred slightly to elevate a handsomely tanned face capped with thick, wavy dark hair. He, too, wore shorts and a polo shirt.

"Buck represents England in our W.O.N. He's going to offer the motion of censure," she added, digging into a fancy tin box of sour lemon balls. She chewed one thoughtfully while surveying the littered table. "Hm-m-m. These are good! Want one, Pop? Buck's dad gets them." She offered the box.

"Get 'em through the W.O.N. Commissary. Right from England," Buck added proudly. He groped absently under the chaise for a half-consumed bottle of beer—my beer.

I drew up a chair next to Peggy and helped myself to a lemon ball, which was tastier than I had remembered. "How are you coming?" I asked.

"I'm stuck, Pop." She pursed her lips and blew like a winded tomboy. For an instant she reminded me of how she was as a little child whenever a toy would not work or she could not find a piece to a picture puzzle—a perplexed kitten. "I have to give an opening address. I know what I want to say, but I don't know how to put it down. And it has to be good, really good."

"It's too broad, that's your trouble," the young man said flatly. His eyes were still half closed.

"Well, it's supposed to be that way. Mr. Thomas said so." She reached through the litter for her can of beer which had been hidden behind an open magazine and took a generous swig.

Beer and lemon drops! I thought. Oh well, never mind.

"What's it on, honey?"

"Poverty, Pop. Poverty. The elimination of world-wide poverty… our theme for next year."

"I thought peace was," I said.

"That was last year, silly." She helped herself to another lemon ball and picked up a sheaf of mimeographed papers. "The peace is won, and see right here … it says ninety percent of the people of the world are in poverty and it's up to the rich nations to share their re-sources and things." She pointed to a lengthy paragraph on a sheet entitled "Procedural Instructions for Student World Order of Nations, Revised." "There's an outline here," she fumbled through the papers, "but I want my speech to be really mine. So I wanna juggle it around some, and yet it has to pave the way for Buck's censure."

"Censure?"

"Sure, Pop. You know. Censure. Like… bawling out someone, only it's a country instead."

"I know the meaning. What kind of censure?"

"Well, Buck," she turned to include him in our conversation and straightened her trim body in lithe indignation. "Buck, for god's sake, sit up and take a few notes! You know we have to have this done by Monday. Jesus! Come on!"

The youth popped his eyes wide open and swung his feet to the patio floor as if someone had jabbed him with a pin. "Gimme some paper and quit hollering! You don't own me, you know!"

"Huh! Who wants you!"

"O.K., kids." I interjected.

"Well, Buck … if he ever gets going … is supposed to censure the United States," Peggy continued briskly.

"About what?"

"That's what we're trying to figure out… specifically, I mean." Again she made a face. "It has to fit the poverty theme, and it has to show that the United States is not doing its fair share yet. But we don't know where to begin."

I shifted in my seat. One of the slats in the redwood chair was missing. I looked out over the yard. Showing an ugly brown during the day from lack of water or fertilization, it looked lush and cool in the closing twilight. The neighborhood had grown quiet. From behind us the voice of television was intoning, "And now, live from Moscow…." Peggy had asked my help, a rarity, and I had to deliver some sort of a suggestion.

"Why don't you start outlining your speech, Peggy, and Buck, you follow along and outline your censure motion to fit. Of course you'll have to be more specific. For instance, Peg, what is the first point you want to make?"

She fussed through her notes, squinting in the dusk. "Well," she sighed. "The rich get richer and the poor get poorer, I suppose." "All right. Now, that's a general statement, and you probably have some general statistics to prove it."

"Yeah ... a whole batch."

"Now, Buck, maybe your lead-in would be to pick up this point and apply it specifically to the United States. Like… the gross national product."

"That hasn't gone up much. That's what our advisor said," Buck replied. "But," he brightened, "government spending has. Maybe I could use that."

"Fine. You could say we are spending more on ourselves than ever before," I said.

"Don't know. We're spending more overseas, I think. The point is we're still spending too much on ourselves, even though it's less this year than last."

"Well, Buck. Don't you see? You've got it! Simply say the United States is spending too much on itself."

"Sure! I get it! Hey, how 'bout that, Peg!" And Buck came to life. We lit the patio candle and settled into a surprisingly serious working session.

By now it was almost dark. A nearly full moon had begun its climb through the spotless sky, turning the rooftops into patterns of pale yellow and shadow. Here and there fireflies dotted the heavy dusk. Inside, the lights shone from the bedrooms where David and Annie were getting ready for bed. Through open windows came the sounds of their nighttime preparations—the splashing of water, a door slam, the play of the dog, an occasional yelp, and finally, the soft tones of good night.

Buck had drawn another chair to the table close to Peggy, and the two bent close to the flickering candle. They scrawled notes and squinted at pieces of paper from the mass of materials fanned out before them. Two serious youngsters, now, wrestling with issues and problems that, even at my own age, were beyond my depth. Youngsters put upon by the adult world to solve adult problems, make adult judgments and indulge in adult practicalities. Youngsters caught in a net made by other hands and forced over their heads. Yet, the very flexibility of their youth makes them susceptible to the demands heaped upon them, and they seemed to be having an easier time of it than I. Youngsters no more, much too soon. A man and a woman now at the table, etched in soft light, busy at adult work. Who can blame them, then, if in their off hours they also behave like adults?

"I can probably say that the danger ... let me look again ... is that the private economy is gaining too much at the expense of government." It was my daughter speaking in a matter-of-fact way, reading from a magazine article.

"How about *world* government?"

"Well, maybe..."

"Well, at least say ... at the expense of *some* governments, but don't say who. Then I can point specially to the United States in my censure motion. There's a whole book of statistics and stuff." Buck poked around the table and finally produced a slim volume entitled *The Public Haters, An Analysis of the Abuses of Private Capitalism.*

"Good. But not too many statistics."

"It's all summarized."

"Uh..." once again Peggy made a face and shuffled more papers, "I should hit this point pretty hard... that the only sure way to banish poverty is to increase public services."

"W.O.N. services, don't you think? After all, this is the W.O.N." said Buck, and he laughed softly, almost obscenely. "And don't forget you want a scholarship out of this mush."

"Yeah. Sometimes I wonder if it's worth it. But..." she sighed softly and took another lemon ball. "The things you have to do to make points with them."

"Hey!" Buck exclaimed. "Look at this Lincoln quote. You could use that."

"Too nationalistic. Let me look." And the two heads bobbed close while they both read. "But you could! Look ... it says, 'As Lincoln once said: The government should do for the people what they are unable to do for themselves.' You could say that and then say that Americans are violating their own heritage. Put all the leftover Belltollers right in their place."

"Good." Buck scribbled briskly for a moment. "Ought to get a hand on that."

"When you read it, be sure to pause. I'll prime some of the kids to clap."

"How about debt and all?"

Peggy shrugged wearily. "I never did understand that stuff. Our country's in debt, and they say the W.O.N. is in debt.[63] Yet there seems to be plenty of money." She shook her head. "What's the difference if we're in debt or not, as long as we have money?"

"Mr. Thomas told us we'd have to deal with debt."

"The hell with him!"

"Well, here … try this quote." Buck flashed a newspaper clipping. " 'Our economic difficulties are the direct result of an economy—world economy—that produces too little—rather than governments that spend too much.' Also, you can bring in savings accounts."

"People who save are depriving the world of…" Peggy made another face.

"Desperately needed financial resources," Buck finished.

"That fits. But I just can't get into all that junk."

"Well you can certainly mention Peace Bonds. In fact you gotta, because I'm supposed to lay that on real heavy."

"Oh, sure. Easy," Peggy replied amiably.

So they worked, while the moon rose. Finally they stopped, pleased that their assignment was well in hand; pleased, too, with me.

"Mr. Little, you sure saved our hides." Buck's voice held faint traces of admiration.

"My pop knows the ropes!" She rose then and gave me a big hug. "Thanks, Pop. You're smart! I'll bet you're tired."

---

63 World Order of Nations debt during the period was about eight hundred billion dollars.

294

"Yeah. I'll bet you're real tired. Well, thanks for helping us," Buck added, like a gracious host about to nudge me out of his front door.

It was, of course, a hint to clear out. The budding adults had done their adult work and now they were demanding a little free time to themselves. It was already past eleven.

So I left them, feeling a little closer to Peggy. She, too, has her own world of pressures. School must be as rough a place in which to survive as anywhere else. Nancy was already in bed, though not asleep, by the time I had seen to the dog, secured the house and checked David and Annie. All the while I was preparing for bed I kept listening for telltale sounds from the patio below. Buck and Peggy were still there. They had extinguished the candle the moment I left. They had moved one of the chaises close to the house, in the deep shadows out of reach of the moonlight and out of sight from the bedroom window. Not a sound anywhere, except the distant whine of a jet streaking somewhere. The rooftops stretching down the long hill behind us now showed dull silver—eerie like a field full of tombstones. Once I thought I heard someone utter a long, satisfying sigh.

"David! Get away from the window and come to bed." Nancy spoke sleepily. "You're like a maiden aunt. Don't be so nebby!"

"All right. It's just that ..." I paused awkwardly. I have never been good at discussing intimate things with Nancy, and whenever Peggy was out late I had one worry worse than all of the others. "I worry sometimes."

"About what?"

"Peg. Every time she's alone with a boy I ... I just don't want her to get herself in a jam." I finished belligerently.

Nancy laughed softly. "You're always so bashful about things. Are you talking about Peggy getting pregnant?"

"Yes!"

"Relax. You remind me of the irate father type of a century ago." Nancy pulled herself up. The moonlight revealed only her lightly clad torso, leaving her face hidden in the shadows, so that she looked like an exotic but headless spirit. "Peggy and I have had our talks, strictly woman to woman. She understands things. Besides, she has pills,[64] and she knows she must use them at all times."

"But how do we know she will?"

"Oh, we talked it all out when we first went to the doctor. He explained everything and prescribed a double supply. So, David, believe me, nothing will happen. Besides, they're both good, hardworking kids, and maybe," she slid back down and yawned cozily, "they're smarter than we were at their age. How can we condemn then for seeking happiness whenever they have the chance. Don't they deserve at least that?"

How does one argue a point like that, or even question it? The world is the world, and who am I—any longer—to judge what others do? Whatever Peggy is, she has long since been cast into her mold. In this new world she fares well.

It was a congenial evening, in itself a rare occasion, and on the whole most pleasing. So I could sleep content with our lot.

4

Last Saturday evening Nancy and I went to the PTA dance. It was our first dance in over a year, and I had fun. The orchestra was not too good. Only four pieces, which was all the PTA could afford. But there was a large turnout. Nancy was chairman of the dance committee. The new PTA president, Mrs. Edmundson, had suggested the dance as a means to boost the Foreign Underprivileged Scholarship Fund as well as to push the sale of Peace Bonds. Mrs. Edmundson is nice enough. She is a rather plain-looking woman of 40. I have heard she is an actual member of the Communist Party, although she apparently never mentions it. She certainly does not behave like anything sinister. I managed to spend a little time with her and her husband, an equally plain and mild-looking fellow. They made an austere couple, somewhat out of keeping with the setting. When I found out they were close friends of Leon Tidings, I decided that the less said the better, and I put aside my image-making efforts for the evening and went in search of Nancy.

---

64 Anti-pregnancy pills similar to present day chemicals used in birth control.

We were in the high school gym. It was festooned with ribbons and balloons, with the lights dimmed. But it was uncomfortably warm, especially if you had been dancing. And I felt like dancing for a change. No heavy problems hanging over my head. The week had been a good one. So why not unbend a little? For once I paid some attention to Nancy. She was dressed in black, and without a doubt was one of the handsomest women there.

I suppose in my headlong rush to escape the world, I have neglected her. I have too often wanted to criticize her and the things about her that have irritated me. I have been unwilling to look at the positive side. But she is an asset. She knows the things one must do to get along in the world, and while she has been sometimes awkward and overanxious, she has weathered the crisis of this past year better than I. She has emerged with more poise and more direction. Possibly this is because of her work at the BWP, and Larry, I think, has been a source of inspiration to her. She has become avidly interested in public affairs, and while she has never seemed especially bright, she has, nonetheless, acquired a great deal of knowledge, mostly by listening and reading. She has always been ambitious for both of us to succeed. The difference of late is that she seems to know better what to do with this drive for achievement. No longer do I resent her proddings. I have come to realize that she probably has been more right than I; that success is won only on the terms made available by the world about you—a world over which you have no control. So I took her to the dance floor with a new sense of appreciation.

My first date with her had been in the college gym, not too unlike this one. We were sophomores, and she was a blind date—arranged through Larry—for the Homecoming Hop. Next to the proms it was the biggest social event on campus and, I suppose, like most college dances. There was no student union in those days, only the gymnasium which the student committees managed to camouflage with balloons, streamers, and potted palms. But the grey brick walls were still there, along with the wooden folding chairs ringing the undisguised basketball floor. Still, when packed with elegant couples, all prettied, slender and shining, with the big band sound echoing with tumultuous grandeur, the college dance is worth keeping as a memory, particularly if you have a date. I was never over-aggressive with the girls in either high school or my freshman year at Western College, yet I was lured to school dances in a timid sort of way; so I would, often as not, go stag, hoping somehow to meet and charm with bon-vivant nonchalance some as yet undiscovered beauty, also stag, which never seemed to work out, and I would spend hours leaning against the cold brick walls or chatting with the biology teacher sitting in a depressing wooden chair.

It was Larry who took a hand in things to put an end to "this waste of virile masculinity" by providing a date for me, a simple matter arranged through the girl he had staked out. It turned out I knew my date, who was in Sociology 101 with me. Her name was Nancy Blazer. While she was not stamped with glamour, she was quite pretty—with gently curling dark hair and soft, sometimes pleading brown eyes. She was medium height and just enough on the plump side to give subtle validity to the pleasant fullness of her figure. She was nice to look upon, which I did at every opportunity in class. But I do not recall that we had ever actually spoken. I was generally shy and a trifle unsure and she was the same; although there was perhaps an ounce of anxiousness about her, as if she were seeking, almost desperately at times, to break out of her shell. She had the mixed characteristics of being at once standoffish and yet anxious to make a hit with someone—anyone—worthwhile. While I was not the greatest catch in the class, still I held my own. I was a fair student and performed with reasonable skill. Also, most everyone identified me as a pal of Larry's, whose star already had begun to zoom upward. I rather enjoyed this distinct identification and, while I did not consciously use my friendship with Larry, still it gave me a social platform from which to operate in a way that served to strengthen our relationship. I offered no competition to Larry in his struggle for achievement. Rather, I sincerely enjoyed tagging along. He made me feel good by including me in many of his social and academic excursions, and I made him feel just as good, because I was satisfied to listen and follow. Thus, I, was able to rub shoulders with the college elite without disturbing

anyone. While I formed few close friendships, still I earned no enemies and managed to get along sufficiently well with everyone so that
I had a substantial number of acquaintances. Nancy was just barely an acquaintance, but at least we nodded to each other from time
to time, and occasionally we would smile at each other from across
the classroom (we sat in a huge circle to stimulate togetherness)
only to look quickly away. Once Larry had broken the ice ("She's on
the telephone now, Dave. Here, talk to her, damn it!") the barriers
came tumbling down.

The day after the date had been set we grinned openly at each other in class, and I walked her back to her sorority house. I liked her
because she added to my sense of well-being; in truth, she made me
feel more important than I actually was. Of course, I did nothing to
destroy the illusion that Larry and I were active and equal partners
in the effort to catch the world by the tail and fling it wide. I liked
her, too, because she was something of a catch herself. She belonged
to one of the better sororities, and she, too, had her fair share of
acquaintances, including a substantial number of boys who were acceptable enough, but not of the Prime Mover Class. I can understand
now where Nancy might well have considered me more of a Prime
Mover than I actually was. Anyhow, before the week had passed we
had become good friends. In fact, she had by then begun to take a
he-belongs-to-me attitude toward me which was quite pleasing. She
was a good gal and won Larry's immediate approval.

So the dance that sophomore year was a mighty big occasion. I
had to rent a tux and buy flowers, which crippled my allowance, but
it was worth it. Nancy, though she has never said, must have gone to
some considerable pains, too. For she was devastatingly dressed in
an amber gown that showed her to maximum advantage. She came
down the circular stairs at her house like a proud queen, her eyes
bright with expectation, and I stood at the bottom twenty pounds
lighter than I am today and slicked into gleaming black and white.
It was a flawless scene right out of the movies, only it was real. I had
come into my own at last! I was a wheel—well, sort of—and I had me
a girl. We cut a path that night. For Larry and his date (the sorority

president no less) were with us, and I think they were pleased with their match. We nodded hello to everyone and there was a "Hi, Dave" and "Wha'd'ya say, Nancy" at almost every turn.

The first dance was awkward and threatened to tarnish the image, but the big band number was fortunately slow, an old standard, Moonlight Becomes You—so we survived with my stepping on her toes only a couple of times. The next number was a fast Latin step, which we started and then abandoned in favor of a beer. But the one after that, a slow, swinging version of Georgia on My Mind, put us in unison, and halfway through, with confidence restored, I pulled her close and she responded. The big moment on the big date—to pull the girl close for the first time and find that she does not mind in the least. The first time is the best time, when cheek meets cheek and bosom meets bosom and thigh meets thigh and there is the scent of freshly applied perfume and the faint breathing of another warm in your ear. The exaltation of discovery! Strangers no more, nor were we ever again quite as we were. For a while we spoke little. Midway along we talked.

"I love this song, don't you, David?"

"I'll say! You can call me Dave if you like."

"I like David much better."

"No one ever calls me that."

"Well, it suits you much better. Whenever I think of you ... I always think ... David. Dave, somehow, doesn't fit. It's too casual for someone like you."

"Think of me? Sure you do... I'll just bet!"

"Honest! I shouldn't say it... what must you think of me... but I do!"

"Aw, you're just being nice."

"Oh, David. I am not. I don't say things I don't mean."

"Well ... I think of you, too... 'times."

"Really."

"Uh-huh."

"What about?"

300

"Oh, I don't know… just sort of… oops, sorry… did I hurt your foot?"

"No. Of course not. You dance very well."

"Not really very well…"

"You are with me. I just love to dance with you!"

"Me, too—with you, I mean!"

"What do you think when you think about me?"

"What do you think when you think about me?"

"You tell me first, and I'll tell you."

"Nice things. I don't know how to explain it."

"Me too… David?"

"Ummm?"

"Can I call you David?"

"Uh-huh."

"You don't mind?"

"Gee no. Kinda like it, I think."

"I'm glad… David, do you like me a little?"

"Gosh, yes! I mean… sure."

"How much?"

"Lots … I guess."

"You guess?"

"Lots… Nan."

"I like you lots, too…. David, do you mind calling me Nancy, rather than Nan?"

"Of course not."

"Oh, good! Nan always seems so… informal. I mean … do you understand?"

"Sure, Nancy."

"I like the way you say my name… David."

The last number was Goodnight Sweetheart. We did not talk but hung on to each other for dear life, for tragedy was closing in on us; the night was ending and there would never be another one quite like it, and even in our unconscious we must have known it.

Nancy's folks came the next day, Sunday, to catch the end of the Homecoming, and she had assumed that I would want to meet them.

It was a beautiful fall morning, the bright blue and gold kind with an icy clear sky, magnanimous sun and patchwork trees. The air was bracing, but the sun was warm enough for Nancy and me to lean against the porch railing of her sorority house for better than an hour to await their arrival. The magic of the night before was still at work so that we barely noticed the door-slamming traffic of coeds with brightly polished mothers and fathers in tow as they went about the business of flinging themselves into organized campus fun.

My parents could not come. The store, of course. Originally, it was to have been a glum weekend for me. But now with the discovery of Nancy I was just as glad Mom and Dad had stayed put. For Nancy's folks, I was learning in bits and pieces of chatter, were—by my standards, at least—of impressive substance. She spoke of them with genuine pride, the way a good daughter ought. Mr. Blazer sold insurance and was "definitely on his way up." Her mother, while "sometimes a little nervous," was a real pal to Nancy and wanted her to have every advantage that a good, solid and enriching marriage could provide. They belonged to a country club—just barely I was to find out later, for her father had to struggle some with the bills... but they did belong. They lived in one of the better sections of Columbus, Ohio—again just barely as I was to discover ... but it was sufficient to impress me at the time. Her mother belonged to three clubs. The family belonged to a good church too, "lots of company presidents, vice presidents and bankers just sit all around us, and Father and Mother know many of them personally!"

I did not discuss either my parents or where we lived, except to say they owned their own business, a rather large and successful supermarket. So we babbled and waited in bright morning, ignoring the feverish flow of people, cars, bicycles and dogs that wove a cocoon of bedlam about us on the great porch and the broad and long walk to the narrow college avenue in front. And then they arrived, Mother and Father Blazer. They drove a Cadillac, "a demonstrator but so new looking that people would never know," Nancy had said as she tugged me down the steps and moved us through the Homecoming hoopla to a spot at the curb, which fortunately had been vacated a second before by a very tired-looking man and a teary-eyed woman, doubtlessly victims of a quarrel with their offspring. After four tries, Father Blazer put the car in place.

"Careful of the whitewalls, Douglas!" a rather frail-looking woman screeched nervously. But she was too late. The tires were already ground hard against the cement with ugly black streaks carved into the wedding-white rubber.

"Son of a…" the florid and heavy-set man cursed. His two chins quivered under the strain.

They regained their composure hastily. Mother Blazer took one last quick look at a mirror she had flashed from her purse, while Father eased himself out of the driver's seat, which caused a precarious traffic jam, as he moved with portly ease around the car to the sidewalk, first to embrace Nancy with unmistakable relish and then to help Mother from the car. Nancy introduced me with a clinging warmth that made me tingle, which neither parent seemed to mind. In fact they were delighted.

"Delighted to meet you, young man." Father boomed. His handshake meant business.

"Indeed. You are just what we expected. Nancy has described you very well," Mother Blazer said, with a slight tremor. She half offered her hand, quickly withdrew it and then offered it again. Her hand was damp and cold. She was fairly tall and thin about her face which was noticeably made up. She was dressed in a gay suit that probably was an expensive one.

Nancy, it appeared, had given them a full account of me the day before. They had phoned her to say that they had to attend a party at The Club and so could not even hope to be here before Sunday. "Such a dear. Nancy understands these things."

"Yes. Remarkable girl, our Nancy. Quite a catch for some lucky fellow who's going places, eh, Dave?"

"Father!" Nancy blushed, while Mother scowled. "Don't embarrass me! And call him David. He likes that, don't you dear?"

"Sure. That is… sure."

"Well. Who's for breakfast? Bet you kids are starved. Been three hours since I've had a thing."

"Douglas! It's eleven o'clock."

"Yes, Daddy. Lunch is at twelve-thirty."

"Well. A little snack then. Where can a tired old man get some energy?"

So we went to the Hub and managed to squeeze into a booth for donuts and coffee; then back to the sorority where I stood uselessly to the side, next to the cloak room in the entry while Nancy made her parents known to fifty-odd other parents and their aspiring daughters strewn through the huge livingroom. I was trying to find a way to leave gracefully when Father Blazer's voice boomed out well above the Sunday chitchat. "Say! Where's that good lookin' beau of Nancy's?" In the next moment Father had beckoned me into the room and proceeded to introduce me to the elders while the young ladies looked up and down with dead-panned approval, I suppose. Father personally arranged with the housemother, Mrs. Gibbs, for me to stay for lunch. The moment was an awkward one since I was the only boy friend in the room, the rest having discreetly departed. But Mrs. Gibbs rose to the situation by ordering one more place at the table.

Lunch was a sweaty affair. First came the jibes from the other girls, kindly jokes and friendly pokes like, "He is cute!" "The way you two carried on last night!" "Better watch them, Mr. Blazer!" Teehee. They sang songs dedicated to "Nancy and her love." I was embarrassed until I found the courage to look directly at her at my side, instead of at the pumpkin pie. She was radiant. Father was radiant. Mother was radiant. Even Mrs. Gibbs was radiant, and the soft dreamy chorus sang Sweetheart of Sigma Chi. Then I did not mind any more.

Three weeks later I gave her my newly won fraternity pin, and was promptly ushered into the family. "We're gaining another son. Yes sir, Martha, we've always wanted one of our own but we have this fine, aggressive young man, too. Makes a fella feel proud to know he's done right by his daughters." (Nancy has an older married sister who lives in Seattle.) So spoke Father not long after, when the Blazers paid us another visit. Mother cried a little. Nancy just hugged me all the more. I felt wonderfully good, anxious to be worthy of the "great trust" that was bestowed upon me.

In the flush of new love it had not occurred to me that I had not even suggested an engagement, let alone marriage. The pinning just seemed to happen without any great fuss and not too much discussion about what it meant. It was just one of those things that seemed to grow out of nowhere. First it was an implied understanding. (I don't want to rush you into anything, dear.) Then came the window shopping. (I like that, don't you?) Soon, career planning. (I can teach when we're out of school.) I spent part of Christmas at the Blazers, in what I would now call a relatively modest but neatly kept home located adjacent to estate-type dwellings of imposing size, and by New Year's Eve the understanding was firm. Nancy and I would marry upon graduation. (I don't want a ring until our senior year.)

As I say, it just happened. It was all most agreeable, even to putting up with some of Nancy's anxieties that began to show here and there. (David, supposing we don't get invited to the Empire Club outing? Please check with Larry.) She urged me to run for Student Council once, and when I lost she was terribly upset for days. I began wearing ties and sport coats to class, sweaters being too informal. I tried out for track and sprained my knee, which still troubles me some. She begged me to write for the newspaper, which did not work out; so I sold advertising. I tried the debating team (David, you've got to perfect yourself. Be fluent to be affluent. That's what Larry says.) I was chopped to pieces. The effort gave me chronic headaches and stomach trouble, so I gave up the attempt and took more of a firm attitude that I would not fight the world. We argued some over this, particularly during the senior year.

But when I landed a respectable job as a sales trainee at the company after graduation, Nancy seemed to settle down, for a time at least, confident that in time I would be every bit as successful as Larry.

But she had one overriding quality that made up for any momentary qualms I might have had about her. It was her complete loyalty to me. She had staked me out as hers, and she let the world know this, without apology, in sweet, patient ways that said: "He's mine ... for better or worse."

And that is what I was thinking this past Saturday night at the PTA dance. I might complain about her—even bitterly resent her at times, with justification. Yet, through it all here she was, more slender and possibly even more attractive than ever. Nancy, trusting and eternally hopeful. Nancy, whose dream of ultimate success in a cruel world has never dimmed. Nancy, who sees the bright ending with "just a little more effort." She was the best that this world could offer me—now. On that note, I pulled her close and closed my eyes to pretend that the flat, uncoordinated rhythm of the four-piece orchestra was, in fact, the big band sounds of another year.

"David, it's hot, and you'll wrinkle my dress."

I'm sorry.

"Did you read Mother's letter?" The Blazers had long since moved to the West Coast, and Father was now retired. They lived in Golden Haven, California, a planned community for senior citizens. Letters came weekly, crammed with advice and questions about "David's progress" and broad hints for funds to cover some new emergency.

"They're in trouble."

"How so?"

"Their food allowance ... it isn't near enough with the way inflation is going."

"I'm sorry, Nancy."

"Can't we send them something?"

"Of course."

"David ... we should have spent more time with Mrs. Edmundson. There's no one with them now... see?"

"Nancy, PTA president or not, I can't risk it. She knows Tidings."

"So what. That little runt. You can outfox him."

"Not hardly. He's my only VIP contact that I can use for ..." "Leverage, David. Leverage."

"I start palming my buddy-buddy line on her and she's sure to mention it to Tidings and he'll set her straight, and then we're done for sure."

"So we don't mention Tidings. Look, David, we've got to get to know her. She actually belongs to the Communist Party."

"Are you sure?"

"Of course! We've got to become friends with people like her ... now, dance on over... careful, my feet! Oh, damn! The music is lousy. Come on! Let's walk."

"Nancy?"

"What?"

I held her still in the center of the gym floor while the perspiring sea of middleagers pumped their way around us."

"Remember our first date?"

"David! How could I, after all this time? I suppose it was a movie or something. What a silly thing. Come on! Mrs. Edmundson is looking our way .. . smile . ... come on!"

We visited with Mr. and Mrs. Edmundson for nearly an hour, before I took her to the dance floor, while Nancy danced with Mr. Edmundson.

I am not sure it was worth it. Nancy tried to land a luncheon invitation, but Mrs. Edmundson did not oblige.

Oh well, you can't win them all. On the whole it was a mighty fine evening.

It is the end of July. Actually I have nothing to write about. Life goes on well enough. Whatever it was that drove me to write all this has ceased. Maybe I was searching for a clue as to what it is I think I am. Once I thought I was an all-right guy who could go his own way undisturbed. But it did not work that way. I was disturbed, plenty. And I find I am like all the others—he who is the cleverest wins, and you do anything to win. That is what I am. If there has been any value to this journal it is that it has taught me to face myself squarely and live through it. Occasionally, I think of Harry and Mom and Mary—and even Miss Lee. Sometimes I wonder why. Sometimes I get terribly afraid. But I push it all away. I have learned to do this very well indeed. I am neither happy nor unhappy. I am simply here, living each day as it comes. If I have any security, it is in the fact that I am becoming more used to the idea of being clever. The old ways must go, along with all of the old ground rules. All is new now. This I have come to accept. I will get along with Communism or any other ism because that is all there is for me to do.

So there is no further need to keep this account, for it can only be more of the same. Tonight, then, I put it away with mixed feelings. How can one otherwise file away an old friend? I commend to these pages another life set in another time. It is proper to have an appropriate closing line. It is the least I can do for an old friend. I have more or less given up God, but every now and then the urge to acknowledge Him seeps back—part of the old world. Perhaps the past should stay with the past. So let my closing line be one last fervent backward glance before we plunge into the faceless future:

May God please find us again!

VII

The Seventeenth Month

Sleep is out of the question. For the third straight night I have fought the urge to steal down here to my fallout-shelter-turned-den with its lovely scarred makeshift furniture and dig into this tired footlocker like a starving man searching for bread; dig down through moldy old knickknacks to a plastic wrapped bundle and tear at the strings like the addict rips into his packet of heroin or the alcoholic undoes his cleverly hidden bottle. Were I seeking dope or bread or whisky, I would have more sympathy for these compulsions. But to reach again for this cursed journal. How I wish I had destroyed it! I crawl like a beaten dog on its belly to his master, and the journal is my master. Or is it my refuge? Who can say and who cares? Fully a dozen times these past ten months this urge has crept toward me like a sneak thief and as many times I have struck it from my mind with contempt and disdain. For I have made my peace a hundred times. I am done with this silliness! I know where I stand, and I am doing all right. Not as well as some; better than most.

But the still, small voices do not let me alone. They whisper that I—we, all of us—are being slowly destroyed, sickeningly slowly. Why do they not think positively? Confidence makes the world anything we want it to be. Every knowing person—politician, government leader, and newsman—says in a great thundering chorus: Be confident! Confidence wins jobs. Confidence cures inflation. Confidence gives us prosperity. Again and again, on posters, on television, on radio, in newspapers, the word is confidence!

Why do the small voices laugh?

Their laughter drives me finally to this place tonight and to this smeared ledger.

Now that I have the rage out of my system, I see that it is still my old friend.

Ten months or ten years. The time makes little sense any more. You bargain for the next minute, the next hour and the next day, and let it go at that. Sometimes you win. Other times you lose.

Lately I have lost, but not as much as I could have. I swear it. Small voices, go away! I have had to make an adjustment or two, nothing serious, mind. Just temporary situations, until the dust settles. That is what I tell the neighbors and other friends and associates. Larry is the toughest one to tell. He has such a curious way of looking at me, a slightly quizzical expression tumbled in with a dash of disbelief and both laced together with flickers of easy confidence. "Y' don't say, old boy! Well, well, now. My point exactly. Never depend on people. Temporary bad run of luck. But, we'll get things cranked up again. Well, well!" And his bright eyes stare unblinkingly in and around but never at me. He is clearly disappointed, but in what? Me? Or is it something else?

That is how it was the day my career at the steel company was abolished this past March, just a few weeks ago. It was a breath-sucking blow. I had already been through an earlier job "adjustment." That is the new phrase these days. One is not "demoted" or "fired" any more. One suffers, instead, a temporary setback involving "a bit of an adjustment."

My troubles began last September when the entire sales department was simply eliminated, and I was demoted. We got the word in a group meeting at a quarter-to-five. Sixty percent of the sales department—out, effective immediately. But I was spared and was pooled into a new function with some leftover marketing, advertising and public relations people, whose departments likewise had been eliminated. We were to be "allocators." Since there was now a

310

full and predetermined demand for all of our products at new low prices, promotion and selling no longer were necessary. The need was to allocate the steel. Besides, the company had suffered severe losses and had reached a point where even government loans were almost impossible to get. Someone had to go, and they did by the hundreds. But I escaped the initial purge. While I had to take a thirty percent salary reduction, still, I reminded myself, I was one of the lucky ones. My contacts and image building had paid off. Poor Sam. Poor Pete. Poor Joe. Let's keep in touch, fellas. Sure you're gonna get something. Let's get together often— pal.

So, initially, I was not among the glazed, shuffling men in sincere blue suits who suddenly had nothing left to be sincere about. Thus, winter passed with relative pleasantness. I allocated like hell. No more fancy stuff, like trying to bail out a Rug-Bilt Company. Stick to policy and stay busy. Write lots and lots of memos based upon lots and lots of directives. Create problems, and handle them with confidence.

But the magic formula did not work. They did not need as many allocators as they had thought. So, six months later, at four forty-five on a bright day in young March, I was given fifteen minutes to clean out my desk. No gold watch, but I got a firm handshake. Let's keep in touch, fella! Call me for lunch sometime.

I have never been out of a job before. It is a little like death; no one likes to think of it. Life without a job. What man is there who, while he works, has the guts to contemplate this possibility? Who has the courage to sit some rainy evening cozy in his snug home and mentally remove his wealth; to pretend away his income and then play the game of how to feed young bodies and an anxious wife? How does one tell the neighbors? What does one do? But then, I never thought about it, any more than I think about death. That is not the way. For confident men anticipate living and working forever. They do not ponder unpleasant things. They kill off the still small voices that whisper, as easily as lionesses eat their newborn cubs. History must be strewn with wreckage made by confident men.

In my case it was a clean shot in the head. I never knew a thing, not even a rest-room rumor. I was at my desk in my half-partitioned cubicle. It was a busy scene. No less than a half-dozen thick books bearing columns and black paragraphs of regulations lay open on the desk, on the file, on the single guest chair and even on the floor. And the forms! I had a little trick of fanning them out in a haphazard sort of way across the desk, which along with an assortment of customer files and two or three tablets, made a fine exhibit for anyone who happened by. As an added touch, I always managed to have a pamphlet or two on world affairs lying casually off to the side, but clearly visible—"The W.O.N. Peace Enforcement Task Force in Britain"[65] or "Mercy Kill: The Answer to the Population Explosion?" Every three or four days I would change the booklets, an easy task since the W.O.N. bookstore had quantities of free pamphlets. At least one of these always had a business card clipped to it: Smith Armstrong, Chairman, JCFLA, South West Region, Commonwealth of Pennsylvania, Skyway Building, Pittsburgh. I got the card from Larry some time ago and, on a hunch, kept it. There is no doubt that this was the touch, a real show stopper.

Into this auspicious mess, then, came the boss, Adam Stringer. (My other boss, Frank, was let out with the other salesmen, a fact that gave me a secret pleasure. I am told he is an alcoholic derelict and hangs out somewhere across the river.) Usually Adam liked to pick up one of the pamphlets whenever he came around to check up, which was seldom. This time he did not. That should have tipped me off. For they were new pamphlets that I had picked up that very noon. I had even gone to the trouble of thumbing through them to underline a few passages in case someone took a look.

"David, could I see you in my office, please?"

That was another storm signal I missed. Usually he said things like "pal" or "buddy" or "tiger," anything to convey warmth and respect.

---

65 Great Britain also signed a Treaty of Friendship with the Soviet Union about a year after the United States did. At that time the full British Commonwealth was not involved in this action. However, England, Scotland and Ireland, except the Free State, agreed essentially to the same conditions as the United States.

Each month employees evaluate the bosses on their performance as part of a joint directive from the JCFLA and BWP aimed at "developing a true sense of democracy, individual responsibility and job performance consistent with a sound relationship between employers and employees."

"Sure, Adam. What can I do for you?" It was a bigger-than-life answer that failed to bring forth the friendly climate.

"If you'll just come along over to my place, we can talk," was the cold reply.

I followed him to his office, a corner room with four windows—an achievement in itself—and a sofa, some chairs and a conference-type desk. On the walls hung several so-so steel mill photos. Beyond this there was nothing that pointed to any particular affluence. In fact, for a recently created office, it had too much of a used quality to it. The desk was scratched and the fabric on the sofa and chairs was somewhat soiled, even frayed in a couple of places. Doubtless it was part of the progressive austerity that has cut successively deeper into the trappings of corporate officialdom, this due in large measure, I suppose, to all the fuss made at election time last year. And, of course, with the government buying up the company, the past few weeks had been a nightmare of scrambling to cut costs to the bone, including another salary reduction, ten percent across the board for everyone. I had thought that was why Adam wanted to see me, and so I geared myself to the news of less pay.

Editor's Note: In reading through this passage the first time, the editors missed the full significance of what Mr. Little writes here; or what he does not write. The assumption was that he would pick up and expand at some later point one of the more critical turning points in United States history. Even present-day world history students know, without too much prompting, that two major events occurred during the particular period to which Mr. Little devotes this section.

The first involved the presidential election held the preceding November. Recall that Mr. Little stated earlier that the Communist Party of America had been growing in scope and influence, which has been verified by any number of scholars. What he has failed to mention anywhere is the tremendous burst of energy that occurred in establishing a Communist Party of America headquarters in virtually every county in and around the great urban centers, such as New York, Chicago, Los Angeles and so forth, which took place suddenly during the preceding July, August and September. Further, Mr. Little makes no mention (other than to use the term "fuss," above) of the vigor and purpose with which the Communist Party entered into the presidential election. While this party technically fielded token candidates with little popular appeal for elective offices (the party was still a minority party at the time of the primaries), its main thrust was to inflict upon the voter community a full "Slate of Support" eight weeks before the election in which certain Democrat and Republican candidates were given "unqualified" CPA support. Party demonstrations became commonplace in those weeks. Also, riots were widely reported in which "unpopular" candidates were stoned or otherwise prevented from moving freely through the streets. There were several assassinations which at the time were blamed on "right-wing extremists." Election issues centered upon measures to enforce the peace and upon means to boost industrial and agricultural production; namely, nationalization of all basic industries, banks, transportation, power, basic communications and agriculture, farms of one hundred acres or less excepted. Both peaceful demonstrations and the riots appeared to have been used to apply pressure calling for the election of candidates who would vigorously support such programs. The riots seem to have been inspired through the CPA, if their own official writings are to be believed. Following the election, the CPA boldly announced that they now controlled forty percent of the House of Representatives and twenty-eight percent of the Senate. They made no claims regarding the President, who was reelected, except to offer support in the formation of a coalition between the CPA his administration and his party. Immediately after the inauguration the following January, the coalition was achieved.

One might ask how it was that the CPA could claim such a high percentage of successful candidates without entering candidates of their own. The answer is best described in Thomas MacHenry's study, Communist Strategy: Successes and Failures, 1848-2007 (Freeman Press, 2185). He quotes from numerous papers written by CPA officials detailing the various strategies employed by them. One section deals comprehensively with this particular election, termed "the beginning of the end for both the American bourgeois and their tools, the Reformists." In an essay written some years later, one official, Smith Armstrong (presumably the same as the one to whom Mr. Little refers), points out that the selection of candidates began immediately after the Treaty of Friendship was signed and "International Communism clearly had control of the power apparatus of the World Order of Nations which, in turn, gave them basic control over the United States; this ten months before the election."

The CPA activity began with the selection of certain key people, called sleepers, i.e., Communists who worked underground over a period of many years. They filed petitions for the various primary elections, beginning in the spring of the year. These candidates were registered as either Democrats or Republicans. Second, using hidden pressure tactics through the JCFLA units across the country, the kind Mr. Little describes earlier in his encounters with Leon Tidings, "certain unwanted candidates were asked to withdraw, and in most instances they did." It was a maneuver that went unnoticed. Third, those candidates who were "permitted" to remain in the primary elections were subsequently indoctrinated into Communism. The plan did not work perfectly. "We did well with this in the cities," Armstrong relates, "but were largely ineffective in the rural areas where there was still a preponderance of property holders. Fortunately, the apportionments for the House were overwhelmingly in favor of urban areas so that, even without the help of rural areas, we achieved a highly successful first step in solidifying our power position. From then on it was merely a matter of our sleeper candidates keeping silent until we could popularize the CPA and consolidate our growing power."

The other significant occurrence was the nationalization processes that took place almost immediately after the new Congress convened. The President in his Inaugural Address had called for the nationalization, as listed above, as well as the "elimination of private charity which for generations has been abused by the wealthy few who give their income away in order to escape the payment of their fair share of taxes, which has placed greater burdens upon those of lesser means who must make up out of their wages the additional taxes that the wealthy should be paying." Congress did not delay for long. Within three weeks after the opening session, Congress enacted the National Prosperity Act.

Better than five hundred major firms, power, steel, aluminum, petroleum and the like, were nationalised under the direction of the Department of Commerce. Mr. Little's company was included, and it is this point in time about which he now is writing.

It was only when the editors were studying this passage for the second time that they realized Mr. Little has omitted much from his account. Either he deemed these matters of little importance, or he was ignorant as to their meaning, or perhaps he no longer cared. In any event, he chose to ignore them and dwell, instead, upon his more personal problems.

But the news which Adam Stringer had for me involved more than a slight reduction in pay. It was no pay at all.

"Sit down, David. We've got a problem which you can help us with." Adam had moved to the scarred desk and stood behind it in a pot-bellied posture of monumental care.

"You know me, Adam. Let's just lay it on the line and have a look at it," I replied. Might as well win a few Brownie points by showing how easy I am to deal with, I thought.

"Knew you'd say that! We know, of course, that you, as much as anyone, are vitally interested in the success of our Peace and Prosperity Program."

"I certainly am! I try to keep up on things as best I can. Try to be helpful where I can, and all," I replied confidently.

"Well, then you're aware of all the problems of trying to get this peace-prosperity stuff off the ground."

"Yes."

316

"Well, we're just not measuring up under our new budget."

"Way over, eh?" Might as well beat him to the punch, I reasoned. A little gamesmanship.

"Way over is right! And that's where we need your help."

"Shoot."

Adam paced once completely around his desk to stand staring out one of his four windows at the city below. The ice was just breaking up on the rivers, and the late afternoon sun played tricks on the endless train of the white chunks as they drifted aimlessly down the river.

"David, I have to cut my payroll by one-third. The greatest service you can perform for your company... and you've been with us now for nearly twenty years... would be to give up your position here."

"Give it up for what?" I asked, the light beginning to dawn. I did not feel cute any more.

"Well, just give it up." He flicked some lint from his blue suit and stared absently at his frayed shirt cuff.

"You mean you're letting me... go?"

"That's about it." Adam sighed and sat wearily behind his desk to toy with a file folder which I then noticed was my personnel record, while all sorts of things darted through my mind. Then he brightened, his soft, square face alive with optimism. "Of course, you won't have any trouble. A man as good as you ought to be able to write his own ticket anywhere. That's what I'm going to say in my BWP recommendations, yes sir!"

"You think I do a good job then?" I asked, a new ploy coming into my mind, which was working desperately.

"Excellent. In fact... outstanding work!"

"If I'm so good, then why fire me?"

"Who's firing you? That's a poor word to use, David. Mighty poor," Adam cautioned with tones of personal hurt. "We're asking you to leave because of circumstances completely beyond your control. After all, you're not responsible, society is, for the pickle they've got us in. Of course, under the new plan we will get things straightened out again, but that's going to take some time. In the meantime. ..." He flapped his arms helplessly.

"If I'm so good, then why am I being asked to leave?" I'll pin him yet, I thought.

"Who better to leave than you!" he cried, as if he were delighted I had asked. "Look at it from my point of view. I've got 77 allocators. Now, all of 'em do their jobs pretty well, which means that I can use any or all of them and get by. Right?"

"Suppose so."

"O-kay! Employee welfare is one of my responsibilities, I'll tell you! It's no easy matter trying to meet our production quota and look after everyone's interests. But," he sighed with martyred care, "I do my best to have a well-rounded, balanced department. Right?"

"Right."

" 'Kay. Now, sure I could let someone else go who isn't as good as you. That's the easy way. But supposing they're not good enough to get a job on the outside? Think, for a moment, what this would mean. I would be conscience stricken."

I fought desperately to find some way of responding intelligibly, but failed utterly.

"Now. On the other hand, if I let my best men go I know they will do all right. Everyone is looking for good men, and I won't have to worry about you fellows. See?" He leaned back in his chair, beaming with brotherliness.

"You mean you're letting me go because I do a good ... an outstanding job?"

"Natch. By five o'clock tonight, I have to let 26 men go. If I part with the best ones, then at least I've let guys go who have the guts to land on their feet okay. Otherwise, I couldn't sleep nights knowing that I put someone out who just might not be able to make it. See?"

"You're willing to keep the poorer men and let the best men go?"

"That was a tough decision," Adam went on bravely. "I'll be shorthanded as hell, which is going to be rough as it is… mighty rough. And then on top of that, I'm giving up my best men, which will make matters even worse. But we can take it. I'm making a real sacrifice, but it's the only humane way."

318

I am not skilled enough with words to describe adequately the torrents of feelings that ripped through me. Once again, as so many times in the past, I was fighting a soft, billowy cloud. I strike at it and nothing happens. It is not hurt. It does not go away. I swing hard, but the cloud stays, peaceful and unperturbed. I knew there was absolutely nothing I could do to alter Adam's decision. It was too late to try to sell him on how poor a worker I was, not after all my efforts to create an image of superiority. He would not buy it, because—and we both knew this—he had made up his mind that I must go. The reasons he gave were of no consequence.

But I could still take one more tack. I could refuse to leave, thus forcing him actually to fire me, which no manager ever likes to do.

For one thing it goes into his BWP record as being "unable to resolve employee problems satisfactorily," a grave offense for those who hope to earn promotions. I know of one instance where a fellow pulled such a bluff, and his boss kept him on and let someone else go.

"All right, Adam, but you'll have to fire me."

Adam did not like that. He shifted uneasily. Beyond him through the windows and down over the rooftops the ice continued its relentless journey down river. People and lumbering busses began to flow steadily over the bridges. It was close to five. Quitting time.

"All right," he sighed. "Have it your way. I'll fire you. Of course, don't forget what goes into your record ... an obstructionist to the Peace and Prosperity Program and, therefore, a bad risk. Of course, you know if you resign by letter pointing out that you are leaving voluntarily for patriotic purposes there's a little bonus of two months' severance pay. Otherwise, you get nothing, other than this check here."[66] He picked a slip of paper from the file and waved it lazily in front of me. It comes to the penny, your salary as of five p.m. today... and no more."

He had me, and that was that.

---

66 Since one of the goals of the Treaty of Friendship was full employment of "responsible, freedom-loving people dedicated to peace and prosperity," and, since under this definition such desirable people already were fully employed, all forms of unemployment compensation had been abolished. Company life insurance fringe benefits also terminated with Mr. Little's job.

My letter of resignation was effective—at least on the stenographer, who had tears in her eyes after I dictated it. "Oh, Mr. Little, how fine of you to do this for us. But then you must really have something big going on outside…"

Like death, the loss of a job takes a little time to sink in. For a while the past pattern hangs together so that the teeth-clenching reality is numbed. Leaving the building at approximately five-o-five, for instance. Nothing unusual in that pattern. Carrying my briefcase and a paper bag. I have done that lots of times—important papers and a new shirt. So while the mind jabbered that I was leaving the building for the last time, the twenty-year habits that a fellow acquires going home from work pooh-poohed the whole thing. Nodding good night to the floor guard. Picking up a newspaper from tired Joe. Waving cheerfully to Miss Tucker, the ironing board spinster whose path I crossed nearly every night for more years than I care to remember. Patterns that said: This is all a joke; tomorrow will be the same as always. And the briefcase and paper bag were closed tight against prying eyes. Even my own mind could forget that inside were all of the earthly effects of a lifetime of work; outdated pictures of Nancy and the children in a tarnished double frame; a desk pen; a pencil cup; a couple of old cigars, big expensive ones left over from a posh company dinner; an hour-glass gimcrack that advertised "Time to Refinance Your Bills?" There were, too, a couple of file folders, labeled "personal," in which were my BWP papers, life and health insurance papers, now void, and a few personal letters of commendation that I had saved over the years. That was it.

I could walk out the door at five-o-five and not really believe that I would not be back tomorrow. I could go to the parking lot, pull the car from its slot, curse my usual curses and not feel a thing. At least, I did have the car. When the sales department was abolished in September I lost my right to a leased car but was given the opportunity to buy, which I had done. So here, too, the pattern still hung together. Even the sun low in the sky was the same, as were the people, the busses and the other cars all bluffing their way out of the city to choke the ramps to the tunnel and the South Hills beyond. Home as usual. No pain yet.

At home. Same greetings. Kids on top of kids, so that you have to look hard to spot your own. The cluttered driveway. Wagons, bicycles and roller skates to be moved. Lots of interesting things to keep the mind still. Nancy, in the kitchen, of course. Where else at this hour? Home from her office fifteen minutes before me and scurrying to throw some kind of an evening meal together. Too busy to talk then, of course, so you put the whole thing off until after dinner. And the pattern hangs together still. So you might as well be chipper—even a little silly, if the family will tolerate it, and enjoy dinner. It is ground beef patties, and for a moment there is a twinge. For you know you can no longer afford ground beef, not pure anyway. But Nancy has splurged on this, of all days, and it strikes you extremely funny.

Then, naturally, there is television after dinner. A comedy show. Now, who would want to miss that? So you sit and watch. You laugh and laugh. Funniest show in ages! The pattern hangs there, yet. Now it has become sort of a game. Perhaps if you ignore the plight it will go away.

Bedtime. Why get Nancy all upset and waken the children? Tend to it in the morning. So the pattern remains discreetly undisturbed. You see to the house, same as always. You brush your teeth in the same lazy way and stumble over the same clothes hamper after you turn out the light. You even set the clock. Then you rush headlong into sleep, because you know sleep is the most blessed of all balms. Here you are safe.

Morning, and the pattern shatters. The children have left for school and it is time to get up from the breakfast table. Time to grab the briefcase. Time to go to work.

"David, for heaven's sake, hurry with you hot milk so I can get the dishes in the sink." The matter-of-fact voice of Nancy. Hear it for the last time. Good-bye, old world! You had better say goodbye to it, too, Nancy.

The end of the road.

So you tell her, finally.

There is plenty of hell to pay. But it was worth the wait. One last, luscious hour squeezed out of the old ways before they are discarded. Actually, morning is a good time to break bad news. I recommend it highly to all those whose wives work. They cannot tarry to rant and cry. They must catch their ride. For they still have their patterns. See?

This gives you the whole day to mourn the dead, to figure how to explain things to friends and neighbors and plan next steps. You make no overt moves, but steel yourself for the onslaught of the three children as they charge across the yard and bang through the front door after school. They screech to a halt in mild surprise. Daddy is home! You shoo them away with the simple statement that you are in the process of changing jobs and are taking a little time off.

Hey. That's it. The official line to hand out to neighbors and friends. Changing jobs. Of course, Larry will be told the truth, because his help is desperately needed.

By and by comes Nancy flashing through the door with her face all bent out of shape with anxiety. She has had the day to think, too, in the central filing room at the BWP.

"What shall we do, David! What shall we do?"

We were in the bedroom, the only place where we could talk without being interrupted by the children. Ordinarily, it would have been a pleasant enough room. Nancy had done it herself in cheery yellow and white a couple of years before, and while faded here and there, it still ranked as our most elegant room, even surpassing the living room which never had been "done" in anything except odd pieces of furniture collected over a long period of installment payments and subjected to hard use. We were seated on the bed. She tugged at a floppy doll-type thing that ordinarily graced the coverlet. She was, naturally, crying, but not loudly. "Why? Why you?"

"I've told you. I'm too good to stay on," I replied, feeling a twisted kind of amusement at this irony.

"But, it doesn't make sense!" She spun the doll-type thing, its eight legs, or whatever, whirring like confused propellers.

"It's your world. You figure it out."

"I'm scared … awfully scared."

322

For a while we sat silently, watching the dying sun slip across the floor and up the wall into dusk. Dinner was a forgotten item.

"First, of course, you've got to start drawing some more pay .. . instead of working as a half-volunteer," I said, finally. "Or else find another job that really pays something, until I can get on my feet." "How can I?" Her reply quaked with nervous shame. "What will people say? It's considered the thing to offer your services for patriotic work. I just. .. can't... change all that."

"Somebody at BWP draws full salary."

"Oh sure, the executives and the," she paused unhappily, "less successful people. But David, how can I just go in and beg for money? I mean..."

"Because we'll starve unless you do, and you might as well get used to the idea. For god sakes, you know Tom Shade! Used to speak of him often enough. Tom this and Tom that, until I was sick of hearing his name!"

"That was a long time ago. I really haven't seen him since the hearings, when you got into all that trouble with Tidings, and I was put back in central filing."

"Well, hunt him up, then." My voice was less than sympathetic. The woman did not seem to understand. She fingered the doll-like thing again as if she thought the answers lay there.

"David," again she paused, her moist brown eyes big and somber. Her voice trembled slightly. "I never told you this but Tom sort of took a... well... liking to me. In some ways I was pleasing to him."

"So?"

"So. He used to make passes at me."

"And?"

"I always told him... no." She sat back, trembling slightly and waited.

I am not certain what sort of reaction she expected. Most bosses make passes at office girls. It is part of the game and a lot of women land some fine jobs. I only made one pass, myself, and that years ago. My ego could not take the rebuff when the young lady looked at me unblushingly and told me to go to hell, that I was not important enough and that she was already being nicely cared for by an assistant vice president. As far as Nancy's probable encounters, I knew that she had neither the courage nor the inclination for store-room hanky-panky. Too stand-offish. Too demeaning to her dreams of glamor and glory. A Larry Best type would be more to her tastes if she thought she could get away with it. But to my knowledge the opportunity never presented itself, in the past year or so, at least. And who can think back beyond a year and a half ago?

"You never did learn how to cope with men ... or boys ... in things like that, did you?"

"What an odd thing to say!" She put down the doll-like thing. The tears were now gone, replaced with surprise. "You sound... almost disappointed."

"No," I replied. An idea was beginning to take shape in my mind. "It's just that sometimes a woman can have her cake and eat it, too, if she plays her cards right. In your case, Tom Shade likes you, or used to. What's the harm in warming up that friendship— not too much, mind, but a little bit maybe—just enough to get you on salary for a while until I can get located. And, oh, incidentally, let's just tell everyone that I'm in the process of changing jobs."

"I like that about what to tell people but, David," her heart-shaped face furrowed, perplexed, "do you think I should lead him on ... in case he should..."

"Damn right! It'll serve them right. All of them. And in the meantime I'll get down to the BWP first thing tomorrow and set things in motion. I've got a good record. Shouldn't have much trouble... especially if you nudge things along. Get yourself reestablished with Shade on salary and then maybe you can steer me toward a job ... in case I luck out."

"You don't know what you are saying!" she cried. "You can't expect me to behave like the rest of those bitches! All my life I've wanted to live in dignity and in good taste. And now you want me to throw myself at a man, in order to get money!"

"All right!" I exploded. "We'll sell the house. Can't you understand that I have exactly two months' pay, and there is no more! There is

324

no job! There is no anything and there won't be, unless we get busy and use our wits. That's what Larry said, remember? We can win, he said, if we use our wits. Now, damn it, it's your turn! I've carried the load as far as I can alone. Call it what you will! Call me weak! Call me a coward! I don't care, now. I know what I am. A lousy nothing just like you've said. Well, all right! Now it's your turn to get dirty with the crass details of trying to live in this stinking world. You don't like what I say? Well, get used to it! This is your world, Nancy. Now get dirty in it like the rest of us. Do that... or starve."

I spoke as if someone else were inside of me now; that the old David Little had been cashed in along with his last pay check and a whole tub full of wooden nickels had come tumbling out. The breadwinner without bread, shoving the wife out into the streets. But then I would begin tomorrow to find a job on my own through the regular channels of the BWP Employment Division.

2

The still, small voices said that finding a new job would not be quite as easy as my polished outside self kept proclaiming. They were right. Getting inside the BWP for a job referral interview, in itself, was a major undertaking. I was three days just getting inside the doors, and another two were spent waiting for the interview. A week of standing in line, leaning against walls and maneuvering for a place to sit on a hard bench. The long grey line of job seekers, hundreds of them in assorted sizes, shapes and spirits. Some people had had baths. Some had not. Most were sober. This was the sight that shook me on the raw, rainy morning this past March, as I swung around the corner at the base of the Federal Building. People! A double line weaved out of the mouth of the building and up Liberty for almost two blocks. At first I did not connect the people with jobs. Blandly, I went past them into the lobby to the elevator bay where the line terminated, only to be accosted by one of the dozen or so guards who wanted to know where I thought I was going.

"Sixth floor. Employment," I said, testily.

"Got a card?"

"A what?"

"Skip it, you're not going up there, sonny."

The guard was, perhaps, ten years younger than I, but he had a mustache and was smoking a cigar that he kept poking at me. Better that than his night stick. "Where do you think all these people are going?"

"Yeah!" a half dozen voices added. The faces at the head of the line, waiting as I now saw for their turn in the elevator, were dark with rage. "Throw the rat out! Yeah! Yeah!"

"You mean that's the line?"

"That's right, buddy boy. Now get the hell out of here and wait your turn, before I run you in."

Yeah. Yeah. Yeah. The chorus followed me all the way back.

By four o'clock I had made it into the building lobby again, where at least it was dry and warm. I was quite wet and a little tired. I had been fortunate, though. About a dozen of us standing together had made deals to spell each other off. So I was able to get a sandwich about noon and go to the rest-room four times. At first neither the woman in front nor the man behind me would hold my place, that is, not until they and a few others had to go. Then we worked out the plan. So the day went smoothly enough. But the rub came at five o'clock when the office closed. I was sixth in line to the elevator. They shoved us all out of the lobby and told us to come back tomorrow.

The next morning I was there at seven-thirty, an hour-and-a- half before the office opened. But others had the same idea and so, again, I was too late to make the elevators. Still it rained. This time I did some thinking.

The following day I was at the doors at five a.m. I managed to signal the night guard who unlocked the door cautiously and belligerently. We had a few whispered words, and I slipped him a twenty dollar bill. He turned his back, while I climbed the stairs to the sixth floor. I was in! But not really. The night guards must have been making sizable fortunes; the whole corridor was packed with people, some standing, some sitting, some sleeping on the floor. Now

326

I understood why the line moved so slowly at street level. It was stinky, for the air conditioning was off. At nine o'clock some neat, official-looking people got off the elevators, and the big double doors leading to the employment waiting room were thrown open. The mob surged forward to the completely inadequate counter space, where the bank-teller-like clerks began filling out name cards in duplicate. The applicants kept one and the other went into a big box to be dispatched, ultimately, to one of a battery of desks in the huge open room beyond, where the interviewers sat.

Ever try to order drinks at a banquet with a thousand people moving in on one bar? That is child's play compared with trying to work your way to the BWP counter. It was nearly noon before I could get my name filled out on cards. That was a major breakthrough. Even if no interviewer got to me that day, I still would have the right to come back the next day and go directly to the waiting room, merely by showing the card to the guard. That is what happened, for no particular order was being followed. Cards were scooped up out of the big box every now and then by interviewers. It was like a giant Bingo game, only my number was never called.

Nor was it called on the fourth day. But I did find a bench to sit on fairly close to the counter gate where interviewers came and went occasionally for coffee or lunch or whatever.

My luck changed on the fifth day. A young girl had ridden up on the elevator with me the day before (there was no longer any need to be there before nine). She was having difficulty with some packages obviously destined for the Post Office. So I had helped her through the crowd. Now on this morning we met again in the elevator and smiled a greeting. Several times during the morning I saw her. She was an interviewer, and twice noticed me. At noon she came through the gate on her way to lunch. The interviewers worked in shifts so it was not wise to leave long enough to get something to eat, lest I be called. She was going to pass me by, I am sure, but perhaps because of my good deed the day before, she stopped and smiled down at me.

"I know you can't leave. Could I bring you a sandwich?" Her voice was warm and alive with the eagerness of youth. She was perhaps twenty, a tall, slender girl with a wholesome face. She had spoken the first genuinely kind words that I had heard in perhaps a year—the simple, direct offer to do something for somebody else without a price tag. I suppose I let my gratitude show, mostly in my face. I remember looking up at her for a very long time before I stood up.

"Forgive me for staring, but you're quite a shock," I replied finally.

"Me? Have I done something wrong?"

"No! No!" I laughed. An honest laugh of pleasure, not pain. "I am as hungry as can be, and I appreciate your thoughtfulness, but you've no reason to..."

"I know, sir. But I've noticed you all morning... yesterday, too... just sitting there and not moving. I'd feel better if you'd let me bring you something." Her eyes were searchingly big and bright and brown. Hers was a young face that somehow had escaped the iron locks of cynicism. She had a simple, madonna-like quality that gave her a timeless substance and a plain kind of beauty. She was neat but not flashily dressed, as if clothes were an important event to her, in the sense that they must be made to last and to suit a variety of needs.

We drifted toward the big double doors, working our way around the weary, dejected bodies that shifted senselessly back and forth. A few people talked, like two toothless old men who were cackling in low tones while their beady eyes roved. Elsewhere a man and woman argued, husband and wife doubtless. There were younger people, too—as many women as men—quiet, mostly, in prayer-like attitudes of desperation. One imagines they had young families at home to feed, clothe and comfort. We talked, the young lady and I, as we sought the elevator. I gave her my name and learned that she was Marie Salvatoria.

"Believe me," I said, "I could eat a dozen sandwiches, but not in this! There isn't enough room to blow your nose!" She laughed. It was light and musical and suggested that perhaps she was a person who would hum or sing a lot to herself around the house or walking down the street. "And you're right, I can't leave this swamp. It took me five days to claw my way in here."

"Five days!" She was genuinely shocked. "That's awful! And no one has called you yet?"

"I'm still at the bottom of that barrel you've got over there, and if I left here it would be just my luck…"

"Excuse me, sir. I'll be right back." And she darted back through the gate, lithe and quick. She was back in five minutes, heels clicking in triumph. She held a card between long, slender fingers. Her eyes radiated the pleasure she felt in successfully performing her deed.

"They can't call you now, Mr. Little, because I've got it right here. And after you have something to eat, I'll fill out your papers!"

"Then lunch is on me!"

She perked her head for a moment, as if deciding if this would be all right. Her full lips were pursed in a half-smile. "I eat a lot."

"You should. You're almost as tall as I am!" I quipped.

"All right. Close though."

"Of course, I can't risk missing my interview."

She nodded, her face ponderous with mock gravity, "And I have to be on time for my appointment."

We both laughed then, the only ones on the floor who, on a somber March day, could find a light side in an otherwise dark world. We found a stand-up sandwich shop, and she had two hamburgers (mostly cornmeal or sawdust; we could not tell for sure, a puzzle that triggered more laughter). Then we walked in the rain—a drizzle, really, that carried the sweetness of spring—down along the river and back up to the Federal Building, all in fifty minutes.

Her remarkableness was, paradoxically, her simplicity, because she was not simple. Rather, she put things into perspective because of the uncluttered way she could look at them. For instance, her job as interview clerk with the BWP was her second one, full-time that is. Her first had been in the steno pool at the Litemetal Corporation, a job she had held for two-and-a-half years before it was abolished just a month before. Apparently she had befriended someone at the BWP when she applied there for new employment; holding the door open for a department head or someone, an older woman anyway; a simple, unplanned act, I gather, that was so out of keeping with most youthful behavior that Miss Whatever-her- name (Marie was talking too spiritedly for me to catch all of the detail) hired her on the spot

329

as a "temporary." This means no civil service protection and no notice or severance pay required for dismissal.

"Doesn't that make you uneasy?" I asked. She had volunteered this information without any sign of particular concern. Yet, there was nothing about her that implied smug confidence or arrogance, just a straight away recitation rattled off between bites of her hamburger, her second at this point. While she chewed, her eyes took over; big, bright and expressive—too young and innocent to know the terrors of a grownup world, I thought.

"What makes me uneasy?"

"A temporary job?"

"M'm'm," she gulped. "Aren't all jobs?"

I was about to explain seniority and the other technicalities of stable employment, when the still small voices reminded me I had no job to which to refer. "You're right!" I found myself laughing again, because her eyes were laughing too, while she consumed the last bite of her sandwich. "But some jobs are, shall we say, less temporary."

"Yes. I had one of those, too, at Litemetal, but it's gone. So now I'm here. Tomorrow I'll be somewhere else."

"You really believe that, don't you?"

She wiped her lips thoughtfully on the little slip of paper they give you for napkins nowadays. The stand-up eatery was packed with people and loud talk. High-pitched, over-dressed girls who, like Marie, were newcomers to the business world but who, unlike her, were out to make it the easy way; slick-suited men of all ages ranged in and about the new crop, puffing, strutting and staring to impress someone enough for a drink or two after work. So what she said next was jarringly out of context with the atmosphere, enough to set her in sharp relief against the scene.

"Yes. God helps those who help themselves. I try always to help myself, so I know God will help me. I worry about what I should worry about and let Him take care of the rest." She said it as if she were giving me the time from the plain but tastefully serviceable watch she wore.

Coming from anyone else, except possibly Mary Best, I would have laughed, particularly had it been the Reverend Mr. Sandmeyer. I had heard the phrase used many years ago by my parents. I was intrigued that one so young should not only know it but speak it with such soft, firm conviction. "Who told you this? Rather, who taught it to you?"

"Our Mother Superior at St. Ann's."

"A school?"

"Used to be. It was closed right after I graduated. It was too small I guess. Besides, I heard they wanted to split up the nuns. They were all Orthodox, you know."[67] "Are you still a Catholic?"

"Yes, I suppose. Father Herbert understands and never makes me say too many beads."

"You mean for saying God helps those who help themselves." She nodded, eyes and mouth in smiles. "He winks at me and says, 'Confidentially, you're right! Only don't give the Lord away, or they'll be transferring Him, too.' He says not to be afraid. So I'm not."

"He must be quite a guy, this..."

"Father Herbert. They've transferred him four times, somebody said. Of course, I'm glad, because he's at our church now."

We were walking in the drizzle now, down along the drab Liberty Avenue, with more shops closed than open. Here and there were a few stores doing brisk business selling secondhand merchandise under garish signs labeled: "Discounts! First-Class Items Specially Selected!" Loudspeakers blared "giveaway bargains!" Toasters like new beginning at sixty-five dollars. Irons at forty-five dollars and TV parts at new low prices. We peered at the gleaming array in one window.

"Who needs a toaster when you can fry bread in a pan," she scoffed.

"You have no toaster?"

---

67 Roman Orthodox Catholics. Not to be confused with either Greek or Russian Orthodoxy. Refers to Catholic Traditionalists who subscribed to original Christian values and who fought extensive changes in their church but who lost to the Moderates who redefined God as an impersonal force whose sole role was to create the universe and who revised church teachings toward more direct participation in political affairs.

"Daddy dropped it last year. He doesn't walk very well or hold things, either."

It was a comfortable opener that permitted me to ask questions and her to answer them matter-of-factly, as we completed our damp walk. She was the youngest of six children, three of each sex. All were married, except for her. Two of her brothers were in the W.O.N. Peace Keeping Force and the third was a mechanical engineer with an auto plant in Detroit. Her two older sisters lived in New England and California. This left Marie to care for her father, widowed some years earlier and in recent times the victim of a stroke. They still had their home, an old dwelling squeezed in with others like it on a narrow, cobbled street on top of Mount Washington. They lived in the downstairs and let the upper floor to another Italian family, with only three children (a young couple, Marie laughed). Other than the rent, Marie was the sole keeper, except for odd sums her brothers and sisters dutifully sent home more as a token of respect than anything else. Marie has always known work. At ten she started in the kitchen at her uncle's pizzeria after school and Saturdays without thought of child labor laws. (The work wasn't hard. Uncle Jerry saw to that. Besides, to work is good, and the money went for clothes.) The pizzeria was sold when she was fifteen, so she took care of children and later became a grocery clerk, waitress and, finally, worked as a part- time typist in an insurance agent's office. Then, after she was graduated from high school (a college prep course, just in case) she got her big chance, a job as mail girl in the vast, coveted corridors of Litemetal Corporation. Competition for the job was keen, and her whole neighborhood celebrated with pride this accomplishment. From there she had enrolled at William Penn, nights, with the dream of taking eight or so years to earn her degree. ("I guess I couldn't qualify for a scholarship. Dad didn't have much pull and St. Ann's didn't have much of a reputation.") But her father suffered a stroke, and he had to retire from his craft as a stone mason. That ended William Penn ("for now, but I'll get an education somewhere").

"Boy friends?"

She flushed a slight bit and smiled. "No. I date some, but I'm too busy. Besides, there's no one I care about, really."

"But what of your future. I thought all girls worked toward the day when they could marry... anyone... for," my voice took on mock hearts and flowers, "the sanctity and security of a home?" I was thinking of my own elder daughter, Peggy.

"I have a home, and I have a job."

"Not forever."

"Perhaps. But I'll make out. As long as there is work to be done, I'll work at any job that I can do. Some day, perhaps, there will be a man who will attract me, and I him, for keeps. But in the meantime I have to live as best I know how."

"Not everyone feels that way."

"I do."

Another lesson from your Mother Superior?"

"My father."

"You love him."

"Yes. I respect him, too. Women should respect their men." "What is your greatest ambition?"

"To live my life as if I were going to die tomorrow."

"Another lesson?"

She smiled broadly, her cheeks streaked with moisture, as dew on a rose, and her brown eyes rich with the promise of life that, again, stood her in sharp contrast with the grim parade of harried and hopeless men and women who moved along the wet street; curiously bent figures wrapped in worn clothing whose images were weirdly reflected from the shiny pavement in the dull light of cloudy mid-day.

"Father Herbert. Some day, maybe you'll get to meet him."

We went back inside, then. Back to the living dying, where the turn of a piece of paper into this stack or that would make the difference. Back to the oracles at BWP where the fate of the employables is decided. The steps are simple enough. First, the employable's 2020F (Basic Job Request Form) is filled out by an "interviewer" such as Marie. The employable then returns home to await word in writing on the next step; namely, the impartial review of his application by a "classifier."

333

Here his entire work history file, including all tests, personal aptitude, attitude, and so on is re-examined, and—under normal circumstances—a minimum of two potential job classifications is "suggested." The employable then is advised of his area of potential employment, and his entire file is forwarded to a "coordinator" who determines what jobs are available to fit the assigned classifications. Here priorities are assigned or, rather, "suggested," and the file goes to the "evaluator." His job is to match all job openings with potential job holders in each situation and, from this, select the top three "competitors." At this point it used to be that the competing employables then would be notified to report to Company X at a given time for an interview. However, this provision has been eliminated. Instead, only one employable is selected, this done through the newly created function of "selector," who then so advises the employable and company. The new method, we are told, has greatly streamlined the whole employment process and has resulted in a considerable reduction in ill-used time and effort. For those employables who do not make it the first time, their records are returned to the coordinator who takes another stab at matching another job opening and the file goes back up the line. If that fails, the file then is returned to the classifier for another run. And if that fails—but then it never does. No employable is ever told "no," unless he is mentally or physically ill. His file simply keeps moving on the theory that something may develop.

And while this process goes on, the employable waits at home. It used to be that he could draw unemployment compensation for as long as three years, but that provision was abolished last fall. He may now, however, apply for relief, providing he can prove he has no assets of any kind, save clothing; in other words, show that he's a pauper, which requires court certification. All employables have the right of appeal and also have the right to visit the selector personally, provided it is merited.

Time lapse for a new job: six weeks minimum and no one knows the maximum.

There are a lot of people waiting. The streets are full of aimless wanderers, many of them panhandlers. A favorite trick is for a man to have his wife and at least one child at his side. Others scavenge for junk and, occasionally, for scraps of food around eating places. This is always a depressing sight.

Marie got things rolling in a hurry as soon as we returned from our outing. It had done us both good. We had become friends, a novelty these days. No one makes friends, unless they have to. It puts you under too much obligation. You never know when your friend will come around to your door some evening with family in tow looking for a place to stay or possibly a meal. It's tough to say no under such circumstances. Nancy and I have had to say it twice already, just in the past month. With Marie it was different. Her own sense of pride and purpose would forbid her to become a burden on others, even with an ill father. Once back at the BWP she was all business. She ran the 2020F into her typewriter with smooth energy and set to work.

"Name ... oh, I've got that!" She had to raise her voice to an unnatural pitch to fight the bedlam about us. Date of birth and place, father's occupation, race, nationality and religion (if any), spouse, children, previous occupations, education, references, and so on. She clacked away as fifty others were doing.

"And... let's see. Organizations? Like unions? Wait. You won't need that, or will you?" she asked, stumped for a moment. All hourly rated jobs in manufacturing and industry require union membership. Without it, no job.

"I hope not. I don't belong to a union." I replied. But it occurred to me that I had better join one, and soon.

"Other organizations?"

I gave her my church, the Boy Scouts and threw in the PTA for luck.

"Is that all?" There was mild surprise in her voice. "Usually, I fill this blank to overflowing."

"I'm not a joiner."

She looked at me pensively for a moment. "You know, I'm glad, but we've got to think of something."

"How about Chairman, Greater Pittsburgh Industrial Association for Peace?" I asked, struck with the inspiration that I might as well take advantage of my investment with Leon Tidings, too.

Her face fell, and for the first time her spirit seemed to falter. "Of course," she said. "You're the Little who led the demonstration. I remember, because I had to watch it on TV when I was at Litemetal. Father Herbert says you helped to destroy our leadership."

"Would you believe me, Marie, if I told you I was forced to do that?" I think I asked the question quietly enough, without trying to defend myself.

Once again her great brown eyes looked directly into mine. I did not look away. She read my pleas.

"I believe you," she replied.

"Won't you tell your Father Herbert?" I asked. She nodded, pleased, I like to believe. One person out of all of this, I thought, looking around the crowded BWP office, who maybe will believe the truth.

"Let's put the committee down, anyway." And we did.

In another half-hour we were done, and Marie performed another act of kindness. She hand-delivered Form 2020F to the classifier urging that it be processed as quickly as possible. "Mr. Carter is a good man. He's the only classifier I really know, and he'll do everything he can."

"Uh-huh," I replied wryly. This brought a gentle protest from her.

"Really, Mr. Little, he is a lot like you, only a little older and a very distinguished and kind person. He's like me, a temporary, but he used to be vice president of a bank. So he knows what it means not to have a job."

A brave young girl, straight and tall, still, going to bat for the likes of me. A breath of sweet air sweeping across a foul landscape to lift the heads and hopes of the desperate few whom fortune flings at her battered desk day after day. A youth serious in the job given her, this itself something of a miracle. She still is capable of trust but, I note, trust in a Supreme Being. Whoever the Mother Superior had been, she had outfoxed the system. For she had managed to slip through the rank upon rank of faceless system-makers another breed, for whom there was no mold, a throwback, perhaps, to another time. And the college and universities had not yet put their hooks into her to undo what St. Ann's had taught her. Marie Salvatoria, I had no doubt, would somehow survive, not by wit or cleverness or opportunism but through a kind of basic simplicity stronger than any force that could be turned on her. At least this was my hope as I left the BWP after a five-day siege.

3

As well-meaning and helpful as Marie Salvatoria had been, I knew it was unrealistic to expect much. For one thing there were too many former salesmen on the loose. Steel, aluminum, chemicals, oil, fabrication; wherever one turns, salesmen have had their jobs abolished as companies are nationalized and their products more and more are allocated by prearrangement to fill overseas Treaty commitments. Only the leftovers are being piecemealed out to hungry manufacturers and businesses here at home. Privation in the midst of plenty. For production in the basic plants continues at record pace, while less and less of our products are consumed by us, leaving empty store shelves and great multitudes of unwashed salesmen. For another thing, Marie could not know how most job placements were being auctioned off. One favor deserves another, and BWP job evaluators and selectors hold perhaps the most coveted positions in the community. They live well. One hears stories of bribes and other less savory kinds of accommodation. Of course, nothing is ever proved. Strangely enough it is the Communist Party that has begun calling for reforms among "fat BWP officials." There is no denying that the Communists carry considerable weight. Their charges are being aired openly in the press and, once more, whether one likes them or not, on this particular issue of corruption in the BWP they do make sense. It is difficult to keep from going along with them. My dilemma is that I have neither the resources nor the contacts to gain a favorable decision on a new job. While I had left it with Marie that I would contact her periodically to determine the progress of my file, the real effort depended on Nancy.

Unless I found employment soon we would lose everything. My savings had long since been eaten up by a series of Peace Bond drives that occur about once a month now. Mr. Jamison has been to our house five times since last fall, each time with a "suggested" pledge card all neatly made out. We have had no choice but to cooperate. Beyond this, a portion of my salary also had been committed to Peace Bonds. We were, in short, absolutely broke.

Nancy, of course, was tearfully aware of this. And while I conducted my five-day siege, she set herself to go a whole new tack. I was not fully aware of the extent to which she drove herself in this effort. Women are funny creatures. They will go to pieces over a leaky faucet, but let a crisis arise, and it is as if a chemical change has taken place in them. Their bodies become rigid with an inner and uncommunicated resolve. Their faces shape themselves into whatever expression is demanded at the moment—gaiety, fury or grim determination. They switch emotions on and off with a calculated swiftness that is chilling to observe.

I noticed it first in Nancy the Monday morning after my BWP stint. The initial chore was done and all I could now do was wait at home. I was watching her dress for work. She had not chosen to discuss her progress with Tom Shade, and I chose not to ask. She had been for the most part quiet over the weekend, except to snap at the children more than usual. Occasionally, I would catch her in the midst of silent tears, which she would quickly wipe away and go about her business over the kitchen sink or wherever. Only once did she refer directly to our plight and this to say, "If I have to sell my soul to the devil, I will get you a job." It was the way she dressed herself with cold, reluctant care, standing first for a long time at the closet studying the row of dresses and suits that hung there and then selecting her good black dress. It was the one that cost us one hundred and ninety-five dollars two years ago. It was her very best, and she nursed with frantic care to keep it like new. She was careful where and how often she wore it. She did not wear it too often before the same people because it would be the tip-off that we could only afford one good, dressy dress. The black dress, then, was a symbol.

338

It was the ultimate weapon, brought into play only on very special occasions. The last time she had worn it was at the PTA dance last summer. She put it on now with painstaking care, standing before the mirror turning this way and that to observe herself. It fitted her well. The neck line was modest, as dressy dress neck lines go, cut to her waist with only a narrow V, rather than the open V's that most women wear. Her hair was done with extra care, and after a long look, a slow smile crept over her face.

"Well?" she asked, her eyes catching mine in the mirror.

"You are truly a beautiful woman," I said.

"Now you tell me," she said flatly, the smile fading.

"Maybe you haven't always deserved it."

"I could argue that point," she replied coldly.

"You would find us on two different wave lengths. So an argument is pointless. The past is dead, Nancy."

"Not if I can help it." She spoke with a trace of bitterness ringing her full, moist lips. For an instant her eyes became mystic flints. She turned from the mirror and faced me. "I shall be working late. Can you get dinner for the children?"

The matter-of-fact way she said it began to seep under my skin. Her brittleness made her a stranger. She might, I thought, have expressed some kind of warmth or regret or something.

"Sure, but is it so damned necessary for you to... work late?" I emphasized.

"Yes, because... dear Mr. Shade, Tom, that is ... is taking me to dinner."

"When did he ask you?"

"He hasn't," she said softly, "but he will," Her eyes glittered. She left then, after giving terse directions as to where I could find potatoes and a ham hock she had been saving. The children had gone on their way without much help from either of us. Then I was in the quiet house with no one but Peppy, our beagle, who had no interest in anything except to sleep. I did the breakfast dishes, made the beds and tidied up as best I could. The vacuum was broken—parts are not available—and so I used a broom. I wet it to keep the dust down, an

339

ironic twist, for I had learned that trick as a child in my father's store. A lifetime spent traveling full circle from one broom to another.

By ten o'clock I had done all I could, and the quiet, empty house was eating at me. I was accustomed to noise and people, and my mind was struggling for some kind of exercise. I tried reading, but the magazines and newspapers were too depressing. Everywhere it was the same old story—peace and prosperity for all, new performance standards and government programs and, always, "hope for the future!" as soon as this emergency or that problem is solved. The formula was the same for everything, be it juvenile delinquency, education, business or marriage and the family. Television also was a total loss. Quiz shows were ever present, as they have been for a very long time, offering pots of gold to a few privileged housewives and workmen. "And now, ladies (they leave off gentlemen during the daytime shows), our plumber from Lincoln, Nebraska, meets Mrs. Jones, a housewife from Boston...." Enough! The radio was worse. Terrible music, endless public service commercials on the Peace Keeping Force and Bonds, and lengthy taped interviews with W.O.N. and Communist Party leaders revealing plans for all the peoples of the world. That was the phrase most consistently used in spoken word or print, "For all the peoples of the world!" It was the one that finally drove me to fling a book at the radio, smashing it to the floor. I was momentarily stricken with panic and remorse, until I remembered that radios were still easy to get, at very low cost as a government educational subsidy. I tried solitaire and gave up quickly.

It was inevitable that my mind should turn to Mary and Larry Best. I had managed to stop by their home after the first day of waiting in line at the BWP, to break the news of my resignation. I thought of Mary first, because this was the time of day when we used to be together. At odd moments I am concerned about her. For ever since that day in the parking lot after the hearings, she had been too—too gay, too energetic. She always is busy doing something; fidgeting with an object picked absently from a table top or painting a room or washing down a wall; too casual; too funny with her wit; too much on the go. She seems to have taken on a sudden burst of speed in everything she does and cannot slow down long enough to see where she has been or where she is going. She has never once mentioned our interlude of false hope. She is like the light bulb that burns suddenly too brightly, and a sixth sense tells you it will soon burn out in one last brilliant flash. Thus, every so often, come the disquieting thoughts of Mary. So on this empty morning I phoned her.

"It's me," I said, after a too bright hello at the other end of the line.

"David?"

"None other."

"How's the job hunt?"

"Fine." There was a long pause. "How are you?"

"Busy. Don't know why there's always more to do than there is time." She breathed as if she had just come running from some place. "I'm redoing Larry's study. Finding paint has been an awful chore, and I can't get the right color. I wanted a nice warm brown tone, but I'm afraid I've got one with too much pink." She spoke like a machine gun.

"I thought I might stop by," I cut in.

"Why, that would be very nice, except everything is in such a mess, and Larry's not here and I know he would love to see you too…"

"I mean, to see you. Look, do you realize that we haven't had a chance to talk … well, for some time… you and me, I mean." I was floundering, because the words were taking me nowhere. "Damn it, Mary! Don't you remember anything that happened between us?"

"Well," she laughed too gaily, "we were a little foolish, weren't we? But it happens I guess all the time, so we can certainly be forgiven our little affair."

"Have you ever told Larry?"

"No, of course not. That's not polite. I think he probably suspects I had an affair with someone, but then I suspect he's had one or two himself … a coed or two. So we're even. Besides, it's the fashion. Everybody's doing it you know!" She laughed, too lightly.

Then there was another pause. The conversation was exhausted. There was nothing else to do but wish her well and hang up. Who was it who said: "You can't go home again?" If Mary had any message, that was the one.

I tried to read a book. Nancy belonged to the One-A-Month-Club, so the book shelves were loaded with all sorts of fancy titles: *Affair in the Garden; Poor Man's Passions; The Inner Cross*. Nearly all dealt with peace, poverty, and sex. But, like the magazines, they were too depressing. As I searched frantically for something else to do, the cheerful countenance of Larry hovered ghostlike at my side. As the clock neared noon, I phoned him.

"Well, Well. David, m'boy! How's it all going?"

I said things were fine and suggested I drop by his office. I knew he had no classes Monday afternoon.

"Come ahead. Only make it at two-thirty. I've a lunch on, y'see." It was a cordial enough invitation, only there was an unidentifiable vagueness in his voice, as if he were overtired.

I had a lonely sandwich, peanut butter, and some powdered milk. I also found an apple that I knew Nancy was saving for the evening meal to be shared with everyone, but I ate the whole thing anyway. Then I debated whether I should take the bus or the car. The tank was half full, which meant I would not have to buy gas for a while, if I made each trip count. The bus would save on the gas but the fares are so high. I finally took paper and calculated which would be more economical. It was a tossup. So I took the car, timing my arrival in the parking lot behind Grant Hall at exactly two-thirty.

Larry's office was on the third floor of a fairly new building of straight, functional lines, like so many of the later buildings on the William Penn campus. The exterior still looked presentable, although the patchwork of different colored panels had begun to fade, and the sidewalk and steps were cracked. The lower two floors were classrooms, filled with the low buzzings of learning. The automatic elevator was out of order, so I walked to the door of room 303 which bore a plastic plate: Professor L. A. Best, Political Science. Behind it was a small reception area where a coed, a provocative creature with classic Greek features, sat typing some sort of manuscript. I was able to go right into Larry's office, a big comer room that bore the stamp of academic affluence, faded but still impressive. The walls were lined with books and jumbled stacks of papers, and Larry's desk had its usual untidy look. He was in the midst of writing on a long yellow tablet. His handwriting was neat and thoughtful even in comfortably large scrawls. He was thinner, and his usually serene face bore the marks of fatigue. His hair and suit were as rumpled as ever, but there was lackluster about these trademarks. He was the same, and yet he was not. His tall frame, usually at ease in an awkward sort of way, was more stooped than his personality called for. His greeting was warm enough, but his blue eyes were not quite in it. They kept looking over my shoulder.

"Well, well! Have a seat." He did not offer to move over to his sofa as he had so often done in the past. Usually, too, Larry took the lead in setting the conversation. He most always had a bit of news or some cryptic comment about the affairs of the nation or some other profound thought. But not today.

"Doing some writing? Hope I haven't cut you up by barging in," I said.

"Not at all. Fact is, I was wondering how things are going."

Something in his manner told me he could not take the truth. I gave him an optimistic picture. He seemed a little more relieved of some inner tension when I finished extolling the list of contacts that my imagination had quickly summoned.

"That's fine. You'll make out. Only thing…" he hesitated almost guiltily, "I would have liked to have gone to bat for you, only," he ran his large bony hands through his hair, "exam time, y'know. Been so busy I haven't seen much of Smith Armstrong lately. He's busy, too," he added hastily.

I now saw that Larry had been afraid that I might ask his help. "Understandable. Don't worry. I've several solid leads. Tell me," I probed, "are you still as active with the JCFLA as you used to be?"

For an instant his eyes clouded and then fought to become clear and steady. "Well, well. Things have tapered off. To be expected, y' know. Can't do the whole thing myself!" he laughed, like Mary, with too much ease. "Told Smith he'd have to learn to rely a little less on me for the next few months. So I don't see him as often as I should."

He's lying, I thought. Larry Best is lying to himself. He's being dumped, like the rest of us. They're moving in on him now. And he's been dreading to see me, because he's afraid I'll ask him to do me a favor that he can no longer deliver. But he'll never admit it, because he won't allow himself to believe it.

"Larry, we've known each other for more than twenty years. You've never lied to me... knowingly, anyway... but you're lying to me now."

For a moment he straightened himself, and his face broke into buoyant confidence. "Nonsense, m'boy! Ought to know better than that!"

"You ought to know better." I looked at him hard. And he melted. He sagged. The forced sparkle in his eyes was washed away by weariness. He pushed the yellow tablet from him and rose painfully from behind the still faintly elegant desk, his tall, bony frame gaunt. He turned away to the window, as if somehow to hide his shame that the old image had faded, even as the drapes before him had from a rich brown to a dingy beige.

"They've no reason to act this way!" There was hurt in his voice.

"The 'children' are acting up?"

"Eh? Oh, yes. Once I did compare them to children, didn't I? A million years ago," he said almost in a whisper. "Yes, Dave... now why should I call you that after all this time? No matter. They've got their recognition. They've got equal status. Did I say equal?" He laughed with harsh contempt. "They have almost godlike prestige everywhere they turn. No longer do they have to be suspicious of us. Why, my god, look what we're sending them! And this is right. It's the only real answer. You know that, Dave."

"Sure, Larry."

He turned back to me, his face a crazy quilt of emotions. "Then, why do they talk like..." he paused, his long arms exploring the empty air, "like 1917?"

"Like how?" I kept my voice gentle so as not to scare off his train of thought.

"Revolution! They talk revolution, as if it hadn't occurred yet!"

"Maybe for them it hasn't."

"Nonsense! We've had the greatest revolution the world has ever seen. A peaceful revolution that is bringing justice to everyone. It's

344

what they've always preached, and they've been part of it. They don't seem to realize that violence is no longer necessary. They've got everything they could possibly want, and yet they keep talking about..." He stopped again and sought his chair.

"Tell me, Larry."

"It's how they say it." He was speaking vacantly to the wall of books. "Over and over. Matter-of-factly, like you and I might discuss football or a fishing trip."

Not any more, I thought. I sold my little boat late last summer, at a loss, too.

"What, Larry?"

"*Liquidation!* Bourgeois liquidation. Can you imagine? They still use those terms!" He laughed in some kind of deep pain.

"Maybe they're just kidding or something." I fought to keep my voice low.

"Not the way they say it. I know. Look," he explained, "you know I've been trying to join the Party."

"Communist. Yes, I know. Only, I thought you had."

"No. Not quite. You see, they have study groups. Been going to one since last December. You see...I've explained this ,,, I felt I should... well... show them that we could all live together. I figured if I became a member of the Party they would see that we really are sincere in what we're trying to do. I thought I could give them something of myself. Exchange of views. Reasonable men going forward together and all that. You see what I was trying to do!" he gestured, a trace of the old Larry returning for an instant.

"Sure, Larry."

"Well, at first the study group was all right. We spent some time getting acquainted. Twenty or so of us and the instructor, a Mrs. Edmundson. We got into the history of Marx, Lenin and so on. Very interesting stuff... about the terribleness of their oppression and the great days of the Revolution and how they won. All that, y'know." He stopped again to reach for a water jug from which he filled a glass and drank deeply. He grinned sheepishly as an afterthought. "Excuse me. Not myself. Want some?"

I was not thirsty. Down below, classes had let out, and the campus echoed the hurdy-gurdy of spirited youth. Kids headed for fun. Kids who have a life in front of them, as Larry and I once had. The clock screamed to be turned back so that he and I could join them for a cup of coffee somewhere to laugh and scheme our way through the rest of the day. But the clocks adhere rigidly to their forward move and can be stopped only if they are smashed.

"It was fascinating, really. The struggle to achieve a place in the sun. The dedication and discipline of their people. The beauty of purpose and achievement and victory against such terrible odds. The masses struggling upwards! Only ... it hasn't stopped with history. They still speak of the struggle here as if it's only begun. They still speak of the next steps in the Revolution."

"Which are?"

"To kill off," he waved his arms again at the world outside, "anything and everything that smacks of the old capitalistic society which is largely gone. We've got socialism... humane socialism. But that doesn't seem to satisfy them. They talk as if liquidation is still their pattern. I could sympathize with it before... when they weren't understood, but now there's no need to talk that way any more. They still hate! They hate anyone who owns anything... farmers, bankers, businessmen, or even socialists. They call us 'reformists.' They accuse people like me of being tools of capitalism because I'm not willing to go far enough."

"And how far is that?"

"To kill off everyone except the youth. To erase our society without trace and rebuild it... totally. I could swear allegiance to their creeds if I had to. I could help them collectivize. I could serve them in many capacities. But to plan and take part in *liquidation* —I wish they had a more humane name for it—I can't do that!" "Are you sure they mean for you to do all of this?"

"Anyone who joins the Party must swear to it. They even have a whole course of study on the role of parliament in achieving a revolution."

"The parliament?" I asked. Larry was beginning to make no sense at all. "What has England to do with us here?"

"Oh, never mind," Larry replied. He was not angry. Just weary. "I don't understand all of it myself. They've got a whole book on the subject. Czechoslovakia and all they did there a long time ago, and we're supposed to study it and apply it here. How to liquidate the bourgeoisie. How they love that word!"[68]

"And how do they plan to liquidate us?" New awareness began to creep into my stomach.

"If you mean specifically, like lining people up and shooting them like the Nazis did...they don't say. They just say it must be done. Any method, I suppose. I only know I've got a paper to do on how I would plan and execute the isolation and liquidation of the bourgeoisie in Pittsburgh." Larry shoved the yellow tablet across the desk along with a much folded sheet of paper bearing a printed outline of the assignment.

The paper made little sense. There were phrases such as national front, pressure from below and pressure from above. Only one thing was unmistakably clear, a sternly boxed note at the top of the page which said: "Workers are warned not to lose sight for a single moment of the aim of a complete socialist overthrow."

"It doesn't make much sense to me, except they seem to want to get rid of a lot of people," I said.

"I can't really believe that they would go through with all that garbage. It's all so theoretical. Even if they wanted to, I can't see how they could possibly do it. There aren't that many of them. Let's face facts," Larry laughed, "we outnumber them considerably. That isn't my concern, not really. It's... how can I possibly sound convincing?"

---

68 As one example of how the Communists preached "liquidation" over and over again see: *How Parliament Can Play a Revolutionary Part in the Transition to Socialism and the Role of the Popular Masses*, by Jan Kozak, Member of the Secretariat of the Communist Party of Czechoslovakia, first presented to Communist intellectuals in 1957 and published in English in 1961 in London by the Independent Information Centre. This thesis was largely ignored by Western leaders and intellectuals. Nevertheless, many of the techniques developed in Czechoslovakia were later applied to the United States and elsewhere. (See Appendix.)

"Can't you just skip it?"

"No." He twisted around in his chair and frowned again at the books. "It's my graduation paper. How well I do determines whether or not I will be allowed to join the Party. They're pretty choosy."

He unfolded himself from his chair and prowled the room. "It's not in me to talk violence. I've never engaged in anything I haven't thoroughly believed in."

"Might as well get used to it."

"Eh?" He spun around and looked at me narrowly.

"We do what we have to do. Don't we... Larry?" I tried to keep irony out of my tone.

Once again he took his seat, chin cupped in his long hands and elbows set on his knees. He stared at a worn place in the carpet. "You're right, of course. I must do a good job. I've got to convince Smith and Nick that I'm important to them." He raised his head and looked at me with desperate eyes. "Don't you see! I've got to be clever enough to get in! Once I'm there, then I can work on them. I can change them. I know I can. I've got to do it! By god, I will do it!"

And suddenly, the old Larry came back. "You do see, don't you, David? We've got to put these people on the track... before something terrible happens."

"Sure."

"By god, I'm glad you came! You're always good for me."

His manner hinted that he wanted to return to work, so I rose to leave. "Good luck."

"Thanks." We stood awkwardly for a long moment, while his face became haunted again. "Only ... I just hope it works."

I frowned, not understanding.

"Even if I do a good paper . .. I'm not sure they want me. Can't prove it. Just a feeling and something Smith said the last time I saw him."

"Which was?"

"We were discussing some problems on the steel nationalization and he said, 'Your ideas don't go far enough.' Nothing more. But he has never called me since."

I left him standing, looking down at the yellow tablet, shoulders bent and arms crossed as if a sudden chill had come upon him.

Mid-afternoon traffic was light. I drove without noticing much of anything, trying hard to conjure up some kind of feeling for Larry's dilemma, but little came of it. I had my own problems. I arrived home shortly after the children came from school and found the ham hock and boiled it with the potatoes. It was a good dinner, even though the children complained. The bread was a little stale, but softened in the broth, it was quite tasty. The evening was a long one. Peggy went on a date ... a fellow I never heard of. David studied scouting, but without asking my help. Annie, though, was glad to see me, and we played Old Maid until it was time for her to go to bed. I turned in early but could not sleep. At one a.m. Peggy came home and slipped softly into her room.

Nancy arrived at three-ten. I could not see the automobile, but it sounded big and powerful, and it stayed in front of the house for nearly fifteen minutes before she fumbled her way through the door and up to the bedroom. She smelled badly of stale smoke and liquor.

"How was work?" I snapped on the light. She squinted at me in the sudden glare. She was pale with faded makeup and her face sagged around the lips.

"Turn that damn thing off!" She struggled doggedly with her clothes, peeling them off in unsteady jerks, leaving them where they had fallen. She fished inside the closet for her nightie, slipped into it unsteadily and flung herself into bed. "God, I'm tired!" And then she was asleep.

When one works one seldom notices things about the city, except possibly the nuisances; like the pokey pedestrian who gawks his way from curb to curb after the light has turned green; or if you are the one on foot, the wild motorist who shaves you within an inch. The impossible clerk or the stuck elevator. The long lunch line or the rain that slows the city to a halt. These are about all one ever sees of his town when he works. He sees only what he must to get from here to there in a hurry. But when there is no work to do there is time to look around, and in the two weeks that followed I had plenty of time. It is like looking in the mirror with extra attention to detail one morning to discover with genuine amazement that you have changed. So has this city. Two years ago it still had gilt and sparkle in places, and if you did not look too closely at empty windows and office vacancies in the tall, gleaming buildings, there were outward signs of heavenly prosperity. A year ago the bustle of people hellbent on one mission or another hid the growing physical decay—the once-bright buildings singed with stains of grime and corrosion; the parks and promenades with dead trees, flowerless planters and weedy, ragged grass. And the litter! Even then, sticky dust swirled with gum wrappers, newspapers, rags, broken bits of glass and endless cigarette butts. And now, all has become grey. Even in the sun the city is dull and sluggish. Its buildings are weary with broader streaks of dirt. The forests of cement planters—once the pride of urban redevelopment—are chipped and eroded into free forms of weird sculpture and slopping over with dead plants and unplanned trash. Once bright patches of grass are now mires fed by unusually heavy rains. The streets are like giant slabs of Swiss cheese, with deep, metal-wrenching, bone-shattering potholes. The buses are dismal, whining, smoke-trailing drags on the soul. And the automobiles, few new models. Few old models. Few limousines, except for the old-timers, they at least are shined, but they are not fun to watch. For their very cleanness, and the fact that there are so few, make them jarring contrasts to the rest of the city—shiny badges that scream: "How dirty you are!"

And the people. Does the city make them grey, or do they make the city grey? No matter. There are more of them out these days. It is like it used to be when everyone was on his lunch hour, the sidewalks and parks choked with the ebb and flow of people leisurely taking their measure of relaxation. Only the lunch hour is all day now. Beginning in the mid-morning, they drift into the Golden Triangle; the traditional bums of other years, shabby and dirty, who have always been part of the city, and the new bums. Nouveaux riches in reverse. They stand apart from the old bums, because their ways are different, as are their clothes. The old bums wear just any old thing and do not care how they look. The new bums have not graduated

350

down to that level yet. Most of them still wear matching suit coats and trousers and reasonably pressed topcoats. Their shoes still are in one piece. And the new bums are shaved and hatted and combed. They still look and act as if they are stealing one last moment of leisure before returning to their offices, poking through stores or ambling down streets or chatting on corners. Only they have no offices to go to. So the process lasts all day. There are few among the new bums who are—or were— hourly wage earners. For the mills still run at peak production, and while union men work at reduced wages, they do work. Most of the new bums are like me, former management and professional men whom society no longer needs; men who have not quite made the transition yet; men who still have not forgotten what they once were and who still hope. They come into town simply because there is nowhere else for them to go. Besides, they have been doing so for years. Only, instead of the office, it's the park now, especially with spring almost here. There is a pattern for most new bums. They check the BWP probably three times a day, to see if there are any new developments on their job applications. In most instances there are no new developments. The new bums do have one thing in common with the old. Neither breed eats lunch. Except a fortunate few.

A fair number of the new bums are women, former secretaries, bank tellers and store clerks who also have pinned their hopes on the BWP job forms, or if not that, other things. Most are single and try to dress with some degree of taste, depending on how hard up they are. This, perhaps, is the most moving sight. Being a single career girl living alone in the unfriendly city has its lonely moments at best, but being without a job—one sees it in their thin faces and bodies, the growing desperation born of frantic fear. Some have made up their minds to a new career, that of seeking men, for a fast fifteen minutes in a cheap hotel room or in the back end of a car. As with the factory worker there is demand for that kind of woman, and while the price is low, it is paid work, enough to keep things going for another day. But not all are nouveaux prostitutes. Many still stay the sweet stenographer on her lunch hour, shopping perhaps, for a man, as has been the time-honored custom of stenographers since women began to work. These are nice girls, bright, dull, thin, fat—each hopeful that some employed man (single, of course) will suddenly see her sitting on the park bench, rain or no, as the girl of his dreams. Their faces betray their hurt when the men they have spotted 50 feet away pass them by without a look. Finally, there are the prim and the coldly proud females, not women as a man thinks of women. They are the real misfits of bum society. For they will not even pass so much as the time of day with anyone, man or woman.

There is a certain common denominator that runs through most of the new bums. They are grey people, neither fish nor fowl, black nor white. They are the link between two conflicting ways of life; neuters standing midway between perpetual success and chronic failure. On the one hand, they wear the leftovers of success but, on the other, they face the life of failure. They are shabby, but it is a matched shabbiness hardly to be compared with the gunny-sack kind. Their faces still flicker hope but there is a grey tautness to their features that comes with being half sick, scared, and desperate.

Plainly, they do not yet know how to act like bums. I spent every other day in town to monitor my situation in the BWP. Nancy had grown irritable and uncommunicative. She was working—a polite phrase for going out on the town with VIP guests—late, very late, almost every other night. The rest of her time at home either was spent trying to keep house or else she slept. She could expect no help from Peggy, who has never cared for housework, and I did more harm than good trying to help. At the end of the first week Nancy went on the payroll as a full-time employee of the BWP at a small salary of one hundred dollars a week, plus an overtime allowance. She was assigned to Tom Shade's office, which she revealed without much emotion. Ever since my forced resignation from the old job, she had grown progressively more wooden. Every bit of her energy, every instinct, every thought was focused on one thing; the battle to survive. The price she was paying in hostessing pasty bureaucrats was only a sickening guess, for she would not say. Whatever was involved, it all went against her grain. Yet, with silent stubbornness she went each morning to her office, being careful to look as well groomed as she could, even to practicing a smile in the mirror, until she could switch winsomeness on and off like an electric light, like the professional models do just before the camera clicks. Nancy and I both understand two things. We have children, and we have to eat. One cannot eat pride or principles. If someone is pawing Nancy, I know she will permit no more than she absolutely must to achieve her goal—bread in the house. It is this harsh realism that keeps me still.

To stay sane, then, I went to town every other day. Each of these days I would phone my only contact from a pay phone booth in the lobby of the Federal Building. Marie Salvatoria usually was at her desk. She always made time to talk for perhaps half a minute, long enough to give me a status report on my application, which was working slowly up the long line, and to say something pleasant by way of a greeting. The rest of my day was spent walking, looking and listening, observing for the first time the city and its grey people. I could still hold myself aloof. For I was not yet a bum, because I could still buy lunch, but only one, not two. So I would call Marie in the early afternoon, in order not to create an awkward situation. By the second week, guilt had taken hold, particularly after Nancy went on payroll, so I began calling Marie at eleven with an invitation for lunch. At first she hesitated but finally accepted. So it was that we established a friendship that lacked malice and was completely moral. Unusual. We had nothing to offer by way of influence or affluence. We each accepted the other at face value: two people pleased to engage in simple dialogue. We had our sandwiches, and we would walk down to the river. There we would comment on the passing scene, like the hopeless people who stood or sat alone on stone benches and stanchions near the water.

"Why do they stay here in the wind when it is so raw?" she asked once and then shivered against the damp March wind, still unseasonably cold, and pulled her neat coat up tightly.

"The river moves... the only thing that moves for them. And if you stare at it long enough you begin to imagine that it is taking you with it, down through the warm southlands and out to sea to another land, perhaps where things are better." It was our second time at lunch. She had seemed pleased to see me again.

"Is there a land like that?"

"Not any more. Some day for you, maybe. But not any more for me ... or them."

"How I wish that I could help them." She rested her arms on a bridge railing and looked soberly at the wharf below where assembled the new bums. Her eyes were wide and brown, carrying traces of sunshine that otherwise were hidden behind the cold, grey clouds. She added luster to a gun-metal day.

"There's nothing you can do for them, because they have already done it to themselves. They've been helped to death, now."

"I don't mean handouts. There are other ways to help." She paused to search my face. "You have suffered, haven't you?"

"Do I show that?"

"Yes. But not like so many others... bitter, swearing, screaming sometimes... even begging. You don't do these things. But it's in your eyes and the way you talk."

"Thank you for that. I chose what I have. I have no right to complain."

"And you don't. You're so cheerful..."

"No. I am not cheerful."

"Not much!" She poked me with timid playfulness. "Look who kids me about how tall I am and how much I eat!" Her eyes sparkled, and we both laughed, again at nothing other than ourselves.

"If I strike you as being cheerful, full of fun and honest wit, then you must take credit for that."

"Me? How?" Her face probed mine.

For a moment the tenderness of her eyes and her soft, plain beauty lured me almost to put into words her worth as a human being and her worth to me. But her simplicity would never let her understand.

"Because one person is to another what that person allows him to be... and because you're tall and a little skinny. Also you eat like a horse!"

"Pooh! And you're losing your hair!"

"Ah! But think how much less I spend on haircuts so I can buy you sandwiches!"

That was a Monday. There was Wednesday with even more nonsense and random commentaries that revealed still more of Marie Salvatoria. Her curiosity is endless. She seems starved for knowledge. "I want to know things… really, anything at all. I'm not fussy. All this big, wide world and people thinking and doing things! It's like Christmas every day … if I can only find something new to learn, even sad things, because if enough of us learn about sad things then maybe we can be wise enough to do away with them." She has her own self-improvement program. "Books. I'm so slow at reading. The Mother Superior gave me a list. I read one a month… well, sometimes it takes two or three months, like the Punic Wars and Thomas Aquinas." She is learning to sew, and she hopes to find someone to teach her chess. She sings to children whenever she watches them. She cooks and cleans and practices ballet positions in her room. She studies her manners from an ancient etiquette book. And she writes poetry. "But I tear it up." She designs dresses and wallpaper patterns. And she sees to her father with reverent care.

Then came a Friday and the pattern of our little visits changed with savage abruptness. A new World Order of Nations Building was going up farther up along the river where an older building had been razed. It is to house the District World Court[69] that will serve Western Pennsylvania and West Virginia. It was Marie's curiosity that led us to the fenced edge of the excavation, where fifteen or so feet below a group of mudcaked men struggled in the water-soaked day with shovels and wheelbarrows to load a dump truck which sat near a power shovel. Only the shovel was not in operation. Broken wire ropes dangled uselessly from the boom, and tell-tale signs of rust indicated the shovel had not worked in some days. It was murderous work. Twenty or so men chopping into the morass of clay with picks and shovels and heaving the soggy mess into the wheelbarrows. Then

---

69 The World Court had become increasingly involved in local affairs having to do with enforcing provisions of the Treaty of Friendship. Treaty violations across the nation numbered in the hundreds of thousands. Thus, District World Courts were created to handle the growing backlog of indictments.

came the abysmal trudge to move them to the trucks; weary feet sucking up a gentle clay incline and arms straining to keep the load even on a flimsy plank runway. Faces streaked with mud and grimacing with pain. Panting. Coughing. But otherwise, not a sound except the slurp of metal on clay and the rasping of tired wheels. Perhaps a hundred persons stood along the excavation, as many men as women, watching silently. Suddenly one of the men, younger and thinner than most of the others, collapsed. His wheelbarrow spun crazily out of his hands and toppled, spewing the clay back where it came from. He lay face down, motionless, and a beefy, red-faced man in a yellow raincoat charged out of a small shack and stooped to his side. He nudged the form with his boot. The body responded in loose wiggles, like jelly. The work stopped, and the spectators shifted with growing interest. "God damn you! Get your tail up! We're on penalty now with three weeks to make up. Here, you. Give me a hand with this bum. The rest of you go back to work!" The man bellowed like a wild bull, his voice ringing off the deserted buildings that surrounded the hole. Another streaked and weary man joined the foreman, and together they dragged the body to the sidewalk above. The spectators shifted slightly to make room, but there were no moves to offer assistance. A patrolman appeared just as they laid the body out on the pavement.

"Been weavin' around all morning like he's drunk as a skunk," the foreman gestured to the blue uniform.

"I'll call a wagon."

"Well, get him out of here fast." And the foreman slopped back into the hole muttering one oath after another.

The body stirred and then fought to get up. It was caked from head to foot with drying clay. It looked like a statue coming to life. Its thin face was set with awful determination. Its arms flopped loosely, trying to push upward, while the legs moved back and forth in a slow, mechanical motion, like a wind-up toy that had run down. The patrolman prodded the body with his shoe. "Stay there, boy, till I get you in the wagon. No funny stuff."

And Marie took it all in with growing shortness of breath, her eyes brimming with tears.

356

"No," she sobbed. "Don't do that." She pushed her way through the motionless spectators and dropped to the side of the body, still trying to rise. She ran her hand quickly over its head. "Why, he's burning with fever. He's not drunk at all. We've got to help him!"

"Jail's as good as anywhere. Doubt if he has any place to go. Most of these men don't," the patrolman said, gesturing at the men now busy again with the clay.

The young girl shifted to cradle the head in her lap. She fished in her purse for a handkerchief and began to wipe the face and the hair, revealing a head with ice blue eyes fighting to stay open, while she spoke low words of comfort.

"You watch him, Miss, if you like, while I get the wagon."

"Never mind, officer. I know this boy. I'll take care of him." I had moved up behind Marie. I had noted the leather jacket. And when his face had been wiped clean, I knew its owner. It was the struggling remains of the fighter with hands that would once have looked comfortable wrapped around an iron bar—Chip Baker.

The sight of me roused him. He struggled to a sitting position, his eyes forced open at last. "Let me up," he breathed harshly. "Got to go back!"

"You're not going anywhere. And watch yourself. I'm the only friend you have right now—except her. So cool it!"

He blinked at me a couple of times and then fell back into Marie's lap and looked up into her face. Slowly he lifted his caked hand and touched a lock of her long dark hair that had fallen carelessly around her neck. Her eyes softened into a steady, even look as he searched her features. His face lost its harshness to become boyish. His breathing became less labored, and he smiled. "Hello."

"Hello, yourself. Now you do as Mr. Little says." Marie's voice had a queer catch in it as if she wanted to cry but did not dare.

And the two were motionless, neither taking his eyes from the other, until the patrolman shifted uneasily. "If he's a friend of yours, get him out of here."

We got him to a nearby bus shelter. It had a bench where we sat Chip between us. His eyes had closed again. While he rested, my mind worked. I would have to take him home, at least until he could recover from whatever it was that plagued him. He was obviously ill with pneumonia or some other equally fierce virus infection. The thinness of him testified to malnutrition, as well, and his exhaustion was complete, for he slumped against me as a dead man. Only the rattle of his breathing revealed the life still in him. Fortunately, I had driven the car in, since I had planned to visit Larry that afternoon.

He stirred again, restless and tormented. "Let me up. Dr. Rodgers... got to get him."

"Dr. Rodgers! Where is he?" I asked, holding firmly to Chip who was trying to lift himself up from the bench. The memories dashed out at me; the old white-haired gentleman as he sipped his brandy beneath a pinpoint of light in a restaurant—the original Mister X; as he was when he beat the examiners at their own game at the hearings; as he looked upon Mary Best in his pathetic attempt to order an English muffin.

"We were evicted this morning... he's to meet me at five... fountain... Ohio Park," Chip gasped, as a fever chill ripped through him. Between quick takes of his breath he explained that he and the doctor had been sharing a basement room in an old tenement across the river. Neither of the two apparently had any money at all, and the only way they had managed was through the small sums that Chip was able to earn working each day in a labor pool run by the BWP, until Chip had fallen ill a week ago. Both were evicted, then, and Dr. Rodgers had taken their earthly possessions into the street with him before the landlord had thought to stop him. Chip had little choice but to try to get work that day in the labor pool.[70]

"Please! Dr. Rodgers has nowhere to go!" He fought again to move off the bench. Tears began to well up in his burning eyes.

---

70 It was "unlawful for any commercial, educational or non profit organization to hire or otherwise compensate for employment or services any person who does not hold a proper authorization from the Bureau of Wages and Prices"—from the Federal Fair Wages and Prices Act. However, persons without such authorisation were free to work in manual labour pools organised in most urban areas for various menial construction and maintenance jobs.

"Chip! Listen! I will get Dr. Rodgers. Do you understand me?" I spoke with harsh clarity repeating the words over and over again, until he ceased to struggle. Finally he nodded and then moved to look at the girl.

"Chip Baker, meet Marie Salvatoria. He is a student of Dr. Rodgers, a very important man." I explained hastily to Marie what I knew of the doctor.

"Hello." Chip managed a wry grin.

"Hello, again. You're sick. We will get you some place to stay ... and your precious doctor, too."

"I have plenty of room, Chip. Now, take it easy until we get organized," I said.

"How can they both stay with you?" Marie asked, concern marking her young face. "With three children and a wife who works and yourself looking for work. No!" she said firmly. "They will come to my house. Father is there all day with nothing to do, and we have room. I know just how to fix things up."

I protested, but she would have it no other way. Besides, she was right. Her home would be more suitable for many reasons. Chip and Dr. Rodgers were her kind of people. They would get on well. So it was agreed that both would stay with Marie and her father until Chip was sufficiently recovered to seek more permanent quarters. Marie phoned BWP for a lunch hour extension, pleading family illness, while I went for the car.

The Salvatoria house was a weathered, red-brick structure, perhaps seventy-five years old. It stood crowded in with others like it on a steep street of old stone that twisted through Mount Washington. The yard was almost vertical, hardly more than a flight of crumbling concrete steps flanked with small patches of grass trying to turn green. A porch ran the full width of the house. The dim outline of a male figure peered through the wide front window, straightened abruptly and vanished into the shadows. An instant later the faded yellow front door was yanked open and Victor Salvatoria stood staring out first at the half-collapsed Chip and then at Marie and me. This he did over and over without a sound as we struggled up the steps.

He kept silent until we had gained the front room, a combination parlor-bedroom. The furniture was old and dark, but still presentable. We laid Chip out on the studio bed which had been neatly made with a colorful quilt coverlet. I stuck a silk throw pillow under his head. It bore the words, "Niagara Falls—1938."

"There is some kind of trouble, Daughter?" the man asked. His voice held traces of virility and purpose. He was a slight man of medium height, in his sixties, and he moved with cautious uncertainty due to his stroke, steadying himself on whatever substantial object was at hand. He had elements of Marie's features, prominent cheekbones and an equally prominent, but not unsightly, nose; except he was quite frail. His hands were rough and while not large must have once been both skilled and powerful. His hair was still largely black with hints of white. His eyes were a stern, unwavering brown, but cordial. He was dressed in a white shirt and a pair of brown trousers, worn but spotlessly pressed. A gold watch chain hung from his waist. He wore worn but polished leather slippers. He gave all the signs of a proud and determined man who, in spite of his near-invalid condition, was fighting to stay that way.

Marie explained, and the old man listened gravely, his eyes narrowing occasionally at the more significant parts of her story. "And I thought they could come here until Mr. Baker is well, Papa."

He nodded. "Of course. It is what Mama would have done. I can watch out for him."

Chip, by this time, had fallen into a fitful slumber.

"And who is this Dr. Rodgers?" he asked, and again I explained. Marie's father nodded. "It would be an honor to have such a distinguished man in our home, but can we know that he would want to stay with people like us who have never been to great universities? Though it had been my dream that Marie should at least go. But such was not to be." He spoke with a slight shrug of his shoulders.

I looked at the plain, shining honesty of the room, slightly overcrowded with knickknacks that had been collected over the past 50 years—colorful shells, Venetian glass, an Italian box, a religious figurine. A glass front bookcase held a few volumes of ancient and

360

rich-looking vintage, many with foreign titles. A couple were World Books, and there were others—*A Child's Garden of Verses*, *Swiss Family Robinson*, Shakespeare. I looked at the man trying to keep himself erect without revealing his struggle to remain steady on his feet; then at Marie and the sparkle of expectancy in her eyes.

"I do not know Dr. Rodgers well, except that I think he knows how to measure that which is worthwhile."

"You are kind, sir," Victor replied. "You are as Marie had described you."

"You overestimate me. If I have shown any kindness it is because your daughter has brought it out in me. And now," I said, "I must find Dr. Rodgers, and Marie must return to work. I will drive her and bring Dr. Rodgers back."

It had begun to rain again by the time I reached Ohio Park, a long narrow mall running between rows of government apartments of stained brick and dirty windows, some of them broken. The benches were filled with people, old bums mostly, huddled together in a vain attempt to keep dry. The fountain, a huge chipped bowl, empty, save for the litter of old newspapers, tin cans, and broken bottles, stood in the center. I moved toward it with eyes straight ahead, lest I attract a beggar. I circled the fountain twice, checking each face on the benches out of the comer of my eye. But no Dr. Rodgers. Of course, he would not be looking for Chip this early so he could be anywhere. He would probably want to keep moving. I cruised the whole park without a sign of him. I tried the side streets next, older sections of the city that had not been redeveloped—ramshackle houses of stained brick and dirty windows, some of them broken. I found him sitting on the stoop of one, jammed rigidly against the deep recess of the doorway where it was dry. Two heavy-looking suitcases, scarred and soaked, sat alongside the stoop. He wore a heavy coat wrapped tightly about his big, slightly hunched frame. A hat, shapeless with wet, was pulled securely over his head. His eyes were closed, and his face, creased with ageless dignity, held a half smile, as if he were recounting days more pleasantly spent—or perhaps more pleasant to come. His great head bobbed slightly, and he roused himself to look at the watch on his wrist.

"Dr. Rodgers."

He started, his eyes searching me for some familiar sign.

"I am David Little, You may not remember me."

"Ah! Yes." And he struggled stiffly to his feet, gathering my proffered hand into both of his which, in spite of the rawness of the day, were steady and warm. "What brings you here?" he asked. His voice had lost none of its timbre. He seemed unaffected that I should find him thus.

"Chip Baker told me where to look for you."

"You've seen him?" The lined face brightened.

"He fell ill this noon, but we have him in a safe place," I finished quickly.

"Bad, I suppose." The grey head wagged, and the serene composure of the doctor broke. "I tried to tell him! Months ago... after I lost my place... Chip insisted that we live together. Can you believe," he shifted his big frame to emphasize his words, "that I cursed that boy to get him to forget all about me? And he cursed me right back. Left his own boys, so he could find a roof for me." The big face sniffed. "Punk, no-good rascal! Can't obey his elders! And now he's..."

"Going to be all right." I explained the circumstances, and slowly Dr. Rodgers regained his composure.

"You're sure? Thank God you were there!"

"I've come to get you, at Chip's request, a very strong request. And he said to tell you 'No nonsense.' " I outlined the plan and described Marie, her father and the Salvatoria home. The doctor did little to hide his relief about Chip. It was plain that he had been tormented with worry that had worn even deeper creases upon his face than there had been when we last had met. But as I spoke a smile of thanksgiving gave back to him the look of agelessness that had so set him apart from other men.

"I did not know that such wonderful people still exist, but it is unthinkable that I should burden them further," the doctor mused. "This is no place for the old and unproductive."

362

"And where do you think you will go?" I asked.

"I have friends."

"Maybe you do. Maybe you don't. But you won't use them. You'll wander around here until you collapse like Chip." I took him by the arm. "I'm hardly qualified to tell you what to do, but you're coming with me if I have to carry you!"

"You've changed, Mr. Little." He searched my face intently, but not unkindly. "I guess I called you Davey when we last met."

A passing patrol jeep grinding at high speed smacked into a chuck hole, spraying water on us and a trio of young men who were poking noisily down the narrow street in search of something to do. I studied them intently, wondering if there was a parallel between them and me.

"I've changed only to the extent of knowing now what I am… a louse, and since I am one, I'll not hesitate to strongarm you into my car. Now let's go!"

So we went, the doctor protesting in a muttering sort of way, but beneath it all there was an undercurrent of relief.

As I had suspected, the meeting between Victor Salvatoria and Dr. Rodgers was instantly cordial. First we moved Chip to what used to be a pantry off the kitchen but had at sometime been transformed into a small, guest sleeping room. There were plenty of blankets, which were hauled out of a deep closet under the stairs and tucked snugly around the youth, who was having violent chills. We debated the possibilities of medical care, but concluded it would be impossible to bring a physician to the house. A clinic would be useless since Chip no longer had valid evidence of a permanent residence.[71] All that remained was the workhouse clinic, and he would have been in far more danger there.[72] Drugs were impossible to get, except aspi-

---

71 By now the only way a person could get government medical care was to produce his Residence Permit to give proof that he was not "an irresponsible itinerant who seeks to freeload off the production of the gainfully employed," as was stated in a Bureau of Health directive.

72 Medical care in labour camps, prisons and jails was more attuned to letting a patient die than to supplying the necessities for his recovery, according to a number of official records that have been uncovered.

rin, which I found in good quantity a block away. While Chip slept, I strung a wire across part of the dining room. From the same stair closet I found two bedspreads which I fashioned into a curtain by fastening them with safety pins to the wire. A basement shelf yielded an old canvas cot, which I installed behind the curtain. This was to be Dr. Rodgers' quarters. Marie was to keep her room, the only true bedroom on the first floor. And while I worked, the floor above came alive with the stirring of three young children and a harassed mother. Victor wanted to quiet them, but Dr. Rodgers only smiled and shook his head.

"No," he said. "The sounds of children playing are sounds Chip will want to hear. For it tells him he is in a home again where there is love and life. These are forgotten sounds that will do him more good than any medicine."

Then I drove home with the promise to return again tomorrow. I left five dollars for food on the bookcase where I was sure it would be found. It was my allowance for the next two weeks. But who needs an allowance? It was not yet five p.m., but it seemed as if weeks had passed since breakfast.

Nancy came home at the regular time, exhausted and in an ill humor. She picked at her dinner, more boiled potatoes and ham hocks, too weary to eat. She had worked late the night before. "What did you do today outside of roaming around town?" "Nothing much," I replied.

5

Neckties, bold patterned and jarringly bright. Shirts, sleazily cut and paper cheap. Plastic belts, not a leather one anywhere. And the shoes! The few with any lasting quality—ninety-two fifty. Then there are the suits. Three single breasted styles only: Budget, Prep and Exec, ranging from one hundred and thirty-nine dollars to four hundred even. The fabrics, a mixture of synthetics and wool from Japan, are available in twelve shades and patterns of blue, grey, brown and green. Most United States fabrics are shipped to Europe under the new "resource agreement." Japanese fabrics are shipped here to balance out the deficit. I picked this up in the *Clothiers Journal*. A beautifully written and handsomely illustrated article does not mention the difference in quality between the fabrics we make but cannot use and the imported fabrics which we must use. I was given the magazine to read on my first day at work as a clerk (Salesman—Dry Goods, class three) in the Men's Shop at Barnes' Department Store. It is the last full-fledged department store left in the city. Even now there is talk that, rather than have it go bankrupt, the government will buy it so that "Pittsburgh is assured a continuing supply of quality consumer items," as the newspapers stated.

Nancy—alone—got me the job. Marie and her friend at the BWP contributed only the filled-in forms, while I contributed nothing at all. How could I? I have not built a life around selling neckties. Pull got me the job, the best one in the hopper. There were nineteen sales openings for Allegheny County. One involved a concessionaire at the stadium. Three were for selling cemetery lots. Eleven were sales positions in small secondhand merchandise shops. The remaining four were at Barnes', the top of the heap being the Men's Shop. Marie tells me that better than three hundred applicants were being considered for these jobs. When I phoned her the news, I did not tell her that she had nothing to do with my good fortune. Elapsed time between jobs—only 44 days. It must be a record of some sort.

There was no wild celebration of achievement. No beaming friends, neighbors and associates to whack your back and crush your hand. No gee-whiz expressions on the faces of the children. No special little supper with candlelight and perhaps a bottle of wine. No internal expansiveness to allow a man to lean back and look fondly upon himself and the world. No cloud nine.

Nancy had come home especially tired, her face hard around the edges with traces of hate about the eyes and mouth. The children had the television on too loud, and she had to scream her ultimatum to turn it down. I was in the kitchen trying to fix potato pancakes and sausage. I had spent the afternoon at the Salvatoria house where Chip Baker had recovered sufficiently to think about joining another labor pool, and Dr. Rodgers was making himself busy with household chores. It had been a good afternoon full of warm fellowship. On my way home I discovered the sausage in a nearby neighborhood store, and so I was prepared to greet the evening with exceptionally good humor.

"What are you burning now!" Her greeting was harsh. She dropped her handbag on the kitchen table and flopped heavily, almost slovenly, onto a chair. A loose bolt holding a chrome leg in place plunked to the floor. "Oh, god! Everything we own is falling apart!"

"Poor day?" I asked.

She shrugged. "Like all days. Smile. Cajole. And kick them when they're not looking. Or sell a little more of your soul," she added vacantly. She sat for a long moment, watching me trying to shape cold mashed potatoes into a cohesive patty, a leering halfsmile rising over her face. "Try flour ... up there on the top shelf. I got you a job." She said it casually with a pinch of bitterness. "Not too much grease in the pan." And she kicked off her heels and moved to my side as if I had just unwittingly pulled the pin on a hand grenade. "God, can't you do anything right?"

"What sort of job?" The tide of elation that had begun to rise in me quickly ebbed, and I matched her dreary tones.

"Suits... men's suits. Hardly a vice presidency, but you wouldn't know what to do with a job like that anyway."

The afternoon glow was all gone now. I felt as if two lead weights had been placed on my shoulders. "You talk as if I could have done better."

"Yes, you could, like hell! Here, let me." She nudged me aside and with deft hands brought the sizzling frying pan under control. "Give me your apron and go sit some place."

"What else could I have done to get a job, Nancy?"

For a moment she was hunched over the burners, her hands gripping the counter top. Finally, she turned. "If you hadn't frittered away your life you would have had contacts, and I wouldn't have had to...." She stopped abruptly and jabbed viciously into the pan.

"To have done what?" I asked. She had been out quite late the night before. She had, during the past couple of weeks, dropped the working late routine and ... to her credit... simply said, every other day or so, that Tom Shade was asking her to dinner with himself and important guests, usually officials of the W.O.N., our own government or the Communist Party. Only twice had she gone into particular detail to explain that there was no wrongdoing—that all she had to do was look charming and be a good listener —something she felt obligated to say, and I felt obligated to accept. But knowing Nancy's prudishness, I saw no useful reason to question her. But her manner this time was different. "What did you do last night?"

My face, and what must have been written on it, softened her. "David, why think about it?" and she burst into tears. I did not move to comfort her. "Look. Last night Smith Armstrong had a small dinner party, and it involved Tom Shade and some big men from New York, I think. I was invited... and you said yourself I should use charm... and one of the men, a Mr. Jorgensen from Sweden, well we got to talking, and he asked what you did and... so I told him, and he told Mr. Armstrong that he should do me a favor, and he told Tom to do something, and today you got the best job open for salesmen. Please... please don't ask about anything more."

But my eyes must have betrayed the ugliness in me.

Her tears stopped then and for a brief second her eyes hardened. Slowly indignation began to work through her. "So you think me some cheap tramp! Do you think I've been having fun trying to get you a job? Listen. I love my children, however good or bad. I love them, because I bore them and cleaned their bottoms and wiped their noses. There are little bits and pieces of me in each of them. They're scared and confused just as I was and always have been. They've got their dreams just like I had mine. All my life I've had my nose pressed against the window looking into somebody else's world, and I don't want that for them. I know I'm not clever or brilliant and no real match against... against anyone, I suppose. But I'm going to try. Maybe the best I can hope for is a few stinking crumbs to keep us alive until those kids can learn to claw their own way—up! I'm not made for this kind of life, but I'll do it again and again if that's what it takes. What I did is my business. But I did it, and you've got a job. I'd make a pact with the devil if I thought it would help!" And she turned back to the stove and poked furiously into the frying pan.

"What you are really saying is that if I had the stuff... contacts in the W.O.N. or maybe joined the Communist Party years ago... that none of this would be happening. Well, maybe so. Maybe I should have really gone all out during those first hearings and denounced everybody I've ever known. Maybe I should have," the acid of bitterness ran through my mouth, "denounced my own brother! Maybe then we'd be on Easy Street! Is that what you mean?"

She sagged as if I had struck her. "No. I don't know what I mean. And how could you say that about Harry and your mother? You've no right to bring that up. Not after all these months ... not when you wouldn't even talk about it when the accident happened. I know it must drive you crazy at times trying to figure out why all of them... especially your mother... were out over the lake, but it doesn't fit here, David. Look, I'm tired and a little disgusted. I know you've done your best, but don't you see I'm trying to do my best, too!"

I went to her then and gathered her up in my arms as gently as I knew how.

So I went to work in one of the few remaining busy centers left in the city and, while the pay was less than half of what I had been making, I looked forward to the new job with more than passing interest. I have always liked men's clothing stores. This attachment stems from some of my earliest memories when my father used to take me to Morrison's Men's Store while he searched carefully through the racks for a new suit for himself. The ritual occurred about once every year-and-a-half. Buying a suit was a thoughtful, unhurried process that most always began at the breakfast table at about the time my father was midway through the morning paper. "I think I'll buy a suit," he would announce, and it inevitably drew a respectful silence from the rest of us, for such decisions were not to be taken lightly. "A suit," he used to say, "is a man's only way to wear on the outside what he is on the inside."

368

And so the plan would be laid out. A weekday afternoon would be selected—the grocery business made Saturdays out of the question—and my mother would be commissioned to take over the store. Even before I was old enough for school, the plan involved me. "I shall take Dave. It is important that he know how to buy clothes properly." Mother never went with us. This was a man's business, which she understood. And I thrilled at the prospects of being included. Before I became old enough to be involved in managing our store, these were the only times my father and I ever went into downtown Cleveland to shop. For an occasion like this we always took the car rather than the bus, and even parked it in a parking lot, instead of trying to seek out a free space at the curb. Then we would walk down Euclid Avenue, Father taking big, purposeful strides, while I trotted to keep up and wished he would slow down long enough for me to look in the store windows. And then there it would be: Morrison's! It was a tidy black-glass storefront with the letters spelled out in elegant gold above a window that held a sweeping array of crisp new things for men; nothing for little boys, except to hold out the bright promise of what manhood one day would permit them to wear. Then we would pause to look, and Father would always say, "Hmm. Don't see what I want here. Hope Sam can do better inside." In we would go then, and the sounds of the city suddenly would be muffled away in the folds of rows of suits and coats that lined the walls. How quiet, with voices strangely muted, and how good the smells of wool and the occasional traces of a fine cigar! For Morrison's was a good store, not elaborate, but solid with quality, an enterprise that had served the city for more than a hundred years. Always there were one or two customers in the rear of the store, studying themselves in three-way mirrors, while the harried little tailor moved deftly about them. But always one of the attending salesmen, usually Sam Morrison, would detach himself long enough to welcome us and invite Father to look. So we would poke and feel and "hmmm," first him and then me, until Sam was finished with his sale. Then Sam would brighten, sweep towards us and clap his hand.

"Now then, Mr. Little, what have you found? Is it to be brown?"

"No," Father might reply. "That one is good for at least another year. Grey, I think."

"Ah! Of course! The brown you got the last time. Let's see. Your present grey would be… my goodness… four years old!"

Father kept a balanced wardrobe of blue, brown and grey suits. He was always careful to have at least one of each on hand at all times. So he and Sam would poke and try on and look and feel and reflect, until, finally, there would be the one. Not too loud. Not too old fashioned. Not too young and not too plain. It would be just right with a pinch of dash and a clean, functional cut. The material would "wear like iron, believe you me." Then came the fitting and no nonsense. Cuffs—so. Back—pull in. Waist—perfect. Send it out next Monday? Of course, you can have it on Friday! A new tie? Of course. Right this way. Then the magic hour would end, capped with one last look around at some of the luxury items that one never buys. But still it's fun to look, isn't it, my son? Then Father would always light up a big, expensive cigar that he had secured for the occasion, and we would stroll leisurely back to the car, taking in the sights of a city preparing to go home for dinner.

The biggest day of all came when Father took me to Morrison's for my first suit at the age of twelve. Sam brought everything to a standstill in the store. For the decision was complex. Should I start with a blue or a brown or a grey suit? Father was in command most of the time, while Sam and his help moved among the racks pulling this and that and laying them aside. The final decision was a plain dark blue suit. I remember particularly how tall and straight and still I tried to stand in front of the mirrors while the tailor fussed. And I remember—now—the image of my father moving behind me to rest his hand upon my shoulder and then smiling into the mirrors. "You look just fine, Son."

"Indeed, he does," Sam Morrison had said. " 'Tis the third generation of Littles now who have bought in this store. Happy birthday, Dave. May there be a fourth generation for you to send to see old Sam!"

Only that never came to pass. Morrison's went bankrupt a year after I graduated from college.

Until recently, the habit of cruising men's stores, at noontime especially, never left me. Seldom did I ever buy, except a budget suit perhaps once a year. It was enough just to look and poke and feel. But with all of the shortages the fun of it was gone. So, it had been better than a year since I had been near one. Then came the new job.

I reported in a half-hour early the first day, anxious to be useful again. Mr. Kloomer is the department head, a very tired and flighty man of possibly 35, although he sometimes looks 60. He does not speak. He moans. He moans, because there are too many non-buyers cluttering up the already hodgepodge of racks and cases that have been jammed into one corner of the cavernous third floor. He moans because the paint is flaking off the ceiling, creating aggravating dust problems. The lights occasionally go bad, and there are only three clerks now, instead of nine. So he moans about this and the fact that he has no time to do the paperwork, particularly the ration slips and requisition forms that all customers must present for processing. And when one of us takes too long with a customer he groans openly, "There are three styles and twelve colors. Surely, that much time is not needed to make a simple decision."

Finally, he has no time to study his lessons properly. For Mr. Kloomer is trying desperately to join the Communist Party, and he goes to his study group every night of the week, plus Sundays. And my two fellow clerks have caught Mr. Kloomer's spirit. They moan too. About long hours, 48 hours a week; low pay, and fickle customers, especially the emerging bureaucrats who demand all sorts of attention. For members of the Communist Party or for recognized members of the Coalition,[73] Mr. Kloomer has set aside a small room back behind the partitions that once was used exclusively by the tailors. Here, under lock and key, he keeps his "special stuff." It consists

---

73 The JCFLA and Communist Party made much publicly of "cooperating with our learned friends in the coalition." By the following May after the presidential election, remnants of both the Democrat and Republican parties had organised into the Coalition Party, and its leading politicians were given many privileges, until they were no longer regarded as a major force to be dealt with.

of leftover merchandise, stashed away bit by bit over the past year—premium shirts and suits, jackets and slacks of rarest American and English fabrics. Holdovers. An open secret between Mr. Kloomer, the store, and certain select people who come eagerly to buy. Only Mr. Kloomer handles these special customers, and it is by appointment only, one at a time. The prices are steep, but then the limited clientele can afford it. It is only in this function that Mr. Kloomer can find time to smile.

For the rest of us, the Hearty Three, as we call ourselves, selling men's clothing is a grim business. Witness my first day. The noon hour is particularly heavy with foot traffic. It is hard to distinguish the looker from the shopper, just as it is still difficult to tell the employed white collar from the new bums. In comes the reasonably dressed man of 45 or so; that is, his suit coat and trousers match, and he wears a worn white shirt and tie. His shoes are scuffed and perhaps a little mud-stained (this is the tipoff to the non-buyer, I now know). But he has the still presentable air of a man of affluence, the vice president of a bank or a corporation or perhaps a lawyer (if he still wears round glasses). It is in his face and his posture, as if he expects to be paged at any moment over a non-existent loudspeaker, "Paging Mister X. Your board of directors is awaiting your return!" So he both preens and looks and pokes into the racks. And you clap your hands together in the spirit of Sam Morrison.

"May I help you, sir?"

"Why… as.…" And the face, until now so carefully molded in self-importance and pretense, takes on a hungry look, and the eyes seem almost to beg for mercy. "How much for these suits?"

"That's the Exec line. Four hundred, plus tax. The blue is especially nice." A lie. The blue is too bright and harsh. It leaps at you, but less so than the other colors.

"No. That's a little steep."

"Well." Clap those hands. "We have some nice heh-heh threads for only one thirty-nine. Over here." And you nudge him along to another rack of flashy plaids and stripes.

And he looks some more, and the same hurt comes into his eyes that must have come into mine when I first toured the floor during my briefing. "These? For one thirty-nine, did you say?"

At this point: Enter Mr. Kloomer.

"Mr. Biddle…"

"That's Little."

"Well, whatever. Trouble?" Mr. Kloomer fidgets with pen and papers that he holds crumpled hysterically in his hands. He looks at the growing lunch-hour mob, wondering if somewhere there might be at least one buyer. Then he looks at Mister X with a cold, disdainful eye.

"This person. You, sir," he addresses the haunted eyes of Mister What-Used-To-Be. "Are you buying today?"

And the man—men, actually, because there are dozens—loses his affluent pose. He slumps and stammers. "Well, no. Not today. But one day soon, I expect.,."

"On your way," says Mr. Kloomer, and for one instant the face of the almost buyer turns dark with how-dare-you anger. The eyes burn hate. The mouth quivers. The cheeks sink. But Mister X leaves, slinking in shame.

"Let's keep moving, Biddle. Don't get taken in by those jobless time-wasters." And Mr. Kloomer stalks away.

So you try. Here comes one. Looks as if he slept in his suit. Needs a haircut especially bad. "Ah, you, sir. Unless you are planning to buy something, I suggest you move on." Politely, but firmly put. Neat touch.

"Mind your manners and get me that pirate Kloomer," is the unexpected reply. ·

When Mr. Kloomer at length is brought to the scene he is all smiles. "Ah! Mr. Jones. How good of you to stop by." And into the back room they go. A special customer. I should have looked at his shoes first. They were neither scuffed nor muddy. They were, in fact, quite new.

On that first day I recognized only one person, Mr. Sanders, the V.P. for production of my old company who, as with me, had testified so effectively against Avery Brown at the hearings a year ago. At first I did not know him. His suit coat did not match his trousers. His shoes were terribly worn, and he had not shaved that day. But he had a shirt and tie on. I was about to ask him to leave when he recognized me.

"You're David Little, aren't you?" The face that spoke was sallow and flabby. He had been drinking beer, lots of it.

"Yes?"

"Well," his face brightened. "By golly! You certainly remember me! I'm Sanders. I used to be…"

"Yes. I remember now." The cool, confident Mr. Sanders, who once turned awed heads in office corridors and elevators, who used to make million-dollar decisions on the back of country club napkins (a corporate legend), who used to be too busy to see any but the most mighty in the hierarchy. Mr. Sanders, who made his calculated decision against Avery Brown but who lost anyway, right along with the rest of us. And in this moment of meeting—he never once gave me the time of day back when—he struggled to pull himself upward for my benefit.

"I'm shopping a bit. Guess you know I left the company. Resigned, of course. In the process of changing jobs. Taking a little time off, you see."

Enter Mr. Kloomer again coming up fast on my left, but I beat him to it. "Mr. Sanders, are you buying today?"

"Well, as a matter of fact, no. But… one day soon, I expect. .."
"Sorry, I must ask you to leave." I say this loudly so Mr. Kloomer hears, nods and turns away. "Please go now before I catch hell."

Sanders lingers, traces of envy on his face. "You're lucky. Mind telling me how you got this job?"

"Pull," I said, thinking of Nancy. "A one-time-only pull. I couldn't get you … or Jesus Christ … in here if my life depended on it. Now please leave."

"Sure." But he hung back still. "Say, Dave. For old times sake. I'm a little short. I mean…"

"Take this and leave." I gave him a dollar. He did not thank me, and I did not want him to.

Selling clothes is grim business. Except for the first day, I have never come to work early. The faint wisps of memory about the magic of men's stores I must forever put behind me.

What is a home?

To the very young it is the whole world, where the front doorstep is the jumping-off place into the terrible unknown. To the explosive teenager it is a repair and refueling stop or—occasionally—a prison. To the young collegiate, home is a place one can still go back to and feel warmth and comfort for a short time, before the restless lure of unfettered freedom beckons anew. To the young marrieds, it is the nesting place that cuddles new life, where fresh paint and newly turned flower beds hold a sacred promise of happiness unbound.

But to the middle-agers, and for all I know beyond, home is a drudge. It is a washing machine that does not work and grass that does not grow and storm windows that are cracked. It is the Seat of Noise where children from everywhere, it seems, gather for no other apparent reason than to scream in your ear or bang loudly on something. It is the scene of hasty breakfasts with bedlam all about and quarrels in the bedroom. It is the site of illness and despair. It is what conventioneers—when we had conventions— used to like to get away from. It is the tangled morass of trying to keep going with one tiring generation pitted against a new and growing generation that in time will become equally old and tired. Home is peeling paint on the outside and dingy walls and sagging furniture on the inside.

Until.

It slips away.

Then.

You look again, and home is you and yours, such as they may be. Pain, boredom and work. Sure. But here and there, out among the weeds or from the cracks in the wall, come occasional whispers which are echoes of the past to remind you of other things of home. A laugh, for instance, from little Annie playing with the dog right out there in the yard where the grass used to be thick and green. Or the hoopla of an informal neighborhood party that years back celebrated a birthday—yours. The time Peggy had pneumonia, and Nancy and I prayed. Or take the moment when David plugged in his homemade radio and it worked. Nancy fixing a suitcoat button, thread between her teeth and fingers working swiftly. A familiar bed when you are bone weary. Being able to move around the house without turning on the light. And occasionally touches of tenderness—even traces of affection—from wife, from husband, from children in a hundred little ways, memories that still echo between dingy walls.

Home is the familiar, then, at whatever stage of life. It is different from any other home, because it is yours.

And when you must give it up, it hurts.

It was bound to happen. There is simply not enough money. Inflation on the one hand. Low wages on the other. And in between, a bank that demands payment. The situation was grave even before I left the steel company. I had hoped to borrow enough money at least to supplement the mortgage payments. "Our regulations forbid this, you know." The new job could not begin to cover our living costs. For a while we pretended, but the mortgage and store credit notices began to come, and so finally we faced it late one night over the kitchen table. The good old kitchen table, the scene of more joy and grief than any other item in the house. We will have to sell it or leave it behind, now. But that night Nancy sat folding and unfolding a defunct bank book. Her brown eyes were wide and wild, but her voice was low and cracking.

"It's true, then. Whatever shall we do?"

"Find an apartment." I held my voice even and soft, lest I trigger her into hysteria.

"They must not understand. This is our place!" She laughed vacantly. "Don't they know? Somebody should tell them! We'll just write them a letter. Or better yet, we'll go see somebody! That's it, isn't it? That's what everyone does. See somebody! There's always somebody to fix things."

"Not any more. We are at the end of the line." I interjected. She seemed to be teetering on the edge of reality, ready to plunge into the darkness of her own dream world.

"Maybe they're punishing me, because I'm not a nice girl any more. But. Yes! Maybe if they knew I do naughty things because I want to keep my babies in a nice home with nice flowers and nice people all about... maybe they'd fix things. Maybe Momma can tell them how hard I try to be a nice girl. She used to read me stories... such wonderful stories... about how the fairy godmother would do nice things for good little girls. And I was a mommy sometimes, too, with my dolls, and I would tell them this and they would listen and I had a big house for them and lots of pretty clothes to dress them in. What shall I do with my babies? Once I left my dollies outside under the big tree and it rained all night and they were cold and spoiled." Her voice trailed off, and she sat staring past me.

"It is time for bed," and I steered her gently up the stairs. "I promise your babies will never have to sleep in the rain. Everything will be all right."

"You'll fix it so it's all right? David." And she moved against me, her body trembling and sagging in weariness. Her heart-shaped face was pale, like fragile porcelain, and pinched together by a plea.

"I'll fix things. We may not be able to keep the house, but we'll have a home just as nice... some place."

So she slept deeply, lost, I hope, in a dreamland of gingham, calico and the vistas of enchantment. For she had earned that much. The realities would come soon enough, and she would face them, ultimately, with the same dogged practicality that is so much a part of her character, a trait that I have come to respect.

More easily said than done—a home just as nice. For there was the Bureau of Housing to reckon with. It, too, is located in the Federal Building, but on the second floor. It is more thoughtfully oriented toward the convenience of its clientele, which includes everyone who owns or rents any sort of domestic dwelling.[74] For example, the

---

74 The Bureau of Housing had absolute control over the renting and purchasing of all dwellings, whether privately or government owned. Private realtors no

office is open from nine to nine, in order to allow persons employed during the day the opportunity to "avail themselves of the wide variety of services offered," as the brochure states. Result is that the line is delightfully short. I was in the waiting room less than two hours after I quit work at five. Even the surroundings were pleasant. The chairs all matched, and I was able to sit down almost immediately. The walls were a pleasing green, and large, colorful architectural renderings of elegant looking homes and apartment buildings were hung with obvious care. It was pleasant to sit back and look at prints of new dwellings being planned for Pittsburgh. The most striking was the rendering of Unity Center, which is to be a carefully balanced selection of single story homes incorporating a variety of designs employing suspended roof systems and hyperparaboloids and some geodesic structures. Construction has been delayed for more than a year, but apparently they will begin soon.[75] By eight p.m. I was being interviewed by a pleasant banker-type "processor." There are perhaps 50 of them occupying a huge open area, but unlike the BWP, the desks here are spaced more widely apart so that everything is more neat and efficient looking. Mr. Long greeted me pleasantly enough and invited me to be seated in an armchair at the side of his desk. It took him but a moment to secure the complete file on my home.

"A very nice house," Mr. Long mused. "A trifle small but in a sound enough neighborhood... where, incidentally, the cultural ratio is very much in your favor." He consulted a sheaf of papers labeled: Cultural Index—Pennsylvania. "We can sell to either Negro or white."[76]

---

longer were permitted to operate.

75 There is evidence that the government unveiled many bold plans for lush housing projects, but few were even started, much less completed. Private home builders were no longer allowed to function on the grounds that they "were selfishly motivated to serve the self-seeking interests of an equally selfish minority," according to a BWP directive.

76 In order to assure "absolute equality and free choice," the Bureau of Housing established racial quotas. One area, for example, might require tenants and/ or home owners to be sixty percent white and forty percent Negro. Houses occasionally stood vacant for long periods waiting for the right color to occupy them. (From various Bureau of Housing records.)

"That is good news!" I replied, genuinely pleased on two counts. First, it is important that one's personal rapport with the Bureau of Housing be as cordial as possible if one is to get the best kind of deal, and Mr. Long looked and acted as if he would prove sympathetic to my problem. Also, the fact that there would be no restrictions race-wise on who might be allowed to buy the house obviously provided the widest possible market, which would almost assure top dollar. This was my key concern. How much could I clear on the sale?

"Now," Mr. Long studied the papers in my file. "That's 1443 Sunshine Lane, Southern Estates. And purchased seven years ago at twenty-five nine, and the present mortgage is sixteen-eight, thirty-two. Uh-huh."

An equity of nearly ten thousand dollars! I thought. Not much, especially the way the bottom has dropped out of the dollar, but enough to get even again and make a fresh start. And counting the inflation—you could not build that house for under forty today. The resale could be that much, so I might clear as much as twenty-five thousand! Provided Mr. Long and I can hit it off. For he would have some influence on the Bureau's appraiser who would visit the house. I hitched myself forward, expectantly.

"What do you think it will go for?" I asked.

Mr. Long pondered, his moon face placid and thoughtful. "Well, that will be up to the appraiser, of course. But," he brightened, "you should make out all right… considering."

I could get no more out of Mr. Long. He dialed the appraiser and after a brief conversation turned back to me with the news that the man would examine the house the following Thursday afternoon.

"Any chance he could come, say, after six? You see, my wife and I work," I said. It would be psychologically important for me to be there.

"Oh no! No! All appraisals must be made during the day," was the cool reply. I did not press the matter.

As I knew she would, Nancy had adjusted to the idea of moving, and so when I reported the interview later that night she was delighted.

"Oh, David, if we could clear twenty-five thousand! Think! We'd have enough to pay bond on, really, a pretty nice apartment ... or maybe another house, an older one." Her enthusiasm had returned, and her eyes gradually began to lose their dullness. "You know, an apartment might be nice for a change. No yard to worry about. Like the Gardens on Washington Road. The rent is reasonable, even though the bond is high."

"Worth a try," I replied. "But there's a hell of a waiting list and I think the bond is about twelve thousand. But we will see."

The next few days passed pleasantly enough. I had adjusted to the horrors of the new job. The way ahead began to appear successively brighter. On Thursday we left the house key with a neighbor, and the appraiser came that afternoon and stayed for better than half an hour. A good sign, we thought, since fifteen minutes is the usual time allotted. My second appointment with Mr. Long was for the following Monday. Again he greeted me pleasantly. The excitement pounding within was almost more than I could hide from him. I had inquired at the Rental Section and found the Washington Gardens was a definite possibility, based largely on the fact that Nancy was employed at the BWP with a good record.

Mr. Long studied the closely typed report for a long moment. "Hm-m-m. I see you've suffered extensive damage from vandalism. I had overlooked that matter. Should have read your file more carefully."

"Any damage ever done... and we've only had no more than maybe a half-dozen incidents... always has been repaired good as new. And there's been no vandalism[77] at all in at least eight months," I replied, uneasily.

"Well, the records show nine incidents. Mostly windows, I see. And," he thumbed back through the file, his moon face tilted upward so that he looked down his nose, "paint damage twice and internal damage three times."

---

77 There is overwhelming evidence that vandalism and other kinds of street violence, particularly home damage by roving bands of youths, was widespread in all cities in the United States. The local police authorities were limited in several respects due to tight legal restrictions making the apprehension of suspected criminals almost impossible. Police also were not allowed to carry arms.

"That was mostly furniture damage. We were away on a little holiday each time. There was practically no damage to the walls or floors. Couple of broken lamps. Some kids had a party, we think. But I've always made prompt repairs."

"Yes. Mr. Little, you have a good record on that. I suppose you are right. Still," he paused anew to check yet another index lying on his desk entitled, *Juvenile Crime Data—Pennsylvania*. "You are in a particularly vicious area for vandalism, and that's bound to affect the over-all worth of the house."

"Just what is it worth?"

"Well ... all things considered... you've been appraised at... ah... eighteen-five," came the unruffled reply. "A fair appraisal, considering depreciation."

"Depreciation!" My head was beginning to throb. Another fluffy cloud bank of a mind to deal with. "You know that house couldn't be built today for under forty! My god, look at the inflation!"

"Exactly! I was just coming to that." Mr. Long's moon face looked even more friendly, as if we had just discovered that we had mutual friends. "You're aware, I am sure, of the new government program to combat this awful inflation. Cut to the bone. That's the word everywhere you turn. Now," he admonished gently, "how can we hope to bring this awful thing under control, unless everyone does his part! Under the old system of private home building one, indeed, would have to pay at least forty. But that's being changed with the new public housing program. So we could hardly authorize your house for forty. That would be feeding the fires of inflation! And that's why the new regulations clearly state," he picked up yet another book, Housing Price Index— Pennsylvania, and began to read from it, "that 'under no circumstances shall the selling price of a used dwelling exceed the original purchase price,' so you see . .

"Yes, I see!" I countered. For Mr. Long had left himself wide open. "My purchase price... and it's right there ... is twenty-five nine! That's better than seven thousand dollars more than your appraisal!"

"So it is," Mr. Long mused. "Hm-m." The round face assembled little lines of perplexity, and the slightly overweight body slouched wearily in the new black suit it was wearing; a suit not part of the authorized line and so a product of the black market. "I never make it a point to discuss my problems... people have so many of their own, you know... but the fact is that the appraiser assigned to me is a most difficult person to work with. Ordinarily, I wouldn't suggest this, but you seem like a pretty solid looking fellow. It's almost nine. What say we slip away for a little nightcap and ... a ... a quiet chat."

I made no attempt to hide my delight at the suggestion and my relief that maybe some sort of adjustment could yet be made. Mr. Long has excellent taste. We took a cab at my expense to the Drawing Room in the Hotel Royal. It is the most plush cocktail spot in the city, boasting sofa-chair combinations around low tables and a concert grand piano and harpist. The headwaiter recognized him instantly and, taking his cue from a curt nod of Mr. Long's magnificently spherical head, seated us in a quiet corner. Few people were in the place, an occasional couple snuggled together and only one large group, of government men probably, who were making discreet eyes at three women parked nearby. All had one thing in common. They were well dressed and, judging from the smooth flow of tray-bearing waiters, well off financially. We ordered drinks, and Mr. Long came right to the point.

"My appraiser ... no point in mentioning his name. Kind of sticky, this is, and you wouldn't know him anyway... he's a real cross to bear. In a word, he's just plain mean. He deliberately sets his appraisals low, and there's nothing I can do about it."

"Can't you report him?"

Mr. Long began toying with a cocktail napkin that bore the slogan, "World Peace Through Unity of Purpose." His hands were nimble and well manicured. "No, sir. They encourage low appraisals ... so long as it isn't below the mortgage value; otherwise the government would have to pay the difference. No," he sighed, long and hard, "there's only one way."

"How much to get him to reappraise my house," I asked, weariness sweeping over me.

"Ah! You are a most perceptive person, Mr. Little. You do believe in coming right to the point... and on such a delicate subject, too."

"I've had lots of practice. Your appraiser would like a cut. How much?"

Mr. Long pursed his lips and cocked his moon face in his friendly manner. "Fifty percent of the difference between the old and new appraisal figure."

"Your appraiser friend doesn't fool around. What would the new appraisal be?" I spoke almost without any kind of feeling, which impressed Mr. Long.

"You're a remarkably cool customer."

"Skip it. How much?"

"Well, I could probably talk him into, let's say, twenty-five, two. Got to show a little depreciation to look right on paper." Mr. Long signaled a waiter for another round. Neither of us spoke during the interlude, until we were replenished, and then he continued. "Wish I could do better for you. Still... that would boost your profit from a little over fifteen hundred to over five thousand. Not bad at all! Of course, I should mention another fee, you might say, of probably a thousand ... for the records clerk, since a couple of reports will have to be changed and, unfortunately, she's as bad as my appraiser."

"Down to four thousand. Hardly worth it, and we haven't got to the big one yet... your cut."

"Heavens!" Mr. Long exclaimed. "You don't think I would engage in such a disgusting display of greed. I am hurt ... yes hurt... that you should even consider the thought." The moon face dipped into an oval as he pouted. "I'll take none of your money."

"Aren't you grand," I replied. "If you are so distressed with this transaction, why not tell me who this bird is, and I'll deal directly with him."

"And place myself in jeopardy! Let my appraiser know I'm revealing his dirty deeds! I simply can't!"

We drank in silence. He had me, and he knew it. A simple proposition. Fifteen hundred one way. Four thousand another, and better than that much for the "appraiser." It was beautiful. Here was one man who would survive as long as the new world continued to hang together.

"You are a sly one, Mr. Long. Agreed. Now, where do we go from here?"

"As soon as the papers are... ah... adjusted, we go to the bank."

"We?"

"Of course!" was the friendly reply. "We are required to issue checks, and we couldn't have any slips... like you forgetting your end of the bargain."

"An interesting thought. How do you plan to keep me honest, like you?"

"Well," he sighed. "At the bank we exchange checks. I give you one for the full appraisal... less the mortgage... and you give me a check made out to me for exactly," he calculated rapidly on another Peace napkin, "four thousand, three hundred and fifty dollars. Then we go to the window together... you first, of course."

"A little risky for you ... a check in your name."

"Ah! You are indeed perceptive!" Mr. Long finished his drink, and we ordered again. By this time the three women had joined the group of men and occasional waves of laughter and brazen words drifted in our direction.

"You see," he continued finally, "I also make loans on the side ... to unfortunate chaps who are unable to deal through regular channels. Just before we cash our checks I will ask you to sign a little loan agreement, pre-dated to, say, six months ago... but all ready to be marked paid. That way if anyone asks any questions, my answer is simple."

"I am paying off a loan using the proceeds from my house."

"Exactly. Now, shall we have another little touch from the bar to celebrate?"

So we did. Then Mr. Long had to get home to the wife and kiddies. He made a clean sweep. He left me with the bar check, sixteen dollars plus tip.

My first impulse was to stay on in the opulent Drawing Room and consume four thousand dollars' worth of liquor, but some sense of decency prevailed. I went home to Nancy instead.

384

The news broke her in two. She grabbed a kitchen knife and tried to stab herself. I had to strike her to get the knife away. Then she collapsed in a heap on the floor and cursed God in low murmurs, rocking back and forth, eyes closed and dry of any tears. I half dragged her to bed. She uttered scarcely a sound so the children were not awakened. When I turned the lights out she was still staring dry-eyed at the ceiling. Some time during the night I fell asleep.

Mornings always have been my preferred time of day, because things look better then, even if the night before has been a bad one. This is especially true in the month of May on those days when the sky is a deep blue, and the early sun bathes young leaves and newborn grasses in sidelights of gold to underscore the lush green of the rolling hills and give sparkle to the carpet of houses that stretch from horizon to horizon; while the fresh breeze of the new day brings the songs of birds busy already with their happy tasks. And the children are rested and, thus, gay and tumbling in a pleasing way. Morning is that time of day that insists on bringing us hope, even when we know that by noon or, certainly, by late afternoon the work day will have taken it away from us in some new, unexpected, diabolical way, leaving no other recourse but to drink the evening away—if you can afford the price of a drink—and then to tumble deep into the escape hatch of sleep, again to awaken to the sun and a new round of hope.

So Nancy was up first, as always, and there she stood before the mirror, nursing the pleats and buttons of her dress. For her clothing was beginning to show signs of wear, a pulled stitch or a loose button that requires quick service with needle and thread. The same old Nancy, well almost anyway. The porcelain face has been glued back together. But there are faint cracks. The face is no longer as soft and pretty, and the brown eyes are not so wide with the determination to get on with things. The new lines in the face show weary resolve, void of sweetness, while the eyes are guarded with a film of cunningness. The mouth is twisted downward, as if it would give voice to some darkly kept thoughts. A woman nearly 40 having an early morning conference with herself on how she was to make another desperate bid to go on living—the only brand of hope the new sun could give her on the day after the awful night before. She did not tell what this hope might be, and I did not ask. At breakfast—corn-flakes and toast—however, she did speak, finally, in a voice steady but flat and cold.

"You will find us a place to live ... or must I do that, too?"

The sun had been more generous in its measure of hope to me. We still would have four thousand, enough to clean up our debts and a little left over for moving expenses. Also, we could sell some of our furnishings. Beyond this there were lots of older apartments closer to the city. In the Salvatoria neighborhood I knew of several, nothing fancy, but we could make it work. Somehow we would hang on, until things got better. So I was convincing in my reply.

"I know exactly where to look. I will handle all arrangements." The children, of course, wanted to know how things stood. They knew of the move, but the details had been kept from them. They had been upset enough with just the news that we were leaving the neighborhood—Peggy storming with anger damning—god damning—me for ruining her life "just when I was getting in big at school." David muttering darkly about going to live at Bob Johnson's house. Little Annie crying softly in her pillow, and then bravely pushing back the tears to turn her sweet, wet face upward to comfort me, "It's all right, Daddy. I'll help you…"

So I told them that I would make everything nice. And we went our separate ways to classrooms, bureaucratic forms and loud neckties, each carrying his own private brand of hope.

Good-bye, then, to this split-level wonder of the twentieth century. Three bedrooms, a living room and dining room. A kitchen with its electric stove tops, miracle ovens, garbage grinder, automatic ice dispensing refrigerator and deep freeze that we cannot take with us. So long, clever hanging lamps and nifty bread drawer. So long, game room with the glass wall that slides open. And the basement, where I write for this, the last time; the sleek gas furnace with its gadgets and washing and drying machines that think of everything, when they work—good-bye to you, too. And the hedges outside. Annie's swing and the brick barbecue. The whispering trees, oak, maple and locust, and the budding bushes all pink and white. The hills around us and neighbors, too; the mean ones and the nice ones. Whatever there is in view from this plot of ground, all of it is the familiar site of home, your home that no longer is.

For a week ago I found a place. An ancient building of stained, chipped yellow brick midway down the side of Mount Washington in the heart of the city near the rivers. But its roof lines are still reasonably straight, and the windows are whole. Six apartments set in three stories, and we have the one on the right side, top floor. A living room, a little snug; a dining room with a broken brass chandelier of some god-awful vintage, just a wee tight for five; two bedrooms, kind of close and, besides, son David can sleep on the couch; the kitchen, two at a time can move around just fine, and the gas hot plate and crumpled refrigerator—well, maybe we can replace them when things get better. There is a sun porch, too, but the flooring is rotted, so it is boarded up.

Day after tomorrow, we move. All about are the boxes marked "Keep" or "Sell." For there is not room for everything. Besides, the used household goods market is booming, and we anticipate a handsome profit. I already have sold the playroom furniture, including Annie's little rocker and the two chairs and table, as well as a bed and three chests. I made a separate deal with a hardware store for the lawn furniture, the mower, hose, tools and other odds and ends from the work bench. All told, we will add better than six hundred dollars to our resources. We are keeping the car, our ace in the hole. It can still bring a good price, if I am careful not to drive it much.

While we grumble some about the turn of events, the family is beginning to pull more closely together. Even Peggy has seen that if we are to build for the future we must all help each other. Perhaps this is a blessing. For stripped as we are of the gilt of carefree living, we are forced to mingle with ourselves.

That is one thing they cannot take from us—the sanctuary of the family, however ineffective it might have been in the past.

IX

The Twenty-Fourth Month

It is still snowing. If it keeps up we will have nearly a foot by morning—one of the worst December snows on record. It is nearly impossible to move around. Still, one manages. Excuses for absences are not acceptable, excepting in cases of a family death or a severe personal illness, either one of which must be certified by a public health official, this by order of the JCFLA. Purpose is to eliminate malingering, in order to boost productivity,[78] and to enforce more strict attention in school classrooms. So, even children dare not be absent. This morning all of us were late. The buses could not get through because of the hills, and we barely had three inches of snow then. So Nancy and I walked into town. We were better than two hours late, and I was fined twenty-five dollars, as were my two companion clerks in the Men's Shop. Nancy suffered no such punishment at the BWP. The children were forty-five minutes late for school. Their punishments were quite light. Annie and most of the rest of her class were not allowed to go to lunch. David was assigned to do an extra essay on World Revolution. Peggy was called to the principal's office and suspended from her duties as

---

78 As a result of the National Prosperity Act, production quotas were set which, in addition to agriculture and dairy products, included tonnage quotas for the basic metals industries, certain of the higher priority metal fabricators and manufacturers, as well as elements of the chemical and petroleum industries. Records indicate their quotas were widely publicised using the most advanced methods in "motivation propaganda." A few of the quotas were met, initially, in agriculture and chemicals, but elsewhere the quota system was a failure.

secretary of the senior class, which has upset her some. She fears that this black mark will ruin her chances for a JCFLA scholarship next June, but in light of her achievements over the past year, I think not.

If only the snow were a little less wet, we could manage better. My overshoes do not help much, and Nancy's boots are ripped down the back. The two girls are in good shape with boots that ought to hold up over the winter, but David had his stolen, and now the wetness has rotted the soles of his shoes loose. I must find a way to fix that. I know where I can get an old inner tube, which should take care of Nancy, too.

It is a chore to keep this journal up to date. I can only write when I am alone, and there is no place in the apartment. Even nighttime is out, since a light from the dining room—the only possibility— would keep David awake, and he has difficulty enough sleeping on the sofa in the living room. Last week I finally found a private place, a small storage area in the basement latticed off behind the boilers. Through a complicated set of maneuvers I rearranged the cubicle for a wooden box to serve as a desk, and I found an old stool. I also have candles. It is unlawful to burn electric lights past ten o'clock, unless a special permit is secured.

Life has been smooth enough. We get by with a reasonable amount of food, and while we are unable to save any money, at least we are not too deeply in debt, since we still have left a number of odds and ends to sell. The transition from home to apartment at first was difficult, particularly since we were in a completely strange neighborhood. The people are mostly workers' families, and their ways are different. The men do not wear suits, for example, and I do. Once, shortly after we came here, a gang of teenagers jostled me around a bit as I came home from work one evening. I solved that by removing my coat on the way up the hill each day and carrying it over my arm so as to be less conspicuous. With cold weather the top coat tones me down enough.

Our major concern was the children. For we moved just as the summer was beginning, and there is no yard. The only open space is a city play yard six blocks away, but there were so many frightening things happening there that we feared for the safety of the children and so forbade them to go there. This happened after our first week when little Annie came home with her underwear ripped from her. The park director, an oily college freshman, could not identify the "curious boys," as he put it, and the police merely laughed. Fortunately, we thought at the time, the Youth Camp Program[79] became official, and—thanks to Nancy, again—permission was granted for all three children to attend, each one at a different camp, for the entire summer.

I went to camp once. It was the summer I was thirteen. I was a Boy Scout then, but not a very good one, largely I think, because I spent so much time working in the grocery store. So I was slow getting my merit badges and for that reason was always behind the rest of the fellows in the troop. Initially, I had not wanted to go to camp. The idea of being away from home in unknown and wild surroundings left me sleepless at night. But Father had insisted. While he did not talk about it, I knew that he had set aside small sums of money each week all through the winter and spring to pay the cost of two full weeks at Camp Rolling Green. It was unthinkable, then, to say or do anything that might have dampened Father's enthusiasm. "Never had the chance to go when I was a boy," he mused several times, "and my boys are going to go—at least once. You can bet on that!"

Had I wanted to, I could have stopped the whole operation by simply turning Mother loose on him. She was worried about the damp air, insects, snakes and the possibility of drowning in the dammed up creek that the brochure said served as a swimming pool. She fussed about what kind of clothes I should take and how many blankets I should pack, too. But Father was adamant and pooh-poohed every negative suggestion she put forth. "Nonsense! He'll be as safe as if he were in church, and besides he wants to go, don't you, boy?" What other answer could I give except yes?

---

79 The National Prosperity Act also provided for the reorganisation and expansion of the government youth program, to coincide with a World Order of Nations directive. In order to end all forms of economic and social discrimination, all private, municipal and state summer camps were abolished.

So one horribly hot Sunday in July we loaded me into the car. Much of me was in a huge, wooden foot locker which Father had built, heavy with clothing to cover every possible emergency, including a sub-zero blizzard. There were four blankets, plus cooking utensils, a hatchet, a hunting knife, a compass, a flashlight with two spare batteries—all newly purchased—and an assortment of emergency health aids, aspirin, nosedrops, band aids and cough syrup, plus a year's supply of toilet articles. Father, obviously, had compromised a point or two, so that Mother, at least, was resigned to my going. It took us half a day to get there, south and west from Cleveland. We went off the main highway and took narrow, less traveled country roads. Even in the heat, the air was sweet and heavy with cut clover, and the corn stood knee-high and rich green, while the fields of ripening grain rippled in the faint breeze like oceans of gold. We sped by neat farm houses, either of white clapboard or red brick, with huge trees shading portions of big front yards that ran to the edge of the road. There, stretched out on the cool looking grass or rocking back and forth in wooden, high-backed chairs, the farmers and their broods relaxed in pastoral splendor—still dressed in their Sunday best, minus heavy suit coats. I remember so well those scenes for the sense of openness they gave me. There was the land, green and gold, stretched mile on mile, and there were the people at peace with it. As we drove, bobbing up and down the steaming macadam road, the specter of camp became less and less foreboding. Almost too soon we were there, pulling off the pavement to rock gingerly down a rugged dirt lane delightfully cool in the shade of the tree arches that protected it. We came out of the woods to a meadow that sloped gently down to a sparkling stream flanked by more trees. Automobiles were everywhere, and milling about were dust-streaked papas, harassed mamas and bawling babies and pre-camp children— all come to take Junior to camp or to return him home. The human stream eddied, flowed and swirled over the meadow to neat rows of screened tents set with precision at the lower end. In the midst of the tumbling herd we found a perspiring counselor who consulted a wilted list of names taken from a shapeless hip pocket and pointed out Tent Three. The distance, measured in foot-locker-bearing steps, was impossible. Half way along the route, Father and I gave up and undid the lid to the heavy box. Out came all but one blanket, the woolen jacket, the boots, the long socks and heavy shirts. Even the sheets went back to the car. Thus lightened, the burden of the foot locker was less dangerous and much more hopeful. In due course we made it to Tent Three, which, shaded by more great trees, was almost comfortable inside. By and by they left, Father, Mother and nine-year-old Harry, who had turned up missing four times—once up a tree—before the family car slowly turned and bumped out of the meadow. The momentary pang of loneliness vanished with the business of learning new names that went with new faces, of learning where the latrine was and the mess hall and the hobby center. To cap things off, supper featured hot dogs and ice cream, as much as you could eat. The air was good that night, and the sounds of woods and water and the shadows of moonlight enveloped me so that after a few turns to get used to the canvas cot, I slept the sleep of true peace.

Looking back on it, I liked camp best because every effort was made to fit it to me and not fit me to it. Of course, there were the rules, such as up at six-thirty and lights out at nine and hikes and nature study classes. But in terms of personal achievement it almost seems that there was a deliberate plan to give each boy an opportunity to be himself. I have never been absolutely certain of this, since I was only there that one time, and of course, I was too young to know. But never again did I ever have the same kind of experience; not in school or college or in my old job in the steel company.

I did not sense this immediately, however, since camp life—from the boys' point of view—centered around baseball. Every bright young boy likes baseball, and it was so when I was young. You liked it—or else you were a social outcast. But I did not like baseball. I could not hit the ball. I could not throw it with any sort of accuracy, and I got tired and bored standing out in center field, because nothing much ever came my way. At home this was not a particularly severe social problem, since I worked in the store most of the time and was something of an outcast anyway. But camp was different.

There was no store to tend and everyone played ball. There was the Blue Jay Team and the Red Birds, the Indians, the Pirates and several more. Competition among them was fierce, and by luck I wound up with the Blue Jays which, even during the first game with the Pirates, showed definite promise of being the camp champs. I was determined to try, and I went at it too hard. I struck out repeatedly and otherwise fumbled badly, so that by the third day I already was known as "The Hex," and the success of my entire stay at camp hung dangerously in the balance. I was pondering this late one afternoon after a particularly disastrous performance that gave the Jays their first defeat. I had sought the top of a wood pile behind the tents and sat hunched with the world resting squarely on my shoulders. My counselor found me there half way through the evening meal. He was what every counselor ought to be: young, perhaps twenty, with an apple cheek face and slim, lithe body that was made for the woods; soft-spoken but firm when necessary, and patient and good-natured with the tumbling free-for-all boys fresh from the city. He had charge of my tent section, and his name was James Murray from Galion. He was an Eagle and an Explorer Scout. We all idolized Jim. He was the last person I wanted to see.

"Aren't you hungry?" he asked. He stood hands on hips, with feet planted widely like a Royal Mounted Policeman in a poster I once saw. "Better come on."

"Think I'll stay here," I mumbled, not daring to look him in the face.

"Well," he stepped lightly to the top of the wood pile and sat beside me, "suit yourself. Kind of a rough afternoon."

"Yeah. Wish I were dead."

"Don't blame you. You sure were lousy." There was the hint of a smile that edged into his clean features now bathed in gold and shadows of the setting sun. From somewhere a frog croaked. As Jim looked at me the smile on his face broadened into a grin. "Come on! It's not the end! Not all of us are baseball players."

"What am I gonna do, Jim?" I flung the words at him, fighting tears and a choking lump in my throat.

"Don't know." He paused, and we both listened to the woods for a while. From the other end of the camp happy voices drifted back as the boys prepared the nightly camp fire. Finally he said, "Noticed you swimming yesterday. Not too bad. Like it?"

"Oh sure. It's easy," I replied. And this was true. I always had liked water, and my father had taught me to stroke and breathe properly when I was quite small.

"You know we've got a swimming meet Saturday. I didn't notice that you've signed up for it yet." Jim said with studied casualness.

"Who, me! In a regular meet? I've never been in one." The thought, particularly after my bout with baseball, chilled me with panic.

We sat in more silence as deep and gloomy as the dusk that was fast overtaking the woods and meadow. Here and there flickers of light popped up in the tents, to rhyme with the fireflies that were unveiling themselves.

"Suppose you're right," Jim mused. "Still, I just was thinking… suppose I arranged for a substitute for you on the ball team tomorrow and, while the games are going on, maybe we could slip down to the river. Been in a couple of meets, myself, and if a fellow knows a little bit about swimming… well, it's not bad at all . ."

We did that. No one was around. We slid into water that was bone shivering cold and swam between the markers. Then we raced, and while I did not win, I came close. We raced again and again, faster each time. Still I did not win, but I always came close. Then I was getting friendly tips on how to make a diving start and how to turn without missing a stroke. So passed Wednesday afternoon away from the yelling baseball diamonds, and Thursday and Friday, too. No one missed me at all.

Saturday morning, at the last minute, I entered the meet. I placed first in the toughest event of all, six laps of fury with nine other boys ranged against me.. I won, just barely. And I received a golden cup, First Place—Free Style—Camp Rolling Green.

It was the only thing in my life that I ever won. I am sorry we could not bring it with us when we moved, but there was no room. It was sold with other trivia.

No wonder, then, that I was both pleased and relieved when Nancy and I were notified that all three of our children had been accepted for Youth Camp. There was a trace of selfish glee in digesting this pleasant turn of events; for the government was to absorb all costs, and perhaps I could begin to get even with the board again. In the brief span of a week the cares of daily life were pushed aside as we readied the children to go, and if one did not care to look too closely around the edges, it could have been 25 years ago, back in the days when we were still an unenlightened nation. For the little, dingy apartment sang with the preparations. From crammed chests and cartons stored under the beds and on closet shelves came assorted clothing—shorts, slacks, dresses, trousers, sweaters, shirts, and blouses to be refitted in some cases or simply repaired in others. The hunt was on for thread and patching material. The dining room table became a tailor shop, and the tiny living room became the marshaling area. The place was a bubbling litter of chitchat and odd corners of cloth and useless bits of thread. Even the heat of the emerging summer that soaked into the peeling walls to hang stagnant and heavy did not stifle the reborn spirits. Camp! Even Nancy dropped some of the brittleness, and she began to soften about the face as her fingers flashed back and forth with needle and thread. She made it a point to be home from work as early as possible for a change, and after a quick and simple supper everyone got to work. The children's daytime chores were double checked, and the nighttime clothing repair work was conducted with good humored precision. I was occupied for the most part with shoe repair. New shoes were out of the question, but through my connections at the store I was able to pick up synthetic shoe soles. I fashioned an awl from the head of an old hammer and, with some tacks I still had, did a creditable job, including the heels.

Since getting ready for camp was so important to us, a trip to the Youth Bureau seemed logical and necessary. (Don't forget to ask about blankets, David!) So, on my lunch hour I made yet another trip to the Federal Building, this time to the seventeenth floor. Doubtlessly, they would have a check list of some sort and some brochures showing

395

pictures of the camps. The reception room was not as jammed as most bureau offices. I waited less than an hour so that even though I missed lunch, which is never much anyway, I was back at work on time. The atmosphere of the reception room was pleasant. Huge color photographs of scrubbed children at play in "nature's playground" graced cool green walls. Most government posters are much more somber, usually showing peace soldiers in action somewhere in the world against "the enemies of freedom."[80] Or grim pictures of impoverished people of other countries bearing the message of "stamp out poverty—buy Peace Bonds," a rather unnecessary message since most working people are simply given bond quotas based on their "fair shares." But here at the Youth Bureau the scenes on the walls were ones of happiness and delight. Splendid looking camp buildings of brick and stone with lush woods in the background played host to glowing youth—the kind that every parent and social worker dreams about. There was a color photo showing girl-next-door and boy-next-door type teenagers sitting together in "summer seminars under the trees," while a dashing young instructor in crisp blue shirt and shorts outlines the blessing of materialism neatly spelled out on a chalk board. There was a picture of wide-eyed moppets at the kindergarten camp clustered around a trim, sweet-looking young woman, almost Madonna-like, explaining an ant farm and the virtues of "teamwork begins with the little things." There was another photo scene showing jaunty boys of grade school age marching in perfect unison through a country meadow singing lustily, "Oh let us be strong, boys, for the world!" A new youth song, as the caption explained. The fact that everyone, children and adults alike, wore blue uniforms failed to register at the time I was waiting my turn at the long counter.

---

80 World Order of Nations Peace Keeping Forces, at this time about sixteen million soldiers, airmen and seamen, were on active duty in central and south Africa, Egypt, Turkey, India, France, Great Britain, Canada, the United States, Central and South America. This excluded the Soviet Union and Chinese military forces numbering an estimated twenty-one million troops, who were permitted to remain intact as "special World Order of Nations auxiliary forces." A special amendment to the Treaty of Friendship was required which was agreed to with little or no opposition by the other member nations of the W.O.N.

And it was the counter that offered a weird contrast to the pictorial decor of the room. For there were possibly a dozen women seated behind it answering questions and filling out forms for the lines of parents who waited patiently for their turns. Unlike the Employment Bureau, these people, like me, were reasonably well dressed in the sense that their clothing, while showing signs of wear, still was neat and fairly clean. Also the people, themselves, were better kept. The men were shaven and most women wore lipstick. But the women behind the counters conflicted with the naturalness of the men, women and children in the pictures; nearly all of them were sticks of flesh, looking mannish in tailored summer suits and void of any noticeable emotion. They did not smile, but they did not scowl, either. Poker faces without makeup of any sort. Some women had long hair pulled securely back, while others had theirs cut close to their heads. All seemed to have the same rawboned build. Indeed, when I first entered the room it took me a moment to be absolutely sure of their sex—or lack of it. For they looked not man or woman but neuter, from their voices and faces to god knows what kind of shoes they were wearing.

Finally, my turn came, and I was confronted with the face of a woman that reminded me of a horse.

"Yes?"

"My children have been selected to go to camp… Sommerset, numbers One, Three and Four… and I would like information on clothes to take and… what the places are like… brochures, if you have any."

The woman frowned ever so slightly. "What clothes?"

"Clothes for the children to take."

She leaned forward to rest a bony elbow on the counter, her body bowed like a willow sapling. "None of the children take clothes, except of course what they're wearing. The government provides everything needed."

"Everything?" I was plainly astonished. I thought of the long hours of preparation we already had put behind us.

"Didn't you get the instructions?"

I told her I did not think so. The woman scowled and muttered something about the inefficiency of men. She picked up a phone and dialed a number.

"Record checks, please," she said crisply into the mouthpiece. Biddle. David ..."

"That's Little."

"Make that Little. David..."

"Q."

"Q. Little. Three children."

"Peggy, David and Annie."

She repeated the names and waited in silence for a moment. "What's your departure date?" she asked me finally.

"This Sunday."

She relayed that information and waited some more. Then she hung up. Her manner had changed slightly. She seemed almost to smile. "You're a special applicant. Direct through the BWP. Our people probably assumed you got the information, sir."

"Well, we didn't. Now what's this about clothes?"

"Here." She reached under the counter to produce a mimeographed sheaf of papers fastened together under the heading, "Instructions, Rules, Regulations—World Order of Nations Youth Camps in the United States. Official. World Order of Nations." "Read this," she continued. "It states quite plainly that civilian clothes are strictly forbidden. The children are issued uniforms, blankets... everything, including towels and undergarments. Also, sir, be sure you get your children to the right departure areas. There are seven stations in the county, and every child is assigned to a particular bus. It would be easy to get mixed up." "Thanks, but we were planning to drive the children up to Sommerset."

"Oh, no, that's not necessary."

"But we want to!"

"The rules are quite explicit on that. All children must leave their parents at the designated departure area. Children must begin

on an equal footing and with proper organization. Also it is bad for morale to have parents at the camps. Besides, some parents don't even have cars, and their children must go by bus. Such discrimination would work against the spirit of the whole summer... unless you are an official of the JCFLA or one of the bureaus," she added hastily, "because there are special arrangements..."

"No. I am not."

The woman's face stopped all attempts to smile. "Oh, I see. Departure for you is station seven, Sunday noon, exactly." She looked past me. "Next, please."

Thus, the family sewing bee came to an end. The children were delighted, but Nancy only bit her lip and became brittle again. On Sunday, then, we loaded them into the car. Sweet Annie clutching her favorite stuffed doll, her constant companion since infancy. Son David alive with a hundred questions, his freckled face as wholesome as any of the boys in the color photographs. And in her mind Peggy had left us already. "You say there'll be boys there my age?" she had asked, and then settled back to look dreamily out the car window while her fingers toyed absently with the top button of her very tight, almost transparent blouse. We said good-bye to them at a picket fence which held back a muddled mob of parents all saying similar good-byes that ran the emotional spectrum, from tears and wails to laughs and shouts of good riddance. Uniformed counselors quickly separated the three children to different waiting areas. The last we saw of them was when one of the counselors—a brutish-looking woman in thick walking shoes —plucked the doll from Annie's bewildered arms and handed it over to another blue uniform hovering nearby to be deposited quickly in a trash can. Annie had tried to cry out to us, but the woman grabbed her roughly by the shoulders, shook her violently and spun her quickly out of sight into the swirling pool of other youngsters.

I had to tug at Nancy to get her to come to the car. For she stood statue still, gnawing the knuckles of her hand, eyes spilling tears down her cheeks.

The snow is still with us, although not falling with the same brutal consistency as it did the other day. Most of our street now has been cleared, so it's easier to walk to the bus. They say, now, that it is the worst snow on record for December. The result has been that I was late two more times for work, but I was not fined in either case—the result of my first successful attempt to deal with the system. The day after I was charged with the twenty-five dollar fine, I was late again despite my efforts to be on time. I left the apartment at six-thirty a.m. It was a miserably dark[81] morning, and the snow was clinging wet and another two inches deep. Nancy had elected to leave a little later, since she was positive that she would not be fined. There were many people afoot with me, slip ping and slogging down the twisted cobblestones. Men and women of all ages traveling for the most part singly or in couples and saying very little. The air and the city both were still so that each slopping step, each intake of breath and each muttered curse rose to an oozing, wheezing clamor. I had not taken a dozen steps before I was soaked to the knees. By the time I had covered a city block I had to shake the peaks of sticky snow from my hat to keep it all from sliding down my neck. By the time I reached the bridge my legs had no feeling, and my back ached so that it was bent. I had to lean on the railing in order to force my body upright to rest some. Another long haul brought me to Barnes' Department Store. I was not, therefore, in the best frame of mind when I arrived on the floor in the Men's Shop at nine-thirty. Mr. Kloomer was waiting for me, as well as for my two fellow clerks who had not yet arrived.

"Ah there, Little!" Mr. Kloomer flitted through the maze of display tables and racks like a nervous moth. He was biting his thin lower lip, trying to control his relish at catching me late a second time. "Thirty minutes! I see my lesson of the other day is not enough. You're all alike. Discipline means nothing. Well," he quavered, "we'll just see if another fine won't teach you better."

Mr. Kloomer had installed a cot in his special back room so that he was spared the rigors of morning travel on the city's Miracle Transportation System that had broken down almost entirely. Since

---

81 Electrical generating equipment was beginning to fail more and more frequently in all of the major cities due to the shortage of fuel and parts. Hence, electricity was severely rationed. Street lighting, for instance, was discontinued in all but the most elite sections of the cities.

rank has its privileges, we clerks had been denied this convenience, more due to a sadistic whim of Mr. Kloomer's than to store policy.

There was little point in discussing the situation. Kloomer obviously was not looking for a bribe, for there was nothing to offer —or take. He was not the charitable type, so it was pointless to plead with him. Reason was also out of the question, since he was an unreasonable person. He was vulnerable only in one area, that of fear, and I could think of nothing at the moment to hold over him. So I merely nodded and, simply because he would not expect it, grinned openly at him. Then I stared hard into his water-blue eyes, and he ducked away like a rabbit. The other two clerks dragged in shortly afterwards and got the same treatment. All morning long I squeezed from my brain dozens of possibilities that might successfully generate fear within the fidgety soul of Mr. Kloomer. I could threaten his life and mean it, since I could easily hire the deed done for as little as twenty-five dollars. But he would have me jailed on the spot. I could shoo some of his special customers away by saying, "Mr. Kloomer doesn't like you any more." But it would take several days for the reaction to trickle down, and, while he might be fired, I would probably go, too. I could report him to one of the bureaus for some misdeed, or I could threaten to report him, except I had nothing to report. Unless, I thought finally, a situation could be created. Kloomer, himself, supplied the solution shortly before noon. A special customer had come in, and I had ducked behind the curtains into the back room to alert him. He was at his desk reading, with obvious difficulty, *The Works of Karl Marx*. He was not happy to see me or to be interrupted by a customer. "Damn!" He snapped the book shut. "I've got an impossible exam tonight, and if I miss that I'm cooked! Oh, well, send him in."

All the lights went on in my head at once. A plan unfolded in all of its splendid detail. During my lunch hour I visited a small secondhand book store that I have come to know quite well. It was set in a crumbling brick building. All of the windows were boarded up, save a few on the street level. Behind those windows, so grimy that one could scarcely see through them, lived a very old man who kept barely alive by selling battered volumes and magazines of this and that. No one was about, and after a brief conversation he grinned toothlessly and bolted the front door. Then he led me back through his dreary living quarters to the filthy basement below. He shifted a few empty packing cases to uncover another door which led to a small, windowless, booklined room that was tidy and orderly. A quick search produced exactly what I was looking for, and I paid him ten dollars. My coat was a perfect shield, and I wore it right up to the Men's Shop deliberately ignoring the employees' locker room. I simply told my fellow clerks that I was looking for the tailor to do some quick mending on my coat and walked boldly into the back room. As I had hoped, the place was deserted. Neither Kloomer nor the tailor had returned from lunch. It took only a moment to lift the pillow on Kloomer's cot to make my deposit and then replace the pillow over it. Perfect concealment! Then I marched back to the locker room, indignant that the tailor could not be found. The foot traffic was heavier than usual, non-buyers seeking the warmth of the store, so that the afternoon slipped by quickly. All of us, including Kloomer, were busy moving the new bums out, at least to another department, so that any recollection of my visit to the backroom would by the end of the day be completely forgotten.

Forty-five minutes before quitting time I made my move. The foot traffic had ceased, and Kloomer had moaned his way back through the curtains to do his morning paper work and to make a last bid to understand Marx. I pulled the other two clerks in close behind a clothes rack and suggested we have one more try at talking Kloomer out of recommending another fine, a paper chore he had not yet completed. So we entered the back room.

"Mr. Kloomer," I said, careful to keep my voice humble.

He jumped like he had been stung, spilling notes out of his lap. "What now!" he shrieked. "I'm due at Party headquarters in two hours! Handle it yourselves!"

"We're here to ask you… please … to reconsider the fines you hit us with this morning," I continued. The three of us edged closer to the tensely hunched figure, who was now biting his upper lip, teeth showing ugly stains of yellow.

402

The figure relaxed slightly, and the mouth flowed into a flat smile. "Wondered when you'd come begging, Little. The answer is no. Now, get out of here before I fire all of you!"

"Mr. Kloomer... sir." I moved wearily to his cot and sat down.

"Off my cot!" He rose from his chair, twitching with rage.

"Surely, I could rest here a moment. I'm quite faint." Slowly I reclined so my elbow rested on the pillow. "Can't we... please... discuss this?"

"No!" And off my cot before I have you thrown out. You're fired, Little!"

My two companions gulped and began to move away, leadened with fear.

"All right. Fire me for sitting on a lousy cot! You act as if I'm sitting on some state secrets or something." Slowly, disgustedly, I started to get up, and in so doing my hand tumbled the pillow to the floor.

"Now you've done it!" Kloomer squeaked. His hands fidgeted a long arch through the air.

"I guess I have done it!" I said, staring hard at the exposed head of the cot. For on the blankets lay a book, a very old book. I picked it up and handed it to my two companions. "*The Enduring Works of Thomas Jefferson*"! I said, awed by the discovery. "Mr. Kloomer is a very brave man to read such a dangerous book."[82]

"Wha . . The fidgeting hands snatched wildly at the volume, turning it over and over to make sure it was real.

My fellow employees were at once stunned and delighted. Both, thanks to the example set by Kloomer, were likewise studying to join the Party, and both recognized instantly the worth of the discovery. Their stature could only go up in the eyes of the Party were they to denounce Kloomer for the dark, treacherous deed of studying Jefferson while pretending to revere the Party.

---

82 The writings of the Founding Fathers of the United States—Jefferson, Madison, Jay, Adams, Paine, among others—were banned as being "too readily misinterpreted by right-wing extremists who twist the utterings of these great men to serve their own selfish purpose, which is to plot revolt against peace-loving people."

Kloomer saw it, too. "L-look," he stammered. "I've never seen this... trash... this poison!"

"Relax, you tired old man," one of the clerks said. "Now you sit, and you listen."

And Kloomer sat, while the two clerks talked in soft tones that ate him up.

Fifteen minutes later a very humble Kloomer squeezed my hand lovingly with both his, as he had done with my companions. "And you, Dave... hope you understand I've been on edge. How could I have been so stupid and thoughtless even to suggest a fine... after what you boys have been through. And don't think I don't appreciate your willingness to forget about the book ..."

I was two hours late the next morning, but Kloomer only waved a cheery hello.

3

The thought of recruiting Thomas Jefferson for this most recent skirmish with Kloomer never would have occurred to me had it not been for Dr. Hamilton Rodgers. Ever since that day last March when Marie Salvatoria and I found Chip Baker more dead than alive, I have visited the Salvatoria home regularly. At first I went there every other day to see to their needs. Our resources—mine and theirs—were slim. Except for Marie's modest earnings, the Salvatorias were destitute. The little bit of rent they charged the family upstairs—unofficially, since they were not listed with the Bureau of Housing, an illegality which the neighbors protected with stony silence—was months overdue. Dr. Rodgers' pension, upon which he had counted so heavily, had long since been abolished on the technicality that, because of his admissions of Treaty violations at the hearings, he was no longer eligible as a law-abiding citizen. It was a situation he had accepted quite philosophically, convinced that one way or another they would have taken the pension from him anyway.[83]

---

83 Most "bourgeois pensions" ultimately were rescinded as money "ill-gotten
    through a capitalistic system that exploited and discriminated against the peo-

404

With Chip and me not working, the situation posed many problems, especially during the first two weeks when Chip was so severely ill. For his fever would not break. It stayed at about one hundred and five for nearly a week. Aspirin was all that we could find for medication, along with cold sponge baths. Food was the big problem, enough to feed all of us, my family included. Occasionally, I would bring from home a couple of slices of bread and perhaps an apple or an egg, but I had to be careful so that Nancy did not notice. I compensated by eating less myself. While some food items were becoming more and more scarce, it was the ever-rising prices that plagued us. Citrus fruits were almost non-existent. Meat stock to make broth, which was about all we could force down into Chip's wasted body, had doubled in price. Milk and eggs were impossibly high, as was margarine—as everything still is now, nine months later. Beans, however, were cheap, and they could be made into a fairly hearty gruel when combined with ham broth and seasonings, a large selection of which the Salvatorias still had on hand. Spaghetti could be had too. So my days initially were spent helping attend to Chip and shopping for food. The people upstairs were able to help some with potatoes and cabbage. Once I thought of calling Mary Best for help, but Dr. Rodgers would not hear of it, saying that "I should not want her to see us like this, particularly myself."

There were some grim moments, but we made it through the first two weeks, and then Chip was able to sit up some. Following this came my job in the men's shop, and my visits dropped off, but at least I was now able to supply five or ten dollars a week, which helped some. Early in May, Chip, against everyone's protest, returned to the manual labor pool. It was difficult for him at first. He would collapse the instant he stumbled through the door after a day of digging or hauling trash or cleaning industrial sewers, and he would sleep the evening and night away. But by June Chip had regained his strength so that he could earn small amounts of money on a regular basis.

---

ple by charging unjustly high prices in order to reap huge profits for the benefit of a few people."

It was obvious from the start that the four of them—Marie, Chip, Victor and Dr. Rodgers—were good for each other. For Victor, the lonely days at home were gone; Chip had a solid home under his feet and the steadying influence of Marie, who seemed to be happiest of all, for she viewed the new arrivals as an omen of hope. And Dr. Rodgers had his fondest wish realized—students to teach, not only Chip but both Marie and her father and on occasion myself. We all had something else, too. It was a bond of mutual acceptance that gave us new strength to deal with the tumbling world about us.

In my case, of course, the loss of our home and the children gone to Youth Camp had left Nancy and me suddenly—as the summer began in earnest—with no place to go as far as each other was concerned. The mainstays of our life together had been chopped away; neither children nor home to worry about. Nothing now but an intolerably hot June to make worse an intolerably hot apartment on an intolerably noisy street with intolerably noisy neighbors.

Six apartments with six families bound together by a single, ugly yellow-brick building. Six units of loving togetherness with windows and doors thrown wide open to vent the breath-sucking heat that causes babies to cry misery and children to scream dirty remarks, while the men and women swear at their ill luck or bat each other around. Crash, bang, thump and gurgle. Somewhere a pan clatters to the floor or a toilet is flushed or someone belches. Televisions and radios screech all sorts of messages. The odors of cooked cabbage or something being fried in lots of grease. The stench of stale beer. The voices, sounds and smells of human activity, shut up no more but collected and driven by the heat three flights up the stairwell where it is all assembled in one giant ball of noise and stink at the threshold of our own open doorway; to be joined by more noise and stink from the hot street supplied by the open windows—homey little things like boys tormenting girls, not in fun either, or mixed groups of teenagers throwing sticks, stones and garbage at other teenagers. With our own children gone and the resulting deathly stillness of our apartment, it was as if some diabolical power had dumped all of the outside noise right in the middle of the living room where we sat, during those first three nights, numbed and nauseated listening to this slice of life.

The first evening after the children left for camp was not unbearable. The full impact of the children's absence had not yet occurred. So it was a relief, almost, to sit quietly to keep from sweating too much. Besides, it was intriguing to listen to what the Joneses had to say about sex or Communism or the inlaws. It was even slightly amusing to hear toilets flushed, and the adventures in the street below offered more realism than anything on television, assuming one might have been able to hear it.

The second evening was old hat, and the noise began to thump inside my head.

The third evening shattered us. Nancy went first. The little bit of supper we had was finished by seven, right on schedule with everyone else in the building. And all of a sudden it was not funny or even boring any more. The noise, the heat and the cracked walls had become uncompromising enemies. We sat in the living room in the growing dusk; a square room that barely took the old nine-by-twelve rug that had once been in our game room; a crowded room that bulged with two over-stuffed arm chairs, the sofa, a coffee table, two floor lamps, three occasional tables and the radio-television—residue from our old home. We sat without talking, each screened off from the other by the noise and each thinking of the same things. We had expected to hear from the children at least by the third day; nothing much, a brief post card or two or perhaps a short note to tell us how fine things were. But the mail had brought nothing, not even a bill or an official directive from the JCFLA. It was the kind of a letdown that made the emptiness of the apartment all the more empty, the noises all the more noisy and the heat all the more hot. There suddenly loomed before us nothing at all save a perpetual living hell of dreary, ill-paying work and an even more fruitless existence in what was now our home. If there was a purpose to all of this, it had escaped us. Our life, such as it was, had been built around the children, the home and—at least in Nancy's view—social and economic achievement. On all of these counts we were beaten. The noises and the heat and the cramped little room told us this over and over and louder and louder.

She had been sitting rigidly on the edge of the hot over-stuffed chair, work-roughened hands gripping the arms as if she were expecting a bomb to go off in the middle of the room. Her heart shaped face was pale and moist. Her eyes had the glaze of a hypnotic trance. The late evening shadows highlighted the deep lines of her features to make her look far older than she was, a thought that must have been in her mind, too. For she rose suddenly as if jerked up by strings and moved woodenly to the still fancy mirror that hung on the wall, a leftover reminder of better days. She stared at herself for a very long time, until the daylight was nearly gone. She had grown quite thin so that the lines of her body were slumped in some areas and angular in others. Once or twice she patted at her hair, which was straight and tangled from the dust that occasionally was swirled up from the filthy street below by the hot wind. Shampoos were expensive items, and she had been rationing her supply to one hair shampoo per month, relying on plain water rinses in between. Soap, toothpaste, deodorants and other toilet articles were equally expensive, especially with the one hundred percent luxury tax, and in short supply, so that the whole process of body cleanliness was a carefully rationed procedure. We used salt and soda in place of toothpaste. Soap was used only once a day, either the morning or evening as had suited each member of our family. Deodorant had to last four days minimum. Makeup, the most expensive item of all, was used only on special occasions by Nancy, and she had had no such occasion since we had moved, another thought that must have been unwinding behind her glazed eyes.

"The beautiful, gay, successful Little family!" she spoke in mock cheerfulness to herself. "How fortunate we all are, and how well I look! Don't you think I look well, David? Aren't you pleased and proud? I know my mother would be pleased and proud! A lifetime of effort, of being nice people. Nice people get nice things. Nice Nancy gets nice David. And how well David looks, don't you, David?"

"We're still alive."

"Are we?" She turned, her mouth tense with hurt. "You would be happy to sit in this stink and rot! To sit and let the rest of the world go by. The story of your life... our life."

"What do you suggest?" I would like to have felt pity, but it was too hot and noisy to feel that. Besides, I had retreated to an old dream of mine, the cool, pine-scented air of Canada with trees all about. "Would you like me to join the Party and help them eliminate all the non-producers? I could think of any number that I should like to liquidate."

"Me?" She laughed with a grotesque pitch to her voice. "You haven't even the guts to join the Party, let alone do anything else!" "You really want me to join the Party, don't you, Nancy?"

She stared hard at me, defiance smeared across her face. "Yes, I do. They're got brains. They know how to do things. They know how to live. Do you see any poor Communists running around? Not any more. Look at me." She screeched. "Look! Look! I'm 40 years old! All I have left is my looks, and look at me!"

She swung around and began pulling at the mirror. "Make fun of me, will you!" The hook came loose from the plaster. She held the mirror in its antique white frame high over her head and then smashed it to the floor. Glass sprayed across the room in a noise that outdid all other noises. She stood panting, glaring at me. "Well, I won't be a hag... not now or ever! Other women get what they want, and I'm going to get what I want for a change. I'm tired of looking at you and listening to you. You're a nobody, and I'm not going to let you drag me down to look 60 when I'm only 40!"

"Stop it!" I jumped from my chair and slapped hard at her face. She shuddered into silence, still glaring. "We've got to live with all of this, because that's all there is."

"Oh, no." She cooed, mockery again on her face. "There are ways, but you're too nice to acknowledge it." And she laughed. "Men! I'm going to start going out again with men. The right men. Make them happy, and they make you happy. The smart women know this, and I've learned a lot."

"You... frigid you ... so cold and proper all your life... going to bed wholesale with men? That's what you mean, isn't it?"

"But of course, darling!" she purred, mocking me still. She ran her hand along her hip, and her eyes flicked into warm coyness as if I suddenly had become the most devastating kind of male. "I've had practice... darling."

Outside noises pounded against my head and from the dark recesses of my mind came the picture of Nancy acting like other women I see operating regularly out of hotels and bars; a vision I had fought to keep out of my mind by ignoring the obvious; an agony to complement handsomely all of the other hells that we have been flung into which she now would no longer allow me to ignore.

"You know how I got that job for you." She bit the words off in sharp accents and spat them at me. "Only you never want to talk about it, do you? And I let us both pretend that all is sweet and pure because I thought it was the nice thing to do. But now I want you to know, because I like the look that's beginning to show on your face!"

She had touched all of my nerve endings, and I twitched all over. "Don't talk about it!" I yelled.

"I want to make you suffer the hell I've suffered," she replied, her face now twisted in a wild smile. "I let them do everything they wanted. First it was Tom Shade and then..."

"Stop it!"

"Later on it was a nice man from New York. At first I hated it. Oh, how I hated it!" She paused. Her body was drenched in perspiration, and her face had the look of madness. "But you know what?" Her voice had dropped to a harsh whisper. The twilight had turned her face a pink that made her all the more unreal. "I got so I liked it. Do you hear? I like men! And I'm glad you know, because I can come and go as I please without all this polite silliness about working late. I won't die in this miserable place!" She stopped and cocked her head birdlike at me, puzzled now that I showed no reaction. For I was too sick and empty inside to show anything.

"I suppose you want to throw me out now that I've got you a job... *darling*... but you won't, because you caused all of... *this*. Well?" She

410

paused again. "I'm going to make myself available *again* to Tom Shade and any other *man* so long as he's strictly VIP. And I'm going to get clothes and food and perfume. Do you hear? Well?"

I must have looked at her a long time, because she kept changing form. I saw her as a young college coed, with a sensitive face, eager to please and anxious to be recognized. I saw her prettily dressed for church and then fresh and white in her wedding gown. I saw her holding our first child to her, glowingly. I saw her fragile and anxious, as she has been countless times in twenty years—a growing woman trying to live in a bewildering world. And I saw her as she was now, with her soul burned out.

"No. I won't throw you out. And I can't stop you, because there is nothing I could say that would make sense to you."

"Get out of my sight!" She spoke still in a whisper.

I nodded and left the building on rubber legs. Halfway down the stairs I nearly stumbled over a heavy-looking man oozing out of his undershirt, sitting in the shadows on a step.

"Boy, do you have troubles, buddy!" he said and then laughed.

4

Once, I might have turned to Larry Best and let his calm, confident ways pull me up out of the cesspool in which I foundered that night when Nancy smashed the mirror. But this reflex was dead, and in its place a new set of muscles, that had been slowly developing over the past three months, took hold of my trembling frame and steered me elsewhere; out of the ugly, yellow building and onto sidewalks that still radiated heat; past knots of boys and girls slinking through the shadows of late June dusk performing a variety of misdeeds; up the hill and over a block or two to the Salvatoria house with its vertical front yard and high, cool-looking porch. It was not planned. It just happened. It was dark when I arrived at the foot of the steps. The street lights no longer are burned and most houses were dark. One sensed, rather than saw, that most people either were lurking in the streets or on the stoops and porches or behind wide-open windows,

411

not talking aloud—not in this neighborhood of clannish Italians—but brooding quietly to themselves. The big front window at the Salvatoria's, though, was alive with the flicker of light. As I stepped gratefully onto the porch I could hear the steady, low voice of Dr. Rodgers through the open window.

"What's it all about, anyway?" There was a half-angry growl in his tone, as if he had caught a trusted friend searching through his bureau drawer.

"I don't think I understand your question," came the puzzled response from Chip Baker. Over the weeks his manner and actions had lost their hostility. He had even progressed to a point where he greeted me warmly whenever I came to visit, the last time being two weeks earlier.

"Victor has asked what went wrong and we owe him an answer, don't we, boy? For five years I've had you under my wing, and you've traveled the route all the way from Plato and Aristotle to Coke and Keynes. You've sawed your way through the Bible and John Dewey. You've studied Marx and Jefferson, *Das Kapital* and the *Federalist*. You've picked apart the Magna Carta, our Constitution and Declaration, The Rights of Man and the Treaty of Friendship. You've even combed through Beard and Schlesinger. Pope, Mather, Lenin and Kozak... you've made all sorts of academic visitations. And now Victor asks the payoff question. What went wrong with the wonderful American Dream? And before we can answer it we must first ask another question. What is all of *this* about?" The shadow of an arm gesturing swept across the window. "Life! What is life all about ... to begin with? Until we know that, we can't very well determine what has gone wrong with us, can we?"

There was a pause, and I rapped softly on the screen door, which still was in good repair. Someone said, "Sh-h," and padded footsteps moved cautiously through the parlor door to the screen. It was Chip. His body was wary, as he peered into the darkness. Then he recognized me and quickly motioned me inside.

"It's all right," he announced, "it's only Dave."

412

"Only! I bet he likes that!" It was Marie who spoke, and there was warm, gentle laughter from everyone at her peppery cheer. They were sitting in a semi-circle... Victor, Marie and another person dressed as a cleric. Dr. Rodgers was standing in the archway leading to the dining room. Next to him was a battered card table, and propped up on it was a chalk board. Two candles stood burning on the table. The room was cool and neat in the soft light, and the people were at ease. Their faces were open and expectant.

"How pleased we are that you visit us." Victor rose slowly and steadied himself to clasp my hand in his. The strength still flowed from them, in spite of the stroke that was trying to age him beyond the vigor of his 60 years.

And Marie greeted me with a hug, while Chip grinned and tapped me on the arm. Dr. Rodgers—who was now known to me as "Ham," his old academic nickname—also left little doubt about his delight at seeing me. "You're late for class. I ought to dock you for that," he quipped.

To stand in a friendly room and know that you are welcome; to feel the richness of human spirits alive, as they replenish your own; these are rare moments to be hoarded, and you do nothing to chase them. So I said nothing about the sickness that must still be raging at home.

"You look terribly tired. Are you ill?" Marie asked.

"I'm absolutely tops! But that walk ... the heat."

"Before you sit, come," Marie took me by the arm and steered me to the cleric who stood silent in the moving light. A half-smile was on his broad, open features. He was of medium size and wore his coat and collar without seeming to mind the heat. "I want you to meet Father Herbert," Marie added softly. Her voice crowded pride and reverence into this simple introduction.

"So, you are Dave Little, the man responsible for the new happiness of Marie and her father." His voice was warm and easy, like the rest of him. He had a certain firmness about him, too, that revealed his probable ability to preach courageously, as well as coach a tough game of football and still be sympathetic to troubled parishioners.

"We all owe you a debt for bringing Dr. Rodgers and Chip among us. I have passed many wonderful hours here in the evenings, and we are all richer, because of you. But we will talk another time. Ham is beginning to fidget," he added lightly.

The doctor coughed meaningfully. Marie settled me in her chair, rather firmly, and then seated herself on the floor, where Chip joined her. Then all eyes turned to Dr. Rodgers, who had resumed a lecture stance by the rickety card table.

"Now, then." His voice was steady and low again, with the faint trace of a growl. "There is one question that one time or another we ask of ourselves… and of others, too. Men write books about it, and drunks mumble it out loud to bartenders. 'Why am I here?' Indeed, why are any of us here?" The doctor paused significantly, to await a response.

"There are a lot of reasons why we are here," Chip ventured again. "It would take all night to go over them."

"True. Many reasons, but really only one basic reason… upon which all of the others rest."

"To serve God." Father Herbert spoke flatly.

"To Christians that would be part of the answer, but only part of it, and to non-believers it would be no answer at all," the doctor continued evenly. He pushed his glasses—forever in need of polishing—back up his nose and mopped his ageless face clean with a handkerchief held in his big, lumbering hand.

"Well," Marie spoke hesitantly, as if shy to enter such a discussion, "I'm a Christian and shouldn't a person live …"

"Stop!" Dr. Rodgers commanded, and his hand flew up like a traffic cop's. "You are right if you say no more." He shifted his stance so as to emphasize what he was about to say. The room was very still. Somewhere in the distance a siren wailed.

"We are put on this earth … to live," he breathed softly. "Ah! I see by your faces that you are disappointed. You expected something more profound and less elementary. Yet, may I suggest that this most basic conclusion is, in fact, so basic, so taken for granted that we tend to overlook the true impact of it."

414

He was right. The stirrings of the room indicated a guarded sort of disappointment. For we knew by this time that the doctor had a way with words. The more unassuming and innocent his manner, the more likely he was to strike hard with some point of logic where it was least expected and which had usually the most universal kind of impact. Such verbal booby traps had exploded in our faces before. So we waited, while Dr. Rodgers studied us one by one, his lips compressed in a doltish, downward line. Then he sniffed—another habit that had little to do with nose trouble and much to do with projecting, momentarily, the image of an imbecilic clod, fresh from the barnyard.

"Because," he continued, "unless we establish this point firmly, there is nothing solid for us to build upon. So, let us agree that we are put upon this earth to live until some force beyond our control… one might argue the same force that gave us life in the first place… sees fit to take life from our bodies. Until that time, however, we are obligated to survive. What does this tell us?"

The room of flickering yellow was burdened with heavy concentration. Father Herbert had pulled forward, his eyes shadowy slits of thought. "Our actions should be calculated to sustain life," he said, finally.

"Where is your proof?" the doctor inquired.

"Proof?" The square face of the priest began to glisten with faint traces of moisture. "It's obvious."

"That won't do," Dr. Rodgers admonished. "We've gotten out of the habit of asking ourselves and others for proof on matters of importance to us… that, Victor, is part of what has gone wrong. Besides, I don't think it's all quite that obvious. At least, the condition of the world out there," his arm swept the room in a monstrous shadow, "indicates that not everyone shares your view. So prove it, Martin."

The priest shifted to the outermost edge of his chair. "How do you prove something as obvious as daylight?" A locker-room toughness began to creep into his voice.

"By establishing the absence of darkness. That's one way," the doctor shot back.

There was another pause.

Then a voice cut the silence. It trembled slightly, as if its owner had just embarked upon some new and bold journey. It was neither fear nor nervousness that caused the tremor. It was a sense of growing discovery, where the spokesman simply had mechanical difficulty in meshing a racing brain—not at all used to racing— with a wagging tongue—not at all used to shaping words such as these. The voice was mine. The terror of Nancy was all gone, as were other terrors. Something had happened to time and place, so that as my mind bent and twisted under the stern eye of Dr. Rodgers, I ached to reach back to something that drifted aimlessly just behind my eyes. Then I grabbed it, and it came to me as a friend.

"If it were not so ... if our actions were not calculated to sustain life... then... everything we do would be calculated to achieve death."

"Excellent. Exactly, Dave." Dr. Rodgers was a sunbeam, his white head nodding with warm approval. "Now think it through some more."

"If our purpose on earth were to achieve death... then we could achieve it quickly in any number of ways. And if all of us rushed out and killed ourselves then there wouldn't be anything. Besides, if death were our goal on earth why would we be placed here in the first place? So, our purpose must be to survive as long as we can."

"Ah! As long as we can," the doctor repeated slowly. "I'm glad you added that. What do you mean?"

I was still groping behind my eyes to scoop up other formless fragments that drifted just out of reach. It seemed as if I were stretching every muscle in my body beyond endurance, pulling and wrenching to capture and form something into words that made sense.

"I suppose how well we do something determines ... or at least helps to determine... how long we can do it. Yes, I think that's what I mean. How well we feed ourselves or treat our illnesses could have much to do with how long we survive."

"Would that apply generally?" The big man shuffled forward, the dry wooden floor creaking under his feet. He had hunched his head forward, and his glasses had slipped much too low. But he did not seem to notice. The room was so still that it ceased to be a room.

"Yes." I fished some more in the black sea behind my eyes, and the net strained with a new catch. "Swimming ... I used to swim some. How well or how skilled you are at staying afloat will help determine how long you can survive in the water. Another way of putting it is..." I groped again but with less success.

"Quality," the doctor prodded softly. "You are talking about quality. The higher the quality, the better."

"Of course! How well we do something... that could be quality. Good. Bad."

"If I may ride along on your thought," the doctor sniffed again, "would it be fair to suggest that quality... being a universal sort of a word that can be applied to all that we think and do... determines the kind of life we live, within our natural limitations to live it, and that, finally, the kind of life determines in great measure the manner in which we survive? And may I suggest further that it is not merely a question of how long we survive, but how well we survive ... so that the matter of quality is of some considerable importance?"

Again there was silence. Chip had been seated on the floor with his knees drawn up like a child listening to a bedtime story, while Marie, beside him, had kept flashing her large brown eyes first at the doctor and then at me with unabashed delight. Now the young man stirred in the flickering shadows. "I missed it, Doctor, and I should have known better after all of the time we've spent on this one." There was rueful apology in his voice. "May I try?"

"Certainly, my boy. But you can't do it from there. On your feet. Up here." The doctor had shed his softness to become abruptly gruff. "Time I had a seat. M' feet hurt." He searched out a wooden chair from the dark opening to the dining room and turned it so he could sit astride with his arms resting over the back. He waved a big hand. "Proceed. What can you tell us of quality, Mr. Baker?"

And it was Mr. Baker, now. A slim young man standing at ease by the wobbly card table that barely kept the chalk board from crashing to the floor. Even in the dimness of the candles his eyes showed clear and steady. It was not much of a classroom in which a promising scholar might try his wings—a frayed parlor that held a curious

417

mixture of crumbling men and yearning youth—but it was all his, this place and these people, and he honored us by addressing us in the manner of a university classroom.

"Man is presumed to be at present the highest form of life. What gives him this superiority?"

Chip did not wait for an answer, since I am sure, he did not wish to appear presumptuous. Nor did anyone want to speak just then.

"A higher form of life is distinguished from a lower form in that it has greater and more varied sources of energy and a greater variety of suitable surroundings to which it can adapt, grow and reproduce. Man's sources of energy are greater and more varied, and he is able to adapt to almost every kind of surrounding...

even outer space. That man has this flexibility is due to the fact that he is a more complex creature than any other on earth. His physical dexterity and his intellect are both vastly superior to other forms of life. In other words, he can do more than any other creature.

"Now, quality means excellence..."

"Ahem," the doctor coughed softly. He shuffled his feet to tuck them under the chair. "Couldn't you say... before you get on to quality... that the greater the variety available to a creature, the higher its form of life?"

"So! Man has greater variety than any other creature ... so that makes him superior to other forms of life." It was Victor Salvatoria who spoke. He had not ventured one sound since my arrival but had sat absolutely still with his powerful hands resting stiffly on his knees, as if he had been waiting for a photographer to snap a studio portrait in the manner of 1880.

Chip looked expectantly at the doctor, who merely nodded his head. "Go on, boy."

"Yes, sir," he replied with a professional flourish. He fumbled across the table for a tiny piece of chalk and printed the word "Variety" in large neat letters upon the board. "What makes variety .. . variety? What does it involve?" This time Chip waited for an answer, but none came. A small smile of triumph played around his lips which, until now, had been frozen in a straight, tight line. With deliberate slowness he printed a second word under the first. "Choice."

"When any creature is confronted by variety he must exercise some sort of choice. Man, having the greatest variety in what he can do, therefore, has the greatest degree of choice available to him. Agreed?"

The room nodded.

"But what does choice involve?" Chip continued. Once again he moved to the board. He was fully caught up in his subject now, so that he did not notice the anxious rumble of an automobile jerking to a hasty stop in front of the house. Its doors slammed and footsteps sounded. Marie, who had been curled up in a rapt silence, uncoiled like a cat and extinguished the two candles.

"Quiet!" And she crept to the window to peer from behind the curtains into the hot night. We waited, our ears making mental maps of footsteps moving—thank heaven—away from us to the house across the street. "They're at the Gabrielli's, Father."

"God protect them," said the stroke-haunted voice.

The room had become suddenly hot, and Father Herbert stirred from his seat. "Perhaps I had better go see . .."

"No!" Marie spoke in a harsh whisper that betrayed her usual good humor and optimism. "You'll only make things worse. I heard the labor unions are conducting new hearings on more Treaty violations, and Mario Gabrielli is secretary of his local. They think he's a Nazi."

"For fighting the ten-hour day.[84] Yes, I know," the priest replied equally harshly. "There have been rumors all week that they might arrest him now... before the hearings."

"Wait until tomorrow, when it's light and you can case the situation," Dr. Rodgers rumbled. His attempt to whisper sounded like distant rolls of thunder.

---

84 Until the Treaty of Friendship, a six- or seven-hour work day was considered normal, with the government favouring the six-hour day, while certain industries still held out for the seven-hour day. The JCFLA viewed this as a "capitalistic waste of human resources" and almost immediately sought to reinstate a ten-hour working day, which was practised nearly a century earlier in the United States. This drew heavy opposition from organized labour, but these objections were soon overcome.

"It's too late anyway. They're coming back to the car," Marie said.

And the auto rumbled away as it had come, leaving behind a sullen, silent and sick-at-heart street.

"Damn! Damn! Damn!" The pitch black could not hide the teeth-gritting anguish that had swept over Chip Baker. His fists must have been balled at his sides. The vision of him as I saw him on that New Year's morning eighteen months earlier towered like a ghost, filling the room. Leather jacket. Tortured face. A kid of the streets.

"Light the candles!" Dr. Rodgers commanded. When this was done he rose sternly to his feet. Gone was the coyness and humaneness that endeared him to us, and in their places the cold granite of ageless resolution had transformed him into a human fortress against which no man would dare storm.

"We have business here... not out there! Not tonight. And we will be about our business, lest our energies be needlessly drained from us, and the battle lost forever. Are we clear?"

The knotted figure of Chip shook under the doctor's thundering voice. His hands balled one final spasm, and his jutted jaw relaxed with a shuddering sigh.

"Clear."

"As you were, then." The Fortress lumbered to his seat, and we settled ourselves as an audience settles itself into Act III of a play — after a fire scare.

Slowly Chip retrieved the bit of chalk and studied it with painful care. Then he turned quickly to face us, once again the young scholar.

"The recent incident involving Mr. Gabrielli, a former labor leader, lends some degree of credibility to the point I was about to make... before the interruption." He spoke with exaggerated formality and with a hostile coldness directed to a world outside that would never hear or see Charles Comer Baker. He jabbed viciously at the two words on the chalk board. "Variety involves choice and," he scratched a new word furiously, "choice involves ... will! If a man ... Gabrielli, for example ... does not, or cannot, have the will... the desire, the urge, the drive, the courage ... to make choices, then that person does not take full advantage of the natural variety available to him

420

as a member of the human race. And right now," Chip breathed, "the quality of Mr. Gabrielli's life has been downgraded to equal roughly that of an ape... captured and dragged behind iron bars."

"So we learn," Marie spoke in a flat, half-aloud tone meant mostly for herself, "that variety involves choice, that choice involves will, and all three determine the level of life... the quality of life. And Mario Gabrielli has had choice and will taken from him... and he might as well be at Highland Park Zoo."

"He might better be at the zoo," I replied. "At least there, apes are not forced to betray fellow apes in order to live, to survive as long as possible. And how do you answer that one, Doctor? How do you explain a man who betrays his fellow men in order to survive? Where's the quality in that?" There was no mistaking the bitterness in my voice. The shadows in the room had become the familiar faces of my dead mother, Harry, his family, and Mary Best.

"Dave," Chip spoke with a soft concern. "I'm sure none of us meant..."

"Wait a moment," Dr. Rodgers spoke. He rose slowly. "My feet are rested. Why don't you rest yours for a moment, Chip. You've done well, boy. But Dave has addressed a question to me that deserves a most careful answer."

A candle sputtered out, leaving only one lonely sentry of wavering light to illuminate the pensive features of the old teacher. He had put away his lecture stance and mannerisms. His eyes were not upon us but upon the deepened shadows around us, as if he were about to address some timeless tribunal we could not see. Yet we could feel presence in this old house. Not hostile. It was a comforting presence. He removed his glasses and placed them on the table, as one might remove a hat on entering a holy place. His words were wrought slowly. "We have been speaking here of the quality of life... which implies doing things well or progressively better, so that in addition to our being able to survive, an enrichment process can take place to give greater value and importance to the things of human life." His voice was heavy with the mixture of might and wonder. His hair seemed to grow whiter in the near darkness, and the wrinkles of his face were smoothed by faint brushings of candle flame.

"This is the miracle of man.

"He has the ability to effect great changes in the world on a scale that can be duplicated by no other creature.

"Provided—that the will and choice exercised strengthen the human race and not weaken it. To upgrade and not to downgrade.

"These past eight thousand years," the voice rumbled, oblivious to all but the shadows it addressed, "quite clearly, I think, reveal that man has not always exercised wisdom in his choices. We have but to call the roll of ancient Egypt, broken Greece, burned Carthage and wasted Rome ... of Hitler terror ... of our own terror now… and there is a consistent pattern. Choices were made that led both to triumph and tragedy. But above all else, whenever a society, a civilization, chooses to place unnatural restrictions upon the will and choice of its people… whether through the exercise of power or simply plain apathy… the quality of that society is downgraded; indeed, if carried far enough, destroyed."

The face smiled. "But the reverse is true. Let the unnatural restrictions be lifted, and the quality of life can abound. History and our own senses tell us this, too. So let us choose to remember this above all else."

Only then did he look at each of us, slowly, one face at a time, to be sure that we might comprehend his plea.

"But a question has been asked. Betrayal! What of this?" His voice firmed to the classroom climate. With a lumbering move he retrieved his glasses and popped them midway upon his nose. "When a man betrays someone he exercises a form of will and choice right enough, but one that denies other men their opportunities to exercise will and choice, and in so doing he downgrades the quality of life about him. In so doing he downgrades his own intellect. And while his body, as the reward for betrayal, may survive in terms of food, clothing and shelter, his intellect, his mind, his soul—the very force that separates and uplifts him above all other creatures—dies a little. So he is a lesser man for all of his pains. And if his betrayal is devastating

422

enough to affect great multitudes of people, then one might wonder if he still is a man at all, or merely another upright creature not too unlike the ape at that.

"There are two parts to man, Dave, his mind and his body. To sacrifice one for the continued survival of the other merely reduces him as whole being. That is not survival, but a more subtle, more prolonged form of death... the wasting away of the human spirit."

I tried to keep it out of my face—the anguish now rekindled. But they all saw it. So I spoke it. "I have betrayed."

"Aye. You have." The doctor replied. "And tell us, how went the quality of your life?"

"Down, I suppose. Or perhaps it merely stayed even with what I have been all along."

The others in the room were growing uncomfortable and were trying not to listen.

"I will accept that," the doctor rolled on. "And now, I suppose you will crawl out of here tonight with your tail neatly tucked beneath your legs, eh?"

"Doctor! How can you say this?" It was Marie, rising to her feet, slim, tall, and angry. "He has helped to feed us! He has..."

"Stop... please!" The doctor's hand flew up. "You comprehend well, m'dear. I should have liked to have had you in my logic class, but no matter now." He moved to my side now, for I had risen, uncertain whether I should go or stay. For a moment his eyes held mine with a faint twinkle that suggested pride. "At those memorable hearings you did, indeed, exercise will and choice. Admittedly the choices were few. But you did make a choice on that particular occasion ... to betray! But I should remind you, dear lad, that there have been other occasions since where you, likewise, have exercised your own will and choice... such as is available these days."

He looked for a moment at the others. "To pull Chip from a muck-cluttered sidewalk when he was more dead than alive. To drag me from rain-soaked steps ... so that a night like tonight could be made possible. I cannot speak for the quality of your own life, but I can of mine, and I can guess about the others. You have uplifted us using the very limits of your abilities so that we continue to grow both in mind and body. Do you not think that perhaps you have begun to redress the balance?"

A swelling in my throat denied a reply.

"We all are betrayers at one time or another. But it is how a man responds and acts after his poor deeds that measures him. If he seeks to redress the balance, to offset, indeed, outweigh a bad choice with several good choices, then he might rest peacefully at night.

"I have betrayed," the white head wagged gently. "When I was working on my doctorate, I tailored my dissertations to fit the angry whims of the department chairman who believed that society must eliminate all industrialization and return to a pure agrarian life… peasants all, tilling the soil with sticks. Only I fancied myself brilliant, and I feared that the world would not recognize my genius, unless academic honors were heaped on me from all sides. So I turned my back upon the knowledge I had so painfully acquired and the beliefs I was only then beginning to cultivate. I constructed… fabricated … a beautifully developed thesis which was published and enjoyed wide circulation among men of letters. And I was patted on the head when I should have been whacked on the behind. For it was rubbish! I spent the next 27 years trying to redress the balance … to get even with where I was before I made that awful choice."

"The *Quality of Life?* That is the book that came out of it, isn't it?" Chip asked.

"Yes," Dr. Rodgers chuckled. "And you know, I did it knowing full well it would never enjoy academic status, in my lifetime at least."

"Would you have written it if, well, you hadn't behaved so badly with your thesis?"

"I don't know, Chip. I doubt I would have had the drive otherwise."

"Thank God for it!"[85]

---

85 *The Quality of Life*, by Hamilton M. Rodgers, today is regarded as a standard reference in the study of political and social philosophy. At the time of publication, however, it was met with a storm of angry criticism from leading intellectuals of the day. The result was that it was not carried in most university libraries. Indeed, only three copies of the original edition of this work are known to exist. However, close to one million copies have been reprinted and distributed in

"It is nice of you to say that, Chip. Victor, do you begin to see?"

"Yes. I think I see some. I am glad, for I think I see hope."

"Hope? Sure!"

"Ah, Chip! Perhaps it takes an old man who no longer can do anything but recall all that he has ever been, or might have been, to know where hope is possible," Victor replied.

So the evening ended on tiptoe, as softly as it had begun when I had stood on the outside of the window looking in. My mind was a whirlpool where thoughts had no beginning or end—save a vortex in the middle. A hole leading nowhere. But I had resolved to try to understand better the course of the evening. Dr. Rodgers gave me the name of a book store—an underground store—where precious volumes of knowledge still could be had. Thus I came to know many of the books that had been banned as fascist, including *The Enduring Works of Thomas Jefferson*. And in the weeks that followed I would do more reading that I had ever done in my life. Possibly I read in an honest search for knowledge. But I also read to forget. To forget the stinking heat and noise boiling up through the ugly yellow brick apartment. To forget where the children might be in their sojourn to carefree summer camp. To forget Mary Best and Larry too; for I could not face them, each though for a different reason. To forget what madness Nancy might be up to; for I would see little of her

recent years to university centres here and at a few newly established centres of learning in Europe and Southeast Asia.

In summary Dr. Rodgers, through sequences employing both inductive and deductive logic, establishes that life, liberty and property comprise the behavioural natural laws upon which depend man's existence as a human being. He states that the requirements to human life are (1) energy and (2) protection for both mind and body. He submits the argument that the quality of life is determined by will and choice available to the individual, i.e., the greater the will and choice, the higher the quality of life. A reduction of will and choice leads to a lower quality of life. He concludes that will and choice demand liberty. He also submits that will and choice, in great degree, are manifested through the possession, use and disposition of things of value (property). Therefore, "property is necessary if we are to have liberty, and liberty is necessary if we are to have life."

He admonishes all would-be reformers that "Man must first learn to obey the laws of nature before he can hope to conquer nature."

during the balance of the summer. I would watch her harden into a garden-variety harlot, building bit by bit, night by night, a brand new wardrobe of cheap and flashing clothing intended for someone half her age. I would become used to heavy perfume, stale cigarette smoke and whiskey that would follow her into our bedroom at four a.m. or later, depending.

But on this particular night—the third after the children had left for camp, the night she had smashed the mirror—I returned home by a full moon to find her already asleep, an anguished sleep.

And her moans all but drowned out the purposeful voice of Hamilton Rodgers that still rang in my ears.

5

To me there always has been something especially significant whenever a person finally achieves his sixteenth birthday. Of all the birthdays it is the longest coming. The ones that follow occur more rapidly with each passing year, while the ones beforehand perhaps are as much fun, but they are not nearly as important. The youngsters approaching the sixteen-year mark know this, or at least knew it in my day. For the sixteenth birthday was for us in my era the first important birthday. It departed from mere childhood frivolity and became the first firmly established bridgehead into the adult world, because an unwritten law—established more through sufferance than anything else—decreed that the celebrator, in addition to receiving the usual childhood gifts, became the possessor of some highly significant symbol of adulthood. Henceforth, the now budding young man or young woman would never again be fully one and at ease with, say, a fifteen-year-old, or worse, someone far younger, like a twelve-year-old. Sixteen was the age when one sought the company of the elders as equals and was allowed to do so. For some boys it meant being allowed to play baseball in a vacant lot with the older boys of seventeen, eighteen and, on coveted occasions, worldly men of nineteen. For girls it meant a formal dress and white gloves or a trip to a beauty parlor or perhaps seeing an evening performance of a play at a theater.

In my father's case, his sixteenth birthday was marked with a formal visit to the First Citizens Bank of Cleveland. There in the presence of great marble pillars, lofty windows and gleaming cages he opened his first *personal* bank account. It was one of his favorite stories, a Sunday dinner special. He used to describe in living detail how, in the company of his father, he met the president, first of all, who gave a precise accounting of how his money—an initial and quite substantial birthday gift of five dollars—would be put to work as capital to build great new industries and so provide employment for thousands *and* earn a thing called interest. Next, he was shown the vault, this in answer to his question regarding the safety of his money. Finally, in a solemn ceremony witnessed by an assortment of clerks in celluloid collars, he placed his signature with painful care upon a variety of papers and forms, thereby becoming known henceforth as *Young Mr. Little.*

The particular importance of attaining sixteen years of life was observed with similar pomp in my Grandfather Quincy's day, though in a far different manner. For Grandfather Quincy's father, being a sailor aboard a whaleback iron ore carrier, was tuned to the more rugged and overt aspects of manhood. His boat, a steam-sail vessel, the *Henry Johnson,* was tied up along the Cuyahoga River flats at the ore yards beyond the blast furnaces, and his special birthday gift was to take my grandfather aboard to meet his mates who, in turn, accompanied the father and his son to a waterfront saloon. There to the cheers of stocking-capped seamen of a dozen different nationalities he ordered his first drink—beer.

The occasion surrounding my birthday was equal to that of my forebears in adult-giving stature—driving the family automobile on my own. To be sure, I had had a learner's permit, and my father had spent many anxious hours teaching me to operate our seven-year-old Ford. But the agreement was that upon achieving the magical age of sixteen I would be allowed to apply for my license and on occasion use the auto to perform a growing number of chores. It was remarkable that I found so many convincing reasons why this had to be done, else the entire family structure might well have fallen apart. But more remarkable, still, was the fact that Father seemed to agree. He would purse his thin lips and nod his head while I talked at a breathless pace of the carefree life that could be his if only his son knew how to drive. When he said quite unexpectedly one day, "Well, maybe when you are sixteen ..." it was my first clue as to the potential importance of that birthday. Thereafter his casual phrase became a contract and the source of considerable bargaining that centered around how well I did my chores at the store, my grades and my behavior towards my brother, Harry. How delightful were those last months as they closed upon my sixteenth birthday! What dreams and expectations! And as I ticked off the final days the waiting became an immense burden. I thought of little else. I had nightly visions of me behind the wheel of one of the new British sport cars that were just beginning to make their way back into the country again. I saw myself smeared with grime and parked heroically in my own specially designed racer out at the winner's circle of the dirt track south of the city, the roaring of motors and derring-do still whirling through my head. From my lumpy bed I followed my flawless and casual movements as I steered a sleek new cream-colored Cadillac through congested streets while traffic cops waved me on with flourishes of tribute to my superior driving skills. Of course, somewhere in the background of each carefully constructed scene was a girl, Mary Beth Hanselmier, to be exact. She was my current love, a rather one-sided affair, since she was going steady with Varsity Ed, a senior, and, worse, the football star. But with a car and me in it, well, that would change sure enough! So Mary Beth was always on her front porch whenever I would choose to varoom down her street in the sports car. I would never stop, just slow up a little and wave. Or Mary Beth was always on the edge of the crowd that would begin to close in on me as I purred to a stop in the winner's circle at the track, bone tired but determined not to show it. In every one of those dreams I would ask the judges to let Mary Beth hold the cup, while I conferred with my pit crew on repairs that would have to be made before noon tomorrow. Or Mary Beth would be beside me in the Cadillac as we would roll into Bernie's Drive-In out on Route Twenty. Of course everyone would be there, including Varsity Ed, who would be sulking all alone in his crummy Model A. It is well that my birthday came when it did or else my dreams would have become more grandiose than my system would have permitted.

The birthday came, appropriately, on a Sunday, my father's one day off. Weather permitting, we always went for a little Sunday drive out along the lake, east if we wanted to see new, dramatic plant construction, west if we wished to ogle new homes fast rising on windswept farm lands that were now being eaten up by Cozy Acre Developers—Estate-Type Homes of Distinction. Sometimes we drove south to see farmlands still being farmed. We used to joke about driving "north for a swim." My father always drove, although my mother functioned every bit as well behind the wheel as he. But the Sunday drive was different from the other trips in the "machine," as Mother called our auto. Sunday was Dad's day to do with us as he chose to do and, perhaps, symbolically to remind Mother, Harry and me—and others who might look upon our scarred maroon Ford as it moved sedately along—that he, after all, was head of the household and thus expected to occupy the driver's seat. Besides, Father enjoyed driving on Sundays.

So even my wildest dreams did not anticipate his pronouncement at the Sunday dinner table ladened with prime roast beef, hefty baked potatoes, crunchy green beans, hot rolls and crisp lettuce, topped off with a rich, moist chocolate cake buried in a superabundance of creamy icing. The gifts—a pocket knife, another flashlight, a model airplane kit, a tie and socks—had been opened and the birthday greeting sung. He pulled his watch from his vest, which he always did after Sunday dinner, and suggested that we take a little drive. Then he said:

"David will drive us today."

I nodded with lightheaded gravity, and while Mother stacked the dishes and found her hat, I went alone to the garage, my father's keys warm in my hand. I found the auto newly washed and shined with wax, a little surprise, I later learned, that twelve-year-old Harry had carried out all on his own. I backed the car out and then waited, sitting alone in the front seat and running my fingers over the steering wheel and dashboard, just to be sure this was not simply another dream.

They came out through the back door—the three of them, Dad in animated conversation with Mother, doubtlessly reassuring her now that this moment had to come, while Harry slammed out behind them carrying a cigar box containing Uncle Ned, his pet frog. I got out then and one by one held the doors open for them, just as Dad always did.

How neat and clean and upright we all looked that day! With the exception of stalling the engine once at a traffic light, all went well. My father said not a word about my performance, choosing to look out his window at the world passing slowly by us and to keep whatever thoughts he may have had to himself. All he ever said was, "A fine job, my boy." And that was all a sixteen-year-old could want from his dad.

Because these and other similar recollections more and more have been in my mind of late, perhaps I had expected too much when it came time to celebrate my own son's sixteenth birthday, which occurred this past September. Actually, I began thinking about it in August while the children were still away at camp. There had been no opportunity to teach young David anything about driving an automobile. Gasoline rationing had become more and more severe. Also, fewer people own cars these days partly because of fuel problems but mostly because spare parts for repairs seldom are made available for privately owned vehicles. Owning a new car is out of the question. The few new ones that occasionally appear are state owned and are in the possession of high officials.

There is one highly desirable aspect to owning a car, though, if it is seldom driven. It represents money in the bank. Unlike the old days, the worth of an automobile goes up, instead of depreciating as each month passes. I very wisely had kept ours, even though late last summer I could have sold it for twice what I paid to any number of government and Party officials in search of a second car—this in spite of the shape it was in. For it lacked a right front tire, which had simply gone to pieces one day shortly after we had moved, and I had long since been without a spare. The one favorable thing about the apartment building in which we now live is that it has a garage with it built of the same ugly yellow brick but still in good repair. So I was able to bump my way home and lock the car away securely after draining the tank and setting the wheels up on blocks. Barring any critical emergencies I decided to keep it thus until absolute necessity would force me to sell it at the highest possible price. Therefore, I had not even attempted to find a tire, until it occurred to me one hot stink-laden evening that my son would soon be sixteen. I had hoarded a modest supply of gasoline coupons which I had intended to sell on the black market, but it might be worth it to use them to give David driving lessons for this important occasion. What youngster would not jump at a chance like that!

I wanted to have the car in shape by the time the children returned the Sunday before Labor Day, but I could not find a tire of the right size. Then I decided it was just as well to hold off until the birthday itself, two weeks later, so that David's day truly might be marked with a surprise he would long remember. I would keep my preparations a secret.

The children were returned home more or less on schedule, and for the first couple of days it was difficult to detect any real changes in them. A Labor Day demonstration calling for longer work hours, along with a parade later in the day, had commanded their full attention. Each had a Unit Master to report to early in the morning of the holiday, so that their first night back home was spent in learning lines to slogans as well as a variety of instructions concerning demonstration responses, signs to be carried and other items governing the "quality of spontaneity that must be achieved," as one instruction sheet stated. The strain of these preparations, plus the long, hot bus ride, I assumed to be responsible for the children's distant, almost hostile greetings. David had lost weight, which he needed to do, and he looked tan and strong. Only his eyes betrayed the possibility of fatigue. For they appeared sunken and cold. They wavered furtively whenever I tried to look into them. Peggy had achieved complete womanhood, figurewise at least. Her face had lost all trace of childhood and had acquired an aloof beauty. She kept both her forehead and lips pinched in some unexplained distaste. Her coquettishness was gone, replaced with an automated sleekness that suggested full confidence in herself and little in anyone else. She seemed more like twenty-eight than nearly eighteen. Little Annie had grown most of all. All of her baby fat was gone, especially in her fingers which were no longer as pudgy. Her face had narrowed. Her cheerful and sweet disposition that had so marked these first eight years of her life had waned. Her eyes seemed larger, almost perfectly round, and the brown in them looked to be darker and sad. At first she seemed afraid, but a few hours later she did come to me and catch hold of my hand for an instant before Peggy called to her sharply to come and rehearse for the Labor Day program.

All three had one particular thing in common. None talked very much—to me or to themselves. None offered to discuss the summer, the three saying only that they found the "experience stimulating" and had "learned much that will be useful in building the New World." I quote these phrases because each used them as if taught to recite them—like a line in a Sunday school Christmas pageant. They kept essentially to themselves. They were polite but guarded. They did not laugh nor did they sulk. They behaved as if they were someone else's children sent to visit with near strangers.

How much of this Nancy observed I do not know. With the return of the children she had curtailed most nightly prowlings. We, of course, no longer lived as man and wife, and we did not discuss things.

Clearly, something had to be done to reestablish contact with the children—particularly David and Annie; for I had long ago resigned myself that Peggy was gone for good with no hope of ever getting her back. But I was reluctant to see the ground washed away between David and me. A man wanted his only son to think well of him, even as he wished to think well of his son. Annie was too young and too precious to go anywhere—save only next to the heart of her father.

432

She was not ready for the world, and I did not want her to grow up any more for a time.

If something was needed to reestablish pride in us as a family—and I suspected that elements of shame lurked behind my children's eyes—the car was the answer. Not only would I teach David to drive, but once the word got around and the family was seen cruising around a few times, then things would change for the better. Other children at school and in the youth organizations doubtless would be suitably impressed, just as they were in my day when we had more cars available. If I could work things right both David and Peggy might even be able to drive the car to school once or twice. If that would not perk them up, then nothing would.

Thus fortified I redoubled my efforts to locate a usable tire. The swap shops,[86] of course, had nothing. That left the black market. Since the authorities are particularly touchy about the illegal sale and use of tires, making the right contact proved difficult. It took me nearly a week, and then I found my contact right under my nose. An unassuming little clerk in what was left of the housewares department at Barnes' had a going business on the side. He specialized in risk items, tires, as well as other auto parts—piston rings, spark plugs, points, voltage regulators, bearings and some gears. He also sold knives and a wide variety of firearms, ration books and forged certificates of one sort or another. Occasionally he would come into possession of medicines which were quickly sold at very high prices. He could get a brand new tire for me for only four hundred dollars. Even if I had had the money, the new tire would have attracted the attention of the nearest policeman. We settled on a used tire with about thirty thousand miles on it. It cost me ninety dollars. I raised the money by selling two matching table lamps, both in excellent shape, which I removed from our tiny, overcrowded living room. With the ban on electricity they were of little use to us. Since government officials were exempt from this edict, I reasoned that perhaps there would be any number of potential buyers. I was right. The Swap

---

86 Barter became increasingly important as a means to conserve and exchange real wealth. Growing shortages of consumer items gave rise to barter centers which flourished across the country.

Shop on Liberty Avenue jumped at the chance to take the lamps off my hands. We had trouble over the price, but when I threatened to smash them in the gutter outside, the horrified proprietor came through with ninety dollars. The tire was delivered late at night via a panel truck much too old to attract attention.

I could only work on the car nights, since my days off—Sundays —were spent attending block lectures that usually lasted four or five hours.[87] Installing the tire was fairly easy, but pumping it up was another matter. All that was available was an old hand pump which I borrowed from Victor. The battery was dead, and I used Annie's old coaster wagon to move it to one of the few remaining service stations for recharge. Finally, the night before David's birthday I succeeded in starting the engine. Then I rubbed the dust away with some old rags, and there she stood! One automobile in working order, clean inside and out.

David's birthday came on a Wednesday, and I had succeeded in rousing Nancy from a trancelike existence so that we could have a birthday dinner. By taking an advance on my wages I was able to get a brand new sweater for David. I also found some used slippers, and Annie—the only one who revealed any sign of excitement over the event—made some birthday cards out of scrap paper with crayon pictures. So we wedged ourselves around the table featuring a meat loaf, which took up our full week's ration, and boiled cabbage and potatoes. We bought a small pound cake, and Nancy made a gelatin dessert. Then David opened his gifts, while Peggy sulked in exaggerated boredom and Nancy sat listlessly playing with a fork on the empty cake plate. Only beloved Annie let her eyes turn bright. David liked the sweater, I think, but seemed not to care about the slippers.

Then we came to the Big Moment. The sun was almost set, and the evening was cool and clear, with the beginnings of autumn in the air. The trees had begun to turn so that the hills stood out boldly

---

87 The JCFLA insisted that all "patriotic citizens demonstrate their dedication to peace, prosperity and freedom" by attending indoctrination classes sponsored by the Communist Party on the "ideals of state socialism compared with the evils of capitalism."

in banks of bright brown and gold. It would be an ideal evening to go for a drive.

"What say we go downstairs. I have something to show all of…
you.

No one moved.

"It's a surprise for David."

"Oh god!" Peggy snorted. "What's with all of this? It's egotistical to celebrate birthdays… and wasteful."

"Why don't you shut up!" David snapped. Then he flashed me a grin, the first of the evening. "What you got, Dad?"

"Let's go see, eh, son? The rest of you can come or not … we don't care, do we, boy?" The growing grin on my own face had stirred, finally, some interest. Nancy, roused from wherever her thoughts had taken her, frowned, genuinely puzzled. Peggy threw me a wary look, and Annie squealed in delight, momentarily losing her little-girl-lost look that had haunted me ever since her return.

So down we went. A family off for a little drive.

I threw the garage doors open in undisguised triumph. "Now how about that?"

"You've fixed it," Nancy managed woodenly.

"Sure! And she's all ready to take us for a little ride. But that's not all… no, sir. David, I'm going to teach you to drive. Think of it! And you, Peggy, we'll see that you get a chance to use the car, too. Of course it can't be too often… not right away… but things are beginning to look up for us. Yes, sir. How about that, David?"

Both Peggy and David exchanged nervous glances, and then both froze with dead-pan expressions.

"Dad," the boy sighed heavily, "it wouldn't be right." The golden twilight etched the solemnness of his face so that he looked far older than his years. Fear and doubt had crept into his eyes— and shame, too.

"Of all the foolish things!" Peggy stamped in raw disgust. "You would come up with something like this."

"Silence! How dare you address me this way? I am your father, and you had better remember it."

"A mere biological happenstance," Peggy replied. There was biting cold in her words. "You're part of the backwash, or you would know that no worthwhile person ever would deliberately embarrass his children by such a vulgar display of materialism. Don't you realize that if I'm ever seen in a car owned and operated for purely selfish reasons, I would have to go before the student council and suffer all kinds of hell?"

"Dad," David interrupted gently. "Most patriotic citizens have gotten rid of their cars. Besides, I've had driving lessons at camp. I know how to drive a truck and a tractor, too. I did so well that I've been promised a job driving a limousine for the JCFLA. But if I'm seen... like Peggy says. Don't you see, Dad? People would think that I'm against the ...," he fished nervously for more words.

"The Treaty?"

"Yes. You understand, don't you? I just can't. I've got a chance to be a unit leader in the Scouts. I've done real well, and I just don't want things messed up. The private sector should walk more... it's good for people. Even Comrade Syerov walks a lot. You've seen the pictures."

Then he fell silent. Nancy began to laugh softly to herself. "You see, your children, at least, have learned something," she cooed softly. "Sell that pile of junk before we all land in a discipline camp.[88] Come, children. Let's get back inside before the neighbors see us."

They all left, except Annie. She had crept to my side, and now her little hand found mine.

"Take me, Daddy."

I looked down at her, and saw that she would not be a little girl for much longer. One golden treasure left, standing with upturned face in the soft light. One bundle of human flesh that still radiated warmth and trust. One hour left until darkness.

So we went for the drive, Annie and I. We chatted some and looked and chatted some more—about trees and the shape of leaves and cows. Then on the way back she snuggled close, hugging my arm.

"Will you teach me to drive some day, Daddy?"

---

88 There was a shortage of prisons, so that camps were created for Treaty offenders. At least 62 such camps were in operation during this period.

"Sure."

"I love you so, Daddy!"

6

Early in October I saw Larry Best once again. This time it was not my idea. He came to the store. It was mid-afternoon, and most of the non-buying foot traffic had been cleared away. Kloomer had scurried into his backroom sanctuary like a scalded squirrel to do some paper work, leaving me to complete an inventory account. Larry came poking along the racks of garish clothes. He looked absolutely splendid. To be sure his lean features were haggard, and his frame more bony than ever, but he was neatly dressed in an old English tweed suit that I had seen him wear many times. A raglan coat still in excellent shape hung cloakwise about his shoulders, and he wore his hat continental style, with one side of the brim up and the other side down to give a cavalier effect. He stood erect with shoulders well back to give further emphasis to his natural tallness. His head moved in the old familiar birdlike patterns as he poked at this suit and that. Then our eyes met, and his face erupted into the old buoyant grin that I have known for more than twenty years. His ways were still commanding, and I found myself grinning back.

"David, m'boy! What a delight! I was wondering if I might not see you."

We belted each other as brothers would.

"Where have you been keeping yourself? No address. Not even a phone call," he chided. "Good thing I remembered you were working here." He searched the room with his clear blue eyes and squeezed his face into an elaborate squint. "God! The brilliance of this place! Are these things for horses or people?" Then he sobered. "How's the family... Nancy, the kids and all?"

"Fine."

"Good. Well. The job's agreeing with you. You look great."

"How's Mary?"

"Fine. Just fine. You bet. She's been a little tired lately, but she'll be back on her feet in no time."

"And how are you?"

"Couldn't be better," was the bubbling reply. "Still at it out at the old skull factory. Don't have to carry that awful teaching load I used to have. Had a chance to drop the day stuff and teach only in night school. A real blessing. Gives me time to branch out and do something I've always wanted to do."

"Uh-huh. Like what?" Long ago Larry had told me that night school was for beginning teachers or for incompetent old timers who had to be removed from the mainstream of education.

"Well," he pondered a moment. "Reading. I'm way behind. And I've been wanting to do more writing. Also," he jabbed a long, bony finger at me, "Politics. Remember how I always wanted to get into the fray? Used to be pretty good at it, remember? Well, now I have a chance of a lifetime to really get into it."

"Don't tell me you're running for office." Elections were but a month away—local this time, for city and county offices. The Communist Party had fielded a blue-ribbon slate. The only opposition was the Coalition Party, but it was so much in the minority that its hopes for success were in vain.[89] "You must have made it into the Party, after all?"

"No. Nothing like that... yet," he cut in hastily. "I'm staying behind the scenes. I'm in charge of things in the Fourteenth Ward for the Party. My job is to get that vote out for our man."

"But you are in the Party now?"

"Not exactly." Larry faltered for a moment, and haggard lines crept over his face to take charge of everything. "Fact is my membership approval hasn't come through yet, but I expect to hear right after the elections, as soon as things settle down."

---

89 Once it began operating in the open, the Communist Party of America quickly became the majority party. The two previous major political parties, Democrat and Republican, for a time merged to become the Coalition Party, which functioned as a minority party until it became extinct one year later.

"I understand. One last test to pass—how well you deliver the vote. I assume that has something to do with how soon you and the Party become one?"

"Well, bluntly put, yes, I suppose. But they're really very nice. Anxious to help and all that, but, well, they're just all filled up and understaffed. They've got lots of problems. After all, going from a minority party… hell, a secret party at one time … to the largest party in the country .. . that takes some doing. So, patience. But in the meantime there's work to do, and I've got to convince them, David, that all of us can work together." He paused, his eyebrows oddly raised. "You do see, don't you?"

"Yes, Larry, I see. Of that you can be sure." Suddenly I wished he would go away.

"Good. Then you'll help?"

"Help what?"

"Me. Who else? Just like old times. Remember how it was back at school. You and I stumping the campus together. And we won, old boy! Had 'em eating right out of our hands. So, why not again, eh? I can sure use you out in the Fourteenth, and you'll get a big kick out of it. Besides, your efforts will not go unnoticed in the Party, and that kind of recognition comes in mighty handy these days." He nodded and winked like a carnival pitchman, which was completely out of character.

"Oh Christ, Larry! Lay off. Count me out. Look, it's been nice talking . .. and we've got to get together real soon… but I've got to get back to this damn inventory." I started to move back to a blizzard of white papers jumbled across the counter, but the bony fingers clutched at my arm. There was a frantic plea in them.

"Look, old man. I need you."

"No, not me."

"But David, you've got to. I've already told them that you'd help. They're expecting you."

"Who?"

"Why, Leon Tidings. You remember him."

"You signed me up without even asking?" I grabbed Larry's shirt front into my fist, and jammed him against a clothes rack. "I'll kill you for that!"

"Easy, old man." He shook loose from me and gathered himself together. He was perspiring, and he breathed unevenly. "Look, I never would have done it if I honestly thought that you wouldn't do it. They asked me for names, and I couldn't think of enough. Your name just popped into my head, and when I saw how pleased Tidings was… well, I just," he faltered miserably, "got carried away and made a big thing out of it. I told him you were second in command… that you were anxious to get active."

Beware of your friends, the saying goes, and I knew that if I backed down on this one that Leon Tidings would be after me for certain. With no job I could not hope to keep the family together any longer.

"Will and choice," I mumbled aloud. "I exercised choice, but someone else exercised the will, so my choice is now his."

"How's that?"

"Never mind, Larry. When do you want me?"

"Tonight, my place. At eight." I pulled away from him, but once again he sought my sleeve. His face had lost its image of strength and confidence. He looked like a grateful dog. "You'll not regret this. I promise. If I miss this one, I've had it. David, for the love of god, help me."

"Good-bye, Larry. I'll see you at eight."

And he finally left.

I arrived early, not because I wanted to, but because I misjudged the time it took me to walk from downtown to Oakland, a task which spared me the necessity of going home to eat. By ignoring the buses that wheezed and snorted past I saved enough in fare to allow for a sandwich and some powdered milk. The walk up the long hill with its wretched, agonized houses, shops and streets was made all the more dreary by a cold, vigorous October rain that lashed after me in the early evening gloom. One does not poke along under such conditions. I turned in at the familiar red brick colonial house set back between two towering Victorian mansions, surprised that the light over the door burned in defiance of the otherwise darkened street. The door

440

opened before I could ring the bell, and Larry ushered me inside with a sweep that he traditionally reserves for the more special occasions.

"Mary! Come quickly and see who is here." He shooed me into the foyer that, as with everything else in the city, had grown more dreary and worn. The ivory walls that once glowed so elegantly under a twinkling light of delicate prisms were peeling and the chandelier was gone, leaving a small ragged hole in the ceiling from which naked wires protruded in twisted designs. The cheerful, gold cherub that had hung on the wall was gone, too, with only a ghostly outline remaining. Only the Vermont slate floor retained its warm gaiety, and Larry seemed bent on matching it. "It's really splendid of you to come out on a night like this. Say, you're soaked. Surely you didn't walk? I'm sorry. Why on earth didn't you drive?" His voice piped upward in sing-song tempo.

"I'm in the process of selling the car, as soon as I'm sure I've got top money."

"Oh, of course. Sensible. Damned nuisance, I've always said. You ought to get a fortune for it. Wish I had one to sell," he sighed and then looked upward expectantly. "Ah, Mary."

She had come to the head of the stairs, her small, tomboyish figure wrapped tightly in a faded white gown revealing her frail thinness. Her honey-colored hair showed hints of grey, and where she once wore it with a tousled disregard of what others might think of her nonconformity to style, she now wore it short, neat and straight in the latest vogue that had swept the city, the Victory Do. Her oval face with its button nose and full lips, which used to be perked most of the time in open inquisitiveness, was taut and etched with little lines that suggested a deep weariness rather than age. She moved slowly down the stairs with a smooth poise that revealed listless calm. Only her eyes, looking larger than they should, gave hints of a smile. They were clear and steady.

"Good evening, David." She offered me her hand, which conveyed neither hope nor hostility.

We exchanged pleasantries—the three of us who had known each other for so long—as one might have in a theater lobby during intermission. Then Larry excused himself to make last-minute kitchen preparations to meet the needs of other guests yet to come. Mary made no move to follow.

"Larry is so sweet to put up with me. He said I need not come down tonight, so I plan to go to bed quite early, but of course I wanted to see you for a moment." She paused to look at me thoughtfully and for an instant inquisitiveness returned to her face. "You look remarkably fit. How are Nancy and the children?"

"Fine."

Her fingers, still smooth and tapered, traced a pattern on the stair rail. "Tell me ... by any chance... have you any idea what might have become of Dr. Rodgers?" She turned her eyes quickly into mine in a gesture of tentative hope.

I told her where he was and that he was happy and productive. Perhaps I embellished the circumstances some, but it was worth it; for her face broke into an honest smile that warmed the hall, the house, the world.

"God has not let me down! He is safe," she murmured. "Do you see him much?"

"Yes, a little. We've become good friends."

Then her hand reached to mine, and there was warmth. "I can tell." Her voice was soft with pleasure. "He will do you good. When you see him," she paused and straightened herself as if she were about to go on stage, "tell him how well I look. Tell him I am happy, and that all is well."

"Why don't you tell him yourself? I can bring him here any time you wish."

"No! I don't want him to see me... like this." She gathered her gown more tightly about her. "I must go now. Tell him I think of him much and what we used to talk about and that I am happy when I think those things. And David ... I truly am glad to see you again."

And she was gone as she had come.

The others came then. Four men and three women, I think, and I am sure all of them must have had names. But my mind was not on them, their looks, or what they thought or said or did. They were "ward hacks," as Larry called them privately to me in the kitchen during a beer recess. I wanted only to find out what I was to do and leave. Everyone had his shoe boxes,[90] and the first hour was hopelessly boring as they pored through the lists and cards. They had taken over the living room which still retained an air of easy grace with its clutter of modern paintings and super-extreme gewgaws of one sort or another that occupied tables and shelves. The decor was predominantly white, or what used to be white but which now leaned more toward tattletale grey. The room was large and served by a big bay. Its furnishings were £ scramble of traditional, modern and period pieces. Yet all came together in what at one time was one of the most congenial, intellectual residential settings in the whole university area. In the old days it was something to be invited to Professor Best's house. The hacks did not fit. Like me, none was actually a member of the Party, but like Larry, each was trying to get in by the simplest, most direct route—loyal service on the political battlefront.

At nine precisely the door chimes sounded. The main event had arrived, and there was a frantic scramble to reassemble papers, cards and books into more orderly patterns while Larry attended the door. And there he was, unchanged from the last time I saw him, wearing his tinted, rimless glasses, his heavy facial features still showing signs of stomach distress—Leon Tidings. He took us in one by one, pausing to study the semi-circle of assorted faces frozen in assorted degrees of suspicious expectancy. He did this without once changing his own expression, except when the tinted glasses reached me. His eyes, made large by the glasses, were like those of an owl. My god, he's nearsighted! I thought. Pity I had not really noticed this before; perhaps he would not have seemed quite so overpoweringly sinister then. I must have smiled, and he did not expect this. His face wrinkled into prunelike puzzlement and then broke into what I suppose was meant to be a grin.

"Mr.... ah... Little, I believe." He spoke in a soft, silken voice.

---

90 Shoe boxes were easily acquired for precinct workers to use as a card file to hold names and other data on eligible voters who were assigned to them for follow-up.

"The same, Mr. .. . ah… Tidings."

"Here to help us, I understand."

I nodded. "That is right, Mr. Tidings."

"Ladies and gentlemen," Larry cut in with forced breeziness. "For those of you who haven't met him, this is the newly appointed Regional Director of Field Operations for the JCFLA, Leon Tidings. Leon's very presence here is a tribute to all of us, and I think emphasizes the importance of our job. For the Party does not take lightly this idea of dedication of duty…"

"Thank you very much, Professor Best. Perhaps we should get on with matters." The voice had grown frosty. The heavy-lidded eyes closed in a slow blink like signal lamps, and Larry shifted gears.

"Righto, Mr. Tidings! I was about to say… well, why don't you… heh, heh… take over, so to speak. We're all ready to go. The Party must win the election."

The heavy black brows over Tidings' tinted glasses rose up and up. His short stature did not make him any the less formidable even in the shadow of Larry's extra-tall frame. "Must win, Professor Best? Is there any doubt but that the Party will win?"

The adam's apple now so clearly evident in Larry's scrawny neck moved slowly up and then down the long line of his throat. "Not at all! No, sir. It's in the bag. Right, gang?"

The assorted heads bobbed. We were still standing, and there were nervous shifts, discreet hints requesting that some sort of sign be given for permission to be seated.

"Be seated, please." Tidings spoke with quiet authority. He moved with measured slowness to the edge of a baby grand piano in the comer of the room where he paused to examine with critical care the elongated head of an African wood sculpture. He shook his head slowly in dour distaste. "Oh, well," he sighed heavily to himself and from his slim briefcase withdrew several sheets of yellow paper covered with close, orderly writing. He studied these for a moment while the room hung in silence. Then he turned to face us with his tinted searchlights.

"Listen carefully, for I do not like to repeat myself." His voice crack-led like a live wire, and the silence grew hectic. "Get this absolutely straight. The Party will win. Your job is to make sure that the mar-gin of victory against the Coalition Party is the greatest margin ever achieved in this city. I don't mean a ten percent margin, or twenty or thirty." He paused to look at the assorted faces which had begun to mold into a unanimous expression of stupefaction.

"Ordinarily we should require a margin of ninety-eight per cent, but since we are still in the process of liberation there are a few prob-lems to be overcome. Accordingly, the Party will be quite lenient. We will be satisfied with a ninety percent margin... provided no less than ninety-eight percent of your eligible voters cast their ballots."

"But sir," a nervous voice piped up, "it's never been done. The best we've ever done is to register seventy-five percent of the eligible vot-ers and of these, usually only about sixty percent even vote."

The tinted glasses seemed to grow larger as if they were x-raying everyone in the room. When they reached me I felt a particular sat-isfaction in being able to look directly into them.

"Be patient, friend. Mr. Tidings will tell us how," I replied.

"Quite right," Tidings said. "In a true social democracy voting is of critical importance. It is a duty that must be exercised by all eli-gible citizens. In a social democracy a small majority of votes cast is an evidence of weakness of the government in power. A close elec-tion, therefore, breeds suspicion and doubt on the part of the people which in turn affects their capacity to work, to serve and to be abso-lutely loyal to the government."

He paused to look again at each of us. "The people always need to know the strength of their government. In the days of kings this strength was made known without the participation of the people. But today governments are a reflection of the people. It is the people's government that rules, and the people must speak overwhelming-ly and convincingly. What more direct way is there than one man... one vote? Every person, therefore, must vote or he is not fit to ben-efit from the people's government, and with his vote he must stand with the will of the people, lest he be guilty of deliberately trying to destroy their efforts to achieve true and lasting peace and prosperity. Do I make myself clear?"

All nodded as if their heads were pulled by the same invisible string. Tidings favored them again with the frostiest of smiles, and then turned his tinted rays on Larry, who sat stone still. "I trust you understand this, Professor Best, since you are the... ah... leader here."

"Of course!" Larry's long arm moved in a sticklike gesture. "That's exactly what I was about to say. I..."

"Yes, of course. And now let us review the means by which the electorate can be... ah... reminded to perform this duty in the proper spirit of dedication and singleness of purpose. We cannot have a shabby showing, such as the last election in which there was only a sixty-eight percent majority for Party candidates. As the final stage of our first phase of operations, this election perhaps is the most critical.[91] Any evidences of sloppiness or weakness on the part of the people in carrying forward the great programs of liberation will not be tolerated." The hissing ring of Leon Tidings' voice carried back and forth across the shabby white living room with a force that belied his meek, swarthy stature. His dour face was darkly flushed in open rage, and his whole person shook. Then, while the room contemplated the full meaning of his words, he composed himself, and in a soft, silken tone he outlined the several "reminders."

Eviction was one of them. Any eligible voter who failed to exercise his precious franchise to vote, won through the sacrifices of the masses, would lose his Residence Permit.[92] A penalty fine was another, and if a recalcitrant voter was caught influencing others to shun the polling place, then loss of his job and or a prison sentence would almost surely follow. Any questionable voter attitudes detected prior

---

91 The Communist Party of America could not hope to consolidate its power until it achieved total control of all local elective offices. Hence, the local elections—mayors, councilmen, commissioners, etc.—were of critical importance to the perpetuation of International Communism. (See Appendix excerpts from *Achieving the Revolution in America*.)

92 Under a directive from the JCFLA, the Bureau of Housing issued Residence Permits as a prerequisite to anyone seeking either to rent or buy a dwelling. This was "to protect the people from opportunists who work against the public interests through attempts to undermine the goals of the Treaty of Friendship."

446

to election day were to be promptly reported. And as far as election day itself was concerned, there were the "quality patriot" checks, a series of voluntary declarations that gave every voting citizen a means to evaluate and judge the intentions of every other voter, "a free and open exchange which no man of sincere good will and concern for his fellowmen would ever think of avoiding."

The test was a simple one. Americans, Tidings said, still clung to the sinister tradition of voting in secret—a process that could only generate distrust. It was a carryover from the days of seeking personal gain at the expense of others. During the preceding weeks several citizens' groups had begun demonstrations around the city calling for an end to the secret ballot. "If a man's intentions are for the public good, why should he want to keep them secret?" That was one of the slogans that had been appearing repeatedly on billboards and on television. Another was: "Only the guilty have something to hide—abolish the secret ballot!" Leon Tidings reviewed the problem, saying that the secret ballot could be eliminated only through Constitutional change which was not presently possible. So, since we must all stay within the law, he admonished, each voter would be asked, voluntarily, to proclaim publicly the candidate of his choice and—once in the polling place—would be asked to leave the voting booth curtain open, so that all might see.

"What greater proof of a man's good intention than for him to share his innermost political views with his fellowmen ... to repudiate voluntarily the secret ballot in favor of free and open action? To do otherwise would clearly mark him an enemy of the people, to be dealt with as all enemies must," Tidings concluded softly. "Is that not so, Professor Best?"

The others in the room were looking at Larry now, their faces glazed and expressionless.

"Why... ah..." The tall, bony man, who once could command a roomful of people with one upward turn of an eyebrow, faltered miserably. Clearly he could not honestly determine whether Tidings was right or wrong. "Of course."

"Of course, what?" Tidings prodded.

"Only the guilty have anything to hide. People should welcome this opportunity!" Color started to flow into his taut cheeks again, and Larry began to assume something of his old manner. "Can't be any other way... not really! All of our lives we've hidden behind curtains of one sort or another, each man cut off from the other by fear and distrust. And all we have to show for it is violence and hatred in the world. But now we have a chance to achieve real understanding." Larry was looking straight at Tidings now, smiling, confident and spilling over with sincerity. "If we all open our hearts and work together. That is what you mean, Mr. Tidings... it is, isn't it?"

Leon Tidings returned the pleading look with unblinking eyes. Then after a long moment the heavy eyelids closed sleepily and opened again with a tinted glint of unnamed triumph. His lips formed a slow, silken smile. "Of course, it is, Professor Best."

At length it came time to leave. Each of us had been assigned streets to cover, and Larry and I were made responsible for supervising the small work force, now deeply dedicated. Throughout the evening I had remained strangely calm and markedly unaffected by Tidings. Similarly, Larry had failed to stir anything in me. Only Mary, thin and pale in her wrapper, had moved me, but she was out of my reach now, and so I had locked thoughts of her conveniently away in the darkest recesses of my mind. Instead, my thoughts had turned inwardly to an imaginary debate between myself and Dr. Rodgers. How would my actions over the next few weeks, that of terrorizing helpless old ladies and arrogant young people, square with the wisdom of this gentleman of whom I had grown so fond? The quality of life seemed remote, indeed, to the matter at hand.

"One moment, Mr. Little." The small, quiet voice of Leon Tidings reached out to hold me as I attempted to depart through the front door. Larry had remained behind to heap a few more words of encouragement upon the paper-weary team that now scrambled to pack up and go home. Tidings had retrieved a rich, black Homburg and a new English trench coat. He moved smoothly to catch up with me. The night was shrouded in a cold drizzle that plastered fallen leaves in crazy patterns over the walks and grass that glistened in the reflection of the one porch light that burned—a beacon of light where there was no light. "I will drop you at your apartment." He pointed the way to a new black limousine that sat waiting, bathed in the ghostly glow of dim parking lights. A uniformed chauffeur loomed through the wet to hold open a door for us.

The smell of a new car!

For a long moment I soaked it up, and Leon Tidings seemed content to let me. The car purred away swiftly, almost without sound. Tidings gave my address through an intercom and then settled back to observe me.

"I am puzzled, Mr. Little, and I am not used to being puzzled." His voice was measured and supersoft. "You have changed, and I should like to know why." He removed his rimless glasses and polished them dry with gentle care.

"Your interest flatters me."

He hitched himself forward from the deep cushions of the big car and looked at me sharply. A half-smile began to seep through. "And that's it! Your speech has changed. Your manner has changed." He studied me anew. "You have gained something, and I can't quite put my finger on it."

"We all change," I replied. "Besides, why should you be concerned about someone like me whom you seek to destroy?"

"Oh, I expect change. Indeed, I count on change. I predict it... precisely. That is my job. But you do not fit the pattern I had selected for you. You have gained an element of perception, I think, yes, and even a small amount of poise that you did not have when we last... ah... worked together. Most unusual. Suggestions of strength where there should be more weakness."

He hissed a tuneless tune through his teeth. The few lights here and there threw odd shadows across his face as we sped through the city along deserted streets. We might have been the only men left alive on earth. He must have sensed this special kind of intimacy for his mood reflected an inner thoughtfulness that he seemed willing to share. "Of course I am interested in you, as I am in all creatures whose behavior I must govern. And whenever behavior doesn't follow

449

the intended course, I become very interested indeed. For every action, for every thought there is a reason... and an antidote if one thinks hard enough. I was not prepared to see you looking so fit, in spite of your... ah... misfortunes. Why would this be, Mr. Little?"

"Would you believe me if I told you I honestly don't know, but you are right? I am not quite as shaken as I once was, perhaps because so much has happened that I no longer care."

"No," Tidings mused. "You wouldn't have come tonight if that were the case."

"I suppose you're right. But I don't feel particularly brave, so it can't be courage."

"I agree. I wouldn't call you... ah... courageous. Damn! I can't put my finger on it!" He sighed and peered for a moment at the blackness of the river. "You seem more... aware. Ah! Your comment about your... ah ... destruction! Tell me, do you think you'll be destroyed?"

"Who can say? It looks that way, though, in a manner of speaking. "And what about me?"

"How should I know? You know the history of the Party better than I. What do you think?"

"Probably I shall be destroyed... sometime ... to make way for new men, but I am geared to expect it on that day when I am no longer useful. I shall ask no more for myself than I have demanded of others," he replied with chilling simplicity.

"What do you do with your time?" he asked.

"Work and all of those civic study groups that the Party has organized."

"Nothing else?"

"Not of any importance."

Even in the shadows I could perceive the heavy eyelids fall sleepily over his eyes. "I wonder about that. Yes, Mr. Little, you interest me very much. We shall see. Indeed, we shall see," he said ever so softly.

And then I was home.

The next month I was busy with the grim task of motivating the voters in the Fourteenth Ward to give their all in the name of peace, patriotism and plenty. I performed the chore with as much gentleness and sympathy as I could afford without being denounced. I encountered very little difficulty. Not once did I attempt to bribe anyone by threatening to report them, as did most of my teammates. And the stoic, wary faces that peered out at me from doorways along the trash-littered streets, slick with rain and garbage, offered no comment except very definite assurances that they would all be there. And they were. Ninety-eight and one-half percent of the eligible voters were registered, and ninety-six and two-tenths percent voted for the Party. One percent supported the Coalition Party. One old Polish woman asked to be excused because of a heart condition, but, since she could not prove she was a total invalid, she decided to go anyway, rather than pay a two-hundred-dollar fine. She died en route.

I felt no guilt over my part in the election. I even voted openly for the Party and barely suffered a pang. I had worked it all out, as best I could, after a lengthy session with Dr. Rodgers, Chip Baker, the Salvatorias and Father Herbert. I called on them the night after the meeting at Larry's house, and at first there were stormy protests, particularly from Chip. But as the evening wore on the answer began to appear. Had there been but Nancy and myself then—I like to tell myself this over and over—I would have told Larry to go straight to hell. But there were the children. What would happen to the quality of their lives had I not sacrificed my own will and choice so that they could continue to live in a home —of sorts, but still a home— rather than to be taken from us to spend the rest of their youth in the growing number of permanent camps that had become flourishing enterprises of "human reclamation?"

Perhaps I am only kidding myself. Perhaps my friends in the Salvatoria household were only being kind to a soul already lost beyond recall when they wished me well.

How would anyone know for sure?

7

How does a man learn to hate properly so as to do full justice to the torment that rages in the head? Does one curse just God alone, or should he include, say, his mother for bearing him? But mere words salve the tongue only and do nothing to flush out the body, particularly the hands and feet, which need to kick and beat at something. Killing, therefore, might help. Perhaps some fat bureaucrat that one might batter into a screaming mass of sewage? Or maybe poison the whole city and watch it writhe? Or pray to the devil for a nuclear holocaust so that the filthy face of the earth might be wiped clean? Or does one merely sit silently brooding, awaiting death to complete its work?

Ten days ago I was given an Attitude Test[93] at the store. It was a silly test. I did not worry much about it, because Kloomer still feared being denounced for possessing the book on Thomas Jefferson and would, therefore, protect me. I did not count on the fact that he also was required to take the test. We both failed.

Eight days ago both Kloomer and I were released from our jobs and given a permanent classification on our BWP records as "unreliable." Future employment—except perhaps in the common labor pool—now is impossible.

Six days ago I was served a notice of eviction to vacate the ugly, yellow apartment building by midnight, December 31, unless I could produce evidence of permanent employment.

Five days ago Larry Best dropped sobbing to his knees, begging forgiveness because both university regulations and the Bureau of Housing made it unlawful for him to take us in, even though there would have been ample room for Nancy, the three children and myself.

Four days ago I made my first visit to the Salvatoria house since the night following the meeting with Tidings and Larry. A total stranger answered the door, a big, unshaven fellow who smelled of factory sweat and whiskey. He had never heard of the Salvatorias or Chip Baker or Dr. Rodgers. They had simply vanished without a trace; yet the furnishings, from what could be seen from a half open doorway, still were there. Father Herbert's church was deserted, and

---

93 The Attitude Test was a psychological test to determine the feelings of a person toward his job, politics, economics and social behaviour. Persons judged "neurotic, unstable or disloyal" were discharged from their jobs.

there was no trace of the priest. No one in the neighborhood would talk. It was as if none of them ever had existed.

One day ago Nancy swept wildly from these horrible rooms and has not been home since.

And three hours ago they came in a station wagon and took the children away. The official papers served on me stated plainly that "the said minor children shall be returned to the custody of the Father whenever he shall establish proof of his ability to support said minor children in a manner to provide adequate food, clothing and shelter along with a proper home environment."

I was not particularly moved to see Peggy leave, for she had been complaining bitterly for weeks about having to live with us when she could enroll at any one of a dozen high school camps, most of which offered full college scholarships to deserving students. She would have left us anyway.

It hurt quite a little to see my son packed away like a drunk being hauled off to the precinct station house. He is in the middle of the awkward age, and I hope they will be patient with him. I console myself some with the knowledge that he is nearly grown and that he will retain memory of his home and, perhaps, manage to hang onto a few traits that he acquired from his father. Lots of boys go to boarding school. His camp could be like that.

But it was little Annie who ripped away all the muscles of my chest. For they had to carry her out of the building. And all the while she screamed, "Daddy, don't let them take me away! Daddy! Please!"

The Bureaus, when they want, can work quickly.

Tomorrow is Christmas Eve, but Christmas no longer is a holiday, since there are new moves to be absolutely certain that Church and State remain properly separated. The Church says the ban does not affect true believers.

And tonight I am absolutely alone, with not even a God to lean upon, for I have cast Him aside—even as the Little family has been scattered like ashes in the wind never to be whole again.

X

The Thirty-First Month

It is pleasantly cool this afternoon, for July, due to a heavy thunderstorm that passed last night sweeping with it the muggy filth that has hung over us for days. I am sitting on the rusted, bent steel deck of a tired barge, long ago abandoned as useless. From here, looking across the river, the Point of the city looks sharp and fresh against a deep blue sky. The water sparkles in the sun, and a midsummer stillness seems to have settled upon us, so that the sounds are muted and far away. Most everyone is gone from below, ashore on a variety of missions and jobs. I was out all morning trying to swap a pair of women's shoes for some fresh vegetables or perhaps an egg or two, but no luck. I should have selected something else from our central stores. Shoes are not in much demand right now. Besides, these have high heels which no one likes. My legs got awfully tired, so I called it quits. I am glad, because it gives me an opportunity to sit quietly and enjoy the day. It has been a very long time since I have done such a thing, and it gives me a steadying sense of calm that allows me to reach back to sort through all that has occurred these past six months.

For example, I have not seen my children since they were taken away, except one of them very briefly, and I am now fully reconciled that I shall never see them again. This has been the most difficult to accept. With Nancy it is somewhat easier, now that time has dulled the edges of memory and I can think about her again. She came home to that ugly yellow apartment by and by, tattered, tormented and soiled. Her heart-shaped face, once smooth, white and fragile with an appealing sensitiveness, had shattered into a hundred lines as a mirror after it has been dealt a smashing blow. Her hair, once brown and glowing, stood every which way. The harsh bleaching which she had tried weeks before now was well grown out, so that her hair did not make any sense at all. She was mostly all bone, her flesh withered in want of food, instead of drink. She was not drunk, but clearly she had been. One of her front teeth was missing, a sight not too unusual these days. I have lost four myself in this past year. But it was startling, all the same, for it made her that much uglier. And her hands, especially about the shredded fingernails, were rough and grey with dirt. Her eyes were hollow sockets of brown.

Were we on the street I should not have recognized her.

It was nearly noon on the second or third day after the children had been taken. Somewhere in the midst of things Christmas had come and gone without exciting any particular notice. We had been given until the end of December to vacate the apartment, and I had turned to the weary task of seeking to dispose of our possessions and finding some sort of shelter against the bitter winter. All across the city growing numbers of broken forms—the "residue of the bourgeoisie"—huddled homeless in alleyways and tight against building walls to try to live one more day, and I wondered if Dr. Rodgers and the others were now among them. It would be useless to look for them. They could do nothing for me. I could do nothing for them. And there was the matter of our furniture to attend to. I would need to sell it for cash, which presented two problems. Most items are simply swapped back and forth, a coat for shoes and shoes for food, and even if I could get cash I did not see how I could possibly cart it around, unless I could find bills of large denomination—or possibly silver coins. But the latter carried certain risks, since they had to be exchanged behind the backs of the authorities.[94] The matter of

94 Inflation had progressed to a point where it was almost impossible to carry one's total worth around in currency. Yet banks were not trusted, since funds were thus too easily available for confiscation should the JCFLA find a reason to do so. Silver coins had not been used for many years, being replaced first by coins of other metal and then later by paper money. Many Americans, however,

shelter was as much a dilemma. Having no Housing Permit, I would have to find an unofficial boarding house at a reasonable enough rate to keep us out of the weather until spring. Then perhaps things would get better.

I was sorting through a chest of drawers in the living room when she came up the stairs. The agony and weariness of her footfall could not disguise her step. She opened the door tentatively and then moved inside to lean against the wall. Her coat was sodden with snow, and she shook out of it slowly. After a very long moment she spoke in a flat voice as if she had just returned from the store.

"I don't hear the children."

"They are gone. They are gone for good. Do you understand?"

Her eyes became glazed. "Of course. That was it, wasn't it? They'll be taken care of .. . well taken care of?"

I nodded. The sight of her was overpowering, and I grieved for her as one might for a dear, dead friend. I offered her my hand. She hesitated, and slowly her rough fingers found mine. They were cold and lifeless, but as my hand warmed hers they stirred and grew stronger.

"May I come home again?" she asked.

"Of course."

"I have no job. I am not as pretty as I once was so the BWP let me go."

"I expected it."

"Funny. I don't really care."

"You are tired. You must rest now." I pulled her to me that I might support and comfort her, this human being that once was, and I put her to bed.

The next few days were frantic ones, so there was little time to ponder events. The decision of what clothing to keep and what household items to carry with us was sufficiently complex so that Nancy roused herself to help. Blankets, sheets, towels, dishes, irons and toasters. Chairs, tables, books—and toys. What does one do with

---

managed to hoard some of the silver, and as inflation worsened, they found the coins to be worth many times their face value. Also, they were relatively easy to carry, compared with an equivalent amount in paper money, and could be hidden without fear of deterioration.

them? I was able to sell most of the smaller items to people on our street. The word, of course, was out, and the good neighbors—many of them newcomers who were union laborers[95]—came by the third-floor flat to look, poke and haggle. It was cash on the spot and no nonsense. Oftentimes belligerent words were spoken, but I held firm. I only had to bribe one official. He was from the BWP. We gave him two old silver half dollars worth twenty-five paper dollars each. I did well on selling the smaller items, particularly blankets. We had saved two of the heavier ones to take with us. But I had no luck finding buyers for the furniture. I covered the city with no success. But on our last day in the apartment good fortune came our way. The new tenants, a young workman and his wife and five children, lacked furniture of their own. He had been promoted from some place down the valley and had succeeded in joining the Party. From some source he had acquired considerable cash—including four silver half-dollars and three silver quarters. He balked some at the price, but when I threatened to heave all the furniture down the stairs, he paid well. He was not cheated, though, for the furniture was of a quality that few people in the area could ever hope to have.

And there we were late in the afternoon of the last day, New Year's Eve—Nancy, me, three suitcases, two blanket rolls, a footlocker and better than five thousand dollars in cash, enough to keep us for three, perhaps four months, provided we could locate cheap shelter. I also carried my Peace Bonds, eleven thousand dollars worth, but I could not cash them for another fifteen years. As yet we had found no place to go, and no one in the neighborhood offered to take us in. One does not invite a swimmer to share an already dangerously overloaded life boat. One neighbor did, however, offer to keep the footlocker for a time. It was in here that I placed this journal, along with some old family records, a few pieces of silver tableware, some cotton clothing and an old silver embroidered tablecloth that had belonged to

---

95 It should be pointed out that rank and file members of organised labour were left reasonably intact, provided they offered public support of the Communist Party and were willing to accept jobs as assigned, longer working hours and reduced pay. Most had skills that were still much in demand, so that employment for them was steady so long as they met these conditions.

Nancy's grandmother. Since I had money we were able to stay in an all-night movie, which was far less expensive than a cheap hotel. It was crowded, but we found seats together and spent the next eleven hours watching a film on the "Miracles of State Socialism." Actually we dozed most of the time. At eight the next morning they kicked us out into the snow so the inside could be hosed down and the place aired for the next day's worth of eager theater-goers. Happy New Year.

The daylight brought winds bearing slashing sleet to burn our faces. We set out across the Ninth Street Bridge—near where I am now—to the north side of the city. It was one of the few places where the authorities let the "transients," as they call the homeless, alone to do pretty much as they please. Only the Stadium-Housing project area was off limits.

Elsewhere the narrow, crooked streets with their patched, rickety houses and beatup stores and shops were surging with people. It was a melting pot of nightmare proportions. The snow was all slush mixed with human waste and trash. Here and there rusted oil drums belched up smoke and fire while people fought to get nearer to the life-giving heat. Every shade of humanity was there, shoving, screaming, sobbing, slinking and sulking on the sidewalks, in the streets and alleys and inside the dozens of swap shops, saloons and what were supposed to be lunch counters. Here and there a form lay huddled against the wall of a building too ill to move or too weary to care—or dead.

There was an absence of children. The relatively few younger people were at least in their early twenties and by their dress and manner were part of the growing number of street gangs who thus far had successfully defied the authorities. Their presence in this awful sea obviously was in the role of predator—to steal or to bargain with stolen goods or just to torment whoever looked the weakest. Most of the pulsating throng were middle-aged and up. It was difficult to determine from where they might have come originally or what they had been. There were as many women as men. They were dressed in a wild assortment of coats or sweaters or tattered blankets. Nearly all were unwashed, and the men unshaven.

458

We moved with difficulty toward a saloon that someone had said I should try. Twice groups of young toughs accosted us. The suitcase and blankets we carried marked us clearly as newcomers. Both times they let us pass. This was possible because each time I fished a small bottle of gasoline I had saved and a cigarette lighter from my pocket and said: "One move from you birds, and I light this and blow us all to hell!" A path would clear then. Throughout our journey Nancy kept stoically still, eyes fastened to the ground just in front of her. She carried the lightest of the suitcases. It was necessary to rest often. Only once did she take note of the scene. That was when I spotted two wretchedly dirty people—a man and a woman—struggling with perhaps half-a-dozen persons who were trying to dislodge them from their warm, dry spot next to one of the fires. It was Leroy and Beth Silkmore. Nancy and I had gone to their house once for cocktails and a buffet dinner that I recall over and over again with increasing clarity. It was there that Nancy had blown her serene, suburban housewife image by decrying her shame of me.

"Hurry along, now. The Silkmores! They're right over there." I quickened my pace lest they see us, but Nancy stopped and turned to watch Leroy and Beth, as they swore and kicked out at the angry group. Slowly a smile grew across Nancy's haggard face. It was a smile of unchecked pleasure, and it swept the lines on her face away. A glint showed like pinpoints of light from her eyes.

"I wonder how many more of our friends are over here. Don't they look grand?" These were the only words she had spoken throughout the morning. Then she moved quickly to catch up with me, and in a moment the Silkmores were out of view.

Finally we reached the saloon. It must have been built in the 1890's. The Golden Hour. It was crowded inside, but I found a quiet comer where Nancy could sit on the suitcases. Then I found the bartender, looking like a bartender should.

"Where can I find a room?"

"How would I know? Either order up or get out."

I slipped a five dollar bill across the bar. The man merely glared at me. I added a sister bill. The man smiled. He gave me two addresses.

He was agreeable to letting Nancy wait while I checked them out. The first place was an old brick house that looked reasonably solid. A hawk-faced woman opened the door and I explained my plight. The answer was short and mean. A room would cost two hundred and fifty dollars per week, payable in advance.

The second place, some ten blocks away back up the hillside, was an ancient clapboard house long since blackened by the elements. It stood squeezed tightly between a row of a half dozen like it on a narrow cobbled street that hung on the hill. Most of the windows were replaced with cardboard or wood. A battered and baldheaded man in a grimy sweatshirt opened a sagging door that faced directly onto the narrow sidewalk that was more mud than cement.

"Two hundred and fifty bucks per week," he growled.

"You're out of your mind." I turned away.

"So, a guy can try. Two twenty-five." "One seventy-five."

"Get out!"

I turned away again.

"Two-fifteen."

"Two hundred."

The man rubbed a thick, dirty hand across his thick, dirty face. "You're a robber! Bet you used to be one of them bankers. Two-ten. That's it."

"Two hundred," I replied.

"Go to hell!" And he slammed the door.

I started to walk away. The door flew open with a screeching wrench. "OK! OK! Goddamn robber. But pay me now."

"When can I move in?"

"Soon as I get the other people out."

I stopped short. "Why me over them?"

"You pay more. And them that's got the most gets the room. Remember that, bud." He growled again. "I'll have 'em out in fifteen minutes. Pay me a week in advance."

I paid and waited in the street. Shortly the door squeaked open again, and a man and a woman came out bearing two cloth sacks and a blanket. Both must have been in their sixties. The woman was in tears. I did not want to see any more, so I turned the other way.

"What will happen to them?" I asked the burly man, named Hennessey, moments later as he led me up the narrow, creaking stairs.

"They'll find a place. 'Course, won't be as good as this. But they still got money… unless the gangs get 'em."

There were four rooms on the second floor and one room that passed for a bath. Nancy and I had the right rear. The room was terribly small. A sagging, tattered sofa bed, two wooden chairs, a bureau, a frail table and two bottles bearing candle sticks; two narrow windows, glass intact, framed by ripped lace curtains that once might have been white; walls that still bore wallpaper here and there that had not come loose, a nifty rose pattern. This was the new home, our little cottage for two. When Nancy saw it she only shrugged.

"By spring things will be better," she said softly. There was a bite in her voice, as if she had made a vow that she meant to keep.

It did not take us long to get settled. The biggest problem was where to keep the money. Fortunately, the room, being part of a very old house, had a small fireplace originally designed to burn coal. Somewhere along the way it had been remodeled to hold a small gas heater. Since gas is now heavily rationed, the heater had been wrenched to one side and the hearth reopened to permit an open fire. I was able to loosen several bricks at various places on the inside of the fireplace wall and dig out spaces big enough to hold tin cans padded tightly with rolls of bills and silver coins. So long as we burned only charcoal our resources would be safe and certainly no one would search on the inside. There were nine other adults living on the floor, besides us. Two men and two women in one room, family related in one way or another. I think they once had been school teachers. Three men of questionable character shared another room. They did not care for girls. They had been in some kind of sales work. The room adjacent to ours was occupied by two young women, once secretaries, and a baby girl about eight months old. I never did learn who was the mother, because they each took turns watching after the child while the other was away.

They were fullfledged prostitutes, of course, their only way to secure an income now. They did not seem to mind, but then, who does? The world has always had its prostitutes, probably ever since the days of the cave. One never thinks about the subject except the vague feeling that such women are different and, so, remote from the day-to-day life of a proper and orderly society; until you become enmeshed in the particular world of the ladies in red. Then the perspective is different. Suddenly you understand that some of the gals, at least, are in the business for a very simple, straightforward reason. They want to survive. That takes money, and there is nowhere else for them to go. When evaluated from this most basic viewpoint—to eat or not to eat—prostitution loses much of its unsavoriness and becomes, instead, a perfectly logical pursuit. I have to feel this way, because Nancy became one, too, in earnest. No attempts were made to develop fancy justifications in which I and the system were to be blamed. No guilt. No angry words. All that had passed. Even the lure of fancy clothes or a more comfortable life no longer figured in the reasoning that went on in Nancy's mind. It was real simple.

"It's this ... or starve," she said with a cold flatness. "If the positions were reversed, what would you do?"

One does not answer a question like that, but looks, instead at the floor and says nothing.

For I had tried, once again, to have another go at cooperating with the new order of things. I went first to the union headquarters —there no longer being any sort of market for non-technical white collar workers—to make application for membership.[96] They were nice to me. They found a chair for me to sit on. They brought me coffee. They listened sympathetically to my story. They commended me for my desire to be more useful in perpetuating the cause of peace. They shared my view that all of our human resources must be more efficient producers, including myself. I have never been more gently

---

96 By this time, in order to be eligible for food allowances, medical care and the like, a person had to show evidence of at least one member of his immediate family belonging either to the Communist Party or a labour union. As an alternative, a Certificate of Good Citizenship was often used to reward workers not belonging to either one, which would still entitle them to "full government services." (From JCFLA records.)

treated. It made them sick—and you could see it right on their fac-es—to have to tell me, but, well, they were filled up just right then; more members than they could handle. They were so sorry, but could I come back in, say, six months?

I begged. The answer was still no. Gentle, honey-sweet to the end.

I went to Leon Tidings. I still had one good suit which I wore for the occasion. He was located, now, on one of the upper floors of the Skyway Building, and his office was very large. At first the guard would not even let me approach the information desk, but a ten dol-lar bill changed that. Another five got the pert receptionist on the phone, and to our great surprise Tidings agreed to see me immedi-ately. He rose to greet me, his dark features showing a slight trace of puzzled amusement.

"Let me guess, Mr.... ah... Little. You would like to join the Party?"

My laugh was honest in its admiration. "Yes."

"Why?" He removed his tinted glasses and polished them with elaborate care.

"You know why. I want to live."

"Understandable, of course." He sighed and moved back to his big desk to slip easily into his big chair. I could not keep myself from looking around his office. Neat, clean and tastefully furnished with all of the accouterments of top executivehood.

"The pigs are eating with the farmers," I said, and he responded with a laugh that was also honest in its admiration.[97]

"Well stated. But let's stick to the subject." He spoke with a re-laxed easiness. "You want to live, but I want you to die. Quite an impasse, isn't it?"

"Why not shoot me and get it over with?"

"Too messy and too many bullets. Your kind... any bourgeoisie ... is not worth the trouble. Better to ignore you and keep you out of our way. Events do the rest, you see?"

"Why not give me a chance? I will work hard."

---

97 David Little was referring to the last chapter of Animal Farm, by George Orwell, a satire on Communism written in the late 1940's. Tidings recognized the refer-ence.

"Impossible. Your whole background is against you. Only a very few who have ever been a product of the bourgeoisie can ever serve our cause with the dedication and discipline we must have, and you are not one of us. Personally," he paused a moment reflectively, "I shouldn't mind you in the Party. I could almost like you, Mr. Little, but, you see, it doesn't work. If our system is to survive and work, every particle of the old life… your old life… must be liquidated without a trace. Hence, you and all others like you must be liquidated as soon as you have served your purposes. You people have never understood this fact, so there is no point in my trying to explain further."

"I'm going to fool you. I will live … if for no other reason than to see you… ah… displeased."

He looked at me for a long moment not without a suggestion of respect. "You might. You probably will … for a time. But in the end, no."

"Tell me, what became of the Salvatoria family?"

"Ah! I wondered if you would connect me with their departure. I told you I was curious. I had you followed, and I evicted them. I do not know where they are."

We parted then, and the next day I went to my last hope—the labor pool, the only place where neither union nor Party membership was necessary for employment. Two dollars an hour and ten hours a day, seven days a week, if you could stand it. The headquarters is a huge open area near Dome Center. I had hoped that somewhere among the thousands of desperate faces I might see Chip Baker. But I did not. I was assigned to a work detail. We are transferring a huge, mountainous slag dump south of the city into railroad cars. The slag will be used to make cement. David Little working in a slag dump and wearing an old business suit— Corporate Blue—a dark top coat and oxford shoes.

I laugh at the moralists, if there are any left. I laugh at the reformers,[98] too; there were enough of them shoveling slag with me.

So we lived for nearly three months, well into March, and the quality of our lives sank lower and lower as we found less and less

---

98 Reformers was the Communist term for the so-called Fabian Socialists, i.e., those who believed in achieving socialism by gradual, constitutional means, rather than by revolution.

to choose from. At first we talked of returning to the good old days—the ugly apartment, now not so ugly; we never even considered the hope of returning to a home in Southern Estates. In spite of our earnings, the money slowly drained away for food and clothing that both of us urgently needed for our respective trades. It was not long before our highest aspiration was to remain exactly where we were, and whatever individual will we could summon was directed solely to this frantic ambition to stay even with the board; so that we rarely thought of the children or Larry and Mary Best. We tried once to locate the children, but it was hopeless, for we could gain no information as to their whereabouts. Even the puzzle of what happened to Marie Salvatoria, her father, Chip Baker, Dr. Rodgers and Father Herbert was slowly pushed to the back of my mind, as I concentrated more and more on how I could keep pace with a shovel that was forever under the sadistic eyes of a most brutally ambitious "project director," once referred to as a "straw boss"; to concentrate on frozen slag, biting wind, clinging snow and hands raw and blue with cold pain. At least we were transported by trucks to and from the dump. Otherwise I would have perished.

I seldom saw Nancy, since she worked nights mostly. With luck she could clear a good two hundred a week after payoffs. The two girls in the adjacent room had taken a liking to her and cut her in on some of the prospects that were not at all easy to come by. Even had she been home, I would have been too tired to have been conscious of it.

We cooked in the fireplace over charcoal. Potatoes, corn meal, beans and ham bones were the most plentiful items. Sometimes we could get chicken, ground beef and salmon. Once I picked up some sausage through the black market. Even powdered milk had become scarce, and what we could get we saved for the baby next door. The bathroom toilet that served all of us worked only when water was carried upstairs from the one working faucet in the kitchen below, which seldom happened. We carried washing water, too, unheated. I slept, and soundly, whenever I had the chance. I seldom saw Hennessey, the landlord, or the remarkable mixture of people who

465

lived on the first floor, but I have a suspicion that Hennessey saw Nancy and the two girls every now and then.

Ultimately, the days came to be longer, and the darkness of night shorter. Occasionally, there would be a break in the bitter weather, and warm winds would suggest the possibility that spring might come almost any time. It was something to perk us up, something to talk about. But, of course, March always has a last whopper before it lets loose. It came right after St. Patrick's Day, a well celebrated event, still; a nice six-inch snow that lasted but a day.

It was close to six by the time I was back from the slag dump. Nancy had not departed as yet. The two girls were away on a little "errand" and Nancy was looking after Sally, the baby. There was no powdered milk, and little Sally was hungry. I agreed to try to find some and set out on the search. I had gone but a few steps along the street when Nancy came calling after me. She had recalled a place where I might find the milk. She had no coat about her but wore only a simple sweater and skirt that she had had for many years, and in that brief moment she looked every bit the Nancy of old—a comfortable, suburban housewife dashing outside to flag down her husband for one last bit of instruction; a scene repeated a hundred times in my memory of her and our twenty years of life together. She was pleased with herself that she had recalled this important bit of information, and I took pleasure in seeing her thus.

At that moment a station wagon spun slowly up the street and stopped beside us. A window, sticky with snow, was rolled down and a voice called, "Hey, old man! Y' gonna make out with her, huh?" Then came cackling laughter in assorted shapes and sizes.

Half a dozen or so youths dressed in Boy Scout uniforms leered out at us.

"You better hurry, or you'll be late for your meeting," I replied.

"Lots of time, old man!" a voice shouted back. For a moment I had the wild idea that one of the boys might be our own son, so I stepped close to the window and in the dying light of the day looked closely. David was not among them, and they looked like no other Scouts that I had ever seen before in all my years of scouting. Their eyes all had the same cold hardness about them. Their faces were harsh with expressions of contempt mixed with boredom. Their bodies were restless in their neat uniforms and snappy hats, for the boys kept shifting this way and that as if they were itching to get out of the car and have at something. They were bad news, pent-up boys looking for trouble on the wrong side of the tracks, and I backed away quickly, too quickly; for they sensed my assessment of them, and as if a mental telegraph had dispatched an urgent message, they got out of the car with deliberate slowness.

"Where are you running to, old man and nice lady?" One voice squeaked in a display of supermanliness.

We stood still then. The other persons on the street—and there were many—froze where they were and waited with approving expectancy to see what the boys would do next.

So they had an audience, and what growing young teenager does not appreciate an audience all his? They strutted a bit, looking here and there at the people, the street and, finally, the old houses.

"Kinda cold today, eh, old man," one of the Scouts called to me. I did not answer. "Yes, cold. Hey, fellas, have we done our good deed for today?"

"No-o-o," a chorus of voices mocked.

"These people look cold."

"Yeah, cold," the chorus replied in grinning cadence.

"Let's warm 'em up!"

"Yeah, yeah."

"Who's got a little paper?"

"Right here."

"Who's got a little match?"

"Right here."

"Gimme." And the Scouts formed a tight circle while one of them fashioned a torch from stray pieces of cardboard and paper that someone had fished from a dry spot in an overflowing junk barrel.

The Scout lit the torch and held it aloft until it burned brightly.

"Nice, huh?"

"Pretty!"

Then the Scout very calmly opened the front door of our house and touched the fire to tattered lace curtains that hung over the narrow windows flanking the doorway.

Before anyone could move they scurried back into their car and spun away, their laughter clear and sharp on the new night air. For we had not yet begun to scream.

That was that. The flames rippled upwards, to dance along the walls and ceiling, while the smoke gathered in modest little billows that grew and grew and then drifted lazily out the still open door. By now we were able to give the alarm, which no longer was necessary. Being mealtime, the twenty or so persons who occupied the ancient house must have all been inside, save for the two girls, Nancy and me. So they started out the door, a panic-stricken file of them; white faces, clawing hands and bodies shoving one another. Before I could stop her, Nancy bolted into house. "The baby! Please, somebody get the baby!" she cried over and over again. But not one of the onrushing adults heard—or maybe they did not care. She bounced and spun her way, to go against the frantic line that cursed her, back into the house and up the narrow stairs that had already become a chimney.

I tried to follow, tried to snag her sleeve, tried to convince her that I should go. But she ignored my pleas, and the hellbent line would not tolerate yet another mad body crushing against it, so that I fell farther behind her, until in the end the tide had swept me back into the street, from where I watched the flames slowly eat up the front of the house. At length I got back to the front door, but the stairs by now were impassable and the heat beyond endurance. I raced through the narrow passageway between the houses to the back. The rear yard was small and piled high with junk, rusted bits of steel and iron parts from automobiles, construction and plant equipment. I saw Nancy at the window above. She held a blanket tightly bundled against her.

"The front of the house! Go to the front!" I yelled, frantic that she might jump into the twisted metal. She nodded and vanished from the window. I made my way back. Twice I fell, smashing my legs and arms against jagged objects hidden in the snow, and then I stumbled drunkenly out onto the street. The crowd had grown thick and stood well away from the inferno in an awe-struck silence to watch the figure of a woman silhouetted against the yellow light, half hidden by smoke. She had smashed a window and stood frozen in a trance.

"The baby! Drop it!" I cried. She did, and little Sally, well wrapped in the blanket, fell softly into my arms. The action prompted several of the bystanders to move in to help.

"Jump!" voices screamed, my own among them.

"I can't!" she replied, her words a soft wail of fear.

The house was a mass of flames now, little savages of pain doing their war dance, darting in and around Nancy to torment her. Finally, she plunged over the flaming window sill and fell into my outstretched arms. We both crumbled into the slush of the street. Other hands moved to help beat out the fire that was consuming her clothing. We lifted her limp form and moved her away from the flames which were beginning to work on the neighboring houses. The fire sirens and bells that had been sounding in the distance grew deafening as the fire fighting equipment fought its way up the choked street. We found a quiet spot for her, a patch of somebody's front yard that was still angel white in the falling snow. We laid her on my coat.

"I've got to get her inside... some place!" I looked anxiously at the house before us, another shabby wooden box, but one which was for the moment out of danger. A tattered old man with a gentle face had been among the few who tried to help me with Nancy.

"Let her be where she is. Snow. We'll cover her with snow. That will be best," he said.

"Can't somebody please find a doctor!" I spoke to the growing group of persons who were gathering to watch with morbid interest.

"Are you kidding?" a voice drawled quietly. "I'll try, but it won't do any good."

She stirred then, a shuddering, jerking movement, and opened her eyes. The dancing flames in the background gave off a soft, steady light. She was terribly burned all over.

"I hurt," she said.

We packed her in the snow. Then she lay still for a long moment, her eyes searching my face in wistful sweeps.

"The baby?" she asked. I had to bend low to hear her words.

"Safe, and a doctor is on the way. Everything is going to be all right."

"I'm glad she is safe. That's all I ever wanted for any of us … to be safe." She was silent again, her eyes trying to comprehend the scene about us. "I have been a bad person … to you especially. Please forgive me. It has been madness … these months."

"If you have been bad, I have been worse. Perhaps we need to forgive each other."

For a long while she was quiet. While large snowflakes drifted from the heavens to comfort her, I knelt at her side oblivious to all else. Finally, she roused with a sleepy half-smile.

"The pain is gone now," she murmured. "I think I'll take a little nap before the children come home from school." She uttered a long, contented sigh and her eyes closed, never to open again.

By and by they took her away. They would not let me bury her. The rules call for cremation.

You see, land is very valuable, and there is not enough cemetery space for everyone. It would be unfair to discriminate, to pit one bereaved family against another. That is what they said, but they were very nice about the whole thing.

2

Once when I was still a teenage boy, I sneaked a copy of *Real Life* magazine into my bedroom, and whenever no one was about I would read it with heart-pounding care. Confessions of a dope addict. Confessions of an alcoholic. Confessions of a party girl. They were all there in vivid word pictures and photographs, the ugly, sometimes racy thoughts of the dregs of the human race. Men and women owning up to their wayward and wicked ways. I would stare for long moments at some of the more bold and intimate passages where the repentant authors came within a hair of divulging all of the details of their wrongdoings, and my imagination would take over with a cold horror that such people really did exist right out there in the world beyond my window. The lure of the magazine was nested in a titanic struggle between absolute fascination and sickening revulsion. Naturally, I was caught with the goods, by my mother, of course. But while I was severely punished, I never regretted the purchase, and secretly I used to wonder what it would be like—to drift from one exotic adventure to another without caring what others might think.

I am curious no longer, and now that I have reclaimed my footlocker, I can write about it in this Journal, which was still safely tucked away six months after we left it behind.

After they took Nancy away I wandered aimlessly in the growing light of dawn. It was fruitless to report to the labor pool to work for less than livable wages, since all was gone now. Even the money which had been so carefully accumulated had been forever lost in the ashes. Later on that first truly empty day the snow melted, and the sun appeared to warm the air. I recall only that I wanted to mix with people; to be packed in close, but not to stay in any one place long enough to risk having someone speak to me. The streets, stores, shops and alleys had an unreal quality, and I kept walking with a certain desperateness. Later, though, at some point I came to a better part of the city. By then I was hungry, and I ate my first meal out of a garbage can, set carelessly exposed at the back entrance to a large house still in excellent repair. There were grapefruit rinds and some stale bread. Two police dogs chased me away before I had a chance to search further. I sat for a time some place on steps—in a park, I think—taking great care to follow the rays of the sun. It was warm, and I drowsed.

Then it was night, and I went back across the bridge to No-Man's Land, as they called the place of the transients. Lights blazed in every saloon, all of which were packed thick with ragged bodies seeking warmth and cheer. I visited these places all through the night. I had the price of one drink in my pockets, and I spent it quickly. A ruthless kind of gaiety prevailed at every place I stopped. Some men cavorted freely with women, while others were gathered in small groups plotting how they would live yet another day. Occasionally, a fight would break out. Someone had a cigarette that someone else wanted or a woman or a pocket knife or an empty wallet that still might

471

be useful for trade. There was singing. "Roll Out the Barrel." "When Irish Eyes Are Smiling." Croaking, shrill voices raised on high. These places did not close for the night. The mobs would not leave, and the police were content to let matters stand. In fact there were no police—not in No-Man's Land. They patrolled all around the Land, but only to keep us in it. Curfew was enforced in the other parts of the city where the New Society—the government authorities who now ran things, everything—now slept in reasonable comfort. But there was no curfew where I was.

The days and nights were rolled into one never-ending chorus that was the grand finale of Pittsburgh Past. Somewhere I performed my first robbery. Lurking in the shadows among the tall buildings in the heart of the city, I waited for someone to pass. It was very late and from out of a night club down the street came a man and his date. I had a companion, some nameless soul who had done this sort of thing before. We leaped at them out of the shadows. We held clubs high, and they cringed before us. One wallet and one purse, containing two hundred dollars and a flock of ration stamps. This bought food and drink and a knife for me. The saloon was our bed for the night. There were many more robberies.

April brought warmer weather, and there were sheltered places outside where one could spend the night huddled against other bodies of people you did not know—or care to know. May was better yet. By June I had difficulty recalling that I had ever slept inside before, and I did not need warm bodies around me. Rain, whenever it came, was the only problem, but then there were always the saloons, and I had the knife to make my way inside, while some other nameless wretch took my place outside.

I had made a few friends—a wicked old goat named Slinker, plus a one-eyed apparition called Moon, and a rawboned woman whom everyone called Zimbam. They were a cheerful lot, part of the Old Bum set. I preferred the old timers, the vets who knew how to cope effectively with power and poverty. I ignored the New Bums, people like me—greenhorns. Every now and then I would spot someone like the Silkmores, former business associates, neighbors and the like, and I would move away quickly. Slinker, Moon, Zimbam and I made a pretty good team. Thanks to them I learned how to spot a mark and hit and run with remarkable speed. I soon learned how to hide from the police. I learned, too, how to use a knife to protect myself from other gangs. This came the hard way. It cost me several slashes across the face, chest and arms before I got the hang of it. Then, one night I killed a man. He came at me out of an alley. I had learned how to spin, crouch and come up fast from underneath. I got him in the stomach. No one bothered me after that, and Slinker, Moon and Zimbam became my steady companions. By this time the only things left out of my catalogue of experience were taking dope and committing rape.

I drank more than I ate, and one night I slipped off a curb. It was a freak accident. One could expect to become hopelessly ill or to be maimed in a fight, but to be prepared for such a simple happening—never. I did not see the curb, and so my foot crunched down at a grotesque angle that paralyzed me with pain and pitched me helplessly into the street. Ultimately, I was able to stand, but when I tried to walk I found that my right heel dragged. I later learned that I had torn loose all of the ligaments in the back of my leg and that I would never again walk correctly. Fortunately, my companions were with me at the time, and they helped me to an informal little lean-to we had built in a rubble area not too far from the river. It was our operational headquarters. We had sufficient loot buried in various places so that I could allow a few days for my injury to heal. Slinker, Moon and Zimbam took turns seeing that I was fed—stewed chicken necks and old bread mostly. In due course the pain ceased, but I could not eliminate the shuffling of my right leg. So I was invited out of the little group—the iron law being that each person had to pull his own weight, and my days of lightning-swift attacks upon the unwary bureaucrats across the river had come to an abrupt end. The parting was cordial, and I was given my fair share of the loot I had helped to secure. They took on another partner and moved on down the river—Ambridge, I think they said.

So I became a beggar. Each morning I would drag my way across the bridge into the Golden Triangle, and I would spend the day moving slowly among the tall buildings, not daring to stop for fear of being arrested for loitering and not wanting to move too fast, lest I miss an easy mark.

One day in late June I was working lower Liberty Avenue. It was close to noon, and the area around the Skyway Building was packed with people, most of whom looked to be employed, a few of them rather prosperous, judging from the black market clothes they wore. It was the premium spot in the city, and I was trying my luck there when a military staff car cruised to stop in front of the building. A man—perhaps my age, though I looked much older than he—alighted from the rear of the car and held the door for a strikingly attractive girl. He was in the blue uniform of the Peace Force and was obviously an officer of high rank, probably a general. The girl was dressed in a pale green summer dress tightly fitted to her. She wore gloves, shoes and carried a small purse, all of which were matched in dazzling, flawless white. I approached the marks with a sudden spurt of energy, hoping that I could catch them.

"Please, sir! Won't you please help an old Peace soldier?" I cried. It was the only effective approach that could be used on the military, and maybe once out of a dozen tries it would work.

The officer turned and scowled in open disgust. But that was not unusual. Nor was it unusual that the girl turned away in complete revulsion. The well dressed, bright young creatures always did. What made things different was that the girl was my own daughter.

"Peggy! It's your father!" I reached out for her, and her carefully made-up eyes grew round in terror.

"Go away!" she shrieked. "Lew, get this dirty scum away from me!"

The officer hesitated for an instant, his smoothly shaven face plainly perplexed, and then he caught Peggy by the arm and steered her away toward the building. "Out of our way!" he commanded. "Go on! Get!"

But I bumped along behind them, forgetting the people, even the place, and seething with an almighty rage.

474

"Get, like an old dog ... oh, no! I'm her father, do you hear? Yes! Think of that! Her father, see?" I yelled out at them and flailed against a policeman who had come out of nowhere to restrain me.

"Hurry, Lew! Oh hurry, please!"

Those words were the last I heard from her, and as she receded toward the building, I screamed my last to her.

"Your mother is dead!"

Peggy stopped, and her back stiffened as if she had been stabbed. Then she moved on again, head down, her steps clicking hard on the pavement.

"She burned to death! Do you hear? Burned! Burned!"

And they were gone behind the doors, so that all that was left to stare at was the reflection of my own image in the glass. But surely this was not me! Matted hair, long and thick with dirt. A much too narrow face, ragged with old scars and long in need of a shave. A tattered white shirt, smudged black almost, and trousers soiled with dried mud. For shoes, sandals made from an old tire casing. And the eyes could not possibly be mine. They were sunk too deeply into the skeletonlike head. The reflection was playing tricks.

I moved away across the broad sidewalk, cutting through the current of people who turned their heads at me brazenly, contemptuously.

"Listen!" I yelled again. "I wasn't always a beggar ... do you hear?" I stumbled blindly on, looking wildly about that I might catch some friendly ear. "I came from a good family, you hear? I went to college. I'm no ordinary beggar. Why, at one time I had more money than any of you. Do you hear me? Won't somebody please hear me?"

On I went with the pavement reeling in front of me.

"Please!"

"Away, old man!"

"Say, could you..."

"Beat it!"

At length on a quiet comer I stopped and looked back to the Skyway Building, still tall and sparkling in the summer sun. The rage and the shame were gone. Resolution again settled over me.

"There's one more thing for you to know, Peggy," I said softly to the building. "You have no Father, either."

Later in the afternoon I was moving back through No-Man's Land. Three younger men lounging alongside a decaying brick dwelling eyed me with more than casual interest.

"Hey there, Pop. Where are you going?" one of the men asked. He was a rangy fellow but dressed with surprising neatness in a clean white "T" shirt and blue jeans. The other two were dressed likewise. Obviously, they had had a highly profitable day in trading or stealing or both. Their mood was one of seeking amusement. I had seen them about from time to time, but they had never given me any trouble.

"Leave him alone, Ripper," growled one of his companions.

"I'm not going to hurt him. Come here. I got an idea," he beckoned, genially. He looked me up and down. "Seen you before. Old Slinker told me you wuz real good, 'fore you got hurt. Saw you fight once. Yes, sir, you wuz real good."

"Thanks," I replied. I pulled myself straight. "I may be a little slower, but I can still make a pretty good stand."

The man was called Jack the Ripper, and he studied me carefully. "You know, boys, maybe Pop here could watch the place while we're away." The other two nodded in quick agreement. "We got a little shack over in the old park. We're kinda savin' up, you might say, to take over a house someplace. We got stuff, see. It's hid good. I figure if you're sort of around to keep an eye on things, then nobody'd get tempted."

We talked for a bit and then moved on to the shack, which was set prominently in the middle of what used to be a small park. Compared to other makeshift shelters around it, the shack was a mansion. It was made from brand new wooden pallets, stolen from a factory some place and brought to the site without any apparent difficulty, which was a remarkable feat. It had four sides and a roof of heavy plastic material. Inside were three low bunks stuffed with old rags, a rough table and two short benches—all made from the rough, new wood.

"I'll have to think about it," I said finally. Experience had taught me not to jump too quickly.

476

"Well, now. Why don't we all think together?" And Ripper, who proved to be the leader of the trio, fished among the rags of his bunk and withdrew a couple of dark bottles. "Let's have a little think medicine!" He laughed with honest pleasure. I learned that the young men had given themselves both the afternoon and evening off in their search for plunder. They had made a particularly good strike—a military supply truck which, along with its contents of dried rations, clothing, soap and mess kits, had been sold into the black market and, accordingly, had vanished from sight. Even now the truck was probably being dismantled so that the parts could be more easily sold piecemeal. They did not say how much they made on the deal, but it must have been plenty. The bottles contained real, high-grade whiskey, a brand I had not seen for a long time. We passed them around and around. Ultimately the pain within me was all gone. Finally, it was dusk, and we were all delightfully drunk.

"You know, boys," Ripper was saying, "we clean forgot what we wuz settin' out for." "Whazzat?" one of the others asked with a heavy-lidded emphasis.

"Women!"

"Yeah! That's right! Well, let's go."

"What about Pop, here?"

"Take him with us."

"How 'bout that, Pop! Something kinda young and pretty, maybe?"

My head buzzed at the thought, but through the alcoholic vapor I saw myself again as I now was. "Nothing worthwhile would ever take to me. You guys go on."

"I got it! Let's get a woman for old Pop. We'll make it a special 'casion. Something really nice from the good side of town. We'll grab her and hold a knife to her pretty white throat and turn old Pop loose. Man! Can't you just see it?"

"What about us?"

"Oh, hell, we can get 'em any old time. But I can see Pop's got a point. We gonna give'm some help. It's more blessed to give than receive."

"Says who?"

"My grandmaw, that's who. It's some old saying she used to talk all the time."

Before I knew it, we were all on our feet and out on the street again, stumbling along in the twilight of a June night. So it was to be this now. I floated along as we prowled toward the bridge that would lead us to the other world—the world to which I owed nothing. Hate began to work through me. What an adventure this could be!

We were almost to the bridge when Ripper signaled us to stop. "Hold it, boys. Will you look at that, now?" he whistled softly.

A girl was walking briskly across the bridge toward us. The light had faded too much to catch the details of her features, except that she was dark-haired, slender and still neatly dressed. Most appealing of all, she looked clean. And my head pounded in an awful dilemma. If I took this final step there would be no way back.

"Hide!" Ripper shooed us back behind the abutment. From where we stood the ground dropped down to the river bank. There was hardly anyone around, and even if there were, no one would disturb us. "What luck! Ain't nobody gonna bother us here. Man, we can take our time."

We waited. Her steps drew close. And then they pounced on her and began to drag her down the bank. But she fought back hard. They were having trouble, so they called to me. In a trancelike reflex I stepped out to join them. There was still some light. I saw her face, then.

In one single, mighty shudder my whole being came to a stop. Awareness slapped me awake. *In the name of anything left that is decent, what have you become, David Little?*

"Stop it!" And I flung myself at the three men, who pulled away, bewildered. "I know her! Please! Let her be! I know her, I tell you!"

I took hold of her then. She was trembling and sobbing in low tones. "Praised be!" She spoke it over and over again, her eyes tightly closed and hands clenched to her thin body. We stood there all of us silent and immovable, while she recovered herself. Finally, she opened her eyes and looked at me. By now I was the one who was trembling, barely able to stand. This, in truth, had been the final straw. I had hoped Marie Salvatoria would not know me, so that I might slip away and put an end to this misery once and for all, but slowly recognition came into her eyes.

"Dave! Is it really you?" And she embraced my stinking clothes. "Sonofa ... he really does know her." Ripper said, his voice choked with disbelief. "You don't need us, Pop." And the trio melted away, babbling happily that their hunt could continue without further obligation.

Marie led me to a spot along the river bank where she insisted that we sit. She had composed herself almost completely and had taken a quick measure of my general state.

"You are ill. Now, sit," she commanded.

"Don't you know better than to be out alone like this!"

"Of course, but I was looking for work and I misjudged my time. It was quite a scare, but when I saw you.... What are you doing here? Why aren't you at home?"

"I'm just passing through. I'll be on my way, as soon as I get you... where?"

"A barge!" she managed to laugh at my surprise. "Up the river at Fords Landing."

I knew the place. It was a defunct shipyard. River derelicts— old tow boats and barges—for years had been nested along the shore, desolate, half-sunken scrap heaps. What a perfect place for shelter!

"We're all there... except Father. He's dead. But Chip and Doctor Rodgers and Father Herbert and a few others are there. Come! I'll show you. They'll want to see you. Oh, I'm so glad." And she tugged me to my feet. Her face was gay with youthful expectancy, as it had been so much of the time when I used to visit her home.

"I'll take you there so that you will be safe. But I don't wish to see them, any of them."

"But why?"

"Marie... don't you realize what almost happened here?"

"Of course," she replied soberly. "I'm so grateful to you. I'll never be able to thank you."

"Thank me? You blind fool! Don't you understand I was with them? They were doing it for me! I'm not even a human being any more. Don't you see that?"

"I see only that you are a wreck, and you need rest." She looked at me carefully. "And you have nowhere to go, have you? Don't lie."

"My home is here, now. I rob and kill and beg. And tonight.. "Tonight you kept me from harm."

"Sure. But only because I recognized you. Had I not..."

"You still would have saved me." She smiled softly, and took my hand in hers. "You say you've killed someone. Did you do it for fun?"

"No. Of course not."

"Then you would not have harmed any girl... not really. You may have done other things... bad, all of them... but only because you had no other choice, except perhaps to die. But where you still can choose... how would you act? No, you would not deliberately bring harm to anyone ... for fun."

"But I was ready... "

"Were you?"

"I suppose I don't really know, but I know I can't face you or them."

"Face me now." She clutched both of my arms, her fingers digging deeply into my bones. She did not recoil at my face. Her eyes were large and steady. I looked into them, finally. She saw me for what I was and did not flinch.

"Do you think you are the only one who ever had a wicked thought? Don't we have enough... just struggling with things that

have happened, without also struggling with things that only might have happened?"

We walked on then, along rusted railroad tracks. I had the sensation of awaking from a particularly bad dream—groggy, but relieved that it was only a dream. All of this could not have happened. Or did it? In the darkness, outlined against the spotty non-rationed lights of the city across the river, the jumble of wrecked barges and towboats came into view. Once they were useless derelicts, but now they were giving shelter and thus life to people who themselves are derelicts. It was a good omen.

480

Marie led the way around jagged holes in rusted decking and over flimsy planking from one hull to another. Somewhere out of the night a voice called softly, "Halt!"

"It's Marie."

"Oh! We were worried. Come ahead."

We crossed over the last rusted bit of railing onto a barge that stood farthest from the shore. A young man holding a pistol greeted us and waved us below. A soft glow of light filtered out a small hatchway at the stem. We moved down some steep iron steps to the hold below. In the near comer was a large table where candles burned, and elsewhere there were a variety of sleeping accommodations. There were perhaps a couple of dozen persons in the hold.

As we neared the bottom of the steps, a large white-haired man looked up from his book at the table, as did a younger man at his side. The two had been in earnest conversation.

"Ah! There you are at last, Marie." Dr. Rodgers growled. "You missed supper."

"Did you have any luck?" Chip Baker asked.

XI

The Thirty-Second Month

It is quite late, and I sit now at the big table, with one small candle at my elbow. All else is still, save this dancing little flame that wants to be my friend. Above me the rain still beats its exotic tunes upon the rusted deck which, except for a few weak places, keeps us dry. The August storm has brought fresh coolness to this stuffy hold and to the warm, weary world outside. It is as if Nature has turned another page in her book, a fresh new page.

Today, Dr. Rodgers and I visited Larry and Mary Best. The newspaper has been particularly good at covering events of the Great Liberation, which is the latest designation of the new hearings and, of late, the purges that go on nearly every day somewhere in the area. It is not so much the businessmen and bankers any longer. They are all gone. Most of the activity has centered around craftsmen, such as plumbers, carpenters and the like; mill and factory workers, especially the Negroes; wholesale lots of ministers—particularly rabbis and all of the Jews now—and college professors and even a few Party members themselves. It is as if the world out there, once being upheaved, cannot seem to resettle into any orderly pattern.[99] At any

---

99 The author fails to mention agriculture. During this period a massive campaign was underway to collectivise beef and chicken ranches, as well as farms, especially dairy, wheat and corn. Initially the pressure was exerted on the large landowners in the middle west and in the southwest. The effort was not nearly as effective in the northwest, due largely to the mountainous terrain which made resistance to the program easier.

rate, a couple of days ago Larry Best was good for a two-column head-line near the bottom of page one: "Professors Demand Best Resign; W.O.N. Functionary and Teacher Ousted on Treason Charge."

> Dr. Lawrence A. Best, Chairman of William Penn's Political Science Department and prime mover in the early stages of The Great Liberation, today was discharged from the University.
>
> "Professional incompetence" was given as the official reason by Dr. Amos C. Mocker, newly appointed President of the University
>
> The action came after an emotion-packed meeting between the school officials and faculty members late yesterday in which recent JCFLA charges of "treason" were aired.
>
> More than 300 area professors had signed petitions demanding Dr. Best's dismissal, following published findings that the noted educator had "conspired to overthrow the solemn agreements as expressed by two great nations in the Treaty of Friendship."
>
> Specifically, Dr. Best was cited for ...

We get our papers a day or two late these days, so that Dr. Rodgers and I were not at all certain that Mary and Larry would still even be in their university-sponsored home.

"Got to do something about this, Dave," the doctor had said. "It's time you and I saw them again. Think you can walk it?"

I assured him that my strength had returned—a half-truth, but it would only take us an hour or so. I had acquired some cheap cotton trousers and a light shirt. Thanks to the daily loan of Dr. Rodgers' old-fashioned straight razor, I was now consistently clean-shaven, a luxury that gives a considerable boost to a man's self-respect and morale. Also, primitive facilities had been constructed on the barge so that one might bathe in river water every day. Thus, we could look reasonably civilized. Dr. Rodgers still was an imposing figure, though his big frame was more bent and his movements more deliberate and slow. The nature of the times, plus his 67 years of life, were beginning to show plainly now. Only his face, capped with the full white hair, seemed unaffected: alert and strong about the eyes, mouth and chin. The seasoned ageless quality was still there.

We set out about noon. It was one of those flat, dull, listless dog-days that is typical of August, where the sun hangs behind a heavy haze, a ghostly disc of hot orange, and there is not even a trace of a breeze. The air was heavy with dampness and the sky was too still, so that the walking was too hot and not at all enjoyable.

"That's an angry sky," the doctor said as we crossed over the bridge. People were everywhere along the railings holding to long lines of string that had been dropped into the sluggish brown water in the vain hope of snagging some fish. "I don't like it. Could be a bad storm coming."

"I don't like this whole business," I replied. The circumstances of my frantic visit last December after the eviction notice came sharply to mind. Even as Larry was letting me in, before he knew of my trouble, the strained expression of fear on his face had indicated that he did not want to see me. There had been a wildness in his eyes that revealed some terrible torment within him, and the sight of me had merely made matters worse. And when I begged him to take us in, he came apart completely, screaming alternately for me to go away and asking my forgiveness. Mary had come but part way down the stairs dressed in her faded wrapper to stand emptyfaced in some numb state of grief; for she neither did nor said anything to dissuade Larry's barely coherent and rambling pleas that I leave quickly, lest I get him in trouble with the authorities. On departing, I had slammed the door so the whole house shook, and cursed them both. I explained all this to Dr. Rodgers.

We walked in silence for several minutes, out along the desolation of Fifth Avenue with its decayed buildings and masses of broken people with no place to go and no further missions to perform. I felt something new today—grief for these poor blundering souls, instead of myself. For, as we picked our way among them, they met us with unblinking eyes of bewilderment and hurt. A dead street on a dead day, bodies packed closely together going nowhere. It was for them, too, the end of the line.

"They don't understand, do they, Ham?"

"No, God protect them, they don't. And what is more, they never will, so that all of this," Dr. Rodgers swept his arms over the scene, "is truly in vain for them. And what about you, Dave? Is this all in vain, or have you perhaps gained some understanding that will make it easier to bear your burdens?"

"Sometimes I think I understand part of it. Other times nothing makes sense. But I want to find out before I die, Ham... and I doubt there is much time left. It almost seems as if fate threw the book at me, just to see how I'd react."

"And how have you reacted?"

"Badly."

The old scholar chuckled warmly. "A good sign, indeed! My students, especially the freshmen, during the first months of the school year, would go around wearing glazed expressions because they did not understand. The signs of learning would come when, one by one, they would come to me and confess how badly they were doing. Thereafter, things became easier. For they had passed the biggest barrier to learning... brutal assessment of themselves, first. And how will you greet Larry and Mary?"

"I don't know," I said bitterly.

"It must have been as terrible for them as it was for you... the specter of conscious betrayal, turning their backs on old friends and knowing it."

"How does a black pot judge a black kettle?"

"Better to leave the judging to a higher power." We had paused to rest for a moment during our climb up a particularly long rise, and now Dr. Rodgers looked at me sharply. His voice was a low growl. "There already have been too many men playing at being God."

We moved on in thoughtful silence. In the west behind us, low over the horizon, ink-black clouds were forming, while the sky above us had turned a hazy orange that gave an ominous glow to the street of broken dreams. The air was heavy now with the pungent smell of sulphur that came from the coke ovens down along the river. In a while we came to the familiar street where the Bests lived. It was nearly deserted. The old, fading houses along the tree-shaded avenue had a shut-up remote atmosphere as if they were in another world immediately adjacent to ours, but completely out of reach. Different people doubtlessly lived in them now—Party members and those who were still regarded as useful in the Grand Design. Then we were in front of the brick colonial. The shades and drapes were drawn. The door was closed, and nailed to it was a large yellow Notice of Eviction. We rang, and gay door chimes sounded in mockery. After a long moment, the door swung slowly open to reveal Mary Best.

Recognition came to her face slowly but when, at last, she perceived us, the light came into her eyes. Like a lost kitten seeks the comfort of its master, she allowed herself to be enfolded in the doctor's arms, and his big work-roughened hands patted her clumsily. "There, there," he said over and over again, while she murmured nothings, her eyes closed, her face released from its burdens.

"You live still! You are not crumbled and destroyed. And David!" She pulled away from the doctor to look upon me with a sweetness of long ago. She came to me then, and for a moment we clung to each other with desperate tightness. I could feel life within her struggling to reestablish itself. We went inside then where it was still and dark.

"Where is Larry?" I asked.

"Upstairs, in his study. He tried to shoot himself this morning… but he lost his nerve." She fought to keep the tears from her eyes. "He is not the same any more." She looked at me somberly for a moment. "You see, we both know about Nancy. Bad news travels fast. Beth Silkmore came by right at that time looking for food. I guess everyone in No-Man's Land knew about it. Larry was gone for three days looking for you. I was out, too. But we couldn't find you. We thought you were dead. And now we have no place to go. It's our tum, isn't it? And Larry is hardly prepared."

"How is that?" the doctor asked.

"His mind. It comes and goes. He still does not see things as they are. When his mind is functioning he talks, as he's always talked, only it no longer makes any sense. When it isn't functioning he merely sits and stares."

"We have a place for you both," the doctor smiled. "Tell me, what about furniture and other possessions? We must help you trade them for useful items."

She laughed then, a dry, mocking sound. "All of the furniture," she waved grandly, "has been judged to be the property of the university, even though we bought it ourselves. A Bureau of Housing ruling... based on what, I don't know. Something about living in a university house constitutes something or other. So there is nothing to sell other than a few tableware items, some knickknacks, and they will let us keep our clothes and bedding. Our savings, the little we had, were confiscated for non-payment of some sort of new tax somebody discovered that we have not paid. All we have are our Peace Bonds. Lots of them. So there is nothing much. Besides, we're not going with you."

"Come now," I said.

"No, David." She dug at my arm. "I could not... cannot... face you. Not after Nancy." She closed her eyes, and a shudder ran through her. She had dressed herself up in an old cotton frock the lines of which had given back to her something of the tomboy, girl-next-door look. "We killed her, and I am haunted by it."

I caught her wrist in a harsh grip. "If you think I'm sticking you with that responsibility, you had better forget it now. Where do you get off being so smug? You didn't run our lives. You're no great benevolent god charged with the care of Nancy or myself or anyone else."

"Easy, boy," the doctor said sharply. In the distance there was a roll of thunder that rumbled on and on like cannon in a savage battle.

I released her wrists and gently took her hands into mine. They were small, and they trembled. "Nancy might have lived if she had not married me, or if she had not gone to college, or if I had selected another place to live, or if I had ignored the Scouts ... or if we all had gone to Canada. Where do you draw the line, Mary? We each made our choices and our reasons made sense to us at the time. That's the way it has always been and always will be. We choose, or else we let somebody else choose for us. But always a choice is made somewhere, from the day we are born right up to the day we leave this place. And

487

one choice begets another until there is a whole network all knitted together. One knitting flaw in a sweater is barely noticeable ... a hundred flaws, and you have a lousy sweater. So it is with our lives. It's not one bad choice but a whole string of them."

"And when you knit a lousy sweater, you can do one of two things... wear it and pretend the flaws are not there, or not care if they are there ... or throw it out and knit a new one with fewer flaws. We may never get our new sweater knitted, but we're going to try, aren't we, Dave?" Dr. Rodgers intoned gruffly.

"So where would I start knitting and with what?"

"With us on the barge," he replied to her. And he told her where we were.

She laughed then, a long wail. "You expect me to live in a dark hold, like a prisoner. Look at me. And listen. I love the soil and the sky and trees and living creatures all about. Is this in your new sweater? Where is the new green and the fresh winds? Don't you see? I love this land, and it is all gone now, and there is no place for me. Why would you want to torture me more by putting me in a rusting iron prison in a sea of foul people? I am not bent that way."

"But bend you must," the doctor said.

"For what reason? To write books for children? To live again in peace with my dear little animals? Where are the children and the animals now? All day long I have had a feeling about these things," and the strained lines about her eyes and mouth softened, "not an unhappy feeling, oddly. Today, I can think about them again. And there is no pain. Imagine! Now that the university has dealt us the final blow... it's as if somewhere in my mind a giant book has been forever closed. I feel as I used to whenever I finished one of my stories. Suddenly, it was all done, and I could think of other things again. And somehow I feel that I'm all done here... that I don't have to think about Larry or this house or eating or rusty barges. That's why I could look at you both again and feel joy at seeing you as people, not as grave markers. And I have this awful urge to be outside, away from buildings and people. To be way up some place high. To be washed clean by new air."

488

She had thrown her head back, and her eyes were closed. She had cast loose for some faraway shore.

Then a pleasant, cheery voice drifted down the stairs. "Halloo! I do believe I hear David's voice. I say, how very nice of you to call. It so happens I've taken a bit of a breather from the sweaty old classrooms. How opportune that you are here. Mary! Guess who's here? Don't keep him standing. Show him up. Show him up. And bring whoever is with him." And Larry Best moved back to his study on the second floor humming loudly to himself. "Fetch some drinks, too."

Mary stood rigid and white, her face frozen in terror. "No!" she cried. "No more! No more!"

She flung herself from the room and out of the house into the street. Dr. Rodgers and I ran after her, but we were no match. We followed as best we could, but she stayed well ahead of us—up the maze of streets leading to the top of the high hill.

There was a wind now bending the ancient trees as slaves cringe before the whip of an angry master. The orange sky had become boiling black, and mighty bolts of fire flashed from one seething mass to another, ripping the air and shaking the ground with jabbing crashes of sound. Here and there raindrops the size of quarters slammed into us and the pavement like bullets. The going became tougher, for we faced into a wind that sucked the air from our lungs and stung our eyes and raised great yellow clouds of debris—invisible nets to hold us back while Mary, possessed with a super strength, pressed onward. Time had no meaning, and the place was no world I ever saw before. We were struggling in a sky that had assembled all of its weapons and then had tumbled in upon us, pinning us to the earth, so that each step was a lead weight. We barely made her out now—a long, slender reed bending but not breaking. She had entered a small park on the hilltop. Off to our left were the blurred outlines of the great broad arches of the stadium—where Mary and I once had stood to fight another battle and to lose that battle.

Now as we came at last over the crest of the hill we saw her standing into the wind at the base of a lofty poplar tree that stood as bravely as she. Her face and arms were raised upwards, reveling

489

in the sheets of fresh, cool water that swept in waves across the tiny plot of parched earth.

Then it came. The blinding flash of light and the crash and the spinning earth and the fresh smell of ozone. Lights twinkled, dazzling across my eyes in a mad symphony of colors, and my head buzzed with a hundred unearthly sounds. Then, some time later, I raised my head from the muddy earth, even as Dr. Rodgers raised his plastered white thatch like a half-drowned ghost. For the bolt of lightning had flung us to the ground in one last mighty gesture.

She lay near the splintered poplar tree, crumpled like a spent rag doll.

We stood over her, then, and saw that she was no more. The book had been closed.

"Nature gave her life, nurtured her, and now she has reclaimed her quickly and mercifully." I could hear the words plainly as Dr. Rodgers spoke. For the wind had passed on, as had the lightning and the thunder, to some distant place.

All that remained was a subdued rain that fell softly, lest her sleep be disturbed.

So it is night now, and my friend, the candle, burns. Beyond in the darkness of the hold Larry Best sleeps fitfully on a rag bunk—mine. There were really very few personal belongings left. They had sold most everything for food already, so it was no trouble to move Larry out of the house.

2

Those with whom I live in the belly of this barge understandably are a haphazard mixture. For they came together through no particular plan but, rather, through a series of chance meetings not unlike my meeting with Marie. Indeed, it was pure chance that put Chip Baker on the barge in the first place. The day after my last visit at the Salvatoria home, Marie and her father were served with an eviction notice. Since they did not want to place me under any further obligation, they made no effort to contact me and, of course, I was busy helping Larry in the local elections. The Bureau of Housing found two legalities for the action. They were advised through JCFLA Security Agents[100] that illegal tenants were on the property and that the Salvatorias profited illegally thereby, and that the owners were unable to pay a special tax assessment to cover the rising costs of regional government. Except for personal belongings, all household items were to be confiscated in lieu of tax payment. They were given a week to vacate. In that time Chip covered every possibility of finding shelter in No-Man's Land, but having virtually no ready cash, the outlook was hopeless.

Then late one afternoon Chip was set upon by three young men— probably the same ones who befriended me with whiskey because it was near the same bridge where we encountered Marie. They came at him out of the gathering shadows of a cheerless fall dusk. Chip slipped away, but they gave chase up the tracks along the river. In one last attempt to escape he cut desperately across the rails and, leaping from one rusting hulk to another, found refuge here—the only habitable structure, since all of the other hulls were completely filled with water. The city had long since acquired Fords Landing for non-payment of taxes, and it had been planned even before the Treaty of Friendship that this floating junk pile by and by would be hauled away as scrap iron for the steelmaking furnaces—only no one has ever gotten around to it. Also, everyone, including the old and new bums alike, assumed that no suitable shelter existed here.

Actually, the bow end of the barge is stove in, probably from a river collision some years back, so that the forward hold is water-filled. However, a solid bulkhead has kept the stern half of the hull dry, an aft hold roughly twenty-five by eighty feet. There were a number of problems involved in making the hold fit to live in, but the most critical was how to hang onto this shelter, once the hundreds of "transients" in the immediate area found out about it, as they were sure to do.

---

100 Secret Police. The Federal Bureau of Investigation by special act of Congress was reorganised, enlarged and transferred to the JCFLA as part of a move to "upgrade both law enforcement and protection of citizens engaged in peaceful pursuits."

"Naturally, we had every intention of accommodating as many homeless persons as possible," Dr. Rodgers explained the day after my arrival, "but we wanted to pick the most responsible persons we could find and also," he chuckled, "we wanted to keep possession of this place without having our throats slit."

The first task was security, and Chip began a weary search for some of his former companions with whom he had lived before Dr. Rodgers was discharged from the university. In the meantime, the eviction took place as scheduled, and the Salvatoria home was vacated in the dead of night. Father Herbert was with them. His church officialdom had seen fit, probably as a result of JCFLA pressure, to dismiss him from the parish as incompetent. Chip had located an old peddler's pushcart, and into this they piled all personal belongings that had any value. Coming down Mount Washington the cart nearly got away from them. There was a cold drizzle that night, Dr. Rodgers explained, and they lost their footing. The cart began to pull away in wild zigzags. But for Victor Salvatoria, it would have careened over the side of the road to go smashing end over end several hundred feet to the bottom, and it would have been virtually impossible to have recovered their possessions. In one mighty spring the aging and frail Victor had caught hold, and with every muscle straining, he slowed the cart so that the others could grab on to stop the mad plunge.

By then, the long walk already was showing itself to be beyond his endurance, and his struggle with the cart and the slow torturous trip to the bottom of the hill left him no longer able to stand. Even then he continued to protest all efforts to make him ride on the cart. But as they were about to cross the Liberty Bridge, Chip Baker and Father Herbert had their way and lifted the proud old man atop the cart, covering him with an old quilt.

In due course they made it to Fords Landing without attracting any particular attention. They were stopped only once by a patrol car which let them pass on, once it was learned they were going to No-Man's Land. Ragged forms huddled against the cold bothered them not at all as they rumbled through the misty streets of the Land itself. At length, they carried all of their belongings into the barge, and in the midst of the rusting dirt of the hold they made a bed of sorts for Victor, who still remained very weak. As the eastern sky grew light with a new day, he fell into a coma, the result of a massive stroke in all probability, and shortly died, while Father Herbert prayed the blessings of a Church and of a God in whom Victor had never lost faith.

They sewed his body in a piece of stout canvas, and before the sun was yet above the horizon buried him in the river. They none of them could find it in their hearts to be truly sad, any more than they could have been glad. They mourned him for his goodness but were thankful that he had been permitted to pass peacefully from a world that no longer had any use for him, while he was yet a whole man.

In the days that followed, Marie, Father Herbert and Dr. Rodgers scrubbed down the deck of the hold and cleaned the sides of the barge as far as they could. Chip continued his hunt and was successful in finding two of his former companions, Tony Weinberg and Tommy Wong, son of a once industrious Chinese family that had operated a restaurant. Their most valuable possession was a pistol and a dozen rounds of ammunition. With these reinforcements they were able to mount a guard around the clock, and just in time. For a day or so later a gang of toughs had attempted to storm the barge. The pistol turned them back.

Slowly the barge became a reasonably comfortable center. Every few days, as chance meetings dictated, one or two persons were allowed to come aboard, but only with the approval of all concerned. For Dr. Rodgers had insisted on maintaining an orderly procedure in all phases of life in the hold. Occasionally, Chip would balk at some of the choices, but when Dr. Rodgers put it squarely to him as to whom he would rather share the barge with, he would relent. Using tools taken from the Salvatoria house, the barge was made into a livable community. The center of the hold became the eating area where a stove, fashioned from oil drums, was installed, complete with a flue. The forward hold held a quantity of forgotten coal hidden beneath the dark water which provided ample fuel. Tables, benches, stools and low bunks were built from scraps of wood collected after painful search. Most of the periphery of the hold was reserved for sleeping areas screened as best as possible into family groupings or dormitory areas. A latrine shack was constructed on the weather deck and bathing facilities installed in a corner of the hold below. All residents had to agree to contribute their tradable possessions to a central store as a condition of living on the barge. Dr. Rodgers created a Barge Council which planned the day's activities—a detail to go out on trade missions for food and other necessities; a kitchen detail and three others for maintenance, guard duty and job-hunting. The more able-bodied were expected to seek work. Grievance and disciplinary committees were also created along with a rules committee. One of the first decisions of the Council was to prohibit stealing, until such time as there would remain no other choice, when it was agreed to review the matter again. One third of the Council members were selected by Dr. Rodgers and the balance elected by the group.

By late December about 30 persons inhabited the barge. They were able to survive the winter with only three deaths, a woman who suffered appendicitis and two others from heart disease and pneumonia. Larry and I were the most recent additions. While Chip was glad to see me, he protested Larry's presence. But when he learned that I had every intention of keeping him with me wherever we might go, Chip voted in favor of letting Larry stay aboard, at least until his mind became clearer and more rational. I was not particularly pleased at how many of the inhabitants I knew. For a number of them, like me, had figured prominently in the hearings. But as Dr. Rodgers says, where are the more deserving?

With us then are Justin Wright, once a prominent lawyer, judge and president of the bar; Benjamin Zanhorst, former publisher of the *Pittsburgh News-Journal* and his wife; David O. Harmes, former Superintendent of Schools, and his wife and sister; Richard

Malcolm Grant, one of his sons, Sanford J. Grant, and wife, Laura, and the family chauffeur; and—how small the world—the good Reverend Sandmire and his wife Rose, and none other than Avery A. Brown.

There are another ten persons of whom I have never heard. Four young women, three of whom have one surviving parent with them, two fathers and a mother; an elderly couple who apparently knew Dr. Rodgers quite well, and Buster Romakowski, former Secretary of the Amalgamated Workers of America.

This is the group then that each day strives to keep life going. It is not a particularly congenial group. There is a continuing under-current of bitterness which oftentimes gives rise to petty quarreling. On the other hand, there is a general climate of cooperation based on the absolute necessity of working together in order to survive. The day begins for all at six a.m. to allow time for policing of personal effects without interfering with the various work chores of the day. Two meals are served from the meager food stores of corn meal, rice, potatoes and scraps of meat when available. Attempts are made to serve chicken at least once a week, usually Sunday, which is more or less our day off from the bigger chores, when we can properly ap-preciate such a fine meal.

Through special arrangements of the Barge Council, Chip Baker has been given all of July, August and perhaps, September, to devote entirely to his studies under Dr. Rodgers. He is being put through a series of exams in economics, political science and philosophy which, the doctor explained, "are really a series of dissertations to deter-mine the scope and depth of his knowledge... and most importantly, his wisdom. It is time we conducted an inventory. These exercis-es will have to pass for what otherwise should have been the usual procedures for completing the work for his doctorate." The Council—composed of Dr. Rodgers, Chip, Father Herbert, Justin Wright, David O. Harmes, Buster Romakowski and Laura Grant—were generally willing to exempt Chip from normal work schedules, although both Harmes and Romakowski thought the exercises to be a waste of time. Chip, of course, balked right from the beginning, saying, "A man who doesn't work shouldn't eat."

But Dr. Rodgers was adamant. "Gentlemen," he said, "for better than six years now I have worked with this lad, under the most dif-ficult of conditions for him and for me. I should not expect you to understand why we chose to do this, nor will I ask you to render a judgment upon its importance or lack of importance. I shall leave that judgment to history. But I do know that time has all but run out, and I must know the general condition of my—shall we say—investment. While you, Chip, may view this as some sort of vacation, I assure you that you will toil as you have never toiled before. All of us, at one time or another, owe an accounting of ourselves. One such accounting now is due from you to me. As far as the others living here are concerned, let me say that Chip already has done far more than his fair share. But for him none of us would be here in the first place."

So began Chip's weeks of ordeal. Day and night now see him either at a remote spot on the rusted deck above or bent low over the big Council table in the hold. In his company are dozens of books which Dr. Rodgers has managed to keep from his once vast personal library, and Chip pores back and forth through these over and over again. He has lost much of his belligerence, though his toughness and resiliency have matured considerably. He is now almost 25 and stands trim and tall. The arrogant nonchalance that once was his manner has been replaced by an ease of self that is neither overbearing nor careless. He has learned to know himself, and that has given him the right amount of self-confidence that marks him as a leader. The underlying wariness that also has been so much a part of his person is still very much in evidence, only it is now a controlled wariness. His cold blue eyes still take in things in irregular flicks, but the perpetual anger is gone. He is like a slim, finished reed of steel—strong but able to bend without breaking, tempered in the fires of adversity and hammered against the anvil of experience. He is strong, highly disciplined and both incisive and decisive in all that he does. He can speak well but, most important, he can listen well. He is slow to render an opinion but when he does there is no mistaking his views. At the same time he will amend his views, if logic and reason dictate that he should. He has somehow also discovered a gentle humor which can only be attributed to his closeness to Marie. It shows around his eyes and mouth the most—a slow grin and a growing twinkle whenever he is with her. For he loves her deeply, as she does him. Even in the midst of his academic ordeal there is talk of a wedding here on the barge with Father Herbert officiating. Chip

496

Baker is a young man who is able to grow at a time when the world places a penalty on growth.

This is no little achievement, considering whence the young man came. His father, a mill laborer, had been disabled in the prime of life when his right arm and leg were severed by a plant railroad train. There were six children in the family, and Chip was one of the middle ones. His mother had died after the birth of the sixth child. She had hemorrhaged and had received transfusions at the hospital. The blood was contaminated with hepatitis, and the disease killed her. The Baker family was a tight-knit one, though, and Chip's aunt and uncle took them in, even before the father was disabled. The uncle owned a small appliance store, and the income from it, as well as the wages earned by Chip's father, kept them from starving. After the plant accident, Chip's father found employment with Handicapped Industries which, along with compensation payments, kept them going for a while. Then the appliance store went bankrupt, and a few months later Handicapped Industries, a private organization, closed its doors through lack of charitable funds. The Baker family then became solely the responsibility of a continuing stream of social workers from various government agencies.

Through a series of aptitude and attitude tests, it was determined that Chip should learn a trade in electronics. Considerable friction developed because Chip did not want to learn that kind of a trade. He was seventeen then and had set his sights on college. But he could not even sit for entrance exams until he had proper authorization from the Bureau of Education. Whether through bribery or belligerence, I do not know, he secured the authorization after nearly two years of effort and surprised everyone by passing the entrance exams at William Penn. One of the classes in which he enrolled was an elective course in a summary of philosophy under one Dr. Hamilton Rodgers. The attraction between the two was, apparently, immediate. Unable to find employment of any consequence, Chip relied upon a government scholarship as the only means of keeping him in school. For a time things went smoothly enough, until he began to oppose the Treaty of Friendship. This finally led to his expulsion from the university, but the association between him and Dr. Rodgers continued strong and steady. He also was a student of Larry's but I do not believe he is aware that Larry figured prominently in his expulsion. Naturally, 1 will say nothing.

Obviously, there have not been many opportunities for me to visit with Chip since my return to this little fold. But I have grown quite fond of him. He lives his life as if he will live tomorrow and the day after that. When I see him bending to his work, when I see the slow, purposeful way he moves his stubby pencil from book to paper and back again without seeming to tire or falter—I see what I would have liked to have been. It is a sight that gives me true pleasure. Our boy is going to make it! I do not know how, but he will whip them one day. He senses my pleasure, and whenever I pass nearby, he always pauses in his concentration to say a pleasant word. Perhaps he knows that the same fires that temper him temper me also. But there is a difference between fresh steel and old iron; even after being reheated and reworked the old iron is not nearly so useful or enduring.

But there is much to keep me busy. I have been given permanent charge of the trading detail. My knowledge of No-Man's Land, acquired at such a high price, has proved most valuable. We have a fairly broad trading base, thanks largely to Malcolm Grant, Justin Wright and Avery Brown. All three once had been quite wealthy and, while most of this wealth has been confiscated, the residue is most impressive by present standards. We have an abundance of clothing and several handsome silver pieces, along with a sizable number of silver coins. While the coins are kept in central stores, we keep a strict accounting in the name of the owners. We also have a wide variety of hand tools and many usable appliances, along with a few cameras and some art objects. We try to balance the items selected in trading for food so that resources of no one donor are unjustly drawn upon; thus, should a person wish to leave the barge he may take with him from central stores whatever remains of his possessions, and we try to hold as many of his possessions as possible. In fact, we trade from central stores only when the wages which some of the rest earn from time to time are not sufficient to provide two adequate meals each

498

day for everyone. I was able to retrieve my old footlocker from our former neighbor and, except for this Journal and a few clothes, contributed the entire contents to central stores.

Also, I have been much occupied with Larry these past couple of weeks. His mind continues its wanderings in and out of reality. One moment after I have carefully explained the circumstances he seems to comprehend fully the gravity of our situation, and he is gratefully anxious to do his part; the next moment his eyes cloud to take him some place else. We let him rest one full day after we brought him here, but the morning of the next he was put under the care of Justin Wright, who is still a vigorous man of tall build, in his late fifties. Justin had staked out a labor pool assignment to enlarge the Pittsburgh Zoo[101] which promised several weeks of employment. Weinberg, Wong, Zanhorst, Harmes, the younger Grant, Romakowski and Father Herbert, as well as Ham, were part of this work detail. Larry accompanied them in a trancelike condition that caused no end of difficulty. For one thing, he kept wandering away from the excavation in which the men were digging, causing the project supervisor to become increasingly angry. Finally, after a half-dozen such flights, Larry was called severely to task and instead of returning to his shovel, he pulled himself to his tallest and loudly proclaimed, "Perhaps, sir, I have not made clear that I am Doctor Lawrence Best, and I warn you that Smith Armstrong and Nicholas Syerov will not take kindly to this disgraceful treatment." That was as far as he got. The project supervisor smashed him one in the jaw and sent Larry tumbling headlong into the excavation, a new bear den.

Another problem was that Larry was not yet used to manual labor. This, along with the hot, muggy weather, made him tire easily. Once he even tried to fall asleep on the ground. Justin Wright had his hands full keeping Larry on the job and the project supervisor properly soothed with a silver dime as a bribe. Larry, bruised, cut and completely exhausted, slept soundly at least that night. So on those

---

101 One of the continuing projects of the Bureau of Culture. The plan was to upgrade zoos in major cities across the country as major show places where "deserving citizens might enjoy the fruits of their labors in relaxed and pleasant surroundings."

days when his mind does not seem too clear I keep him here with me, and we prowl No-Man's Land and the more respectable Golden Triangle in search of profitable trade. It is a new experience—Larry trotting along at my side, anxious to please and fearful that I might lose him in the crowds.

For Larry the adjustment is particularly severe. He had never been particularly in need. His parents, for example, had been quite wealthy. Even during our college days he never seemed to want for anything, not that he ever abused his affluence. On the contrary he was quite good about sharing. He shared his convertible, his clothes and even his dates with a disarming nonchalance that made you love the guy for his generous nature. He even lent money without ever pressing for its return. I never met his parents. They were divorced. His mother spent much of her time in Europe, and his father—a stockbroker, I think—lived on the West Coast someplace. He was an only child. Perhaps this was what had made us friends in the beginning; Larry had things I would have liked, and—now that I think of it—I must have had something, too, that he missed.

Until yesterday evening I had managed to keep Larry well away from Chip, but following the evening meal he got away from me. The sun had not quite set, and Chip had moved to the cool of the weather deck near the bow, where he worked at the tired old card table that had served us so well at the Salvatoria home. The kitchen mess area was being put to rights and some of the younger people were getting ready for a songfest (we find that group singing helps end the day, the oldtime songs mostly) and I was conferring with Avery Brown on the possible disposition of one of his silver candlesticks, whether the item should be melted down into small ingots or traded as is. The matter did not take long, and since I am always at a loss in trying to involve Mr. Brown in any sort of personal discussion, I excused myself and went topside to join some of the others. Larry was midway down the deck ambling in a careless, loose-jointed way toward Chip who was deeply engrossed. I caught up with him just as he sought Chip's attention.

"Halloo," he waved cheerily. "At it, I see."

Chip flashed him a mild look of disapproval and continued to read. It was Dr. Rodger's book. *The Quality of Life.*

"Weren't you in one of my classes? Yes, of course. Very promising, as I recall. Indeed. Must admire your perseverance, young man. Yes, sir. Scholarship. That's what it takes, y'know." Larry moved in a birdlike fashion to hover over Chip's shoulder, like a proctor in an examination hall at some great university. He has lost considerable weight so that he is a jumble of jagged bones. His fair complexion is peeling raw from his days in the sun, which gives him a red glow that makes me wince. Out in the middle of the river a cabin cruiser churned by towing two carefree water-skiers, a man and woman being cheered on by other men and women in blue uniforms who dangled hither and yon in the boat. The wake sloshed sleepily against the hull of the barge. "Personally, I don't see how you can ever get credit for a doctorate. Shame, of course. Perhaps if you were to stop by my office some afternoon...." He faltered vacantly while Chip shifted uneasily on the rough little bench on which he sat.

"Come, Larry," I said. "We're going to have a songfest soon, and we need you to lead us in a couple of rounds."

"Oh? Excellent." His flaming face broke into a grin of expectancy. "Hate those cornball things they sing. A couple of good English hunting rounds will pep things up! But I'm busy at the moment, David. One of my students has a problem. That is," he faltered absently, "he used to be one of my students. I think." "That's all right, Dr. Best. Feel free to run on." Chip had finally given up his careful notemaking and sighed in resignation.

"No-o-o. Wouldn't think of running out on a student. The group will simply have to wait a bit. Now, what was the problem? Let's see." Once more Larry peered over Chip's shoulder. A slight breeze rustled some of the papers on the table, refreshing us as it went. Soft laughter came from the stern where a number of persons had gathered to talk and loaf. The day had been a good one for all of us, and the urge for fellowship was stronger than usual.

The look on Chip's face changed from irritation to a mixture of curiosity and mild amusement. Slowly he extracted a sheet of paper from the litter and handed it to Larry. "I'm having trouble with these. It's part of a series of exams I've been writing. I would welcome your suggestions."

With a slight cough of pleasure, Larry took the paper and studied it eagerly. He read it several times, each time his face grew more and more perplexed. Marie had come upon us then, looking tall, slender and cool in a freshly laundered summer frock. Her wholesome face sparkled from her evening bath, and her large brown eyes were soft with contentment as she brushed her hand along Chip's shoulder and bent to kiss him lightly on the forehead. She said nothing but watched with puzzled interest.

"How would you suggest I answer them, Doctor?" Chip prodded softly.

"Well." Larry waved the paper depreciatively. "Of course... ah. Elementary. My goodness. What's the sense in having questions that are based on..." his long arm waved aimlessly as he fished for a fitting word, "opinions? You should have no problem, at all. They're irrelevant. Hardly fitting for doctoral discussions. Facts! We deal with facts, not this sort of thing." He paused, more perplexed now by Chip's unabashed smile than by the paper. "Well... English rounds, you say? Well, Marie! How nice to see you. I understand the group wants to learn English rounds. Perhaps we should join the others." And Larry ambled away.

"Chip, what have you been up to? Teasing him like that!" Marie scolded. "The poor man is ill. You should be nice to him."

He laughed and his strong bronze arm encircled her tiny waist, which in contrast made his big hand look twice its size. "Nice to him? Why?"

"It costs you nothing, does it?" she replied with the quiet simplicity that so strongly marks her nature.

"Only time." He shook his head in mock agony and sighed, "Ah, Marie, you'll soon have me as sodden as watersoaked bread. Now scat before I swat your little behind."

"Until ten o'clock, and then I'm going to throw those old books in the river. I'm beginning to hate them," she teased.

502

We caught up with Larry, then, and joined the others.

Later, I asked Chip if I might see the paper which was part of a thick packet. It was written in Dr. Rodgers' firm, neat hand and at the top bore a subhead: "Part IV—Value Assessments, continued. Use at least one reference each from the Classical, Romance and Contemporary periods to substantiate each of the points of view given."

Following this was a series of questions grouped as follows:

- *What are the differences between conformity and self-discipline?*
- *To what extent is each a desirable and/or a necessary ingredient in determining the quality of life?*
- *To what extent is the quality of life governed by the ability to distinguish between the real world and the ideal world?*
- *What is the relationship between realism and idealism as it affects the quality of life?*
- *What is a group?*
- *What is an individual?*
- *Which is the basic unit of human society, the group or the individual?*
- *In terms of the absolute, if the function of the group is abolished can the individual remain functional? Likewise, if the function of the individual is abolished can the group remain functional?*
- *What is a principle, and should a principle be a principle all of the time? In the sense of a truism, can a principle be a principle all of the time; in the sense of reality, is it ever?*
- *To what extent is self-help desirable?*
- *At which point should the group take over: that point where an individual cannot do for himself or that point where an individual will not do for himself?*
- *What is opportunity? Of what does it consist? To what extent is the phrase "equal opportunity" valid?*
- *Is materialism the product or by-product of intellectual effort? Should the instruments of political society limit the powers of government (citing what it shall not do) or grant the powers of government (citing what it shall do)?*

3

Every now and then I awaken in the middle of the night, and in those first few moments when the dormant mind struggles to become conscious I give thanks that all of this has been a super-deluxe nightmare and expect that any moment now I will hear the dog bark or the children stir restlessly in their beds; or if my sleep has been particularly deep, I might think myself home in the tiny junk-cluttered bedroom expecting brother Harry to rouse me with some absolutely nonsensical thought. But after a moment of this fools' gold, the realities come flooding back, and for an instant I am suffocating like a drowning man. The others about me in the hold occasionally do the same. They flail in their bunks, call out to someone now gone and then sit up in a slow daze, as if they wish to be absolutely certain they are where they are. And then like me, they stretch out once again, this time not to sleep, but to ponder the alpha, the omega, the whole bit.

Why all of this?

Because of Chip's solitary academic preoccupations, I have had opportunities for quiet discussions with Ham Rodgers that might not otherwise have occurred. I find him easy to talk with and exciting to listen to, because each conversation is like an expedition into an unknown which does not present fear, but where one can be completely at ease to let the mind bobble along, ranging at will. It is paradoxical that in these moments I feel a greater sense of freedom than I have ever known.

The other evening I brought the subject up.

"You've observed us all, I know, bickering with each other and moaning in our sleep ... all of us trying to fathom our lot. There's not one among us who doesn't crave to know why and how all of this came to be. We're suspicious and bitter and confused and afraid. Except you, Ham. You don't bicker. You're not bitter. You're hot afraid."

We were sitting on deck, and the sun was all gone. The night was still, and a big moon fought to shine through the August haze as it climbed over the tall office buildings across the river from us. The white of the old man's hair was iridescent, and the lines marking his big face were softened in the glow.

"I did my weeping a long time ago, and for a long time, too. I fought it... this drift to insanity, this flight from reason. Tell them, I thought. Sound the alarm, and they will respond. But few did, and I could only resign myself to the inevitable."

"But why?" I asked. "Why didn't they listen?"

504

He was silent for a long moment, folding and unfolding his heavy hands. "I finally tumbled to it. They did not understand what I was talking about, because I was unable to communicate with them. You see, each of us has a language all his own, and this is because each of us has values all his own, of one sort or another, even if one of our values is to have no values. Everything we do or say or think stems from these values. If your values and mine are reasonably well aligned, then we have a fair chance to communicate our respective thoughts with some effectiveness, provided we are of a mind to. But if our systems of values are different, then our interpretations of words and thoughts and deeds are different, too. Try as we might, communication is impossible under those conditions."

"I can't believe that. Surely a man with your gifts could communicate... well, with anyone here, for instance."

Again he was silent for a time. In the distance, out from the hills to the east, came faint echoes of rifle fire. It lasted but a moment and then all was still. "Are you game for a little experiment?" he asked.

"To prove me wrong, of course. But you're on. What will it be?"

"Let's find Larry, first. How has he been today?"

I explained that he had been much less vague during this particular day and certainly more fully aware of his circumstances than he had been at any other time since he came among us. This brought a nod of satisfaction to Dr. Rodgers. We found Larry chatting quietly with young Tommy Wong who was standing guard near the stern. After a few pleasantries, Dr. Rodgers got to the point.

"Dave and I are having a bit of discussion on the nature of man. Perhaps you can help us. Is man—when left entirely unto himself without any outside forces acting either for him or against him—inherently good or inherently bad?" resume here ***

Larry's answer was sharp and instantaneous. "He is inherently good, if the forces about him would only leave him alone."

"Yes, I see," Ham replied evenly. "Suppose I were to suggest that man—left entirely unto himself, is inherently bad and that he needs a voluntary system to keep himself both in check and in proper balance with respect to his fellow men?"

505

Again, Larry's response was immediate, the excitement of debate beginning to work through him. "Checks and balances are bloody nuisances. You do an injustice, sir, to the human race." He spoke with emphatic dignity. "To deny the noble aspirations of men everywhere? To accuse man of being despicable and evil? I say, shame on you!" Larry's voice had risen to a vibrant pitch of sufferance. Forgotten was the barge and this world. He was moving back to his old, comfortable, free-swinging universe again.

"I have not said that man does not aspire to be noble," Ham said. "I merely suggest that man might be inclined to commit evil acts ... if he thinks he will go absolutely unpunished. Just for fun, I might even add the possibility that perhaps true nobleness comes only when a man recognizes his weaknesses and voluntarily holds himself in check. And even then," he sighed wearily, "the most noble of men under the right circumstances have been known to betray their fellow men... when they thought they could get away with it." Dr. Rodgers kept his voice deliberately soft, as if in deference to Larry's precarious emotional state. He paused for a moment and then asked, "Back in the days when all of us drove cars, how many of us would have put our nickels in the parking meters if we knew we would not be ticketed for a meter violation? If all the policemen had been ordered to ignore the parking meters, how many people would have still dutifully inserted their nickels into the meters?"

"Not many," Larry managed an easy grin. "But I don't understand what parking meters have to do with the nobleness of man."

"Well, the question is a little academic now, I suppose," Dr. Rodgers smiled. "So, let's assume your position is correct. Man is inherently good. It could be assumed then that environment—and I'm excluding the raw natural environment of climate, geography, soil conditions, the weather and such—creates the character of man..."

"You can include all environment if you want," Larry interrupted.

"No. Hear the rest of the question. That unnatural environment creates the character of the man ... or does man create the character of the environment?"

"There's no yes or no answer to that," Larry replied pleasantly. A spark of his old self was being rekindled.

"Well, come as close as you can with a general statement, recognizing that one or the other obviously has varying degrees of effect on things... still one of them, in my view, must dominate the other, would you not agree?"

Larry thought for a moment and finally nodded. Tommy Wong had been watching the conversation as if it were a tennis match and he was sitting midcourt. His almond eyes were almost round and were bright in the moonlight.

"Environment, of course, dominates. Too much evidence. Look at what slums do to people... hatred, violence, ignorance," Larry responded.

"Ah! Exactly!" Ham beamed. "Take an unproductive man from an ugly listless environment and surround him with a pleasant, stimulating environment, and this will change him?"

"Precisely." Larry replied. "Urban renewal plans are based on that concept. Worked on that for many years."

"Indeed. Some of the public housing projects have shown some spectacular results over the years," Ham said softly. "And take a sensitive, insecure, and sometimes violent Sino-Soviet empire and surround it with a pleasant, stimulating environment, and the empire will forget its wicked ways ... for the forces of the world now leave it alone... and its character will change into sweetness and light. Is that not so, Professor Best?"

"I don't think I understand you." Larry blinked. The spark faded. "You're obviously trying to confuse the issues."

"Never mind. It is no longer of any great consequence."

We moved along, then, to seek out the Reverend Arthur Sandmire, formerly my minister, to whom I had once turned for guidance and whose word was: Endure. And so he himself had thus far endured—none too gracefully, but he was still generally intact. At some point following his dismissal from his church he had denounced God. He had not yet renounced the Creator but had simply charged him with wholesale betrayal of His flock—the faithful, like himself, who had

507

served so well and who clearly did not deserve such foul treatment. "Our God has forsaken us, even as He had once forsaken His only Begotten Son!" the Reverend Mr. Sandmire now intones at least once every day. His voice has grown old and squeaky, and of late he has been making this pronouncement from the bottom of the excavation that he and the others are digging out at the zoo. He does this usually in the late afternoon when the heat of the day is at its ugliest, and the men are exhausted and in deep thirst and soaked in muddy sweat. He has somehow managed to hang unto his round—perfectly round— horn-rimmed glasses. He looks more like an owl than ever, because he has lost much weight, and nearly all of his teeth are gone, so that his face is terribly shrunken, except the roundness around his eyes. There is little about him now to suggest the syrupy, peaceful calm that once was his stock in trade. He never smiles, and he fidgets a lot. He complains much of the time that he is being unfairly treated in terms of food servings, sleeping space and the fact that he is allowed no money for liquor. He regards Father Herbert as a heretic and Marie, Chip, Ham, and me as being godless and selfish. Still, he cooperates and does the work assigned to him. He seldom speaks to his wife Rose, who is a very thin, quiet woman. While she helps with chores, she is almost totally withdrawn and, in all likelihood, will one day soon simply give up altogether and die. I recall they had three children, but the Sandmires never speak of them. We found him also on deck, sitting on the rusty hatch, mumbling at the rising moon.

"How are you tonight, Mr. Sandmire?"

"Eh? Oh, 's you, Rodgers." His squeaky voice was slurred, and he rose unsteadily to his feet. One way or another he had found the means to acquire some whiskey. I made a mental note to check central stores for any missing items. We none of us have any objection to whiskey, except that we have decided to reserve our trading resources only for the bare necessities, in order to keep going as long as possible. "Ahem. Been meaning to talk to you about th' mighty Charles Baker. He threatened me with bodily harm tonight, and that upstart mus' be taught a stern lesson!"

508

"How was that?" Ham asked.

"Throw m' in th' river. Tha's what he wanted to do." Sandmire lurched back to his seat. "I have every right to know what he's up to… all that writin' and me workin' so he can do nothin'." His forefinger wagged upward in oscillating indignation. "Don't disturb me, he says, like some high monkey-monk. Pfsst!" He ran his ragged sleeve over his mouth.

"Endure, Reverend. One must endure," I said.

"Whazzat? Who's pure?"

"Never mind. Dr. Rodgers has a question." I looked at Ham who was working to maintain an absolutely neutral composure. He nodded.

"Dave and I were having a little discussion about Christian ethics. Thought you could help us."

"Pfsst! What do you know about it? And he never supported the church worth a damn." Sandmire wagged his head at me.

"Let's say we know nothing. That's why we're seeking your guidance," the doctor replied.

Sandmire's glasses had picked up the image of the moon, so that two moons were reflected back to us. He straightened himself. "Ahem. Indeed. Proceed."

"Define Christian love."

"Is that all?" He thought for a moment. "Christian love… ahem … is to give 'til it hurts."

"What about denial?"

"Denial? That's what I say. To love is to give to those who are denied."

"No, no. Is love ever in the form of a denial? To deny someone something?"

"You don't make sense, Rodgers," Sandmire growled. "It is more blessed to give than receive. That's love. Now, does that sound like denial?"

"While we're on that subject," the doctor rumbled good-naturedly, "if it is more blessed to give, then it must be less blessed to receive. Surely there must be some heavenly qualifications which

509

the receivers of gifts must live up to ... if they are ever to gain eternal life, and there are lots of receivers these days. What

are the qualifications of the receivers for a Christian life? Ever preach a sermon on that?"

"Rodgers, I don't even understand what you're talking about. You'll have to be a lit' more specific. Are y' gonna do anything about Baker or not?"

"What do you think, Dave? The lash for Chip?" Dr. Rodgers rubbed his heavy hand over his chin.

"Too mild. I think his fingers should be broken one at a time. That way he won't be able to write," I answered, but Sandmire did not think us funny.

"Make light of me, will you! It's selfish people like you who have done this to us. You'll be punished. God will not long keep His back turned to us. He will redeem His children and punish the rest of you. You'll see." And Sandmire moved on down the deck. In the moonlight he looked like a marionette hanging from slack, jerky strings.

"True, and may we all have the wisdom to recognize our punishments," Ham rumbled. "Come, Dave, let's try one or two more and see how well we communicate." And the big man clumped along the deck upon which most of our barge group were now gathered in small knots taking in the fresh night, some sitting, others standing, some talking, others saying nothing—cold, bloodless figures in the white light of the moon, motionless for the most part, like sculptured ghosts. As we passed among them, nearly all had a soft, pleasant greeting for Dr. Rodgers that revealed a measure of respect and gratitude toward him. Perhaps it was the contrast of the white light and shadows that made me more acutely aware of the difficulty the old gentleman had in walking. He seemed to become more and more bent. His step seemed to get heavier and more measured with a growing shuffle, as if his legs were becoming too stiff and weak to carry him too far for too long. I had not realized how thin he was getting, either. But he spurned my suggestion to sit and rest for a moment. He had spied the tall, brittle form of Malcolm Grant standing alone along the bent fragments of a railing on the river side of the barge.

510

The man was almost completely bald so that his head looked like white marble. He was now close to 70 years old and, while dreadfully thin, he seemed to have enormous reserves of strength that could only come from the marrow of his bones, for he had apparently fully recovered from his emotional collapse, following his condemnation at the hearing two years ago, when even his closest friends in the Allegheny Committee for American Action testified against him, as did his sons.

"Good evening, Mr. Grant."

He turned his face slowly away from the quiet city across the sluggish waters, as if we had shattered some recollection out of the distant past. His features were as unyielding as ever.

"Dr. Rodgers. Mr. Little." He acknowledged stiffly. His voice was thin and wavery, but it was still strong.

"We're having a little discussion on the ethics of voluntary association, and we should like your views on one point."

"If you want me to associate with some of these friends of yours, kindly put it out of your mind."

"Nothing like that, I assure you," Ham responded amiably, "although we can't all of us be all bad."

"Voluntary association! Who is there to associate with? A long time ago I swore I would have nothing to do with ignorant dupes who cook up phony issues and phony solutions. There is certainly no reason to change now."

"Sometimes voluntary association can be a very good thing, even with ignorant dupes, if you can get them to understand at least part of your own point of view."

"Association with responsible people, yes, and I pride myself on that, but to tarnish my principles by associating with irresponsible troublemakers ... don't ask me to lower myself ..."

"I repeat," the doctor interrupted sternly. "We do not ask you to associate with anyone here, except as it applies to our respective duties, and you do your share very well. But I wish to ask you this question: Can wholesome change be achieved through prudent compromise?"

511

The brittle old man looked at us with stem disapproval. "Changes, if they must come, take care of themselves. When they are forced through compromise," he waved his sticklike arm at the dying city, "Well, look around you. Compromise? Bah!"

"I said *prudent* compromise to achieve *wholesome* change." "There is no such thing."

"Oh," the doctor answered ever so softly. "You must have courted your late wife some before your married her. You mean to say you never had a discussion, maybe even an argument, over something . .. whether to go on a picnic or not, or sit in the parlor, or go for a walk? No prudent compromise in courtship or married life or dealing with your former customers?"

Malcolm Grant trembled slightly to hold back hints of growing rage. "I'll thank you not to pry into my personal affairs. What has courtship to do with all of this? You don't make sense."

He turned again to stand stiffly at the broken railing, his thin lips compressed into a straight line and his marble face once more intent upon the city.

We found Benjamin Zanhorst sitting crosslegged on the deck talking with young Tony Weinberg and one of the four young women who were staying with us. Her name was Alice Bomer, an attractive redhead. Zanhorst has lost much of his solidarity due to loss of weight. Once a heavyset man of square build, his clothes now hang on him as loosely as the flesh of his arms and face. At some point he had lost his magnificent, heavy shell-rimmed glasses that had done so much to enhance his image of sincerity and integrity, so that now he squints his nearsighted eyes in order to make things out. He was in the process of telling a story about his days as a reporter when Dr. Rodgers interrupted him with another of his questions.

"Would you agree to the proposition that private possessions .. . private property in the most broad meaning of possessing, using and disposing of things ... is indispensable to the quality of life?" "I don't think it's all that important. If anything," Zanhorst chuckled, "the whole idea of private property has done more harm than good."

"If that is so, how does a person exercise the maximum of his will and choice if he is not able to possess, use and dispose of things?"

"Oh, you eggheads. Always trying to embarrass us common people with your fancy questions. So, okay, I don't know what you're talking about. So who cares?"

We saw Justin Wright next, and Dr. Rodgers' question was: "Should laws rule over men or should men rule over laws?"

"I don't think I understand your question," the lawyer replied. "I revere the law, though. I miss it."

"How could you miss it? It has been very busy lately," Dr. Rodgers concluded.

Then the experiment was over, and Ham and I seated ourselves on two iron stanchions. For a long time we did not speak. It was enough to watch the moon in its upward climb. There was no hint of a breeze. The steel deck still radiated warmth that the hot sun had stored there during the day, which meant that the hold was still hot and stuffy so that most of the people were trying to make themselves comfortable on deck for a night of rest.

"Well?" I asked.

"When values become twisted, so do men's thoughts, words and deeds," the doctor rumbled more to himself than to me. "If one man believes that denial is as much a part of love as giving, and another man believes that love is manifested only through giving... how do they both agree on handling the unruly teenager who wants the keys to the family car before he knows how to drive, or the criminal who simply wants out of jail, or the African nation that wants unbridled freedom to live as Western nations do ... or did . .. before it has ac-quired the experience for it?

"If one man believes that the best way to upgrade poverty-strick-en people is through the creation of more private property for these people, and the other man believes that progress is made through the elimination of private possessions... how do they both agree on the orderly procedures of our economic world?

"If one man believes that the character of our unnatural environ-ment is determined by men acting to change the environment and

513

another man believes in inflicting a pre-selected environment in order to improve mankind... how do they agree on the role of government? After all, did Edison, through his intellect and will, choose to invent the electric lamp and in so doing change the environment of the world? Or did a committee of supermen change the environment first in order to direct Edison to come forth with the device?"

"If I recall my history, Edison was thought to be a nut, and he played hell getting the city of New York to cooperate with him," I said.

"There are many others... men and women through the centuries who acted, often in opposition to organized society, to change the environment for the better. No, Dave, if we are ever to regain that which we have lost we must first regain our values. And it will not be easy. There is only one way to assess our values and that is to know the truth about ourselves ... as we are ... not as we think we are. And there are few men willing to accept this kind of punishment but, praise be, there are at least some who care enough to learn."

We talked through much of the night then, for Dr. Rodgers had opened a floodgate in my head and the thoughts and questions came tumbling out.

XII

The Thirty-Fifth Month

It is my turn at the guard. Again, the candle at my elbow seeks my friendship and I, its. For it is drafty cold here at the foot of the companionway—the raw, wet kind that chills and stiffens the bones and makes the flesh numb and blue. I keep my knife ready, lest there be a suspicious sound from those who seem to sleep. They would as soon do me in as not if it enabled them to get to the one I am charged to protect, at least until the trial tomorrow, who sleeps at my feet bundled in a heavy coat and blanket. By dawn it will be dreadfully cold. Our precious supply of coal is nearly gone, and it is severely rationed for use in our oil drum stove for cooking only. The rest of the time we must rely on the dying embers to warm ourselves.

But Father Herbert and Chip Baker must be even more uncomfortable. They both are standing watch up on deck in the cold November rain that for two days now has refused to move on to torment someone else. Three nights in a row attempts have been made by marauding bands of desperate vagrants—now more animal than human—to storm the barge and butcher us for the few remaining treasures we possess. It was necessary to kill one poor devil last night. Tony Weinberg and I were on the guard then. A dozen or so forms came at us through the black wet, slipping silently over the wasted hulks that separate the barge from shore. They were men mostly, we think, although the shrill cries revealed some women, too. "Kill them all!" they called back and forth in harsh whispers to one another. "They deny us food and a place to sleep. They deserve to die."

We warned them again and again. But when the first form gained our railing there was nothing else to do. I waited until the form, hooded against the wet, was close enough so I could shoot between the eyes. Death had to be instant. To have sent this nameless, faceless thing crawling away wounded would have been diabolically cruel. The body slipped between the beached wreckage and dropped like a stone into the water, mercifully without uttering a sound. The band melted away then, and no further attempts have been made since then.

The strain is beginning to tell on some. We are able to entrust guard duty to only seven of us. Larry is too mentally unstable, and while he is increasingly anxious to please these days and keeps offering, we cannot rely on his alertness. And Dr. Rodgers is much too ill—though he keeps demanding that he be given his turn, which presents some major problems in keeping him in his bunk, particularly for Marie and Alice who are the only two younger women we can rely upon to look after him. The rest, all of them, would tear the place—and each other—apart if we gave them the chance. Yet we are reluctant to force them all to leave. For we do have enough space to shelter them, and they still represent probably the best companions that are presently available. So we also keep a guard in the hold to maintain order below deck.

The summer months had created no particularly grave problems in discipline. But in early October the zoo project had been abandoned at least until next spring, and the labor pool requirements were drastically reduced. All that was open now was to volunteer for the IWA,[102] but only a desperate fool would do such a thing, since we hear that men usually die within a matter of months after being as-

---

102 The International Work Army was an international labour pool. Persons unable to find employment could volunteer for manual labour duty at various camps around the world. Records indicate a person had to enlist for at least three years. Based on fairly complete historical documentation, it is established that food, lodging and a small spending allowance were provided, but conditions were little better than those in prison camps.

signed to work camps, most of which are located in South America, southeast Asia and Africa. So many of us went, first, to begging and now a few to the inevitable—stealing.

It began right in our own hold when Avery Brown and David Harmes tried to make off with our small supply of coins. They made the attempt in the middle of the night and would have been successful except that they dropped a few which rained across the steel floor in a resounding crescendo of sound that set people tumbling in every direction. It took the rest of the night to quell the riot. The result was that everyone, including a majority of the members of the Council, wanted his possessions—whatever still remained—returned to him from central stores. So it was decided that from then on each one would do his own private trading and secure and cook and eat his own food. As one might suspect, there was a grand rush to live it up—liquor mostly and some marijuana, which we try to keep under control.

Some, of course, ran through their possessions more quickly than others, so the stealing began. Of our three young women, excluding Marie and Alice, two of them are now pregnant and God knows what else. Since it is too cold for comfortable bathing, people do not wash quite so often, but we still are able to keep the hold reasonably free of litter, one reason being that almost everything has some value as an item of barter, even old newspapers. Also, the seven of us men demand daily policing up.

It has become increasingly obvious that we cannot stay here too much longer. With luck we might possibly last through the winter, but the competition for dwindling jobs and tradable resources will be so severe by spring as to make life in Pittsburgh all but impossible. "Obviously, we must think about moving on," Ham had said one night several weeks ago. Marie, Chip, Father Herbert and I had been sitting with him around the Council table trying to figure out how to make our own resources last. Most of the hand tools on the barge had belonged to Marie's father and represented a fairly respectable trading inventory. To our surprise, Father Herbert went to his bunk and returned with a worn map of the United States. "Here." His thick

517

finger poked to a point on the paper. "I've been thinking about this for over a year now. The Wind River Range out in Wyoming. Used to hunt and fish through there regularly. It's not the easiest place to get to but, unless things have changed an awful lot, there's fish and game, and we would be about as remote as we can be from the power centers."

We sat far into the night discussing the matter, finally agreeing that it might be worth a try. It would be necessary to use the rivers as far west as possible and go overland from, say, the headwaters of the Missouri. This, of course, meant that we would need to find a boat or a raft capable of such a journey—an almost impossible task. But the plan, wild though it seemed, gave us plenty to think about.

During the next several days we combed the city in search of some kind of water craft but without luck. It was then that Ham got soaked in the rains and developed a fever and chest cold which has kept him confined to his bunk for nearly two weeks now. We are concerned, because he does not seem to be getting any better.

Then, to add to our difficulties, we acquired a new guest this morning.

Avery Brown, David Harmes, young Sanford Grant and his wife Laura, in recent weeks, have taken to the camaraderie of carousing almost every night in the blazing heart of No-Man's Land. By present standards they are liberal spenders and seem to care little that their tradable possessions are fast dwindling, a source of great unhappiness to us all and particularly discomforting to Malcolm Grant, who can only watch with mounting fury as his younger and only surviving son—Malcolm, Jr. having died of something—gradually dissipates the only legacy he will ever have on so base an occupation. From all I have heard, the nightly saloon crawling has been helpful to Avery Brown's ego if nothing else. He still owns one suit, blue and of good quality, although a bit stained and rumpled, and he has managed to hang on to his Homburg, likewise somewhat soiled and a bit soft in the crown here and there, but a genuine Homburg all the same. He is not quite as mild-appearing as he used to be back when he was chairman of the board, although he manages to preserve something

518

of his former dignity by wearing a pince-nez he picked up someplace to replace his heavy glasses which had been smashed during a scuffle over the contents of a garbage can—this before he came to the barge. There is little left of his celebrated even temperament. He has acquired a vicious temper of late, demanding, as he puts it, "more respect and consideration for a man of my station."

Mr. Harmes, also once a slight, timid man, has endeared himself to Brown by catering to his every whim, even at the expense of ignoring his still plump wife Doris who, like her mate, is somewhere in her fifties.

The younger Grants have become sloppy and loud. Sanford still has something remaining of his dark good looks. Laura still has an outstanding figure and manages to show it off in the one white sequined cocktail dress she still owns. It, too, is becoming a bit soiled and worn, but when she wears it on these nightly sorties, she looks relatively stunning, considering the environment around her.

Sanford still owns a tux. It is an unbelievable sight when the four of them get decked out for the evening. A Homburg, a pince-nez, a couple of rumpled blue suits, one tired tux and a slinky once-white cocktail dress set against the dreary background of the rusty barge. Like kids playing dress-up on Saturday morning.

As a rule the gay, svelte quartet comes rolling home across the half-sunken hulls before dawn, barely, to clatter down into the hold at the expense of all who are trying to put off as long as possible the chore of facing yet another day. We had ruled out their bringing new-found friends aboard. Both Brown and Harmes were particularly unpleasant about this, since they were acquiring an ever-growing circle of female acquaintances but lacked suitable quarters for informal entertaining which, perhaps, had become their most frustrating cross to bear.

But this morning they were late. Breakfast time was over, and the hold already had been policed up when Tommy Wong called from his guard post on deck. Several of us dashed topside carrying clubs and knives, expecting the worst. The morning was drizzle-grey with everything shrouded in misty, fine rain. And slipping and sliding over

519

the junk steel forms came the quartet, each warning the others in superloud voices to take it easy. Brown led the way, his Homburg jammed on the back of his head and the rain-dripping pince-nez still clinging to his nose. Harmes lurched along at his side, his thin strands of hair plastered to his forehead, while the Grants flailed along behind. But that was not what startled us.

For preceding them was another man, short in stature and wearing a heavy overcoat and new boots. He moved haltingly as if uncertain that his legs could carry him any further. His bareheaded countenance revealed that he had been beaten about the face and neck. Most of him was mud-soaked. A length of rope had been noosed around his neck, the end of which was held by Brown, and his hands were tied behind him.

"Gangway!" Brown called. "We've got a real prize. Get everyone together. Tell them we've got something special."

A dozen eager hands pulled the stumbling prisoner over the railing, while I pushed my way through to quiet everyone against attracting too much attention from the river patrol—which, incidentally, except for one quick halfhearted inspection had never bothered us. Then I was face to face with the bound man, and for a long moment we looked at each other without a sound. While his tinted glasses were gone, there was no mistaking the heavy facial features, the heavy black eyebrows and the uncombed hair. He had borne his ordeal impassively and with a trace of contempt for his captors. And he stood now waiting without any outward emotion, his black eyes looking unblinkingly into mine.

"Welcome aboard, Mr. Tidings."

"Thank you, Mr.... ah... Little."

"All right, Avery," I sighed wearily. "Where did you get him?"

"We won him in a crap game," Laura shrieked loudly.

"A what?"

"She's right," Brown beamed in the first outward show of honest pleasure since coming here. "Tidings got thrown out of the Party, and like the rest of us he wound up in No-Man's Land. Somebody recognized him. So we shot craps for him."

"But why?"

"Why?" Sanford Grant snapped. "To see who gets to kill him! Why else?"

"Are they telling the truth?" I turned to Tidings.

"Yes. You are surprised? Don't be. I did not measure up during this last election.[103] Rules are rules, and they had to let me go. I would have done the same thing myself." A wry half-smile cracked the dried mud and blood on his face. "Pity I didn't have you to help."

Chip had arrived by then, and we hustled the prisoner into the hold. By now the full meaning of Tidings' presence had begun to sink into the consciousness of the barge group. *Think of it! We have one of the enemy to do with as we please!* It was in their eyes, the way they sparkled with half-mad glee as one grinning head turned to another to whisper the Good News. It was in the way their tongues licked their lips, slyly and eagerly, as if a sumptuous feast awaited them. It was in the way they all pressed back into the hold to get a better look at the short, stocky man who had not yet lost his well fed appearance.

The good Reverend Mr. Sandmire set the pace. He pushed everyone aside, his sunken, toothless face cracked in a wide grin. His perfectly round glasses magnified the exalted triumph in his eyes. "So, thou blasphemous wretch, thou agent of the devil, judgment is upon you, eh?"

The group shouted its approval while Chip, Father Herbert, Marie and I held a hasty conference.

"Filth! Doer of evil deeds! Killer of children and men! May you be damned to everlasting hell!" the Reverend Mr. Sandmire shrieked.

"Let's kill him now," a voice suggested.

---

103 This was the second Congressional election after the Treaty of Friendship was ratified. It was imperative to the time table of the revolution that at least "ninety percent of the newly elected House of Representatives be members of the Communist Party of America, instead of the forty percent achieved in the presidential election two years earlier." (See Appendix, excerpts from *Achieving the Revolution in America*.) However, the CPA achieved only a seventy-eight percent majority, which resulted in a substantial purge of Party functionaries. The situation was later corrected through the wholesale use of impeachment proceedings brought against the remaining members of the Coalition Party still serving Congress, who then were replaced by appointees of the CPA.

"No. Wait a bit. We've got to think of a nice, slow way," said another.

"Break his bones one at a time."

"I wanna hear him scream . .

"And beg . .

"Yes, we mustn't be hasty."

"Exactly." I spoke firmly and loudly and pushed my way into the circle next to Tidings. Tommy Wong had slipped me the pistol. "Larry, Tony, Justin Wright and you, too, Romakowski! Get over with Chip Baker and be ready to help me keep order." Neither Wright nor Romakowski moved. They were both transfixed by the wonder of it all; the one, a tall, gaunt man still with the quiet dignity of an English barrister; the other, big and husky still with a florid square face that bore the lines of tough stubbornness.

"Make up your minds, you two. With us or against us... now!" And for a moment our eyes locked in combat—theirs looking like those of cats from whom you are about to remove half-dead birds they have captured. After a moment they shook the spell and moved away from the group. I began to work the noose off Tidings' neck.

"I wouldn't." It was Avery Brown who called out. He shoved Sandmire aside and stood glaring at me. "He's mine, and I brought him back for everyone. He deserves to die."

"Undoubtedly he does, Avery, but we're not going to kill him."

The group shifted in angry protest.

"Then we will kill you, too," Brown said quietly. "You'll not deprive us of the only satisfaction we have left, to see this scum sweat and die like we've seen other people die. And if you use that gun on me, the rest here will see that you die the same way he does."

There was an assenting chorus of voices.

Then from behind the group a deep voice growled. "Enough of this! Aside! Stand aside!" And Dr. Rodgers moved slowly but resolutely to my side.

"So you are about to become what he has always believed you to be—decadent bourgeoisie. You would murder and so prove yourself nothing but a bunch of savages. Look at him! Do you think for one moment you will ever get him to beg for anything? Kill him and who… who, I say … is the final victor in this struggle, you or he?"

Leon Tidings watched intently, his dark eyes moving quickly back and forth from the group to the old teacher, a half-smile still on his face.

"But, Dr. Rodgers," Justin Wright pressed forward. "You can't deprive these people of the justice they seek."

"Yes," voices chorused. "Justice! We want justice!"

"So!" the doctor thundered. "It is justice you want! Ultimate justice … or interim justice?"

"I don't understand . .

"Never mind, counsellor," Ham grunted. "Justice, you say? So be it. Let him stand trial so that we may judge his relevant guilt. I am sure Justin Wright would be willing once again to mount the bench, possibly for the last time. Well?"

"If you insist that it is necessary," the lawyer said with ill grace.

Amid grumbles and curses the group moved aside as Tidings was placed under guard.

So the trial is set for ten tomorrow morning.

Meanwhile, Tidings sleeps at my feet, and the rest sleep too, I think.

2

They were all gathered around the big Council table by a quarter to ten, expectantly silent, waiting while Justin Wright, the Reverend Sandmire and Ham Rodgers conferred in soft tones. There was little that was congenial among the three. Justin Wright was pensive and appeared to be in something of a daze, as if he had sensed a certain magnitude connected with these proceedings that threatened to overwhelm him. The Reverend Sandmire flitted about the table like a lost moth. His toothless face and perfectly round glasses made him look like the Grim Reaper. His lips wore a half-smile of unconcealed triumph. The group, following the leadership of Avery Brown, had asked Sandmire to serve as a kind of prosecutor and to act on their behalf.

It was plain that Dr. Rodgers' illness had worsened. Occasionally he would break into a dry coughing spasm, and he obviously had a high fever. When he moved he did so with slow deliberation as if to conserve as much of his waning energy as possible. He held his face in even composure most of the time, going about things as if he were preparing to lecture a class, but at unguarded moments the great white head would droop momentarily and his eyes would close, and weariness would overtake him. Then he would shake himself upright again to get on with things. For he had agreed to represent Leon Tidings. Chip, Marie, Father Herbert and I had tried desperately to dissuade him. But he only became angry. "I am needed here as much as I have ever been needed by anyone anywhere, even including you, Chip. Please accept my word for it." That left us no choice.

The three men were to occupy a seat at the table, one on an edge, and Mr. Wright in the middle. Neither books nor papers were on the table. Each man was entirely on his own without props of any sort. The three had been conferring about procedures. Even in the daytime the hold is dim, so for this occasion several candles were lit to illuminate in flickering yellow the area around the table.

Meanwhile the group, 27 of us, had gathered about the table where we were seated and waiting. Marie and Chip, holding hands and watching Dr. Rodgers with heartwrenching concern; Father Herbert, his tough, square face also intent upon the threesome; the two young men, Tony and Tommy, sitting next to Chip, and clearly perplexed at what was taking place; Benjamin Zanhorst and Malcolm Grant, both ignoring each other but each wearing complacent looks of confidence that before the day was over Tidings would meet his end.

David Harmes and Avery Brown sat together, impatiently waiting for things to get underway. Buster Romakowski was behind me, mumbling to himself that this whole business was silly. Larry Best sat beside me, politely interested, so his expression said, but not really involved. Laura Grant, half asleep with well-deserved weariness; the four other young women and their fathers and a mother. It had been agreed by all that neither the barge Council nor a jury would be used, but that all would abide by Justin Wright's decision as to whether or not Tidings would live or die.

Last was Tidings. I had provided him with water which, while in reasonable supply, must be purchased and then painfully carried from the outside tap of an old gasoline station now occupied by a dozen or so persons. He was seated on a wobbly, rough bench. The group had insisted that his hands be kept tied behind his back. Like others who had lost their glasses, he had to squint in order to see better. His face was impassively dark with a slight trace of contempt mixed with amusement of some mysterious sort. The only interest at all that gained his heavy features occurred whenever his eyes fell upon Dr. Rodgers, and then he seemed mildly puzzled, as if he, too, wondered why this old man should go to this trouble.

Outside a strong wind had sprung up. The day was a cheerless one—a Thursday, and a few years ago most of us would have been in some cozy warm home frantically scurrying around to prepare an awesome dinner of turkey and dressing with, as the oldtime menus used to say, all the trimmings: Thanksgiving Day. It, too, ceased to be a national holiday some time ago, a move to separate Church and State further in order "to insure complete religious freedom."

Finally, Justin Wright spoke.

"Let us come to order."

"Mr. Wright, if I may speak, may I suggest that we call this the Court of Truth?" Dr. Rodgers asked.

The tall, serious man pondered for a moment and then with a shrug of his shoulders said, "I suppose that is as good as any other, but I question how much truth will be determined here today. However, it's of little consequence what we call it, since it is doubtful that we shall meet like this again. Our rules are these. Everyone here will have an opportunity to speak and ask questions but only after I have recognized each of you. I will ask the Reverend Sandmire to speak first and summarize as best he can the general views of many of you as to how we shall dispose of Leon S. Tidings. I understand you want an all-or-nothing judgment from me... either the man's freedom or his life."

A dozen heads bobbed in assent.

The Reverend Sandmire rose slowly with as much dignity as he could muster. He had spruced up his black suit as best he could for the occasion. He coughed once or twice, the way he used to do just before he would launch into his Sunday sermon in the old days.

"Ahem. Let me say, first, that I think all of this is quite unnecessary, because the guilt of this man in his crimes against humanity is plainly obvious," his voice squeaked. "It is obvious in the fact that all of us are here. We are destroyed. Our loved ones are dead. Our homes are gone. And why?" His voice trembled in a low wail. "Because of him and men like him. All we ever wanted was peace ... and we told them this repeatedly. So, there can be no mistaking our intentions. How many times did we turn the other cheek as the good book says?

"But," the Reverend leveled a quivering finger at the impassive Tidings, "what did he do? He tricked us! He lied! He cheated! And now innocent people everywhere suffer. But for him and the others like him all of us would be safely in our homes and at work in the vineyards of the world doing good for all men. This evil thing must be blotted from the face of the earth. Only then will the eyes of the Lord look upon us again with grace."

The group began to stir restlessly, the fires of anger and resentment smoldering behind their eyes and under their breaths. Justin Wright tapped softly for order. He used an old claw hammer as a gavel.

"Reverend Mr. Sandmire, had you considered asking some of the others to speak?" Several persons had begun to agitate for recognition.

"Why... ahem..."

"Thank you. Mr. Harmes, you were once a superintendent of schools. What have you to say?"

The mild-looking man rose with an encouraging pat from Avery Brown. He, too, had done his best to look as neat as possible in his worn suit. It was as if he and most of the others had gone to special pains to fix themselves up, in order that they might lift themselves up again in one last desperate attempt to regain at least some fragments of their lost worlds and, so, feel some measure of hope, dignity and purpose. They were putting themselves on full-dress review one last time in the hope that there might still be someone left in the reviewing stand to applaud them and tell them that everything will be all right; to tell them that their consciences were clean; to tell them they had nothing to fear or regret; to comfort them and to justify the hatred stirring through their souls toward a man they wanted so badly to kill.

"We were so close, you see, to solving the great problems of the world. So close!" Harmes cried out, his teeth and fist clenched in anguish. "We had worked so hard to eliminate evil and to make all men truly equal and to make them truly free from all wants. Oh, how I despise you, Tidings! For look what you have done." Tears began to stream down his thin, pale cheeks. "But for you, our great work could have continued. Now it's all gone. Death for you is the only way you can pay for your crimes, and even that isn't enough. Don't you see? It could have been so beautiful." Then Harmes stood silent, to cover his eyes with his hands, while his shoulders shook to hold the sobs inside him.

Tidings' impassiveness gave way to undisguised disgust. His heavy features seemed to recoil at Harmes, and his voice cut through the hold with a flat heaviness. "Mr.... ah ... Wright. The sight of a man in tears revolts me. Kill me if you wish. After all, I've had the pleasure of seeing many of your kind die, so I can quite understand your desire to see me die. But please put a stop to this... ah... display of weakness."

The hold exploded in a torrent of noise. Most of the group jumped from their seats in a fury that threatened to obliterate all of our efforts to achieve orderliness. Cries of "Kill him now!" rent the air, and Chip, Father Herbert and I had to use our muscles to hold people in check. Avery Brown pushed his way to Harmes' side and waved the group silent.

"Please! Let us have order!" Even Mr. Brown had retrieved a few shreds of the old corporate mannerisms in his bid to attract the notice of someone in the reviewing stand. Calm had swept his face clean, momentarily. And the group heeded. "May I be recognized, Mr. Wright?"

527

"Indeed, Mr. Brown, and the Court thanks you."

"Thank you. Ladies and gentlemen. For many years private enterprise, that wonderful system of economic wealth for all, had been mindful of the needs of the people. More so, please take note, than the likes of Leon Tidings. I call to your attention the fact that business and industry, mindful of its responsibilities to the total community, long ago decided to put aside their differences with a foreign ideology and cooperate with it to the fullest extent. And what has been our reward?" Brown paused, as I used to see him do whenever he gave a speech before the local Chamber of Commerce. "We have undergone a sneak attack that was completely unwarranted. An attack that has stripped us of everything, as the Reverend Sandmire has said. Tidings and his kind brought this ruin and death without warning and without provocation. Simple justice dictates that he must die."

The group cheered Avery Brown, who inclined his head slightly as he used to do whenever he gave a speech in a fancy ballroom to a fancy audience who applauded the fancy subject which he had discussed with such admirable calm. He stood for a moment, then, in the hold of the barge still inclining his head up and down—even after the group had fallen silent.

"I say... thank you, Mr. Brown," Justin Wright repeated for the third time. And someone pulled him back into the group.

Then Buster Romakowski spoke. He had not decked himself out with quite as much care. Possibly he had not thought of the reviewing stand, or maybe he did not care. The big, husky man spoke in a powerful voice doubtlessly cultivated over the years by making speeches in noisy union halls and outside plant gates. "This is all silly. If you want to kill him, then kill him, but let's cut out all the junk. Me, I don't care what happens to the bum. Sure, I hate his guts. We had things all set up ... a labor government, with labor where it rightly belongs ... in power everywhere. We were willing to cooperate with these monkeys on items of mutual interest... better pay, working conditions and all that. And if guys like this Tidings would have gone along with us... well, we'd all be sitting pretty. But, we both lost, didn't we, Tidings? Looks to me like we all lost. So kill him ... so who cares?"

"Dr. Best. You have long been identified with the peace effort. I think we should like to hear from you," Wright said in a sympathetic voice.

Larry, who had been watching listlessly, slowly unfolded himself from an awkward crosslegged sitting position. His thinness made him seem taller than he was, and he already was the tallest person in the hold, more so than Justin Wright. His face was smooth from a fresh shave, and the fair skin was drawn tightly over the bones of his cheeks and jaws. There was a wistful expression in his eyes as he looked slowly about the hold, his eyes coming to rest on Tidings.

"All I ever wanted to do was to help you ... to show you the way ... to lead you out of your dark, ugly world into something far better. It was all so simple. I don't want you to die, any more than I want to die. I want to be your friend."

"And my leader, too. Isn't that right?" Tidings asked. His voice, steady and casual, gave the hold an unexpected jolt.

"Not any more. Just your friend." And Larry sat down as suddenly as he had gotten up.

Now everyone was silent, and all eyes turned to Dr. Rodgers. He had sat motionless, head resting on his chest, as if he were napping. He had raised up only once, during the scuffle. But now he roused himself, shaking his white head upward. His heavy hand fished his glasses from the pocket of a faded and frayed grey coat sweater. "May I?" he asked, and Justin Wright nodded. He rose carefully to his feet and took a minute to adjust himself to a fully upright, head-up position. Then his shaggy head took in the hold and its curious assortment of people in one single, sweeping glance.

"My purpose is to represent this man in context with ourselves ... not to defend him," and Ham glared at the short, dark prisoner whose eyes had narrowed into sharp, black pinpoints to look unblinkingly back. "If, indeed, one can call him simply a man. I should think *homo sapiens—despicabilis* would be a more fitting description. For his ways mark him so. To him truth is a variable to be used as a strategic weapon in his never-ending war upon the world. His sources of energy are found in violent pursuits. His whole system of values is one vast, multicolored, everchanging arsenal from which he fashions new weapons of deceit every day of his life, which he employs with skillful leverage to destroy the status quo whenever and wherever he can. To eradicate without trace ... to vaporize anything that does not square precisely with his religion. His is a slave psychology, for he is himself a slave... both a worshiper and a subject of tyranny. He thrives on absolute force and obedience. He must be obedient to someone above, and he must have someone who is in turn obedient to him. Remove one or the other, and he withers and is helpless, so that his only peace of mind comes through the perpetuation of violence and force. That is his definition of the word peace ... to be allowed to carry on his quest of absolute obedience without interference. He and his kind have been with us for a very long time. His ancestors have been found in every age in an endless variety of manifestations in every race and color and creed. My task, therefore, is not to plead Leon Tidings' innocence, but rather to determine the relative degree of his guilt."

The group stirred with restless expectancy. Here and there murmurs of approval broke from I-told-you-so faces. Old Tidings was going to get his! Outside, waves of water sloshed against the side of the hull, the result of another string of barges moving down river carrying away still more of the once vigorous heartbeat of this city.[104] Dr. Rodgers shifted slightly to lean against the edge of the table. Again he lowered his head for momentary rest. Then he shook himself fully erect.

---

104 As part of its Treaty obligations, the United States was required to make substantial portions of its capital equipment base available to "underdeveloped eastern European nations," as well as to the Soviet Union. Hence, during this period and after, plant equipment was uprooted and shipped to eastern Europe where it became part of the capital equipment base there, particularly capital equipment used in the electronics, metals fabricating, chemical, petroleum and food-processing industries—ranging from automobile and home appliance manufacturing to computers and heavy machinery. Specifically, in Pittsburgh, metal fabricating, chemical and electronic facilities were dismantled and shipped by water to New Orleans and then to eastern Europe.

530

"Now, how much of a secret has all of this been? One might suppose that such evil schemes would logically be kept hidden from the unsuspecting victims. After all, if I were about to slit your throat you would hardly expect me to tell you in advance. But one of the truly diabolical aspects of Tidings and his masters is the supreme ego that all of them possess, which should not be surprising, for their whole human perspective is based upon ego rather than humility. They want their victims to know what their goals are because it makes the contest of violence all that much more satisfying to their egos ... to succeed even after they have warned their victims. Can you imagine a greater sense of victory? So Comrade Tidings and his associates in this latest form of tyranny have gone to special pains to warn the world. The warning was first sounded in 1848 and at varying times thereafter—in 1917, in the Twenties, again in the Thirties, likewise in the Forties and Fifties. And while the world groveled more and more at their feet, their contempt for us was such that even in the Sixties they dared to offer still more warnings of their intentions. It was a risk, of sorts, but a very well calculated one." The big, lumbering man paused to search the faces in front of him which now stared back like rows of expressionless dots.

"Yet," he continued, "we didn't believe them, and this is exactly what they counted on. Indeed, their entire conquest was based on this absolute assumption. The world never takes the tyrants seriously until after they become tyrants. But I see you are skeptical." The doctor turned stiffly to Leon Tidings, who still continued his watchful observation. "Perhaps Comrade Tidings still has sufficient confidence in his system that he would explain further."

"What is this gibberish?" the Reverend Sandmire squeaked. "You said he was guilty. So let's get on with it."

There was a chorus of yeas, and Justin Wright, who had sat unmoving throughout, suddenly roused himself and tapped for order. "Is it really necessary?" he asked.

"Absolutely not!" a trembling voice called. "He will try to brainwash you even more." It was Malcolm Grant who had struggled to his feet, to stand quaking with rage.

531

"I say yes!" And Chip Baker was on his feet. "How else can you learn about men like him, unless you study them?"

"Very well, let him speak," Justin Wright sighed.

All eyes turned to Tidings, who shifted slightly on his bench to ease the discomfort of his ropebound arms. Even in this posture he had lost none of his composure. He smiled frostily, and the heavy eyelids closed sleepily and then opened as if he had perceived a magnificent dream. "There is no mystery. Bourgeois society was decadent and weak because it grew too comfortable living off the labor of the slaves of capitalism."

"But we were eliminating the evils of capitalism!" Benjamin Zanhorst shouted indignantly.

"The only way you can eliminate the evil is to eliminate all traces of capitalism itself, and five thousand years of tradition and custom that permitted it in the first place. The only way you can do that is to liquidate the past by liquidating the people. There is no other goal, no other way."

Tidings' voice was soft and casual. "This, naturally, is incomprehensible to you. And your Dr. Rodgers is correct. The bourgeoisie have one blind spot which proves how rotten and decayed they are. They fear violence. They seek to avoid violence at all costs. It was therefore desirable always for us to talk openly of our supreme dedication to the Revolution and of our resolve to use violence wherever necessary. The more we threatened violence, the more fearful you became. Could there be any greater proof of your unfitness to be the leaders of the world?" Tidings seemed to forget where he was. His bright black eyes were directed far away. "You are not fit to live, any of you," he spat out at the group.

"What about me?" It was Larry. He had struggled awkwardly to his feet like a sick colt, his eyes frantic in his appeal. "Look, I shared your concern for reform and the elimination of social injustice."

"Ah, you, *Professor* Best." Tidings' voice was thick with contempt. "We hate your kind worst of all. You are the weakest. You *pretend* to our goals, but you want only to change things here and there, in order to preserve elements of the capitalistic world. You are fainthearted impostors, as all democratic socialists are. Reformers like yourself are useful but more dangerous than even the landowners and industrialists. For you are content with only half a loaf. Were we to allow your kind to exist, you would soften our own people, warp their discipline and thus keep them from completing the Revolution."

The words were like whiplashes flailing Larry across the face and the back. For he cringed in pain and flung himself upon me, his fingers digging into my arm.

"Stop him!" he begged. "You've got to stop him!"

Then there was silence. A great deal of it. Dr. Rodgers again shook himself upright, the muscles of his face working to keep the weariness and illness from engulfing him. He fumbled his handkerchief from his pocket and wiped his fever-dampened face.

"So the warnings were ignored," Ham continued so quietly that it was an effort to hear him. "Why? We can read. We have eyes, ears and brains. Our system of values says never trust a stranger until he proves himself. Never give credit to a bad business risk, eh, Mr. Brown? We don't abolish our police system in order to encourage the criminal to give up crime, eh, Mr. Harmes? We don't give power of attorney to an unproven friend, eh, Mr. Wright? Yet we gave our national power of attorney to an unproved world organization and discharged our armed forces in the process. And we gave unlimited credit that claimed all of our resources. Why?" The doctor paused and again searched all the faces.

"Somewhere along the line we took our precious system of values, even including the basic essentials of national security, and made them objects of partisanship. We stuck a tag on them and categorized them and relegated them to only one segment of our society, an unpopular one at that; so that whenever concerned men good and true tried to rise above this rigidly inflicted partisanship, we promptly discounted both normal prudence and common sense as propaganda.

"We became as spoiled children kicking back at their parents. We scoffed at history, at our past, at our traditions, at our heritage ... forgetting that these things begot us, taught us and nurtured us. We poked fun at the past and in so doing tried to dishonor it but succeeded only in dishonoring ourselves. We blamed the system for all of our ills, forgetting that any worthwhile system is only as good as the people who run it. We chose to try to reform our injustices by seeking to destroy our system, rather than by using our heritage as a means to improve ourselves.

"In our grasp for progress, we tried to find a moral shortcut and lost. We created, instead, a new tyranny of convenience. Wherein we created the hucksters of privilege, the hawkers of mass guilt and the cult of expertise. Wherein the individual is either a nuisance or a problem but never an asset... unless he apologizes for whatever it is he might have achieved and, instead, regards himself only as a resource, like a lump of coal or a piece of ore, to be used as a faceless society sees fit.

"We created our own tyranny of slick phrases where personal success is termed failure and personal failure is worshipped as success; where thrift is extravagance and extravagance is thrift; where Christian thought is pagan and pagan thought is Christian; where less money is more money and more money is less money; where defeat is victory and victory is defeat; where big men are made small and small men are made big; where danger is security and security is danger; where freedom is slavery and slavery is freedom; where treason is heroism and heroism is treason; where war is peace and peace is war; where patriotism is bigotry and bigotry is patriotism; where justice is privilege and privilege is justice; where aristocracy of the mind becomes arrogance of the mind!"

"Sit down!" someone cried.

"The nerve."

"Order, please!" Justin Wright banged. His gaunt features showed impatience. "Are you finished, Dr. Rodgers?"

"Almost. In another moment," the big man rumbled. He brushed the back of his hand along his craggy face and then continued in a voice that had lost its thunder, dropping almost to a whisper as if desperately pleading that his words might be fully comprehended.

"We have demanded that justice be done, and so be it. But in judging Tidings we must likewise make a judgment upon ourselves. For there is such a thing called proportional justice, wherein the evil acts of men must be weighed one against the other to determine the relative degree of guilt.

"If Leon Tidings is guilty of the horrendous acts of murder and maiming of bodies and manipulation of minds ... if he has raped and plundered the fruits of six thousand years of labor ... if he has blasphemed the nobleness of nature and the divine spark in human life and the human spirit... and I believe he has done these evils... then his punishment must be in keeping with these terrible deeds.

"But our judgment cannot stop here, because we also are a part of Tidings' world. And we, too, in our own way and in our own setting have likewise committed another form of evil, less horrible perhaps, but still one that cannot go unrecorded... the evil of default. If our flight from reason made us too sick and too weak to stand against the likes of Tidings, then do we not incur a proportionate share of punishment?

"If we demand that justice be done to Leon Tidings, then we must be prepared to accept the justice which is to be done to us."

Then it came. Boiling animal anger. Zanhorst, Sandmire, Brown and Malcolm Grant and some others swept over us to descend, not upon Leon Tidings, but upon Dr. Rodgers. They screamed in his ears, cursing him and brandishing their fists.

Somebody pushed him. The old teacher lost his balance and fell, striking his head against the table.

And they pressed in upon him all the more, still screaming.

By this time Father Herbert had struggled through the knot of violence to gain the top of the table. His voice, locker-room strong, rang out like a cannonade:

"Why don't you just... *crucify him?*"

Only then did silence come, and they stood away so that Chip and I might carry the barely conscious teacher back to his rag bunk.

XIII

The Thirty-Sixth Month

In a few more hours the barge as a place of refuge will cease to be. The salvage crews come in the morning to clean out the rusting junk pile of Fords Landing, and what has been our home will become scrap for the steel-making furnaces up river, themselves grown hungry. The hysteria largely is under control now, and everyone has fallen to the task of pulling together what few personal belongings remain to each of us. We must all be gone from here by dawn. Fortunately, the weather so far has been mercifully mild for early December and if it holds will allow a grace period in which to get resettled before the severe part of the winter comes upon us. All thoughts of holding the group together as a unit are now seen as impossible. Even if there were facilities enough to carry everyone down river, there does not exist the kind of rapport and self-discipline to make such a hard and dangerous journey possible. If nothing else, the attack upon Dr. Rodgers proved that.

"People hate truth more than they hate tyranny," Father Herbert said right after Chip and I had carried the doctor to his bunk. "Ham should have known better."

"He probably knows better than any of us. But I suppose he had to try one more time," Chip replied. His face was taut, white with anxiety and rage.

"He's that kind," Marie said. The four of us stood to one side of where Dr. Rodgers lay. He had lost consciousness, a combination of exhaustion from his illness and the head injury which had resulted from his fall against the table. We had done our best to make him comfortable, and now the young woman who looked down on him was wretched in her sadness. "He did it because, even after all that has happened, he still cares," Marie added slowly.

A stunned silence had enveloped the hold. Larry sat crosslegged in my bunk like a shattered Buddha. Avery Brown, Sandmire, Zanhorst and the elder Grant stood tightly together, still frozen by the Council table. Balanced against them stood the young men, Weinberg and Wong, and Romakowski. Justin Wright still sat at the big table, his face empty and his tall form sagging. The others shuffled quietly in the background, as if the slightest noise from them might trigger yet another unforeseen turn of events. Forgotten momentarily was Leon Tidings, who sat impassively, arms still bound and his dark eyes moving carefully over the scene.

It was as if someone had stopped the clock to await the next steps of fate.

At last the labored breathing of the fallen scholar changed pace, and the shaggy white head, bandaged against a raw wound across the forehead, moved to perceive us. Our eyes met, four pairs searching his for a clue. Dazed at first, his wavered as a soft flame against the wind, as if unsure whether to burn on or simply to go out. Then the flame of consciousness steadied and brightened, and his eyes came to rest on me sharp and strong.

"Dave," the voice rumbled, "I should be much relieved if you would see to the orderly process of things in my place. Chip... Marie... Father Herbert, you will help him." There was no question in his voice any more than there was command. He spoke as if confirming a mutual thought.

I shook my head in silent protest.

"You know what needs to be done," the granite voice continued.

"Balance. We talked of it one night," I replied. "To know where to draw the line between the real and obtainable and the ideal and unobtainable... and once, having drawn that line, sticking to it no matter what. To know that values based upon the two sets of natural laws[105] determine the balance we must strike. Yes, I know what needs to be done ... to keep going and do what must be done to restore that balance."

"To know the difference between trying to understand human nature and trying to change it. To know both prudence and resolve," the doctor added.

"But the others know this, too."

"Indeed. But Chip must now bring order into his own life. He is of the new and must be occupied with new things, and Father Herbert must help him. You are of the old, and you must assume the burden of paving the way." The old gentleman closed his eyes to slip again into sleep.

Across the hold, Avery Brown cleared his throat. "Look... how's the old man doing? Why don't we all just sit down and collect ourselves?"

"You know," the big voice of Romakowski cut in, "I've done some sneaky mean things in my day. I've taken bribes, and I've beaten people up. But I never ground a fine old gent into the dirt because he wanted to do right by me. I think, Mr. Punk Brown, that I'm going to snap you in two right now. Then I'm gonna work on him and enjoy every screamin' minute of it." He nodded his florid, square face at the Reverend Sandmire who jumped as if jabbed by a needle.

I looked again at Chip, Marie and Father Herbert. "You have the pistol, Chip." He fumbled at his belt and handed it to me. Then I faced them all.

---

105 Mr. Little is referring to Hamilton Rodgers' contention that there are "two faces to nature," which he explains in his *Quality of Life* as being (1) the *physical* side, which embodies the laws of physical science and (2) the *behavioural* side, classically defined as "natural laws," which govern the use of man's "intellect and dexterity as exercised through will and choice and manifested in life, liberty and property." Rodgers states: "Let us never forget that nature has two sets of laws; one governing the predictable, which we call the physical sciences, and another set governing the unpredictable behavior of man. Thus, the physical laws which are derived from predictable phenomena cannot be applied as the sole measure of human behavior, since these laws cannot accommodate the unpredictable, i.e., will and choice."

"All right. Enough. I will shoot the first person who gets out of line. Romakowski, I can think of nothing better than to watch you take those two apart one bone at a time, but we can't afford that luxury right now. So, topside! We have no lookout. You take the day watch. The rest of you… particularly you, Brown … let me repeat the rules. The Council will continue adjourned until further notice. Each of you has an assignment, and after we've heard from Justin Wright you'll be expected to get to it. Like it or not, we're going to work together or out you go. If you've got complaints, bring them to me. Those of you who don't like these rules can get out.

"And now Mr. Wright, you have a duty to perform. We've all agreed that it will be all or nothing as far as Tidings is concerned. What is it to be? Do you order us to take his life or set him free?"

The damp, rusting hold echoed the hum of speculation as the group, subdued by a mixture of shame and fear, waited on Justin Wright. The lawyer still had not moved. One might have thought that he had died or been turned to stone were it not for his face. The emptiness was gone, replaced by deep lines of concentration, as if he were trying to distill a whole lifetime of experience and thought into one final, potent drop of wisdom. There must have raged within him some terrible struggle. Perhaps he had met his own Moment of Truth, even as I had met mine at the hearings now so long past. But whatever, the group saw the transformation from a gaunt, empty human shape to something resembling a man who could still recall purpose and fulfillment to his life; a man now capable of decision without vacillation and an unyielding resolve to back it up. All became absolutely still as the transformation was completed and Justin Wright slowly pulled himself erect in his seat at the center of the Council table.

"Dr. Rodgers said that the punishment should equal the crime, and those of you who struck out at him surely by now must know this. Your faces tell me so, and in time, in another place probably, you may come to appreciate that much of the world in which we live is the result of our own efforts … or lack of efforts… and that both our rewards for deeds well done and our punishments for evils committed have a direct relationship to this man-made environment. What more fitting earthly justice, then, than to be required to live in the place we have helped to create for ourselves? You and I possibly are lucky, compared with Leon Tidings ... for most of us have not yet gone so far that we cannot retrieve a little of that which we have lost. Our punishment has been to live in our world... this world... and while our lot is difficult, still there is hope. Because fortunately there is an antidote for default. It is enlightened human achievement, and for those of you who would like to try, it is still not too late. Perhaps you won't achieve much .. . the odds are pretty heavy . .. but what little you do achieve will count a hundredfold over what it used to.

"But the antidote for murder of souls and bodies is not so easily acquired, if it can be acquired at all, so that if we follow the same formula of justice for Mr. Tidings as we have accepted for ourselves, then we may expect that his punishment shall fit precisely the nature of his crime."

The silence hung on as Justin Wright turned to face the heavy, immobile features of the prisoner, who had remained coldly aloof.

"Will the prisoner rise." And Tidings did so with painful effort which he fought to conceal as he struggled awkwardly to his feet, bound arms working grotesquely to help him keep his balance.

"Leon Tidings. I find you guilty as charged," the lawyer intoned and then paused as if he were selecting the right emphasis for his words. "I sentence you to endure the kind of world which you have helped to create... the world that lies immediately beyond this barge. I sentence you to be set free to wander for as long as you shall live among the maimed and the sick, the bitter and the weak... and those whom hate has made strong and vengeful. Mr. Little, set him free."

In the still silent hold I fished a knife from my pocket and cut Tidings free. He worked his arms slowly back and forth, the cold smile gone from his lips and the heavy face working to stay together.

"No!" he breathed harshly. "Shoot me here," he gestured to a point behind his ear. "I have expected that. It is only proper. You would be fully justified. Were I in your shoes ..."

"You were in our shoes," Justin Wright cut in coldly. He had risen from his place now and stood towering above the short, dark man

540

who seemed to get shorter and whose face had become rubbery grey with growing terror. "But you did not put bullets behind our ears."

Then Tidings turned to squint at us in the gloomy candlelight. "Don't you want your revenge? A shot right here." Silence. "Very well. Let me stay on." Silence. "I'll work. You'll have no trouble."

Justin Wright nodded to me. "Tony and Tommy," I called, "escort Mr. Tidings ashore."

Then it came. As the two young men approached, the heavy face with its black eyes convulsed and squinted in supreme agony.

"No!" the face begged now. "Not out there. You know I won't last five hundred yards, and they'll be all over me. Please. They've got knives and fire and clubs." The voice choked into a wretched sob. "And they'll be slow!"

And they hauled him screaming up the rusted metal stairs—a short, quivering, dumpy form wearing brand new boots and a brand new coat. It was a very long while before the screams faded completely.

2

Late in the day after Tidings' departure I turned back to Marie and Chip who, along with Father Herbert, were tending Dr. Rodgers. His fever had worsened and his breathing was steadily becoming more labored. "If you two are serious about getting married and you want the doctor present, it had better be soon," I said.

"Can we wait for him to wake up?" Marie asked.

"I think it best that we try to wake him now," Father Herbert said, and he knelt close to the doctor's head. "Ham, we are going to have a wedding. Come back for the wedding." He called softly over and over again, until the eyes opened once more and the flame of consciousness again burned steadily but no longer as brightly.

So in the dimness of the rusted hold we gathered around while Father Herbert read from his worn book as Marie and Chip knelt together at Dr. Rodgers' side. A few of us drew from the words a new source of energy and hope. But most stood about to crane their necks out of shy curiosity, for—imagine—a wedding, in this day and at this late hour!

When Father Herbert had finished, the teacher gave his blessing to the young man and woman, and then he beckoned me close to his lips.

"How goes it?" he asked in a gruff whisper.

"It goes well. Tidings was forced to go ashore… with the consent of everyone. We're going to manage just fine."

He nodded, and a smile began to gather upon his ageless face as he drifted deeper and deeper into restful sleep.

Still later, at dusk, he died without another backward glance. We buried him late in the night between the railroad tracks. We dug deeply so he will be safe for all time from prying hands who would vaporize even his bones if they could but find them.

Ten days have passed now, and once again the rules of life have changed. Yesterday, the patrol boat came and the captain sought me out with the word that, starting tomorrow, salvage crews would begin dismantling this graveyard of useless steel and iron. He was a nice young man in a well-fitted blue uniform who did not seem to enjoy his mission.

"Hope you don't think I had anything to do with this," he said anxiously. "Some of the people over there in No-Man's Land, I guess, complained for some reason that they wanted you out with them. Word is you're planning a revolution. So the decision was made to clean the place up. I'm sorry." He paused to kick some dirt off his shiny black shoe. "Look. Don't give us away, but sometimes my men and I… well, we like to help if we can."

"How can I get hold of something that will float us down river? You know what one more winter will do to us." The December sky was grey with damp cold, and the harsh wind whipped at the river, still alive with barge traffic.

He nodded and then shook his head. "I know where there are some boats, but you wouldn't get far. Even if you could prove ownership, they'd still take them away from you."

"Rafts... like those two on your boat. They're insignificant enough. I'll buy them."

"I wouldn't dare. Besides, you'd be out of your mind to try and make it on them."

"Why? They're dry inside and solid. If a person is young and strong, he might stand a good chance."

The young police captain scowled in thoughtful concentration. Then he brightened. "The other night one of our boats was robbed during shift change. Some food and flares. They didn't even dock the skipper. Just chewed him out a little." We had been standing on the deck of the barge and now the police captain called to his three fellow officers who still remained aboard.

"Come, there may be trouble here." In an instant they were at his side. "We're going on a little inspection tour below deck," he said to me gravely. Then a small smile worked at the edges of his eyes and lips. "We'll be gone about ten minutes. Sometimes we're a little careless about checking our equipment as often as we should, especially the after part. Probably won't even give things a good looking at until tonight when we go off duty." And he followed his men toward the companionway.

"Captain," I called after him, "why do you do it... this inspection, I mean?"

He turned and he faced me with a slow grin. "I don't really know. Maybe it's because I like you people... especially that white-haired fellow."

It took only a moment to grab Tommy Wong, who was standing his turn as guard, and jump aboard the boat. We loosened the rafts and dropped them into the water. It was no trick at all to paddle them around the stern of the barge and hide them in the murky shadows. Then the police boat was gone.

The unpredictable. That little flaw in the makeup of men. Even the most advanced police state will never eliminate it.

So the preparations have gone ahead. The rafts are small, each able to take only four persons, plus their possessions, and even then the journey will be hazardous. New Orleans is the destination, out of range from the cold and deadly winds of the northern winter. And then in the spring—overland to a mountain peak in Wyoming. The journey may take a year or two, but the strong will make it.

There was some discussion on choosing the eight to make the journey, but with the words of Dr. Rodgers echoing through my mind, the matter was quickly resolved by me alone. Chip and Marie. Father Herbert, Tony Weinberg and Tommy Wong and two of the young women who had proved themselves worthy, Alice and another young lady, Marcia.

"And you make eight," Chip said. His eyes were alive with expectations of the future.

"But I am not going. Buster Romakowski will go."

In time Chip and Marie will understand this. Father Herbert already does. My leg would not permit me to do the job, and I would weaken the whole expedition. Besides, what would become of Larry? He needs me now. We have been together too long for it to be any other way. Once he gets back to his old self and I can explain things so he'll understand clearly, it will still not be too late for us to make a good team. One hears more and more each day about growing bands of guerrilla forces operating out of the mountains to the east of us. With luck Larry and I should be able to join up with them before the heavy snows come.

But I see Father Herbert is getting anxious. He has asked to take this Journal with him. He wants to seal it in some plastic material to keep it dry. He caught me as I was about to drop it into the river this afternoon along with some other family trivia. Both he and Ham, of course, knew of these writing efforts, though they always remained discreetly aloof by seldom ever discussing the matter.

"Hold on! What are you doing?" he had said.

"Dumping some junk."

"Not *that*."

"This?" I turned the heavy ledger over in my hands. Its pages, flipped open by the wind, revealed the words crowded one on the other in a small, tight, irregular hand. "You already know what's in here, though you haven't read it, and there is no one left to care."

544

The priest nodded and chuckled. "True. But someday... who knows?"

Perhaps.

The dawn comes soon. I must wake Larry now. I have arranged everything into two bundles, so that we can slip away quickly before the others miss us.

All of my life I have reached out. Only now have I learned to reach up.

XIV

The Forty-Third Month and Thereafter

(Publisher's Commentary)

During the month of July following David Little's final entry, a Constitutional Convention was held in Philadelphia, Pennsylvania. Duly elected representatives from the fifty states gathered "to continue the great work of our Founding Fathers through the process of revising their handiwork so as to perpetuate the Constitution as a truly living instrument of a peaceful, democratic society for all times and for all of the people; an undertaking which the Founders, themselves believers in change, would have applauded." The new Constitution was ratified by each of the states during the following September, and on the twenty-fifth of that month the United Socialist States of America was born. (See Appendix, excerpts from *Achieving the Revolution in America*.)

Concurrent with these efforts was a general strengthening of the Communist Empire throughout the Western world. The year following, the entire Commonwealth of Great Britain formally adopted Communist governments with the exception of Australia, which withdrew. The continent of Africa, the Middle East, Southeast Asia and South America likewise were formally drawn into the Empire. As a final touch, the World Order of Nations was completely restructured as the World Order of Socialist Democracies, to become the official seat of International Communism, "a sovereign World State comprised of 131 nations and states." Thus, approximately five years after the time of David Little, the Empire of International Communism reached its zenith.

But almost as quickly, the Empire began to fall apart, in spite of the use of the most sophisticated scientific and electronic equipment ever devised for the control of men's minds. Purge after purge was recorded during that period historically known as the Decade of Blood. For by this time the capital resources of the Western civilization, which once comprised eighty percent of the world's capital wealth, had been nearly dissipated. Dr. Edison Tyler explains this as the "dissipation of capital resources at an ever increasing rate into nonproductive areas until nothing was left to prevent the most catastrophic economic collapse in the history of the world." The Empire thus was unable to sustain itself, and by the early part of the twenty-first century it had broken up into warring factions, which over the next one hundred years crumbled into anarchy that swept much of the world, forcing the revival in many areas of the ancient city-state system of mutual protection.

On the North American continent, the USSA was one of the earliest of the socialist democracies to disintegrate. This was due basically to two factors: its capital resources were swiftly drained from the country, leaving it impoverished, and its sources of water had been greatly restricted due to the lowering of the water tables on the continent. Also, geography and distance made centralised control extremely difficult, since there was no longer an economic base capable of supporting a highly automated technological society that might have been able to enforce the discipline of the state. But most important of all was the growing human resistance that swept over the land in thunderous waves.

One of the outgrowths of these circumstances is the Wyoming Federation. Capital of the Federation is the thriving city of Rodgers Center, located at the western base of the Wind River Range and within a day's journey of the St. Luke's Mission of Hope located on Mt. Victor, where this journal was discovered by Dr. Jason A. Doyle.

There is ample historical evidence to establish beyond any doubt that a Charles Comer Baker, his wife and a Father Martin Herbert arrived at this Christian mission accompanied by three other persons, about two years after David Little made his last entry. Baker became commander of guerrilla forces which for more than fifteen years operated from a number of mountain strongholds. In time he won the whole of Wyoming and Montana.

He became provisional governor of these areas for about five years, while the instruments of a more stable government were being reinstituted. He chose Boulder Lake as the site for Rodgers Center, which he founded early in the twenty-first century. Shortly thereafter he was elected the first governor of the Federation and served two terms. Both of his sons, Hamilton and David, had distinguished military careers in which they played major roles in the restoration of Seattle, Washington; Portland, Oregon; and San Francisco, California, in a series of campaigns against the weakened forces of the World Order of Socialist Democracies.

Nothing is known of David Little after his final entry in this journal. It is difficult to speculate on this matter, since it has been estimated that between sixty and eighty million Americans died through violence, exposure, starvation and disease during this period.

Indeed, other than this journal, there is no known record to show that David Little and many of those whom he mentions ever existed at all. However, scientific examination shows this account to have been written during the latter twentieth century. This journal must therefore be regarded as an authentic historical document.

Mr. Little would be pleased to know that after his lifetime search for fulfillment, he now has made a permanent place for himself in the history of world affairs.

—A. A. Grace, Ltd.
Publishers

There will always be those who care; those few who carry it on, this thing we call civilization; those few who have always been with us, whom adversity and failure only strengthen; those few who weary along, doggedly at it, who are neither bought nor sold; those who still care and who even this day labor behind closed doors and in the brush of the hills.

They are the tiny bands of resolve who, as did their forebears, struggle to rise up again; who have dotted the landscape since the days of the mastodon; doughty beings who stagger to their feet to stand yet again as their Creator meant for them to stand, to pick up the threads of life long after the Pharaohs and the legions of Rome and the elite of Hitler and the Mongol hordes have perished and are dust.

Each civilization has its Carthage, with its great masses of the uncaring, which becomes agony and ash. But the spark stays, somehow, in spite of all we do to kill it. Life goes on, even as before. Everyman lives to sift from the ashes the simple logic and reason that has been his since the Beginning. And so it shall be, until He—and none other— shall write Omega.

> —Charles Comer Baker, on the occasion of the
> Founding of Rodgers Center, Wyoming Federation
> (As recorded by Jason A. Doyle on his visit to
> Rodgers Center)

APPENDIX I

ACHIEVING THE REVOLUTION IN AMERICA
By
Smith Armstrong
Member of the Secretariat
Communist Party of
The United Socialist States of America

(Following are excerpts from a scholarly paper on the tactical moves used to transform the United States of America into the USSA. The paper makes reference to tactics preached by V. I. Lenin and Jan Kozak. It also stresses that other tactics had to be developed because of certain peculiarities of the United States' government, namely, its system of checks and balances found in its Constitution. The paper was written approximately five years after the final entry in the Journal of David Q. Little. *The editors.*)

* * *

The classics of Marxism-Leninism and the later brilliant work of Jan Kozak never cease to point out that the inexorable revolutionary transformation of capitalist society into a socialist one does not preclude the possibility of various forms and roads of the proletarian revolution. ...

In spite of the fact that throughout the world exceptionally favorable circumstances for the socialist revolution have existed for two generations, the political situation in the USSA before the revolution made it difficult to exploit fully the feelings of the working class and accordingly to establish a broad national front and adopt full pressure-from-above and pressure-from-below tactics. The bourgeois Constitution, the most evil force ever created to crush workers in their struggle for democracy, had been one of the greatest exceptional difficulties of our proletarian revolution. Because strong bourgeois traditions, inherited from the Anglo-Saxon exploiters which Marx originally described, comprised the heart of this anti-proletariat weapon, it denied the right of the proletariat to function openly in working for its goals of a socialist revolution. Similarly it permitted its bourgeois police and press to function without centralized restrictions in persecuting the worker class unmercifully and even went so far as to establish double standards of freedom by prohibiting Party members from organizing even for peaceful pursuits; while at the same time holding no restrictions on the movements of bourgeois groups such as the Chamber of Commerce and the National Association of Manufacturers, and tools of the bourgeoisie such as unions, the League for Industrial Democracy and the Rand School.

The unfortunate circumstance understandably lay beyond the control of dedicated socialists since the Constitution had been drawn 75 years before Marx. The strong and extreme bourgeois elements behind the American Revolution were successful in creating legal machinery that allowed them iron control over all sectors of the nation's political, social and economic life. But even this control failed to keep courageous elements of the working class from establishing the beginnings of Popular Fronts based on socialist doctrine largely through pressure-from-below. It is true, too, that for nearly a half century Reform Socialists helped to neutralize and isolate certain of the extreme bourgeois tyrannies and thus help build slowly over the years greater sympathies for the proletariat. Effectiveness of these "reformists," who practice the "democratic way to socialism" by calling for the coexistence of capitalism and socialism, was limited. For as Lenin states, the reformists deny the necessity of a socialist revolution and therefore reformism cannot "in its consequences ever lead to the building up of socialism, is not in its substance a socialist program." It is not capable of "smashing capitalism." And "capitalism cannot collapse but through a revolution." This is not achieved until all bourgeois forces, including our unreliable allies, the reformists, are liquidated. So reformists were of limited benefit to the later revolution....

551

One factor in our favor was the condition of the American bourgeois themselves. Like those in the other nations, the American bourgeois showed strong fears of pressures of the popular masses and an equally strong dislike for armed conflict, two factors which at the time of surrender helped to prevent bloodshed and ensured the undisturbed course of the revolution and their ultimate liquidation....

Thus, while the climate was favorable for revolution, the bourgeois Constitution stood in our way. Because of the tremendous concentration of domestic power in the hands of the bourgeois and because, too, of deeply engrained bourgeois traditions, overt revolution could not be considered. Only subverted approaches could be used to follow up on the gradualist efforts of the unreliable reformists. Hence, we were unable to bring Lenin's and Kozak's tactics into full play.

We knew that before we could do this a strategy employing gradualism must somehow be employed to isolate the Constitution and neutralize it. Fortunately, because of the reformists' successes in building a pressured sympathy for socialism and the bourgeois' fear of pressure and aversion to conflict, the then United States became increasingly docile in its relationships with the World Order of Nations. This welcome development wrote our strategy for us: while we would continue our efforts with the USA we would focus our efforts to gain control of the W.O.N. through gradualism. Here, without the barriers of a strong bourgeois constitution, we could give full employment to the tactics of Kozak, i.e., coexistence and cooperation, while building the pressure pincers toward ultimate control over the W.O.N. through neutrals and all Communist nations. Full employment of Lenin's revolutionary tactics in the W.O.N. was to be withheld until successful conclusion of the New Revolution in America....

Through steady applications of pressures and isolation techniques, both by ourselves and the reformists, the bourgeois gradually gave in, again largely due to fear of conflict, and voluntarily placed themselves and their Constitution subservient to the World Order of Nations and to treaties....

The final step was to pressure the bourgeois Americans into a treaty designed to circumvent their Constitution and to clear the way for overt revolutionary activities. Only when this was achieved could the full tactics of Lenin and Kozak be applied to complete the liquidation of the bourgeois and capitalism and create the dictatorship of the proletariat....

The strategy of circumventing and neutralizing a hostile constitution does not replace or conflict with our Father, Lenin; on the contrary, it merely adds dimension to his tactical philosophies by providing a relatively quick means to achieve the revolution....

The Interim and Overt Tactics for the Achievement of a Revolutionary Climate for the Transition to Socialism can be summarized as follows:

1. USA Constitution outlaws overt tactics of Communist revolution.
   a. Constitution weakness binds it and makes it subservient to treaties.
2. Interim tactics follow two broad roads:
   a. Control the W.O.N.
   b. Pressure the USA into a treaty which permits overt tactics of revolution and which neutralizes and/or controls all other instruments of power, i.e., military, police, press, right of assembly, judicial, executive, legislative, political parties, finance.
3. Carry out overt revolution based on Lenin-Kozak.
   a. Rebuild state apparatus through control of legislative bodies.
   b. Create new work disciplines.
   c. Create new forms of organization of working people.
   d. Complete assumption of power and total liquidation of capitalism.
4. Consolidate the new socialist state into its final form: The United Socialist States of America. ....

Once the Treaty of Friendship was ratified by the fearful and anxious bourgeois and their treacherous reformists, the revolution was achieved in only 45 months to become the greatest feat in Communist Party history....

APPENDIX II

HIGHLIGHTS OF THE TREATY OF FRIENDSHIP

Treaty emblem: The American Eagle in its peace posture set within the frame of a star. The eagle is gold; the field of the star is red.

Excerpts from the Preamble:

In the name of humanity and in the cause of just and lasting peace and tranquility for all peoples of the earth we, the people of the Union of Soviet Socialist Republics and the United States of America, do hereby enter into a Treaty binding upon us both to ban war and eliminate sources thereof, first, within our own sovereign states and, second, through mutual effort with all peace-loving peoples of the nations of the world; to protect the liberty and welfare and to guard vigorously the rights and privileges of all people sincerely desiring peace; and do hereby pledge the fruits of our daily labors to the welfare of our respective peoples, even as we pledge our fruits to benefit people everywhere, to the end that the poor shall know comfort, the meek and mild shall know honor, the unknowing shall be made wise through learning, the rich shall know the virtues of charity, the sick and lowly shall be made whole men, and the councils of men shall know good will and harmony to make both real and pure the eternal hope for peace, prosperity and spiritual growth for all mankind on earth forever....

Excerpts from Articles of the Treaty:

Article One: We hereby subscribe to the World Order of Nations' Mandate of Principles "that war, hereinafter defined as armed conflict, is outlawed under World Order of Nations' Statutes and that any persons, groups or governments found guilty of seeking to practice it shall be punished according to the statutes of the injured nation, nations and/or the World Order of Nations...

Article Two: To help assure peace for all time and freedom for all peoples, we do hereby agree to immediate disarmament and disbandment of all military personnel, excepting those forces necessary to keep the peace which shall serve under the authority of the World Order of Nations and shall be used only for defense against aggression... the disarmament shall be subject to World Order of Nations' control....

Article Three: We hereby subscribe to the World Order of Nations' Mandate of Principles that "all nationalistic goals considered to be in conflict with broader democratic interests of the peoples of the world shall be considered contrary to the interest and purposes of the World Order of Nations and hence are made void for legal considerations...."

Article Four: To ensure civil peace and tranquility no firearms or other instruments of violence shall be permitted in the possession of civilians.... only authorized personnel, as prescribed through this Treaty, shall possess arms as necessary to keeping the peace and shall be empowered to search and seize all persons suspect in violating this provision....

Article Five: Through economic cooperation we pledge a fair share of new and peaceful production resulting from this Treaty to aid further the underdeveloped nations of the world to eliminate the poverty resulting from imperialism... under the auspices of the World Order of Nations....

Article Six: We guarantee the free and open operation of all political parties which foster true democratic principles and shall protect said parties from fascistic and/or other undemocratic forces which seek to destroy true democracy....

Article Seven: The right of free speech, press and assembly shall be enjoyed by all freedom-loving persons, who shall be protected against abuses of speech, press and assembly wherein truth is distorted by persons threatening the power and sovereignty of the people. ...

Article Eight: We hold that the practice of fascism, imperialism and any other form of anti-democracy shall be deemed a treasonable crime... any persons or groups suspect shall be subject to search and seizure....

Article Nine: It shall be deemed a crime for any person and/or persons to exploit or profit wrongly from the labors of others... any persons or groups suspect shall be subject to search and seizure....

Article Ten: We do hereby agree to merge our productive resources to fulfill our mutual obligations hereinabove described to better the lot of freedom-loving peoples in accordance with need....

Article Eleven: A fair and just share of the productive wealth shall be made available to those who contribute their labors to this production....

Article Twelve: We agree to the immediate establishment of the USA-USSR Joint Peace Commission which shall be under the supervision and final authority of the World Order of Nations. It shall be the expressed purpose of the Commission to enforce with vigor and justice all provisions of this Treaty.... The Commission shall be comprised of three accredited representatives each of the USSR and USA, plus a neutral chairman who is an accredited representative of the World Order of Nations.

The Commission shall have under it and by its authority such regional units as shall be deemed necessary by the Commission in enforcing provisions of the Treaty. These regional units shall be named Joint Committees for Local Action, hereinafter known as JCFLA

CPSIA information can be obtained at www.ICGtesting.com
Printed in the USA
LVOW100706180413

329777LV00001B/1/P